BUDDHIS

As the first comprehensive study of Buddhism and law in Asia, this interdisciplinary volume challenges the concept of Buddhism as an apolitical religion without implications for law. *Buddhism and Law* draws on the expertise of the foremost scholars in Buddhist studies and in law to trace the legal aspects of the religion from the time of the Buddha to the present. In some cases, Buddhism provided the crucial architecture for legal ideologies and secular law codes, while in other cases it had to contend with a pre-existing legal system, to which it added a new layer of complexity. The wide-ranging studies in this book reveal a diversity of relationships between Buddhist monastic codes and secular legal systems in terms of substantive rules, factoring, and ritual practices. This volume will be an essential resource for all students and teachers in Buddhist studies, law and religion, and comparative law.

REBECCA REDWOOD FRENCH is the Roger and Karen Jones Faculty Scholar and Professor of Law at the SUNY Buffalo Law School and a former director of the Baldy Center for Law and Social Policy (2008–2010). She is the author of *The Golden Yoke: The Legal Cosmology of Buddhist Tibet* (1995). Her recent work focuses on the intersection of Buddhism and law in relation to feminism, natural law, and comparative law.

MARK A. NATHAN is Assistant Professor in the Department of History and the Asian Studies Program at the University at Buffalo, the State University of New York (SUNY Buffalo). A specialist on Buddhism in Korea, his research focuses on Buddhist responses to the changing religious, social, political, and legal environments since the late nineteenth century. He is currently at work on a book project entitled *From the Mountains to the City: Buddhist Propagation and Religious Reform in Modern Korean History.*

BUDDHISM AND LAW

An Introduction

EDITED BY

REBECCA REDWOOD FRENCH

MARK A. NATHAN

CAMBRIDGE
UNIVERSITY PRESS

CAMBRIDGE
UNIVERSITY PRESS

32 Avenue of the Americas, New York, NY 10013-2473, USA

Cambridge University Press is part of the University of Cambridge.

It furthers the University's mission by disseminating knowledge in the pursuit of education, learning, and research at the highest international levels of excellence.

www.cambridge.org
Information on this title: www.cambridge.org/9780521734196

First published 2014

Printed in the United States of America

A catalog record for this publication is available from the British Library.

Library of Congress Cataloging in Publication Data
Buddhism and law : an introduction / Rebecca Redwood French, State University of New York Buffalo Law School; Mark A. Nathan, University at Buffalo, The State University of New York.
pages cm.
Includes bibliographical references and index.
ISBN 978-0-521-51579-5 (hardback) – ISBN 978-0-521-73419-6 (paperback)
1. Buddhists – Legal status, laws, etc. – Asia. 2. Buddhism and law – Asia. I. French, Rebecca Redwood, editor of compilation. II. Nathan, Mark A., 1969– editor of compilation.
KNC615.B83 2014
342.508'52943–dc23 2013040362

ISBN 978-0-521-51579-5 Hardback
ISBN 978-0-521-73419-6 Paperback

To Frank E. Reynolds
for his lifelong work in the field
and his steadfast commitment to establishing
Buddhism and Law as an accepted academic pursuit

Contents

Maps and Illustrations — *page* xi
Contributors — xiii
Preface — xvii
Abbreviations — xxi

Introducing Buddhism and Law — 1
Rebecca Redwood French and Mark A. Nathan

PART I THE ROOTS OF BUDDHISM AND LAW IN INDIA

1. Society at the Time of the Buddha — 31
Kumkum Roy

2. What the *Vinayas* Can Tell Us about Law — 46
Petra Kieffer-Pülz

3. Keeping the Buddha's Rules: The View from the Sūtra Piṭaka — 63
Rupert Gethin

4. Proper Possessions: Buddhist Attitudes toward Material Property — 78
Jacob N. Kinnard

5. On the Legal and Economic Activities of Buddhist Nuns: Two Examples from Early India — 91
Gregory Schopen

PART II BUDDHISM AND LAW IN SOUTH AND SOUTHEAST ASIA

6. Buddhism and Law in Sri Lanka — 117
Sunil Goonasekera

7. Flanked by Images of Our Buddha: Community, Law, and Religion in a Premodern Buddhist Context 135
Jonathan S. Walters

8. The Legal Regulation of Buddhism in Contemporary Sri Lanka 150
Benjamin Schonthal

9. Pāli Buddhist Law in Southeast Asia 167
Andrew Huxley

10. Genres and Jurisdictions: Laws Governing Monastic Inheritance in Seventeenth-Century Burma 183
Christian Lammerts

PART III BUDDHISM AND LAW IN EAST ASIA

11. Buddhism and Law in China: The Emergence of Distinctive Patterns in Chinese History 201
T.H. Barrett

12. The Ownership and Theft of Monastic Land in Ming China 217
Timothy Brook

13. Buddhism and Law in China: Qing Dynasty to the Present 234
Anthony Dicks

14. Buddhism and Law in Korean History: From Parallel Transmission to Institutional Divergence 255
Mark A. Nathan

15. Buddhism and Law in Japan 273
Brian Ruppert

16. Relic Theft in Medieval Japan 288
Bernard Faure

PART IV BUDDHISM AND LAW IN NORTH ASIA AND THE HIMALAYAN REGION

17. Buddhism and Law in Tibet 305
Rebecca Redwood French

18. Buddhist Laws in Mongolia 319
Vesna A. Wallace

19. Karma, Monastic Law, and Gender Justice 334
Karma Lekshe Tsomo

20. Buddhism and Constitutions in Bhutan 350
Richard W. Whitecross

A Selection of Readings 369
Index 373

Maps and Illustrations

Ruins of the Nālandā Monastic Complex, Bihar, India	7
Map of Northern India, c. 500 BCE	30
Wheel of Dharma	70
Map of Sri Lanka, c. 1450 CE	116
Gal Vihāra Monument, Sri Lanka	134
Map of Mainland Southeast Asia, c. 1400 CE	166
Map of Ming China	216
Map of Korea in the Three Kingdoms Period, c. 500 CE	254
Map of Medieval Japan	272
Map of Himalayan Plateau and North Asia	304
Cover image of the Constitution of Bhutan	362

Contributors

T.H. BARRETT is Professor of East Asian History, Study of Religions, at the School of Oriental and African Studies, University of London. A specialist in Chinese religions, he has written widely on the history of religion in East Asia, most recently *The Woman Who Discovered Printing* (2008) and *From Religious Ideology to Political Expediency in Early Printing: An Aspect of Buddho-Daoist Rivalry* (2012).

TIMOTHY BROOK is Professor of Chinese History in the Department of History and Institute of Asian Research at the University of British Columbia. He has many publications on different aspects of Chinese history, especially the Ming dynasty. Among his recent books are *The Troubled Empire: China in the Yuan and Ming Dynasties* (2010) and *Death by a Thousand Cuts*, with Jérôme Bourgon and Gregory Blue (2008).

ANTHONY DICKS is Emeritus Professor of Chinese Law at the School of Oriental and African Studies at the University of London. He received his M.A., LL.B., and B.A. from the University of Cambridge. He is an editor for the Law in East Asia series and has written extensively on Chinese law.

BERNARD FAURE is Kao Professor of Japanese Religion in the Department of East Asian Languages and Cultures and the Department of Religion at Columbia University. His research focuses primarily on East Asian Buddhism. Faure publishes widely in both English and French, and his most recent English-language books include *The Power of Denial: Buddhism, Purity, and Gender* (2003); *Double Exposure: Cutting across Buddhist and Western Discourses* (2004); and *Unmasking Buddhism* (2009).

REBECCA REDWOOD FRENCH is the Roger and Karen Jones Faculty Scholar and Professor of Law at the State University of New York at Buffalo Law School. She received her J.D. from the University of Washington and her LL.M. and Ph.D. in Anthropology from Yale University.

Her research interests include anthropology of law, comparative law, Buddhism and law, and property law. She is the author of *The Golden Yoke: The Legal Cosmology of Buddhist Tibet* (1995), in addition to many articles and book chapters.

RUPERT GETHIN is Professor of Buddhist Studies in the Department of Theology and Religious Studies and Co-Director of the Centre for Buddhist Studies at the University of Bristol. He has served as President of the Pali Text Society since 2003, and his main research interest lies in the history and development of Buddhist thought in the Nikāyas and Abhidhamma. His publications include *Sayings of the Buddha: New Translations from the Pali Nikāyas* (2008) and *The Foundations of Buddhism* (1998).

SUNIL GOONASEKERA is currently Visiting Assistant Professor in the Department of Religion at Bowdoin College. He obtained his Ph.D. in Anthropology from the University of California, San Diego, and his J.D. from the University of California, Hastings College of Law. His areas of research include religion, art, law, political violence in South Asia, and pilgrimage studies. He is the author of *Walking to Kataragama* (2007), as well as many journal articles and book chapters.

ANDREW HUXLEY is Professor of Southeast Asian Law at the University of London. His academic work focuses on Burmese law and Buddhism. He has published widely on topics related to Southeast Asia and religion and law, including *Religion, Law and Tradition: Comparative Studies in Religious Law* (2002) and an edited volume, *Thai Law, Buddhist Law: Essays on the Legal History of Thailand, Laos, and Burma* (1996).

PETRA KIEFFER-PÜLZ is a Research Fellow at the Academy of Sciences and Literature in Mainz, with the project *Scholastic Pāli* of the German Research Foundation. Her research interests include the Pāli language of the commentarial literature, the cultural history of South and Southeast Asia, and Buddhist law. In addition to numerous articles on Buddhist monastic law, her recent book is *Sīmāvicāraṇa: A Pāli Letter on Monastic Boundaries by King Rāma IV of Siam* (2011).

JACOB N. KINNARD is Professor of Comparative Religions at Iliff School of Theology. His current work focuses on the relationship between Hinduism and Buddhism as it is played out at shared pilgrimage places in India. He is the author of *The Emergence of Buddhism* (2006, reissued 2011) and a coeditor of *Constituting Communities: Theravāda Buddhism and the Religious Cultures of South and Southeast Asia* (2003).

CHRISTIAN LAMMERTS is Assistant Professor of Buddhist Studies in the Department of Religion at Rutgers University. His research focuses on the history of Buddhism in Burma/Myanmar and Southeast Asia. He published "Narratives of Buddhist Legislation: Textual Authority and Legal Heterodoxy in 17th–19th Century Burma" in the *Journal of Southeast Asian Studies* (2013) and is currently working on a book project entitled *Buddhist Dynamics in Pre-modern and Early Modern Southeast Asia*.

MARK A. NATHAN is Assistant Professor in the Department of History and the Asian Studies Program at the University at Buffalo, the State University of New York. His work centers on Korean Buddhism and religion in the modern period, and his article "The Encounter of Buddhism and Law in Early Twentieth-Century Korea" was published in the *Journal of Law and Religion* (2010). He is currently at work on an annotated translation and a book project entitled *From the Mountains to the City: Buddhist Propagation and Religious Reform in Modern Korean History*.

KUMKUM ROY is Professor in the Center for Historical Studies at Jawaharlal Nehru University, where she has taught since 1999. Her areas of special interest include early Indian history and gender studies. She is the author of *The Power of Gender and the Gender of Power: Explorations in Early Indian History* (2010) and *The A to Z of Ancient India* (2010).

BRIAN RUPPERT is Associate Professor of Religion at the University of Illinois at Urbana-Champaign. His research interests include Buddhism in Japan, Japanese religion and politics, and Buddhist treasuries and study in premodern Japan. He is the author of *Jewel in the Ashes: Buddha Relics and Power in Early Medieval Japan* (2000), as well as many book chapters and journal articles.

BENJAMIN SCHONTHAL is a Lecturer in the Religion Department at the University of Otago in New Zealand. His research examines the intersections of law, politics, and religion in late colonial and contemporary Southern Asia, with a particular focus on Sri Lanka. He is the author of "Translating Remembering," which appeared in *The Sri Lankan Reader: History, Culture, Politics* (2011), and his dissertation "Ruling Religion: Buddhism, Politics and Law in Contemporary Sri Lanka" won the Law and Society Association's Dissertation Prize in 2013.

GREGORY SCHOPEN is a Rush C. Hawkins Professor of Religious Studies at Brown University. His research focuses on Indian Buddhist monastic life and early Mahāyāna movements. He is the author of several books, including *Buddhist Monks and Business Matters* (2004) and *Figments and Fragments of Mahāyāna Buddhism in India* (2005).

KARMA LEKSHE TSOMO was ordained in the Korean Buddhist tradition and practices Tibetan Buddhism. She is an Associate Professor in the Department of Theology & Religious Studies at the University of San Diego. Her research interests include women in Buddhism, Buddhism and bioethics, religion and cultural change, and Buddhism in the United States. She has authored and edited several books on Buddhism, including *Into the Jaws of Yama, Lord of Death: Buddhism, Bioethics, and Death* (2006) and *Buddhist Women and Social Justice: Ideals, Challenges, and Achievements* (2004).

VESNA A. WALLACE is Professor of Religious Studies at the University of California, Santa Barbara. Her research interests include Indian Mahāyāna, Vajrayāna Buddhism, and Mongolian Buddhism. She is the author of several publications on Buddhism and Asian Religious Studies. Some of her most recent work includes *The Kālacakra Tantra: The Chapter on the Sadhana together with the Vimalaprabhā* (2010) and "The Legalized Violence: Punitive Measures of Buddhist Khans in Mongolia" in *Buddhist Warfare* (2010).

JONATHAN S. WALTERS is the Ball Endowed Chair of Humanities and Professor of Religion at Whitman College. His work centers on traditions of South Asian and especially Sri Lankan Buddhism. He has authored numerous articles and books, including *Constituting Communities: Theravada Buddhism and the Religious Cultures of South and Southeast Asia*, coedited with John C. Holt and Jacob N. Kinnard (2003) and *Querying the Medieval: Texts and the History of Practices in South Asia*, with Ronald Inden and Daud Ali (2000).

RICHARD W. WHITECROSS is Lecturer of Law at Edinburgh Napier University. He received his Ph.D. in Legal Studies and Anthropology from the University of Edinburgh, in addition to his LL.B. and LLM. His research focuses on anthropology and law, comparative law, Bhutan, and constitutional and family law. He is the author of several publications, including most recently "Bhutan" in *Countries at the Crossroads: A Survey of Democratic Governance* (2012) and "Separating Religion and Politics? Buddhism and the Bhutanese Constitution" in *Comparative Constitutionalism in South Asia* (2013).

Preface

The genesis of this volume lies in several workshops and conferences that took place over the past decade. The first, "Locating Law in Buddhist Societies," was held in June 2004 by the Baldy Center for Law and Social Policy of the University at Buffalo Law School. Organized by Rebecca French and David Engel, the workshop brought together scholars from a range of disciplines whose work focused on different areas of Asia. The attendees included José Cabezón, Leslie Gunawardena, Andrew Huxley, Brian McKnight, Mark A. Nathan, Frank Reynolds, and Winifred Sullivan. In addition to the participants, we would like to extend our gratitude to Lynn Mather, Director of the Baldy Center at the time, who generously supported the workshop, and to the staff who helped make it a success.

At the conclusion of the workshop, plans were made to follow up with a more formal conference organized around some of the themes identified in the discussions that had taken place. The result was an international conference in March 2006 at the Rockefeller Foundation's Bellagio Study and Conference Center in Bellagio, Italy, organized by Rebecca Redwood French where scholars from around the globe presented papers and engaged in discussions on Buddhism and Law related to several topics: how to think about Buddhist law, modern Buddhist nationalism and law, textualism, theft, and religious institutions and the state. Among those who attended were several scholars who had participated in the previous workshop and many who were new to the project, including Timothy Brook, José Cabezón, Bernard Faure, Leslie Gunawardena, Andrew Huxley, James Ketelaar, Petra Kieffer-Pülz, Justin McDaniel, Ryuji Okudaira, Frank Reynolds, Peter Skilling, Winifred Sullivan, Vesna A. Wallace, and Richard W. Whitecross. Some of the papers in this volume resulted from drafts prepared for the Bellagio conference. We thank all those who participated and the Rockefeller Foundation and the Baldy Center for funding the conference.

The third conference, "Law, Buddhism, and Social Change: A Conversation with the 14th Dalai Lama," was held later that year in conjunction with the visit of His Holiness the Dalai Lama to the State University of New York at Buffalo. In a remarkable and noteworthy event, Rebecca French brought together a group of distinguished scholars who posed questions to the Dalai Lama on the relationship between Buddhism and law. This was followed the next day by several panels: "The Buddha as Lawgiver: Monastic and Secular Communities," "Social Change and Buddhism: Buddhism's Effect on Different Legal Systems in Asia," and "Social Change and Conscience, Self and Society." Transcripts and several of the papers prepared for this event were published in 2007 as a special issue of the *Buffalo Law Review*, vol. 55. Enormous thanks goes to His Holiness the Dalai Lama, who has long been a supporter and mentor for research and writing on the topic of Buddhism and law. This conference was also responsible for bringing the subject of Buddhism and law to the attention of Kate Brett, who was then the Religion Editor at Cambridge University Press.

The papers and ideas herein have been presented by both the co-editors and the authors at many venues over the last ten years, and while it is not possible to name them all, we would like to thank all of the presenters, participants, and discussants for their intellectual engagement with the ideas as they have greatly enriched this volume. We would like to acknowledge all of the editors and staff who worked on the volume at Cambridge University Press, particularly Kate Brett, Anna Lowe, Laura Morris, and Alexandra Poreda, for their help and encouragement with the project. We are additionally grateful to the Rockefeller Foundation, the Baldy Center for Law and Social Policy, as well as the numerous scholars who acted as anonymous readers for the volume and patiently helped with editing and suggestions. Several research assistants – Gretchen Frank, Katie Grennell, Chloe Hall, Anne Rosenbaum, and Rob Vanwey – helped with footnotes and initial editing. Josh Coene was instrumental in helping shape the volume by doing extensive final edits and checking, even though the topic was far from his area of scholarly expertise (the history of prisons). Linda Kelly has been a superb help with transcripts and typing. Nancy Babb of the UB Law library worked tirelessly on the index while mastering words in several foreign languages. We would also like to thank Walter Hakala, Devonya Havis, Teri Miller, Drorah Setel, Winnie Sullivan, Vesna Wallace, and Richard Whitecross for reading and commenting on drafts of the Introduction. Clara Redwood deserves special mention for using her computer skills to create the maps and Peetie Van Etten and David Engel for the contribution of their photographs.

Rebecca French would like to thank her family and, of course, her two daughters, Emo and Clara Redwood, who have turned into perfectly wonderful young adults while she was working on this book. She would also like to extend her deep thanks to her mentors, each of whom has contributed in his and her own way to this book, including Donald Chisum of UW Law; Leopold Pospisil, Stanley Weinstein, Harold Conklin, and Mirjan Damaska of Yale; Bob Thurman at Columbia; Gyatso Tsering and Thupten Sangye of the LTW&A; the late Michael Aris, Bill Alford and Jordan Lama at Harvard; Michael Walzer and the late Clifford Geertz at the IAS; Frank Reynolds of UC; the late Hugh Richardson in Fife; Stephen D. Smith and Karma Lekshe Tsomo now at the University of San Diego; and Dzogchen Ponlop Rinpoche. She is also grateful for the continuing support of Kristen Van Ausdall, Nancy Black, Susan DeReimer, Devonya Havis, LaReine Hungerford, Isabel Marcus, Teri Miller, Mia Morabito, Drorah Setel, as well as attendees of the Friday night potluck dinners.

Mark Nathan would like to thank his two children, Dylan and Sarah, whose love serves as a constant reminder of what is really important in life. He would also like to thank his colleagues in the Department of History and the Asian Studies Program at the University at Buffalo, as well as his mentors at UCLA: Robert Buswell, William Bodiford, Gregory Schopen, and John Duncan.

Finally, we want to remember our friend and colleague, Leslie Gunawardena, who passed away in November 2010 at the age of seventy-three. He brought both a keen intellect and an infectious smile to our discussions at the conferences leading up to this volume, and his untimely death cut short his important work on Buddhism and law.

Abbreviations

A	*Aṅguttara Nikāya*
Abhidh-k-bh	*Abhidharmakośa-bhāṣya* edited by P. Pradhan (Patna: Kashi Prasad Jayaswal Research Institute, 1967)
BL	British Library
D	*Dīgha Nikāya*
Derge	The *Sde-dge Mtshal-par Bka'-'gyur*, a facsimilie edition of the 18th-century redaction of the Si-Tu Chos-kyi-'byuṅ-gnas.
Dhs	*Dhammasaṅgaṇi*
Divy	*Divyāvadāna* edited by P.L. Vaidya (Darbhanga: Mithila Institute, 1959)
Ja	*Jātaka*; Viggo Fausbøll (ed.), *The Jātaka together with its Commentary*, 7 vols. (London: Trübner, 1877–1897)
M	*Majjhima Nikāya*
Mhv	*Mahāvaṃsa* edited by Wilhelm Geiger (London: Pāli Text Society, 1912).
Mil	*Milindapañha*
MPS	*Mahāparinirvaṇsūtra* edited by E. Waldschmidt (Berlin: Akademie Verlag, 1951)
Mvu	*Le Mahāvastu* vol. I, edited by É. Senart (Paris: Imprimerie Nationale, 1882)
NL	National Library of Myanmar
Pālim	*Vinayasaṅgaha-aṭṭhakathā-pāṭh* (Yangon: Pyi Gyi Mundyne, 1954)
Pālim-nṭ	Tipiṭakālaṅkāra, *Vinayālaṅkāra-ṭīkā*, 2 vols. (Yangon: Buddhasāsanasamiti, 1984)
Peking	*The Tibetan Tripitaka, Peking Edition, Reprinted under the Supervision of the Otani University, Kyoto,* Vols. 1–169 (Tokyo and Kyoto: 1955–1961)
Ps	*Papañcasūdanī*

S	*Saṃyutta Nikāya*
SBV	*Saṅghabhedavastu* edited by R. Gnoli and T. Venkatacharya, 2 vols. (Rome: Istituto italiano per il Medio ed Estremo Oriente, 1977–1978)
Sp	*Samantapāsādikā*, Takakusu, Junjiro and Makoto Nagai (eds.), *Samantapāsādikā: Buddhaghosa's Commentary on the Vinaya Piṭaka*, 7 vols. (London: Pāli Text Society, 1924–1947)
Spk	*Sāratthappakāsinī*
Sp-ṭ	*Sāratthadīpanī*, 3 vols. (Yangon: Buddhasāsanasamiti, 1960)
Sv	*Sumaṅgalavilāsinī*
T	*Taishō shinshū daizōkyō* (Tokyo: Taishō Issaikyō Kankōkai, 1924–1932)
Tikap	*Tikapaṭṭhāna*
Tog	*The Tog Palace Manuscript of the Tibetan Kanjur*, Vols. 1–109 (Leh: 1975–1980)
UBhS	U Bo Thi Manuscript Library, Thaton
UCL	Universities Central Library, Yangon
Vin	*Vinaya*. Editions of Pāli texts are those of the Pāli Text Society, originally published Oldenberg, H. (ed.), *The Vinaya Piṭakaṃ*, 5 vols. (London: Williams and Norgate, 1879–1883)
Vjb	*Vajirabuddhi-ṭīkā*. (Yangon: Buddhasāsanasamiti, 1960)
Vmv	*Vimativinodanī-ṭīkā*, 2 vols. (Yangon: Buddhasāsanasamiti, 1960)

Introducing Buddhism and Law

Rebecca Redwood French and Mark A. Nathan

Some edited volumes are self-explanatory and others need a substantial introduction to the material; the latter is the case with this volume. While the title is intriguing, many readers will need a guidebook to explain much of what they are encountering here. And it is well worth the effort as the material is some of the most exciting and unorthodox both on legal systems and in Buddhist Studies. Therefore, the task of this introduction to the volume is to provide readers with a road map to define the object of study, and to offer ways to think about the field of Buddhism and Law.

This introduction is divided into three main sections: Buddhism, Law, and Buddhism and Law. The first, Buddhism, presents a brief account of the life of the Buddha before turning to an examination of *dharma*, a fundamental term in Buddhism that has long been translated as law. A discussion of Buddhist monasticism and some of the misconceptions that have surrounded the place of the monastic community in society comes next, followed by a consideration of the *Vinaya*, the canonical Buddhist law codes that have served to regulate the religious life of Buddhist monasteries. Buddhist traditions also possess a wealth of other legal texts and materials, most of which reflect attempts to devise supplementary rules and regulations that fit local conditions, and these are introduced last.

The second section, Law, is intended to show how Buddhism and Law might fit into the legal scholarly world, perhaps the most difficult connection for legal academics and scholars of Buddhism. This section begins with a definition of law that moves beyond a simple denotation of state regulations and permits a more expansive view of legal practices. In this section, three more ideas will be broached. The first is the concept that Buddhism, when viewed as an otherworldly religion, does not seem to have law. The second is a discussion of a strong, centralized state model of law that European and North American scholars might be working from, and the third is the idea of Legal Orientalism. Following this, four areas of legal academics are introduced: Religion and Law, Law and Society,

Comparative Law, and Legal History. The central question for each of these discussions is how the new field of Buddhism and Law can be integrated into current legal perspectives.

The final section, Buddhism and Law, offers possible ways to think about the scope, distinctive characteristics, and possible directions for the field. Rather than defining Buddhism and Law at this early stage of its development, it offers observations drawn from the volume. The idea is to ask what the characteristics and scope of Buddhism and Law might be. The first observation is that the subject of Buddhism and Law is very diverse, as the papers in the volume demonstrate. Second, there are three geographic areas that are most pronounced in terms of their similarities: South and Southeast Asia, East Asia, and North Asia and the Himalayan region. These resemblances become quite apparent in Parts II, III, and IV. Finally, the broad range of possible future topics for research within Buddhism and Law is delineated.

Buddhism

The Life of the Buddha

Siddhārtha Gautama was born the son of a ruler in an area that is now southern Nepal and, according to the tradition, was raised in a life of princely luxury. Although the dates of his life are uncertain, a majority of scholars place his birth in the sixth century BCE. As it was foretold that his son was destined to become either a great king or a great religious teacher, it is said that Siddhārtha's father shielded him from any painful elements of life that might lead him along the latter path. However, the sacred biographies say that the prince eventually became curious about the world outside the walls of the palace and, leaving behind his wife and newborn child, studied under a number of teachers and experimented with different forms of ascetic practice that were common in India at the time, including some extreme austerities. Finding none of these methods efficacious, he finally sat down beneath a *pīpal* tree and determined not to move from the spot until he had achieved his goal. In the course of one evening, the canonical texts say he progressed through successive stages of meditative insight before arriving at a perfect understanding of the way things truly are, rather than how they might appear to the unenlightened[1] – that is,

[1] As Don Lopez has noted, "Accounts differ as to precisely what it was that he understood, and, indeed, Buddhist schools throughout history have looked back to this night to claim their particular view of reality to have been discovered by the prince." Donald S. Lopez, Jr., *The Story of Buddhism* (New York: HarperCollins, 2001), 40.

an understanding of causality and karma, impermanence and the absence of self, suffering and liberation. The Buddha's awakening that night and his subsequent teachings and discourses based on that experience are both referred to as dharma.[2]

The Buddha's teaching career began a few weeks after that event, we are told, and lasted some forty-five years. Over the course of that time, many people gathered around Śākyamuni, an honorific title meaning "the sage of the Śākyas," and the teachings called "turning the wheel of law" have continued to attract followers for 2,500 years. His first disciples were his five fellow ascetic practitioners. Significantly for the development of Buddhism as a religion and for the purposes of this volume, among those who became followers of the Buddha during his lifetime and thereafter, some left home to join the *saṅgha* (or *saṃgha*), while others remained householders and provided support for those who had "gone forth" into the religious life. At times the word saṅgha is used more inclusively to encompass both groups, but most often it refers to a community or an assembly of monks or nuns who, upon full ordination, take a vow to uphold the precepts and rules contained in the Buddhist law codes, which are called *Vinaya*. The basic dynamic at the heart of the link between the saṅgha and lay society has long been recognized as a type of reciprocal relationship. Laypeople earn karmic "merit" for themselves or loved ones by donating food, land, or other necessities and gifts to the saṅgha, while the monks and nuns serve as teachers of dharma and "fields of merit," especially through their observance of the *Vinaya*.

Buddhism emerged in a particular sociocultural, economic, and political context. In Chapter 1 of this volume, Kumkum Roy examines the archeological and textual evidence for a variety of changes and developments in commerce, agriculture, and polities taking place in northern India around the time of the Buddha. To understand how law developed within Buddhism in the early stages of the religion, Roy asserts, these contexts are important. She draws attention in particular to the increasingly common practice of textual codification during this period for things like grammar, rituals, and social norms. Citing the work of Patrick Olivelle, Roy notes that the Buddhist appropriation of dharma may have influenced the development of the Dharmaśāstras, a genre of Brahmanical literature that codified certain customary practices and became the basis for ancient Hindu

[2] Pāli, *dhamma*. Sanskrit and Pāli are the two classical languages of India in which the "word of the Buddha" (*buddhavacana*) was initially set down in writing. Sanskrit pronunciation of this and other Indian words – with the exception of *saṅgha* – will be used throughout this introduction and in most chapters. The authors in this volume who focus on Buddhism in South or Southeast Asia, where the Pāli-language Buddhist canon was adopted, prefer Pāli.

law.[3] In turn, these texts and the social norms they expressed exerted influence on Buddhism, particularly the monastic codes. This type of interaction reminds us that the terms like dharma and saṅgha were not unique to Buddhism alone, but widely shared in religious, ethical, political, and legal discourses at the time of the Buddha.

Dharma as Law

The word *dharma* has a broad range of meanings in the wider Indian social, religious, political, and legal discourses. It can signify the natural order of the universe and society as well as one's duty or ritual obligations within that order.[4] The nineteenth-century founders of Buddhist studies in Europe, notably Eugène Burnouf and Brian Hodgson, recognized that the word *dharma* had multiple meanings and was difficult to translate, but they considered "law" an acceptable or even preferred translation.[5] As T.H. Barrett briefly discusses in Chapter 11, the word *dharma* was also translated into Chinese more than a millennium ago as *fa*, one prominent meaning of which is unquestionably law. However, Barrett notes that despite this early choice, over the long term the connection between them becomes less clear. Similarly, as Frank Reynolds points out, "'Law' when it was used as a translation for Dharma, was used with cosmic, philosophical, and/or ethical connotations that were never associated – in any really intrinsic or crucial way – with legal systems or codes."[6] Although the term "Buddhist law" in this volume is used to refer to the monastic law codes, whereas "Buddhism and Law" alludes to the secular legal systems of communities that are Buddhist, it is still worthwhile to consider briefly "law" as dharma.

One attribute shared by dharma and law may be universality. The law of cause and effect and other central doctrines described as the Buddha's dharma can be applied to all people – and all sentient beings, for that

[3] For more on Hindu law, see the previous volume in this series, Timothy Lubin, Donald R. Davis, Jr., and Jayanth K. Krishnan (eds.), *Hinduism and Law: An Introduction* (Cambridge: Cambridge University Press, 2010).

[4] For more on the history and meaning of dharma, see the articles in Patrick Olivelle (ed.), *Dharma: Studies in Its Semantic, Cultural, and Religious History*, special issue of the *Journal of Indian Philosophy* 32 (2004). For more on the connection to law, see Robert Lingat and J. Duncan M. Derrett (trans.), *The Classical Law of India* (Berkeley: University of California Press, 1973), 3–17.

[5] See, for instance, Eugène Burnouf, *Introduction à l'histoire du Buddhisme indien* (Paris: Imprimerie Royale, 1844), 37, n. 1, where he cites the definitions of *dharma* provided by Hodgson, discusses the problems of translating the word, and gives "law" as one of his preferences.

[6] Frank Reynolds, "Buddhism and Law – Preface," *Journal of the International Association of Buddhist Studies* 18.1 (1995), 3.

matter – at all times. The conditioned nature of all things holds true no matter what a person's station in life or what beliefs that person may hold. Moreover, dharma also possesses a prescriptive aspect in addition to its descriptive component, or as Rupert Gethin points out in Chapter 3, "The 'law' (*dharma*) is what is right, and our behavior should conform to it." In other words, the Buddha did not simply describe reality as seen from his enlightened vantage point; he also laid down a number of principles for correct moral and ethical conduct based on his perfect insight and profound wisdom. Karma Lekshe Tsomo in Chapter 19 links the "law" of karma and principle of cause and effect to Buddhist ethical prescriptions, noting some of the factors found in Buddhist commentaries on causality that were influential in Buddhist legal reasoning as well: "the nature of the action, the intention behind action, the agent of the action, the mindset of the agent, the object of the action, the *modus operandi*, and the factors or the circumstances surrounding the event."

One final way in which dharma enters this discussion of Buddhist law is through Buddhist textual references to a *cakravartin*, a "wheel-turning" king, the Buddhist image of an ideal ruler. While a number of essays in this volume mention the historical example of Aśoka, who lived a century or two after the Buddha in India and is seen by later Buddhist traditions as the personification of a cakravartin king, Gethin explores the origins of this concept and its possible connections to law. Like so many other central concepts in Buddhism, this notion of a "wheel-turning" king was common to Brahmanism and Jainism too, but in Buddhist teachings, Gethins tells us, "where *cakravartin* kings are described as conquering and ruling the whole earth not by violence or by the sword, but by righteousness (*dharma*), the wheel has also the connotation of 'the wheel of truth' (*dharma-cakra*)." In numerous places throughout the Buddhist scriptures, the Buddha is depicted as interacting with contemporary kings, instructing them in dharma and sometimes giving them advice. Although the texts clearly contain scattered views on kingship grounded in Buddhist ethics and virtue, Gethin cautions against reading a Buddhist form of constitutional law into them, as some have done, and concludes that at a minimum, discussions of kingship and the ideal of a cakravartin "have been used by Buddhists to reflect on how a king should behave."

Buddhist Monasticism

The relationship between those who leave home to become ordained monks and nuns and those who remain lay householders is central to an understanding of Buddhism as it spread throughout much of Asia. The establishment of a functioning and viable monastic community, which inevitably involved the establishment of monasteries and eventually the adoption of a monastic code to regulate the community, was an indispensable part of the transmission of Buddhism into new regions of Asia.[7] This basic distinction is also important for any consideration of Buddhism and Law for two closely connected reasons. The first relates to persistent presumptions about the degree of distance separating these two groups of Buddhist practitioners, while the second concerns the set of rules or precepts that function as a Buddhist law code for individual monks and nuns and for the saṅgha as a communal body or organization.

Although the monastic ideal within Buddhism, as portrayed in some canonical sources, was peripatetic, solitary, and austere, echoing perhaps the paradigmatic story of the Buddha leading up to his awakening, a more sedentary lifestyle clearly became the norm early in the history of the saṅgha involving tight-knit communities of settled religious practitioners. These monasteries in time grew to become quite large and complex institutions, as the example of the famous monastery and university at Nālandā located in the present-day Indian state of Bihar shows. Having been founded a century or so after the start of the Common Era, at its peak between the eighth and twelfth centuries, Nālandā housed several thousand monks (including some from faraway lands like China) and lay students, taught a wide range of subjects, hosted famous Buddhist teachers, and contained numerous buildings and elaborate structures. Equally large, wealthy, and sophisticated monastic institutions could be found playing prominent roles in society and politics wherever Buddhism became established in Asia. Monasteries functioned as corporate institutions that owned property, could engage in commerce and trade, entered into sophisticated financial arrangements, acted as centers of learning for monastic members and laypeople alike, and were regulated by a set of formal rules and punishments. In other words, to function socially as a communal organization, the saṅgha could not avoid interacting with, and having an influence on, the legal culture of the societies in which they became established.

One reason for the perceived disjuncture between saṅgha and society was the false assumption that Buddhist monasticism is marked by otherworldliness and the complete separation from society. The biases that

[7] Charles S. Prebish, "Varying the Vinaya: Creative Responses to Modernity," in Steven Heine and Charles S. Prebish (eds.), *Buddhism in the Modern World: Adaptations of an Ancient Tradition* (Oxford and New York: Oxford University Press, 2003), 45.

Ruins of the Nālandā Monastic Complex, Bihar, India.

Western observers and generations of Buddhist scholars brought to bear on their conception of Buddhist monasticism, which was almost invariably compared to Christian forms of monasticism, certainly played a role.[8] This has begun to change, however, in the last few decades. Changes in our understanding of Buddhist monasticism were spurred by two important trends in Buddhist studies in recent decades. First, there was a turn away from the normative descriptions found in Buddhist scriptural texts and more focus on the lived tradition as it is practiced in Buddhist monasteries and temples throughout Asia. Many of the preconceptions concerning Buddhist monasticism have come under scrutiny from the 1970s as more anthropologists began to conduct field studies of Buddhist communities in Asia. There is now a greater awareness and sensitivity to the institutional realities of life in a Buddhist monastery, and less criticism of deviations or devolutions from the ideal religious life described in the *sūtras*.

[8] James Robson, "Introduction: 'Neither too far, nor too near': The Historical and Cultural Contexts of Buddhist Monasticism in Medieval China and Japan," in James A. Benn, Lori Meeks, and James Robson (eds.), *Buddhist Monasticism in East Asia: Places of Practice* (New York: Routledge, 2010), 1–3.

The second trend that has begun to reshape our understanding of Buddhist monasticism is the increased scholarly attention being given to *Vinaya* materials. The *Vinaya* is a set of canonical law texts containing rules, descriptions, case studies, definitions and punishments, and some ancillary material that was used to regulate the saṅgha. The more scholars scrutinize the contents of the *Vinaya*, the more shibboleths previously held by Buddhist Studies scholars concerning the nature of Buddhist monasticism have faltered. Gregory Schopen has been a leading voice in this endeavor, and his body of work demonstrates that there is much the *Vinayas*, together with epigraphic evidence, can teach us about what we can know – and what we still do not know – about Buddhist monasticism in early India. In Chapter 5 of this volume, Schopen takes aim at the textual image of nuns as "hierarchically or ritually subservient to monks," noting that if this were true, then it "had . . . no bearing on their legal or economic status: for the *Vinaya* nuns had equal legal rights of ownership and economic independence." Schopen's use of a variety of *Vinaya* materials to arrive at a more accurate picture of the lives of monks and nuns in ancient India, particularly their economic and legal capacities, has provided a necessary corrective to misperceptions of monastic life in Buddhism.

Just as the prevailing notions of Buddhist monasticism have been built on faulty assumptions about the degree of separation between saṅgha and lay society, so too have perceptions of Buddhism and law rested unsteadily on the incommensurability of monastic law and secular law. The monastic-lay distinction has been interpreted as severely limiting the conclusions that can be drawn about the relationship of Buddhism to law. Some might go so far as to suggest that it precludes even the possibility of studying Buddhism and Law, unless we are talking strictly about the *Vinaya* and the monastic setting. Most scholars of Buddhism recognize that the *Vinaya* is imbued with strongly legal characteristics and would agree that it can certainly be seen as a law code. Nevertheless, because this code and the legal practices or procedures associated with it are portrayed as peripheral to the life of the laity, it is often considered tangential to the wider social ethics and secular legal norms that bear on their daily lives. This perception has allowed Buddhism and Law to be dismissed for the most part by both legal academics engaged in the study of religion and law, as well as by Buddhist Studies scholars.

Vinaya as Law

The *Vinaya* comprises one-third of the Buddhist canon and is the first of the three "baskets" (*piṭika*) to appear, followed by the discourses of the

Buddha (Sūtra Piṭika) and scholastic treatises or commentarial literature – the "further dharma" (Abhidharma Piṭika). The use of the word *Vinaya* in singular form is quite common, especially when referring to it as part of a singular Buddhist canon, but this usage is merely conventional because, just as there are multiple canons, nearly a dozen *Vinayas* existed at one time. Six of these *Vinayas* have been preserved in a more or less complete form to the present day, and several more have survived only in fragments,. Of the six that are extant, three are still in use today by monastic communities in Asia, and for simplicity they can be identified by the language of the Buddhist canon in which they are found: Pāli, Chinese, and Tibetan.[9]

The core of the *Vinaya* lays out rules for monks and nuns to uphold individually and for the order to follow collectively. The tradition credits the Buddha himself with the creation of these rules on a case-by-case basis, but we may never know which (if any) of the rules can actually be traced to the time of the Buddha. The extant *Vinayas* almost certainly went through a sustained period of development before arriving in the written form that we have them today.[10] Nevertheless, Petra Kieffer-Pülz observes in Chapter 2, "Scholars generally conclude that prescriptions preserved in all monastic legal codes had been enacted already at an early time, probably sometime after the demise of the Buddha." The unresolved issues and problems surrounding the origin, dating, and development of the *Vinayas*, however, should not obscure the significant fact that in every *Vinaya* scholars have examined, the Buddha is depicted as the lawgiver. After hearing accounts from others and thoroughly investigating the "causes and conditions" surrounding a suspected transgression or moral lapse on the part of monks and nuns, the Buddha decided on cases as the highest spiritual and legal authority concerning what is good and true. On that basis, he is said to have created a substantial body of law for the community of monks and nuns, making Buddhist law in this sense quite unique among the major world religions. A process of accommodation or adaptation to the legal, political, and social environments is plainly evident in the

[9] The Pāli canon contains the *Theravāda-vinaya*, which is used in Sri Lanka and most of Southeast Asia. The *Dharmaguptaka-vinaya*, commonly known as the *Four-Part Vinaya*, became authoritative in the Chinese-language canon used throughout East Asia, but a number of *Vinayas* were known, studied, and preserved in Chinese. Lastly, the Tibetan canon has the *Mūlasarvāstivāda-vinaya* as the basis for its monastic law.

[10] Gregory Schopen has argued elsewhere that placing the *Vinayas* in their current form during or close to the Buddha's life "would mean that Buddhist monasticism had little or no real history or development" and would contradict "what little we actually know about the various vinayas and the history of Buddhist monasticism." See Gregory Schopen, "Deaths, Funerals, and the Division of Property in a Monastic Code," in Donald S. Lopez, Jr. (ed.), *Buddhism in Practice* (Princeton, NJ: Princeton University Press, 1995), 475.

development of *Vinayas*, yet the existence of a complex law code gave the saṅgha sophisticated legal tools necessary to engage with lay society, political systems, and secular law wherever it became established.

All versions of the *Vinaya* have a similar structure. The material is divided into two main parts: the *Sūtravibhaṅga*, which contains the core list of rules called the *Prātimokṣa* that individual monks and nuns vow to uphold on full ordination; and the *Skandhaka*, which lays out the organizational procedures to be followed by the monastic community as a whole. The number of rules in the *Prātimokṣa* range from 219 to 371 depending on the school and gender of the practitioner. Women were initially excluded from joining the saṅgha, we are told, but after several years the Buddha reluctantly agreed to admit them. He did so, however, only after handing down a set of eight rules that appears to establish the subordination of nuns individually and collectively to their brethren, and additional requirements. In her chapter, Tsomo discusses the establishment of a *bhikṣuṇī* saṅgha as portrayed in the canonical texts, and questions the historicity of these eight special rules and more importantly their necessity for nuns today. She spotlights the difficulties that contemporary women have in becoming fully ordained members of the saṅgha in many places, especially where the order of nuns was allowed to die out. The tension that she identifies between, on the one hand, the authority of laws and the weight of tradition and, on the other hand, social justice or gender equality in conformity with changing sociocultural norms is an issue all legal systems must confront.

Other Buddhist Legal Texts

When Buddhism spread to other parts of Asia, differences in local and regional conditions necessitated additional legal regulations at both the local and state levels. In India local rules were often developed at the level of individual monasteries, and according to Kieffer-Pülz, these additional temple ordinances (*kriyākāra*) were decided on by all members of a particular temple or monastery and promulgated within a single *vihāra* (monastic dwelling). While local temple ordinances in India are known mostly through references to them in canonical sources, examples of the ones used in Sri Lanka, where they are known as *vihāra-katikāvata*, are available in abundance.[11] Closely related legal texts called *sāsana-katikāvata*

[11] Ratnapala states that the word *katikāvata* and the Pāli word *katikāvatta* from which it was derived do not appear in the Pāli canon, but that *katikā*, which has the same meaning, is well attested the

were issued by a ruling Buddhist king, inscribed in stone, and applied to all monasteries in the island. In Chapter 7, Jonathan Walters analyzes the first *katikāvata* of this type in Sri Lanka, promulgated by King Parākramabāhu I (1153–1186). Written in the vernacular, the legal texts were addressed to the saṅgha of the entire kingdom and followed a fairly standard form, including praise for the ruler and his Buddhist ideology in addition to the actual regulations and enforcement clauses. King Parākramabāhu's inscription, located at the center of Gal Vihāra, "enacted momentous change in the Sri Lankan religious community" and "gave birth to a regulatory genre that lasted for hundreds of years." Interestingly, like the *Vinaya* itself, this *katikāvata* is concerned above all else with maintaining the purity of the saṅgha. Walters's analysis provides further evidence of why the prevalent view of Buddhist law as operational only inside the monastery and unrelated to lay and state concerns is in such need of revision.

The many commentaries on the *Vinaya* provide a window into legal exegesis in Buddhism. The *Samantapāsādikā*, an extremely influential fifth-century Sri Lankan commentary on the Pāli *Vinaya*, is one of the best known. Written by Buddhaghosa, the most celebrated commentator of the Theravāda tradition, this wide-ranging commentary also contains historical narratives and geographical information concerning Buddhism in India and Sri Lanka. A number of chapters in this volume mention Buddhaghosa's Pāli commentary, including Andrew Huxley and Christian Lammerts in Chapters 9 and 10, respectively, on Burma, where it was an influential and authoritative source of legal reasoning for judges and *Vinaya* jurists (*vinayadhara*) who drew on multiple sources of law. Huxley calls it "the central law text in the Pāli legal tradition" and discusses the interrelationship between the *Vinaya* and other legal texts known as *dhammasat* and *rajadhamma* (the dharma of kings). Lammerts examines the way in which the first two sources handled the question of inheritance of monastic property in Burma, and he concludes: "Calling into question any strict divide between lay and monastic legal spheres, it shows that monastic inheritance did not fall under the exclusive jurisdiction of *Vinaya*, and also that *Vinaya* laws regulating monastic partition were appropriated by *dhammasattha* for application to the lay community." These findings challenge the idea of a strict separation of monastic law from the secular law of the laity.

literature. According to him, "Originally katikā referred to an agreement made by either a lay or an ecclesiastical assembly, but in canonical Pāli texts it is used to refer exclusively to ecclesiastical agreements or pacts." See Nandasena Ratnapala, *The Katikāvatas: Laws of the Buddhist Order of Ceylon from the 12th Century to the 18th Century* (München: Kitzinger, 1971), 6.

Further examples of legal exegesis and local sources of Buddhist law are abundant in China and the rest of East Asia, where *Vinaya* masters translated, studied, and commented on several different versions of the *Vinaya*. Although not covered in this volume, another type of Buddhist legal text worth mentioning has stood alongside the *Vinaya* in many East Asian monasteries for centuries. These texts, which contain monastic regulations known as "pure rules" (*qinggui*), were initially drawn up to regulate Chan monasteries in China and later imported and adopted for use in Korean Sŏn monasteries as well as Japanese Zen temples. The *Pure Rules for Chan Monasteries*, an eleventh-century text purportedly based on rules composed earlier by the Tang-dynasty monk Baizhang (749–814), consisted of seven fascicles comprising seventy-seven chapters. A recent study by Yifa compared the Chan monastic codes to the *Vinaya* and found that the former was "directly influenced by the vinaya texts, vinaya literature, and the Chinese cultural milieu of the times."[12] The proliferation of these local rules allowed the monastic communities that adopted them to create "new organizational forms and institutional structures better adapted to the demands of local culture and history," while at the same time addressing problems over how "to legitimate Buddhist orders according to some kind of vinaya."[13] The Pure Rules, it should be noted, were meant to supplement rather than replace the *Vinaya*, and monks and nuns were still expected to receive and abide by its precepts.[14]

Bodhisattva precepts were also used in China and Korea as supplements to the *Vinaya*, much like Pure Rules for individual monasteries. The Bodhisattva precepts and Mahāyāna ordination platforms that became popular in East Asia were an additional source of Buddhist law in East Asia, but they were not derived from any *Vinaya* sources. Instead, they were found in Mahāyāna sūtras and apocryphal scriptures that were popular in East Asia, but were, for the most part, unknown in South and Southeast Asia. While the Bodhisattva precepts are not treated much in this volume, they do offer an interesting contrast to the *Vinaya*, since monastics and laypeople alike took the Bodhisattva precepts.[15] In Japan, however, as Brian Ruppert explains in Chapter 15, the *Vinaya* was actually replaced. This

12 Yifa, "From the Chinese Vinaya Tradition to Chan Regulations: Continuity and Adaptation," in William M. Bodiford (ed.), *Going Forth: Visions of Buddhist Vinaya* (Honolulu: University of Hawai'i Press, 2005), 134.

13 William M. Bodiford, "Introduction," in Bodiford (ed.), *Going Forth*, 2.

14 T. Griffith Foulk, "*Chanyan qinggui* and Other 'Rules of Purity' in Chinese Buddhism," in Steven Heine and Dale S. Wright (eds.), *The Zen Canon: Understanding the Classic Texts* (Oxford and New York: Oxford University Press, 2004), 294.

15 Bodiford (ed.), *Going Forth*, 5.

process was started by the extremely influential Tendai Buddhist monk, Saichō (767–822), who criticized the *Vinaya* as "Hīnayāna" and not fit for Tendai monks. As Ruppert says, Saichō "interpreted [the Buddhist ordination practice] primarily in terms of the Mahāyāna 'perfect precepts' (*endon kai*) based on the *Brahmā Net Sūtra* (Ch. *Fan-wang jing*) in place of the traditional *Four-part Vinaya*." However, the Bodhisattva precepts that were derived from this text and others that became popular addressed more generalized ethical behaviors, and this too had to be supplemented with detailed temple laws, the development of which Ruppert describes.

Law

Definition of Law

While definitions are often avoided in scholarly work owing to the difficulties and ambiguities inherent in the endeavor, it is important in this introduction to indicate the scope of the term "law" as it is being used here. The history and possible reasons for translating law as "dharma" have already been discussed. Therefore, this second section opens with the definition of law as it is more commonly used and includes additional components, which may be more expansive and inclusive than some would expect. There are four other initial points made here: the general view of Buddhism as an other-worldly religion devoid of law; the "strong" centralized, religious legal system model in our current legal culture; the immense diversity and range of legal systems in most religious communities; and the new ideas of Legal Orientalism being advanced in the legal academy that may prove useful for this endeavor.

For the purposes of this volume, the term *law* has several connotations, the first of which is the written secular laws of a nation-state, that is, the statutes, cases, rulebooks, law codes, judicial processes, and decision documents of a political entity. Under this rubric, law can be defined as "(1) a body of rules considered binding on a particular political or social unit, and the principle of justice underlying it . . . ; (2) a code or canon of such rules . . . ; (3) institutions and practices for the creation and application of such rules and for the adjudication of disputes."[16] Several of the authors in this volume have employed a similar understanding of law. However, law also includes other practices, such as (4) the social customs, practices,

[16] Lubin, Davis, and Krishnan, *Hinduism and Law*, 5. The authors of the previous volume in this series note that Hindu Law had all three of these.

and rules that constitute a form of social control for the maintenance of a group; and (5) social manners, customary practices, etiquette, and general behaviors regulating silence, speech, and interaction. These last two definitions of law are more expansive and encompass many of the rules encountered in the *Vinaya* and other parts of Buddhist law.

The historic view of Buddhism as an otherworldly religion, unconcerned with affairs of state or a mundane life, is one that has proven to inhibit the study of Buddhism and Law. Frank Reynolds has pointed out that early in the history of Buddhist Studies, the dominant view was that "*true Buddhism* was not a religion that had a strong legal component." This conclusion was primarily based on its image as an other-worldly and contemplative religion, or at least one "concerned with individuals but not with issues of social, political, and economic order." The consequence was that "Buddhist secular law was given even less attention than the study of monastic law. The Buddhological community as such was hardly aware either of the presence of Buddhist secular law or the influence Buddhism had had on the legal systems in the countries where the *sāsana* had been established."[17] Conversely, the essays in this volume demonstrate that Buddhism was very concerned with issues of social, legal, political, and economic order.

For most European and North American scholars, the iconic religious legal system is the canon law of Medieval Catholic Europe, a complex set of legal principles and formal procedures largely incorporated from the Roman law code of Justinian. Measured against this standard, Buddhist legal systems will perhaps seem weak because they lack divine revelation, a law code that applies to an entire society, a centralized body for enforcement, and many of the other aspects of canon law. But a strong model of religious law, like canon law, can overemphasize unity while deemphasizing multiplicity and difference. The Buddhist tradition has always been known for its wide diversity in terms of its vast store of sacred texts and different canons, multiple buddhas and bodhisattvas, and accommodation to local religious beliefs and worldviews. The Buddha is seen as the lawgiver who personally sat in judgment on hundreds of cases during his forty-five years of teaching that were compiled into the *Vinaya*. The purity and scope of this formation of the Buddhist law code is a source of great reverence within the religion.

And finally, Legal Orientalism has become a subject of interest in Comparative Law. Edward Said's original point was that scholars come to think of their superior knowledge of particular languages, texts, and cultures

[17] Reynolds, "Buddhism and Law–Preface," 2–4.

of Asia as licensing their ability to rule over and colonize or dictate to those groups. Law professor Teemu Ruskola has presented his idea of Legal Orientalism a bit differently. He proposes that the framework of Legal Orientalism allows scholars to examine their tendency to designate which countries have law and which do not, how much they have, and how images of those Orientalist societies will be viewed.[18] But a lack of knowledge is also central to this problem. Ian Harris has stated of politics that, "... despite high-level interest in the political manifestations of the great monotheist traditions of Christianity, Islam and Judaism, little sustained attention has been given to this crucial aspect of Buddhism, Asia's most important religion."[19] He goes on to emphasize that Buddhism was central to the formation of several states in Southeast Asia and has had a lasting influence on the political – and we would add, legal – processes that are used in these countries today. The purpose of the rest of this section is to provide a set of contexts in law for reading these essays and also for future research.

Religion and Law

Current work in Religion and Law looks at legal issues in large nation-states such as human rights, state control of religion through law, the free exercise of religious belief and expression, the economic and political conditions that affect religious stability, secularism in the modern world, and constitutions.[20] Scholars such as Harold J. Berman have bemoaned the lack of available information on Asian religious legal systems, noting that "the influence of Buddhism on the law of a country such as China where for centuries Buddhism was the predominant belief system," needs investigation. He goes on to state that "most classical works on comparative religion have also ignored or minimized connections between various types of religious belief and various types of law."[21]

[18] Teemu Ruskola, *Legal Orientalism: China, The United States and Modern Law* (Cambridge: Harvard University Press, 2013). See also Piyel Haldar, *Law, Orientalism and Postcolonialism: The Jurisdiction of the Lotus Eaters* (London: Routledge-Cavendish, 2007).

[19] Ian Harris, *Buddhism, Power and Political Order* (London: Routledge, 2007), 1.

[20] Other topics include charity laws, religious movements, clergy privilege and confidentiality, freedom of religion, abortion and assisted suicide, religion in prisons, ordination of women and gays, multi-faith societies, state establishment of religion, hermeneutics and translation, gay rights, the financial relationships between religion and the state, human rights, and religious associations and education.

[21] See Harold J. Berman, "Comparative Law and Religion," in Mathias Reimann and Reinhard Zimmerman (eds.), *The Oxford Handbook of Comparative Law* (Oxford: Oxford University Press, 2008), 740–41. He cites two exceptions: Werner F. Menski, *Comparative Law in a Global Context:*

Anthony Dicks' paper (Chapter 13) presents Buddhism and Law in China, from the Qing state in 1644 to the present, as a continuous history of strong state regulation of religion. Mirroring much of the current literature on secularization, Dicks and other scholars of Chinese law or Buddhism look for the subtle interplay between the state and religions. Dicks demonstrates that the statutory record in China concerning the regulation of religious groups changed very little over the centuries. The state gave recognition to some established religions, but withheld it from other religious groups, maintaining what he calls a "carefully balanced ambivalence," which remains the government's attitude today. In his paper (Chapter 12) on the theft of Buddhist monastic lands in the Ming period, Timothy Brook points out that changes in the political and economic environment are central to the stability of Buddhism vis-à-vis the state. The theft of monastic property increased greatly when the Ming economy became monetized and transactions of all kinds were available at every level of the economy. As land was extremely valuable, "the economic reality of the Wanli-era commercial land market was that the acquisition or disposal of land operated in complete indifference to claims to moral or religious benefits accruing to specially designated parcels of land." However, to the great Buddhist master Yunqi Zhuhong (1535–1615), "it seems, what made Buddhist property vulnerable was the political climate of the Wanli era, not the economic environment. The latter was simply an unexceptional fact of institutional existence."

Richard Whitecross has written extensively on the constitutional process, another popular topic in Religion and Law, in the Buddhist state of Bhutan, a concept that he points out was not considered in Tibet or Bhutan until the middle of the twentieth century. Buddhism and the state have always been intertwined in Bhutanese history as the state "sought to balance its traditional values informed by Buddhist teachings with major political and social change." The drafters of the Constitution decided to include the Buddhist monarchy and the concept of Gross National Happiness in the new Constitution of Bhutan, but they excluded the Central Monk Body from the legislature and did not declare Buddhism the official religion. "The creation and enactment of a written Constitution in 2008 highlights the problem of untwining the interrelationship between the religious and secular systems," while not losing sight of "how deeply held values . . . have shaped and defined the Constitution."

The Legal Systems of Asia and Africa (Cambridge: Cambridge University Press, 2006) and H. Patrick Glenn, *Legal Traditions of the World: Sustainable Diversity in Law* (Oxford: Oxford University Press, 2010).

Law and Society

A group of scholars working on legal issues from a social science perspective – anthropologists, sociologists, linguists, political scientists, historians, lawyers, economists, and psychologists – came together in the 1960s to create the Law and Society movement. The founders of this interdisciplinary organization were committed to looking at a wide range of legal processes within specific social contexts rather than just the official cases and statutes studied in law schools. Understanding law as culture, seeing *law-in-action* as separate from *law-on-the-books*, looking for legal consciousness, taking the perspective of a legal professional working in a global law firm, tracking resistance to racial discrimination in a criminal procedure, describing the narrative behind a First Nations case in Canada, listening to how illegal aliens in Los Angeles interpret the immigration process, and asking prisoners their views on gun control – these are all typical of work done by scholars in Law and Society. Several of the scholars in this volume write from this perspective.

Rebecca French presents ethnographic findings in Chapter 17 on Tibetan law in the 1940s. Describing the daily practice of legal administration in Lhasa, she discusses the formal style of documentation, including the way staff were trained to draft documents, the process of decision-making, and the use of standardized phrases praising Buddhism. The Tibetans that she interviewed outlined four different legal processes in the 1940s in Lhasa: internal dispute settlements, a conciliation between two parties, visiting a judge at home, and official legal proceedings in court. Interviews with Tibetan refugees were used to construct this picture of Tibetan legal procedures and cases in the 1940s.[22] Benjamin Schonthal opens Chapter 8 with an interesting problem in current courtrooms throughout Sri Lanka when judges and monks find themselves in a standoff. Civil procedure requires that all participants rise for the judge, but Buddhist custom demands that monks never stand to greet anyone but another monk. As he states, "[r]eligious and civil authority collide, before a word is even spoken." The long history of competing views of religion and politics has been acted out in all the "modern nation-states with Theravāda Buddhist majorities," namely Sri Lanka, Thailand, Laos, Cambodia, and Myanmar/Burma. Schonthal points out that this conflict is now encoded in two types of laws: "[O]ne set of laws gives states powers to manage the conduct and wealth

[22] See also Rebecca Redwood French, *The Golden Yoke: The Legal Cosmology of Buddhist Tibet* (Ithaca: Cornell University Press, 1995).

of Buddhist monks; another set of laws obligates the state to protect the welfare of 'Buddhism' generally."[23] Andrew Huxley has also been centrally concerned with the historical ethnographic record of the legal profession and daily interactions in the courts in Burma. He recounts that Burmese lawyers in the eighteenth century were called *she-ne*, wore red or green turbans depending on their client, carried a cotton briefcase, drinking cup, and fan, and were expected to vigorously defend their client's case. In court, they boasted, laughed, slapped their shoulders or thighs, pounded the floor, and even bet on who would win.

The ethnographic recording and comparison of legal disputes in modern nunneries and monasteries is another fertile area for ethnographic scholarship. Some of this work has already begun with monks and nuns who have recorded legal processes in their monasteries[24] or written treatises on their *Vinayas*. As pointed out earlier, how Buddhist monasticism actually functioned in a society and its relationship both historically and currently to lay supporters and political rulers is another interesting area for investigation. Comparisons can then be made of these findings across historical periods, traditions, and regions to fill out the picture of Buddhist law and its associated practices.

Comparative Law

The inception of Comparative Law is usually dated to the growth of national legal systems in Europe at the turn of the nineteenth century, when the great codifications of law in Prussia, France, and Austria provided a rich field for comparison. Based on its history of investigating ways to compare and contrast separate legal systems, Comparative Law offers analytical categories for making sense of the details uncovered in a new sub-discipline. Conversely, including Buddhism and Law challenges the quasi-universalist rubrics on which the commensurability of European legal systems are based. In particular, the theories of Legal Traditions, Legal Subject Matters, and Legal Transplants, which are frequently used by comparative legal scholars, may help explicate some of the ideas encountered in Buddhism and Law.

Legal Traditions theory in Comparative Law drew from the scientific categorizations of the eighteenth century such as Linnaean botany to create

[23] Benjamin Schonthal just won the 2013 Law and Society Association Dissertation Prize for his thesis, *Ruling Religion: Buddhism, Politics and Law in Contemporary Sri Lanka* (PhD diss., University of Chicago, 2013).

[24] George Dreyfus, *The Sound of Two Hands Clapping: The Education of a Tibetan Buddhist Monk* (Berkeley: University of California Press, 2003) is just one example.

taxonomies of law called legal traditions, or legal families, that are still in use today.[25] Efforts to achieve full inclusion and universality notwithstanding, comparative legal scholars have struggled to comprehend Buddhist legal systems within these taxonomies. In a recent work in 2010, Patrick Glenn outlined seven different legal traditions: the chthonic, Talmudic, Civil, Islamic, Common, Hindu, and Confucian legal traditions.[26] Buddhism, however, was singled out in this otherwise excellent work as spreading

> in a non-political, non-institutional way, just telling people about the way of the world and achieving some kind of political consensus only in Tibet. Generally, it was only within the communities of Buddhist monks or *saṅgha* that some type of formal order developed, leaving external societies free to drift or even to enact positive (though not necessarily unreal) law.[27]

There are two interesting possibilities for Buddhism in terms of taxonomies within the Comparative Law method. The first would be to include Buddhism as a legal tradition in Comparative Law discourse. The robust, influential, and enduring legal systems described in this volume provide ample evidence of Buddhism's indispensable position in the Comparative Law world. The second possibility is for scholars in Buddhist Studies and related disciplines to consider what different types of traditions arise when looking at the breadth of Buddhism and Law across Asia. Here, the idea is to understand how and why various patterns of Buddhism and Law arose in different geographic areas and periods.

A second central topic in Comparative Law is the investigation of Legal Subject Matters across nations. The basic subject matters of law have been divided into two main areas: (1) private law, or the legal relationships between individuals in terms of contracts, torts, and property and (2) public law, that is, legal relationships between individuals and the state, such as criminal, constitutional, and administrative law. In Buddhism, any comparison of private law must first be related to the different rules in the various *Vinayas*. For example, notions of property in a *Vinaya* are determined, first, by what a monk or nun is allowed or forbidden to handle and, second, by what a member of the laity can give to a religious institution. In either case, a subject for future investigation is the degree to which the

[25] See John H. Merryman and Rogelio Perez-Perdomo, *The Civil Law Tradition: An Introduction to the Legal Systems of Europe and Latin America* 3rd ed. (Stanford: Stanford University Press, 2007); Mary Ann Glendon, Paolo G. Carozza and Colin B. Picker, *Comparative Legal Traditions* (Eagan, MN: West Publishing, 2006).

[26] Glenn, *Legal Traditions of the World* (Oxford: Oxford University Press, 2010). This is a change from the types of René David and John E.C. Brierley or Zweigert and Kotz.

[27] Ibid., 331–32.

public-private dichotomy enshrined in Comparative Law discourse is of heuristic value in Buddhism, and also whether or not these putatively universal constructs are too culturally and historically determined to be useful.

Property law, a central concern for comparison between legal systems, is the subject of Chapter 12 by Timothy Brook. According to Brook, while private property had no karmic weight, monastic property had the "capacity to generate merit" for the one who donated it. As a result, giving private property away or selling it in general entailed no Buddhist consequences, but giving it to a monastery or nunnery, created great merit for the donor. But, "[o]nce land that had been given to the saṅgha was no longer supporting Buddhist practice, the karmic value of the original donation was cancelled. Thus there were interests on both sides of the monastery-donor relationship to accumulate land and prevent its loss."

Indeed, the simple possession of property appears to present a conundrum in Buddhism because the Buddha had to first give up his family, position, and all of his possessions in order to become enlightened. And yet, giving to others and not retaining property for one's own benefit results in the accumulation of merit, meaning that greater wealth affords more opportunities to earn karmic merit in Buddhism. Jacob Kinnard writes specifically on this private law issue and explains the tension in the Buddhist view of property. As part of Chapter 4, he describes the mythic story of King Vessantara, a wealthy monarch who was so serious about his Buddhist precepts that he gave everything away – including all of his possessions, his kingdom, and his family – much to the horror of everyone around him. These acts are often taken to be the very embodiment of perfect generosity in Buddhism. Much as the possession of property was depicted as a hindrance in the life of the Buddha, Vessantara's giving of property, while denounced by some in the texts, allowed him to generate immense Buddhist merit and good karma.

The study of private law can also help to understand how the *Vinaya* actually worked. It has generally been presumed from the early texts that nuns were subservient to monks and had a reduced economic status with no legal rights, especially with respect to property. Gregory Schopen argues in Chapter 5 that early nuns were as active as monks in their donations, possessed financial resources, went to court to press their causes, and had equal legal rights of ownership and economic independence. Using evidence from the *Mūlasarvāstivāda-vinaya*, closely related texts and a variety of other sources, the intriguing image he offers of nuns who engage in contractual and property matters involving complex financial instruments is completely at odds with our usual picture. In Chapter 16, Bernard Faure asks two different private law questions: What constitutes property for the purposes of theft? Is a Buddhist relic "property" in this sense? Although both the Japanese Bodhisattva precepts and the *Dharmaguptaka-vinaya* make theft illegal, Faure shows that thefts of important relics have taken place throughout Japanese history. Since the saṅgha is identified with the Buddha, theft of monastic property such as relics is, in effect, an act of theft against the Buddha himself. After describing the monastic, secular, and after-worldly results of theft, Faure demonstrates that theft of an important Buddhist relic can go unpunished when the relic is then used to enhance the power of a religious site.

A third topic in Comparative Law, the study of Legal Transplants in general – rather than simply the reception of Roman law into Europe – began in the 1970s and rapidly became a major theme with the important work of several scholars including Alan Watson's *Legal Transplants: An Approach to Comparative Law* in 1993.[28] Legal Transplants, defined as the importation of rules between different legal cultures and societies, looks at how law codes and legal rules are introduced, translated, received, or rejected in whole or in part in another society, and the role of power, legitimacy, and authority in their transmission.[29]

The movement of Buddhist legal ideas throughout Asia over a long span of time can be viewed as a series of Legal Transplants. While the spread of Buddhism has been a subject of interest in Buddhist Studies and Asian history, the emphasis has generally been on how the doctrines in the religion were transmitted and adapted to fit new cultural environments.[30] The papers in this volume point to several interesting twists for Legal Transplant theory. First, the Buddhist legal ideas contained in the *Vinaya* were embedded in the monastic institutions that invariably provided a vehicle for the transmission of Buddhism. The saṅgha was a type of religious corporation that in most cases functioned unlike other social institutions present in the receiving countries, and therefore presented a legal anomaly. Several of the chapters in this volume address the strategies that various societies and states deployed in comprehending and interacting with this

28 Alan Watson, *Legal Transplants: An Approach to Comparative Law*, 2nd ed. (Athens: University of Georgia Press, 1993 [1974]).

29 For example, the introduction of the German model in the creation of a civil code in Japan in 1898 is an example of a Legal Transplant in Asia that has been the subject of many studies. See Wilhelm Röhl (ed.), *History of Law in Japan since 1868* (Leiden: Brill, 2005). Legal scholars have also referred to Legal Transplants as transfers, circulation, influences, formants, and inspirations.

30 See, for example, the collection of papers published in Ann Hierman and Stephen Bumbacher (eds.), *The Spread of Buddhism* (Leiden: Brill, 2007).

unique institution. A second point in that, once established within a society, the maintenance of this new corporate institution required extensive economic, social, and political support, with some of the aspects of this support requiring new legislation and legal regulation.

A third aspect of these Buddhist Legal Transplants was that they were often accompanied by and encased in a "cultural package" – an idea first introduced by Andrew Huxley,[31] such as Pāli cultural ideas, Confucian administrative ideas or Tibetan culture – when Buddhism moved into a new area. For example, Andrew Huxley mentions in Chapter 9 the ways in which the Buddhist laws that came to Southeast Asia were intertwined with a larger Pāli cultural package, which included the *dharmaśāstras* and *dharmasūtras* from South Asia. Mark Nathan (Chapter 14) explains how the transmission of Buddhism to Korea was inextricably bound to other aspects of Chinese culture and statecraft, including administrative law codes. This transmission process was then repeated when it travelled to new areas: "The dissemination of Buddhism from the ruler of one state to another through official diplomatic channels in conjunction with a wider transmission of culture, people, institutions and knowledge, including law, also characterizes the way in which King Sŏng of Paekche officially introduced Buddhism to the Yamato ruler in Japan in the sixth century." A fourth point is that, in some cases, while the Buddhist legal rules were transplanted to a new culture, they could perdure within monasteries for hundreds of years without necessarily being incorporated into the secular legal systems of the new culture (and in spite of the vicissitudes of state support and acceptance) as the history of Chinese Buddhism outlined in this volume demonstrates.

Legal Transplant theory also looks at the underlying causes for the spatial expansion of a legal system examining the roles played by military force, cultural innovation associated with social prestige, emergent opportunities afforded through networks of trade, political advantage through elite networks, or the conversion of high-status individuals or communities. These causal factors affect the transmission, the degree to which it is accepted, and the depth of the reception of the law by the receiving society. Pierre Legrand has pointed out that there may be great variation in Legal Transplants; their impact at the point of reception may be limited, they may be received but not produce change; some laws may only be useful in particular cultures,

[31] Andrew Huxley, "Sanction in the Theravada Buddhist Kingdoms of S.E. Asia," *Recueils de la Societe Jean Bodin* 43 (1991), 335–70; see also Huxley, "Legal Transplants as Historical Data, Exemplum Birmanicum," *Journal of Imperial and Commonwealth History*, 37, 167–82.

and the transplants themselves cannot move into a new site without being significantly altered as the process of transplantation requires a significant amount of interpretation and critical reflection.[32] It might be noted also that neither the monks nor the laity were simply passive actors in the Legal Transplant process.

Legal History

Several of the chapters in this volume are histories of Buddhism and Law in different parts of Asia: Sri Lanka, Burma, China, Korea, Japan, Tibet, and Mongolia. Although not all of the countries in Asia where Buddhism became established are covered, those that are included here tell the story of the introduction of the religion and its legal system, how it was affected by and influenced the area into which it moved, and how the relationship between Buddhism and Law evolved over time. In these chapters, the authors present Legal History through the intellectual, social, and economic climate of each period, the roles of legal institutions, major players and symbolic objects, and the ways in which the laws of these religious institutions affected civil life. It must be stressed that compiling a legal history of Buddhism within a specific area is not an easy task. What follows are a few core themes from the many that emerge from these Legal Histories.

In each of these chapters, the saṅgha develops particular relationships with the lay population that often changed over time. While the monastic community has the *Vinaya* for its internal legal discipline, the lay population has legal customs that are then directly and indirectly influenced by the *Vinaya* rules to a greater or lesser degree. As Sunil Goonesekera points out in Chapter 6, while the *Vinaya* had no direct authority over the laity in precolonial Sri Lanka, it was very influential in setting out proper standards for social conduct. Surprisingly, in some historical periods, members of the laity openly criticized other laity when their own behaviour violated eating, etiquette, and cleanliness procedures articulated for monks. He states, "[i]n practice, the Buddhist monastic order of Sri Lanka has been informally involved in the legal system of the country from the earliest times."

[32] Pierre Legrand, "What Legal Transplants?" in David Nelken and Johannes Feest (eds.), *Adapting Legal Cultures* (Oxford: Hart Publishing, 2001). He states on page 64: "Inevitably, [Legal Transplant theory] fails therefore, to treat rules as actively constituted through the life of interpretive communities."

T.H. Barrett (Chapter 11) makes a very different claim about the situation in China. The *Prātimokṣa* rules found in the *Vinaya* were restricted to monks and not read outside of China's monasteries, except perhaps by some very serious monarchs. He goes on to state that

> [t]his communication barrier between religious and secular law means that we should not necessarily expect to see direct reflections of the former in the latter, nor assume Buddhist influence unless it can be demonstrated. Some seemingly Buddhist traditions of clemency within Chinese Legal History, for example, are in fact older than Buddhism and eventually withered under regimes more Buddhist than Chinese.

One final aspect of Legal History displayed in these papers is the construction of a myth of the state to explain the relationship between Buddhism and the state. Vesna Wallace, in Chapter 18 on Buddhism and Law in Mongolia, suggests that this construction of a legal mythic history for a Buddhist state can be extremely important in establishing a regime's historical legitimacy. In Mongolia, the dual-law notion from India – dharma law and state law – was propagated as early as the late-sixteenth century. To make a claim of legitimacy, Mongolian historians identified the Golden Clan of Chinggis Khaan with the Golden Clan of the mythical Buddhist King Māhasammata, who was the emanation of the Buddha Samantabhadra. Richard Whitecross similarly argues in Chapter 20 that the legitimacy of a constitution-drafting project in Bhutan rests, in part, on the origin myth of the nation-state. Zhabdrung Ngawang Namgyal, the religious hierarch of the Drukpa Kagyu, a Tibetan Buddhist sect, wanted to create a "new state based on religious laws, as well as the legends and laws of the early Tibetan monarchy." Fleeing from Ralung Monastery in south-central Tibet, he came to Bhutan to create a "religious estate" in 1616. This history both validates the origin of that nation-state and creates an important place for Buddhism in the modern drafting project. Legitimation appears to occur in both directions – that is, the religion is legitimized by connection to the early history of the state and the state is legitimized by connection to a universal, high-culture religion.

Buddhism and Law

Thus far we have considered ways to think about law in Buddhism and ways we might approach Buddhism from a legal perspective. This still leaves some questions unanswered: What is "Buddhism and Law"? What does the study of Buddhism and Law entail? How do we define this object of study? These questions are as important as they are difficult to answer. Yet to try to define Buddhism and Law at this early stage would needlessly delimit an important new area of research. Instead, we would like to offer a few observations drawn from this volume as a whole to see what it can tell us about the subject.

The first observation is that Buddhism and Law is extremely diverse. As the papers attest, much like Buddhism itself, the study of Buddhism and Law covers a wide range of geographical areas, historical periods, cultural contexts, and textual layers. Another way to say this might be that Buddhism and Law is rooted in specific contexts, all of which overlap and mutually influence each other. The papers in this volume have been grouped into sections that for the most part follow the geographic patterns in the spread of Buddhism in Asia. Each of these groups shared a common Buddhist canon written in the same language, followed the same Buddhist monastic code, and often had extensive interactions.

The papers in Part I deal with the Buddhist texts, foundational concepts, and social environments related to the origin and subsequent development of Buddhism in India. They look at a wide range of materials and subject matter, from Indian society around the time of the Buddha to canonical literature as it relates to law, both in a general way and more specifically in terms of textual analyses of *Vinaya* passages on nuns or legal concepts. All are connected to India, although not exclusively, during the period spanning roughly 1,000 years (500 BCE–500 CE).

Part II of the volume covers South and Southeast Asia. Sri Lanka received the *Theravāda-vinaya* and the rest of the Pāli Buddhist canon from India and later established links with Buddhist communities in mainland Southeast Asia, where Buddhism was adopted as part of a cultural package. This meant that, as these states unified and developed complex political, legal, and administrative procedures, Buddhism played a formative role. The *Vinaya* provided a model for legal regulation and an authoritative source of law when deciding cases not only within the saṅgha, but also those involving the monks and the laity and even, on occasion it seems, among the laity themselves. A tripartite model of government – king, saṅgha, and laity – appears most common in precolonial Sri Lanka and Burma as described in these papers.

Part III examines Buddhism and Law in East Asia. It begins with three papers on Buddhism and Law in China, which collectively cover nearly 2,000 years of history. China presents a unique case in the history of Buddhist transmission outside of India, because China possessed a written language, literary and philosophical traditions as old as India's, and, most importantly for our purposes, a codified law and a well-established legal system prior to the entrance of Buddhism. The conclusion that has frequently been drawn given these circumstances is that Buddhism played little or no role in law in China. While this may be true for the formation or development of Chinese law codes, this view fails to take into account the persistent and pervasive interactions between the saṅgha, lay Buddhist communities, and the established law in China. The legal regulation of Buddhism by the state is a valid area of study for Buddhism and Law, just as much of the current research in Religion and Law investigates precisely the issue of state regulation of religion. Researchers might also investigate possible influences of Buddhism on Chinese law.

Buddhism in Korea and Japan are also covered in this part because the Buddhist traditions of those countries share a number of affinities with Chinese Buddhism in terms of the canonical sources, Buddhist commentarial literature, indigenous schools, and monastic codes and precepts. Over time their trajectories diverged as the emerging saṅgha and states in those countries developed under different conditions. The *Four-Part Vinaya* became authoritative in Korea and Japan following its official adoption in Chinese Buddhist monasteries, and Chinese and Korean monasteries claimed to adhere to that *Vinaya,* usually in conjunction with additional precepts and temple laws. Moreover, Korean states were historically much more centralized along the lines of the Chinese civil bureaucratic model and employed many of the same legal and administrative tactics for regulating the saṅgha. On the other hand, many Japanese Buddhist schools largely abandoned the *Four-Part Vinaya* or replaced it with other types of ecclesiastical law or precepts. Unlike the centralized, civil bureaucratic states in China and Korea, in Japan during the Tokugawa period, the state's ability to impose uniform regulations on the saṅgha was very limited. Instead, three different entities shared power – the government, the shrine-temple complexes, and the domains of warriors.

Part IV brings together chapters that examine Buddhism and Law in North Asia and the Himalayan region where the Tibetan-language canon and *Mūlasarvāstivāda-vinaya* were used in the monastic communities of Tibet, Mongolia, and Bhutan. Tibet adopted a dual patron-priest model of Buddhist government rule, at times with an outsider acting as the patron. The leader of Tibet from 1650 to 1950 was a Buddhist monk and secular law codes had citations to the Buddha and employed Buddhist reasoning. There were ecclesiastical courts manned by monks, and secular courts manned by both monks and secular officials. The Mongolians imported the Tibetan Buddhist teachings and adopted the dual model of Buddhist government. In several different periods, the Mongolians had full-fledged Buddhist states with monks acting as the supreme political leaders as well as secular law codes drafted to create a Buddhist polity and to enforce the obligations of the *Vinaya* on monks. Bhutan also closely mirrors the Tibetan model of Buddhism and Law, and as we learn in this volume, has sought to maintain the links between Buddhism and the state through the drafting of a constitution in the twentieth century.

While the above comments establish the rich diversity that typifies Buddhism and Law, a few more observations can be made about possible future research in this new subject matter.

First, understanding the basic framework of Buddhist law and how it evolved is an essential first step. What was the *Vinaya* and how do all the various *Vinayas* compare? Several of the papers in this volume have concentrated on this important issue. The Buddha has a unique position as a lawgiver within the tradition that warrants future study. Furthermore, a serious examination of how the *Vinaya* affects the relationships among, first, Buddhist monasteries and nunneries, second, the local populations of lay Buddhists that support the saṅgha, and third, the political complexities of the local, regional and state governments, is essential to the study of Buddhism and Law.

Second, collecting and cataloguing all of the Buddhist canonical and other historical and modern writings that were used as legal documents including other governmental documents, local ordinances, statutes, case law, legislation, and constitutions, is very important. As the authors demonstrate, reading directly from the historical and modern texts provides the best opportunity for assessing legal issues. Many of these documents blur the line between lay and monastic legal spheres and jurisdiction, others strongly delineate them. In some the *Vinaya* serves as a model for non-monastic law (Burma, Mongolia), in others the *Vinaya* is disregarded and replaced (Japan). Some cultures have numerous other documents in addition to the *Vinaya* used in legal decision-making (Sri Lanka, Burma); others appear to only use secular law codes (China). The nature of these Buddhist legal documents also needs to be described: Are they collection of rules? Do they reflect local customs and traditions? Are they filled with lists, administrative regulations, technical terms, stories, quotes from religious works? Who drafted them and what was their intended purpose and actual use?

Third, each of these papers stresses the need to understand context: the geographical, economic, social, mythical, symbolic and other aspects of each of the cultures into which the religion traveled. This includes the reasons for introducing the new religion, basic social stratification, the historical development of law, repression, persecution and colonialism, internal sectarian factionalism, local traditions of legal codification, and many of the other specific aspects of the cultures described by the authors in this book. Most of these communities were legal pluralities with a range of different forms of laws, with the authority of each shifting through history. Examining the source of law to which historical actors turned in order to deal with a specific problem during a particular historic period tells us a great deal about Buddhism and Law on the ground.

Fourth, the wide variety of methodologies that were used in the articles in this volume should be seen as a strength. Authors translate and compare ancient texts; they examine archaeological evidence; they look at historical records, literature, gazetteers and current case law; they interview legal actors, observe legal decision-making processes, and look at the media results of political occurrences involving Buddhism. Equally important, the subject matters under investigation range from specific legal subjects, such as theft (Faure), property (Kinnard, Brook), and inheritance (Lammerts), to legal reasoning (Huxley), legal consciousness (Wallace), the position of women (Tsomo), changes in legislation through time (Dicks), the roles of individual actors, local customs, and many other topics.

It is our general hope that the papers collected in this volume will provide the impetus for further research and writing in the area of Buddhism and Law. One of the more pressing tasks is the need for data, which will require more scholars to devote time and energy to investigating Buddhism and Law. More empirical information on all of the different societies where Buddhism has played a significant role opens up the possibility of more comparisons, theoretical analyses, and perhaps models of interaction. This would be a welcome addition to this exciting new area of scholarly inquiry, and if this volume makes a contribution toward that, however modest it may be, we trust that our efforts to provide an initial roadmap will quickly be eclipsed and surpassed by the accomplishments of a new generation of Buddhism and Law scholars.

PART I

The Roots of Buddhism and Law in India

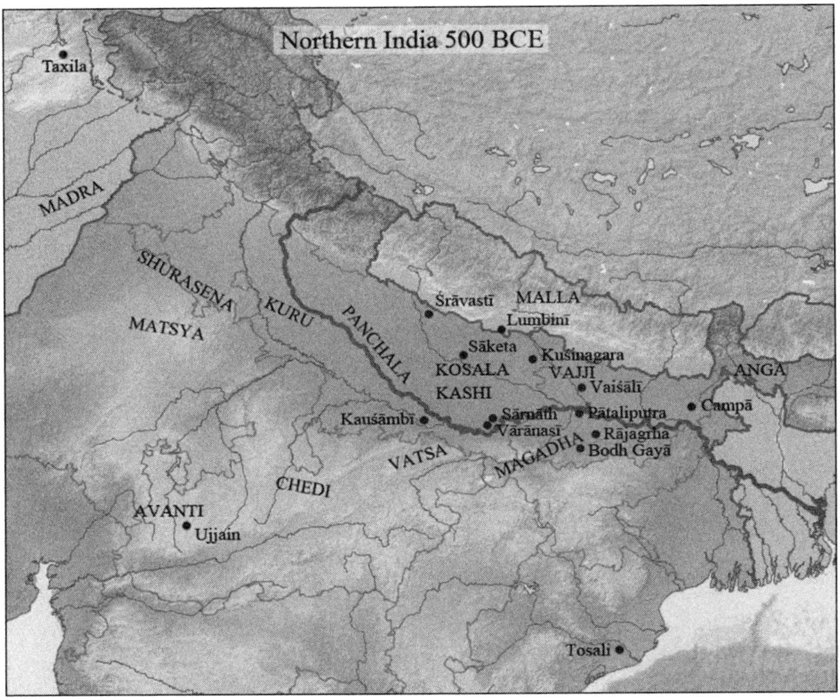

Map of Northern India, c. 500 BCE

CHAPTER I

Society at the Time of the Buddha

Kumkum Roy

Introduction

How do we understand the contexts within which notions of law were developed in early Buddhism? We first need to localize early Buddhism within the geography of the Indian subcontinent. We can then turn to traditions of codification that were in dialogue with one another, remembering that Buddhism was not an isolated phenomenon. Next we will contextualize these traditions in terms of the key economic, political, and social developments that characterized the region at the time.

Historians attempting to reconstruct the milieu of early Buddhism have drawn on a variety of sources. These include texts considered to be part of the early Buddhist Pāli canon, later Vedic and post-Vedic Brahmanical works in Sanskrit, as well as a range of archeological evidence. The latter includes finds from explorations and excavations at sites associated with early Buddhism and elsewhere, along with some of the earliest inscribed material. Not all the sources tell the same story, nor have scholars approached them with the same sets of questions. Consequently, our understanding is fragmentary in more ways than one. This is a limitation that we need to acknowledge at the very outset.

To understand society at the time of the Buddha, it is necessary to delineate certain broad spatial and chronological contours shaping his life. It is well known that the early Buddhist tradition refers to the birth of the Buddha in Lumbinī (in present-day Nepal), his attaining enlightenment in Bodh Gayā (in present-day Bihar), his first preaching at Sārnāth (near Vārāṇasī in present-day Uttar Pradesh), rounds of teaching and periodic residence in groves and monastic settings during the rainy season, and finally attaining *parinibbāna* at Kuśinagara (in Uttar Pradesh). These sites have been mapped, explored and excavated by archaeologists since the second half of the nineteenth century. Textual traditions, with all their limitations, have been used to identify sites and specific architectural features, many of which have been corroborated through inscriptions on seals, sealings, and other artifacts. We suggest that present-day Nepal (or certainly its sub-Himalayan tracts), and parts of the present-day states of Bihar and Uttar Pradesh within India, formed the core area for the development of Buddhism in its earliest phase. It was probably this area that was regarded as the central land, the *majjhimadesa* in the Pāli textual tradition.

What distinguished the *majjhimadesa* was the emergence of as many as sixteen state-like, political formations, the *mahājanapada*, which ranged from Gandhāra in the northwest of the subcontinent (present-day Pakistan) to Aṅga in the eastern Ganga Valley (near the borders of present-day Bihar and West Bengal). Virtually all these states were located to the north of the Vindhya Mountains; the sole exception was Asmaka in the Deccan Plateau. According to texts and archaeology, each of these *mahājanapadas* incorporated a range of settlements – there are indications of small hamlets, villages, as well as a variety of towns and cities.[1] Buddhist texts are replete with references to these different categories of settlement – the *gāma,* or village, occasionally a settlement of craft specialists in the vicinity of a city, the *nigama* or commercial settlement, and the *nagara* (town or city).[2] The *mahājanapadas* also included monarchies or *rajjas* as well as *gaṇas* or *saṅghas,* often described as republics or oligarchies. The latter are thought to have provided models for the organization envisaged within the Buddhist saṅgha or monastic order. Buddhism, and the notions of law within it, developed in the context of these incipient state structures.

Although extensive horizontal excavations have been few and far between, in part because many of the sites continue to be inhabited at present, two artifacts are particularly significant and evince certain elements of shared material culture across the *mahājanapadas.* The first is punch-marked coins, the earliest coinage in the subcontinent. Minted in both silver and copper, their distribution indicates the existence of complex networks of exchange and implicitly several other processes and institutions. Silver is relatively rare in the subcontinent, although copper is fairly common. Thus, procuring raw materials as well as processing them required organization. It is likely that these activities were organized, controlled, and

[1] Useful summaries of the major historical developments of the period can be found in F.R. Allchin, *The Archaeology of Early Historic South Asia* (Cambridge: Cambridge University Press, 1995), and Upinder Singh, *A History of Ancient and Early Medieval India* (Delhi: Pearson Longman, 2008).

[2] Uma Chakravarti, *The Social Dimensions of Early Buddhism* (New Delhi: Munshiram Manoharlal, 1996), 23. See also George Erdosy, "City States of North India and Pakistan at the Time of the Buddha," in F.R. Allchin, *Archaeology Historic South Asia*, 114, and F.R. Allchin, *ibid.* 194–95.

supervised by the issuing authorities – probably associations of dominant urban groups and/or guilds of merchants as well as rulers – who could both regulate and standardize weights and measures and control the quality of the metal used. In all likelihood, the symbols punched on the coins represented those who issued them. The second archeological marker, Northern Black Polished Ware, consists of fine pottery, especially bowls and dishes that were probably used for serving and consuming food. The widespread distribution of this deluxe pottery, which, in spite of its name, is found throughout the subcontinent, indicates both contacts among elites across the subcontinent, as well as the existence of socioeconomic differences.[3]

Ratnagar notes the extensive list of other products and commodities, pointing to the coexistence of complex and diverse practices of production and consumption. She observes:

> All in all, by the time of the Mauryan empire (322–185 BC), there was in place in South Asia a series of agricultural systems, each with a range of crops and its own water supply methods; clothing comprising cotton, linen and silk textiles with the use of indigo (and other) dyes; horticulture including the tending of mango orchards; a varied diet with, for the rich, venison and the meat of peacocks; developed bead, shell and glass industries; a metallurgy that comprised not only iron but also the mining and production of zinc and brass, its alloy with copper, plus silver and lead mining and a resultant metallurgy for the striking of coins.[4]

Within the spatial framework of the *mahājanapadas*, which consisted of overlapping and intersecting frontiers rather than firmly entrenched boundaries, the chronology of the Buddha has been thrown into some disarray. While there was a scholarly consensus locating the Buddha in the sixth century BCE, this has been seriously challenged by Bechert, who argues for a somewhat later date.[5] In any event, given the Maurya ruler Aśoka's close engagement with Buddhism, the Buddha can safely and securely be regarded as pre-Mauryan. Thus, we can work with the assumption that a discussion on society at the time of the Buddha may be located within a time frame of the sixth to the fourth centuries BCE.

By the mid-third century BCE, the distribution and contents of Aśokan inscriptions testify to a wider spatial network, focused on the capital, Pātaliputra (present-day Patna, in Bihar), and including provincial centers

[3] For the problems in dating the Northern Black Polished Ware, see Erdosy, "City States," 104.

[4] Shereen Ratnagar, *Makers and Shapers* (New Delhi: Tulika, 2007), xviii.

[5] Heinz Bechert, *When Did the Buddha Live?* (New Delhi: Sri Satguru, 1996).

such as Taxila in the northwest (present-day Punjab, Pakistan), Ujjain in central India (present-day Madhya Pradesh), Tosali on the eastern coast in present-day Orissa, and Suvarnagiri in Karnataka.[6] It is within this broad spatial and chronological context, at once diverse and connected, that we can locate attempts to codify a range of practices developed within Buddhism and other contemporary traditions.

Traditions of Codification

The Buddhist creation of laws within the early textual tradition was part of a general tendency to codify and systematize a wide range of knowledge during this period. One example is provided by the famous Sanskrit grammar, attributed to Pāṇini, composed circa fifth to fourth centuries BCE in the northwestern part of the subcontinent. This text laid down rules of grammar that were cited, commented on, and continue to be used extensively by Sanskrit scholars.

Other codifications are apparent in the compilation of Brahmanical literature – the *sūtras* – which included codes on major rituals (*Śrautasūtras*), domestic rituals (*Gṛhyasūtras*), texts codifying geometrical principles used for building the sacrificial altar (*Sulbasūtras*), and social norms (*Dharmasūtras*). The last named come closest to our understanding of legal texts and have frequently been translated and interpreted as such by modern scholars. Among other things, their authors attempted to regulate social intercourse, providing for both punishments – including fines and corporal punishments – as well as penances for violations of norms.

Many of these texts were later designated as *śāstras,* a category at once amorphous and multivalent. This classification represented a claim to authority that would have been particularly important in situations of sociopolitical and economic heterogeneity. It was also part of an attempt to monopolize the power of creating and enforcing definitions, and of standardizing ritual, social, political, and cultural/aesthetic practices. As Pollock observes:

(1) *śāstra* could be viewed as offering a real blueprint for practice; (2) as merely describing, *ex post facto*, a cultural product and thereby explicating its components for the benefit of a cultivated public; (3) as providing, in the guise of normative injunctions, something like a standard of taste and judgment to critics, that is, as defining, the

6 Allchin, *Archaeology Historic South Asia*, 198.

> 'classic'; (4) even as functioning in some cases to 'invent' a tradition; (5) as constituting, in the hegemonic manner of high cultures elsewhere, practices as 'sciences' for theoretical or actual control; (6) or – last in order but perhaps first in importance – as endowing a practice with status, legitimacy, and authority directly conferred by any 'Vedic' charter, something most *śāstras* aspire to become.[7]

It is in this context that an exploration of the content and form of early sūtras and śāstras, and their relationship with early Buddhist ideas on law, acquires significance.

The early Dharmasūtras, composed in Sanskrit, are almost invariably in prose and didactic. This is in marked contrast to the dialogic mode employed in early Buddhist texts, as well as, to a lesser extent, in the later Dharmaśāstras. Some of the earliest instances of such dialogues occur in the early Buddhist Pāli canonical texts, as well as in the more or less contemporary *Upaniṣads* within the Brahmanical tradition. The dialogic format may have been a communicative device for drawing in the listener, who would have had the sense of eavesdropping on an ongoing conversation. It may also have created a sense of space, allowing for the logical development of a clinching argument as opposed to the imposition of a diktat. Besides, it may have served to convey a sense of authenticity in a milieu where the spoken word that was heard was often valued more than the written document – as, for instance, exemplified in the notion of the *śruti* used to designate Vedic compositions. In a sense, the use of the dialogue as a marker of authority ties in with questions of defining, interrogating, and redefining the concept of *dharma*. In this context Olivelle states:

> I want to propose the hypothesis that the authors of early Dharmaśāstras were working both within the model provided by the Buddhist texts and in response to the Buddhist appropriation of *dharma*. The Buddhist theory of *dharmapramāṇa,* that is, the way one knows whether a particular oral text is authoritative, is articulated in the doctrine of *buddhavacana* ('Buddha's word'). Either proximately or ultimately all pronouncements on *dharma* must go back to the words of the Buddha himself for those pronouncements to have any authority or validity. This conviction is encapsulated in the opening words of every Buddhist text: *evaṃ mayā śrutam* (Pāli: *evam me sutaṃ*); 'Thus have I heard.'[8]

[7] Sheldon Pollock, cited in Patrick Olivelle, *Manu's Code of Law: A Critical Edition and Translation of the Mānava-Dharmaśāstra* (New Delhi: Oxford University Press, 2005), 63.

[8] Patrick Olivelle, "Exploration in the Early History of the Dharmaśāstra," in Patrick Olivelle (ed.), *Between the Empires: Society in India 300 BCE to 400 CE* (Oxford: Oxford University Press, 2006), 177.

Olivelle also draws attention to the dialogue between Buddhism and Brahmanism, suggesting that:

> . . . once *dharma* had become a central concept in the religious discourse of Buddhism, and once it had penetrated the general vocabulary of ethics, especially through its adoption by the Maurya emperors, certainly by Aśoka and possibly also his predecessors, in developing an imperial theology, Brahmanical theologians had little option but to define their own religion, ethic and way of life in terms of *dharma*.[9]

As Olivelle points out, the Brahmanical texts operate with a wide definition of dharma, including "all aspects of proper individual and social behavior as demanded by one's social identity according to age, gender, caste, marital status, and order of life."[10]

The texts deal with rites of passage, the ritualization of daily life, and lay down the ideal social order, including the king's duties in terms of the administration of justice, even as they provide for penances.[11] While some of these clearly overlap with the concerns of early Buddhist texts, there are also marked differences.

Olivelle points out that while the Brahmanical texts explicitly recognize the Vedas as the source of dharma, they also acknowledge the existence of customary practices that were not textualized. These include *deśadharma,* practices specific to regions, *jātidharma* or those of distinct communities, and *kuladharma,* those of distinct lineages or families.[12] Moreover, some texts, such as the *Āpastamba Dharmasūtra* recognized women and *śudras* as sources of authority, even as their knowledge was expected to supplement that of the Vedas.[13] This is significant because both women and *śudras* were conventionally denied access to Vedic learning. There were other variations as well – *dharma* was recognized as context specific, dependent on the age (*yuga*) in which one lived, and as derived from the practices of the *śiṣṭas,* those recognized as ideal men, worthy of emulation.[14]

While a detailed comparison between Buddhist and Brahmanical "laws" is beyond our present purview, I will flag some areas where such an exercise may be fruitful. These include prescriptions pertaining to initiation into Vedic learning and the rules prescribed for the student in the Dharmasūtras, which can be compared with the provisions for initiation and probation within the early Buddhist tradition. This would facilitate an

[9] *Ibid.*, 171.

[10] Patrick Olivelle, *Dharmasūtras: The Law Codes of Ancient India* (Oxford: Oxford University Press, 1999), xxi.

[11] *Ibid.* [12] *Ibid.*, xxxix. [13] *Ibid.*, xl. [14] *Ibid.*, xli.

understanding of both traditions as well as their dialogic relationship. In addition, the Brahmanical texts were preoccupied with violations of sexual norms, different kinds of assault, and regulating access to property, even as these "rights" were defined in terms of the varṇa hierarchy.[15] These concerns would again find resonances within the Buddhist tradition, in terms of regulating both relations between the laity and renouncers, as well as internal relations within the saṅgha.

Interestingly, Brahmanical texts prescribed penances for several of these offences.[16] At the same time, there were provisions, which were elaborated in the more or less contemporary *Arthaśāstra* and the later *Mānavadharmaśāstra*, for the enforcement of punishments by the king. If we turn to the *Āpastamba Dharmasūtra,* there is a preoccupation with punishing violations of sexual norms, as well as with the protection of property.[17]

Patton has convincingly argued that the strategies of listing adopted in the *Arthaśāstra* resonate with those developed within the Vedic tradition.[18] This indicates that the relationship between the sacred and the secular was less polarized than we tend to assume, and that the author(s) of the *Arthaśāstra* perhaps deliberately adopted strategies of communication developed within the Brahmanical tradition and adapted these to lend a sacral aura to the realm of the king.

Even though the dating of the *Arthaśāstra* remains a vexed issue, we may note that it recognizes four sources of authority: the complex of philosophical traditions, the three Vedas, works on economy, and polity.[19] The text recognizes the judicial role of the ruler as the wielder of *daṇḍa*, or the rod symbolic of authority, as crucial. If the injudicious use of the rod, we are told, angers the proto-ascetics settled in the forest and wandering ascetics, which would have included Buddhist monks, then how much more so the householders?[20] An entire section of the text is devoted to the judicial process, including the criteria for selecting judges and witnesses, documentation, and delineating areas for judicial intervention, such as marriage, inheritance, property, debts, deposits, slavery, sale, and various kinds of injury.[21] In other words, the text attests to the development of a complex understanding of the judicial process in terms of institutional mechanisms as well as content of proceedings, and the need to standardize

[15] *Ibid.*, 56–57. [16] *Ibid.*, 34–39. [17] *Ibid.*, 70–72.

[18] Laurie L. Patton, "Speech Act and King's Edicts: Vedic Words and Rulership in Taxonomical Perspective," *History of Religions*, 34 (1995), 329–50.

[19] *Arthaśāstra*, I.2.1. [20] *Ibid.*, I.4.12. [21] *Ibid.*, Book III.

these. It is also interesting to consider the Aśokan inscriptions, including the well-known schism edicts,[22] which suggest that the king could and did intervene in the affairs of the saṅgha, advocating expulsion for dissenters.

Agricultural Intensification

Let us now return to the spatio-temporal framework during the life of the Buddha as outlined earlier. The *majjhimadesa* is marked by heavy monsoon rains, which decrease as one moves westward.[23] Because of this, and the perennial rivers including the Ganga and its major tributaries, vegetation tends to be dense, thinning out toward the west.

This period and region is characterized by the intensification of agriculture, particularly rice cultivation. The transplantation of paddy was both productive and extremely labor intensive, requiring the use of *dāsa-kammakāras*, literally slaves and workers, mentioned both in early Buddhist texts and Aśokan inscriptions.[24] Wealthy landowners depended on the labor provided by these servile groups for cultivating their vast land holdings.

Apart from labor, there are two issues that have been considered significant for agriculture. One is the use of iron tools – including the iron-tipped ploughshare used to turn the heavy alluvial soils of the mid-Ganga Valley, the axe, used to clear the relatively dense vegetation of the eastern Ganga Valley, and the sickle, for harvesting.[25] This position has been critiqued and qualified by scholars such as Ratnagar, who are wary of an overtly technologically deterministic analysis.[26] She has drawn attention to the need to be sensitive to the varied contexts within which iron technology was discovered, and its many uses. At present, it is evident that while the neat equation between iron equipment and intensive agriculture requires testing in specific contexts, the possibility of a connection cannot be altogether overruled.

The second issue, highlighted by scholars such as Sharma, relates to the changing significance of cattle wealth.[27] Sharma argues that in an agro-pastoral society, the ritual sacrifice of animals, as enjoined in the Vedas, would not have posed a serious problem in terms of depleting productive

[22] For example, at E. Hultzsch (ed.), *Corpus Inscriptionum Indicarum*, 7 Vols. (Delhi: Indological Book House, 1968), vol. I, 160.

[23] Ram Sharan Sharma, *Material Culture and Social Formations in Ancient India* (New Delhi: Macmillan, 1983), 89.

[24] *Ibid.*, 96. [25] *Ibid.*, 118. [26] Ratnagar, *Makers and Shapers*, 184–87.

[27] Sharma, *Material Culture*, 118.

resources. However, in a situation where cattle were increasingly valued for purposes of traction, whether for plowing or for the bullock cart, it was likely that animal sacrifices may have seemed counter-productive. In any case, they were condemned within both Buddhism and Jainism. Again, it is likely that the opposition to animal sacrifices was made on more than such functionalist or instrumentalist grounds. Nonetheless, one of the features that distinguished early Buddhism (and Jainism) from later Vedic precepts was an explicit condemnation of animal sacrifices.

Sharma also draws attention to the vivid use of imagery in Buddhist texts drawn from the practices of the *gahapati* (householder) engaged in agriculture.[28] The *gahapati* was expected to prepare the soil, plant seedlings, irrigate the land, drain out excess water, reap, harvest, thresh the stalks, and winnow the grain in order to obtain rice. Clearly, early Buddhist monks were familiar with this busy world of the agriculturalist.

The *Aggañña Sutta* of the *Dīgha Nikāya* contains an interesting discussion on how kingship originated in order to resolve disputes pertaining to rice fields.[29] Although not literally true, it is evident that a specific form of agriculture and state formation were visualized as related developments. The king mediated disputes, and thus was located above the rest of the population. The conceptualization of disputes as originating from agricultural practices suggests how significant these were, and how rice cultivation was viewed as being virtually synonymous with subsistence.[30]

The rural population was obviously differentiated – slaves and hired laborers were at the bottom of the hierarchy, but there were also small and large peasants, and kings who claimed access to a range of resources. Both early Buddhist and Brahmanical texts justified the *bhaga* (literally share, often specified as the *sad-bhaga* or one-sixth[31]), a standard term for regular taxes as remuneration for services, especially protection, rendered by the king. Even though the king was occasionally viewed as the owner of all his territory, and thus the legitimate claimant of payments in the form of rent, the notion of wages persisted and was reiterated fairly often.

Both Buddhist and Brahmanical texts also acknowledged practices such as the gifting of land, and its sale and purchase, thereby indicating a developed notion of property in at least some kinds of land, including groves and arable tracts. However, other natural resources, such as forests, were claimed collectively or regarded as the property of the state. Allchin

[28] *Ibid.*, 120–21. [29] Singh, *History Ancient India*, 276.
[30] See, for instance, Sharma, *Material Culture*, 127.
[31] For instance, *Arthaśāstra*, II.15.3.

draws on the *Arthaśāstra* to argue that the state may have also adopted a policy of active intervention to extend agriculture.[32] If true, the state was one of the agencies involved in the extension and intensification of agriculture.

Towns and Trade

Buddhist texts describe a set of six great cities (*mahānagaras*): Campā, Rājagṛha, Śrāvastī, Sāketa, Kauśāmbī, and Vārāṇasī.[33] The first three were recognized as the capitals of the *mahājanapada* states of Aṅga, Magadha, and Kośala, and the fifth as that of Vatsa.[34] Explorations and excavations at these sites have yielded evidence, albeit not always securely dated, of significant architectural features. These include traces of fortification walls at Rājagṛha (present-day Rajgir), Kauśāmbī (near present-day Allahabad), and Pātaliputra.[35] While the walls at Rājagṛha were of undressed stone, those at Kauśāmbī were of brick, and the remains at Pātaliputra suggest the extensive use of timber. The walls also point to the mobilization of labor and resources and indicate the existence of political authorities involved in the process. In part, their function may have been defensive; it is also likely that they symbolized the power of the kings who oversaw their construction. In other words, they indicate a complex, hierarchically ordered society. Other elements indicate the building of networks of communication and contact, evident in the location of cities. Pātaliputra, for instance, was situated on the banks of the Ganga River, near its confluence with the Son and fairly close to the Gandak and the Gogra.[36] Thus, it was ideally located in terms of riverine communication. Not surprisingly, it emerged as the capital of the first large empire in the subcontinent. Cities such as Taxila in the northwest, famed in early Buddhist tradition as a site of learning, have also been excavated. The city functioned as a provincial capital of the Mauryas, and was subsequently a major Indo-Greek settlement. Like Pātaliputra, it occupied a nodal point on routes of communication, the northern path or the *uttarāpatha* that ran all the way to the Bay of Bengal after traversing through the major settlements that dotted the Ganga Valley. Some of these cities play a role in early Buddhist traditions. Rājagṛha, for instance, was recognized as the site of the first Buddhist council, whereas Vaiśālī, the capital of the Vajji saṃgha, was the venue of the second, and Pātaliputra was

[32] Allchin, *Archaeology Historic South Asia*, 192–93.
[33] Singh, *History Ancient India*, 279. [34] Sharma, *Material Culture*, 106.
[35] Allchin, *Archaeology Historic South Asia*, 111. [36] Singh, *History Ancient India*, 273.

regarded as the site of the third.[37] Others, such as Śrāvastī and Kauśāmbī, both in present-day Uttar Pradesh, have yielded archeological evidence of Buddhist monasteries. Despite being later structures, they are indicative of the close links between Buddhism and early urban centers. As Sharma points out, cities often functioned as "administrative/commercial/craft/or religious centres."[38]

Ratnagar draws attention to certain distinctive features of urban architecture that point to the work of specialists, especially carpenters and masons.[39] These include the use of materials like timber, mud brick, and baked brick for construction. Moreover, some of the equipment used by carpenters, such as the iron nails to hold tiles in place for sloping roofs, underscores the importance of the blacksmith. Additionally, unique waste disposal systems were devised, consisting of jars or rings made out of pottery, carefully inserted into wells dug within residential and other spaces. Ratnagar also focuses on transport technologies – the bullock cart, used to transport bulk commodities, and the chariot, the vehicle of the elite.[40] Making these vehicles required close cooperation between carpenters and smiths. It is obvious that urban life depended not simply on the kings and merchants who dominated social life, but on a range of service providers who made urban existence possible. None of these crafts could have been practiced within a self-contained domestic setting.

There is evidence for links with the Achaemenid (c. sixth through fifth centuries BCE) and subsequently with Macedonian (c. fourth century BCE) and Seleucid (c. fourth through third centuries BCE) polities through the northwestern part of the subcontinent. Scholars have suggested that the Achaemenid model of rulership may have influenced Mauryan practices.[41] One domain where this is most clearly demonstrated is in the use of the Kharoṣṭhī script, derived from Aramaic,[42] in the northwestern part of the subcontinent. The link between writing and urbanism has been discussed extensively in the context of early civilizations. In the early historic context in the subcontinent, the major earliest surviving examples of writing are provided by the Aśokan/Mauryan inscriptions, found from Afghanistan in the northwest to present-day Bangladesh in the east, and from sites along the Ganga Valley as well as in the Deccan, with a major cluster in Karnataka. While most of the inscriptions are in Brāhmi – the script from which many of those in use in the subcontinent at present evolved – those

[37] Sharma, *Material Culture*, 117. [38] *Ibid.*, 94.
[39] Ratnagar, *Makers and Shapers*, 74, 78, 87, and 92. [40] *Ibid.*, 129–40.
[41] Allchin, *Archaeology Historic South Asia*, 238. [42] *Ibid.*, 212.

in the northwest are in Kharoṣṭhī, Aramaic, and Greek. As Allchin observes, it is likely that these official documents had their predecessors in secular writing, probably used by merchants.[43] The *Arthaśāstra* also contains a section discussing the uses of writing.[44] While the dating of the text remains uncertain, it is obvious that the use of writing to document complex economic and political transactions was significant for the development of legal procedures.

Political Relations

Both Buddhist and Jain works contain narratives about conflict among the sixteen *mahājanapadas.*[45] Present-day historians have tended to explain these conflicts in terms of access to resources – such as fertile land, mineral wealth, forest produce, and elephants, which were highly valued as a part of the military entourage of rulers – and in terms of control over riverine and land routes of communication. However, early Buddhist narratives suggest that conflicts also arose because of contestations related to status. For instance, the conflict between the Śākyas, the gaṇa or saṅgha to which the Buddha belonged, and the Kośalans, who were governed by kings, stemmed from a dispute over a marital alliance. The king of the Kośalans had demanded the hand of a Śākya woman. The proud Śākyans, however, passed off a slave woman instead. When the son of the Kośalan king discovered this ruse, he exacted revenge on the Śākyans.[46]

Buddhist texts provide insights into the internal functioning of the saṅghas.[47] There were to be frequent meetings, unanimity, an upholding of established traditions, respect for elders and women, and for religious traditions and institutions in the ideal saṅgha. These strengths of the ideal saṅgha were recognized in other texts such as the *Arthaśāstra.* Within the saṅgha, kṣatriya (Pāli, *khattiya*) warrior nobles evidently exercised power collectively.[48] Yet, these were by no means egalitarian societies; as Chakravarti demonstrates, the *kṣatriyas* dominated the *non-kṣatriya* population, which included a range of laborers and producers.[49]

The rulers of *mahājanapadas* evidently shared certain common concerns, as noted by Erdosy.[50] These included claiming power on the basis of birth, providing leadership in warfare, procuring booty, affording a modicum of protection to their acknowledged dependents, and enforcing norms

43 *Ibid.*, 210–11. 44 *Arthaśāstra*, II.10. 45 Singh, *History Ancient India*, 260–69.
46 *Ibid.*, 266. 47 *Ibid.*, 268. 48 Chakravarti, *Social Dimensions*, 12. 49 *Ibid.*, 15.
50 Erdosy, "City States," 116.

or dharma. Chakravarti draws attention to the ways in which kingship was conceptualized within early Buddhist textual traditions, focusing on origin myths, and the seven jewels (symbols) of kingship, which are the wheel (*cakra*), the elephant, the horse, the gem (*maṇi*), the female, the householder, and the advisor.[51] Scholars such as Allchin argue that the *Arthaśāstra*, which conceptualized the state as consisting of a different set of seven elements, provides us with insights into the nature of the state in the fourth century BCE.[52]

A Changing Social Scenario

According to the Brahmanical tradition, as codified in the Dharmasūtras, occupations were determined by birth in a particular caste or varṇa. Thus, the priest or the *brāhmaṇa* was expected to study and teach the sacred texts, the Vedas, prepare and perform sacrifices, and give and receive gifts. Three of these activities – studying the Vedas, performing sacrifices, and offering gifts – were technically open to men of the second and third varṇa as well. However, they also had specific "duties." These included – for the kṣatriya or warrior, who was ranked second – participating in warfare, administering justice, and protecting people. The third varṇa, the vaiśya, were to earn their livelihood through agriculture, pastoralism, and trade, with money lending also occasionally mentioned. Finally, the fourth varṇa, the śūdra, were ideally expected to serve the three preceding categories. The division of labor thus envisaged was by no means watertight. It is evident from later and post-Vedic texts that kṣatriya claimed knowledge of the ultimate reality, the *ātman* or *brahman,* thus "encroaching" on the preserve of the *brāhmaṇas.*[53]

Buddhist texts recognize social stratification, although on different principles, thereby dividing occupations into high and low prestige. Moreover, Buddhist narratives attest to a wide range of professionals – from those who participated in the administration, manning various levels of an increasingly complex bureaucracy, to those involved in the militia and standing armies of the more powerful *mahājanapadas.* Other professionals included doctors and scribes, and an array of entertainers, ranging from courtesans, who often epitomized urban culture, to acrobats, musicians, and those who

[51] Chakravarti, *Social Dimensions*, 151–76.

[52] Allchin, *Archaeology Historic South Asia*, 190–91. The seven are the king, the minister, the people and land, the fort, the treasury, the ally and the *danda*, which literally means 'stick', encompassing notions of coercion and justice.

[53] Sharma, *Material Culture*, 81.

were skilled in handling a variety of animals, birds, snakes, and so forth. Also mentioned are several craft specialists – weavers, potters, smiths – whose presence is attested to in the archeological record as well. Thus, the texts convey the sense of a vibrant social world.

Buddhist texts mention two particularly significant social categories: the *gahapati* and the *seṭṭhi*. The *gahapati* was literally the male head of the household. Although the term was used in earlier Sanskrit texts, such as the *Ṛgveda*, Buddhist Pāli literature redefined it in significant ways, as pointed out by Chakravarti.[54] She notes that it was used to indicate a wealthy landowner, as well as peasants. The association with land and prosperity was a defining element of the successful *gahapati*. Significantly, in Buddhist representations of the social order, the *gahapati* was, more often than not, grouped with the kṣatriya and brāhmaṇa, indicating that he was considered both respectable and powerful. This category was represented as constituting "the backbone of the lay following of the Buddha."[55] Chakravarti rightly cautions against attempts to reduce the *gahapati* to the vaiśya mentioned in Brahmanical sources. She argues that it is important to recognize that alternative modes of constituting and representing social identities were available and created by those who participated in this changing social world, and that the search for equivalences between Brahmanical and Buddhist representations often misses the complexities of these processes. This precaution also applies equally to the other category, the *seṭṭhi*. Often translated as banker or treasurer, the *seṭṭhi* was clearly a wealthy merchant, sometimes functioning as an advisor to the king. This position was attained and retained on account of wealth, more often than not acquired through commercial success. As in the case of the *gahapati*, it is best not to assimilate this to the category of the vaiśya. In post-Mauryan inscriptions, both the terms, *seṭṭhi* and *gahapati* were adopted as markers of identity by donors making gifts to Buddhist institutions.

Also significant, and often appearing as a compound word, were the *samaṇa-brāhmaṇa*. The former signified a diverse range of renunciatory orders, including, but not confined to, Buddhism, while the latter stood for the Brahmanical priests, especially those who depended on gifts for their livelihood. As Chakravarti observes, the texts represent, among other things, a constant tension between producers and non-producers – those who depended on gifts and alms that were offered, more or less willingly, by the former.[56] At the other end of the social hierarchy, Buddhist texts

[54] Chakravarti, *Social Dimensions*, 65–93. [55] Sharma, *Material Culture*, 4.
[56] Chakravarti, *Social Dimensions*, 28.

mention the *dāsa, kammakāra* and *porisa*.[57] These terms, often translated as slaves, workers and men, designated a range of poor laborers, often engaged in agriculture. The texts also refer to the poor, the *dalidda,* drawing attention to sharp socioeconomic differences.[58]

Chakravarti also draws attention to sets of overlapping hierarchies recognized within the early Buddhist tradition.[59] These were defined in terms of *jāti* (birth), *kula* (family), *kamma* (work) and *sippa* (craft), each of which encompassed categories of high and low prestige. While the details need not detain us, the complexity of classificatory categories is remarkable. Another category often deployed was that of the *ārya.* Within the Brahmanical tradition, the term was generally used to refer to a member of the first three varṇas. Within Buddhist texts, we find it being used to designate the true, genuine, or noble – as in the conceptualization of the four noble truths, which formed the core of early Buddhist doctrine.

While recognizing, if not valorizing, a differentiated social order, early Buddhist texts contain arguments in favor of mitigating conflict and tension, advocating that kings help pastoralists, agriculturalists, workers, and merchants, and that others treat their parents and dependents with respect and care.[60] In fact, charity was valorized as a substitute for the sacrifice within Buddhist tradition.[61] Sharma points out how these provisions mitigated the harshness of social differentiation, but did not overturn it.[62]

Contexts in Conclusion

Finally, we suggest that early Buddhist attempts to generate laws can be contextualized in a variety of ways. On the one hand, there was a situation of increasing socioeconomic differentiation, related to a complex agrarian formation and a world within which towns and trade were acquiring significance. Regulating social interaction in such a situation would have generated pressures to develop legal mechanisms, among other things. Also, as we have noted, there were new political institutions, where, once again, rulers both claimed and were expected to assume judicial roles. Clearly, there would have been models that were available to members within the saṅgha. We can then visualize a situation of dialogue, competition, and conflict, within which issues that were regarded as subjects of law were framed in a variety of ways.

57 *Ibid.*, 26. 58 *Ibid.*, 27. 59 *Ibid.*, 101.
60 Sharma, *Material Culture*, 109–10, 128.
61 *Ibid.*, 121. 62 *Ibid.*, 129.

CHAPTER 2

What the Vinayas *Can Tell Us about Law*

*Petra Kieffer-Pülz**

"Whatever Dhamma and Vinaya has been taught, made known by me to you, Ānanda, will, with my passing, be your Teacher."[1]

Introduction

When the Buddha entered Nirvāṇa, he is said to have left his adherents with what he had taught, that is, with *dharma* (Pāli *dhamma*[2]) and *Vinaya*. No central body headed the Buddhist community. As the highest legal authority, the Buddhist monastic legal code, *Vinaya,* served as a guide for the daily life of monastics of the Buddhist community (*saṅgha*): Buddhist monks[3] and nuns[4] and, to a lesser degree, male and female novices[5] as well as female probationers.[6] The *Vinaya* forms the first part of the Buddhist canon, the so-called *tripiṭaka*[7] – the authoritative Buddhist writings believed to be the "Word of the Buddha." It contains the rules and regulations that govern the life of monastics both as individuals and as a community. Unlike the discourses, *sūtra,* which are directed toward lay people and ordained alike, the *Vinaya* is an internal document meant for monastics.[8] Since the community of the Buddhists split into two branches – Mahāsāṃghikas and Sthaviravādins, which subsequently split into further schools, all transmitting the word of the Buddha – we have not one, but several canons and,

* I thank Shayne Clarke for his valuable suggestions to an earlier version of this article, and the editors of the present volume for their suggested rearrangements and improvements.

1 T.W. Rhys Davids and J.E. Carpenter (eds.), *Dīghanikāya* vol. 2 (Oxford: Pali Text Society, 1903), 154, 156–58.

2 Hereafter in this text, Sanskrit will generally be used in the text and Pāli translations in the footnotes, except where the description is solely based on the *Theravāda-vinaya,* in which case the Pāli terms are used in the text.

3 Sanskrit *bhikṣu*; Pāli *bhikkhu.*

4 Sanskrit *bhikṣuṇī*; Pāli *bhikkhunī.*

5 Sanskrit *śrāmaṇera, śrāmaṇerī*; Pāli *sāmaṇera, sāmaṇerī.*

6 Sanskrit *śikṣamāṇā*; Pāli *sikkhamānā.*

7 Pāli *tipiṭaka.*

8 Shayne Clarke, "Family Matters in Indian Buddhist Monasticism," unpublished Ph.D. dissertation, University of California, Los Angeles (2006), Introduction, 2.

consequently, several *Vinayas*. The *Vinayas* are not systematically planned and arranged law books. Rather, they are based on case law. They constitute one of the oldest self-contained legal systems, of which the Buddha is thought to be the lawgiver. Unlike the primarily prescriptive Brahmanical law codes, the *Vinayas* contain narrative portions, commentaries, and casuistries, albeit to different degrees. These additional portions shed some light on the historical realities of the religious communities in which they were authored and subsequently redacted.[9]

In this essay we first sketch the origin and development of the *Vinayas*, their composition and dating, and discuss what the *Vinayas* can tell us about law. We then proceed with an overview of the major legal principles underlying monastic law, followed by a depiction of the role of the king, and the intersections of monastic and secular law. The subsequent section will address local monastic ordinances as complements to the *Vinayas*, followed by a consideration of the ambiguities arising from certain interpretations of the *Vinayas*.

The Origin and Development of the *Vinayas*

The *Vinayas*, as anonymous literature, were handed down orally for centuries by reciters, *bhāṇaka*,[10] before being written down and commented on. Their origin lies in the common fundamental rules of ascetic groups in the Buddha's time, prohibiting things such as killing, sexual intercourse, stealing, and lying. Questions of property were also of central importance, since those who entered the Buddhist community, saṅgha, as monastics neither had to give up their property nor take a vow of poverty. Furthermore, the saṅgha owned real estate, cattle, and slaves. With the growth and spread of the Buddhist community and a shift from wandering mendicancy to settled monasticism, the number of new requirements, prescriptions, and regulations increased. Before the texts were redactionally fixed by being written down or receiving commentary, new prescriptions could be added to the *Vinayas*; similarly, old ones could be deleted.

The several *Vinayas* transmitted by various Buddhist schools in different areas of Asia share a common core.[11] Scholars generally conclude

9 *Ibid.*, Introduction, n143.

10 There are no reciters for the whole *Vinaya*, but reciters who memorized the first (*Prātimokṣa* and *Vibhaṅga*) and the second parts (*Khandhakas*).

11 This holds true especially for the *Prātimokṣa* rules. For a comparative presentation, see W. Pachow, *A Comparative Study of the Prātimokṣa on the Basis of its Chinese, Tibetan, Sanskrit and Pali Versions* (Santiniketan: The Sino-Indian Cultural Society, 1955). For investigations regarding the common

that prescriptions preserved in all monastic legal codes were enacted at an early date, probably sometime after the demise of the Buddha. Although only three *Vinayas* are followed today, those of defunct schools have been handed down complete and in fragments in different languages: Sanskrit, Pāli, Gāndhārī, and Tocharian, as well as in Chinese and Tibetan translations. Six seemingly complete *Vinayas* belonging to the Dharmaguptakas, Mahāsāṃghikas, Mahīśāsakas, Mūlasarvāstivādins, Sarvāstivādins, and Theravādins are extant. Additionally, we have fragments of the *Vinayas* of the Haimavatas (ascription contested), Kāśyapīyas, Mahāsāṃghika-Lokottaravādins, Saṃmitīyas, and of several other unidentified schools.[12] Many of these schools are referred to in inscriptions, and in the reports of the Chinese pilgrims who visited India between the fifth and seventh centuries.[13] The *Vinayas* still in use today include the *Dharmaguptaka-vinaya* in East Asia, the *Mūlasarvāstivāda-vinaya* in Tibet and Mongolia (and it seems in some circles in Japan), and the *Theravāda-vinaya* in Sri Lanka, Burma, Thailand, and other countries. Those of the Theravādins and the Mūlasarvāstivādins have received the most scrutiny and study by scholars to date.

The Composition of the *Vinayas*

Common to all *Vinayas* are two large sections: the *Vibhaṅga*[14] and the *Skandhakas*.[15] The *Vinayas* usually begin with the *Vibhaṅga*.[16] It contains

core of the *Skandhaka* section, see Shayne Clarke, "*Vinaya Mātṛkā* – Mother of the Monastic Codes, or Just Another Set of Lists? A Response to Frauwallner's Handling of the Mahāsāṅghika *Vinaya*," *Indo-Iranian Journal*, 47 (2004), 77–120 (with reference to earlier literature).

12 Akira Yuyama, *Systematische Übersicht über die buddhistische Sanskrit-Literatur/A Systematic Survey of Buddhist Sanskrit Literature*, Part 1: *Vinaya-Texte* (Wiesbaden: Franz Steiner Verlag, 1979); Charles S. Prebish, *A Survey of Vinaya Literature* (London: Routledge, 1994); Thomas Oberlies, "Ein bibliographischer Überblick über die kanonischen Texte der Śrāvakayāna-Schulen des Buddhismus (ausgenommen der des Mahāvihāra-Theravāda)," *Wiener Zeitschrift für die Kunde Südasiens*, 47 (2003), 37–84; Clarke, "*Vinaya Mātṛkā*," 77f.; Nobuyuki Yamagiwa, "Vinaya Manuscripts: State of the Field," in Konrad Klaus and Jens-Uwe Hartmann (eds.), *Indica et Tibetica. Festschrift für Michael Hahn* (Wien: Arbeitskreis für Tibetische und Buddhistische Studien, 2007), 607–16; Ingo Strauch, *The Bajaur Collection: A New Collection of Kharoṣṭhī Manuscripts. – A Preliminary Catalogue and Survey* (Online version 1.1, May 2008), 22ff.

13 For the distribution of the different schools, see Petra Kieffer-Pülz, "Die buddhistische Gemeinde" in Heinz Bechert, Johannes Bronkhorst, Jacob Ensink, Jens-Uwe Hartmann, Petra Kieffer-Pülz, Hans-Joachim Klimkeit, Siegfried Lienhard, and Ian William Mabbett (eds.), *Der Buddhismus I. Der indische Buddhismus und seine Verzweigungen* (Stuttgart: Verlag W. Kohlhammer, 2000), 285ff.; Oskar von Hinüber, "The Pedestal Inscription of Śirika," *Annual Report of the International Research Institute for Advanced Buddhology at Soka University for the Academic Year 2007*, vol. 11 (2008), 34; Karl-Heinz Golzio, *Die Ausbreitung des Buddhismus in Süd- und Südostasien. Eine quantitative Untersuchung auf der Basis epigraphischer Quellen* (Frankfurt am Main: Peter Lang, 2010), 55ff.

14 Sanskrit *Vinayavibhaṅga*, Pāli *Suttavibhaṅga*. 15 Pāli *Khandhakas*.

16 One exception is the Tibetan version of the *Mūlasarvāstivāda-vinaya*, beginning with the *Vinayavastu* (i.e., the *Skandhaka* section).

the disciplinary law and has as its core the list of prescriptions, *Prātimokṣa,*[17] to be kept by the monastics of the Buddhist community, the *Bhikṣu-prātimokṣa* for monks and the *Bhikṣuṇī-prātimokṣa*[18] for nuns. The number of prescriptions varies among the schools. The Mahāsāṃghikas hand down 219 and 277 prescriptions for monks and nuns respectively, whereas the Mūlasarvāstivādins have approximately 262 and 371. All other schools fall within these limits.

The *Prātimokṣa* of the monks is divided into eight sections and that of the nuns into seven. Of these, the first seven (six for nuns) comprise prescriptions. The last section contains the seven legal procedures for settling disputes. The *Prātimokṣas* start with the gravest infractions and end with the lightest.[19] For infractions of the first category, *pārājika,* monks and nuns are expelled from the saṅgha, or, according to the Indian *Vinayas,*[20] may stay in the community, albeit with reduced rights.[21] Transgressions of the second class, *saṃghāvaśeṣa,*[22] require a meeting of, and investigation by, the saṅgha. Monks are given a six day and night probation in addition to, where applicable, a similar penalty for as long as they have concealed the offense. All other infractions can be removed by confession; some additionally require relinquishing the unlawfully obtained object.

In the *Vibhaṅgas*, individual *Prātimokṣa* rules are presented by an "introductory story"[23] giving details of the alleged incident that occasioned its establishment; the "prescription"[24] and, where rules are either tightened or slackened, one or several "secondary prescriptions,"[25] sometimes with further introductory stories, come next. These prescriptions are followed by a "word analysis"[26] in which each word of the prescription is explained, and then a "casuistry" (in some cases more than one) in which the severity of the infraction is determined depending on the intention and completion of an offense. For example, the legal opinions in this section distinguish a difference between touching and then moving an object with the intention of stealing it, and touching an object with the intention to steal it and then not actually moving the object. Following this section, there is

[17] Pāli *pātimokkha.* [18] Pāli *Bikkhu-* and *Bhikkhunī-Pātimokkha.*

[19] See also Oskar von Hinüber, *A Handbook of Pāli Literature* (Berlin: Walter de Gruyter, 1996), § 22ff.

[20] "Indian *Vinayas*" is used here for all *Vinayas* except the *Theravāda-vinaya,* also known as the *Pāli-vinaya,* a name given based on the language in which it is written. Although the *Theravāda-vinaya* originated in India as well, it was orally transmitted for a longer period in Sri Lanka, and hence faced influences different from the rest. All other *Vinayas* are differentiated according to their school affiliation.

[21] Shayne Clarke, "Monks Who Have Sex: *Pārājika* Penance in Indian Buddhist Monasticisms," *Journal of Indian Philosophy*, 37 (2009), 1–43. The *Theravāda-vinaya* does not know this status.

[22] Pāli *saṅghādisesa.* [23] Pāli *vatthu.* [24] Pāli *paññatti.* [25] Pāli *anupaññatti.*

[26] Pāli *padabhājaniya.*

a "list of exceptions."[27] For the first nine prescriptions, furthermore, the *Theravāda-vinaya* has supplements with additional cases.[28]

The second section, the *Skandhakas*,[29] deals with the procedures performed by the Buddhist community as a whole. Here the formulas, *Karmavācanā*,[30] to be recited in the legal procedures of the saṅgha are considered the oldest part. The *Prātimokṣas* and *Karmavācanās* were also handed down separately. Unlike the *Prātimokṣas* with their fixed number of rules, no authoritative or binding number and selection existed for the *Karmavācanā* collections.

The supplements to the *Vinayas* vary considerably. The *Theravāda-vinaya* has as a third part, the *Parivāra*, which was probably compiled in Sri Lanka in the first century BCE or CE.[31] This appendix, which discusses mere legal issues, casually refers to matters not dealt with explicitly in other parts of this *Vinaya*.[32] The *Mūlasarvāstivāda-vinaya* contains an additional part, the *Uttaragranthas*.[33] They often present material earlier than that found in the *Skandhakas*, and are mostly taken as a base by the later commentarial tradition.[34] Little work has been done on these supplements, still less regarding those of the other Buddhist schools not mentioned in this connection.

The Dating of the *Vinayas*

The *Vinayas* belong to the class of anonymous literature. In constant use, memorized, and preserved orally for centuries, they suffered alterations, additions, and perhaps omissions. Therefore, it is not possible to give one date for a whole *Vinaya*. Once they were written down or commented on, the *Vinayas* reached a final stage – at least to some degree. Hence, we

27 Pāli *anāpattivāra*.

28 Pāli *vinītavatthu*. Whether other schools have similar sections needs further investigation.

29 Pāli *Khandhakas*. 30 Pāli *kammavācā*.

31 Von Hinüber, *Handbook*, § 40–42; K.R. Norman, *Pāli Literature including the Canonical Literature on Prakrit and Sanskrit of all the Hīnayāna Schools of Buddhism* (Wiesbaden: Harrassowitz, 1983), 26ff.

32 Petra Kieffer-Pülz, *Die Sīmā. Vorschriften zur Regelung der buddhistischen Gemeindegrenze in älteren buddhistischen Texten* (Berlin: Dietrich Reimer Verlag, 1992), 143ff.

33 For the two versions, see Shayne Clarke, "Guṇaprabha, Yijing, Bu sTon and the Lack of a Coherent System of Rules for Nuns in the Tibetan Tradition of the *Mūlasarvāstivāda-vinaya*," unpublished conference presentation (Buddhist Nuns in India, University of Toronto, April 15–17, 2011), 11.

34 For example, Guṇaprabha's *Vinayasūtra*. See Shayne Clarke, "Towards a Comparative Study of the *Sarvāstivāda-* and *Mūlasarvāstivāda-vinayas:* Studies in the Structure of the *Uttaragrantha* (1): *Kathāvastu* – A Preliminary Survey" (unpublished manuscript); Gregory Schopen, *Buddhist Monks and Business Matters: Still More Papers on Monastic Buddhism in India* (Honolulu: University of Hawai'i Press, 2004), 124ff.

have to reckon with various chronologically different textual layers in each of the *Vinayas*. The time frame for their origination is delimited by the dates of their translations into Chinese and Tibetan, which form the *termini ante quem*. Thus, the *Vinayas* of the Dharmaguptakas, Mahīśāsakas, Mahāsāṃghikas, and Sarvāstivādins were translated into Chinese in the first decades of the fifth century CE; that of the Mūlasarvāstivādins were translated into Chinese in the beginning of the eighth century and into Tibetan in the end of the eighth and beginning of the ninth centuries CE. The *Theravāda-vinaya*, according to the Sri Lankan chronicle *Mahāvaṃsa*,[35] was committed to writing and commentaries on it were produced in the first century BCE, thus probably predating the redactional closure of the other *Vinayas*.

Within the time frame thus delimited, only the analysis of the texts will allow us to identify earlier and later textual layers. Content changes and linguistic considerations are essential in this context. Within the *Theravāda-vinaya*, several chronological layers have been determined by the following observations: several versions of one *Prātimokṣa* prescription;[36] discrepancies between the *Prātimokṣa* prescriptions and the corresponding "introductory stories," casuistries, and so forth;[37] diverse ordination formulas;[38] deviating descriptions of one ceremony (e.g., the *kaṭhina* ceremony);[39] and the innovation of the legal terminology.[40]

Within the same school, more than one version of its *Vinaya* (in the case of the Mūlasarvāstivādins), its *Prātimokṣa* or its *Karmavācanā* collection could exist. In the case of the *Prātimokṣa* and the *Karmavācanās*, this probably was an effect of their additional external transmissions. A comparison of such versions clearly shows developments within one school. The Central Asian manuscript tradition of the *Sarvāstivāda-prātimokṣa* may serve as an example here. Traces of at least three chronologically and perhaps

35 *Mahāvaṃsa* 33.100.

36 H. Oldenberg (ed.), *Vinayapiṭaka*, 5 Vols. (London: Pali Text Society, 1879–1883), IV 71, 18–74, 27.

37 Dieter Schlingloff, "Zur Interpretation des Prātimokṣasūtra," *Zeitschrift der Deutschen Morgenländischen Gesellschaft*, 113 (1963), 536–51.

38 *Vinaya* I 56, 10–32; 57, 9–25; 95, 16–34. See also Oskar von Hinüber, "Sprachliche Beobachtungen zum Aufbau des Pāli-Kanons," *Studien zur Indologie und Iranistik*, 2 (1976), 27–40, 32. English translation in *Selected Papers on Pāli Studies* (Oxford: Pali Text Society, 1994), 62–75; Kieffer-Pülz, *Sīmā*, 46–52; Jin-il Chung and Petra Kieffer-Pülz, "The *Karmavācanās* for the Determination of *sīmā* and *ticīvareṇa avippavāsa*," in Bhikkhu T. Dhammaratana and Bhikkhu Pāsādika (eds.), *Mélanges offerts au Vénérable Thích Huyên-Vi à l'occasion de son soixante-dixième anniversair* (Paris: Editions You-feng, 1997), 13–56.

39 *Vinaya* I 253–67; V 172–179. Heinz Bechert, "Some Remarks on the Kaṭhina Rite," *Journal of the Bihar Research Society*, 54 (1968), 319–29.

40 Kieffer-Pülz, *Sīmā*, 46–52.

regionally different versions are preserved: one predating the canonical version embedded in that school's Chinese *Vinaya* translation, one corresponding more or less to the canonical version, and a third representing a younger stage.[41] Another example is the two distinct *Bhikṣunī-prātimokṣas* of the Mūlasarvāstivādins.[42]

A comparison of the different *Vinayas* sheds further light on the relationship between these texts and their relative age. Thus, comparisons of the *Prātimokṣas* have shown that older words in the *Prātimokṣas* of the Mahāsāṃghikas and Theravādins are replaced by younger ones in those of the Sarvāstivādins and Mūlasarvāstivādins and that explanations preserved in the "word analysis" of one school slipped into the *Prātimokṣa* prescription of another (Mūlasarvāstivādins).[43] Moreover, locative or ablative rules in the *Prātimokṣa* of one school are replaced by younger formulations in another.

What the *Vinayas* Can Tell Us about Law

As the overview of the *Vinayas* made clear, it is important to specify which *Vinaya* we rely on and which textual layer within it. Basing claims on text portions forming a common core of all *Vinayas* increases the possibility of reaching a relatively early stage. Drawing information from younger textual layers may reveal deviations between various *Vinayas*, which are the result of regional influences, temporal modifications, and diverging degrees of developed secular law in their original environment. Since Buddhist communities depended on lay people's support for their subsistence, the redactors of their monastic codes had to adapt monastic law to the legal systems that governed the societies in which the Buddhist communities lived.[44] The *Mūlasarvāstivāda-vinaya*, which was redactionally closed in India probably around the fourth–fifth century CE[45] and "redacted by a

41 Georg von Simson, (ed.), *Prātimokṣasūtra der Sarvāstivādins*, 2 vols. (Göttingen: Vandenhoeck and Ruprecht, 2000), 2ff.

42 Clarke, "Guṇaprabha," 16.

43 Oskar von Hinüber, "Review to: Georg von Simson, Prātimokṣasūtra der Sarvāstivādins," *Orientalistische Literaturzeitung*, 98 (2003), 581ff.

44 Schopen, *Buddhist Monks*, 210.

45 According to Schopen (*Buddhist Monks*, 20ff.), the *Mūlasarvāstivāda-vinaya* contains much information corresponding to the time of the Kuṣāns. This, however, does not imply that the *Mūlasarvāstivāda-vinaya* was redactionally closed in the second century CE. As Claus Vogel has shown, the Mūlasarvāstivādins used "the novel lunisolar calendar gradually gaining ground in India from the fourth Century A.D. onwards" in their *Vinaya*. If this is true, then the *Mūlasarvāstivāda-vinaya* could not have been redactionally closed before the fourth and fifth century CE. Claus Vogel, "On the date of the Poṣadha Ceremony," in P. Kieffer-Pülz and Jens-Uwe Hartmann (eds.),

community deeply embedded in the larger Indian, brahmanical world,"[46] had to come to terms with an "established, competing system of nonecclesiastical law in the brahminical milieu."[47] The *Theravāda-vinaya* redacted in Sri Lanka, on the other hand, was shaped in an environment with little formal law and legal literature.[48] Therefore, monastic law was not delineated from secular law as it was in India, and thus there exist subjects discussed by the Mūlasarvāstivādins that the Theravādins never dealt with – for instance, loan contracts.

Vinayas sometimes also shed light on unexpected facets of secular law. Thus, we learn from the *Mahāsāṃghika-vinaya* that "divorce" was possible in certain regions, namely by selling one's wife – forbidden in *Manu's Law* book – or by divorce before the king's face.[49] A comparison of *Vinayas* with the civil laws of Buddhist states may also disclose influences of Buddhist monastic law on secular law. Two allusions may suffice here. The Theravādins developed a system of twenty-five kinds of theft in their fifth-century commentary on the *Vinaya*, the *Samantapāsādikā*,[50] and four variables of value in the fifth-century commentary on the *Prātimokṣa*, *Kaṅkhāvitaraṇī*. These are met with again in Burmese secular law books (*Dhammathats*), many of which were written by Buddhist monks.[51] Ian Harris has traced the "Cambodian border obsession" to the dominant influence of the concept of the Buddhist monastic boundary (*sīmā*).[52]

General Legal Principles Found in the *Vinayas*

Seven general legal principles underlie early Buddhist monastic law.

The first legal principle is no crime or penalty without a law (*nullum crimen, nulla poena sine lege*). According to this principle, the first person to effect a prescription is never liable to punishment, a fact mentioned in the *anāpatti* clause of each *Prātimokṣa* rule.

The second is the principle of inculpability: insanity or mental disorder protects one from punishment. There are several other causes for

Bauddhavidyāsudhākaraḥ. Studies in Honour of Heinz Bechert on the Occasion of His 65th Birthday (Swisttal-Odendorf: Indica-et-Tibetica-Verlag, 1997), 673–88.

46 Schopen, *Buddhist Monks*, 81. 47 *Ibid.*, 210.

48 Andrew Huxley, "Buddhism and Law – The View From Mandalay," *Journal of the International Association of Buddhist Studies*, 18 (1995), 42, 82; Schopen, *Buddhist Monks*, 186.

49 Clarke, *Family Matters*, chapter 2.3. 50 Sp I 302.

51 Huxley, "Buddhism and Law," 47–95; Petra Kieffer-Pülz, "The Law of Theft: Regulations in the Theravāda Vinaya and the Law Commentaries," *Journal of the Pali Text Society*, 31 (2012), § 3.2.

52 Ian Harris, "Rethinking Cambodian Political Discourse on Territory: Genealogy of the Buddhist Ritual Boundary (*sīmā*)," *Journal of Southeast Asian Studies*, 41 (2010), 215–39.

inculpability, some of which appear frequently (for example, illness), but none of them is as general as mental disorder;[53] this is also found in the *anāpatti* clause of each *Prātimokṣa* prescription.

The third principle is the differentiation between intentional and negligent acts. Intention is a central topic in Buddhist monastic law. Intention is so significant that the negligent commission of an intentional crime does not result in an offense, whereas the negligent or intentional commission of a negligent crime leads to an offense. If, for instance, a monk were to sit down on a child who happened to be lying on a chair but concealed by, say, a blanket or piece of cloth, and in so doing the monk kills the boy, no offense involving expulsion (*pārājika*) occurs, because homicide is an intentional delict, and intention is missing here. But if a monk drinks a glass of fruit juice, thinking it to be fruit juice, while the fruit juice has become alcoholic after being left in the sun for too long, he commits the offense of drinking alcohol because this is a negligent delict, and one becomes guilty of transgression with or without intention.

A fourth legal principle is the gradual differentiation of offenses, the central subject of the casuistries in the *Vibhaṅgas*. Because determination of the appropriate offense depends on whether all factors for a certain offense are in fact present, offenses may vary. In the case of theft, for example, one precondition for a *pārājika* offense is that the stolen goods have to be worth more than five *māsaka*. Now, if one steals an object worth less than five but more than one *māsaka,* the most serious possible offense is a "grave offense"; if it is less than one *māsaka,* the offense is simply one of "wrongdoing."

The fifth principle is the absorption of offenses. In the *Vinayas*, early signs of absorption are found in the category of the *yāvatatiyaka-saṅghādisesa* offenses (matters requiring a formal meeting of the Order, which are only completed with the third admonition). Infraction of these rules does not immediately lead to a *Saṅghādisesa* offense. Only after the completion of the recitation of the formula for admonishing does one incur a *Saṅghādisesa* offense. If the perpetrator resists when the motion is recited, an "offense of wrongdoing" arises; if he still resists when the first two resolutions are recited, "grave offenses" arise. But all these offenses are absorbed by the *Saṅghādisesa* offense, which occurs with the completion of the third resolution.[54] In Pāli commentarial literature from around the first century

[53] Hellmuth Hecker, "Allgemeine Rechtsgrundsätze in der buddhistischen Ordensverfassung (Vinaya)," *Verfassung und Recht in Übersee*, 10 (1977), 89–115.

[54] For example, *Vinaya* III 174, 9–12; Kieffer-Pülz, "Theft," § 4.

BCE onward, various systems of absorption are described and applied to the case of theft. There, other offenses commonly related to the perpetration of the main offense (theft), such as breaking into a house or damaging furniture, are treated according to some model of absorption, and not concurrently.[55] It remains to be investigated whether these younger forms of absorption are also described in other schools.

A sixth legal principle is the equality of all ordained members of a local community independent from the hierarchy of positions within a local saṅgha. Almost all aspects of the communal life, such as the allocation of seating, food, clothing, and so forth, were regulated according to one's position in the monastic hierarchy. However, seniority had no bearing on the value of a vote regarding formal procedures; all votes were of equal value. At least in the *Sarvāstivāda-* and *Mūlasarvāstivāda-vinayas*, however, there are examples showing that monks of great merit and virtues or the leader or elder of an assembly enjoyed the privilege of special immunity from prosecution, even for one of the most serious offenses in monastic legislation, namely *Saṃghāvaśeṣa*.[56] Here the principle of equality has obviously been given up, at least partly.

As a seventh legal principle, every decision of a local saṅgha had to be reached unanimously by consensus. In case of differences of opinion, the majority decision ruled.

The Role of the King

Religious communities, guilds, corporations, and other groups that also had their own local rules or charters were generally subordinate to secular law, and the king remained the highest level of jurisdiction.[57] The relation between secular and monastic law was subject to change and depended on the respective kings' attitude vis-à-vis Buddhism. The king determined what rights were granted to Buddhists and whether and to what degree monastics were exempted from secular law. The Buddhists had to respect secular law when creating their own local monastic law. The *Mūlasarvāstivāda-vinaya*, with its many concessions to Brahmanical law, is the best example of such a consideration. We have fewer samples from the

[55] The system of absorption is mentioned in the lost *Mahā-Aṭṭhakathā*; see Kieffer-Pülz, "Theft," § 4.

[56] Shayne Clarke, "One Rule for All? Saṃghāvaśeṣa Indemnity for the Sarvāstivādin Monastic Hierarchy," in Publication Committee (eds.), *Buddhist and Indian Studies in Honour of Professor Sodo Mori* (Hamamatsu: Kokusai Bukkyōto Kyōkai, 2002), 396.

[57] Joseph Walser, *Nāgārjuna in Context: Mahāyāna Buddhism and Early Indian Culture* (New York: Columbia University Press, 2005), 93.

Theravāda-vinaya, but the following stories of King Bimbisāra are telling. The king asked the Buddhist monks to postpone their entering of the rains' retreat for one month.[58] As a result, a general allowance for monks to obey kings was placed in the mouth of the Buddha: a statement so general as to allow commentators to apply it to a wide range of legal matters.[59]

However, the *Vinayas* also report cases demonstrating that secular law was not always the overarching legal category for Buddhist monastics. King Bimbisāra, for instance, decreed that nothing was to be done against those who went forth among the recluses, the sons of the Śākyans, even if they were thieves.[60] He complements this by stating that "kings, who are of no faith, not believing . . . might harm monks even for a trifling matter."[61] This clearly indicates that the kings' personal attitudes were crucial.

In the commentary to the *Theravāda-vinaya*, the *Samantapāsādikā* (fifth century CE), a statement attributed to King Bhātiya (possibly the Sinhalese King Bhātikābhaya, 38–66 or 98–126 CE) is reported in the context of theft. The king declares that as long as he lives, law cases decided by the Elder Godha – an expert in *Abhidhamma* philosophy – are to be followed. He also declared that he puts persons who do not abide by Godha's decisions under the jurisdiction of the king. The king even extended this to lay people, making monks decide cases of secular law.[62] Thus, this king granted one monk absolute authority and placed any monastic who did not accept this monk's decision under his own jurisdiction. These examples indicate that kings interfered in legal matters of religious groups, that they made conventions regarding the application of monastic law, and that the authority of monastic law depended on a single ruler's attitude.

The most prominent historical example of a king who interfered in the internal affairs of the Buddhist community is King Aśoka (third century BCE). Wishing to purge the Buddhist community, he had monks who led a non-virtuous life expelled. Royal interference is also documented in a letter from a king of Krorain (Loulan) to a magistrate in Niya (third century CE) with clear instructions as to the behavior of the monks' community in Niya. Not only the names of the monks appointed by the king to

58 *Vinaya* I 138, 31–36.

59 See Oskar von Hinüber, "Buddhist Law According to the Theravāda-Vinaya: A Survey of Theory and Practice," *Journal of the International Association of Buddhist Studies*, 18 (1995), 29f.

60 *Vinaya* IV 74, 36–75, 2.

61 I.B. Horner, *The Book of the Discipline* (Vinaya-Piṭaka), vol. 4 (London: Pali Text Society, 1952), 92.

62 Takaksusu and Nagai, *Samantapāsādikā*, vol. 1, 306, 29–307, 22; see also von Hinüber, "Buddhist Law," 25f., 28.

administer the monastery are mentioned, but also the fines levied by him for bad behavior.[63]

The Intersection of *Vinayas* and Secular Law

Secular and monastic law intersected, particularly in the areas of property, inheritance, contracts, and the two capital crimes of theft and murder. The *Prātimokṣa* rule prohibiting theft (second *pārājika*) is couched in terms clearly reflecting the definitions and values of common or secular law.[64]

> Whatever monk should take away from a settlement or the wilderness (i.e., from ground which does not belong to settlements) what is not given in a way which is called theft, in such manner of taking what is not given that kings, having arrested a robber, would beat or would bind or would expel him, saying: 'You are a robber, you are a fool, you are stupid, you are a thief.'[65]

The words of this prescription are relatively similar in all of the *Prātimokṣas*.[66] They clearly mirror some common or secular law in India sometime after the Buddha's demise – also reflected later on in the Dharmaśāstric law books – and thus reveal that this early secular law had precise juridical definitions of theft, of the characteristics of an object of theft, of who was called a thief, and of the corresponding penalties. With respect to homicide (third *pārājika*), the prescription contains definitions of killers of human beings, including – besides those who kill with their own hands or using an instrument – those who incite others to kill and those who instigate the victim to self-destruction or speak praise of death, thus causing the victim to commit suicide. The texts also present detailed lists of known methods of killing somebody, including killing by digging pits or traps or by frightening someone to death.

According to the Theravāda tradition, monastic thieves and murderers who committed *pārājika* offenses are excluded from the Buddhist community and rendered liable to secular law. In other schools they remained within the community in specific cases. However, the "introductory story" to the second *Saṅghādisesa* rule for nuns illustrates that, at least in some regions and at certain periods, a lay thief or murderer could obtain some

[63] Walser, *Nāgārjuna*, 104f. [64] von Hinüber, "Buddhist Law," 13.

[65] *Vinaya* III 46, 16–20; for other versions, see Pachow, *Comparative Study*, 74f.

[66] Cf. Oskar von Hinüber, *Das Pātimokkhasutta der Theravādin. Studien zur Literatur des Theravāda-Buddhismus II* (Stuttgart: Akademie der Wissenschaften und der Literatur. Abhandlungen der geistes- und sozialwissenschaftlichen Klasse. Jahrgang, 1999, Nr. 6), 41ff.

immunity from secular law by being ordained in the Buddhist community. In this story, a man whose wife had committed adultery and ran away with precious goods asked King Pasenadi of Kosala for permission to prosecute her. After the king learned that she had gone forth among the nuns, he declared that nothing could be done against her.[67] The chapter on ordination in the *Khandhaka* section of the *Theravāda-vinaya* describes similar cases.

In some cases, there is substantial agreement between Buddhist monastic law and secular law. For example, in monastic law, a person living in dependence – in royal service, in debt, or enslaved[68] – could not be ordained into the order. It is an infraction, according to the *Vinaya*, if a nun "sponsored a woman thief found to deserve death, without having obtained permission from a king or a saṅgha, a group (*gaṇa)*, a guild (*pūga*) or a corporation (*seṇi*)."[69] This prescription is clearly made in deference to secular law, as the reference to various grades of secular courts, beginning with the king and ending with the corporation, indicates.[70]

Most research regarding such intersections to date has been done with reference to the *Theravāda-vinaya* and the *Mūlasarvāstivāda-vinaya*. These texts have been shown to differ.[71] Although monastics were permitted to own property by all traditions, the law of property was not very detailed in the *Theravāda-vinaya*, but rather comprehensive in the *Mūlasarvāstivāda-vinaya*. Thus, for example, we know from the Mūlasarvāstivādin tradition that the person who gives a monastery to the Buddhist community remains the owner of that monastery, *vihārasvāmin*, and retains some rights regarding his monastery.[72] In the Theravāda tradition we have to look intensely for such information. The term *vihārassāmi* is not used often in Pāli literature, and never, as far as we know, in the *Theravāda-vinaya*. Nevertheless, there are traces of the ownership of monasteries, when at least monastic buildings with and without an owner are differentiated.[73] In the "introductory story" to the first *Saṅghādisesa* rule for nuns,[74] the donor also seems to have kept some rights regarding his gifts. Therein, a layman had given a

[67] *Vinaya* IV 226, 4–5. [68] *Vinaya* I 74, 76. [69] *Vinaya* IV 226, 18–22.

[70] Cf. P.V. Kane, *History of Dharmaśāstra (Ancient and Mediaeval Religious and Civil Law)*, vol. 3 (Poona: Bhandarkar Oriental Research Institute, 1973), 281.

[71] As Schopen (*Buddhist Monks*, 130) formulates with respect to the *Mūlasarvāstivāda-vinaya*, the lawyers wanted to avoid social criticism, and this "appears to have prompted . . . any number of rulings that would accommodate and bring its version of Buddhist monasticism into line with brahmanical values and concerns."

[72] Pāli *sassāmika/assāmika*; Schopen, *Buddhist Monks*, 219ff.

[73] *Vinaya* III 144, 149f., 156; IV 47. [74] *Vinaya* III 223–224.

building to the nuns' community, and yet when he passed away, it was still part of his estate. The son who inherited it did not favor Buddhism, and, therefore, tried to take it from the nuns. The case was decided by secular judges in favor of the nuns, who were able to produce eyewitnesses to the former transfer of the building to the nuns' community.

The law of inheritance in the *Mūlasarvāstivāda-vinaya* is closely connected with the proper attendance to the funerary rites, *śarīrapūjā*, for deceased monks, which is how the Buddhists paid regard to the ideas of purity in Brahmanical society. Only one who had attended the funerary rites was entitled to participate in the estate,[75] and, as in dharmaśāstric law, the heir also has to discharge potential debts of the deceased.[76] Although the *Theravāda-vinaya* and *Mahāsāṃghika-vinaya* discuss questions of inheritance,[77] they do not deal with it in a manner as detailed as that of the *Mūlasarvāstivāda-vinaya*. The question of participation in funerary rites seems to have played no role in either of the former two. With respect to the law of contract, a close agreement is observed between Dharmaśāstric law and the *Mūlasarvāstivāda-vinaya*, especially regarding the contents of written loan contracts.[78] The position of other schools still remains to be investigated.

The Importance of Local Communities and Local Ordinances

Since no central ecclesiastic institution existed that could decide legal matters or enforce rulings, decisions were reached by local communities, which were defined by a monastic boundary (*sīmā*). Each local community reached its own decisions, which were not necessarily relevant for or accepted by other local communities. Each Buddhist school had numberless local communities. In addition to the *Vinayas*, local communities had agreements or local ordinances, *kriyākāra*,[79] the jurisdiction of which did not extend beyond their own monasteries.[80] Such ordinances may perhaps have arisen along the lines of ordinances common in secular life. The *Theravāda-vinaya* tells us that townspeople made the agreement that

[75] Gregory Schopen, *Bones, Stones, and Buddhist Monks: Collected Papers on the Archaeology, Epigraphy, and Texts of Monastic Buddhism in India* (Honolulu: University of Hawai'i Press, 1997), 209; Schopen, *Buddhist Monks*, 285–328.

[76] Schopen, *Buddhist Monks*, 131.

[77] *Vinaya* I 308, 31–309, 21; Walser, *Nāgārjuna*, 143–46.

[78] Schopen, *Buddhist Monks*, 62f.

[79] Pāli *katikā, katikavatta, katikasaṇṭhāna*.

[80] Gregory Schopen, "Counting the Buddha and the Local Spirits in: A Monastic Ritual of Inclusion for the Rain Retreat," *Journal of Indian Philosophy*, 30 (2002), 360ff.; Walser, *Nāgārjuna*, 91, 93, 110ff.

someone who comes late for the town's assembly has to pay fifty of some unspecified currency.[81]

Agreements or ordinances mentioned in the *Vinayas* pertain to a wide range of topics. In the *Theravāda-vinaya*, each monastery seems to have had such an ordinance regulating at least the time for entering and leaving the monastery.[82] In the commentary to the *Theravāda-vinaya*, one local ordinance refers to the agreement of a monastery that specific tanks are to be used for specific purposes – one for bathing, another one for fetching water[83] – and another describes how to make an ordinance regarding common income.[84] The *Mūlasarvāstivāda-vinaya,* on the other hand, reports of *kriyākāras* prohibiting nuns to enter the local monastery, or "not to leave the equivalent of sufficient toilet paper" for the next person after having used the privy,[85] or to use beds belonging to the community without a cover.[86] It states in addition that monks had to accept the specific local ordinance of a monastery they wanted to enter for the rains-retreat,[87] a regulation not found in the *Vinayas* of the Mahāsāṃghikas, Mahīśāsakas, Sarvāstivādins, or Theravādins.[88] The *Mahāsāṃghika-vinaya* makes plain that ordinances' conformity with the rules had to be checked by means of the "four great instructions" (*mahāpadesa*).[89] The *Theravāda-vinaya* gives an example of an illegal ordinance – namely, not to let anyone go forth during the rainy season retreat.[90]

In addition to these literary testimonies, there are epigraphical specimens of ordinances from Turkestan (third century CE), from South India (Andhra Pradesh, fifth/sixth centuries CE), and from Sri Lanka (called *vihāra-katikāvatas*) starting from the tenth century.[91] In Sri Lanka, kings enacted ordinances (called *sāsana-katikāvata*) extending over the whole island dating from the twelfth to eighteenth centuries.[92] The organization and administrative structure of monasteries – not regulated in the

81 *Vinaya* III 220, 24–26. 82 *Vinaya* II 76, 30–32, 208, 26–27, 211, 7; III 160, 9–11.

83 *Samantapāsādikā* II 389,14–18. 84 *Samānalābha*; *Samantapāsādikā,* vol. 5 1138, 13–26.

85 Schopen, "Counting," 360.

86 *Varṣavastu* § 1.6.1 quoted according to http://fiindolo.sub.uni-goettingen.de/gretil/1_sanskr/4_rellit/buddh/vinv04_u.htm (last accessed October 21, 2012).

87 Schopen, "Counting," 360. 88 Walser, *Nāgārjuna*, 111 and n. 61.

89 Against Walser, *Nāgārjuna*, 108, these *mahāpadeśas* are not those transmitted in the *Suttapiṭaka* (*Dīghanikāya* II 123, 30–126, 5), but the four *mahāpadeśas* are relevant in a legal context (*Vinaya* I 250, 31–251, 6; *Mūlasarvāstivāda-vinaya,* Derge, Dul-ba PA 252b3–253b4). Information courtesy of Shayne Clarke.

90 *Vinaya* I 153, 21–22. 91 Schopen, *Buddhist Monks*, 355f. n. 45.

92 Nandasena Ratnapāla (ed., trans., annotated), *The Katikāvatas: Laws of the Buddhist Order of Ceylon from the 12th Century to the 18th Century* (München: Kitzinger, 1971).

Vinayas – may also have been an issue of such ordinances. These questions included whether there was a head, and if so, if he was a monastic or a lay person; whether he was elected or simply appointed by other monastics, by kings or by the owners of the monastery; whether the senior-most monk automatically became head; whether the monastery was organized strictly hierarchically or all had equal rights; and whether the tasks of a monastery were taken up by a few elected monastics or distributed generally. All these matters depended on various factors: the owner of the monastery, the community's ideas of how to administer a monastery, local usage and other factors not yet known to us.[93]

Conclusion

It is dangerous to draw conclusions from a single passage of one *Vinaya* because prescriptions referring to the same or similar subjects may be scattered throughout a single *Vinaya*. Reading, for instance, the prescriptive *Prātimokṣa* on its own could lead to wrong impressions regarding the application of monastic law. One might, for example, assume that pregnant women were excluded from ordination, because the *Prātimokṣa* makes it an offense to ordain them. The *Vinaya* texts, however, show that they were ordained.[94] Already the word definitions in the *Vibhaṅga* allow for a wider range of interpretations than the strict wording of the *Prātimokṣa*, as do other portions of the *Vinaya*, and even more so the commentaries. The *Skandhakas* present further examples of persons not allowed to be ordained as Buddhist monks or nuns, like someone in a king's service, a person with debts, thieves, slaves, and so forth. But the Mūlasarvāstivādins allowed people with debts to be ordained, if they gave assurances that they were able to repay the debts after ordination;[95] some Theravādins allowed slaves to be ordained, if they were not called slaves.

In order to learn about law from the *Vinayas*, we have to be aware that there is not just one *Vinaya*, but several, and they stem from distinct schools, from different time periods, from different regions, and were adapted to their environments to different degrees. To be able to make still more definitive statements regarding Buddhist monastic law, many philological investigations regarding legal terminology and textual layers are still necessary. As a corrective, information obtained from the texts

[93] Kieffer-Pülz, "Gemeinde," 327f. [94] See Clarke, *Family Matters*, 3.6.

[95] Schopen, *Buddhist Monks*, 124ff., 131, 160f. n. 12.

has to be checked against external sources (archeological, epigraphical, and numismatical). General statements on the basis of only one *Vinaya* should belong to the past. Future studies will need to bear in mind the many discoveries and findings of recent years, which have shown quite plainly a surprising variety with regard to Buddhist monastic law that will certainly continue to grow with further research.

CHAPTER 3

Keeping the Buddha's Rules
The View from the Sūtra Piṭaka

Rupert Gethin

Early in the history of Buddhist literature, "the word of the Buddha" (*buddha-vacana*) was arranged in three basic categories: monastic discipline (*vinaya*), sayings of the Buddha (*sūtra*), and systematic thought (*abhidharma*), giving us the traditional "three baskets" (*tripiṭaka*).

The "sayings" or "discourses" (sūtra) that make up the Sūtra Piṭaka characteristically begin with the phrase: "This is what I have heard. The Lord was once staying at [. . .]" Some circumstance is then introduced which becomes the occasion for (usually) the Buddha to give some teaching, often in the form of a dialogue. The texts of the Sūtra Piṭaka comprise four principal collections (*nikāya/āgama*): Long (*dīrgha*) Sayings, Medium-Length (*madhyama*) Sayings, and two collections of shorter sayings, Grouped (*saṃyukta*) and Numbered Sayings (*ekottara*). A number of other miscellaneous (*kṣudraka*) texts are also usually classified as belonging to the Sūtra Piṭaka.

Our knowledge of the Sūtra Pīṭaka is less complete than in the case of the Vinaya Piṭaka, versions of which belonging to six ancient Indian schools have come down to us. One version of the Sūtra Pīṭaka, from the Theravāda school, survives complete in the ancient Indian language of Pāli. Parts of the versions of two other ancient schools, the Dharmaguptaka and Sarvāstivāda, survive variously in Sanskrit, Gāndhārī, and in Chinese and Tibetan translations. The differences between the versions usually concern matters of detail rather than substance.

Dating the material contained in the Sūtra Piṭaka is problematic. Early Buddhist texts were composed and transmitted orally, and do not seem to have been systematically committed to writing before the first century BCE. Something of what is contained in the *Nikāyas* and *Āgamas* may go back to the fifth century BCE and to the Buddha himself, but we have no independent corroboration that the material existed in its present form until the appearance of the Pāli commentaries and Chinese translations of the *Āgamas* in the fourth and fifth centuries CE. Still, much of what is contained in the *Nikāyas* and *Āgamas* must stand at the beginning of the development of Buddhist literature, in which case it seems reasonable to think of it as approximating to its present shape by the end of the third century BCE. In the centuries that followed, further sūtras were composed that came to be characterized as *mahāyāna* ("great vehicle") and whose claim to the status of "word of the Buddha" was contested by the Buddhist schools in India. The process and extent of their acceptance as part of the Sūtra Piṭaka in India still remains unclear. Thus, the Mahāyāna sūtras are excluded from the present discussion, which focuses on materials generally accepted by the ancient Indian schools of Buddhism.

While the contents of the *Vinaya* and Sūtra Piṭakas broadly fit the categories of "monastic discipline" (*vinaya*) and "teaching" (*dharma*) respectively, there is some overlap. For example, the *Vinaya* contains an account of the career of the Buddha incorporating material that is found in the Sūtra Piṭaka;[1] a section of the Mūlasarvāstivādin *Vinaya* contains a version of a long *sūtra* that has no immediate relevance to the specifics of monastic discipline that is also found in the collection of long sayings of the Sūtra Piṭaka.[2] Likewise, the Sūtra Piṭaka includes discussion of specific *Vinaya* rules as well as more general *Vinaya* issues.[3] There is also material in the Sūtra Piṭaka that touches on the basic principles of the *Vinaya* legal code that is absent from the Vinaya Piṭaka itself. An example will form our starting point.

Obedience, Authority, and Spiritual Progress

Should a monk or nun follow monastic regulations blindly in all circumstances, or are there occasions when it is appropriate to break the rules? A text from Medium-Length Sayings tells of the monk Bhaddāli who publicly refuses to follow a training rule announced by the Buddha.[4] The rule concerns not eating after midday.[5] Bhaddāli's refusal to comply is based not on a matter of principle, but simply on the fact that he does not find the rule congenial. Prompted by his fellow monks, Bhaddāli eventually agrees to discuss the matter with the Buddha. The Buddha reprimands Bhaddāli

[1] Cf. Vin I 4–10 and M I 168–73. [2] SBV II 216–54 corresponds to D I 47–86, T I 107a–109c.

[3] For example, M I 130 relates to Pācittiya 68 (Vin IV 133–36), S II 218 to Pācittiya 32 (Vin IV 71–75); D I 4–12 relates directly to matters of monastic discipline. See also Oskar von Hinüber, *A Handbook of Pāli Literature* (Berlin: Walter de Gruyter, 1996), 13–14.

[4] The Pāli *Bhaddāli-sutta* of the Majjhima Nikāya (M I 437–47), corresponds closely to the *Batuoheli-jing* of the Chinese translation of the Dharmaguptaka Madhyama Āgama (T 26.746b18–749b29).

[5] In the *Theravāda-vinaya*, Pācittiya 37 (Vin IV 85).

and puts to him a hypothetical question: Suppose the Buddha was to ask one of his spiritually accomplished monks to act as a bridge so that he could walk over some mud, would that monk refuse? Bhaddāli answers that he would not. The Buddha goes on to suggest that not following the rules is a reason why a monk might not make progress and reach the goal of the path: the destruction of all mental defilements. Bhaddāli then asks the Buddha why there used to be few rules but many accomplished monks, and now there are many rules but few accomplished monks. The Buddha answers that this is because the institution of the Buddha's teaching (dharma) is in decline; in the past there was no need for training rules, but now that the community of monks has become large, qualities that are the cause of various corruptions have become more prevalent among monks, hence the need for more rules.

This story might be read as advocating a blind obedience to rules, whose authority lies in the fact that they have been laid down by a buddha, an infinitely wise teacher whose only purpose in making rules is to help unruly ascetics on their way to liberation. The ancient Theravādin commentary,[6] however, is at pains to point out that, in fact, the Buddha would not order a monk to lie down in the mud for him, and even if he did, it would not be appropriate for monks to act on such an order. The hypothetical command to lie down in mud should be understood as a piece of rhetoric illustrating how spiritually accomplished monks are easy to talk to, whereas a monk like Bhaddāli is difficult to talk to. Since the rules have been laid down by the Buddha, and he would not lay down inappropriate rules, we should follow them. And yet the commentary does perhaps provide us with a possible pretext for disobedience: If a rule is inappropriate, then it could not have been uttered by the Buddha, and so it can be ignored.

The issue of the authority of the Buddha and of the rules of the *Vinaya* is taken up in the narrative of the events leading up to the Buddha's death. The Buddha informs Ānanda that after his death the community can abolish the "minor" (*kṣudrānukṣudra*) training rules if it so wishes.[7] The follow up to this story is found in the *Vinaya* accounts of the first Buddhist Council at Rājagṛha: Since no one could say just which rules qualified as minor (and following the logic that *all* rules laid down by the Buddha must be for the good of his followers), Mahākāśyapa proposed that the *saṅgha* should undertake to keep all the training rules.[8]

The material considered so far appears, for the most part, to advocate an unquestioning trust in the rules and regulations of the *Vinaya* as thought

[6] Ps III 151–52. [7] D II 154; MPS, 386. [8] Vin II 287–88.

out by a wise and compassionate teacher. Yet other, perhaps more subtle, attitudes are also evidenced in the texts. A common list of ten "bonds" or "ties" (*saṃyojana*) considers the three general categories of defilement – namely, greed (*rāga*), hatred (*dveṣa*), and delusion (*moha*) – by way of ten types distinguished by their intensity and object. One of the grosser forms of greed manifests as "attachment to precept and vow" (*śīlavrataparāmarśa*). Although in some contexts this seems to be taken as referring to the attachment of non-Buddhist ascetics to their inappropriate training rules and precepts (such as the vow to live as a dog or a cow), elsewhere it seems also to encompass a Buddhist monk's possible attachment to his *Buddhist* precepts and vows. This becomes explicit in the canonical Abhidharma literature of the Theravādins.[9] The point appears to be that mere adherence to precepts and vows, and rules and regulations, is insufficient to bring about enlightenment. Indeed, an unthinking attachment to rules and regulations is an obstacle in the way of progress along the path to enlightenment, and has to be abandoned along with other forms of attachment. There is thus a tension between, on the one hand, a practical approach of unquestioning adherence to the Buddha's rules and regulations as integral to his system of spiritual training, and on the other hand, the recognition that simple obedience to a set of rules is not the goal and may even get in the way.

Related to this is a distinction between universal moral faults (*prakṛtisāvadya*) and conventional faults (*prajñaptisāvadya*), which appears later in the commentaries on the *Vinaya* and Sūtra Piṭakas.[10] Thus, the infringement of certain rules of the *Vinaya* comes to be seen in certain instances as not necessarily a wrong in itself (that is, as not necessarily motivated by greed, hatred, and delusion), but as merely the transgression of a conventional rule. Indeed, enlightened *arhats* who are completely free of greed, hatred, and delusion may on certain occasions break a rule of the *Vinaya* that is considered merely conventional (rules concerning the proper way of building a hut, for example) for entirely selfless, compassionate, and wise reasons.[11] Yet other rules, such as intentionally depriving a living being of life, are always faults because it is considered impossible to break such a rule without hatred and delusion arising in the mind.[12]

9 See M I 387; A I 224–25; Dhs 198; Tikap 154–55, 157–58.

10 See Mil 266–67, Sp I 228, Abhidh-k-bh IV 33–35; see also Rupert Gethin, "Can Killing a Living Being Ever Be an Act of Compassion? The Analysis of the Act of Killing in the Abhidhamma and Pāli Commentaries," *Journal of Buddhist Ethics* 11 (2004), 175; Oskar von Hinüber, "The Arising of an Offence: *Āpattisamuṭṭhān*. A Note on the Structure and History of the Theravāda-Vinaya," *Journal of the Pāli Text Society* 16 (1992), 66–67.

11 Saṃghādisesa 6; Sp 574.

12 Pācittiya 61; see Gethin, "Can Killing a Living."

To the extent that early Buddhist texts are interested in the law, the focus is on monastic law. Nevertheless, secular law is not entirely absent. Just as the Buddha lays down rules that protect the way of life of Buddhist monks and nuns, so, it is acknowledged, a king lays down laws that protect the well-being of his subjects. Yet, whether we can find a coherent social and political philosophy articulated in the texts of the Sūtra Piṭaka has been disputed, and as we shall see, matters of spiritual training dominate the discussion of secular law in various ways.

From the middle of the last century it has been common to make three claims in this regard: (1) that early Buddhist texts set out a social contract theory of kingship, (2) that they establish specific guidelines for the behavior of kings that constitute a political philosophy; and (3) that they exhibit a preference for a republican political system rather than monarchy (reflecting and perhaps influencing the constitution of a number of small, ancient Indian republics contemporary with the Buddha).

The evidence for this last claim is limited and inconclusive,[13] and to the extent that the issue concerns the nature of the constitution of the Buddhist Order as embodied in the Vinaya Piṭaka, it lies beyond the scope of the present discussion. The rest of this article will be concerned particularly with the first two questions.

Origins of Society

Buddhist ideas developed in a society infused with Brahmanical ideology. A series of Brahmanical "law books" (*dharmasūtra*), dating in their present form from perhaps the third century BCE to the second century CE, set out the Brahmanical theory of society that seems, at least in part, assumed by early Buddhist texts. According to this theory, society is hierarchical and made up of four basic classes (*varṇa*), each with their own specific roles: at the top is the priest (*brāhmaṇa*), followed in order by the ruler (*kṣatriya*), the trader (*vaiśya*), and the servant (*śūdra*). According to this scheme, the ruler's role is to protect his subjects by meting out just punishment to those who disregard the law.[14] The texts of the Sūtra Piṭaka do not seek to

[13] Steven Collins, *Nirvana and Other Buddhist Felicities* (Cambridge: Cambridge University Press, 1998), 436–48.

[14] See the *Dharma Sūtras* of Āpastamba (2.10.6), Gautama (10.7–8), Baudhāyana (1.18.16), and Vasiṣṭha (19.1–8) in Patrick Olivelle, *The Dharmasūtras* (Oxford: Oxford University Press, 1999), 53, 94, 159, 299–300; *Mānavadharmaśāstra* 1.87–91, 7.1–31 in Wendy Doniger and Brian K. Smith, *The Laws of Manu* (London: Penguin, 1991), 12–13, 128–31.

challenge directly the idea that society is constituted by these four classes, nor the idea that the ruler should govern.

They do, however, offer an alternative account of the origins of the four classes and also of their hierarchical relationship. This account – from the collection of Long Sayings, the *Aggañña-sutta* and its parallels[15] – accepts the basic duties and roles of the four classes as set out in Brahmanical sources, except in the case of the brahmins. The Buddhist account of the origins of the four classes seeks not to subvert the political power of the ruler, but rather to usurp the clerical power of the priest. This is achieved by first putting the ruler above the priest in the traditional hierarchy of the four classes, and then by redefining the brahmins' ideal duty, suggesting at the same time that they have failed in it while Buddhist ascetics have in fact fulfilled it, making them the *true* "brahmins." This, it is claimed, is even acknowledged by King Prasenajit in getting up from his seat for the Buddha. The Buddhist account also explicitly subordinates the Brahmanical hierarchy of birth to a universal moral hierarchy: What matters is not the class one is born into, but how one behaves (that one refrains from killing, stealing, lying, and sexual misconduct).

The Buddhist account satirizes a specific Brahmanical claim about the origins of the four classes. The "Hymn of the Man"[16] states that the original brahmins were born from the mouth of Puruṣa (identified with Prajāpati and Brahmā in the *Śatapatha-brāhmaṇa*) during the course of the primordial sacrifice from which the world was created. The other three classes are said to be born from his arms (the ruler), his thighs (the trader), and his feet (the servant).[17] The Buddhist counter to this is that, in fact, brahmins are seen to be born from women just like everybody else, and that the four classes evolved as a natural by-product of the development of human society. This development represents a gradual fall from a primordial state when human beings could live without the social and political institutions required now. Just as when the Buddha first established his order of monks, their nature was such that there was no need for the rules of the *Vinaya*, so when beings first appeared in this world they were self-luminous, constantly beautiful, and able to nourish themselves by feeding on joy alone.

Yet, as time passed they became greedy for solid food, and this was the first step in a gradual process that led to the establishment of cultivated

15 D III 80–98; Mvu I 338–48; T. 1, I 36b–39a; Konrad Meisig, *Das Sūtra von den vier Ständen: Das Aggañña-Sutta im Licht seiner chinesischen Parallelen* (Wiesbaden: Harrassowitz, 1988).

16 *Ṛg Veda* 10.90.

17 Sv 254 (= Ps 418 = Spk 397) suggests *kṣatriyas* from his chest, *vaiśyas* from his navel.

rice fields and separate stores of harvested rice. Then came theft, which resulted in lying, punishment, and finally the appointment of the first king who, in return for a share of rice, took responsibility for justice and keeping order by meting out punishment to those who deserved it. We are then told how brahmins originated as a group who wished to reverse this gradual decline. They renounced immorality and took to the forest to practice meditation. But not all were up to the task; these gave up their meditation, and as "non-meditators" (*ajjhāyaka*), returned to the villages to become "students" (*ajjhāyaka*) of the Vedas, precisely the duty traditionally prescribed for brahmins in Brahmanical texts. Thus, by a play on the word *ajjhāyaka*, the *Aggañña-sutta* suggests that study of the Vedas is in fact the occupation of those brahmins who have failed in precisely the way of life that Buddhist monks now successfully pursue.[18]

Buddhist Theories of Kingship and the Concept of the Wheel-Turning King

Some modern scholars have seen a Buddhist "social contract" theory of kingship in this account of the origins of kings that is opposed to a Brahmanical "divine will" theory, as expressed in the *Mahābhārata*.[19] This narrative describes how in an earlier age men lived without kings, but when their behavior became increasingly motivated by greed and passion, the gods Brahmā and Viṣṇu established the institution of kingship. Andrew Huxley has argued that such a reading of the ancient Indian accounts of the origins of kingship is problematic.[20] In the first place, it is anachronistic: the European notion of "social contract" involves the application of the specific legal notion of contract, which did not exist in India in the early centuries BCE. We would do better, he suggests, to characterize the *Aggañña-sutta* as presenting a "popular consent" political theory. In the second place, such a reading tends to set up an unhelpful contrast between "Buddhist" and "Hindu" theories that assumes Buddhist texts propose limitations on royal power and provide justifications for defiance of a king perceived to be unjust, while Hindu texts do not. Yet the *Mahābhārata*[21] tells how, after the first kings rule justly, things deteriorate and the sixth king, Vena, rules

[18] D III 93–94; Steven Collins, "The Discourse on What is Primary (*Aggañña-Sutta*)," *Journal of Indian Philosophy* 21 (1993), 373–74; Meisig, *Das Sūtra von den vier Ständen*, 146–49.

[19] 12.59.

[20] Andrew Huxley, "The Buddha and the Social Contract," *Journal of Indian Philosophy* 24 (1996), 407–20.

[21] 12.59.

as an unjust tyrant, prompting the ancient seers to assassinate him. This Hindu story thus provides a precedent for the defiance of an unjust king, which the Buddhist *Aggañña-sutta* does not. We can add to Huxley's point by noting that elsewhere the *Mahābhārata*[22] also mentions the choosing of the first king Manu by popular consent in terms not dissimilar from those of the *Aggañña-sutta*, while the Brahmanical *Arthaśāstra*[23] discusses both a divine-will theory of kingship and a popular-consent theory. Huxley points to another Buddhist sūtra, the *Cakkavattisīhanāda-sutta*, as more relevant to the question of a Buddhist justification for defying an unjust ruler.

Wheel of Dharma. Photo taken by David M. Engel

Like the *Mahābhārata* legend, the *Cakkavattisīhanāda-sutta* also mentions a succession of kings.[24] These kings are styled "wheel-turning righteous kings of truth, sovereigns of the four quarters who maintain the

[22] 12.67. [23] *Arthaśāstra* I 13.5–7. [24] D III 58–79; T I 39a–42b.

stability of the country." The notion of the *cakravartin* or "wheel-turning" king is shared by Buddhism with Brahmanism and Jainism. The term can be interpreted in various ways: the wheel in question may in origin refer to a symbol of royal power (such as the god Viṣṇu's discus, or the wheel of the chariot of state), or to the circle of the earth, or the circle of subjects and nobles, at the center of which sits the king. In Buddhist texts, where cakravartin kings are described as conquering and ruling the whole earth not by violence or by the sword, but by righteousness (dharma), the wheel has also the connotation of "the wheel of truth" (*dharma-cakra*).[25]

Beginning in a mythical past when humans lived for 80,000 years, the *Cakkavattisīhanāda-sutta* tells how each king, after ruling for many thousands of years, renounced his kingdom to become a homeless ascetic, handing over sovereignty to his son. Each son subsequently sought instruction from his father on how to rule as a cakaravartin. This process of succession continued for seven generations, but the eighth king failed to go to his father for instruction, governing instead according to his own opinions. His ministers suggested that he should seek their advice in the ways of a cakravartin, which he duly did. However, even though he was then able to fulfill some of the duties of a cakravartin, he omitted to give money to the poor. This set off a chain of events: poverty led to theft, lying, and murder; the decline in morality led to ever shorter lifespans and further decline in morality. Eventually the present situation emerged where immorality is widespread and beings live at most 100 years.

Things will get worse before they get better. The sūtra goes on to tell how humans by degree will become more and more depraved and short lived, until with a lifespan of just ten years and consumed by anger and hatred, they will see and attack each other indiscriminately like animals. At this low point some will hide away in fear of their lives, but when they eventually emerge again to find others still alive, they will feel such joy that they will reflect on the course of events that led to this sorry state. This will be the start of an upward spiral: gradually, generation by generation, morality and the lifespan of humans will increase, until once more we will live for 80,000 years and once more a cakravartin will conquer and rule the whole earth by righteousness rather than violence. At this time, too, the next buddha, Maitreya, will appear in the world.

The account of the Buddhist cakravartin set out in the *Cakkavattisīhanāda-sutta* and other texts of the Sūtra Piṭaka has been read as setting

[25] I. Armelin, *Le roi détenteur de la roue solaire en révolution (cakravartin) selon le brahmanisme et selon le bouddhisme* (Paris: Paul Geuthner, 1975), 3–5.

out a specifically Buddhist vision of the ideal king and of the consequences of a king's failure in good government – that is, as preaching a Buddhist form of constitutional law and monarchy.[26] Steven Collins has argued that a reading along these lines fails to bring out much of the significance of the tale, which, he suggests, is found in the way it induces in its audience a sense of ascetic distance from the affairs of the world, a sense of their ultimate futility. Following the inevitable pattern of things (exemplifying the Buddhist law of "dependent arising"), sometimes the affairs of the world amount to a set of circumstances that are almost heavenly, sometimes hellish, but both extremes are ultimately fleeting.[27] The only real hope for relief is to leave them behind by becoming an ascetic and seeking *nirvāṇa*; this, after all, is what even the cakravartins of the tale themselves do. This understanding of the narrative is enhanced by the manner in which it is framed by the Buddha's instructions to his monks to keep to their own ascetic practice. Somewhat similar themes are evident in the tale of another cakravartin from the distant past found in the *Mahāsudassana-sutta*.[28]

Just as the Buddha himself, while not acknowledging anyone in the world as his superior, acknowledges the dharma,[29] so in one place in the Sūtra Piṭaka, in answer to the question, "who is king for the *cakravartin*?" we are told that it is dharma.[30] Steven Collins has usefully distinguished two approaches in early Buddhist texts to the duty of kings.[31] In the first place, dharma or "what is right" functions as an ethic of absolute values that characterizes all forms of violence as wrong, even those carried out by a just king administering punishment in accordance with his duties as king; the advice to kings is thus not to be one with the world, but rather to renounce the world. But in the *Jātaka*, the collection of stories of the Buddha's previous lives as a *bodhisattva* (a being on the way to enlightenment), dharma sometimes functions as a practical moral framework for justice in which, depending on circumstances, violence is allowed; the advice to kings in this case is "not to pass judgement in haste or anger, but appropriately, such that the punishment fits the crime."

[26] See Balakrishna G. Gokhale, "Early Buddhist Kingship," *Journal of Asian Studies* 26 (1966), 15–22; Uma Chakravarti, *The Social Dimensions of Early Buddhism* (Delhi: Oxford University Press, 1987), 150–69; Huxley, "The Buddha and the Social Contract," 416–19. See also Trevor Ling, *The Buddha: Buddhist Civilization in India and Ceylon* (Harmondsworth: Penguin, 1976), 178–80; S.J. Tambiah, *World Conqueror and World Renouncer* (Cambridge: Cambridge University Press, 1976), 39–53.

[27] Collins, *Nirvana*, 480–96.

[28] Rupert Gethin, "Mythology as Meditation: From the Mahāsudassana Sutta to the Sukhāvativyūha Sūtra," *Journal of the Pāli Text Society* 28 (2006), 63–112.

[29] S I 139; A II 21; T II 321c–322a; T II 410a.

[30] A III 149. [31] Collins, *Nirvana*, 419–20, 451–66.

A number of *Jātaka* stories speak of kings who "rule righteously and fairly," establishing just levels of taxation,[32] and they also provide a list of ten virtues of a good king: charity, moral restraint, generosity, honesty, gentleness, religious practice, good temper, mercy, patience, and cooperativeness.[33] But the classic example of the implications of the first understanding of dharma for kings is the story of Temīya, a young prince (the Buddha-to-be) who feigns dumbness in order to avoid becoming king and having to act as judge and condemn criminals.[34]

Another *Jātaka* story, the tale of a frog (again, the Buddha-to-be), illustrates an acceptance of dharma in its pragmatic form.[35] A water snake inadvertently swims into a fishnet where it is attacked by the fish that is already trapped there. The snake manages to escape and reach the bank where he presents his case to a frog. The frog rules that the fish's behavior is perfectly acceptable: Since the snake eats fish that stray into its territory, he has no right to complain if they attack him when he strays into theirs. On seeing the snake diminished by the frog's judgment, the fish find the strength to escape the net and kill the snake. The frog judge is identified with the Buddha-to-be, the snake with King Ajātaśatru, who, according to Buddhist legend, seized the kingdom from his father (a just king), imprisoned him, and eventually starved him to death. In addition to illustrating the notion of dharma as pragmatic justice, this story indirectly provides some justification for defying an unjust king.

It is not easy to gauge the manner in which these early Buddhist texts reflect the actualities of the legal and political world in which they were composed or the kind of influence they had upon it. Certainly the Buddha in a number of places is represented in conversation with several contemporary kings: both Bimbisāra and Ajātaśatru, successive kings of Magadha, as well as Prasenajit, the king of Kośala.[36] But the accounts of these interactions seem less like occasions for the Buddha to preach his political philosophy and policy advice to such kings, who appear more like supporters and followers of the Buddha.

We should be cautious about reading a text such as the *Cakkavattisīhanāda-sutta* as preaching a Buddhist form of constitutional law and monarchy. Nevertheless, as Collins himself notes, the literary material found in the Sūtra-piṭaka provided resources that could be drawn on both

[32] Ja IV 399. [33] *Ibid.*, 460–61; Ja III 320, 412, 274; Ja V 378.

[34] Ja VI 1–30; Collins, *Nirvana*, 425–36; Gethin, "Can Killing a Living Being," 175, 177–78, 183; M. Zimmermann, "Only a Fool Becomes a King: Buddhist Stances on Punishment," in Michael Zimmermann (ed.), *Buddhism and Violence* (Lumbini: Lumbini International Research Institute, 2006), 213–42.

[35] Ja II 237–39; Collins, *Nirvana*, 451–52. [36] M II 118–25; S I 68–70, 75.

to contest and justify military and political power, with the same text sometimes being used in both ways.[37] At the very least, the tales of kings and cakravartins found in the texts of the Sūtra Piṭaka have been used by Buddhists to reflect on how a king should behave.

Basham has suggested that the notion of the cakravartin assumes the actuality of empires and specifically the emergence of the Indian Mauryan Empire toward the end of the fourth century BCE.[38] Gombrich takes the view that the myth of a ruler of the four quarters can be extrapolated from earlier Vedic and Brahmanical ideas, as well as from the manner in which certain kingdoms of eastern India were expanding and absorbing other kingdoms in the fifth century BCE.[39] Alternatively, we might consider as sufficient stimulus some early awareness in eastern India of the vast Persian Empire to the west, dating back to the sixth century BCE. The significance of these possibilities relates to the question of the relationship of the literary concept of the cakravartin to the actual ruler of the Mauryan Empire in the third century BCE, Aśoka (269–232 BCE).

Aśoka as the Ideal Buddhist King

Unlike earlier Indian rulers, Aśoka is known directly to us through a series of rock and pillar edicts. In the thirteenth major rock edict, he tells how he expanded his territory eastward into Kaliṅga. He goes on to speak of his remorse at the deaths and suffering caused by his military campaign, and speaks of his preference for conquest by means of dharma, expressing the wish that his successors will be restrained in their use of force.[40] The extent to which we should read Aśoka's inscriptions as inspiring or as inspired by the Buddhist notion of the cakravartin may remain uncertain, but certainly Buddhist ideas had some influence on him.

We know from a minor rock edict that Aśoka regarded himself as a Buddhist layman (*upāsaka*).[41] Other inscriptions speak of his pilgrimage to Buddhist sites and indicate a particular concern with Buddhist affairs.[42] But there continues to be scholarly debate concerning the extent to which Aśoka might be regarded as a "Buddhist" ruler, and to speak of the Aśokan state as Buddhist with Buddhism as its established religion is inappropriate. Aśoka

[37] Collins, *Nirvana*, 419.

[38] A.L. Basham, *The Wonder That Was India*, 2nd ed. (London: Sidgwick and Jackson, 1967), 83.

[39] R.F. Gombrich, *Theravāda Buddhism: A Social History from Ancient Benares to Modern Colombo* (London: Routledge and Kegan Paul, 1988), 82.

[40] Jules Bloch, *Les inscriptions d'Asoka* (Paris: Les Belles Lettres, 1950), 129–32.

[41] *Ibid.*, 145–46. [42] *Ibid.*, 157.

seems to have approached matters of religion in the spirit of protecting his subjects and promoting dharma generally. His vision of dharma is not explicitly Buddhist; there is no mention of such Buddhist doctrines as the four noble truths, the noble eightfold path, or nirvana. Yet, while Buddhist values share something in common with ancient Indian ethical values more generally, the spirit of tolerance encouraged among different groups of "ascetics and brahmins" and the ethical slant of Aśoka's dharma – especially the emphasis on respect for parents, teachers, and elders – might be read as reflecting the kind of material found in the Buddhist Sūtra Piṭaka, such as passages of the *Sāmaññaphala-sutta* and especially the *Sigālovāda-sutta*.[43] The emphasis on refraining from religious ceremonies involving the slaughter of animals and the promotion of a dharma involving morality and public works might be interpreted as a disavowal of the efficacy of Vedic animal sacrifice and its replacement by a different sort of "sacrifice" in the manner of the *Kūṭādanta-sutta*.[44] This sūtra tells of a brahmin who is instructed by the Buddha that proper sacrifice involves not the slaughter of animals, but the practice of generosity, morality, and meditation.

In his edicts, Aśoka repeatedly exhorted his subjects to avoid anger and killing and injuring human beings and animals, and he also spoke of himself and his huntsmen as giving up killing. However, the argument that he abolished capital punishment remains inconclusive, and certainly flogging as a form of punishment was not excluded.[45] In the mythic kingdoms of the cakravartins of the Sūtra Piṭaka, however, government seems possible without recourse to the violent punishment of criminals. Thus, from the perspective of the Sūtra Piṭaka, if Aśoka was a righteous king, it was only in the more limited pragmatic sense of one who follows dharma as a practical moral framework for justice in which violence is, if possible, avoided, yet still considered an appropriate form of punishment for convicted criminals.

Aśoka's actual empire may have fallen somewhat short of the Sūtra Piṭaka ideal, yet later Buddhist literature nonetheless sought to assimilate Aśoka, and other kings, to the Buddhist ideal of the cakravartin. This was achieved in part by modifying the ideal and talking of a "wheel-turning" king of a

[43] Cf. *Ibid.*, 90–93, 156, 121–24; D I 53, 62; D III 180–193; T I 70a–72c.

[44] D I 127–48; T I 96c–101b.

[45] See Ananda Guruge, "The Evolution of Emperor Aśoka's Humanitarian Policy: Was Capital Punishment Abolished?" in Asanga Tilkaratne and K. Dhammajoti (eds.), *Recent Researches in Buddhist Studies: Essays in Honour of Professor Y. Karunadasa* (Colombo: Karunaratne, 1997), 258–75, which responds to K.R. Norman, "Aśoka and Capital Punishment," in *Collected Papers*, vol. 1 (Oxford: Pāli Text Society, 1990), 200–13.

single continent, like Aśoka or the king of the island of Laṅkā.[46] By using the concept of the cakravartin, later tradition was able to evoke the vision of the ideal king of the Sūtra Piṭaka, and suggest that he is in some sense actualized in real kingdoms of the past and present.

Conclusion

Our starting point was the attitude evinced in some texts of the Sūtra Piṭaka to the Buddhist monastic law. This might be summed up as one of acceptance and obedience on the grounds that the rules have been laid down by the Buddha, the teacher, out of wisdom and compassion in response to the failings of his followers and are there for their benefit. In other words, keeping rules will help them in their progress toward liberation, while disregarding them will not. At the same time, there is recognition that attachment even to good rules can be a hindrance. The arhat is free of such attachment and does what is right, behaving in accordance with dharma not because he is keeping the rules, but because freedom from greed, hatred, and delusion means that he cannot do otherwise.

The attitude toward secular law reflected in the Sūtra Piṭaka is in some ways very similar. Laws arose in response to a general failure in morality, and they safeguard the general good; disregarding those laws means that society will slip further toward chaos. Kingdoms where the king and all his subjects live for a time by the moral precepts come and go. In the end, it is the nature of things that the failure in morality affects the lawmakers themselves; although they may hope to rule justly and fairly, in practice they can only uphold the law by the threat and use of violence. Following Collins, we suggest that such considerations in early Buddhist texts amount not so much to a political philosophy as a reflection on the affairs of the world from the perspective of ascetic renunciation. Nevertheless, the vision of the cakravartin, the righteous king of dharma, seems to have had some impact on the world of real and actual kings.

There is a tension running through all this. The "law" (dharma) is what is right, and our behavior should conform to it. The Buddha's monastic law helps us, yet attachment to it may become an obstacle to overcome. Similarly, the secular law of kings keeps us from wrongdoing, yet it is ultimately upheld by the threat and even enactment of violence. But these

[46] Sp II 309; Pj I 227; Divy 232, 234, 239, 258. For Aśoka and the cakravartin ideal, see John Strong, *The Legend of King Aśoka: A Study and Translation of the Aśokāvadāna* (Princeton: Princeton University Press, 1983), 44–56.

acts of violence are ultimately *adharma* – not right, immoral – and their perpetrators, even legitimate rulers seeking to uphold the law in their kingdoms, must suffer the consequences of their bad acts (*karma*).

This tension is not a peculiarly Buddhist affair. It is the dilemma, for example, that Yudhiṣṭhira, himself the son of the personification of dharma in the form of a god, wrestles with in the great epic poem of the *Mahābhārata*. Yudhiṣṭhira is a king and his duty (dharma) as king is to punish wrongdoers and protect his subjects. Yet an individual's highest dharma lies beyond this in restraint of the senses, lack of greed, kindness, and nonviolence. Yudhiṣṭhira is a king, and yet he is constantly torn between his duty as king and his personal inclination toward renunciation and the ascetic life in the forest.[47]

The world of early Buddhist texts is no doubt more firmly situated in the forest away from kings and their affairs than that of the *Mahābhārata*, thus the dilemma takes on a different dimension. The values of renunciation represent in some sense a critique of the values that the rest of us (including and perhaps especially kings) live by; and yet without the support of the rest of us (including and perhaps especially kings), life in the forest cannot be expected to flourish. Proclaim the values of renunciation too uncompromisingly, and the renouncer risks alienating those whom he seeks to persuade. Proclaim them halfheartedly, and the renouncer risks compromising the ideals that are the very basis of renunciation.

[47] John D. Smith, *The Mahābhārata* (London: Penguin, 2009), xx–xxi, xxx–xxxi.

CHAPTER 4

Proper Possessions
Buddhist Attitudes toward Material Property

Jacob N. Kinnard

"House life is crowded and dusty; going forth is wide open. It is not easy, living life in a household, to lead a holy life as utterly perfect as a polished shell. Suppose I were to shave off my hair and beard, put on saffron garments, and go forth from home into homelessness?"

– *Majjhima Nikāya* I.240

"[A]mong all the religions of India it went furthest in declaring the illusory nature of the world and individual self, and the necessity for salvation through detachment."

– Stanley J. Tambiah[1]

Introduction

It is one of the distinctive features of the Buddhist tradition that the Buddha's life story serves as what can be understood to be, with a nod to Clifford Geertz, both a model of the ideal Buddhist life and a model for all Buddhists to follow. In other words, the Buddha's life is both descriptive of and prescriptive for the proper Buddhist life. At the heart of this story is the young prince's decision to abandon his wife and child, his parents, and the kingdom he is to inherit, in order to seek the enlightenment that will alleviate the suffering that is inherent in the human condition. He goes forth from home to homelessness – *anāgāriya* in Pāli – and becomes an ascetic without attachment to people, places, or things. "Homelessness," thus, denotes more than the literal state of being without a home in Buddhism, but serves as a kind of synecdochic marker for the monastic life. The life of the monk is, fundamentally, described in Pāli canonical texts as the life of an ascetic, devoid of all worldly attachments and property, because such things engender grasping, which is the underlying cause of all suffering.

[1] Stanley J. Tambiah, "Buddhism and This-Worldly Activity," *Modern Asian Studies* 7.1 (1973), 1–20, 3.

Buddhist attitudes toward material property and wealth are not, however, quite so ascetically straightforward. In fact, although it is typically portrayed as having a deep strain of austere renunciation running through it, there is also an ambiguity about property that runs through the tradition. It is generally agreed that monks are required to renounce virtually all material possessions – although, as we shall see, even this assumption is not quite as clear as it may seem – but it is not the case that Buddhism simply holds that all material property is negative. Lay Buddhists, who have been frequently overlooked in Western studies of the tradition, must, by necessity, engage with the material things of the world. Undo attachment to property is certainly to be avoided by the laity, but the possession of personal wealth and property is, in many cases, portrayed as highly virtuous because the possession of property enables the layperson to support the monks, and to donate the money and things that are necessary for the maintenance of the monastic institution. Furthermore, for the layperson, the giving of property and wealth allows for the cultivation of nonattachment, and is understood to be a kind of domestic asceticism. There is thus a symbiotic relationship between the laity and the monks: The monks depend on the laity to donate various material goods, dwellings, robes, food, and so forth, whereas the laity, in turn, both practices nonattachment through such giving (*dāna*) and, in the process, generates positive kamma, merit (*puñña*).[2]

The ideology of *dāna*, however, is more complicated than it may appear. For the monks, in particular, the possession of the property that is given by the laity leads to a whole range of ethical and legal complications, and there is a substantial – and substantially complicated – portion of the monastic codes of conduct, the *Vinayas*, that address the issue of property. Although the *Vinaya* is often understood to be a single, monolithic ethical (and legal) code, there are, in fact, several different versions of the *Vinaya*, and they do not present a simple or singular view of property. There is no similar document for the laity, although ethical guidelines dictating property can be found throughout the Buddhist canons, and these, like the monastic codes, effectively serve as Buddhist laws governing property.

This chapter is not an attempt to cover all aspects of property and law across the Buddhist traditions; such a herculean task is neither appropriate nor possible in the present context. Rather, this chapter will be quite limited in scope: I will first discuss some general understandings of property in the broad Buddhist tradition, attitudes that inform the legal ethos regarding property; I will then look more specifically at some of the particular

[2] Unless otherwise noted, the Pāli form of Buddhist terms will be used here.

ethical and legal issues involving property that may have arisen in monastic communities in South Asia.

Proper Owning and Proper Giving

Property itself is neither a good nor a bad thing in Buddhism;[3] like all things of the world, property is ultimately an illusion, ultimately not "real," but that does not necessarily mean that it is therefore a bad thing. Rather, the issue is how one relates to property. Indeed, Buddhists hold a characteristically middle-way attitude toward property – it is only a problem when one has too much and is too attached to it, or when one has too little and thus craves more of it. Not only should property be possessed properly, it is equally important that property be acquired in the proper manner – that is, through ethical and moral means – such as a layperson, who "by means of wealth acquired by energetic striving, amassed by strength of arm, won by sweat, lawful and lawfully gotten, both enjoys his wealth and does good deeds therewith."[4] The term "lawfully gotten" here means that one has not attained one's property or wealth through theft or trickery and that no living beings were harmed in the acquisition of the property.

This same basic principle holds for monks as well. Indeed, the second of the five precepts, which hold for both monks and laypeople, is "no taking what is not given." This does not mean simply that monks should not steal, although that is part of the meaning of the precept; it also means that monks must not ask for specific things to be given, and that they must accept what is given to them by the laity. Although this may, on its face, seem relatively straightforward, it can lead to complications with regard to property given to the monastery. For example, a prominent monastery in Colombo, Sri Lanka, was given a Mercedes Benz by a wealthy layperson in the mid-1980s. Consequently, the head monk was driven to religious functions in this rather luxurious car – complete with air conditioning and hand-tooled leather seats and a rosewood dash – and laypeople would often remark, upon seeing the head monk emerge from the vehicle, that the monks in that particular monastery must be corrupt, living so luxuriously

[3] Frank Reynolds, "Ethical Analysis and Wealth in Theravaada Buddhism: A Study in Comparative Religious Ethics" in Russell F. Sizemore and Donald K. Swearer (eds.), *Ethics, Wealth, and Salvation: A Study in Buddhist Social Ethics* (Columbia: University of South Carolina Press, 1990), 59–76; F.L. Pryor, "A Buddhist Economic System – In Practice," *American Journal of Economics & Sociology* 50.1 (1991), 17–33.

[4] *Anguttara Nikāya* II.68.

in contrast to the people they serve. The head monk, for his part, invoked the second precept in response to such charges, and said that if he were not to use the car he would be rejecting the layperson's gift, in the process denying him (in this case) the merit (*puñña*) generated by his act of *dāna*. Furthermore, the monk maintained, the car in this case was merely a means to an end, merely a mode of transportation; he was not in any way attached to it, and, indeed, he pointed out, if he were to reject it he would, in fact, be demonstrating a form of attachment. He maintained that the only proper attitude to property was indifference.

Buddhist texts are filled with stories of virtuous wealthy individuals – kings, traders, courtesans – who are also model givers.[5] Frank Reynolds has pointed out that for the layperson, property and wealth "may serve either as a vehicle for achieving greater adherence to dhammic norms *or* as a factor that inhibits such adherence."[6] Sometimes these individuals give huge amounts of money or land; sometimes they give the most humble of gifts. One of the most well-known stories in the entire Buddhist tradition is the story of King Vessantara, a wealthy king who is often taken to be the very embodiment of perfect generosity. Indeed, Vessantara takes this most basic of Buddhist virtues to an almost tragic extreme, giving up all of his material possessions, his entire kingdom, even his family.

In the semi-canonical *Milindapañha* (*Questions of King Milinda*), there is a long conversation between Milinda and the monk Nāgasena about Vessantara's actions. Milinda is troubled that Vessantara's generosity brought hardship and suffering on his own children, and he wants to know how it can be that the giving of material possessions that causes suffering for others can be kammically beneficial for the giver. Nāgesena counters with several examples of meritorious actions that may engender suffering. Milinda, though, is not satisfied, and points out that it is the excessiveness of the gifts that is at issue; Vessantara simply gave away too much. Nāgasena, for his part, defends excessive giving, arguing that Vessantara did so because of his intense desire for enlightenment which, he reasons, was the same motivation of the Buddha himself when he renounced his material and familial life. Nāgasena's response is not particularly satisfying, particularly his invocation of Śākyamuni's renunciation; for the Buddha-to-be, the material world – his family and his property – were a hindrance to religious progress, creating distractions and potential attachment. The

5 Nancy Auer Falk, "Exemplary Donors of the Pāli Tradition" in Sizemore and Swearer (eds.), *Ethics, Wealth, and Salvation*, 124–43.

6 Reynolds, "Ethical Analysis," 67.

possession of property in the Buddha's life story was very much portrayed as a problem; Vessantara's possessions, in contrast, allow him to engage in merit-generating giving, and thus the possessions are "good" because they are a means to a kammically efficacious end.

In an interesting passage of the *Milindapañha*, relevant to the present context, Milinda asks Nāgasena if there are things that should not be given, that should be withheld, despite the worthiness of the recipient. Nāgasena misunderstands the question – understandably – and lists ten things that should not be given: strong drink, women, weapons, and so forth. Milinda puts the question to the monk again, making clear that it was not really the specific objects about which he was asking, but whether there were contexts in which a recipient was worthy of a particular gift, but in which the gift should not be given. Nāgasena says no, there are no such instances. Vessantara's extreme act of generosity is thus primarily understood as a means of gaining positive kamma, merit (*puñña*). Put another way, the discussion about property and giving in the *Milindapañha* addresses the benefits of giving, but does not say much about the problem of property. Vessantara is virtuous because he gives, not because he renounces attachment.

Many other examples of this problem exist. The story of the wealthy layperson Anāthapiṇḍika, for instance, presents what Nancy Falk calls "a complete program of appropriate attitudes and works for the wealthy donor."[7] Indeed, Anāthapiṇḍika appears in a number of contexts throughout the Pāli canon as a model donor; these are also opportunities for the Buddha to articulate the proper attitudes and motivations for acquiring and giving wealth and property. Suffice it to say, there are, in fact, diffuse lay ethical guidelines for attaining, possessing, and giving property that run through the Buddhist tradition. These ethical guidelines are not, however, laws in the strict sense of the term. It is important, nonetheless, that the tradition both recognizes that laypeople will accumulate and possess property, and also that they will give this property to the monks, and that there must be a structure of giving.

Although there is not a single set of ethical or legal guidelines, some basic tenets can be gleaned from the various examples in early Buddhist texts: material possessions are a necessary part of lay life; one should earn one's property through ethical means; one should enjoy one's property, but not to the point of becoming overly attached to it; one should use one's wealth and property to help others, in particular monks; one should give

[7] Falk, "Exemplary Donors," 129.

out of compassion; and one should not be attached to the reward such giving creates. If a certain vagueness characterizes the ethical principles governing property for the layperson, an almost obsessive legal attention to the minutiae of specific conditions marks the monastic discussion of property matters.

Property Matters: *Vinayas* as Laws, Monks as Lawyers

> In fact, 'monastic capitalism' might be more useful to characterize the social and economic organization of large monasteries at that time. Accounts were kept and regularly audited, many lay officials and servants of the monasteries were paid in cash (gold), and interest from capital endowments were used to maintain monk scholars and monastic establishments very much in the same way American Ivy League Universities are operated today. (Hans-Dieter Evers)[8]

> When he died the monk Upananda had a large quantity of gold – three hundred thousands of gold: one hundred thousand from bowls and robes; a second hundred thousand from medicines for the sick; a third hundred thousand from worked and unworked gold. (*Mūlasarvāstivāda-vinaya*)[9]

On one level, the basic issue with property from the monastic perspective can be stated quite simply: Laypeople support monks and monasteries by giving wealth and property to them, and this property and wealth raises issues regarding the ascetic ideal, attachments, and lay perceptions of the purity of the *saṅgha.* As Buddhist monasticism became increasingly institutionalized and monks and monasteries grew, so too did the property they owned. By at least as early as the fifth century CE, many monasteries in India had become large property-owning institutions: they owned land, buildings, supplies, furniture, books, clothing, and so on. Monks, however, are fundamentally supposed to live ascetic lives, devoid of all but the most essential things.

Therefore, monks, from a very early period, necessarily had to develop guidelines – basic principles, rules, laws – for ownership and use of such property. These rules, articulated in the various monastic *Vinayas*, are, not surprisingly, context specific, varied, and at times seemingly contradictory.

[8] Hans-Dieter Evers, "Kinship and Property Rights in a Buddhist Monastery in Central Ceylon," *American Anthropologist* 69.6 (1967), 703–10, 705.

[9] Quoted in Gregory Schopen, "Deaths, Funerals, and the Division of Property in a Monastic Code" in Donald S. Lopez Jr. (ed.), *Buddhism in Practice* (Princeton, NJ: Princeton University Press, 1995), 496.

Some of these rules are very specific, stipulating exactly what sort of property a monk can, and cannot, possess: "An overly short piece of tooth wood is not to be chewed . . . I allow tooth wood four fingerbreadths long at the very least."[10] Others are much more general. Perhaps the most basic, minimal statement about property in the *Vinayas* is in the instructions that are to be given to a new monk upon his or her ordination. According to these instructions, the monk is to possess only four things: begged food or scraps; rag-robes, or robes of discarded cloth; the foot of trees as a place of residence; and urine for medicine. If this were indeed the case on the ground, however, property would simply not be an issue for monks, and there would be no need for the extensive rules governing how monks deal with property.

Gregory Schopen has written extensively on property issues in the different *Vinaya* collections, particularly on the *Mūlasarvāstivāda-vinaya*, and in the process offered up an important correction to the way scholars have typically thought about monks and their relationship with property in Buddhism. In particular, he has demonstrated that in contrast to the way monks are presented in Western textbooks and monographs – as solitary wanderers, strict ascetics – the *Vinaya* texts present a monk who is "caught in the web of social and ritual obligations, is fully and elaborately housed and permanently settled, preoccupied not with *nirvāṇa* but with bowls and robes, bathrooms and door bolts, and proper behavior in public."[11] What Schopen has demonstrated is that not only did monks in medieval Indian Buddhism often own property – sometimes large amounts of property – but also that legal discussions of property matters were quite often highly nuanced and complex. Monks and even the Buddha himself at times seem very much like lawyers in the *Vinayas*, arguing minute details of property possession, acquisition, and inheritance: "They appear to apply to the questions of ownership and inheritance, for example, the same sort of care and precision that their colleagues working on the *Abhidharma* applied to the classification and definition of *dharmas*."[12] Thus, there are rules governing oral and written contracts, loans, endowments, inheritances, and so on.

Take, for example, the seemingly simple issue of a monk's robes, perhaps the most basic of all Buddhist property. If, in fact, it were merely a matter of a monk possessing "rag-robes, or robes of discarded cloth" – as various

[10] Vin 31.2. [11] Schopen, "Deaths, Funerals," 473.

[12] Gregory Schopen, "The Good Monk and His Money in a Buddhist Monasticism of 'the Mahāyāna Period'" in *Buddhist Monks and Business Matters: Still More Papers on Monastic Buddhism in India* (Honolulu: University of Hawai'i Press, 2004), 1–18, 6.

Vinayas stipulate and as the West has generally assumed was the case for Buddhist monks – then the matter would presumably be quite simple. There are, however, long discussions in the Pāli *Vinaya* about robes, about how much cloth a monk should receive in order to make a robe, about what is to be done with excess cloth, about how many robes a monk may possess, about who can and cannot give a monk a robe, about what happens to the robes after his death, and so on. For instance, there are occasions when a monk may request that a layperson give him a robe; however, there are many layers of conditions placed on this seemingly straightforward transaction. Indeed, in some sections of the *Vinaya* collections – the *Nissaggiya pācittiya* of the *Suttavibhaṅga*, for instance – it is made clear that only a relative may give a specific monk a robe. The "laws" here about robes stipulate that a robe may only be properly possessed by a monk if at least one of the following conditions are met: he asks for the robe at the right time; he asks for it from his own relatives; he asks people who have specifically invited the monk to ask for cloth; or if he asks on behalf of a fellow monk. If these conditions are not met, then the monk must forfeit the robe.

Elsewhere, however, it is stated that a monk may receive a robe from a non-relative, but only at the appropriate time, and only if certain conditions are met. The *Mahāvibhaṅga* of the Pāli canon, for instance, lists eight ways in which a potential donor may direct his/her gift of cloth: (1) within the territory, (2) within an agreement, (3) where food is prepared, (4) to the Community, (5) to both sides of the Community, (6) to the Community that has spent the rains, (7) having designated it, and (8) to an individual. Likewise, if a monk accepts robe cloth, he may only accept enough to make a robe – the remainder, if any, goes to the monastery. But, that is not all; there are stipulations about where the cloth should be stored, who may actually make the robe, and so on. The different *Vinayas* also go into great detail about the materials that a monk may accept for a robe, materials that are clearly not limited to the simple rags that are stipulated at ordination. According to the *Mahāvibhaṅga*, robes may be made from linen, cotton, silk, wool, jute, or hemp (a list that is expanded in the modern era to include various synthetic materials). Likewise, the *Vinayas* also stipulate what sorts of materials are not to be worn: there are to be no swallow-wort stalk robes, or robes made of makaci fiber, and there should be no robes made of tirīta-tree. The *Vinayas* do not stop there; there are also discussions of how a robe can be sewn, what sort of equipment can be used, what sort of dye, and so on.

The Pāli *Vinaya* is at least superficially more concerned with internal monastic matters than its Sanskrit *Mūlasarvāstivāda-vinaya* counterpart;

however, it is nonetheless ambiguous and rather confusing on the issue of a monk's ability to possess or to inherit personal property. Thus, even though there are clear rules about what sort of robes or alms bowl a monk may receive and possess, these rules are apparently suspended if that same monk has gotten the objects *attano dhanena* (through his own wealth), indicating, it would seem, that monks did, in fact, continue to possess individual wealth after they had entered the monastery.[13] Conversely, monks could also serve as donors themselves, a tricky proposition, indeed, if they did not continue, in some sense, to possess property and wealth; this is a fact attested to not only in the *Vinayas*, but also in various inscriptions, such as those from Sāñcī and Bhārhut.[14]

These discussions may not initially seem to be about law, or at least not in a sense that would be familiar to those steeped in the contemporary Western legal traditions. Certainly, these are discussions about monastic practice, about ethics and etiquette, and they are, in that sense, about monastic, or religious, law. However, it is important to recognize that these are not simply internal monastic discussions. They are also discussions about the ownership of property, and how such property may or may not relate to the exterior world, outside of the confines of the monastery and the saṅgha. For instance, going back to the issue of the distribution of property after the death of a monk, this is an important legal, and not just monastic, matter, and the various *Vinayas* spend a great deal of time, and expend no small effort, on this issue.

A basic question that the *Vinayas* must address is this: Who actually owns a monk's property? Who receives it upon his death? In the Pāli *Vinaya*, the issue seems relatively straightforward; a monk's property belongs to the monastic community. However, there are, not surprisingly, exceptions to this general rule. For instance, a monk may stipulate that his robe and bowl are to be given to a particular monk, as long as he does not stipulate that the belongings are to be given after his death; if the monk in question did add "after my death" to the gift of his belongings, then the belongings go to the full community. Such a seemingly minute distinction was obviously important to the Buddhist jurists here, even if the import of the discussion is not entirely clear to us from where we now stand.

13 Gregory Schopen, "Monastic Law Meets the Real World: A Monk's Continuing Right to Inherit Family Property in Classical India," *History of Religions* 35.2 (1995), 101–23, 105.

14 Gregory Schopen, "Two Problems in the History of Indian Buddhism: The Layman/Monk Distinction and the Doctrines of the Transference of Merit," *Studien zur Indologie und Iranistik* 10 (1985), 9–47.

Schopen has drawn attention to a similar discussion in the *Mūlasarvāstivāda-vinaya*, in which the Buddha forbids the transfer of a dead monk's robes to a living monk even though the dead monk had explicitly said that they should go to his colleague after his death. The argument goes something like this: the dead monk did not give his robe to the other monk while he was living, and he cannot give it now that he is dead. Thus, the transfer is inappropriate. What is interesting here is that in the case of the Pāli *Vinaya*, the matter seems to be entirely monastic; in the *Mūlasarvāstiāada-vinaya* example, however, Schopen sees an explicit reaction to, or tension with, the larger – and in a sense "secular" – Brahmanical law, which allowed for the living person to state that his (or her) property be distributed in a particular way after death. Buddhist monastic law forbids this. Schopen suggests, then, that in the particular sociopolitical context in which the *Mūlasarvāstivāda-vinaya* was produced, it was important to contrast monastic law with secular/Brahmanical law, and important that monastic law "trumped" secular law in matters of property. Obviously, however, there is much that we cannot, from our vantage point, know about why such legal stipulations were necessary, although it certainly could be as simple as a monastic desire to distinguish, and indeed separate, their laws from the laws of the state.

Another exception to the general rule that the dead monk's property belongs to the community is that such property may be given to the individual monks who cared for the deceased before he died. "The Community is the owner of the robes and bowl of a bhikkhu who has passed away. But those who tend to the sick are of great service. I allow that the Community give the three robes and the bowl to those who tend to the sick."[15] In this case, there is a specific procedure outlined, by which the monk, or monks, who cared for the deceased comes to the community carrying the dead monk's robes and bowl, which he presents to the community; the community then formally gives – or returns to – the monk (or monks) in question the deceased's belongings. Buddhaghosa, in the *Samantapāsādikā*, goes into considerable detail on this matter, discussing who counts as having cared for the dead monk, who should get how much, and so on.

If the dead monk had other belongings besides the basic robe and bowl – again, another clear indication that monks did indeed own personal property – then that property goes to the larger community, the "Saṅgha of the four directions." It may be used, or it may be sold, with the proceeds going to the saṅgha as a whole. This is a significant point that is easily overlooked:

[15] *Mahāvibhaṅga* VIII.27.2.

The saṅgha, both in the large sense of the monastic "institution," as well as in the sense of individual monasteries and individual monks, had no choice but to traffic in property and money.

The *Mūlasarvāstivāda-vinaya* says that before the issue of property can be dealt with, the body must be ritually treated and a variety of ritual actions must be performed, actions that are, according to Schopen, "clearly intended to effect a definitive separation of the dead monk . . . from his personal belongings."[16] Again, it is worth noting that monks clearly were understood to own property here, and not simply the euphemistic robe and bowl that Schopen has noted covered a large range of personal property. Schopen discusses a passage in the *Mūlasarvāstivāda-vinaya* in which the Buddha outlines how and when a dead monk's property is to be distributed, and he concludes that:

> ownership rights were clearly divided in a Mūlasarvāstivādin monastery, a single example that is also consistent across the various *vinaya* collections: property belonged either to the Buddha or the dharma or the community. In each case such property could be used only for specific purposes, and normally could not be transferred to another unit or purpose.[17]

The Buddha's instructions here are quite specific and detailed: certain items are to be distributed to the entire community, certain things for the specific monastery to which the dead monk belonged, certain things are to be sold and the money distributed, and so on.

In the same *Vinaya*, there is a story of the distribution of the property of a strikingly wealthy monk, Upananda, who has died. Several things are worth noting here, the first of which is that, despite the distinct sense that Upananda's property was still "his" even after he had joined the order, upon his death his estate becomes the property of the community as a whole, although individual items are distributed to individual monks. More interesting, however, is the clash between secular and monastic law in this episode. When Upananda dies, government officials hear of his death and go to the king, Prasenjit, who instructs them to seal the monastic cell of the dead monk, thereby intending to take possession of his property.

Upananda's fellow monks go to the Buddha to inform him of the matter, and the Buddha sends Ānanda to Prasenjit on his behalf to intervene. The Buddha instructs Ānanda to ask the king if he consulted the monk Upananda when the king had governmental business or when he took a

[16] Schopen, "Deaths, Funerals," 477. [17] *Ibid.*, 484.

wife? And when Upananda was sick, did the king attend to him? Furthermore, the Buddha tells Ānanda that if Presenjit refuses to leave the matter to the monks, he, Ānanda, should tell him: "Great King, the affairs of the house of householders are one thing; those of renouncers quite another. You must have no concern! These possessions fall to the fellow monks of Upananda. You must not acquiesce to their removal!"[18] Prasenjit is persuaded and leaves the matter to the monks.

Schopen has also drawn attention to a discussion in the same text of a "shaven-headed householder" – a kind of semi-monk, it would seem – who dies after having donated all of his property, via a written will, to the Jetavana monastery. A scene similar to the Upananda case ensues, in which the king's men go to seize the deceased's property. Here the matter is a bit different, in that the issue in part turns on the fact that several monks had attended to the man while he was sick (and would thus receive the dead monk's property), but also, more significantly, that the dead man was not a fully ordained monk. No matter, it would seem. For our purposes, the most significant aspect of this second case is nicely summarized by Schopen, who notes that we have here "yet one more instance where *Mūlasarvāstivādin* jurists appear to be seriously struggling with the relationship and boundaries of monastic and lay law and one more instance where the issues are focused on questions of inheritance."[19]

Conclusion

It is important to point out that the examples presented here are, of course, recorded in Buddhist texts – in the *Vinayas* and their commentaries – and were intended as guides and legal precedents within the medieval Indian monastic context, or, more properly, within several different monastic contexts. The issues discussed in the Pāli *Vinayas* were produced and initially used in Sri Lanka, where Buddhism did not, at least initially, have to contend with the legal precedents established by the Hindu *dharmaśāstras*. They are thus somewhat different from the discussions in the Indian *Vinaya* texts, and tend to be much more inwardly focused on the property matters within the monastic world. There is much comparative work to be done here that would fruitfully include other *Vinayas* as well, from other parts of Asia, particularly Tibet and China. Furthermore, we cannot be sure that on the ground things in fact played out as described in the texts. Certainly, it

[18] *Ibid.*, "Deaths, Funerals," 496; also Schopen, "Monastic Law Meets the Real World," 116.
[19] Schopen, "Monastic Law Meets the Real World," 120.

is significant in the passage just cited that the monastic jurists in the Indian context recognized that there might be tensions with their property law and the secular property law of the state, and such passages can be taken as much as a polemical assertions of the ways in which monastic law trumps secular law as they can be taken as evidence of actual legal practices.

CHAPTER 5

On the Legal and Economic Activities of Buddhist Nuns

Two Examples from Early India

Gregory Schopen

Re-visioning the Indian Buddhist Nun as a "Legal Person"

One of the most obvious limitations of even recent work on the economics and business or corporate law of Buddhist monasticism in early India has been its almost exclusive focus on male monasticism, on male monasteries and monks. Nuns and nunneries have once again been overlooked or dropped between the cracks.[1] There is, of course, no good reason for this, especially since it has been clear for some time from Buddhist inscriptional records that up until the Gupta period, at least, nuns were as active as donors at Buddhist sites as were monks, and must therefore have had very considerable means and economic presence.[2] Even more recently it has also been noted that, although textually nuns may have been hierarchically or ritually subservient to monks, this had – according to at least one *Vinaya* or monastic code – no bearing on their legal or economic status: for this *Vinaya,* nuns had equal legal rights of ownership and economic independence.[3] This same *Vinaya,* the *Mūlasarvāstivāda-vinaya,* or closely related texts, moreover, deals with nuns who engage in a wide range of business enterprises, both licit and – according to the male authors of this code – illicit,[4] and who have at their disposal and use a series of sophisticated

[1] A prime example is G. Schopen, *Buddhist Monks and Business Matters: Still More Papers on Monastic Buddhism in India* (Honolulu: University of Hawai'i Press, 2004).

[2] See the overview and sources cited in P. Kieffer-Pülz's contribution entitled "Die buddhistische Gemeinde" in *Der Buddhismus I. Der indische Buddhismus und seine Verzweigungen* (Die Religionen der Menschheit, Bd. 24, 1), H. Bechert et al. (Stuttgart: Verlag W. Kohlhammer, 2000), 302–03.

[3] G. Schopen, "Separate but Equal: Property Rights and the Legal Independence of Buddhist Nuns and Monks in Early North India," *Journal of the American Oriental Society* 128 (2008), 625–40.

[4] For some of these business enterprises, see G. Schopen, "The Urban Buddhist Nun and a Protective Rite for Children in Early North India," in M. Straube et al. (eds.), *Pāsādikadānaṁ. Festschrift für Bhikkhu Pāsādika*, Indica et Tibetica 52 (Marburg: Indica et Tibetica Verlag, 2009), 375–77, where the urban character of these enterprises is noted.

financial instruments. A comprehensive, detailed survey of all of this would be, of course, of considerable interest and importance for any future view of the Indian Buddhist nun, but such a survey is hardly possible now, and certainly not here. The investigation of these issues has just begun; the sources we must use are in some disarray and more often than not very difficult, and the basic legal vocabulary is barely understood. Here, then, we can only make a start on two topics that will come to form a part of any such future survey: the use of negotiable promissory notes by Buddhist nuns, and their involvement in lending on interest funds that they held as permanent endowments. These two topics alone will amply illustrate the difficulties involved in pursuing these kinds of investigations, and will all too elegantly reveal how very far we have yet to go. But hopefully, too, they may reveal the potential of this kind of work for a badly needed re-visioning of the figure of the Indian Buddhist nun, and show again the perhaps unique importance of *Mūlasarvāstivāda-vinaya* sources for the legal historian.

A First Example: Litigious Nuns and Negotiable Loan Contracts

A first set of texts we might deal with here exemplifies many of the problems; the first of which is, appropriately enough, lexical – law, after all, is very much about the meaning of words. Both texts that follow here deal with Buddhist nuns and "promissory notes," and although neither text has come down to us in Sanskrit and both must be filtered through their Tibetan translations, that promissory note is a reasonably correct translation is fairly certain, even if it is not a literal one. Indeed, in this case even the Sanskrit original might be recoverable.

In the first of our texts – the *Bhikṣuṇī-vibhaṅga* preserved in Tibetan – the term translated as "promissory note" is *chags rgya*. This compound does not occur in Jäschke's still amazing dictionary, nor does it seem to be in use in modern Tibetan. It is, however, registered in both Roerich's *Tibetan-Russian-English Dictionary* and in the *Bod rgya tshig mdzod chen mo* dictionary: In the first it is defined as "promissory note," and the second, explicitly marking it as "old" (*rnying*), says it is *bu lon bda' ba'i dpang rgya*, literally "a witness-seal that calls in a debt," but neither gives a source and both give a referent for the compound, but not a meaning.[5] It is in more specialized studies like Takeuchi's *Old Tibetan Contracts from Central Asia*

[5] Y.N. Roerich, *Tibetan-Russian-English Dictionary* (Moscow: Nauka Publishers, 1985), vol. III, 70; Zhang Yisun, et al., *Bod rgya tshig mdzod chen mo* (Beijing: Mi rigs dpe skrun khang, 1985), 779.

that we get a better sense of what the compound means. He says "*chags* as a transitive verb meaning 'borrow, make a loan'–is found only in Old Tibetan texts, where it also formed a compound noun *chags-rgya* or 'loan contract.'"[6] Obviously, the occurrence of at least the compound in the *Bhikṣuṇī-vibhaṅga* indicates that it is not limited to "Old Tibetan texts," but is also found in canonical Tibetan. In fact, the *Bhikṣuṇī-vibhaṅga* is almost certainly the source for the gloss found in the *Bod rgya tshig mdzod chen mo* dictionary, since that gloss is already found – word for word – in the old word commentary embedded in the former *chags rgya zhes bya ba ni bu lon bda' ba'i dpang rgya'o*. Our second text, which may represent a second distinct redaction of the *Bhikṣuṇī-vibhaṅga* or a developed commentarial gloss, although it is almost certainly rendering the same Sanskrit original, adds an important detail. There the *chags rgya* or "promissory note" is explicitly said to be "a promissory note of debt," *bu lon gyi chags rgya*.

The value of *Vinaya* material dealing with nuns for legal history might already be apparent from the fact that it is only in these texts, it seems, that this important term is explained, and it is this explanation that alone allows a full understanding of, for example, another important legal text preserved in Sanskrit. The *Cīvara-vastu* of the *Mūlasarvāstivāda-vinaya* has a text dealing with the disposition of an estate that is conveyed to the monastic community by means of a written will (*patrābhilikhita*). Among the items included in the estate are two kinds of what are called *patralekhya*. The Sanskrit term refers of course to written documents, but the precise nature of these documents would not at all be clear without access to the Tibetan translation of the text *and* reference to our *Vinaya* texts dealing with nuns. In the Tibetan translation of the *Cīvara-vastu*, the generic *patralekhya* is translated by *chags rgya*, providing another instance of the compound in canonical Tibetan, but more importantly, since the term *chags rgya* is precisely defined in the *Bhikṣuṇī-vibhaṅga*, it can be said with some confidence that the *patralekhya* referred to in the *Cīvara-vastu* were loan contracts or promissory notes that called in a debt.[7] Both the *Cīvara* and *Bhikṣuṇī-vibhaṅga* texts, moreover, allow us to go even further. The first makes it clear that for Buddhist writers, such promissory notes were

[6] T. Takeuchi, *Old Tibetan Contracts from Central Asia* (Tokyo: Daizo Shuppan, 1995), 49.

[7] For the Sanskrit text of the *Cīvara-vastu*, see N. Dutt, *Gilgit Manuscripts*, vol. III, Pt. 2 (Srinagar: The Calcutta Oriental Press, 1942), 143.7; for the Tibetan translation, see *Cīvara-vastu*, Derge 'dul ba Ga 113a.3 (for Tibetan texts, I have used the Derge printing reprinted in *The Tibetan Tripitaka. Taipei Edition* ed. A.W. Barber (Taipei: SMC Publishing Inc, 1991) and all references, unless otherwise noted, are to it, although I have also occasionally indicated where a given text is also found in other versions); for a translation of the full text from Sanskrit, see Schopen, *Buddhist Monks and Business Matters*, 117–19, where *patralekhya* = *chags rgya* is rendered by "written lien."

fully inheritable and could be transferred to unrelated persons, both actual or juristic (i.e., the *saṅgha*); the second shows that for these same writers, these notes were negotiable, that is, they were a "written security which may be transferred by indorsement and delivery, or by delivery merely, so as to vest in the indorsee the legal title, and thus enable him to bring a suit thereon in his own name"[8] – and bring suit is almost exactly what a Buddhist nun does in our first text.

The fact that our first text is found in the Tibetan translation of the *Bhikṣuṇī-vibhaṅga* also raises an issue that must be noted, even though it cannot yet be resolved: No less of a luminary than Bu-ston has expressed doubts about whether or not the *Bhikṣuṇī-vibhaṅga* preserved in Tibetan belongs to the Mūlasarvāstivādin tradition, and some later Tibetan scholars have asserted even more strongly that it does not.[9] This, of course, would be extremely odd, and Bu-ston does not give any reasons for his hesitance, although it is certainly true that there are some significant differences between the versions of the *Prātimokṣa* rules that are found in the *Vibhaṅga* and in the separate Tibetan translation of the *Prātimokṣa-sūtra*. However, since the translation of the *Bhikṣuṇī-vibhaṅga* is already registered in the old Lhan Kar Ma catalog, and was translated by the same team that translated the *Vinayavastu*, a team whose members were therefore not likely to be confused about such matters,[10] these differences could rather suggest that Mūlasarvāstivādin rules for nuns circulated in two different versions and that, in this case, we are lucky enough to have both. Should this be the case, we would not have a problem, but a welcome windfall. However, although clear links have already been noted between the *Bhikṣuṇī-vibhaṅga* preserved in Tibetan and the rest of Mūlasarvāstivādin *Vinaya* literature,[11] and although its reference to "promissory notes" appears to be another such link, the fact remains that the *Bhikṣuṇī-vibhaṅga* preserved in Tibetan has been very little studied, and a great deal of work will be required to sort this out. For the moment, then, and until it can be shown to be otherwise, it can only be a working hypothesis that we have preserved in Tibetan two variant versions of the Mūlasarvāstivādin rules for nuns.

8 B.A. Garner, *Black's Law Dictionary*, 7th ed. (St. Paul: West Group, 1999), 1058.

9 See the sources cited in G. Schopen, "On Emptying Chamber Pots without Looking and the Urban Location of Buddhist Nunneries in Early India Again," *Journal Asiatique* 296 (2008), 231–32 and n. 4 and the discussion there.

10 A. Herrman-Pfandt, *Die Lhan Kar Ma. Ein früher Katalog der ins Tibetische übersetzten buddhistischen Texte* (Wien: Verlag der Österreichischen Akademie der Wissenschaften, 2008), nos. 485, 488; and see also 279, n. 475.

11 See, for example, Schopen, "On Emptying Chamber Pots," 241–44.

One Version of a Legal Tale: A Nun Should Not Take a Debtor to Court over a Loan Contract

Apart from the issues discussed earlier, the text from the *Bhikṣuṇī-vibhaṅga* is, as the following translation will show, reasonably clear in its general purport.

Bhikṣuṇī-vinaya-vibhaṅga

(Derge Ta 123a.5–124a.2 = Tog Nya 165a.3–166a.3)

The Buddha, the Blessed One, was staying in Śrāvastī, in the Jetavana, in the Park of Anāthapiṇḍada.

At that time when a certain householder in Śrāvastī was struck with disease he gave gifts to ascetics and brahmins and the poor and the needy. The nun Sthūlanandā heard about that merit-making and went then to where that householder was. When she arrived she recited Dharma for him, and, when she had finished, she said this to the householder: "Sir, since a woman is one who gets little you should give me at least a little something!"

He said: "Noble One, why did you not come earlier? When it appeared that I was to die I transferred everything to the other world."

Sthūlanandā said: "Alas, one should live a hundred years without any difficulty."

He said: "Noble One, can a promissory note (*chags rgya*) be accepted?"

"Sir," she said, "if you were to give it."

Then he gave it to her.

When Sthūlanandā had accepted the promissory note she went to the other householder (i.e., the debtor) and arriving there, she said to him, "Sir, you must repay this soon!"

The householder read it. When he had read it, he said: "Does this belong to you, Noble One?"

"It is mine," she said.

"I will be financially ruined."

But Sthūlanandā, having seized[12] that householder, said: "If you are not going to give this to me I will take you to the king's court!"

When she had said this he just sat there. A friend of his came along and said to him: "What has happened?"

He said: "I have been seized by a debt collector."

"Who is the debt collector?"

He said: "A nun."

[12] The full or exact sense of "seized" (*bzung nas, bzung ngo*) is not clear. Given what follows, it does not appear to have a literal meaning here – the debtor remains where he was – but seems rather to mean something like "impose a lien or claim" or encumber. The same lack of clarity surrounds the expression "prosecute for seizure" (*len par byed pa*).

> His friend said: "But did you not obtain whatever was borrowed from someone else in the world? – What have you received from a nun?!"
>
> Then brahmins and householders on that account were derisive, contemptuous and critical, saying, "The ascetic practice of Buddhist nuns has gone up in smoke since even a promissory note is prosecuted for seizure!"
>
> The nuns told this matter to the monks, and the monks also reported it to the Blessed One.
>
> The Blessed One, then, determined in regard to this situation . . . and so on up to . . . a rule should be promulgated, said: "Further, when some nun prosecutes for seizure a promissory note, this practice alone would be an immediate offence and, together with its successful realization, it would be a violation involving suspension."
>
> "Further, some nun" means: Sthūlanandā.
>
> "Promissory note" means: a witnessed marker that calls in a debt.
>
> "When one prosecutes for seizure" means: when it is taken.
>
> "This practice alone" means: presenting in regard to what is not good practice the word of good practice.
>
> "The other" means: the one bound (i.e. by the contract)
>
> Here if it is asked in what manner it would be an offense: when a nun prosecutes for seizure a promissory note, in accordance with the conditions it would be a violation involving suspension. In regard to one who gets with some difficulty, is the first to do it, etc., there is no offense.

This is a remarkable little text from several angles. It is remarkable first of all because, as we have seen, it alone allows us to fully understand what the *patralekhya* that were mentioned in the *Cīvara-vastu* were. But beyond that it would seem to indicate that its authors – almost certainly men – took as a given that a Buddhist nun was a *legalis homo*, "a person who has full legal capacity and full legal rights."[13] The Buddhist nun they present cannot only accept a promissory note that is given to her, but is explicitly said to own it. She not only has the right to "seize" its maker, but actually does so, and she has the right to take him to the secular courts, even if doing so results in an offense against Buddhist monastic rule. Notice that there would be absolutely no need or purpose for the monastic rule not to do so if the nun did not already have the acknowledged right to do it. If, in other words, the nun did not have the acknowledged right and capacity to "prosecute for seizure" in the secular courts a debt owed by a layman, then a rule forbidding her to do so would make no sense. Notice also that according to the rule there is only an offense if she prosecutes for seizure. There is no offense if a nun accepts promissory notes or if she owns them. Indeed, the exception clause that ends the rule even allows

[13] Garner, *Black's Law Dictionary*, 904.

prosecution for seizure if she is "one who earns with some difficulty," a status that might be claimed by any number of nuns under any number of circumstances and is claimed, at least obliquely, in our text. This, then, is a remarkable, if inadvertent – even hostile – portrait of the Buddhist nun as a fully independent legal person, and one would like to know the position of non-Buddhist Indian law on such figures since it may well be that Buddhist authors considered their nuns to be particularly litigious: Although there appears to be no counterpart to this rule in the male *Prātimokṣa*, the Pāli *Bhikkhunī-vibhaṅga* and the *Mahāsaṅghika-vinaya* and *Dharmaguptaka-vinaya* for nuns have one.[14] Unfortunately, the Buddhist nun – like the Buddhist monk – is virtually invisible in India Dharmaśāstra.

A Second Version of the Tale: Nuns in Hot Pursuit of Estates or Calling in a Debt

Like the *Bhikṣuṇī-vibhaṅga* preserved in Tibetan, our second text also seems to point to the possibility that Mūlasarvāstivādin rules for nuns circulated in more than one version. It is by title a commentary (*vṛtti*) but in form – as one can see in the translation that will be given below – it looks more like another version of a *Vibhaṅga*. Like a *Vibhaṅga*, it supplies a narrative account of how the rule came to be, and it even contains a word commentary and an exception clause, both again characteristics of a *Vibhaṅga*.[15] It is entitled the *Sarvāstivādi-mūla-bhikṣuṇī-prātimokṣa-sūtra-vṛtti*, and the odd and awkward placement of the *–mūla-* here makes it very hard to know how to interpret the compound. It is, however, clear that the rule it delivers is not that found in the Sarvāstivādin *Bhikṣuṇī-Prātimokṣa-sūtra*, but is essentially that found in the separate Tibetan translation of the *Bhikṣuṇī-Prātimokṣa-sūtra*, which is presumed to be Mūlasarvāstivādin, although there are textual problems here as well. Who translated the text is not known, but it – again, like the translation of the *Bhikṣuṇī-vibhaṅga* – is also already registered in Lhan Kar Ma catalog and shares elements that appear

[14] H. Oldenberg, *The Vinaya Piṭaka* (London: Williams and Norgate, 1882), vol. IV, 223–25 (I.B. Horner's translation of the text is less clear than it might be because she renders the difficult and uncommon *ussayavādikā* as "one who speaks in envy," *The Book of the Discipline*), (London: Oxford University Press, 1942), vol. III, 177–81. See now M. Cone, *A Dictionary of Pāli* (Oxford: 2001), Pt. 1, 516; É. Nolot, *Règles de discipline des nonnes bouddhistes* (Paris: Collège de France, 1991), 88–92; A. Heirman, *'The Discipline in Four Parts': Rules for Nuns according to the Dharmaguptakavinaya* (Delhi: Motilal Banarsidass Publishers, 2002), Pt. 2, 331–35.

[15] On the structure and style of a *vibhaṅga*, see É. Nolot, "Textes de discipline bouddhique. Les *Sūtra-Vibhaṅga* ou 'Classification des *sūtra*,'" in N. Balbir (ed.), *Genres litteraires en Inde* (Paris: Presses de la Sorbonne Nouvelle, 1994), 103–22.

to be characteristic of Mūlasarvāstivādin sources, one of which is, of course, reference to "promissory notes."[16] The narrative in the *Sarvāstivādi-mūla-bhikṣuṇī-prātimokṣa-sūtra-vṛtti* is neither completely different nor entirely the same as that which occurs in the *Bhikṣuṇī-vibhaṅga*, and the same is true of the precise wording of the rule in Tibetan.

Sarvāstivādi-mūla-bhikṣuṇī-prātimokṣa-sūtra-vṛtti

(Derge, bstan 'gyur 'dul ba Tsu 56b.3–57a.3 = Peking, bstan 'gyur 'dul ba Dzu 61a.7–61b.7)

> In Śrāvastī there was a rich householder and when he was struck with a disease, in the face of death, he gave gifts to ascetics and brahmins and the poor, and he made merit.
>
> Sthūlanandā too was going for alms and arriving at the house of that householder said: "Be well, householder! How are you doing? Are you living in comfort?"
>
> He told her exactly how things were.
>
> Sthūlanandā said: "Since, householder, you delight in giving gifts, and since a fool of a woman gets little, you should give a portion to me!"
>
> But the sick man said: "Everything is already given away," and Sthūlanandā said: "But it is not fitting to go away from your house without having received something."
>
> That householder had only a promissory note for a debt and he showed it to Sthūlanandā, saying, "Nothing from this remains – if you wish, take it!"
>
> Sthūlanandā carried away the promissory note. But the sick man then said to the man who owed him: "Son of good family, although you would repay this, since I did not speak falsely, accept whatever I gave you – that must not cause you difficulties!"
>
> When he had said: "Since we are in firm agreement, can Sthūlanandā do anything of importance?",[17] that householder died. But when Sthūlanandā had that son of good family seized, she caused difficulties and other householders being critical said derisively: "How is it that a nun prosecutes for recovery of the property of the dead?"
>
> When what had occurred was reported to the Teacher, he promulgated a rule of training: "Further, if some nun has called in loaned property of the

[16] Herrmann-Pfandt, *Die Lhan Kar Ma*, no. 503; Schopen, "On Emptying Chamber Pots," 232–33, and the sources cited in n. 6; 241–44.

[17] The speech here of the dying householder – both what he said to Sthūlanandā and what he said to the man who owed him – is not entirely clear, and probably intentionally so because it seems to involve some double-talk.

dead, this practice too, from this point, is an offense and it must be given up – it is a *saṃghavaśeṣa*."

"Some nun" means: "Sthūlanandā."

"Calls in loaned property of the dead" means: "she has done it herself."

And how here is there an infraction? When the property of the dead has been given by another – a religious or relative or friend – or when the property of the dead causes difficulties and she pursues it, as soon as it is accepted there would be such an offense. If it is for the Community, or if it is done by one who gets only in some measure without difficulty, there is no infraction.

As already noted, the narrative in the *Vṛtti* is not exactly the same as that in the *Vibhaṅga*, but the two seem to be too close to be unrelated. The *Vṛtti* seems to represent either a variant version of the *Vibhaṅga* narrative, or a commentarial paraphrase of it. Even more important for the question of the sectarian affiliation of both the *Vibhaṅga* and the *Vṛtti* is the virtual certainty that both deliver the same rule and the fact that the rule is peculiar to the presumed Mūlasarvāstivādin *Bhikṣuṇī-Prātimokṣa-sūtra* preserved as a separate translation in Tibetan, and is digested in Guṇaprabha's *Vinaya-sūtra*, an indubitable Mūlasarvāstivādin work. Unfortunately, that rule seems not yet to have been fully understood, in large part, it seems, because it contains our compound *chags rgya*.

We have the rule in three slightly different wordings, the first of which is from the *Prātimokṣa-sūtra*[18] and has been translated several times, most recently by Tsomo: "If a bhikṣuṇī, out of attachment, pursues the wealth or possessions of someone who has died, then she commits a *saṅghāvaśeṣa*."[19] All of the translations are off just enough to conceal the fact that this rule is referring to a very specific practice, and leave the impression that the rule is about what in Roman law and literature is called *captatio*, "legacy hunting" or "inheritance hunting," or something very like it.[20] However, once the technical meaning of *chags rgya* is recognized, and it is understood that the rule is referring specifically to promissory notes or loan contracts, then it is almost obvious that the verbs used in the various versions of the rule

[18] *Bhikṣuṇī-Prātimokṣa-Sūtra*, Derge 'dul ba Ta 6a.4.

[19] K.L. Tsomo, *Sisters in Solitude: Two Traditions in Buddhist Monastic Ethics for Women* (Albany: State University of New York Press, 1996), 85. See also W.W. Rockhill, "Le Traité d'Émancipation ou Pratimoksha Sutra traduit du tibétain," *Revue de l'histoire des religions* 9.1 (1884), 15; E. Waldschmidt, *Bruchstücke des Bhikṣuṇī-Prātimokṣa der Sarvāstivādins. Mit einer Darstellung der Überlieferung des Bhikṣuṇī-Prātimokṣa in den verschiedenen Schulen* (Leipzig: Deutsche Morgenländische Gesellschaft, 1926), 87.

[20] See Schopen, "Separate but Equal," 636 for the suspicion that monks might engage in "inheritance hunting" to secure the estates of fellow monks.

do not have the general sense of "chase after," "seek," or "pursue," but the specific sense of "to call in, to recover" a debt.[21] The rule then – and again, it has no counterpart in the male *Prātimokṣa* – would more accurately be translated: "If some nun were to call in a promissory note from the estate of a dead person . . . it is a *saṅghāvaśeṣa* offense."

In the end, it seems, the differences in our sources come down to two. The *Vṛtti* and the *Prātimokṣa* rules explicitly indicate that the note or loaned wealth that should not be prosecuted for recovery formed part of an estate or belonged originally to a person who was dead – in the *Vibhaṅga*, this is only strongly implied since there the householder is not expressly said to have died. This added qualification would seem to carry important consequences. The rule in this form is only against prosecuting for seizure or recovery of loans that formed a part of an estate. It does not address, and certainly does not rule against, nuns prosecuting for seizure other kinds of loans, whereas the *Vibhaṅga* would seem to forbid any such prosecution. But here the second difference emerges. The *Vibhaṅga* allows for prosecution if the nun is "one who gets with some difficulty" (*tshegs chung ngus khugs pa*). The *Vṛtti* does as well, but it also – and first of all – allows prosecution if it is "for the Community," that is, if the nun does not do it for her own benefit, but to the benefit of the saṅgha. Guṇaprabha's expression of the rule, moreover, seems to follow the *Vṛtti*. He condenses the whole of the rule into: "In regard to calling in [or: recovering what belonged to] an estate [by a nun], there is no offense if it is for the Saṅgha or [done] by one having some difficulty [or: on account of some difficulty]."[22]

But if the differences between the *Vibhaṅga* and the *Vṛtti* are not just reflections of differing degrees of verbal explicitness, and point rather to some development, it is more important for our purposes to note that that development does not weaken the status of the nun as an independent legal person, but strengthens it: Here a nun – a woman – may act on her own, and without the need for a monk or male, to prosecute for seizure or recovery of an outstanding loan *if* it is for the sake of the Community,

[21] Both *bda' ba* and *'ded pa* can, to be sure, mean "to chase after or pursue," but Jäschke, for example, already indicates that when their object is debts or money they mean "call in, collect, recover." And although *len par byed pa* literally means "to cause to be obtained or seized," it is an attested translation of Sanskrit *udgrahaṇa*, a standard Sanskrit legal term for "recovery of debt." In fact, it is very likely that the verb in the lost Sanskrit original of the rule was a form of *ud* $\sqrt{grah}$ since it is under the heading *udgrahaṇa* that Guṇaprabha digests our rule in his *Vinaya-sūtra*.

[22] "*Mṛtadhanodgrahaṇe | anāpattiḥ sāṃghikasya | alpāyāsena cet = shi ba'i nor len pa la'o | dge 'dun gyi la ni ltung ba med do | gal te tshegs chung ngus na'o.*" See R. Sankrityayana, *Vinayasūtra of Bhadanta Gunaprabha* (Bombay: Bharatiya Vidya Bhavan, 1981), 64.29 = *Vinaya-sūtra*, Derge bstan 'gyur, 'dul ba Wu 51a.3.

or *if* she is in need, even if the loan formed part of an estate that had been transferred to her. Indeed, the wording of both the *Vṛtti* and the *Prātimokṣa* would seem to suggest that even these restrictions only applied to loan contracts that had formed a part of an estate, and that therefore nuns could without infraction or restriction prosecute for seizure any other kind of loan contract or promissory note.

A Second Example: An Inscriptional Record of Permanent Endowments and Nuns Lending Money on Interest

A second financial instrument that these same *Vinaya* texts allow – indeed, require – nuns to use is particularly interesting since it links both with a textually required male practice, and with what is found widely in Indian inscriptions from the first half of the first millennium CE and beyond. It links in particular with an important inscriptional record from Junnar that has not received all the attention that it deserves. We might start here with it since it provides an instance in actual practice of what our texts refer to, and since that instance can be placed as early as the second century CE.

The Junnar inscription is not well preserved. Indeed, of the five lines of the inscription, only the first two are all but complete. Ten or eleven *akṣaras* or syllables are damaged or not clearly readable in the third line, and eight or more at the beginning of both lines four and five. Bühler was the first to give a reading of the record, and given the state of its preservation no one –neither Sadakata nor Tsukamoto, for example – has been able to substantially improve on his reading.[23]

> It is unfortunate that this record is so poorly preserved, but fortunate that perhaps the most important, or at least the most unusual, elements are close to certain. Restricting the translation to what is reasonably secure, we might get:
>
> Of the son of Savagiriyāsa of the Apaguriyas, Patībadhaka Giribhūti Sakhuyāru,[24] the cave and a cistern are the religious gift. And for this

[23] Bühler's edition and translation was published in J. Burgess, *Report on the Buddhist Cave Temples and Their Inscriptions Archaeological Survey of Western India* vol. IV (London: Trübner, 1883), 93, no. 3; see also A. Sadakata, "Japanese Translation of Junnar Inscriptions" (in Japanese), *The Bulletin of the Faculty of Letters Tokai University* 48 (1987), 211, no. 3; K. Tsukamoto, *Indo bukkyō himei no kenkyū* [A Comprehensive Study of the Indian Buddhist Inscriptions] Pts. I and II (in Japanese) (Kyoto: Heirakuji-Shoten Ltd., 1996–98), 411, no. 31; but the text in both is essentially that established by Bühler. The record was briefly referred to already in B.C. Law, "Bhikshunis in Indian Inscriptions," *Epigraphia Indica* 25 (1939–40), 31–34. For the date, see S. Nagaraju, *Buddhist Architecture of Western India* (c. 250 BC– AD 300) (Delhi: Agam Kala Prakashan, 1981), 181 and Chart III.

[24] Several of these names or designations were and remain obscure; see, for example, Burgess, *Report on the Buddhist Cave Temples*, 93 and n. 2.

> cave and cistern and the nunnery in town a permanent endowment for the Dharmottarīyas. Kārṣāpaṇas[25] . . . the nunnery in town of the wife of Giribhūti, Savapālitanikā.

Although not translatable with any certainty, the general nature of the damaged parts of the record are not in serious doubt. Bühler (or Burgess) had already said: "The mutilated passages in lines 3 and 4 apparently contained provisions regarding the distribution of the interest accruing from the endowment,"[26] and enough remains of these passages to indicate that they mentioned several different sums (13; 2,000; and 1,000 *kārṣāpaṇas*), interest, and so forth. Moreover, well preserved examples of such provisions can be easily cited from other inscriptions that record the gift of *akṣaya-nīvī* or "permanent endowments" elsewhere – an inscription from Kanheri, for example, reads in Bühler's translation: "And a perpetual endowment has been given to the community (*of monks*, viz.), two hundred *kārṣāpaṇas*. Out of (*the interest of*) that 'a piece of sixteen' (*shall be given*) for clothes [for the resident monks], and the value of one *kārṣāpaṇa* (*each*) month in the season."[27] While by no means always a part of records of this kind, such detailed provisions as our record seems to have contained would therefore not have been unusual.

There are, however, at least three things that are definitely unusual – and perhaps unique – about our inscription from Junnar. First, it unambiguously refers to a Buddhist nunnery, and it may be the only Indian inscription in the period that does.[28] In fact, it refers to it twice. In the

[25] *Kāhāpaṇa* = Skt. *Kārṣāpaṇa* is the "name of a gold, silver or copper coin of one *karṣa* (80 *ratis*) in weight" – so D.C. Sircar, *Indian Epigraphical Glossary* (Delhi: Motilal Banarsidass, 1966), 149; but see also U. Thakur, "The First Coins: A Study in Evolution and Growth," in D.C. Sircar (ed.), *Early Indian Indigenous Coins* (Calcutta: University of Calcutta, 1971), 21–47 for one example of the confusion or obscurity surrounding the term. Given the place and time of the record, it is very unlikely that the *kārṣāpaṇas* referred to here were gold or silver. It is far more likely that the *kārṣāpaṇas* then in circulation were copper, lead, or potin (see more recently the discussion and catalog in O. Bopearachchi and W. Pieper, *Ancient Indian Coins* (Turnhout: Brepols, 1998) 7–174) and Kosambi already long ago recognized that this might well have implications for the limited practical consequences of Buddhist rules against monks having contact with 'gold' and 'silver'; see D.D. Kosambi, "Dhenukākaṭa," *Journal of the Asiatic Society of Bombay* 30.2 (1955), 53.

[26] Burgess, *Report on the Buddhist Cave Temples*, 93.

[27] Bühler's editions and translations of the Kanheri inscriptions are also published in a work of J. Burgess, "Report on the Elura Cave Temples and the Brahmanical and Jaina Caves in Western India," *Archaeological Survey of Western India vol. V* (London: Trübner, 1883) 83, no. 21.

[28] Ironically, there appear to be more inscriptional references to institutions connected with nuns in the second half of the first millennium CE when references to nuns as donors all but disappear – at least one from Nepal, four from Valabhī, and one from Orissa – but there are a number of problems with these. The Nepalese inscription is not dated – M.S. Slusser, *Nepal Mandala. A Cultural Study of the Kathmandu Valley* (Princeton, NJ: Princeton University Press, 1982), vol. II, pl. 450, assigns it to "6th c." – and the published editions appear not to be entirely reliable, but the only photo I have been able to see is so reduced as to be unreadable (see T. Riccardi, "Buddhism

first instance, it uses the term *bhikhuni-upasaya*, and in the second it uses the term *upasaya* without any further qualification. Both the terms and the usage correspond to what is not infrequently found in the Pāli *Vinaya*: there too nunneries are called *bhikkhunūpassaya*, or simply *upassaya*, and sometimes both are used in the same passage, just as in the Junnar inscription.[29] But our inscription just as clearly and explicitly indicates – again not once, but twice – that the nunnery was, just as textual rule and narratives indicate, "in town."[30] It therefore also provides an unimpeachable inscriptional reference to the urban location of a Buddhist nunnery. However, – and this, too, may be unique – our Junnar record provides additional epigraphical evidence for the receipt and presumed use of permanent endowments for Buddhist nuns, although who administered the endowment or how it was used are not clear here. There is some textual evidence, however, that would support the suggestion that the nuns themselves might well have administered the endowment, and might well have themselves lent its funds out on interest.

The Use of Permanent Endowments by Monks in Texts

The cave, cistern, and nunnery that the permanent endowment recorded in the Junnar inscription was meant to support,"belonged," apparently, to the Dharmottarīyas, one of the numerous Buddhist groups about which

in Ancient and Early Medieval Nepal," in *Studies in History of Buddhism* ed. A.K. Narain (Delhi: B. R. Publishing Corporation, 1980), 265–81, esp. 274; D.R. Regmi, *Inscriptions of Ancient Nepal* (New Delhi: Abhinav Publications, 1983), vol. I, 88, no. XC; vol. II, 54, no. XC; vol. III, 160 (where the inscription is dated to the "early" or "mid" 7th century) and pl. XC). Moreover, while the inscription appears to record the gift of an *akṣaya-nīvī* to some Mahāyāna (!) nuns, it does not refer to a *vihāra*, but to a *gandhakuṭī*, and what that term referred to at that time in Nepal is not certain. The Valabhī records all date to the 6th or 7th century and are land grants. They refer to *vihāras*, but where exactly they were, and what their relationship was to the male monasteries at Valabhī is not clear (see A.S. Gadre, "Five Vala Copper-plate Grants," *Journal of the University of Bombay* 3 (1934), 74–91, nos. I–III, V). The Orissa inscription is in some ways the most interesting. It is a land grant made according to the rules of permanent endowments (*akṣayanīvīdharmmena*), but it appears to be granted to a Buddhist temple (*āyatana*) and the nuns it mentions seem to be attached to it (see B. Misra, *Orissa under the Bhauma Kings* [Calcutta: The Vishwamitra Press, 1934], 40–50) – Misra says, "The deed was executed at Jayāśrama Vihāra" (41), but no such statement occurs in the record as he edits it, although it does in his translation – cf. U. Singh, *Kings, Brāhmaṇas and Temples in Orissa: An Epigraphic Study AD 300–1147* (New Delhi: Munshiram Manoharlal Publishers, 1994), 254, n. 72. All the records from the period deserve a more careful and close study. In the meantime, see R.M. Davidson, *Indian Esoteric Buddhism: A Social History of the Tantric Movement* (New York: Columbia University Press, 2002), 91–98.

29 H. Oldenberg, *The Vinaya Piṭakaṃ* (London: Williams and Norgate, 1882), vol. IV, 211ff, 265. Note that in the *Mūlasarvāstivāda-vinaya*, the term used to refer to a nunnery is not *upassaya* but, typically, *varṣaka*.

30 For textual material on the location of nunneries in town, see Schopen, "The Urban Buddhist Nun," and Schopen, "On Emptying Chamber Pots."

we know very little apart from the bits and pieces provided by late doxographical works. Professor Bareau's discussion of the Dharmottarīyas, for example, takes up no more than a single page.[31] This group is also not commonly referred to in inscriptions and, although the founder of the group is said to have been an expert in the *Vinaya*, no texts belonging to the group – *Vinaya* or otherwise – appear to be known or to have survived. So we do not have access to what a Dharmottarīya *Vinaya* might have to say on the subject of endowments, and even if we did, it might not be surprising if it said nothing. At least half of the extant *Vinayas* seem to have been content to let such things go unregulated and make no mention of them.[32] Only one of them – the *Mūlasarvāstivāda-vinaya* – treats such endowments in detail in spite of the fact that they were widely used in actual Buddhist monastic communities. Why this should be so is not immediately clear, and any fully satisfactory answer should probably have to account for the equally curious fact that, although widely used in "Hindu" circles, a treatment of such endowments, and the term *akṣaya-nīvī* or *akṣaya*, are missing from Dharmaśāstra texts as well. In noting this absence, Derrett seems to suggest that it tells us something important about the relationship of Indian legal literature and actual practice, and the same may hold in the case of Buddhist *Vinaya*: Even widely attested practices will not necessarily be treated in the formal literature.[33] About all that can be said for the moment is that we may be seeing here yet another instance in which the *Mūlasarvāstivāda-vinaya* has much more direct and decided links than other *Vinayas* with what is actually found in the Indian inscriptional and archeological records. In this sense, if no other, it appears again to be far more comprehensive and much more useful to historians, especially legal historians, since it can – as in this instance – fill gaps that occur in Dharmaśāstra. However this situation might eventually be explained, the fact remains that there are a number of references in the *Mūlasarvāstivāda-vinaya* to permanent endowments, and some are quite detailed.

The *Mūlasarvāstivāda-vinaya* refers to such endowments once as *akṣaya-nīvī*, more typically just as *akṣayas*, and at least once it describes such an

[31] A. Bareau, *Les sectes bouddhiques du petit véhicule* (Paris: École Française d'Extrême-Orient, 1955), 127.

[32] J. Gernet, *Les aspects économiques du bouddhisme dans la société chinoise du Ve au Xe siècle* (Paris: École française d'Extrême-Orient, 1956), 154–62. The *Vinaya* material preserved in Chinese translations may, however, have to be restudied in regard to this issue. K.K.S. Ch'en, for example, covers some of this same material, but does not always say the same thing – see, *The Chinese Transformation of Buddhism* (Princeton, NJ: Princeton University Press, 1973), esp. 158ff.

[33] J.D.M. Derrett, "Nīvī," *Vishveshvaranand Indological Journal* 12 (1974), 89–90; 95.

endowment without naming it at all. There is a similar terminological variation found in inscriptions as well.[34] References to these endowments that have previously been noticed are also not limited to just one section of this enormous work, but occur in its *Cīvara-vastu*, in its *Uttaragrantha*, and in its *Bhikṣu-vibhaṅga*.[35] They are also treated in some detail in medieval Mūlasarvāstivādin handbooks such as Guṇaprabha's *Vinaya-sūtra*, and its Indian commentaries, and Viśeṣamitra's *Vinaya-saṃgraha*.[36]

The fullest or most detailed treatment of permanent endowments in the *Mūlasarvāstivāda-vinaya* is found in its *Bhikṣu-vibhaṅga*. Because this text has already twice been discussed in some detail, it can here be easily summarized.[37] The people of Vaiśālī built *vihāras* or "monasteries" of several stories, but these were hard to maintain and their donors saw them fall into ruin during their lifetimes. Concerned about what would happen to their vihāras after their death, they approached the monks and offered them "permanent endowments for building purposes." The monks initially declined them because the Buddha had not authorized such endowments. However, when they went to him and he approved, they accepted them but put them in what in effect was the monastery's safe and left them there; note that, in other words, the monks initially hoarded such gifts. When, however, the donors saw that no maintenance or building work was being done, and they found out what the monks had done, they suggested that they should loan the sums involved out on interest. Again, the monks initially declined, saying they could not because of a rule of training promulgated by the Buddha. Again they went to the Buddha, who said: "For the sake of the Community an endowment for building purposes must be lent on interest!" When endowments for the sake of the Buddha and the dharma and the Community were then offered, lending them was also authorized; that these were not limited to "building purposes" is clear from the fact that the Buddha immediately added: "What is generated from that lending, with that accrued revenue, worship is to be performed

[34] In addition to Derrett, "Nīvī," 94, see S.K. Maity, *Economic Life in Northern India in the Gupta Period (Cir. A. D. 300–580)*, rev. 2nd ed. (Delhi: Motilal Banarsidass, 1970), 36–42.

[35] Here only the reference in the *Cīvara-vastu* will not be further discussed – see Dutt, *Gilgit Manuscripts*, vol. III, Pt. 2, 124.11–125.9 where *buddhākṣayanīvi-santakaṃ*, "what belongs to the permanent endowment for the Buddha," is one of a list of things that, although otherwise inviolable, can be used to secure medicine and perform rituals for a sick and dying fellow-monk who is indigent.

[36] For Guṇaprabha's *Vinaya-sūtra*, see Schopen, *Buddhist Monks and Business Matters*, 67–69; 90, which needs revision; for Viśeṣamitra, see *Vinaya-saṃgraha*, Derge, bstan 'gyur, 'dul ba Nu 161a.5.

[37] First by Gernet, *Les aspects économiques du bouddhisme*, 155–56, on the basis of the Chinese translation; then by Schopen, *Buddhist Monks and Business Matters*, 45–90, on the basis of the Tibetan translation, which is there translated in full.

to the Buddha and the Dharma and the Community." Then, however, the monks made a series of unsecured, bad loans – back to the donors themselves, to the rich and powerful who could avoid repayment, and to the poor who were unable to repay. This resulted in the Buddha's final rule, a remarkable and financially and legally very sophisticated piece of *buddha-vacana* or official Buddhist doctrine:

> The Blessed One said: "Taking collateral (*ādhi*, *bandhaka*) of twice the value (of the loan), and writing out a contract (*likhita*) that has a seal and is witnessed, it (the loan) is to be given. In the contract the year, the month, the day, the name of the Elder of the Community (*saṃghasthavira*), the Provost of the Monastery (*upadhivārika*), the borrower, the sum, and the interest must be recorded."

This *Vinaya* text, then, clearly provides us with what is missing from both Dharmaśāstra and inscriptional records: a detailed description of how endowments placed in the hands of the monastic community were – or ought to be – used and administered. Notice here at least that the authors of this text thought or ruled that the monks themselves should both make the loan and administer it, and that such activities involved the senior-most monk and a chief functionary of the Community. Note also that although permanent endowments are initially accepted to address the concerns of donors in regard to what will happen to their gifts after their deaths – to ensure, in effect, that they will continue to be used and therefore generate merit[38] – when it comes to the loans, it is strictly business: There is not the slightest hint here that such endowments were meant to allow the monastic community to function as anything like a "charitable lending institution for people in need."[39] Quite the contrary, lending to the poor is singled out as one form of a bad loan; the requirement of collateral of twice the value of the loan would very likely make it impossible for the truly poor to get one; and, as we will see, making such loans to the poor is also expressly forbidden for nuns. Compassion, it seems, cannot be the main motive here.

A second reference to endowments of this type in the *Mūlasarvāstivāda-vinaya* occurs in its *Uttaragrantha*. It also has previously been noticed

38 On the merit resulting from use, see Schopen, *Buddhist Monks and Business Matters*, 238–42.

39 J. Hubbard, *Absolute Delusion, Perfect Buddhahood. The Rise and Fall of a Chinese Heresy* (Honolulu: University of Hawai'i Press, 2001), 151, referring to the Buddhist lending institution associated with the San-Chieh "movement" in early medieval China that was called "the Inexhaustible Storehouse" or "inexhaustible treasury," and which may or may not have some relationship to what is found in our *Vinaya* – the latter was, at least, translated too late to have directly influenced the founder of this movement; cf. Ch'en, *The Chinese Transformation of Buddhism*, 159–60.

and briefly discussed, but only in the form in which it was quoted in the auto commentary to Guṇaprabha's *Vinaya-sūtra*, and in the Tibetan translation of the latter.[40] Even in that initial discussion, some peculiarities of vocabulary in the text as it was quoted in the auto-commentary were noticed, and now that the "original" of the passage being quoted has been identified, it appears that the chief of these are the result of an idiosyncratic, if not a bad, Tibetan translation. They do not occur in the text that is found in the *Uttaragrantha* itself. Since the "original" has now been identified, and since this text, although found in the same *Vinaya*, clearly represents an approach to our endowments that differs in some important ways from that found in its male *Vibhaṅga*, it is worth citing here. In doing so, moreover, it will be clear that the quotation in the auto-commentary is also incomplete:

> What is enjoined (*samyukta*) for the permanent endowment for *stūpa*?
>
> A merchant of the city of Vaiśālī, after he had made a *stūpa* of the Blessed One, also made a court for the *stūpa* (*stūpāṅgana*), and he gave the monks a permanent endowment (*mi zad pa* = *akṣaya*) for the *stūpa*. But the monks, being uncertain, did not individually accept it.
>
> When the monks reported to the Blessed One what had occurred, the Blessed One said: "Through my orders a monastic groundskeeper (*ārāmika*) or a lay brother (*upāsaka*) must accept the permanent endowment for a *stūpa*. For the sake of looking after (*upasthāna*) the *stūpa,* interest must be generated (*vṛdh*)! Having produced a profit from it, with that worship must be done to the *stūpa*! If moreover there is a remainder from that, with that an offering must be made to the *stūpa*!
>
> This is what is enjoined for the permanent endowment for *stūpa*![41]

In comparison with what is said about endowments in the *Bhikṣu-vibhaṅga*, the presentation here appears to be much more restrained or restricted, and the approach taken to them would seem to be far more conservative. About the only thing the two accounts seem to have in common, in fact, is that both are set in Vaiśālī. The *Uttaragrantha* refers, for example, only to endowments for *stūpa* – there is no mention of such for vihāras or the dharma or Community – and its endowments are to be used, it seems, to generate sums to cover the cost of worship only. There is at least no explicit mention of maintenance. Perhaps the most significant difference, however, may be the fact that the *Uttaragrantha* rule requires that its endowments be accepted and presumably – this is not explicitly indicated – administered

[40] Schopen, *Buddhist Monks and Business Matters*, 67–68.

[41] *Uttaragrantha*, Derge 'dul ba Pa 265a.6–265b.1. On the *Uttaragrantha*, see Schopen, *Buddhist Monks and Business Matters*, 124–28.

by an *ārāmika* or an *upāsaka*, both of which, while being attached to or in some sense employed by the monastery or monastic community, were not themselves ordained monks.[42] Such a requirement would seem to indicate a desire to preclude – or at least distance – monks from direct involvement with these financial instruments, and there is no hint of this in the *Vibhaṅga* rules. When it is also noted that the *Uttaragrantha* knows nothing about – or at least says nothing about – a written contract, it might be natural enough to suggest that the *Uttaragrantha* represents a less-developed or earlier stage in the evolution and use of financial arrangements of this kind by Buddhist groups. Nevertheless, however natural this suggestion might appear, it must remain only one possible explanation for the differences between the two texts, and it is equally possible to suggest that they simply represent two roughly contemporaneous attitudes within the same Buddhist group toward the direct involvement of monks in financial activities, and since the *ārāmikas* or *upāsakas* almost certainly would have acted under instructions from the monks, even in the *Uttaragrantha* the monks would not have been uninvolved.[43]

One Version of a Rule Requiring Nuns to Lend on Interest

Although, then, a number of questions and details remain to be resolved, it should be clear enough by now that these texts from its *Bhikṣu-vibhaṅga* and *Uttaragrantha* demonstrate that the *Mūlasarvāstivāda-vinaya* provides far more material than any other early literary source so far noticed bearing on the kind of financial arrangement that is recorded in our Junnar inscription. However, all these texts deal with monks, or males, and our inscription deals with a nunnery or nuns. Moreover, there may be some resistance to the idea that women in India in this period could have independently engaged in such financial activities or that they had the legal capacity to do so. Happily, on this issue, *Vinaya* texts dealing with nuns that

42 On *ārāmikas,* see most recently N. Yamagiwa, "Ārāmika – Gardener or Park Keeper? One of the Marginals around the Buddhist *Saṃgha*," in *Buddhist and Indian Studies in Honour of Professor Sodo Mori* (Hamamatsu: Kokusai Bukkyōto Kyōkai, 2002), 363–85; G. Schopen, "The Buddhist 'Monastery' and the Indian Garden: Aesthetics, Assimilations, and the Siting of Monastic Establishments," *Journal of the American Oriental Society* 126 (2006), 487–88; P. Kieffer-Pülz, "Stretching the Vinaya Rules and Getting Away with It," *Journal of the Pali Text Society* 29 (2007), 1–51, esp. 15–20, 26–35.

43 Gernet, *Les Aspects économiques du bouddhisme*, 159, cites a passage from the *Sarvāstivāda-vinaya* that places the same restrictions on the direct involvement of monks in lending on interest "les biens des stūpa" as our *Uttaragrantha* text does: there, too, this is to be done by "les 'hommes purs' (*tsing jen*) des monastères ainsi que les upāsaka," but he prematurely limits this restriction to the Sarvāstivādins (160).

are preserved in Tibetan have more than a little to say. In fact, these *Vinaya* texts have explicit rules requiring nuns to use permanent endowments and engage in lending on interest, and they may be the only such texts that do – at least no others have so far been noticed. And as was the case in regard to rules governing the handling of promissory notes or loan contracts, there are two versions of the rules governing the use of permanent endowments: one in the *Bhikṣuṇī-vibhaṅga* and one in the *Sarvāstivādimūla-bhikṣuṇīprātimokṣasūtravṛtti*, both of which are – as we have seen – best taken, *for the moment*, as Mūlasarvāstivādin, until it can be shown to be otherwise.

Similar to the parallel passage in the *Bhikṣu-vibhaṅga*, the passage in the *Bhikṣuṇī-vibhaṅga* that gives these rules immediately follows its presentation of the *Prātimokṣa* rule that seems to contain a condemnation of engaging in certain – indeed, very specific – types of financial transactions and business enterprises, and it is presented both as being required as a consequence of that *Prātimokṣa* rule, and as providing a qualification of it. It might be translated in full as:

Bhikṣuṇī-vinaya-vibhaṅga

(Derge 'dul ba Ta 170a.5–171a.3 = Tog Nya 226b.6–228a.2 = Peking The 156a.8–157a.4)

> The determining event was in Śrāvastī.
>
> When the Blessed One had promulgated on account of the Group-of-Six Monks a rule of training dealing with engaging in various sorts of monetary transactions, then too when the Group-of-Twelve Nuns at that time engaged in various sorts of monetary transactions, nuns of few wants complained and that situation was reported to the Blessed One. Then the Blessed One in regard to that occurrence... promulgated a rule of training...: "If, moreover, some nun engages in various monetary transactions, that is an offence involving forfeiture (of what results)."
>
> "Some nun" means: As before.
>
> "Various" means: Many.
>
> "Monetary" means: Cash or money.
>
> "In transactions" means: In using.
>
> "An offence involving forfeiture" means: As previously.
>
> And how would there be an offense here? There are four kinds:[44] forming a joint venture (*kun tu sbyor bar byed pa*); making loans on interest (*rab tu*

[44] The translation here, especially of the long section describing the four specific forms of business enterprises, is nothing more than tentative, and more 'referential' than literal in some parts, since it bristles with little known lexical items. *bun 'gyed pa*, for example, does not literally mean "a

sbyor bar byed pa); making use of commodity loans (*bun 'gyed par byed pa*); making use of interest on precious commodities (*skyed 'gyed par byed pa*).

Here in regard to forming a joint venture, for the sake of profiting from another region, she joins merchandise and joins transport, and assembles men. From that which results she is to declare "This property is yours. This property is mine." So long as she does not make the profit her own, to that point there is only a misdeed. If she makes the profit her own, there is an offense involving forfeiture. Such is forming a joint venture.

How does she make loans on interest? For the sake of increasing from ten to eleven[45] a monetary sum she makes a loan on interest of the sum. And for the purpose of a contract (*dbang rgya*), she there has recourse to securing a document (*gro ga*) and ink, or a witness. So long as she does not make the profit her own, there is only a misdeed. If she makes it her own, there is an offense involving forfeiture. Such is making loans on interest.

How does she make use of commodity loans? For the sake of the new crop of barley and wheat, she gives on interest wheat and barley using a measuring pot for what is to be loaned, and there she has recourse to securing a measuring pot for them, and a grain meal measure, and a hand measure, weights and men. So long as she does not make the profit her own, there is only a misdeed. If she makes it her own, there is an offense involving forfeiture. Such is making use of commodity loans.

How does she make use of interest on precious commodities? They have interest made through interest-bearing pearls; have interest made through interest-bearing gold. There they endeavor to secure a document and ink and a witness. So long as she does not make the profit her own, there is only a misdeed. If she makes it her own, there is an offense involving forfeiture. Such is making use of interest on precious commodities.

When the rule of training [against monetary transactions] had been promulgated and the nuns did not lend out on interest the permanent endowment belonging to the *stūpa*, and the one belonging to the Community, the Blessed One said: "It must be lent on interest!"

The nuns gave loans to anybody, and when what had been given was lost the Blessed One said: "Money is not to be lent to the poor, nor to those living in the border regions, nor to violent wrong-doers and the powerful."

A first point that might be noted here is that the bulk of this text from the *Bhikṣuṇī-vibhaṅga* is taken up with defining very precisely the types of

commodity loan," but, to judge by its description, refers to one. Likewise *skyed 'gyed pa* does not literally mean "interest on precious commodities," but seems to refer to it. Whoever wrote these descriptions – presumably a monk – must have had a very detailed knowledge of business practices, and that is something we, alas, do not have. For one way forward, see the next note.

45 The expression "increasing from ten to eleven" would almost certainly have been *daśaikādaśa* in the Sanskrit original and "means the lending of ten (coins) on a condition that the borrower should pay eleven. This amounts to the rate of interest of ten percent." H. Chatterjee, *The Law of Debt in Ancient India* (Calcutta: Sanskrit College, 1971), 21.

business enterprises that a nun could not engage in without committing an offense. This list of specific and sophisticated ventures is not, however, unique to the *Bhikṣuṇī-vibhaṅga*. Much the same list is also found in the Mūlasarvāstivādin *Bhikṣu-vibhaṅga*, and, it would appear, only in Mūlasarvāstivādin sources.[46] The fact that the two *Vibhaṅgas* share such specific material, and the fact that this material is not known to occur elsewhere, would seem to suggest that both *Vibhaṅgas* belong to the same tradition, that, indeed, we might have here yet another indication that the *Bhikṣuṇī-vibhaṅga* preserved in Tibetan also is Mūlasarvāstivādin. However, this specific shared material is of interest not just for the issue of the affiliation of the *Bhikṣuṇī-vibhaṅga*.

That a male monastic code would have rules against engaging in these specific business enterprises would not be surprising – they were, as far as we know, primarily male occupations in classical India. Regardless, the inclusion of such rules in a code governing nuns would make no sense or have no function unless their authors – again, almost certainly men – took as a given the fact that Buddhist nuns might or did engage in such activities, and had the independent legal agency or capacity to do so. That these Buddhist authors assumed that nuns had the legal capacity to enter into contracts would seem to be particularly clear in regard to what is said about "loans on interest."

Lending on interest receives special treatment in both *Vibhaṅgas*. Initially, engaging in it or in any of the other listed business enterprises is a *naiḥsargika,* "an offense involving forfeiture," a serious offense, *if it is done for personal profit.* But in both *Vibhaṅgas* the force of this is already mitigated: in both such engagement is only a *duṣkṛta* – a minor offense without clear penalty – if the nun or monk does not personally take the profit. A further mitigation, however, takes place here *only* in regard to lending on interest. According to the much fuller narrative of the male *Vibhaṅga*, this further mitigation, although it might have been anticipated by the previous one, was a direct result of the acceptance by the community of permanent endowments for institutional purposes, and required the modification of the original rule by the addition of a rider. This rider, still visible as such in both *Vibhaṅgas*, not only allowed, but required that funds of this kind be lent out on interest by *both* monks and nuns on the authority of the

46 *Bhikṣu-vibhaṅga*, Derge 'dul ba Cha 152b.7–154b.3. It may eventually be possible to show that the list in the *Bhikṣuṇī-vibhaṅga* is only a slightly shortened variant version of that found in the *Bhikṣu-vibhaṅga*, and a close study of both together may solve some of the lexical problems. Gernet, *Les aspects économiques du bouddhisme*, 155, treats the Chinese translation of the list in its version of the *Bhikṣu-vibhaṅga*, but it also seems not to be entirely clear, and to differ from the Tibetan version.

Buddha himself. Notice also that although the *Bhikṣuṇī-Vibhaṅga* again lacks much of the detail found in the male *Vibhaṅga*, it is clear enough that the community of nuns held their own endowments and were expected to make and administer their own loans: In the *Bhikṣuṇī-Vibhaṅga*, as in the *Bhikṣu-Vibhaṅga*, there is no reference to an *ārāmika* or *upāsaka* acting as an agent, nor is there any reference to a monk or any other male acting on behalf of the nuns. Here again, then, the Buddhist nun appears as a fully independent legal person: Although she may have been ritually subservient to monks, in business matters and legal affairs she appears to have been able to act very much on her own, and could engage in the same financial activities as a monk, and in the same ways. Here it appears they were again on a separate and equal footing. A final text to be cited here would seem only to confirm this.

A Second Version of the Rule Requiring Nuns to Lend on Interest

Our final text comes again from the *Sarvāstivādi-mūla-bhikṣuṇī-prātimokṣa-sūtra-vṛtti* and corresponds to the one just cited from the *Bhikṣuṇī-Vibhaṅga*. In this instance there appear to be even stronger indications that this *Vṛtti*, the *Bhikṣuṇī-Vibhaṅga* preserved in Tibetan, and the Mūlasarvāstivādin *Bhikṣu-vibhaṅga* are all closely related and represent the same tradition: The *Vṛtti*, like the *Bhikṣuṇī-vibhaṅga*, has a version of virtually the same list of very specific business ventures that are not to be engaged in that occurs in the Mūlasarvāstivādin *Bhikṣu-vibhaṅga*, a list that otherwise appears to be unique to it.[47] This, of course, is not to say that there are no differences, and one of the most interesting of these concerns the narrative used in the *Vṛtti* to introduce the rider that requires that permanent endowments be lent out on interest. The male *Vibhaṅga*, as we have seen above, has an elaborate introductory narrative for the requirement. The female *Vibhaṅga* has practically none; the *Vṛtti*, then, falls somewhere in between. Putting aside its list of the specific business ventures for another time when the lexical problems of all three versions can be carefully worked out, the remainder of the text in the *Vṛtti*[48] might be translated as:

> The Teacher had promulgated the rule of training [against using financial instruments] but the nuns' *vihāra* had fallen into disrepair, and when a

[47] The *Vṛtti*, however, only lists the ventures. It lacks the descriptions of each that occur in the two *Vibhaṅgas*.

[48] *Sarvāstivādi-mūla-bhikṣuṇī-prātimokṣa-sūtra-vṛtti*, Derge bstan 'gyur, 'dul ba Tsu 78b.5–79a.1.

donor (*dānapati*) came there he said: "Noble One, why has the *vihāra* fallen into disrepair?"

The nuns said: "The Owner of the *Vihāra* (*vihārasvāmin*)[49] has died."

The donors said: "Many financial instruments are being given to the nuns for repairing the disrepair of the nuns' *vihāra*, but, Noble One, you yourself must make this permanent endowment produce interest, and must use what profit there is to do the renovation work on the *vihāra*," and they gave it to her.

The nuns hid it away, however, and it was commanded: "A nun must make it produce interest!"

They lent it to the poor, but when it was not repaid it was said: "While it must not be lent to poor non-believers and lay brothers, collateral of twice the value must be deposited, and the due date too must be written down, and each month the interest portion must be collected! With that the renovation work must be done! If a nun does not perform this customary rule of behavior as designated, she comes to be guilty of an offense."[50]

The *Vṛtti* narrative is obviously not a copy of that found in the male *Vibhaṅga* of the Mūlasarvāstivādins, but it could easily be a re-gendered condensation or paraphrase of it; both connect permanent endowments and lending on interest with lay concerns about maintenance of vihāras when their donors or owners die, and the title *vihārasvāmin* used in the *Vṛtti* is, as noted, a characteristically Mūlasarvāstivādin one. The stipulation in the *Vṛtti* that "collateral of twice the value [of the loan] must be deposited" could, it seems, only be based on the Mūlasarvāstivādin male *Vibhaṅga* or the same tradition that it was drawing on. The further stipulation in the *Vṛtti* that "each month the interest portion must be collected" appears, however, to be unique to it.

While still other points might be worth following up, for our purposes here the most important would have to be the clarity in the *Vṛtti* text on the role of the nun as an independent legal person. There is again no reference in the *Vṛtti* to a male agent of any kind acting for the nuns. Indeed, the

49 *On vihārasvāmin,* a characteristically Mūlasarvāstivādin term, see Schopen, *Buddhist Monks and Business Matters*, 21, 38 n. 10, 85 n. 50, 220–21, 227–38, etc. Von Hinüber has recently said of the Pāli term *āvāsasāmi* that it "obviously corresponds to the *vihārasvāmin* of the Mūlasarvāstivādins," but also that it "is very rare"; O. von Hinüber, "Everyday Life in an Ancient Indian Buddhist Monastery," *Annual Report of the International Research Institute for Advanced Buddhology at Soka University* 9 (2006), 20 n. 53. However, *vihārasvāmin* also occurs in at least one passage in the Mahāsaṅghika *Abhisamācārikā*, B. Jinananda, *Abhisamācārikā* (Patna: K.P. Jayaswal Research Institute, 1969), 127.14, 128.1.

50 This last sentence also is a characteristically Mūlasarvāstivādin formula. For one of dozens of examples, see R. Gnoli, *The Gilgit Manuscript of the Śayanāsanavastu and Adhikaraṇavastu*, Serie Orientale Roma 50, (Rome: Istituto per il Medio ed Estremo Oriento, 1978), 39.4: . . . *bhikṣur yathāprajñaptān āsamudācārikān dharmān asamādāya vartate sātisāro vartate.*

author of this very short text not once, but three times emphasizes the responsibility of the nun in the transaction: She must initiate the loan, administer it, and collect on it. First the donor explicitly says that the nun herself must lend out what was given to her; then this is repeated as an order that could only have come from the Buddha, and finally it is said that if a nun does not lend to the right sort, does not take the required collateral and record the due date, and does not collect the monthly interest, *she* is guilty of an offense. Obviously, if a nun was not thought to have the legal capacity to fulfill these requirements, she could not be held culpable in this or any other way.

Summing Up the Discussion

What we have seen here are only two examples taken from what appears to be – as far as we can now tell – a single *Vinaya* tradition. But there are others. Reference in a preceding note has been made to what appear to be similar texts dealing with nuns in the Pāli, Dharmaguptaka, and Mahāsāṅghika *Vinayas*, and there are further examples in the Mūlasarvāstivādin *Vinaya* as well, one of which uses essentially the same narrative-frame story as the text in the *Bhikṣuṇī-vibhaṅga* dealing with promissory notes – there the nun Sthūlanandā extracts from the dying householder his one remaining house and when he dies, she seizes and seals it, and will only allow his surviving family to live in it if they pay her rent![51] But the two examples discussed here are hopefully sufficient to show how much might be gained by looking carefully and, in the future, much more broadly not at the religious subservience of the nun in Buddhist textual sources – about which we may have heard too much – but at her legal status and her role there as an independent economic agent. This is a Buddhist nun we need to know more about even if we have to see her mostly through male, and often disapproving, textual eyes.

[51] *Kṣudraka-vastu*, Derge 'dul ba Da 184a.3–184b.5. Translated and discussed in G. Schopen, "The Buddhist Nun as an Urban Landlord and a 'Legal Person' in Early India," in D. Feller et al. (eds.), *Denadattīyam: Johannes Bronkhorst Felicitation Volume* (Bern: Peter Lang, 2011), 627–42.

PART II

Buddhism and Law in South and Southeast Asia

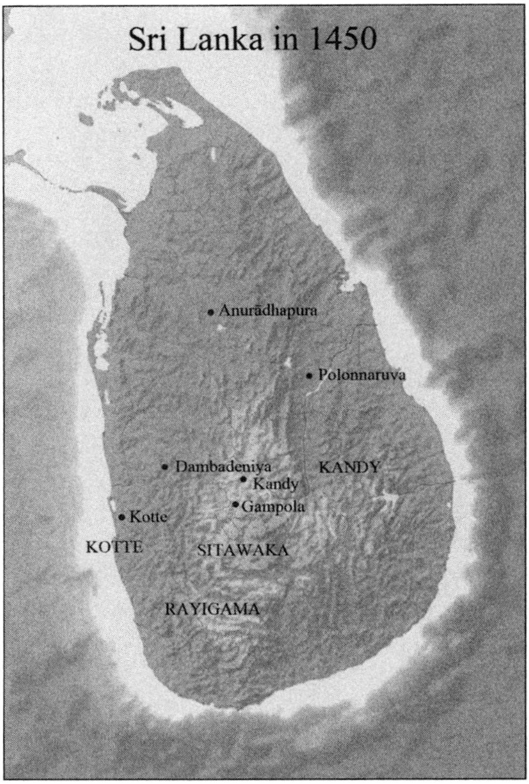

Map of Sri Lanka, c. 1450 CE

CHAPTER 6

Buddhism and Law in Sri Lanka

Sunil Goonasekera

Introduction

In this chapter I explore the interrelationships between Buddhism as a sociocultural institution and the laws of Sri Lanka. Let me first orient the reader to the spatiotemporal trajectory of this relationship and then examine its historical vicissitudes. Sri Lanka is an island nation situated about forty miles southeast of the Indian peninsula. The island has been inhabited from very ancient times and appears prominently in the great South Asian epics, such as the *Ramāyana*. Historical information is available from the Sri Lankan Buddhist chronicles and from various archeological sources. According to the fourth century CE Buddhist chronicle *Dīpavaṃsa* and the sixth century CE chronicle *Mahāvaṃsa*, the capital city of Anurādhapura, was established in the fifth century BCE, and a Theravāda Buddhist monastic order was established by an Indian bhikkhu named Mahinda in the third century BCE. During the reign of King Devānampiyatissa (250–210 BCE), a substantial portion of the population of the kingdom formally accepted Buddhism as their faith. Anurādhapura became the primary stage for the early Buddhist engagements with the law of the land, setting many precedents that are still valid to this day.

The Buddhist community or the *buddhasāsana* in Sri Lanka consists of two basic groups, namely *pavidi* (monastic) and *gihi* (lay). The *pavidi* have a legal system, the *Vinaya*, for the maintenance of discipline in the monastic institution that outlines the formal rules governing monastic conduct involving both injunctions and punishments. Although the *Vinaya* has no direct authority over the *gihi*, it indirectly influences the lay population by setting informal customs for proper social conduct. Lay social ethics and etiquette, ranging from proper procedures for partaking of meals to observance of etiquette in maintaining social relations and cleanliness, can be traced to the *Vinaya* rules, and violating them can result in general opprobrium, open criticism, and even ostracism.

The focus of this chapter will be this relationship between the Buddhist religion as a social system and the lay legal administration. The Buddhist monastic order of Sri Lanka was heavily involved in the politics of the state and the legal affairs of the country. At the same time, the state of Sri Lanka had a right to intervene in monastic affairs and even purify the saṅgha when it failed to adhere to the *Vinaya*. This relationship appears to have developed in various ways over three distinct periods: the pre-colonial, colonial, and post-independence eras. The first two of these will be covered in this chapter.

Buddhism and Law in Pre-colonial Sri Lanka

From the third century BCE, Sri Lankan jurisprudence had to accommodate Buddhist ideals as they exerted a powerful influence on the customs governing the relationships between the state and its subjects.[1] Mahinda established, with royal patronage, the Mahāvihāra monastery in Anurādhapura. Until his demise, Mahinda maintained a close relationship with the court and established a tradition of royal consultation with the monastic leaders whenever a jurisprudential issue conflicted with tenets of Buddhism. From this point, a strong identity developed between Buddhism, the Buddhist community, and the state of Sri Lanka, which compelled the head of the state to protect, maintain, and sustain Buddhism on the island.

By the second century BCE, when many South Indian invaders had occupied Anurādhapura, the saṅgha became deeply concerned about the political structures of the island. The saṅgha supported King Duṭṭhagāmaṇī (161–137 BCE), the Sinhala ruler who fought the invaders, claiming that he waged war for the sake of the *buddhasāsana*. In the following century, King Vaṭṭagāmaṇī (89–77 BCE) had a monastery built within the boundaries of the Mahāvihāra. The new monastery was named Abhayagiri and formed a fraternity within the Mahāvihāra. Soon the relationship between the two fraternities deteriorated owing to a disagreement over an interpretation of the *Vinaya*. King Bhātika Abhaya (38–66 CE) resolved these disputes by employing a Brahman to determine who held the correct view, indicating that the king would intervene in monastic disputes and use independent counselors from the secular government to decide

[1] For details of the impact of local customs on the precolonial legal system, see A.R.B. Amarasinghe, *The Legal Heritage of Sri Lanka* (Colombo: Visva Lekha Publishers, 1999) and M.L.S. Jayasekara, *Customary Laws of Sri Lanka* (Colombo: Ministry of Cultural Affairs, Sri Lanka, 1984).

matters.[2] The Mahāvihāra resisted any attempts to introduce doctrines that revised or opposed the views in the *tipiṭaka*. During the reign of King Vōharika Tissa (269–291 CE), some monks residing at the Abhayagiri attempted to introduce certain proto-Mahāyāna ideas known under the rubric of Vetullavāda, professing that the Theravāda enshrined at the Mahāvihāra did not represent the Buddha's doctrine. The Mahāvihāra responded with much opprobrium and monastically outlawed the Vetullavāda as heresy. The king held an inquisition on these matters on the advice of a minister and Buddhist scholar named Kapila who decided that the Vetulla doctrines did not represent the true doctrines of the Buddha. The king suppressed the Vetullavāda and ordered the Vetulla scriptures to be burned, indicating the authority of the monastic leaders to persuade the king to use the secular law for monastic purposes.[3]

Later, during the reign of King Gothābhaya (309–322 CE), the Abhayagiri adherence to the Vetullavāda reemerged. Many bhikkhus had opposed the Vetullavāda not because they necessarily disagreed with its theories, but because they did not want to suffer the consequences of Vōharaka Tissa's suppression. The Mahāvihāra continued to influence the king who sustained the suppression of the Vetullavādins and had them excommunicated. The *Nikāya Saṅgraha* reports that King Gothābhaya rounded up many Vetullavādins, branded them, and banished them from the island.

During the reign of King Mahāsena (334–362 CE), Saṅghamitta, a Vétullavādi monk who mentored Mahāsena but fled in fear of Mahāsena's elder brother Gothābhaya, returned and convinced the king to declare the Mahāvihāra monastic organization as heretical and proclaim the Abhayagiri as the leading monastery. Under Saṅghamitta's advice, Mahāsena proclaimed that it was unlawful to offer alms to the bhikkhus of the Mahāvihāra. The penalty for the offense was a fine of 100 pieces of money. The Mahāvihāra bhikkhus were thus compelled to flee to regions where the king's rule was not effective. Saṅghamitta invoked the law that ownerless land belonged to the king and, with the approval of the king, set forth destroying the Mahāvihāra by inciting people against it. A minister named Soṇa, together with Vetullavādi bhikkhus, caused much destruction and used materials of the Mahāvihāra to rebuild and glorify

[2] G.P. Malalasekere (ed.), *Vanṃttappakāsinī(Mahāvaṃsatika)* 1935, 2 vols. (London: Pali Text Society, 1936/1935); J. Takakusu and M. Nagai (eds.), *Samantapasadika*, vols. 1–7 (London: Pali Text Society, 1947, 1927); S. Paranavitana, "Civilization of the Early Period: Religion and Art" in Senarat. Paranavitana (ed.), *History of Ceylon*, vol. 1, part 1. (Colombo: University of Ceylon Press, 1960), 246.

[3] C.M. Fernando (trans.), *Nikāya Sangraha* (12), (Colombo, 1908).

the Abhayagiri.[4] An influential minister disapproved of the king's destruction of the Mahāvihāra and, in all likelihood moved by the bhikkhus of the Mahāvihāra, rebelled against the king. The rebellion convinced the king to rebuild the Mahāvihāra, although he continued to support the Vetullavāda.

Mahāvihāra-Abhayagiri conflicts did not end here. An interesting episode illustrates the limitations of the king's authority over the monks. A bhikkhu belonging to a new sect called the Sāgaliya had created an enclave named Jetavana vihāra, presumably with the king's permission, within Mahāvihāra boundaries and asked the Mahāvihāra bhikkhus to shift the boundaries of the Mahāvihāra, perhaps to make the Sāgaliya enclave a separate independent entity existing on premises carved out of Mahāvihāra. The Mahāvihāra bhikkhus refused to shift the boundaries. Some abandoned the Mahāvihāra once again, but some others hid in an underground chamber because as long as bhikkhus remained within the pre-established boundaries of the monastery its boundaries could not legally be altered. They formulated a legal complaint against the Sāgaliya bhikkhu who attempted to have the boundaries moved. The minister who rebelled earlier pursued the case and found the Sāgaliya monk's claims unlawful and, as the *Mahāvaṃsa* states, "according to the right and the law" expelled him from the order, even though this was against the king's wishes. However, this expulsion may not have been effective as the Jetavana vihāra continued to exist within the Mahāvihāra boundaries as an independent monastery until King Parākramabāhu I (1153–86) unified all three sects in the twelfth century.[5] As Geiger notes, "[t]he removal of the boundaries would only have been legal, if the *bhikkhus* themselves had given up the *vihāra*."[6]

The case of the Mahāvihāra points to several legal relationships between the social organization of Buddhism and the state of Sri Lanka. The king, the dispenser of the law and justice, and his subjects had three roles to play from the day Buddhism was established in Sri Lanka and became the de facto religion of the state. These were (1) maintenance of the saṅgha, (2) construction of religious monuments to sustain the religious fervor,

[4] Wilhelm Geiger (ed. and trans.), *The Mahāvaṃsa or the Great Chronicle of Ceylon* (London: Luzac and Co., for Pali Text Society, 1950, 1912), 37: 1–16.

[5] *Ibid.*, 37, 39.

[6] Wilhelm Geiger and Mabel Rickmers (trans.), *The Cūlavaṃsa: Being the More Recent Part of the Mahāvamsa*, 2 vols. 37 (Colombo: Ceylon Government Information Department, 1953), 56–58, 2 n. 2.

and (3) protection of Buddhism.[7] The maintenance of the saṅgha involved provision of alms. Over the centuries, various kings had donated tracks of land including entire villages and the services of the villagers to the monasteries in absolute ownership. Although monasteries could purchase property, their property could never be sold or gifted. Lands granted to individual monasteries belonged to the recipient monasteries alone and not to the Buddhist saṅgha as a whole. The ownership of these lands enjoyed the status of *brahmadeya* (supreme gift), whereby the monastic landlord had complete fiscal and judicial authority over his tenants to the exclusion of state authority over them.[8]

Generally, when land was abandoned for a specific period it reverted to the state. In the episode previously mentioned, the Mahāvihāra bhikkhus knew this rule. Whether this applied to monastic lands or not is unclear, but most probably it did not as they had the *brahmadeya* status. The Sāgaliya bhikkhu who claimed that the king could move the boundaries of the Mahāvihāra had no knowledge of the limits of royal authority over lands granted to monasteries. The minister who disregarded the king's wishes to move the boundary knew the rule.

The case also illustrates the legal relationships between Buddhism and the state over the state's second obligation: construction of monuments. This was done as long as the king perceived that the saṅgha lived by the *Vinaya* rules and respected him. If the king found them to hold heretical views or if they seriously offended him, he could authorize destruction of monastic monuments. On the other hand, while he could authorize construction of monuments, he had no right to shift the boundaries of existing monastic lands for these purposes.

The third obligation of the king, to protect the *buddhasāsana*, permitted the state to become involved in monastic disputes and expel any monk on *Vinaya* grounds. Throughout the pre-colonial era, many kings purified the saṅgha by expelling errant monks. King Vōharika Tissa ordered the first purification of the saṅgha by expelling undisciplined bhikkhus, and his example was followed by several kings through the fourteenth century.

7 K.M. de Silva, *A History of Sri Lanka* (Colombo: Vijitha Yapa Publications, 2005), 60.

8 *Ibid.*, 55–57; R.A L.H. Gunawardana, "Some Economic Aspects of Monastic Life in the Later Anurādhapura Period," *Ceylon Journal of Humanities and Social Studies, New Series* 2.1 (1972), 71–72. By the ninth century, as the inscriptions show, a new kind of land tenure had been developed. This was the *divēl* ownership whereby a functionary of the state or a monastery could be granted land. However, in the case of monastic property, the *divēl* grantee had no claims to the land but to the revenue from the land. The term *divēl* in Sanskrit refers to "for the duration of life," or a "life interest" (de Silva, *History of Sri Lanka*, 54).

King Silāmeghavaṇṇa's (617–626 CE) purification involved much violence. According to the *Cūlavaṃsa*,

> a *bhikkhu* called Bōdhi who had seen many undisciplined *bhikkhus* in the Abhayuttara (Abhayagiri) *vihāra* came to the king and begged him to proclaim a regulative act. The king proclaimed the act and executed it himself in the *vihāra*. The *bhikkhus* who had been expelled from the Order, then secretly murdered Bōdhi and annulled the act. The king punished this action by cutting off the offenders' hands, fettering them, and forcing them to be guardians of the bathing tanks; he also expelled another hundred *bhikkhus* to Jambudīpa. In remembrance of Bōdhi's efforts he thus cleansed the order.[9]

While the king was customarily obligated to protect the *buddhasāsana,* this by no means meant that individual bhikkhus were exempt from the law of the land. One of the most serious crimes was treason. Bhikkhus presumed guilty of committing treason by any means were put to death as common criminals. The king could prohibit provision of alms to, disrobe, brand, and banish monks for violating the laws of the realm or for propagating heresy. Thus, the robe did not protect the individual.

The king's duty to the *buddhasāsana* also had its softer side. Much as the kings built monuments and monasteries to support Buddhism, some of them also enacted laws prohibiting the slaughter of animals, thus upholding one of Buddhism's basic principles. Āmaṇḍagāmanī Abhaya (79–89 CE), for instance, enacted *māghāta* or the prohibition of killing. Sirisanghabodhi (307–309 CE) carried these concerns even further. The *Mahāvaṃsa* states, "[a]t the news: 'Rebels are arisen here and there,' the king had the rebels brought before him, but he released them again secretly; then did he send bodies of dead men, and causing terror to the people by burning of these he did away with the fear from rebels."[10] Geiger notes, "[h]e had the corpses burnt in place of the rebels and thus inspired the belief that he had condemned them to death by fire."[11]

Anurādhapura ceased to be the nucleus of Sinhala Buddhist power in the eleventh century. The kingdom shifted to Polonnaruva where Sinhala Buddhist kings ruled until the mid-thirteenth century, when renewed Cola invasions from South India temporarily ended their sovereignty. Then the kingdom shifted to Dambadeṇiya, situated closer to the northwestern seaboard, to Gampola in the central region south of Kandy, and then to Kotte in the southwestern region.

[9] *Cūlavaṃsa*, 44:75–82; Paranavitana, "Civilization of the Early Period," 382.

[10] *Mahāvaṃsa*, 36:80–82. [11] *Ibid.*, Geiger trans., 262 n1.

Many subcontinental belief systems existed alongside Buddhism in Sri Lanka, including Brahmanism, Jainism, and various other doctrines of wandering mendicants, as well as native tribal belief systems. While Buddhist literature composed in Sri Lanka disapproved of non-Buddhist faiths as soteriologically ineffective, none of the chronicles or commentaries indicate that the Buddhist social organization was hostile toward any of these to the point of compelling the state to prohibit them unless, like the proto-Mahāyāna doctrines mentioned earlier, these non-Buddhist elements were perceived as a threat. Instead, Buddhists advocated the absorption and accommodation of various non-Buddhist, particularly Vedic and post-Vedic beliefs and practices. Although the Theravāda monastic establishment rejected the proto-Mahāyāna and Mahāyāna Buddhist doctrines, many Mahāyāna institutions, including bodhisattva worship, entered the Theravāda Buddhist beliefs and practices, albeit in modified forms.[12] The influence of Brahmanism and Hindu polytheistic ritualism increased during the Polonnaruva era and has gained ground ever since.

In the Kotte kingdom, Brahman priests enjoyed much power and authority in court. Many influential members of the Buddhist saṅgha also came under their influence. Brāhmaṇical law, derived from the *dharmasūtras, Dharmaśāstras*, and the *Arthaśāstras*, informed many matters concerning statecraft and economic management. Buddhism advised that the *pañcaśīla* or the five precepts should be taken into consideration when laws were promulgated and executed, that the ten principles of statecraft or duties of the king (*dasarājadhamma*) be heeded, that the principles of social conduct (*satara sangrahavastu*) be cultivated, and that the four unprofitable directions (*satara agati*) be avoided. *Dasarājadhamma* included principles such as morality, honesty, kindness, and nonviolence. The *dasarājadhamma, satara sangraha vastu* and *satara agati* were normative frameworks for the rulers to follow.

Buddhism and Law in Colonial Sri Lanka: Portuguese Rule

From the sixteenth century, this state of affairs had to include another component: European colonialism and Christianity, which began in Sri Lanka with the arrival of the Portuguese. The first Portuguese ship accidentally arrived in Sri Lanka in 1504 or thereabouts. A second more purposive visit followed around 1513, during which the Portuguese captain met the

[12] On the influence of Mahāyāna Buddhism, see John Clifford Holt, *Buddha in the Crown: Avalokiteśvara in the Buddhist Traditions of Sri Lanka* (New York: Oxford University Press, 1991).

king of Kotte, Dharma Parākramabāhu IX (1489–1513), and discussed the possibilities of doing business. He was accompanied by Franciscan priests who sought to convert the natives, who they believed were various kinds of heathen.

King Bhuvanekabāhu (1521–1551) needed Portuguese support in his wars against his brothers, Rayigam Bandāra of Rayigama in the southwestern inland region and Mayādunne of Sitāwaka that lay between Kotte and Kandy. This allowed the Portuguese to establish themselves on the island as a military power. King Bhuvanekabāhu raised his grandson prince Dharmapāla as the heir to the throne, an unusual procedure in terms of the established rules of succession. The prince was educated by the Franciscans.

In 1540, Bhuvanekabāhu sent a diplomatic mission to Lisbon to secure the support of the Portuguese king, Joao III, for the eventual succession by Dharmapāla. Joao III pledged Portuguese support in 1543 by crowning an effigy of the prince, an act that enraged Mayādunne, who had the right of succession, and made Bhuvanekabāhu unpopular among his subjects. Apparently, the messenger from Kotte misinformed the king of Portugal that the king of Kotte would be willing to convert to Christianity. This was a momentous occasion regarding Buddhism's legal position in Sri Lanka as its state religion and the religion of its monarch, and Mayādunne used this to challenge the legitimacy of Bhuvanekabāhu's rule.

Bhuvanekabāhu died in 1550 and Mayādunne proclaimed himself the king of Kotte. When the Portuguese stood by Dharmapāla and proclaimed him the king, warfare ensued, and in 1557, King Dharmapāla (1551–1597) converted to Catholicism. For the first time in Sri Lanka, its principal Sinhala king ceased to be a Buddhist, thereby breaking a tradition that had the force of law for nearly eighteen centuries. Not only did he convert, he also confiscated all the lands gifted by his ancestors and others to the saṅgha and the various *devales* – shrines dedicated to various local and Hindu gods and goddesses – and gifted them to the Franciscans. Thus, in Kotte the saṅgha and the Buddhist monasteries lost all claims to real property, resulting in Dharmapāla's loss of popular support.

Dharmapāla's misfortunes increased as the Portuguese, who had begun to play the upper hand in Kotte politics, decided in 1565 to abandon Kotte and move their administration to Colombo, which had by then become a Portuguese fortress. In 1580 he bequeathed his kingdom to the king of Portugal, Dom Manuel. This bequest gave the Portuguese legal title to the Kotte kingdom upon Dharmapāla's death, an "inheritance" by deed that was legally inadequate and probably invalid. Dharmapāla had bequeathed the kingdom to the king of Portugal as if the kingdom was his private property when, in fact, it was not. According to the laws of the land, several premises invalidated this bequest. In Sri Lanka, legitimacy of kingship pivoted upon two requirements: The king must be a Buddhist, and only a person of Sinhala or Indian royal descent could rule over the Sinhalas. These requirements invalidated Dharmapāla's right to be the king and his right to bequeath the kingdom to a non-Buddhist king.[13]

When Dharmapāla died in 1597, the Kotte kingdom became a satellite of Portugal. By the end of the sixteenth century, the island had two political systems: the Portuguese colonial administration in the Maritime Provinces and the Kandyan kingdom. For the first time in history, the Sinhala community had two state-sanctioned religions: Buddhism and Roman Catholicism.

After Dharmapāla's demise, the massacres of Buddhists, Hindus, and Muslims, and the brutality and wanton destruction of non-Christian religious establishments by Dom Jeronimo de Azevedo, the Portuguese captain-general, are well recorded by both Sri Lankan and Portuguese writers. Buddhists basically lost legal rights to follow their beliefs and continue with Buddhist practices. The Portuguese soldiers plundered and ravaged the Kalaniya Raja Mahā Vihāraya, one of the most ancient and revered Buddhist temples just six miles east of Colombo. The Buddhist saṅgha and the monasteries lost all of their real property, and the saṅgha had to flee to the Kandyan kingdom where the traditional relationships between Buddhism and state law survived. The Portuguese administration, while rendering Buddhist monasticism illegal, also accelerated their policy of conversion of the natives by offering legal, social, political, and economic advantages to the converts and depriving those who refused any access to such privileges. The Portuguese adopted the local judicial authority system and staffed it with converted natives.

Dutch Rule

Portuguese rule ended in 1658 when the king of Kandy, Rājasinghe II, expelled them with the support of the Dutch, who began to occupy the littoral previously ruled by the Portuguese. Their policy on indigenous belief systems carried the same prejudices, and the Calvinist *predikants* (the

[13] For details, see R.K.W. Goonesekera, "The Gift of a Kingdom," *University of Ceylon Review* 23 (1965), 15–34 and T.B.H. Abeysinghe, "Portuguese Rule in Kotte, 1594–1638" in K.M. De Silva (ed.), *A History of Sri Lanka*, vol. 2 (Peradeniya: University of Peradeniya, 1995), 125–26.

pastors of the Dutch Reformed Church that accompanied the administrators) desired to convert the natives. But they had to reckon with the Catholics, with whom they already had serious conflicts in Europe, before they dealt with other religious groups. Their hostility toward Catholics forced the Franciscans to flee from the Maritime Provinces. Against the wishes of the Kandyan nobility, the kings of Kandy offered them refuge and allowed them to build places of worship and to preach Catholic doctrines. However, by the mid-eighteenth century, when they began to criticize Buddhism and other faiths and publish materials that were offensive to Buddhists and Hindus, the King Śri Vijaya Rājasinghe expelled them from the kingdom.

The Dutch Calvinist impact on Buddhism was felt most strongly in matters of education because conversion was a prerequisite for education and obtaining prestigious and lucrative positions in the administration. It was also influential in matters of real property as anyone who was to inherit land had to be baptized as a Protestant, and the Dutch refused to return any of the property that had been owned by Buddhists. Against the advice of the Board of Church Elders in Amsterdam, they applied coercive practices, including forfeiture of a third of the property owned by a Buddhist if he failed to receive Protestant baptism. They also imposed various penalties on those who did not go to church regularly or did not bring their children for baptism on the day the *predikant* visited the church schools.[14]

The Dutch established a legal system based on Roman Dutch law administered through a system of courts that was a mixture of native systems of dispute resolution and Dutch courts. This system was hierarchically organized with lower levels functioning in accordance with the native legal considerations; litigants could appeal to higher levels. Native converts were appointed as judicial officials of the lower courts. The higher levels consisted of Dutch courts that applied the Roman Dutch laws and the statutes or *placaats* issued by the superior Dutch authorities in Batavia (present-day Jakarta, Indonesia). These courts were known as *Civiele Raad*, *Landraad*, and the *Raad van Justitie*. Appeals could be made from the local *Raad van Justitie* to the *Raad van Justitie* in Batavia.[15]

[14] This legislation is extensive. See K.W. Goonewardena, "Dutch Policy Towards Buddhism in Sri Lanka and Some Aspects of its Impact" in K.M. de Silva, C.R. de Silva, and Sirima Kiribamune (eds.), *Asian Panorama: Essays in Asian History, Past and Present* (New Delhi: Vikas Publishing House, 1990), 319–52.

[15] One might notice similarities with the *adat* systems of Indonesia. The Dutch were interested in the Tamil *Tesavalāmai* in addition to the Sinhala legal system. See D.A. Kotelawele, "The VOC in Sri Lanka 1688–1766 – Problems and Policies" in de Silva (ed.), *A History of Sri Lanka*, 233–80.

The overall legal situation of Buddhism in the Maritime Provinces changed only a little: Buddhist monks could return and preach without harassment, but without any support structures. Buddhist monasteries and practices were illegal in towns, but allowed in the villages. Although the Dutch continued to harass the Hindus and Muslims, unlike the Portuguese, they mostly left the saṅgha alone for they did not want to offend the kings of Kandy with whom they desired cordial, mercantile relationships. Effective Dutch control over Buddhist affairs was limited to a narrow belt along the coast. In the hinterland, Buddhist activities flourished, and although Buddhists had no legal rights vis-à-vis the Dutch administration, bhikkhus from the Kandyan kingdom and religious specialists known as *silvata* visited these areas and provided Buddhist education to children.

Toward the end of the seventeenth century, the Dutch policy changed to allow more freedom to practice religion without hindrance. The Dutch East India Company initially ignored the protests by the *predikants* but later gave in under pressure from the Calvinist clergy. In 1692, the clergy took charge of the vihāra, and the saṅgha were ordered to vacate the premises. A hundred years later, the Kandyan king, Kīrti Śri Rājasinghe, a great patron of the Buddhists who had significant ties with the Dutch administration, had the Kalaniya Raja Mahā Vihāra renovated. The saṅgha returned and the vihāra once again functioned as a major place for Buddhist activities.[16]

The Dutch courts of law at the apex of the judicial system only recognized a Buddhist's rights in disputes between Buddhists. Christians held an advantage in their disputes with Buddhists; for example, evidence provided by Buddhists, and non-Christians in general, was not admissible against Christians. Thus, Buddhists and non-Christians had a dubious legal status in the areas controlled by the Dutch.

Kandyan Kingdom

As the Kotte kingdom became Portuguese property at the end of the sixteenth century, Kandy became the official site of the Sinhala Buddhist kingdom. During the reign of King Vimaladhammasūriya I (1591–1604), Buddhism was still formally the state religion of the Sinhala society. However, as warfare within and without distracted the kings and political leaders, the protection and maintenance of the *sāsana* was overlooked, and monastic practices became lax. It appears that none of the Kandyan kings were

[16] Kitsiri Malalgoda, *Buddhism in Sinhalese Society* (Berkeley: University of California Press, 1976), 28–49; Goonewardena, "Dutch Policy."

particularly religious, but all in their various ways were expected to play normative roles as protectors, sustainers, and maintainers of the *buddhasāsana*. This section examines several events that demonstrate significant interactions between Buddhism and law in the Kandyan kingdom in the areas of monastic property, monastic involvement in succession disputes, treason, and monastic schism.

Monastic Property

From the Anurādhapura period, kings donated extensive tracks of land and even irrigation works to Buddhist monasteries. The chief incumbent of the monastery managed the grants with the help of lay wardens, who employed the tenants and slaves to cultivate the land. Property inheritance was based on a principle called pupillary succession (*śiṣyanuśiṣya paramparā*), according to which the title passed from the chief incumbent to his ordained student (*śiṣya*), who was a resident (*saddhivihārika*) in the monastery and who had sufficient integrity in the eyes of the incumbent. By the tenth century, kings introduced the practice of granting lands as the private property of individual monks. Later on, succession was based less on spiritual bonds between a preceptor (*upajjhāya*) and a resident student than on property interests. The pupils were chosen from the incumbent's own family, usually a nephew, which departed from tradition by instituting a kindred pupillary succession.

This development led to monastic property being tied to property interests of aristocratic families as recruitment was based on the aspirant being of noble birth. This practice resulted in irregularities in training novices (*sāmaṇeras*), the eventual depletion of the ordained bhikkhus and problems with the higher ordination process. However, early in the eighteenth century, a bhikkhu named Välivita Saraṇaṃkara began a movement to counter the moral decay in the saṅgha. He established a group of Buddhists consisting of concerned *sāmaṇeras*, known as the fraternity of the pious (*silvat tanas*), which practiced the *Vinaya* rules to the letter and revived mendicancy. Soon complaints went to King Narendrasinghe regarding the disrespectful attitude of the *silvat tanas* toward their monastic superiors. The dispute was settled in favor of the established monasteries, and the *silvat tanas* were legally compelled to pay proper respect to the monastic superiors. However, the king was impressed with Saraṇaṃkara and appointed him as the mentor to his heir.[17] This takes us to the second event.

[17] *Ibid.*, 60. The *silvat tana* here is the same as *silvata* in Goonewardena, "Dutch Policy."

Rules of Succession to the Throne

King Narendrasinghe (1707–39) lacked an heir for his throne. According to the Brāhmaṇical theory of royal succession, in the absence of a *kṣatriya* heir from the lineage of the king, the successor must be selected from the queen's lineage. Narendrasinghe followed the tradition of finding an appropriate *kṣatriya* queen from South India, but her brother needed an education in Sinhala laws and customs in order to succeed the king, who appointed Saraṇaṃkara to serve as his mentor. After the death of Narendrasinghe, the succession controversy between the Kandyan aristocrats and the foreigner was settled by Saraṇaṃkara, who sided with the Brāhmaṇical tradition, and his pupil was installed as King Śri Vijaya Rājasinghe (1739–47). It is noteworthy from a legal standpoint that the leading Sinhala Buddhist monastic authority ignored the ancient tradition that a Sinhala Buddhist should be the king of Sri Lanka and followed the Brāhmaṇical theory of kingship.

Treason

That takes us to the third event: Buddhists committing treason. As already indicated, when it came to the punishment of the death penalty for treason – conspiracy, rebellion, adultery with a king's wife – the law of Sri Lanka spared no one. Bhikkhu Välivița Saraṇaṃkara's mentor, Sūriyagoḍa Rājasundara, was accused of committing treason against Narendrasinghe. He was executed and his kindred were banished from the kingdom and their property confiscated. Later, Saraṇaṃkara used his influence in Śri Vijaya Rājasinghe's court to have Narendrasinghe's decision reversed. Sūriyagoḍa Rājasundara's relatives were recalled and their ancestral property was returned to them.[18] This indicates two things: The rulings of kings may be reversed by their successors, and influential Buddhist monks could advise kings on Buddhist values and thereby intervene in judicial proceedings.

Saraṇaṃkara himself eventually became involved in a conspiracy to murder king Kīrti Śri Rājasinghe (1747–82). Saraṇaṃkara's great ambition was to reestablish *upasampadā* (monastic higher ordination) in Sri Lanka. He sought King Śri Vijaya Rājasinghe's help in this regard. Twice the king sought Dutch support, obtaining ships to send missions to Siam (Thailand)

[18] *Ibid.*, 61 n149; A.C. Lawrie, *A Gazeteer of the Central Province*, 2 vols. (Colombo: George J.A. Keen, Government Printer, 1898), 801.

to request that ordained bhikkhus be sent to Sri Lanka in order to reestablish higher ordination. Both missions failed. King Śri Vijaya Rājasinghe was succeeded by his brother-in-law, King Kīrti Śri Rājasinghe, who sent a third mission to Siam, again with Dutch help, which succeeded this time. The Siamese bhikkhus reestablished monastic higher ordination in Sri Lanka.

However, in spite of Kīrti Śri Rājasinghe's indefatigable efforts to play the role of a Sinhala Buddhist king to legitimate his rule, he was still a Saivite Hindu and practiced his faith as well. He rubbed ash on his forehead and held Saivite rituals in the palace. This was irksome to some nobility, who resented having a non-Buddhist at the head of the state. They, with the help of several leading bhikkhus including Saraṇaṃkara, conspired to assassinate the king when he attended a function at one of the principal monasteries in Sri Lanka. Their intention was to replace him with a Buddhist prince brought in from Siam. The king found out about the conspiracy, deported the Siamese prince, and executed the laymen involved. However, he pardoned the bhikkhus because, given the political climate of the Buddhist revival, it would have been detrimental to the king to execute the popular bhikkhus.

Monastic Schism

According to the Kandyan treatise on law, *Nīti Nighaṇḍuva*, caste was integral to the Kandyan social organization. The concern with social distinctions based on birth became stronger with increasing Brāhmaṇical influences from the Polonnaruva period. The Brāhmaṇical tradition gave caste an axiomatic position even in the monastic order, which formally rejected it. The *Dambadeṇiya Katikāvata*, a work composed in the Dambadeṇiya kingdom during the reign of King Parākramabāhu II (1236–71), states that only novices of noble birth should be given higher ordination.[19] High-caste laymen were reluctant to pay respect to bhikkhus with low-caste origins, who in turn paid respects to some lay individuals by prostrating before them. This degraded the monastic order, which was supposed to receive highest respects from every layperson.[20] When higher ordination was reestablished, the chief monks in Kandy refused to grant it to low-caste monks and restricted the ordination to high-caste monks. This monastic position was legitimized by King Kīrti Śri Rājasinghe in a royal decree.

[19] D.B. Jayatilaka (ed.), "Dambadeniya Katikavata," *Katikavat Sangara*, (1922), 9–10.

[20] John Davy, *An Account of the Interior of Ceylon* (Dehiwala: Tsara Prakasakayo, 1983, 1821). The Kandyan-period poem *Mandāram Pura Puvata* (verses 823–62) concurs with Davy. Labugama Lankananda (ed.), *Mandāram Pura Puvata*, (Colombo, 1958).

In contrast, the maritime colonial economy was insensitive to caste, and many low-castes – particularly the *karāva* (fisherman), *durāva* (toddy tapper), and *salāgama* (cinnamon peeler) castes – prospered by engaging in mercantile activities and achieved high status in the littoral. Monastically inclined individuals from such groups protested the Kandyan rule on *Vinaya* grounds. These protests culminated in the establishment of the Amarapura Nikāya (1803) for the *karāva*, *durāva*, and *salāgama* castes, and later the Rāmañña Nikāya (1864), which ignored caste considerations.[21] The Kandy based high-caste monastic group, by far the most numerous, became known as the Siyam Nikāya. These nikāyas are not sects but fraternities that held the Theravāda doctrines and practices in common except for the social considerations regarding monastic recruitment. They indicate their separate fraternity identities through dress and other external manifestations. However, these differences are currently disappearing in large measure.

British Rule

The British expelled the Dutch in 1796, and the Kandyan kingdom fell in 1815. Buddhism's legal status under the British rule will be examined through several themes: The Kandyan Convention; missionary intervention; separation of state and Buddhism in 1852; the Act of Appointment; Buddhist Temporalities; and Buddhist education.

The Kandyan monarch's attempts to expel the Dutch power in the maritime regions succeeded with British support in 1796. The Kandyan nobility rebelled against King Śri Vikrama Rājasinghe's rule (1798–1815), hoping to replace him with an alternative king.[22] They then formed an agreement with the British called the Kandyan Convention of 1815, which states: "The Religion of Boodhoo professed by the Chiefs and Inhabitants of these Provinces is declared inviolable, and its Rites, Ministers and Places of Worship are to be maintained and protected."[23]

The British government accepted this clause halfheartedly,[24] but they did not interfere with Buddhist activities in the Kandyan provinces. However, Christian missionaries found this clause unacceptable as the provision "inviolable" would interfere with their activities aimed at

[21] Malalgoda, *Buddhism in Sinhalese Society*, 166. [22] *Ibid.*, 106.

[23] "These Provinces" refers to the Kandyan kingdom and the "Ministers" refers to the bhikkhus and other religious persons associated with the Buddhist establishments.

[24] For details, see Walpola Rahula, *The Heritage of the Bhikkhu* (New York: Grove Press, 1974, 1946), 82–89; Malalgoda, *Buddhism in Sinhalese Society*, 111–12 n.24 and n.25; De Silva, *History of Sri Lanka*, 341–42.

converting Kandyan people. The governor conceded to missionary protests in the aftermath of the 1818 Sinhala rebellion against British rule and extended protection to all faiths, thereby legitimating missionary activities. The various legal innovations introduced by the Proclamation of November 21, 1818 exempted the temple lands (*vihāragam* and *dēvālagam*) from taxation in conformity with pre-colonial times, and allowed the traditional services rendered by the tenants to the temples.[25]

In response to continued missionary protests, the Colonial Office made a crucial determination to sever state connections with Buddhism in 1844, which was reaffirmed in 1847 by Earl Grey, the Secretary of State for the colonies. Throughout the nineteenth century, the British colonial government gradually withdrew government contacts with Buddhist activities, including custodianship of the Tooth Relic, the symbol of sovereignty,[26] and then all religious affairs on the island in 1852, thereby abrogating the fifth clause of the Convention. In 1889, the Colonial Office approved the Buddhist Temporalities Act, which removed all state obligations and interest in Buddhist temple lands that were in serious decline because of poor administration and shifted them to administrative bodies consisting of Buddhist laymen, bhikkhus, and the courts.

Throughout the second half of the nineteenth century and into the early twentieth century, the Buddhists agitated for a return to the status quo ante by having legislation passed for state supervision of, intervention in, and administration of Buddhist properties. This culminated in the Buddhist Temporalities Ordinance of 1931. In the late 1930s, Buddhists began to agitate against the Christian use of education as a means for conversion. They demanded state supervision of education, hoping that the state would secularize the school system, thereby hindering missionary conversion efforts. While denominational interests vehemently opposed the Education Ordinance of 1939, which addressed these issues, the state's role in education expanded considerably in the early 1940s.

Conclusion

This brief historical survey demonstrates how Buddhism and secular legal regimes interacted in many convoluted ways, continuing and changing in

[25] Malalgoda, *Buddhism in Sinhalese Society*, 114.

[26] The Tooth Relic was handed over to a committee consisting of the chief incumbents of Asgiriya and Malvatta monasteries and the *Diyavaḍana Nilamē* – the chief lay caretaker of the Relic in October 1847, thereby divesting the relic of its symbolism of sovereignty and indicating the government's wishes to withdraw from the fifth clause of the Convention. For details, see *Ibid.*, 115–20.

time in a variety of circumstances. In practice, the Buddhist monastic order of Sri Lanka has been informally involved in the legal system of the country from the earliest times. Buddhist monks had the capacity to mobilize the masses in response to the actions of the state, and since this capacity is a political one, any discussion of the relationship between Buddhism and law must include, at least marginally, the monastic involvement in politics. Although the Buddhist monastic system facilitated an existence away from the affairs of the secular society, by its dependence on secular support, it could never stray too far away from society. It had to make compromises, subjecting itself to secular authorities while also asserting its independence. The result was a complex system of legal relationships that is worthy of greater scholarly scrutiny.

Gal Vihāra Monument, Polonnaruva, Sri Lanka. King Parākrmabāhu I's *sasāna-katikāvata* was inscribed on this rock face. Photo by Peetie Van Etten

CHAPTER 7

Flanked by Images of Our Buddha
Community, Law, and Religion in a Premodern Buddhist Context

Jonathan S. Walters

Introduction

This chapter explicates an act of monastic regulation recorded in stone by a powerful Sri Lankan Buddhist king, Parākramabāhu I (1153–86).[1] Stone inscriptions like this one (and parallel incised metal and palm-leaf texts) exemplified the shared form of legal declarations throughout premodern Sri Lanka and much of South Asia. They typically open with an invocation championing the political legitimacy and religious outlook of the responsible monarch or other official, proceed with an operative portion detailing the background and specific political-legal act each concerns, and conclude with an enforcement clause, and aspiration for success. Thousands of such documents still exist today as a major source for the study of premodern South Asian law.

In form, King Parākramabāhu I's inscription is typical of such documents. It invokes the king's royal splendor and Buddhist ideology, proceeds with the regulations themselves, and concludes with enforcement clauses (although not, in this record, a final aspiration). Yet this was not just any inscription. As detailed below, this inscription enacted momentous changes in the Sri Lankan religious community of Parākramabāhu's day and gave birth to a regulatory genre that lasted for hundreds of years. The inscription broadcasts its own significance: It is incised on a 13′ 3″ × 9′ 9″ rectangular rock face in the center of Parākramabāhu's most famous monument, called

[1] For text and translation see Don Martino De Zilva Wickremasinghe (ed. and trans.), "Polonnaruva, Gal-Vihāra: Rock-Inscription of Parakkama-Bāhu (1153–1186 A.D.)," in *Epigraphia Zeylanica, Volume II* (London: Government of Ceylon, 1928), 256–83; Nandasena Ratnapala, *The Katikāvatas: Laws of the Buddhist Order of Ceylon from the 12th Century to the 18th Century* (München: Kitzinger, 1971), 37–44, 127–35. Citations are to line numbers in the original inscription, as published in Wickremasinghe, "Polonnaruva, Gal-Vihāra." All translations are my own, but I acknowledge greatly having benefited from Professor Ratnapala's work and recommend it as a key primary and secondary source for the study of Buddhist law.

Gal Vihāra ("Rock Monastery"), flanked on either side by colossal Buddha images exquisitely carved from a single rock outcropping fifty-six meters long.

The inscription is first and foremost a set of regulations (Pāli *katikāvata*) for the monastic community. The term is an old one that refers in the *Vinaya* and commentaries to sets of supplementary rules for day-to-day life that are agreed upon by the residents of a particular monastery. Some of Parākramabāhu I's predecessors, in the tenth-century heyday of Anurādhapura, had also erected impressive – sometimes enormous – inscriptions formalizing and detailing such regulations of particular, central monasteries. These tenth-century *katikāvatas* have been classed as *Vihāra katikāvatas* (regulations of monasteries[2]), but the scope of Parākramabāhu I's inscription is so much wider – it was meant for application throughout the kingdom – that it can be considered the first in a new genre of texts distinguished as *Sāsana katikāvatas* (regulations of the [Buddha's entire] dispensation).[3] It proved foundational for similar legal texts issued by powerful successors.

In the following three sections, I analyze Parākramabāhu I's inscription for insight into the workings of community, law, and religion. First I introduce the definitions and distinctions of community at work in Parākramabāhu's legislation. Then I explore how the legislation affected the community so defined. Finally, I analyze the underlying Buddhist philosophy of community that motivated this king to regulate the monks in the first place. By way of conclusion, I theorize this case as a set of questions worth asking of any moment in the history of Buddhist law.

Defining Community

"Our Buddha" (l.1) are the first words of Parākramabāhu's legislation, tying it into the whole monument and implying Buddhist community writ large – everyone who belongs to such an *us* – as its audience. After praising his career as Buddha (l.1–2) and his final passing (l.3–4) – the two moments illustrated, as it were, in the flanking Buddha images[4] – the text

[2] See Ratnapala, *Katikāvatas*, 7; Jonathan S. Walters, "Buddhist History: The Sri Lankan Pāli Vamsas and Their Commentary," in Ronald Inden, Jonathan Walters, and Daud Ali (eds.), *Querying the Medieval: Texts and the History of Practices in South Asia* (Oxford: Oxford University Press, 2000), 135–41.

[3] This classificatory distinction is a modern one, first suggested by M. Śrī Rammaṇḍala in 1880 (see Ratnapala, *Katikāvatas*, 6–13 and 14, n. 12).

[4] The images are of a seated Buddha, active in his career, and of a recumbent Buddha, at the moment of his final release from suffering.

quickly traverses the seventeen centuries connecting the Buddha to "the time when . . . Parākramabāhu had been consecrated into kingship over the entire surface of Lanka" (l.6). This delimits the implied audience to the island's own Buddhist community, as does the fact that the inscription, although replete with Sanskrit forms and Pāli quotations, is composed in the vernacular (Sinhala) rather than a transregional language. The citizens who constitute Parākramabāhu's political community or kingdom are assumed to share this vernacular language and to understand themselves as occupying the latest moment in that long history since the Buddha's day. A single event during the reign of an earlier Sri Lankan king, however, stands in for this history. The inscription carefully specifies it to have occurred in the time of King Vaḷagam Abhā (Pāli Vaṭṭagāmaṇī Abhaya, 103 BCE and 89–77 BCE), 454 years after the Buddha's final passing, and 1,254 years before the then-present (l.4–5). However, the inscription does not actually name the event, stating only its result: the dispensation has been broken into divisions and is moving toward destruction. Parākramabāhu's regulations redress this condition.

"Dispensation" (Pāli *sāsana)* or "dispensation of the Buddha" is the closest synonym of Buddhism that Parākramabāhu provides. The term means "command" or "order," and in this context it refers to a legacy or similar ongoing presence of the Buddha whose "establishment" is variously theorized in Sri Lankan historical writings as dependent on the existence of a living local monastic community such that, as the inscription states (quoting Buddhaghosa's Pāli), "even a single son of good family, receiving ordination and higher ordination, establishes the entire dispensation" (l.47–48).[5]

Yet the dispensation is not identical with the community of Buddhist monks, which the inscription consistently designates instead by the term *[bhikkhu]-saṅgha.* The saṅgha, in other words, is constituted as a specialist religious community within a larger Buddhist political community. The inscription is concerned to regulate the saṅgha for its own sake as well as for the sake of the larger political community/kingdom. Parākramabāhu attempted to do this by (re)defining and enforcing boundaries on the saṅgha. He unified those "broken divisions" into a single "great community" (*mahāsaṅgha,* l.14), and thereby, in his estimation, helped protect the dispensation for the 5,000 years that it is predicted to survive (l.16, cf. l.8).

However, this unification of the saṅgha, which is detailed further in this chapter, did not erase other sorts of differences and hierarchies within

[5] The citation is to Buddhaghosa's commentary on the *Vinaya, Samantapāsādikā, Cullavagga, Senāsanaggāha-vinicchaya-vaṇṇanā.* Wickremasinghe, "Polonnaruva, Gal-Vihāra," 272, n. 4.

the monastic community, nor between monks and the general populace. If anything, the regulations entailed a sharpening of such distinctions. The regulations specify numerous different seniority-based ranks or classes within the saṅgha, such that at one point Parākramabāhu must stipulate that he is referring to "every saṅgha" (l.30) rather than just to one or the other of these classes. Underlying the hierarchy was the system of examinations for ordination and higher ordination, as well as special obligations between some junior and senior monks depending on whether the seniors serve the juniors as teachers, or as preceptors. The newly united *mahāsaṅgha* also remained divided according to a system of "groups" (*gaṇa*).[6] R.A.L.H. Gunawardana has argued that the groups were less important than yet another continuing administrative system based on eight fraternities.[7]

These distinctions were consequential for the application of law, which varied depending on the subsection(s) of the saṅgha to which particular monks belonged. Parākramabāhu's legislation treats senior monks differently than it treats junior monks; different rights and responsibilities are placed on relationships with teachers and with preceptors; "outside" monks are treated differently than those in one's own group; the "great elders" hold "elders" accountable for the conduct of the entire group. Similarly, regulations of the saṅgha's interactions with the lay population (l.34, l.44) vary depending on such factors as class, gender, age, and kinship.

Regulating Community

The saṅgha is a self-regulating body. Its laws are encoded in a voluminous literature (*Vinaya*), and adjudication is its own responsibility, according to truly ancient ritual/legal proceedings held on the monthly full moon days (l.28). Parākramabāhu is careful to clarify that the agents who promulgate these regulations are the "great elders headed up by Great Elder Mahākāśyapa" (l.9, 17), not the king himself. These great elders admittedly produced the regulations in response to the king's repeated imploring, made on various occasions when he adopted the Eight Precepts of a pious layman and visited them with appropriate timing and courtesy (l.15–18). However, the great elders dictate what a monk should know and do, and the punishments appropriate to disobeying those dictates.

[6] See Ratnapala, *Katikāvatas*, 189, n. 6.1.

[7] See R.A.L.H. Gunawardana, *Robe and Plough: Monasticism and Economic Interest in Early Medieval Sri Lanka* (New York: Oxford, 1979), 282–312, passim.

Yet the king still looms large, not only for having carved these words in stone, but also as an agent in their production. He is introduced in the invocation before any monks at all – except the Buddha – in full regal glory, "a King over Kings [i.e., emperor] glittering through the rays of [his imperial] fame that are diffused throughout various [foreign] regions" (l.5–6). This opening invocation (l.1–18) is narrated primarily in the first-person voice of the king, who explains how the regulations emerged. Reform is necessary, he maintains, because of 1,254-year-old "dirt" on "the Buddha's pure dispensation." Despite leaving the event unnamed, Parākramabāhu's reference to divisions (*nikāya*) and his mention and dating of Vaḷagam Abhā signaled to his contemporaries his assent to a particular historiographical tradition, which was tantamount to taking sides in a centuries-old sectarian rivalry.

Within the larger premodern Buddhist world, Sri Lanka's Theravāda tradition was known to be split into three divisions (*nikāya*), named for the three main monastic complexes in an ancient royal capital, Anurādhapura: the Mahāvihāra, Abhayagirivihāra, and Jetavanavihāra. Although all three were sophisticated, ancient establishments, they perpetuated a long history of rivalry over matters of practice, interpretation, royal support, and even real estate.[8] Their battles were fought primarily in historical accounts, which sported conflicting versions of a basic template in which the rise of Anurādhapura and of the historians' particular division are linked to each other as well as to the larger history of the Buddha's dispensation abroad. Of the three historiographical traditions, however, only that of the Mahāvihārans survives today. Their ultimate victory over the Abhayagiri and Jetavana monks, which Pārākramabāhu announces in the very inscription under consideration, produced as one of its consequences the loss of all the rival accounts, except insofar as they are discernible within the extensive, surviving Mahāvihāran histories (*vaṃsas*), notably *Illumination of the Purpose of History* (*Vaṃsatthappakāsinī*, tenth century CE), which attempted to adjudicate all the conflicting historical accounts in favor of the Mahāvihāran version.

Vaṃsatthappakāsinī presents itself as a royal practice bringing members of the royal court together with leading Buddhist monks in order to study Buddhist historical precedent – embodied in the Mahāvihārans' core

[8] See Jonathan S. Walters, "Mahāyāna Theravāda and the Origins of the Mahāvihāra," *Sri Lanka Journal of the Humanities* XXII (Nos. 1 and 2, 1998), 100–19; Jonathan S. Walters, "Mahāsena at the Mahāvihāra: On the Interpretation and Politics of History in Pre-colonial Sri Lanka," in Daud Ali (ed.), *Invoking the Past: The Uses of History in South Asia* (Oxford: Oxford University Press, 1999), 322–66; Walters, "Buddhist History."

historical text, *The Great History* (*Mahāvaṃsa*, ca. 460 CE) – as a guide to the proper Buddhist course of action that a powerful king ought to take in the administration of the kingdom, war, trade, ritual, social service, technological development, medicine, or the law. This is, indeed, precisely how Parākramabāhu I appears to have proceeded, as signaled in his allusions to the Mahāvihāran histories. The inscription's depiction of his ongoing association and discussion with the Mahāvihāran "great elders" is likewise reminiscent of *Vaṃsatthappakāsinī*'s royal practice.

In the Mahāvihāran account to which Parākramabāhu alludes, almost 218 years after the establishment of the Mahāvihāra (itself 236 years after the Buddha's passing), King Vattagāmaṇt built the Abhayagirivihāra.[9] Rather than gift it to the Mahāvihārans, however, he gave it to a "splitter" (*nikāyika*) in whose now-private monastery discipline broke down as heresy emerged. Out of that breach, according to the Mahāvihārans (Mhv 37:32–40), a secondary split occurred some centuries later, when an errant king named Mahāsena (274–301 CE) misappropriated Mahāvihāran land and material wealth to construct the Jetavanavihāra, then gave it to a rogue splitter from among the Abhayagiri splitters. Subsequently, according to these historians, the rivals regularly prospered at the Mahavihārans' expense. The archeological and inscriptional evidence substantiates their basic case: while the buildings of the Mahāvihāra truly were older than those of the rivals, Mahāvihāran claims to superiority were made despite the rivals being consistently bigger, richer, and more international.

The rivals presumably narrated alternative accounts, surely plausible ones since they dominated Anurādhapura for most of its history. Their success was likely grounded in precisely what the Mahāvihārans disparaged them for – namely, their cosmopolitan participation in the latest (Mahāyāna and Tantrayāna) Buddhist developments abroad. In the South Asian heyday of these "heretical" Buddhists (ca. third to tenth centuries), the rivals' cosmopolitanism was facilitated by, and in turn facilitated, the cosmopolitan political and economic connections of their kings. These earlier kings' support for the rivals, in other words, was bound up with their own relationships vis-à-vis Buddhist and increasingly non-Buddhist kings abroad, who favored Mahāyāna and Tantrayāna forms of thought and practice if they favored the Buddhists at all. In the Mahāyāna

[9] Wilhelm Geiger (ed.), *The Mahāvamsa* (London: Pali Text Society, 1908); Wilhelm Geiger and Mabel Bode (trans.), *The Mahāvamsa, or the Great Chronicle of Ceylon* (London: Pali Text Society, 1912), 33:79–84 (citations are to chapter and verse).

perspective, the only true awakening is that of a completely accomplished buddha, and the only legitimate Buddhist path is that of the buddha-aspirant (Pāli *bodhisatta).* Kings, like monks, conceived of themselves as so many bodhisattas, transforming the world into so many pure lands. In addition to this profound religious vision and identity, cosmopolitanism benefited Anurādhapura's kings through trade, political alliance, access to cutting-edge technology, styles, and learning, and royal brides from imperial centers on the mainland.

But "having seen the community of Mahāvihāran monks" (l.10–11) Parākramabāhu I came to share their distinctive views, and pushed for reunification "by bringing the three divisions together into a single division" (l.13). This required "expelling from the Master's dispensation various hundreds of evil monks" (l.12), that is, Abhayagiri and Jetavana monks resisting the new order.[10] Yet, since previous kings attempted this and failed, Parākramabāhu worried about the "method by which, in the future, this unification of the saṅgha, effected by me with great effort, might persist unbroken for five thousand years" (l.15–16). This prompted his request of the great elders "to promulgate monastic regulations which do not deviate from the lineages of preceptors, such that those living in negligence have no opening [for inappropriate conduct]" (l.18). The remaining thirty-three lines of the inscription are presented as their response to that repeated beseeching that they thus "protect the dispensation by providing exhortations and instructions according to which future members of the saṅgha can live, possessing virtues like contentment, and being energetic in the two modes of monastic practice, book-study and meditation" (l. 16–17).

Heeding the king's request, the great elders appear to have agreed on a principle that both commences (l.18) and concludes (l.51) the operative portion of the inscription: The elders who are the heads of the monastic "groups" are to be held accountable to the great elders for any infractions that occur on their watch. Thus, even the regulations that seem completely individual – concerning things like the morning toilet, meditation, and bedtimes – are community concerns.

While this centralization of responsibility devolves in some circumstances to individual preceptors (l.28), the elders who lead groups are to make sure that two overlapping mechanisms keep the saṅgha in compliance

10 For a colorful and sarcastic account of their opposition, portrayed as a self-serving attempt by the rivals to preserve their sinful ways, see Wilhelm Geiger (ed.), *The Cūlavaṃsa, Being the More Recent Part of the Mahāvamsa* (London: Pali Text Society, 1925); Wilhelm Geiger and C. Mabel Rickmers, (trans.), *The Cūlavaṃsa, Being the More Recent Part of the Mahāvamsa* (Colombo: Government of Ceylon, 1953), 78:1–27 (citations are to chapter and verse).

with the regulations: (1) the extension of apprenticeship (Pāli *nissaya*) to novices and the concomitant release therefrom, and (2) education and examination. The elders "should not permit" any negligence on the part of those granted apprenticeship, nor on the part of those who have been released from it, but instead should "motivate them to the study of books" that are then specified to include the *Khuddasikkhā* (a compendium of *Vinaya* rules in Pāli verse) and the *Pātimokkha* (the rules as chanted in monastic courts on full moon days) as well as *suttas* (including *Dasadhamma-sutta* and *Anumāna-sutta*) that concern proper conduct (l.19); once these texts have been mastered, monks should put them into practice through meditation and impeccable self-discipline (l.20–22). Those who cannot accomplish such scholarly feats should undertake more limited book study to focus on meditation (l.22–24), while an even simpler version of the same should be the training for novices (l.25). The scholars are presumed to be preparing for examinations associated with higher ordination, but the second subsection should be examined every six months (l.23) and all monks should be thoroughly examined at ordination, higher ordination, and the granting of and release from apprenticeship (l.48–49).

The text then proceeds to highlight specific examples of the monastic conduct it advocates. These examples are of three partly overlapping types: behavior within one's own monastery or group, with monks from different monasteries or groups, and with laypeople. As these involve the nature and legislation of community, it is appropriate to conclude this section with an indication of what each entails.

The first type includes clear regulations for when everyone should rise, and should sleep (l.30–31), a daily schedule of duties and practices (l.31–34), insistence on the restraint of speech in general, and of frivolous or harmful speech in particular (l.35–37, 38, 43–44), discouragement of covetousness with regard to monastic property (l.42–43), prohibition of speaking ill of those who undertake extra ascetic practices (l.49), a stipulation that those studying and reciting texts should not disturb others who are trying to meditate (l.47), and a series of regulations enforcing respect for seniority (l.39–40). These regulations promote the smooth functioning of a local monastic community.

The text highlights two dimensions of the relationship between monastic communities: responsibilities vis-à-vis monks who come to stay in one's own community, and responsibilities vis-à-vis other communities in which one stays. In the former case, a distinction is made between monks who arrive while traveling on temporary business (who should be provided lodging in monastic out-buildings, l. 38) and those who arrive intending to stay permanently, who should not be given lodging without a letter from the elder who oversees the group in which they formerly lived (l.29–30). When visiting other monasteries, and in keeping with the general concern for restrained speech, monks are advised to neither broadcast the legal cases and settlements of their own monasteries, nor to get involved in those of other monasteries (l.42).

Finally, the text enforces boundaries between the saṅgha and lay society. It underscores the *Vinaya* prohibition on entering villages at the wrong times, although in the very process of doing so illustrates its attention to circumstance in the interpretation of law: no permission is to be given to any monks or novices to break this rule "on account of any business whatsoever," unless they need to beg food for their dependent parents or widowed sisters or fellow monks, or in the event that they should fall ill, or need to travel to get medicine or other necessities for one of their fellow monks, or need to journey somewhere to recite protective texts. Even in such exceptional circumstances, preceptors commit an offense if they give such permission to a novice who is not yet well versed in *Vinaya*, but permission may be granted if he is accompanied by a learned monk who at least knows the methods for the monthly legal proceedings and understands what constitutes an offense and what does not (l.25–29). The implicit intention to prevent untrained members of the saṅgha from falling into inappropriate circumstances vis-à-vis lay society is furthered by rules that prohibit secret conversation with females (even one's own mother) and youths (even one's own younger brother, l. 39), discussions about the details of monastic requisites or inappropriate topics with laymen (l.44), and putting one's arms around a boy's body and consoling him (l.47). Much of the concern with monastic demeanor – for example, the prohibition on inappropriate laughter in which the teeth show or a sound is emitted – likewise distinguishes the saṅgha from the larger kingdom.

In the end, the saṅgha is regulated through the self-enforcement of its own high standards, including a practiced aloofness from the larger kingdom in which it exists; this, however paradoxically, is what best serves the interests of that larger kingdom, as well as of the monks. The king's responsibility for the propriety of the monastic community reflects a fundamental overlap of the monks' proper religious vocation with his own religious expectations and practices, and by extension, those of the whole political community. As a later king makes explicit, violating the monastic regulations violates simultaneously the authority of the Buddha and the authority of the king.[11]

[11] Ratnapala, *Katikāvatas*, 121, 183.

Theorizing Community

Parākramabāhu's text is, thus, a regulation *of* the specialized religious community, binding on monks alone. Yet it is nevertheless a regulation partly effected *by*, and *for*, the king and the larger kingdom. It thus behooves us to ask what ideologies of Buddhist kingship and kingdom motivated his actions.

The king provides two explicit reasons for regulating the saṅgha. One is personal: He is "greedy to savor the taste of joy and gladness experienced in beholding the monastic community" (l.14–15). For Theravāda Buddhists such mental pleasure constitutes the operative element of meritorious karma, good actions being efficacious to the extent that they are performed with delight;[12] if the dispensation is stained, the king will not be able to delight when he sees the religious community. Personal religious progress is thus bound up with the existence of a well-regulated saṅgha, which is necessary for beholding the Buddha's pure dispensation.

Parākramabāhu's other reason is ex officio. Dirt on the dispensation means "the sons of good family who follow the dispensation are being prepared as food for purgatory, marinating in the poisonous effects of no religious practice and/or the wrong religious practice, rooted in no knowledge and/or the wrong knowledge." He reasons that, "if one who turns the wheel of authority (Pāli *cakkavatti*), such as myself, repeatedly seeing dirt like this on the supremely pure Buddha-dispensation, were to remain indifferent, the Buddha-dispensation would be destroyed and many beings would be destined for purgatory; [therefore] it would be good if I work for the Buddha-dispensation so it remains for five thousand years" (l.7–8). The soteriological progress of everyone in the community likewise depends on the dispensation's purity, and it is in the very nature of a king to keep it clean for them.

"Wheel-turner" (*cakkavatti*) invokes a Buddhist paradigm of imperial kingship with old roots in the tradition,[13] which also produced parallel, non-Buddhist paradigms across the Indic world. The Buddhist model is developed with reference to primordial times, when various such monarchs are said by the Buddha to have ruled a golden age. Good things magically appeared for them, the world was governed by their mere wish,

[12] Jeffrey Samuels, *Attracting the Heart: Social Relations and the Aesthetics of Emotion in Sri Lankan Monastic Culture* (Honolulu: University of Hawai'i Press, 2010).

[13] For now-standard accounts, see the essays in Bardwell Smith (ed.), *The Two Wheels of Dhamma: Essays on the Theravada Tradition in India and Ceylon* (Chambersburg: American Academy of Religion, 1972).

and everyone was prosperous, healthy, and happy because of the emperors' own meritorious Buddhist activities, and stores of previous merit. The Mahāvihārans understood King Aśoka (third century BCE) as a historical exemplar of such kingship.

On one level, in describing himself as "wheel-turner," Parākramabāhu thus points to his very real political power, but on another level, "wheel-turner" points to the particularly religious orientation of his kingship. His worthiness is evident even before the word itself appears: Parākramabāhu undertakes to effect the present legislation "whilst thriving, enjoying the pleasurable experience of kingship produced through the miraculous powers of [his own] merit" (l.6). Just as previous good karma produces his kingship and its pleasures, he generates more merit, like all the "wheel-turners" of the past, by doing the sorts of things that will save him and his subjects, the whole community, from falling into bad rebirths. After the unification, Parākramabāhu, "built numerous very expensive monasteries at various places . . . caused uncountable thousands of the *mahāsaṅgha* to dwell there, and maintained [them] with constantly replenished gifts" (l.17–18).

The nature of Parākramabāhu's Buddhist kingship is further specified with the epithet "born in the Solar Dynasty in the lineage of Mahāsammata, etc." (l.5). Whereas the reference to the Solar Dynasty was generically imperial – as was "wheel-turner," in the sense that they were deployed by powerful South and Southeast Asian kings, including non-Buddhist ones – the reference to Mahāsammata was a specific, Buddhist historical claim that, like the date "454 years after the Buddha's passing," unambiguously signaled the Mahāvihāran histories. According to those histories and related texts, Mahāsammata was the primordial king of this age, both the Buddha's ancestor and the Buddha himself during a previous bodhisatta life. The Sri Lankan kings (who claimed descent from the Buddha's uncle) were portrayed as the sole surviving descendants of that exalted lineage in which bodhisattas are born. So Parākramabāhu's allusion to this uniquely Mahāvihāran historical interpretation startlingly implied his own bodhisattahood.

But this is not the Mahāyāna ideal sported by Parākramabāhu's royal predecessors and the rival monks. Rejecting the Mahāyāna view that everyone will eventually achieve buddhahood, and hence that all people are (potentially) bodhisattas, the Mahāvihārans maintained that buddhahood is a rare superiority beyond most people, who can escape rebirth only within a buddha's dispensation. Earlier texts had already mapped a complex universe in which, over unfathomable lengths of time, the bodhisatta moved toward buddhahood, establishing karmic connections with vast numbers of beings.[14] The closest disciples had been the bodhisatta's intimate relatives or friends through repeated rebirths; others had been associates of various kinds, quite often as subjects when the bodhisatta was a wheel-turner. Their ultimate salvation under his guidance in this life was the result of having delighted in joining him in his Buddhist pieties during those previous lives. Parākramabāhu's self-presentation as such a king invites his subjects to understand their participation in the kingdom as a practice leading to their own eventual release from suffering in (his) future buddha-dispensation. They form a community now because they share in the merit whose miraculous power effects Parākramabāhu's kingship, already obviously connected to each other in a karmic web that will continue to be spun until the political community becomes, in some future life, the religious community practicing the end of the path, led by its buddha. If such a king remains indifferent to this responsibility, however, then the entire kingdom is scattered to the purgatorial winds, for if there is no dispensation to be born into, then the whole community loses access to further progress on the path.[15]

Underscoring these remarkable revelations is Parākramabāhu's method, a creative, proactive reading of historical precedent apparently learned from studying *Vaṃsatthappakāsinī* with the Mahāvihāran monks. In their historiography, two levels of precedent are distinguished. Because the span of time is so enormous, one level of historical precedent is "incalculable." This corresponds, for example, to the histories of primordial "wheel-turners," mentioned earlier, histories of previous buddhas and their dispensations, and karmic background stories told about historical agents, such as King Aśoka.

But the Mahāvihāran texts are mostly about the other, "calculable" dimension of history, measured in years rather than eons, and based on written and oral records that are examined, interpreted, cited, and debated. Just as he cites this evidence in claiming descent from Mahāsammata,

[14] For a fuller account of this foundational Theravāda Buddhist soteriology-cum-political ideology, see Jonathan S. Walters, "Stupa, Story and Empire: Constructions of the Buddha Biography in Early Post-Aśokan India," in Jason Hawkes and Akira Shimada (eds.), *Buddhist Stupas in South Asia: Recent Archaeological, Art-historical and Historical Perspectives* (Oxford: Oxford University Press, 2009), 235–63.

[15] For further reflections of the communal implications of karma theory in the Sri Lankan Buddhist imagination, see Jonathan S. Walters, "Communal Karma and Karmic Community in Theravāda Buddhist History," in John C. Holt, Jonathan S. Walters, and Jacob N. Kinnard (eds.), *Constituting Communities: Theravāda Buddhism and the Religious Cultures of South and Southeast Asia* (Albany: State University of New York Press, 2003), 9–39.

Parākramabāhu frames unification according to a historical study of division. The huge disruption to the social fabric that must have resulted from driving hundreds of monks away from the two premier monasteries of the previous millennium, and then enforcing stringent new regulations on the entire saṅgha, is further justified on the basis of historical precedent for such legislation. Parākramabāhu says that he made three divisions into one, "just as the righteous Mahārāja Aśoka engaged Great Elder Moggaliputtatissa, crushed the evil monks, defeated the non-Buddhists, cleaned the stain on the dispensation and convened the Third Council" (l.11–12). Parākramabāhu also mentions the comparatively recent precedent of previous Sri Lankan kings who tried strenuously to unify the three divisions. And his actions were cited as precedent in the legislation of later successors.

Parākramabāhu I's theorization of community – his understanding of the kingdom, the saṅgha, and the king's role in promoting the progress of both – appears not to have been revised over all the centuries that subsequent kings encapsulated and supplemented the inscription in their own legislation. All later such texts[16] repeat Parākramabāhu's opening invocation verbatim, and their supplements make clear that the successors operated according to the same basic ideology: Parākramabāhu II claims kingship grounded in heaps of merit; Kīrtti Śrī Rājasiṃha claims to be the supreme bodhisatta and threatens, as punishment for not obeying his regulations, an inability to meet (himself as) the future Buddha.[17]

Yet this was an active, self-revising legal tradition, returning to paradigms and precedents in the face of new situations, like the sacking of the ancient heartland just prior to Parākramabāhu II,[18] and the succession of new, weak, and comparatively short-lived kingdoms that followed it. Although in theory both the political and the religious communities remained the same, in practice the former had to keep regulating the latter in order to keep pace with ever-changing circumstances. The new additions and sometimes subtle changes made as supplements of the original reflect the growth and honing of this legal tradition over all those centuries.[19]

The later successors explicitly state that, in the absence of a strong king like Parākramabāhu I and then Parākramabāhu II, the discipline of the saṅgha declined to even lower standards than those that the predecessor sought to correct.[20] Monks increasingly practiced "animal sciences"

[16] That is, all the later "Sāsana Katikāvatas"; see previous note.
[17] Ratnapala, *Katikāvatas*, 139, 173, 178. [18] *Ibid.*, 138.
[19] *Ibid.*, 219–308, provides a valuable study of this cumulative legal tradition.
[20] *Ibid.*, 138, 166, 172.

such as astrology, fortune-telling, and medicine, and misappropriated the communal property of the saṅgha for their relatives. By the mid-eighteenth century, "the dispensation . . . was in the maw of annihilation," there being no monks at all who possessed higher ordination; in consultation with leading novices, Kīrtti Śrī Rājasiṃha brings ordained monks from Thailand to restart the lineage.[21] Such importation of ordination lineages, which was actually quite common within the network of medieval Theravāda Buddhist kingdoms in Sri Lanka and Southeast Asia, illustrates most clearly the importance of the king, and by extension of the wishes and religious needs of the kingdom, in the legislation of the monastic community. If needed, in consultation with leading monks, the king could jump-start that community from scratch.

Conclusion

Premodern Buddhists did not think about, and their laws did not address, "Buddhism." Instead, they theorized and legislated the specialist religious community (saṅgha) and its relationship to the larger political community or kingdom; the Buddhist king represents the latter in instigating reform of the former. Parākramabāhu I did this in the context of protecting the Buddha's dispensation, his ongoing presence in the living community that memorizes his teachings (book study) and practices them (meditation). Within these terms, this chapter has detailed, respectively, the definitions, regulations, and theories of community that informed Parākramabāhu I's unification and regulation of the saṅgha. In the process, I have argued that this legislation was based on a legal method grounded in historical analysis of precedents in both calculable and incalculable dimensions of Buddhist history to guide would-be wheel-turners.

Parākramabāhu's understanding of community, his standards for a properly trained Buddhist monk, and his version of the bodhisatta-king ideology may have been unique to his own time, or to Sri Lanka, or to Theravāda kingdoms more generally. Especially outside the Sri Lankan and Theravādin milieu, we can expect to find different constructions, controls, and conceptualizations of community at work. But I hope that this close examination of the intersection of community, law, and religion in one moment of Sri Lankan history proves instructive in examining any such moment, especially in premodern Buddhist history. The role of the king vis-à-vis the privileged version of the teaching and subsection of the

[21] *Ibid.*, 166–68.

saṅgha, the relationship of that subsection to the larger saṅgha, and to the whole kingdom, and the religious conceptualization of community's role are all likely to be important issues in any instance of Buddhist community law. While the Sri Lankans may have been especially historical ("calculable") in their outlook, precedent has likewise been a guiding factor for Buddhists everywhere, even those who have tended to focus on history's "incalculable" dimension.

CHAPTER 8

The Legal Regulation of Buddhism in Contemporary Sri Lanka

Benjamin Schonthal

Introduction

Regularly, in courtrooms around Sri Lanka, judges and Buddhist monks find themselves, quite literally, in a standoff. Sri Lanka's code of civil procedure stipulates that all persons must rise when a judge enters the courtroom. However, Buddhist custom dictates that monks, on account of their spiritual superiority, must never rise to greet non-monks, judges included. So, when a judge enters a courtroom with monks present, there is a dilemma: Who stands in deference to whom? Religious and civil authorities collide, before a word is even spoken.

The dilemma of competing political and religious authority has a long history in Buddhism. Pāli Buddhist texts tend to conceive of the relationship in two opposing ways. In certain places, Pāli sources insinuate the dominance of political authority by describing the rights of kings to periodically "cleanse" (*sodheti*) local monastic fraternities of impious or heterodox monks. In other places, Pāli texts suggest the superiority of religious authority by describing monks as assessing the virtues, beneficence, and legitimacy of kings.[1] Taken as a whole, Pāli Buddhist texts portray the links between state and religious authorities as a kind of reciprocity or tension (depending on how one reads it) in which rulers guarantee the piety of monks and monks guarantee the righteousness of rulers – each side claiming to protect, in a broad sense, the vitality of Buddhism in the world.[2]

[1] Stanley J. Tambiah, *World Conqueror and World Renouncer: A Study of Buddhism and Polity in Thailand against a Historical Background* (Cambridge: Cambridge University Press, 1976).

[2] Steven Collins, *Nirvana and Other Buddhist Felicities: Utopias of the Pāli Imaginaire* (Cambridge: Cambridge University Press, 1998), 27 and passim; R.A.L.H. Gunawardena, *Robe and Plough: Monasticism and Economic Interest in Early Medieval Sri Lanka* (Tucson: Arizona University Press, 1979).

In a way, these twin modes of religious governance may be seen as inflecting the legal regulation of Buddhism in modern nation-states with Theravāda Buddhist majorities. In modern-day Thailand, Laos, Cambodia, Myanmar/Burma, and Sri Lanka, laws pertaining to Buddhism consist of two types: One set of laws gives states powers to manage the conduct and wealth of Buddhist monks; another set of laws obligates the state to protect the welfare of Buddhism generally. The first type of laws often consist of statutes, ordinances, or administrative orders, such as the Sangha Act of 1963 in Thailand or the Law Concerning Sangha Organizations of 1990 in Myanmar. These laws govern subjects, such as the ordering of monastic hierarchy, the management of temple property, and the duties and powers of government officials to supervise the conduct of monks. The second type of laws generally consist of constitutional provisions, such as Article 43 of the Cambodian Constitution (which makes Buddhism the "state religion"), or Section 79 of the Thai Constitution (which states that "the State shall patronize and protect Buddhism") or Article 9 of the Sri Lankan Constitution (which awards Buddhism the "foremost place"). These provisions "Buddhicize" political authority by indicating the state's overarching, if vague, commitment to supporting Buddhism.

This congruity between classical and modern forms is not coincidental. Premodern and modern states both needed to establish conventions for dealing with the existence of a group of full-time religious renunciants who were dependent on rulers and laypersons for survival. Moreover, during the twentieth century, as Buddhist polities in southern Asia remade themselves as modern nation-states, lawmakers and drafters of constitutions in these countries deliberately looked to traditional Buddhist sources for political legitimacy and moral authority.

Yet, profound differences also exist between the classical and the contemporary. Unlike various types of "law" pertaining to the ideal conduct of monks and kings that circulated in many pre-eighteenth-century kingdoms (*katikāvata, dhammathat, rajathat*, to give examples[3]), most contemporary Buddhist-majority nation-states have endorsed a particular ideology of legalism, one characterized by the desire for a single authoritative collection of prescriptive law. This body of law, written in the vernacular and circulated widely, details formal principles and procedures that are used by credentialed professionals in specially built courts or tribunals. While the

[3] Nandasena Ratnapala, *The Katikāvatas: Laws of the Buddhist Orders of Ceylon From the 12th to the 18th Century* (Munich: MSZS, 1971); Andrew Huxley, "Studying Theravada Legal Literature," *Journal of the International Association of Buddhist Studies* 20.1 (1997).

actual influence of legal texts and institutions as a limit on political power in modern southern Asia is debatable, this ideology of legalism constitutes a dominant idiom through which political elites – including constitutional monarchs and military juntas – intervene in, engage with, manage, organize, rationalize, control, support, and protect Buddhist persons, actors, institutions, and sites.[4]

In this chapter, I want to examine the contours of the legalization of Buddhism in modern nation-states, by way of a focused case-study of Sri Lanka. In what follows, I examine how the two modes of law previously described – those designed to manage monks and temple lands, and those designed to promote and protect Buddhism – have been embodied in modern Sri Lankan legal culture and indicate the ways in which Sri Lanka's experience is (and is not) unique from other Theravāda-majority states. I will examine statute law, case law, and constitutional law in order to highlight the ways in which the modern Sri Lankan state has both intervened in the administration of monastic life and oriented itself more generally to the protection and support of "the Buddha Sāsana."

Regulating the *Saṅgha*

As already indicated, all modern Theravāda-majority states give the government certain authority to intervene in the lives of Buddhist monks. In Thailand, this authority is embodied in a Sangha Act,[5] which centralizes Thai monks in a national hierarchy under a chief patriarch (*saṅgharāja*) and a Council of Elders (*mahāthera samakhorn*).[6] The Sangha Act also specifies a single system of ecclesiastical administration, which mirrors state administration, routinizes the procedures for disciplining and disrobing monks, and standardizes the content, assessments, and credentials associated with monastic education.[7] In Myanmar, since the 1960s, military governments have enacted a series of orders that are designed to bring Buddhist monks and other religious groups under closer state surveillance. One of the more recent orders is the Law Concerning Sangha Organizations, introduced in

4 See, e.g., Tamara Lynn Loos, *Subject Siam: Family, Law, and Colonial Modernity in Thailand* (Ithaca: Cornell University Press, 2006).

5 First introduced in 1902 and later replaced by different versions in 1941 and 1962.

6 The *saṅgharāja* is ex officio president of the Council, and the Director of the Department of Religious Affairs serves as the secretary to the Council.

7 Tambiah, *World Conqueror and World Renouncer*; Ishii, Yoneo, *Sangha, State, and Society* (Honolulu: University of Hawai'i Press, 1986); Peter A. Jackson, *Buddhism, Legitimation, and Conflict: The Political Functions of Urban Thai Buddhism* (Singapore: Institute of Southeast Asian Studies, 1989).

October 1990, which aims to consolidate Myanmar's monks into a single, official, ecclesiastical hierarchy that remains closely linked to the state in terms of its leaders, conduct, and administration.[8] In Cambodia and Laos, the particularities of state control over the saṅgha have not been elaborated to the same extent in specialized laws, yet, particularly in Laos, government departments and administrative orders give the state significant control over the organization and activities of Buddhist monks as well as other religious clerics.[9]

When compared with other Theravāda-majority states, the Sri Lankan government has not exercised the same degree of control over monastic hierarchy and conduct. Where the Sri Lankan state *does* assert authority is in the way it supervises the use of land, assets, and wealth associated with Buddhist places of worship. Sri Lanka's legal code contains a specific statute for doing so, and because no single, official, monastic hierarchy unites all monks on the island, Sri Lanka's civil courts act as the final arbiter for disputes over temple property. These disputes are frequent and the stakes are high; the island is home to more than 10,000 Buddhist temples, each of which possesses an array of buildings, ancient artifacts, and large tracts of agricultural and urban land.

Buddhist Temporalities

In Sri Lanka, two bodies of legal rules govern the control of temple property, or what many refer to as "Buddhist temporalities": first, a special statute that outlines the specific rules for managing and using temple wealth, and second, a particular body of case law that determines the principles of monastic succession and incumbency. The essential link between these two types of law is that, in virtually all cases, a temple's wealth is controlled by its chief monastic incumbent (*vihāradhipati*).

Sri Lankan temple property differs in an important way from temple property in most of Thailand. Whereas the wealth of most Thai temples is thought to be property of the monastic fraternity-at-large or the Thai state itself,[10] the property of Sri Lankan temples is controlled by the monks

[8] B. Matthews, "Buddhism under a Military Regime: The Iron Heel in Burma," *Asian Survey* 33.4 (1993), 408–23; Peter Gutter, "Law and Religion in Burma," *Legal Issues on Burma Journal* (2001).

[9] For example, in Laos, Decree No. 92/PM for the Management and Protection of Religious Activities, 2002. I. Harris, "Buddhism in Extremis: The Case of Cambodia" in Ian Harris (ed.), *Buddhism and Politics in Twentieth-century Asia* (New York and London: Continuum, 2001); M. Stuart-Fox, "Laos: From Buddhist Kingdom to Marxist State" in Harris (ed.), *Buddhism and Politics*.

[10] Interview with Dr. Amnaj Buasiri, Deputy Director of Buddhist Affairs for the Thai Government, Bangkok, December 21, 2011.

who reside at those temples. In this, the Sri Lankan model of monastic wealth owes much to the fact of British colonial intervention. In colonial Sri Lanka, British governors directed legal draftsmen to produce laws that would prevent the improper use of temple land by corrupt monks and laity.[11] The most significant piece of legislation produced was called the Buddhist Temporalities Ordinance, a revised version of which serves as the main instrument governing the use of temple property today.

The current Buddhist Temporalities Ordinance (most recently amended in 1992) lays out rules for how the property of Buddhist temples (*vihāra*) and important deity shrines (*devala*) on the island ought to be managed. The Ordinance describes Buddhist properties as held in trusts of two types.[12] The first type pertains to special Buddhist sites, and includes the Temple of the Tooth in Kandy as well as other Kandyan region *devales*, Sri Pada (Adam's Peak), the eight holy places (S., *āṭamasthānaya*) in and around Anurādhapura, and any other site designated by the government.[13] For these sites, the management of property vests in special trustees who are appointed or elected in different ways. For instance, in the case of the Temple of the Tooth, the trustee is the Diyawadana Nilame, a chief lay trustee who is elected every ten years by votes from head monks of the Kandyan monastic fraternities, the chief lay trustees of the Kandyan Province *devales* (Basnayake Nilames) and the trustees of large wealthy Buddhist temples in the Kandyan Province.

The second type of trust is the 'ordinary' temple trust, which applies to all other vihāras on the island. These temples, the Ordinance specifies, are managed by a trustee who is appointed for a five-year term by the chief incumbent (*vihāradhipati*), or head monk of the temple. As the chief incumbents may appoint themselves as trustees, today in Sri Lanka most

[11] Steven Kemper, "The Buddhist Monkhood, the Law, and the State in Colonial Sri Lanka," *Comparative Studies in Society and History* 26.3 (1984), 401–27; K.M. De Silva, "The Government and Religion: Problems and Policies, 1832–1910" in K.M. De Silva (ed.), *University of Ceylon History of Ceylon vol. 3* (Kandy: University of Ceylon, 1973); J.D. Rogers, "Religious Belief, Economic Interest, and Social Policy: Temple Endowments in Sri Lanka During the Governorship of William Gregory, 1872–77," *Modern Asian Studies* 21.2 (1987), 349.

[12] According to the Ordinance, Buddhist temples do not have a clear legal status. Unlike deities in Hindu temples in India and elsewhere, Buddhists temples are not juristic persons. Some jurists envision temple property as being held by the *vihāradhipati*, while others, including the Supreme Court in a recent case, argue that property vests in the "temple" itself. H.W. Tambiah, "Buddhist Ecclesiastical Law," *Journal of the Ceylon Branch of the Royal Asiatic Society (N.S.)* 8.1 (1962); Mahinda Ralapanawe, *Buddhist Temporalities Ordinance: Inception, Evolution, Present, Future* (Colombo: Sarasavi, 2011); Citing: *Ven. Omare Dhammapala v. Rajapkshage Peiris and Others* 1SLR1.

[13] In December 2009, Mahinda Rajaksa exempted the Ruhunu Kataragama Devala from the provisions of the Ordinance in order to permit his nephew to serve as Basnayake Nilame of the *devala* while also serving as chief minister of Uva Province.

vihāradhipati also function as trustees for the temple. According to the Ordinance, trustees are prohibited from selling land or property or from using temple income for purposes other than the following: maintaining the temple, supporting monks, paying temple workers, promoting Buddhist education, performing regular rituals, assisting the poor, and covering administration costs and legal expenses relating to the preservation of temple property.[14]

The Commissioner of Buddhist Affairs, who is usually a senior civil servant appointed by the Minister of Buddhist Affairs, is empowered to oversee the implementation of the Ordinance.[15] The Commissioner has wide powers to audit the trustees and manage the temples. He can disqualify trustees who do not meet certain basic qualifications.[16] He can investigate, discipline, and take legal action against trustees who are accused of using temple funds illegitimately.[17] The Commissioner acts as an arbitrator of first instance in all disputes about temple property before they are taken to civil courts.[18] In cases in which trustees fall ill, die, or neglect their duties, the Commissioner has powers to appoint interim trustees himself or "to make any arrangement he thinks necessary for the safe management of the property."[19] Biannually, the Commissioner oversees a review of account statements prepared by the temples, detailing donations, rents, and other income and outlining any expenses made. In consultation with the head monks of Buddhist fraternities, he also maintains a register of all higher ordination monks (*bhikkhus*) and novice monks (*sāmaṇeras*) on the island, which may be used as evidence in legal disputes over monastic succession.[20]

[14] *Buddhist Temporalities Ordinance* No. 19 of 1931, amended most recently by Buddhist Temporalities (Amendment) Act No. 3 of 1992. Sect. 25. In practice, the use of temple income in Sri Lanka seems to vary greatly, with some temples containing elaborate monastic residences, cars, televisions, and other luxuries.

[15] Previously this supervisory position was occupied by the "Public Trustee." But, in 1981, with the creation of the Department of Buddhist Affairs by the government of J.R. Jayawardena, this fell to the Commissioner of Buddhist Affairs. Today, the terms have shifted slightly, with the title, "Commissioner General of Buddhist Affairs" being used to refer to the administrator of the Ordinance (who is also the head of the Department).

[16] All trustees must be male, Buddhist, and older than twenty-one. For laymen, certain minimum requirements for wealth and income apply. Potential lay and monastic trustees are disqualified if they work in the government, have criminal convictions, are greater than seventy years old, or are lessees of temple land.

[17] Neglect of trustee duties is as legal offense with penalties including imprisonment for up to three months. *Ibid.*, Sect. 19.

[18] Interview with Commissioner of Buddhist Affairs, Colombo, Sri Lanka, April 2, 2009.

[19] *Ibid.*, Sect. 11(b).

[20] The reality of the current registration system is more complicated. In practice, not all monks register with the government and, as no record is kept of disrobing or monastic changes, current lists are, in certain cases, not accurate. Interview with Commissioner of Buddhist Affairs, Colombo, Sri Lanka, April 2, 2009.

These registers serve as the basis for issuing official monastic identity cards. In recent years, the Department of Buddhist Affairs has also started to register and issue identity cards to non-ordained Buddhist nuns on the island, called *dasa sil mata*, "mothers of the ten precepts."

Buddhist Ecclesiastical Law

If the Buddhist Temporalities Ordinance is clear at all, it is clear in its specification that the trusteeship of ordinary temple property is to be determined by the chief incumbent of that temple. But how does one determine who qualifies as the chief incumbent? The general rule of thumb is that the chief incumbent is the most senior, qualified successor to the previous chief incumbent, in a system referred to as "student-after-student" succession (*śiṣyanu-śiṣya-paramparāva*).[21] Here, "senior" pertains not to a monk's age, but to the length of time he has spent in robes (or, even more technically, to the number of rainy season retreats, or *vassas*, he has undertaken).[22] Despite this single controlling principle, however, numerous types of disagreements can occur over questions such as: Can a chief incumbent handpick a successor who is not the eldest pupil? How should succession proceed in cases where incumbents or successors disrobe? Are there instances where student-after-student succession does not apply and other forms of succession should be considered, such as succession through the eldest blood relative of the chief incumbent, known as succession "by robes" (*sivuru paramparāva*)?[23] Some monks go to court claiming that certain movable property should not be seen as general monastic property (*sanghika* property), but should be treated as the personal (*pudgalika*) possession of a monk, either because he acquired it through familial inheritance or because it was specially dedicated to him by lay donors. The range of possible disputes is enormous, and monks are not the only ones involved. Laity can also bring legal action against monks regarding succession and temple property, provided they have been regular attendees of a temple.

Unlike the rules for using temple property, which are laid out in statutes, courts assess incumbency claims according to a body of case law that developed from the mid-nineteenth century onward. Jurists in Sri Lanka

[21] An early explanation of this form of "pupillage" is contained in G.W. Woodhouse, "Sissiyanu Sissiya Paramparawa and Other Laws Relating to the Buddhist Priesthood," *The Ceylon Antiquary and Literary Register* 33 (1918).

[22] H.D. Evers, "Kinship and Property Rights in a Buddhist Monastery in Central Ceylon1," *American Anthropologist* 69.6 (1967), 703–10.

[23] Tambiah, "Buddhist Ecclesiastical Law," 87.

refer to this thread of law as "Buddhist Ecclesiastical Law."[24] The size and scope of this corpus is vast. One recent volume, representing the most comprehensive analysis to date, refers to more than 200 Supreme Court judgments![25] The various guidelines for determining succession collected in this law derive from a mixture of sources, including: rules of monastic comportment contained in Pāli texts (in particular, the *Vinaya*), protocols for succession described by the chief monks (*mahānayaka*) of monastic fraternities (some of whom served as expert witnesses in early court cases), and customary practices at temples as described by government officials, monastic residents, and lay patrons. Of course, in determining the correct sequence of succession in specific cases, the assumptions of British and Sri Lankan judges have played an equally significant role.

Promoting Buddhism

While legal disputes over temple property comprise the majority of Buddhism-related legal action (in terms of billable hours and paperwork), the Sri Lankan constitution's explicit commitments to give Buddhism a special, elevated position on the island is a second feature of Buddhism-related law that remains a far more politicized, visible and, for many non-Buddhists on the island, contentious feature of Sri Lanka's modern legal system. Article 9 of the current Sri Lankan Constitution, entitled "Buddhism," reads:

> **Article 9** The Republic of Sri Lanka shall give to Buddhism the foremost place and accordingly it shall be the duty of the State to protect and foster the Buddha Sasana, while assuring to all religions the rights granted by Articles 10 and 14(1)(e).

According to this provision, the Sri Lankan state is obliged to give Buddhism a privileged status ("the foremost place") and it has a responsibility to "protect and foster" the religion's teachings, institutions, and adherents (the Buddha Sasana). At the same time, Article 9 conditions the state's commitment to supporting Buddhism with two assurances for "all religions." The first is that each individual will have the right to "freedom of thought, conscience and religion, including the freedom to have or to adopt a religion or belief of his choice" (Article 10), and second is the right to "manifest" religion in "worship, observance, practice or teaching" in a

[24] A good overview is contained in *Ibid.*

[25] W.S. Weerasooria, *Buddhist Ecclesiastical Law* (Colombo: Postgraduate Institute of Management, 2011).

group or alone, in public or private (Article 14(1)(e)). The special status of Buddhism is further qualified by Article 12 of the constitution, which guarantees that the state will not discriminate against citizens on the basis of language, race, caste, or religion.

Historicizing Article 9

The history of these constitutional protections for Buddhism may be traced back to the attempts of Sri Lanka's post-independence political elites to respond to the demands of the island's Buddhist majority, which constitutes 69 percent of the population. Calls for the integration of special Buddhist protections into the constitution began even before the island achieved independence in 1948 and continued through the 1950s and 1960s. Those who demanded such protections emphasized that Buddhism had been damaged during the island's 450 years of colonial occupation in multiple ways: through the persecution of Buddhists and the confiscation of Buddhist land by the Portuguese and Dutch; through the British overthrow of the last Buddhist kingdom in 1815 and the subsequent reforms made by colonial administrators to the management of temple property (as mentioned earlier); and through the conversion of Buddhists to Christianity and the growing influence of Christians in the elite spheres of politics, government, law, and education. In order to fully realize independence, they argued, the new Sri Lankan state had to rehabilitate Buddhism through a systematic program of state assistance designed to promote Buddhist "values," to encourage closer ties between monks and the laity, to repair Buddhist temples, and to encourage Buddhist education. This rehabilitation, it was insisted, required that the island's new constitution should include explicit guarantees that the state would privilege and protect Buddhism.

Demands for equal religious rights had a similarly long genealogy on the island and, in an interesting way, were linked to anti-colonial nationalism, as well. At the same time that Buddhists were calling for special constitutional protections for Buddhism, many others (Buddhists and non-Buddhists) were insisting that the new constitution ought to include a special chapter of discrete "fundamental rights," among them rights to religious liberty. The nationalistic aspect of such a demand was that it explicitly defied the constitution-making efforts of British legal experts at the time, who, in keeping with an official imperial policy, required that the colonies' new independence charters did not include a bill of rights.[26] Calls for a fundamental rights chapter also framed Sri Lanka's independence struggle in terms of "human rights," linking the island's demand for self-government with nascent international human rights discourses that were taking shape in the 1940s among the Allied forces in Europe and the nascent United Nations.[27]

From these roots in anti-colonial nationalist movements, calls for Buddhist privileges *and* calls for fundamental religious rights remained influential in the politics of the 1950s and 1960s and were blended in the rhetoric of the island's successive prime ministers. The two aspirations were enshrined in consecutive chapters of the Constitutions of 1972 and 1978: the call for Buddhist privileges was embodied in Chapter 2 entitled "Buddhism," while the call for fundamental rights was included in Chapter 3 entitled "Fundamental Rights." Yet, the twin constitutional commitments of specially patronizing Buddhism while guaranteeing equal religious rights have not always been easy to balance. Politicians, lawyers, activists, and many others have criticized the constitution for advocating two schemes of regulating religion: one that charges the government with being a patron, sponsor, and protector of Buddhism, and another that requires the state to be a fair arbiter of fundamental rights all religious communities, including Hindus, Muslims, and Christians (approximately 15 percent, 8 percent, and 8 percent of the population, respectively). At the same time, a number of Buddhist lawmakers, activists, and lawyers have diverged in their opinion of what it means to "protect and foster Buddhism" in the first place.

Giving Buddhism the "Foremost Place"

The question of how the state ought to reconcile its duties to promote Buddhism with its duties to protect religious rights has been raised frequently, but it has become particularly contentious in the last two decades. One major reason for this has been the growing anxiety among Sri Lankan Buddhists about the status of Buddhism on the island. This anxiety comes in the wake of deep political and religious changes that took hold since the 1990s. Since that time, Sri Lanka has seen an increase in the influence of multinational corporations, international treaty organizations (such as the

[26] Charles Parkinson, *Bills of Rights and Decolonization: The Emergence of Domestic Human Rights Instruments in Britain's Overseas Territories* (Oxford: Oxford University Press, 2007).

[27] Benjamin Schonthal, "Reading Religious Freedom in Sri Lanka" *The Immanent Frame: Secularism, Religion, and the Public Sphere*, May 2012, available at: http://blogs.ssrc.org/tif/2012/05/08/reading-religious-freedom-in-sri-lanka/ (last accessed March 2, 2013).

United Nations and the European Union) and transnational aid groups (such as World Vision and the Red Cross). These influences have come in response to the growing demand for Sri Lankan-made consumer goods, international intervention in the island's civil war, and the rapid mobilization of humanitarian assistance in the wake of the December 2004 tsunami. In this globalizing atmosphere, many Sri Lankans have become nervous about the activities of new evangelical Christian groups who, they suspect, have come to the island under the pretense of engaging in humanitarian aid or civil war assistance and have, in reality, been engaged in concerted evangelizing campaigns aimed at converting poor, war-weary Buddhists to Christianity through "unethical" means, including monetary inducements and promises of visas to go abroad.[28]

Between 2000 and 2003, in a climate of heightened public concern about these issues, Sri Lanka's Supreme Court heard three cases in which litigants and judges argued explicitly about the balance between Buddhist protections and general fundamental religious rights in Sri Lanka's constitution. In each case, Buddhists challenged the constitutionality of a proposed bill that, if ratified, would give formal legal incorporation to a Christian organization whose charter linked together social work and religious instruction. In all three cases, Buddhist petitioners argued that, if the state were to permit the incorporation of such a group, it would be tantamount to recognizing and protecting activities that would lead to the "unethical conversion" of Buddhists and would, therefore, threaten the status of Buddhism outlined in Article 9.

While there is much that can be said about these cases,[29] what is significant for this discussion is that over the course of these contests, the court's interpretation of Article 9 gradually shifted toward a more defensive posture regarding the protection of Buddhism. In all three cases the Supreme Court ruled in favor of the petitioners, but its rationale differed in each instance. In the first case, the court based its reasoning almost exclusively on the fact that the proposed corporation would violate Article 10 of the constitution granting citizens "freedom of thought, conscience and religion" because, by mingling religious worship and economic activity, it would introduce a "fetter of allurement" into "the free exercise of one's thought

[28] For an excellent analysis of this, see Stephen Berkwitz, "Religious Conflict and the Politics of Conversion in Sri Lanka" in Rosalind I.J. Hackett (ed.), *Proselytization Revisited: Rights Talk, Free Markets and Culture Wars* (London: Equinox, 2008).

[29] For a good summary of these cases, see A. Owens, "Protecting Freedom of and From Religion: Questioning the Law's Ability to Protect Against Unethical Conversions in Sri Lanka," *Religion and Human Rights* 1.1 (2006), 41–73.

and conscience."[30] In the second case, the court employed a very similar logic, but added to its decision the assertion (albeit without an explanation) that these practices not only violated freedom of conscience, but the protection of Buddhism in Article 9.[31] In the third case, the Supreme Court affirmed its two earlier determinations, but argued further that the acts of conversion that the incorporated groups might perpetrate would "impair the very existence of Buddhism," insofar as converting Buddhists to Christianity would "hinder the very existence of the Buddha Sasana."[32]

Thus, gradually over the course of these three incorporation cases, the Supreme Court chiseled out a specific interpretation of Article 9's balancing of Buddhist prerogatives against fundamental religious rights. A strong interpretation of this arrived-at position would be that it permits the Sri Lankan state to limit legitimately the activities of non-Buddhists in order to protect the interests of Buddhism. This interpretation is championed by a relatively new political party consisting almost entirely of Buddhist monks – the JHU, Jathika Hela Urumaya (National [Sinhala] Heritage Party) – who, since 2004, have exercised a decisive influence in parliament.[33] In 2004, in fact, the group proposed a constitutional amendment that would redraft Article 9 to read:

9.1. The official Religion of the Republic is Buddhism. Other forms of religions and worship may be practiced in peace and harmony with the Buddha Sasana.

9.2. All inhabitants of the Republic shall have the right to free exercise of their worship. The exercise of worship shall not contravene public order or offend morals.

9.3. The State shall foster, protect, patronise [the] Buddha Sasana and promote good understanding and harmony among the followers of other forms of worship as well as encourage the application of religious principles to create virtue and develop quality of life.

9.4. The inhabitants of the Republic professing Buddhism are bound to bring up their children the same.

30 Supreme Court Special Determination No. 2/2001, *Regarding Christian Sahanaye Doratuwa Prayer Centre (Incorporation) Bill.*

31 Supreme Court Special Determination No. 2/2003, *Regarding New Harvest Wine Ministries (Incorporation) Bill.*

32 Supreme Court Special Determination No. 19/2003, *Regarding Provincial of the Teaching Sisters of the Holy Cross of the Third Order of Saint Francis in Menzingen of Sri Lanka (Incorporation) Bill.*

33 M. Deegalle, "Politics of the Jathika Hela Urumaya Monks: Buddhism and Ethnicity in Contemporary Sri Lanka," *Contemporary Buddhism* 5.2 (2004); N. DeVotta and J. Stone, "Jathika Hela Urumaya and Ethno-religious Politics in Sri Lanka," *Pacific Affairs* 81.1 (2008), 31–51.

9.5. To convert Buddhist [sic] into other forms of worship or to spread other forms of worship among the Buddhist [sic] is prohibited.

9.6. No person may be forced to join a religious community, to conduct a religious act or to participate in religious education.[34]

At the same time, the Supreme Court's judgments in the incorporation cases and the actions of the JHU have generated severe criticism among Sri Lanka's more liberal legal experts, who claim that, with these determinations, the Supreme Court has deviated from the egalitarian 'spirit' of the constitution and from what should be the secular, pluralistic, and multicultural values of the modern Sri Lankan state.[35] In a Supreme Court case in which the previously quoted JHU amendment was deemed unconstitutional, one justice offered in a concurring opinion a dramatically different interpretation of Article 9. In her view, the constitution's duties to Buddhists must be counterweighed by the state's general obligation to non-Buddhists to ensure that "there should not be any interference to the equality of all religions in the country."[36] Article 9, on this reading, echoes the broader principles advocated by the constitution as a whole, principles that render the Sri Lankan state as a "secular state . . . [and] a multicultural and plural society" and that require the Sri Lankan state to give "equal importance" to all religious groups.[37]

How to "Protect and Foster" Buddhism

In one way, then, the Sri Lankan state's constitutional obligations to protect and foster Buddhism have been asserted and analyzed with reference to the respective rights of the island's different religious communities. In another way, Article 9 has been used by litigants in a less-structured way: to request the court to "protect" different aspects of Buddhism from state action, private citizens, and other Buddhists. These cases differ from those of Buddhist Ecclesiastical Law in a number of ways. In most cases,

[34] "Nineteenth Amendment to the Constitution Bill," *Gazette of the Democratic Socialist Republic of Sri Lanka* Part II, Supplement, October 29, 2004.

[35] Perhaps the most incisive critiques are contained in an editorial, published in two parts, by Asanga Welikala in the English *Daily News* on October 14, 2003 and October 16, 2003.

[36] J. Tilakwardane, concurring opinion Supreme Court Special Determination No. 32/2004 *Regarding Nineteenth Amendment to the Constitution (Bill)*. It is important to mention that, for reasons I do not know, this concurring opinion (although formally filed officially) was never published by the government, relayed to parliament (as all special determinations must be), or reported in any of the national law reports. Instead, it circulated separately from the main determination, privately and informally.

[37] *Ibid.*

assertions about Article 9 come through strongly in the written submissions of litigants but faintly, if at all, in the judgments of courts. As such, court determinations in these cases have not been compiled into a recognizable body of legal precedents, as they have in the case of Buddhist Ecclesiastical Law. Equally, these cases do not involve questions of monastic succession or ownership of temple property, but rather raise questions about how the state should "protect and foster the Buddha Sasana." Therefore, what is important in this strain of Buddhist-related legal activity is that it tends to bring to the fore important questions about how one ought to define Buddhism, who has the authority to speak for Buddhism, and from whom or what Buddhism ought to be protected.

In this loose category of writ petitions and court cases, the nature of claims are wide and diverse, ranging from questions of whether the state should be given greater powers over Buddhist educational institutions to whether the state should prohibit the selling of retail merchandise with Buddha's image on it. One particularly interesting case from 1978 involves the question of whether, under the rubric of protecting Buddhism, the state can prevent monks from engaging in secular employment. The case involved a Buddhist monk who, having graduated from the national law college, applied for admission to the bar. Venerable Sumana's application was challenged by a number of Buddhist lay activists, who insisted that the monk's actions were contrary to the *Vinaya* and Buddhist custom and, by allowing it, the state would be violating its constitutional obligations to protect Buddhism. In support of the monk's admission to the bar, the head monks of Sumana's monastic fraternity and a well-known professor of Buddhism argued that there were no provisions in the *Vinaya* that forbade monks from becoming lawyers. The Supreme Court assembled a full, five-justice bench to hear the case. Four justices agreed that Ven. Sumana's application should be permitted, and one justice dissented that it should be disallowed.

Two distinct visions of how to protect and foster Buddhism emerged through the litigants' submissions and the judge's decisions. On one side were those who asserted that protecting Buddhism meant preserving the orthropraxy of Buddhist monks as described in Pāli texts, which would ensure that Buddhist monks remained aloof from "material" concerns and "worldly" pursuits. On the other side were those who viewed the act of protecting Buddhism as one of protecting the autonomy and independence of monastic groups to determine their own "ecclesiastical" matters and follow their own customary practices, whether or not they conformed to Pāli texts. In this and other cases, invoking the Buddhism chapter in courtrooms produced arguments (often within the island's Buddhist community) about how, when, and according to what guidelines the state should intervene to "foster" the majority religion.

Thoughts on a Standoff

So, returning to the anecdote with which I began, who wins in the courtroom standoff between monks and judges? The answer is that neither does. Most lawyers in Sri Lanka have gotten around the standoff by leading monastic clients into the courtrooms after judges have taken the bench. As this tactic seems to confirm, in Sri Lanka civil and religious authority both have influence on and claims to law. The Sri Lankan state controls *and* patronizes Buddhist institutions. Civil courts adjudicate monastic disputes over incumbency and temple property. Civil court judges define how the state should protect and foster Buddhism. At the same time, those who drafted, interpreted, and implemented Article 9 and the Buddhist Temporalities Ordinance see themselves as acting in service of Buddhism. It is those very laws, particularly Article 9, which have encouraged and legitimated increased legal activism among Buddhists, including Buddhist monks (some of whom are now in parliament).

In Sri Lanka, as in other contemporary Theravāda-Buddhist-majority states, Buddhism has undergone a process of "legalization" that has sanctioned state intervention in certain aspects of Buddhist life (the management of temple property, for example) and, at the same time, sanctioned Buddhists' claims on the state. These interventions and claims have placed the state neither in a position of authority over, nor subservience to, nor separation from Buddhism. This middling position is unlikely to change. Whereas Thailand and Myanmar have taken measures to centralize and bureaucratize Buddhist monks, it is unlikely that the Sri Lankan state would be able to consolidate and regulate monastic authority similarly in the near future on account of the strong independence of the different monastic orders on the island and the carefully guarded rights of individual vihāras to control their property. At the same time, it seems equally unlikely that Sri Lanka would modify its constitution to make Buddhism the "state religion," as in Cambodia, both because of strong objections by the island's Muslims, Hindus, Christians, secularists, and liberal Buddhists, and also because of the strong opposition by Buddhist monks, who would see such a declaration as a step toward undermining the authority of the saṅgha as the sole organ authorized to speak on behalf of Buddhism. Sri Lanka is also unlikely to pass laws specifying its "secularity" anytime soon, as did Indira Gandhi in her forty-second constitutional amendment to the Indian Constitution in 1976, on account of the continuing significance of Buddhism within the political culture of the island and the growing power of pro-Buddhist activists.

For the foreseeable future, then, monks will continue to appear in civil courts to make claims about temple lands, judges will continue to interpret what it means to "protect Buddhism," and politicians will continue to push the state in three ways: toward greater control over Buddhism, toward greater support for Buddhism, and toward greater separation from Buddhism. In short, it is unlikely that Sri Lanka's courtroom standoff will end anytime soon.

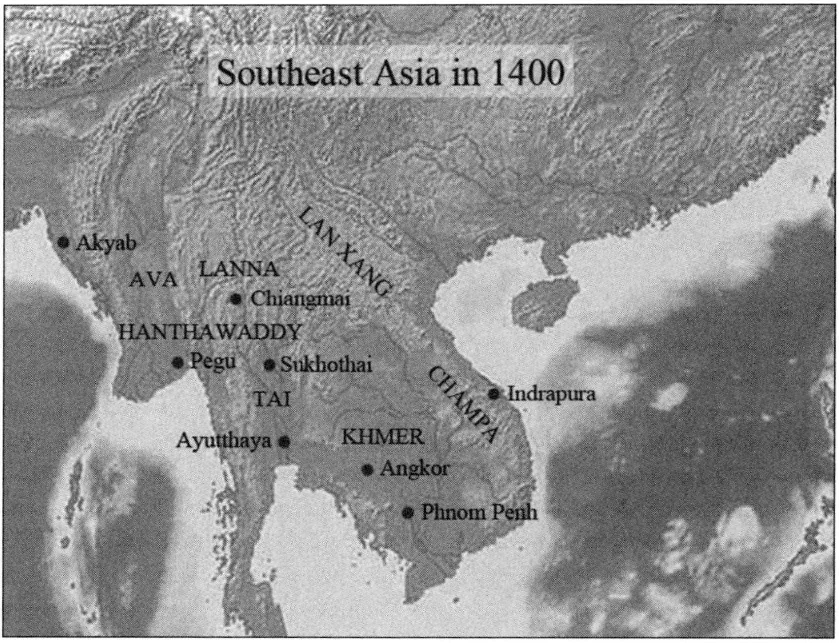

Map of Mainland Southeast Asia, c. 1400 CE

CHAPTER 9

Pāli Buddhist Law in Southeast Asia

Andrew Huxley

Introduction

My title contains an inexactitude and a neologism. The Pāli Buddhist legal tradition's habitat is a lot narrower than the geographic label "Southeast Asia" suggests. Few Buddhists live in the Southeast Asian archipelago. To speak of "Mainland Southeast Asia" as the land of Pāli Buddhism is also inexact, for on the eastern (Vietnamese) side of the subcontinent, Buddhists adhere to the Chinese tradition. It is better, then, to refer to the habitat of Pāli Buddhism as "Laos, Cambodia, Thailand, and Burma, along with the adjoining parts of China, Malaysia and Bangladesh." However, even this unwieldy toponym requires further clarification. Pāli Buddhists prefer to live in the plains and valleys, where they invest heavily in building dams, canals, monasteries, and pagodas. Above them, in the foothills of the Central Asian massif, is a different ecology, suited to swidden cultivation of millet and dry-rice This is where the *montagnards* live, scratching their sustenance from fields that soon lose their nutrients. These mountain people invest little in infrastructure, since every few years they have to move their villages and fields. They have resisted conversion to Buddhism, despite centuries of missionary work.

It is difficult to pin down a belief system onto a set of global positioning service coordinates. My best endeavor is this: The Pāli Buddhist tradition flourishes in west and central mainland Southeast Asia in those valleys and plains where wet rice can be grown. I propose the neologism "Paliland" as shorthand for this region. Buddhists are "Pāli" if the scriptures they regard as normative are written in the Prakrit language called (by them) "Magadhan" and (by others) "Pāli." Some prefer the label *Theravāda* (meaning "the Path of the Elders"), others *Hīnayāna* (meaning "the Lesser Vehicle"). These terms convey too much value to be descriptively useful. The Pāli Buddhists themselves refer to their religion as the *Buddhadhamma* ("The Dharma of the Buddha"), and refer to the kingdoms in which it is the state religion as *Jambudīpa*, by which they meant "India in its widest sense."

This chapter starts by describing the tradition's law texts, then touches on areas (such as the political economy and the constitution) where the law of Paliland is particularly steeped in Buddhism. It ends by asking whether Pāli Buddhist Law has a future or, indeed, a present.

Precolonial Sources of Pāli Buddhist Law

Three separate ethical and legal systems have coexisted in the area of Pāli Buddhist society. Monks, kings, and laity were each bound by their respective legal codes, known as *Vinaya* ("The Training"), *rajadhamma* ("The Dharma of Kings") and *dhammasat* ("The Manual of Dharma"). In its beginnings around the fifth century BCE, Pāli Buddhist Law meant the *Vinaya*. The *rajadhamma* developed from the royal courts and monasteries of Ceylon in the early centuries CE. Southeast Asia contributed the *dhammasats* from the twelfth century onward. Each *dhammasat* is a collection of rules, many of them reflecting local Southeast Asian wisdom traditions. Each is adorned with lists, stories, technical terms, and other odds and ends from the Pāli scriptures, commentaries, and manuals. The *dhammasats* also contain a few elements from Hindu law texts in the *Manusmrti* tradition.

The *dhammasat* is the central law text in the Pāli legal tradition. Its ingredients are numbered lists of rules and short law reports. The idea of topical law reports is borrowed from the *Vinaya*, which includes such collections as *Forty-nine Cases on Theft* and *Twenty-seven Cases on Bad Sex*. The list of 227 monastic vows that Buddhist monks recite each fortnight is found in the *Suttavibhaṅga*, which forms the index to the first half of the *Vinaya*. By the sixteenth century, *dhammasat* and *rajasat* texts were being compiled from Laos in the north down to Malaysia in the south, and from Phnom Penh in the east to Akyab in the west. Many *dhammasat* were written in verse and were probably among the earliest poems in the Khmer, Tai, and Burmese literary traditions. The prose *dhammasat* was typically written in a mixture of Pāli and vernacular languages. Each Pāli Buddhist kingdom (except perhaps for the very smallest) boasted its own local law-text literature. Thus, the *dhammasats* from different areas of Southeast Asia – such as the Tai *thammasats*, Khmer *dhammasarts* and the Burmese *dhammathats* – agree on the fundamental lists and on the genres appropriate to law, but they diverge on such details as the share of inheritance owed to the third daughter of a remarried widow. The *dhammasat* genre contained rules and judgment tales intended to solve disputes within the rice-growing community. The *rajasat* genre contained orders from the king, but this can hardly be referred to as legislation because often the king spoke more as a preacher than as a legislator. He was as likely to urge his subjects to do the right thing as to tell them what the right thing was and what sanction they would incur for not doing it.

These *dhammasat* and *rajasat* texts are now our only path into understanding Pāli Buddhist Law. They were written on fragile palm-leaf manuscripts and kept in the book chests of remote monasteries. Few people now have the language skills to read them, or the necessary visa to consult them. The first step toward knowledge of Paliland Law, therefore, is to get these manuscripts published and translated. The colonial government made a start, but the project then languished for eighty years. In the late 1970s, scholars from Chiangmai in Thailand brought their scanners and cameras to bear on monastic book chests across the Middle Mekong region. The Chiangmai School pioneered a renaissance in the field. Between 1880 and 1990, Europeans knew of only one Siamese law text. Since 1990, however, Pitinai Chaisangsukkul has catalogued hundreds of eighteenth and nineteenth century legal manuscripts from central Thailand, while Sarup Ritchu has collected the distinctive law texts of southern Thailand. Burma has about twelve surviving *dhammasat* earlier than the eighteenth century, and thirty or so more recent works. Two were translated, and seven more were printed in the late-nineteenth century. Within the last twenty years, eleven Mon-language *dhammasats* were published by Nai Pan Hla, and fourteen Shan-language *thammasats* by Sai Kham Mong.[1] Ryuji Okudaira, who helped bring both of these projects to fruition, has transformed our understanding of the many legal traditions that coexisted within Burma's frontiers. Some law texts from Arakan, the fourth Burmese tradition, are known to be in manuscript form, but they await cataloguing and publication. Rumors have emerged from northeast India that Tai language *thammasats* were located in Assam. Cambodia is the only part of the region not to share in this renaissance. Events since 1970 have pushed the retrieval of Khmer legal history low on Cambodia's list of priorities. One collection of Khmer law texts, which was printed and translated during the colonial period, gives the view from the royal palace. It would have been helpful had some law texts from the village perspective survived to give us a subaltern view of Khmer law.

The search for palm-leaf manuscripts that the Chiangmai school inspired has transformed the field. Legal historians of the twenty-first century have access to about twelve times as many Buddhist law texts as the colonial scholars had printed by 1900, and about four times as many as were

[1] Nai Pan Hla, *Eleven Mon Dhammasat Texts* (Tokyo: Center for East Asian Cultural Studies, 1992); Sai Kham Mong, *Shan Thammasat Manuscripts* (Tokyo: Mekong Publishing, 2012).

available in the 1980s, when I started work in the field. This abundance of new material should answer a host of questions about political structures, gender relations, and the economy. With luck it may suggest new answers to two of the big questions of Southeast Asian history: How and why did Paliland adopt Buddhism? When and in what shape did Paliland become Early Modern?

Pāli Buddhist Legal Reasoning

By "legal reasoning" I am referring to argument in open court. What arguments were permissible in Paliland courts, and which of those were favored as representing best practice? It is to the law reports that we must look for answers. Some Cambodian law reports from the eighteenth century and a few Northern Thai reports from the sixteenth century have survived, but they have not yet been scrutinized. From Burma, many precolonial law reports have also survived, and in this case, scholars started to examine them in the 1960s. As a result we know a great deal more about the Burmese legal profession than we do about its Khmer and Thai equivalents. The Burmese lawyers (*she-ne*) were regulated by the king. They wore a cotton briefcase slung over one shoulder and carried an official-issue drinking cup and fan. In the courtroom their roles were color-coded: the claimant's attorney wore a green turban and the defendant's attorney red. The lawyers presented their side's case with gusto and enthusiasm. It would seem that behavior in court was livelier than what I am used to in English courtrooms. As a *dhammathat* compiled in the 1750s discusses:

> [T]he bets of professional lawyers made amongst themselves, laughing and slapping their thighs or shoulders: If a lawyer, on the strength of his client being a man of rank and wealth, slaps the floor or the ground, and bets in anger on the result of the suit, let the bet not be paid. If two lawyers boast of their science and learning laughingly, it is a joke; if they do so regarding the cause under trial and both equally, there is no offence.[2]

This suggests that litigation involved a battle for respect, for "face," for bragging rights. The arena in which such battles were fought was the patron-client system that linked the capital city with rice farmers in far-off villages. Usually it was the individual claimant and defendant who initiated the dispute, but the longer the case went on, the more likely

[2] David Richardson (trans.), *The Dhamathat, or The Laws of Menoo* (Maulmain: American Baptist Mission Press, 1847), 367.

it was that rival patron-client systems would become involved. Cases that were appealed, and then re-appealed, were sure to be heard within the Royal Palace compound of the capital city. In the capital, rival patrons jostled for influence – not just through litigation, but also in spheres as varied as ox-cart racing, reciting-the-scriptures-from-memory competitions, and the organization of festivals. We frequently acknowledge the importance of drama when discussing festivals – the better the costume, music and props, the better the show. We should also make ourselves aware of the dramatic techniques at use in the courtroom.

This awareness, however, should not exclude the reasoning techniques at use in the courtroom. Buddhist lawyers were connoisseurs of legal argument, as well as exuberant displays of self-confidence. The law report of a case decided in Pegu in the 1580s, known as *Lord Kyaw Thu's Precedent*, was preserved because it was considered a model for legal argument. It is a compendium of best practices during the brief decade when King Bayinnaung of Pegu ruled all of Paliland. The dispute concerned the inheritance of the late ruler of Petchabun. The eldest son had been deprived of his share because he was living in Pegu, serving as a royal page and hostage. He sued his other siblings in a Siamese court, and lost. He appealed to Pegu, and lost. He lost two subsequent appeals, also heard in the capital. King Bayinnaung allotted the third appeal to be judged by Kyaw Thu. The *Precedent* summarizes the various arguments (six in all) on which the eldest son kept losing his case. Kyaw Thu, in allowing the eldest son's final appeal, meets all these arguments one by one. For example:

> A maxim has been cited: Parents Rightfully have Authority over their Children. But it is also right that children should be treated equitably, and distribute the wealth so as to achieve equality. Urgent is the rule "Avoid a division where one gets more than the others."[3]

Under other circumstances, Kyaw Thu concedes, the maxim is good law. However, on these particular facts it does not apply because a more urgent rule prevails. These facts fall within the intersection of the sets demarcated by the maxim and the urgent rule. Kyaw Thu gives similarly shaped answers to three more of the arguments he is overruling, for instance:

> True it is that A Formal Written Document Witnessed by Senior Monks, Headmen, Arbitrators and Scribes Transfers the Ownership. But not when

[3] Andrew Huxley, "Lord Kyaw Thu's Precedent: A Sixteenth-Century Burmese Law Report" in Paul Dresch and Hannah Skoda (eds.), *Legalism: Anthropology and History* (Oxford: Oxford University Press, 2012), 229–59 at 242. The two subsequent citations are from the same page.

> one of the heirs was absent. Urgent is the maxim that "A deed of distribution shall not be valid unless all parties to the litigation were physically present."

Kyaw Thu implies that norms come in two different strengths: when played against a "maxim," an "urgent rule" will always do the trick. Evidently the Burmese lawyers analyzed two levels of legal reasoning. Whether or not this is a sign of legal sophistication is an open question. But the manner in which Kyaw Thu deploys his urgent reasons against the other side's maxims is sophisticated in its consistent application:

> It has been said Handing a Thing over is Transferring it. But here the residence pattern of the children differed. It cannot be said that any assets were handed over to the elder son. Urgent is the rule "As your residence, so your share."

The lesson Kyaw Thu gave to Burmese lawyers was this: If your opponent has a good argument, nullify it first with your limitation, then countermand it with your urgent rule.

Twenty-five years after Kyaw Thu settled the Phetchabun inheritance dispute, one of Bayinnaung's grandsons passed a law regulating the *she-ne*. Myint Zan has translated it and linked one of its clauses to a long passage found in the Burmese Encyclopedia.[4] This clause lists the ten forms of argument that were allowed in court. Each of the arguments is named by an agricultural or transport-linked metaphor. I offer my own paraphrase of the cases offered by the Encyclopedia to illustrate them. I understand it to be a list of ten courtroom strategies:

1. *Sending from upstream*: Green Turban asks for more than he will get, knowing that concessions will have to be made.
2. *Grabbing the paddy sheaf by its root*: Green Turban puts forward a lie. Red Turban pretends to accept it, capping it with an even bigger lie.
3. *Sailing the laden raft upstream*: Green Turban prevails by sheer brainpower. He gives an expansive and perspicuous account of the relevant law in its fullest context.
4. *Putting just enough into the rice pot*: Green Turban offers Red Turban one wish. By clever drafting, Red Turban gets three benefits for his one wish.
5. *Grinding and grinding until the oil comes out*: Green Turban reiterates Argument A, whatever other arguments Red Turban introduces.
6. *Ducking away from a charging elephant*: Green Turban does well with argument A. Red Turban diverts attention by introducing Argument B.

[4] Myint Zan, "Woe Unto Ye Lawyers: Three Royal Orders Concerning Pleaders in Early 17th Century Burma," *American Journal of Legal History* 44 (2000): 40–72.

7 *Clearing the undergrowth first*: Green Turban leaves his best argument to the end.
8 *The Game-cock's feint*: Green Turban presents argument C. Red Turban concedes the point, before pointing out that argument C justifies the defendant making a hefty counterclaim.
9 *The Water-strainer*: Green Turban asks a question of Red Turban, such that Red Turban, however he answers it, must lose the case.
10 *Leveling out with the Rice Pounder*: Red Turban refuses to comment on Green Turban's accusations until Green Turban backs them up with evidence.

With the exception of number three, the emphasis is placed on winning the case, rather than on perfecting the law by finding the single best resolution to this dispute.

The Equity of the Rule

In order to do equity in the courtroom, the judge must avoid working iniquity. Europeans understand this to mean that the judge must avoid the evil of applying the rule in circumstances where it does not fit. This way of thinking derives from Aristotle's discussion of *epieikeia* as the skill of knowing when to ignore the rule in the name of a higher justice. The Aristotelian judge knows that *summum ius* ("the strictest application of the rule") brings *summa iniuria* ("the greatest harm"). Cicero developed the idea by incorporating Stoic discussions of hypothetical cases. Aquinas added a Christian dimension, seeing Christianity as the new unwritten equity come to supplant those written rules of Old Testament law whose interpretation had become too strict. Following the English Reformation, equity developed into a separate court system. Lord Chancellor Ellesmere explained that:

> The cause why there is a Chancery is for that men's actions are so divers and infinite that it is impossible to make any general law which may aptly meet with every particular act, and not fail in some circumstances.[5]

The Pāli Buddhist lawyers developed a similar doctrine from an entirely different starting point. As Aristotle was to Europe, so Buddhaghosa, the Great Commentator on the Pāli Buddhist scriptures, was to Southeast Asia. His discussion of theft in the *Great Vinaya Commentary* includes an analysis of the Four Variables of Value. The Buddha had included within

[5] *Earl of Oxford's Case* (1615), per Lord Ellesmere.

his definition of theft a *de minimis* rule that the theft of goods worth less than five dollars is no offense. Buddhaghosa quoted this ancient verse as enabling us to discover the true value of any object:

> The Elders ask what kind of thing it is.
> What time? What place? And was it still brand new?
> Worth less than five? *De minimis* applies.
> And thus they judged the pains that must accrue.[6]

It is by examining the Four Variables (thing, time, place, and use) that we can calculate true value. Buddhaghosa added several pages of exposition, including law reports to illustrate how each of the variables works.

To Buddhaghosa, the Four Variables were part of Theft Law. In Southeast Asia, Pāli Buddhists recast them as a full-blown theory of equity. As early as the 1570s, Judge Kyaw Thu declared that he had "thoroughly inquired" into the Petchabun inheritance dispute "in conformity with the Four Variables" and had based his ruling on them.[7] An eighteenth-century law report tells of a fight between a pet rat and a pet squirrel, which took place on a branch at night. As a result of the fight the rat lost her litter, and her owner sued the squirrel's owner for restitution. The judge's first decision was to award no damages, since a fair fight between animals does not attract liability. The Nats (the local tutelary deities) failed to applaud this ruling, so the judge substituted an analysis based on two of the four variables:

> The time, was night – the place, the branch of a tree. The branch is the squirrel's place; but though this is true, the night is the only time a rat will venture to seek his food; the squirrel makes no distinction as to day or night, in feeding. If we judge by the time, night is the rat's time; if by the branch, it is also the rat's place, as it was in the night time. *Time* outweighs *place*: so a branch at night is rat-territory. Let the owner of the squirrel pay the price of three litters, reckoned at one eue [*ywe*] of silver each. When this decision was given the Nats applauded, and proclaimed it.[8]

Because *time* outweighs *place*, a branch at night is judged to be rat-territory. The text goes on to explain the "four matters – time, place, price, and the thing," which are the Four Variables.

Subsequent Burmese texts treat the Four Variables as a basic hermeneutic to be applied to all rules in all areas of law. Tha Gywe, a barrister trained in the Inns of Court in late-nineteenth-century London, says that they are of

[6] My versification of P. Bapat's translation of the *Great Vinaya Commentary* [Sp 304]. I cite passages in the Pāli scriptures following the standard system, set out in detail in Oscar von Hinüber, *A Handbook of Pali Literature* (Berlin: Walter de Gruyter, 1996), 250–57.

[7] Huxley, "Lord Kyaw Thu's Precedent," 243.

[8] Richardson, *The Dhamathat*, 13.

general application. They "constitute a setting or environment from which no [*dhammasat*] text should be detached."[9] Thus, an economic list taken from a discussion of theft became Pāli Buddhist Law's equivalent of the equity of the rule. It is intriguing that an English lawyer contemporary with Shakespeare discussed his concept of equity by way of the same variables chosen by Buddhaghosa:

> Equity is diversely termed in law: sometimes as a conveniency, because it ministreth among men in a fit proportion, answerable to the persons, the matters, the places and the times.[10]

Equity, like Pataphysics, is a science of exceptions, and therefore it cannot itself be reduced to a set of rules. All we can do, in Europe and in Southeast Asia, is list those variables that affect whether this rule is to be applied to these facts.

Three Pāli Buddhist Legal Systems and Their Interaction

Pāli Buddhists are fond of trichotomies: There are Three Divisions of the Scripture (*Vinaya*, *Sutta*, and *Abidhamma*), Three Jewels (the Buddha, his scripture, and the monastic tradition he founded), and Three Worlds (our Middle Earth, and the levels above and below it). Pāli Buddhist society also was based on a trichotomy. Human society divides between monks, kings, and the laity, meaning everyone who is not a king or a monk. Each of these follows its own code of best practice: *Vinaya* for monks, *rajadhamma* for kings, and *dhammasat* for the laity. Often the codes overlap. Theft laws, for instance, were very similar in all three normative systems: It was equally wrong for a monk, a king, or a rice farmer to commit theft. Often the codes differed: Only monks are duty-bound to urinate from a seated position, and only kings are duty-bound to provide credit to the bankrupt rice farmer.

Even when the content of the three systems overlapped, there were issues of audience, competence, and jurisdiction. Could a layman bring his complaint to a monastic court? Could the king's courts rule on questions of *Vinaya* interpretation? In a Western positivist system, the sovereign decides such internal conflict of law questions from his perch on top of the pyramid of power. But in Southeast Asia, neither Khmer, Tai, nor Burmese

[9] Tha Gywe, *Treatise on Buddhist Law*, 2 vols. (Mandalay: Upper Burma Advertiser Press, 1910), vol. II, iv.

[10] Thomas Ashe, *Epieikeia et table generall a les annales del ley* (London: Society of the Stationers, 1609), 4. Ashe is here quoting from William West's *Symbolography*, published in 1590.

kings possessed the legislative omnicompetence that would allow them to resolve disputes between the three systems. During the final years of the Pāli Buddhist legal tradition, one of King Mindon's ministers suggested that *Vinaya* is the only source respected enough to appeal to all players in the system. He did so in an inheritance dispute, decided at Mandalay in 1877, just five years before the end of the Pāli Buddhist law tradition in Burma.

The report of *Ma Hla v. Ma Wa* contains a very scholarly bouquet of scriptural allusions.[11] The judge was Hpo Hlaing, the leader of the modernizing faction within the Mandalay court. Hpo Hlaing's judgment was copied for circulation at the time, perhaps as a response to British Burma's sudden interest in the Buddhist Law. I concentrate on the fifteen lines of text listing five law reports that appear in the Buddhist scriptures, commentaries, or ancillary literature. Hpo Hlaing gives the cases, without explaining what they signify. If the passage is read as Hpo Hlaing's answer to the British, then he would be urging King Mindon's subjects to resolve Burma's internal conflict of laws problems according to the *Vinaya*, as developed by centuries of *Vinaya* expertise. Hpo Hlaing, the constitutional modernizer, would thus be identifying *Vinaya* as the bedrock on which the Buddhist legal tradition had been built. I paraphrase this list at length, since it is a fine example of how the Pāli Buddhist tradition was able to spin answers to contemporary problems out of its scriptural resources.

Three of the five cases Hpo Hlaing chose are from the canonical *Vinaya*, a fourth is from the *Great Vinaya Commentary* (*Samantapāsādikā*) and the last from a postclassical biography of Buddhaghosa, the reputed author of the *Great Vinaya Commentary*. The first case concerns the reported theft accusation against Ajjuka, one of the *Forty-nine Cases on Theft* in the *Vinaya*. Ajjuka's case wrestled with the question of whether monks can give legal advice to laity. A rich householder living in Vesāli was uncertain whether to leave his wealth to his son or to his pious nephew. He asked Ajjuka, the monk he supported, to invite whichever of the two showed more faith and belief, to a meeting. Ajjuka chose to invite the nephew to a meeting and the latter subsequently inherited his uncle's wealth, upon which the son complained to another monk, Ānanda: "Does not the son have better claims to heirship than the nephew?" Ānanda accused Ajjuka of serious monastic impropriety by interfering with the householder's domestic matters. Ajjuka

[11] Andrew Huxley, "Hpo Hlaing on Buddhist Law," *Bulletin of the School of Oriental and African Studies* 73 (2010), 269–83.

asked Upāli (the first *Vinaya* specialist, and after the Buddha, the second-wisest exponent of the discipline) for a ruling:

> "Is it a crime, Ānanda, to invite a layman to a meeting?"
> "Upāli, it is not even the lightest of offences."
> "Then, Ānanda, Ajjuka has committed no offence."[12]

Upāli's ruling allowed Buddhist monks to advise their lay supporters on the ethical aspects of the family agenda, even if this foreseeably led to the enrichment of the nephew and the impoverishment of the son. Ānanda's view, had it prevailed, would have prevented monks from engaging with such family concerns.

The second case is Godha's precedent on how to determine the value of a stolen item.[13] This decision was made at Sri Lanka's Great Monastery (Mahāvihāra) during the reign of King Bhātiya (143–167 CE). On a deserted island, a monk took a coconut shell and whittled it into a drinking cup polished like mother-of-pearl. He left the cup behind when he returned to Sri Lanka. Another monk visited the island on retreat, and finding the cup in the empty monastery, resolved to make it his own. The cup maker saw him with it later and accused him of theft. At the Great Monastery outside Anurādhapura, the drums were beaten to assemble all the monks to a trial. Those elders with expertise in the *Vinaya* decided that it was theft. But the Elder Godha (Godatta Thera) declared the bowl was worthless, since its raw material could be picked up for free anywhere on the island. When King Bhātiya heard what had happened, he had the city drum beaten and the proclamation made: "As long as I live, any case decided by Godha (whether for monks, nuns, or the laity) shall be regarded as well decided." The economic theory in Godha's decision denies any role to labor in the creation of value. King Bhātiya's jurisdictional claim is that he, *qua* monarch, can decide which conflicting interpretation of the *Vinaya* is correct.

The third case involves the nun Thullanandā's nunnery and an accusation of using malicious speech toward a layperson.[14] A lay donor had given a storehouse to Thullanandā's nunnery. After his death, one of his sons tried to rescind the gift. Thullanandā went to court to question his right to evict them, and won the case. Then the son was heard to disrespect Thullanandā's nunnery, referring to the "shaven-headed women" as "strumpets." Thullanandā went to court to punish this defamation. Finally, the angry son suborned a group of non-Buddhist, naked ascetics to shout

[12] Vin III 45. [13] *Great Vinaya Commentary* (Sp. ii.307). [14] Vin V 222–24.

slogans against the nuns. Thullanandā went to court to get the son put in fetters, but some people disapproved: "First these nuns have his store-room taken away, then they have him punished, then they have him fettered: before too long they will be having him killed!" The Buddha ruled that Thullanandā was not guilty of the offense. His ruling allowed nuns to use the state law-courts to vindicate their collective property rights and reputation, even if this makes them unpopular in certain circles.

The fourth case appears in the Pāli biography of Buddhaghosa. As Buddhaghosa disembarked in Sri Lanka, he witnessed one woman water-carrier accidentally break another's jar.[15] A violent quarrel followed. Knowing that he might be called as a witness, Buddhaghosa wrote down all that he saw and heard. When the king judged the case against the two women, he called Buddhaghosa as a witness. Buddhaghosa sent along his notebook, which the king treated as decisive of the facts. A written deposition is acceptable in court, as long as it comes from a monk. The king became interested in this learned foreign monk, and eventually agreed to help subsidize his project to translate the Sinhalese commentaries into Pāli.

The final case is the consultation by the Buddha of King Bimbisāra's ex-minister of justice. It is taken from the *Vinaya's* discussion of the four most serious monastic offenses:

> Wishing to define the *de minimis* rule for theft, the Buddha consulted a monk who, when a laymen [sic], had been minister and judge of King Bimbisāra. He asked, "For what value of goods stolen does King Seniya Bimbisāra of Magadha, having caught a robber, flog, or imprison, or banish him?" "For 1 *pada*, Lord," was the reply.[16]

Thus, King Bimbisāra's rule was incorporated into the *Vinaya*'s definition of theft.

Hpo Hlaing, I suggest, chose these five classical Pāli Buddhist law reports because they were all concerned with internal conflict of laws. The third and fourth cases concern the appearance of monks and nuns in the king's courts. Buddhaghosa's case implies that a monk could be called as a witness, but that his dignity may be protected by allowing him to submit a written deposition rather than appearing in person. Thullanandā's case confirms that nuns can initiate litigation in the king's courts to protect the nunnery's joint property and reputation. The second and fifth cases concern the influence of dharma of kings on the *Vinaya*. Godha's precedent shows a king of Ceylon broadcasting his appreciation of a particular monastic *Vinaya*

[15] Bu-up 23. [16] Vin III 44.

expert with distinctive economic theories. Bimbisāra's precedent shows, on the authority of the Buddha himself, that the *Vinaya* incorporated useful passages from contemporary, secular laws. Ajjuka's case confirms that it is *Vinaya*, rather than *dhammasat*, which draws the boundary for a relationship between a monk and a layperson and defines the degree of social distance between the two.

The Ethics of the Pāli Buddhist State

Rajasat were the orders that were issued from each palace. They constitute a subgenre within the broader field of *rajadhamma*, which includes manuals for the instruction of princes, sermons preached in the king's presence, and birth stories of the former buddhas. *Rajadhamma* dealt generally with the ethics of kingship. Since monarchy was the only kind of government employed in Paliland, we can think of *rajadhamma* as a guide to best practice in government. To the extent that *rajadhamma* lacked any authority, we may label it as political theory. To the extent it was binding on kings, we may label it as Constitutional Law. Shortly after Burma regained its independence, its leading legal historian argued that some parts of the *rajadhamma* amounted to Constitutional Law. Aye Maung reached this conclusion by raising a question of intellectual history: How did Burmese scholars interpret the many lists contained in the Buddhist scriptures? He examined a list I refer to as the "Four Solidarities" (loosely translating Pāli *saṅghavatthu*/"burdens of companionship"). This list first appears in Buddhaghosa's *Commentaries on the Sutta* as a refutation of a Vedic list of "Four Sacrifices": the hay sacrifice, the human sacrifice, the wedge throw, and the soma sacrifice. Buddhaghosa wrote during the fifth century CE that the good Buddhists of yesteryear had adapted from the Vedic list so as to describe some of the characteristics of their ideal Buddhist state:

> Among them, the *hay-sacrifice* was taking the tenth part from the grain that had been harvested; . . . The *human sacrifice* was the providing of six month's food and wages to great warriors; . . . The *wedge-throw* was taking a written chit from poor people and providing them with money, in the amount of one or two thousand, for three years without interest; . . . The *soma sacrifice* was speaking gentle words such as Daddy and Mummy.[17]

Three of these Four Solidarities reflect the preoccupations of a wet-rice-growing, redistributive economy. The rice cultivators will give the king ten

[17] Mp iv 69; Spk i 144.

percent of their harvest, no more and no less (hay sacrifice). In return, the king will redistribute the kingdom's wealth as interest-free loans to tide the rice farmers over their bad times (wedge throw). When mobilizing the rice growers to become a *corvée* labor force, the king must provide them with a subsistence allowance (human sacrifice).

This approach was much elaborated by Southeast Asian lawyers. An eighteenth-century Burmese *dhammasat* rephrases the wedge throw in legalistic terms:

> If a person has incurred debts beyond his means of paying, and his family are [sic] unable to assist him . . . he shall make a petition to the king, who will say, "On conditions, give him an advance." . . . In three years the king may take back the advances. This he may do in accordance with the *Solidarity Laws*.[18]

A later edition of the same *dhammasat*, written in 1782 to mark King Badon's accession to the throne, portrays the Solidarities as the backbone of the natural law governing Buddhist society:

> The Buddhas reveal the Four Solidarities to every world, so that every king may practice them. Those kings who have founded their kingdoms and practice these Four Solidarities should admonish their subjects in accordance with the law of the *Dhammasat*.[19]

Aye Maung persuasively reads this passage as marking a shift from "moral exhortations to legal obligations binding on the ruler."[20] If he is right, then Burma developed its own Constitutional Law from within its Pāli Buddhist tradition, and the Buddhist kings of Southeast Asia were not the despots painted by Orientalist scholars. The kings in their public pronouncements spoke of their obedience to the rule of law, the dharma that they had sworn to uphold. Perhaps in private their intentions were Machiavellian. In public, however, the king was sometimes trumped by dharma. Here is an instance from the 1850s, when the hay sacrifice was the focus of debate. King Mindon proposed a new tax of a quarter-rupee per household to pay for religious works. One of Mindon's ministers objected, on the grounds that kings may levy no more than ten percent: "To have more on any grounds" would be "an infringement of ancient rights."[21] The minister said that if the king carried out his proposal, he would be like the monkeys

[18] Richardson, *The Damathat*, 106. [19] Ryuji Okudaira (forthcoming) *Pre-colonial Burmese Law*.

[20] Aye Maung, "Insolvency Jurisdiction in Early Burmese Law," *Journal of the Burma Research Society* 34 (1951), 6.

[21] Ma Kyan, "King Mindon's Councillors," *Journal of the Burma Research Society* 44 (1961), 54.

described in the *Ārāmadūsa Jātaka*. These monkeys used to uproot all the fruit trees in their orchard so as to see whether their roots were dry enough to need watering.[22] King Mindon dropped his new tax.

Conclusion: Does Pāli Buddhist Law Still Exist?

Does Pāli Buddhist law in some form or another still endure today? Between 1870 and 1904, France and England eradicated most of the Pāli Buddhist kings. The colonial interlude, although scarcely lasting a century, wiped Buddhist law from the legal map. France had no qualms about the superiority of Napoleon's positivist codification to Pāli Buddhist Law, and applied the Codes in modified form to Cambodia and Laos. British Burma abolished *dhammasat* and *rajasat* in all fields except family law and inheritance. In 1882, the judicial commissioner ordered that henceforth Burmese *she-ne* had to speak English. Thenceforth, the English judges, who barely even understood the Burmese language, followed each other's written decisions. They no longer bothered to have relevant passages of the *dhammasats* interpreted for them. Starting in the 1890s, Thailand switched its law from *dhammasat* and *rajasat* to a system of codes drafted by European legal experts.

Yet, before we concede that the colonial period has killed off Buddhist law, consider the fate of what replaced them, the legal traditions introduced by France and England. In 1973, Burma purged its legal system of all colonial trappings, substituting untrained jurors for the professional judges. Since 1990, there has been some movement back toward trained judges, but it is unlikely that wigs, gowns, and the rest of the common law paraphernalia of justice will ever again grace a Burmese law courtroom. In Laos and Cambodia, French rule was indirect, so that beyond Phnom Penh and Vientiane, villagers had little contact with French officials. Following the end of the 1970s wars, Marxist governments have tried to steer a path out of underdevelopment while maintaining a fragile peace. Since 1980, Laos and Cambodia have promulgated prodigious amounts of legislation and more than one constitution, but none of it seems especially French. In short, the colonial period of Southeast Asian legal history is over.

Southeast Asian Law thus far in the twenty-first century is in a period of globalization. Lawmakers are primarily concerned with foreign investment law, international business companies, and credit institutions. Such issues impinge on Southeast Asia no differently than on Kazakhstan, Bolivia,

[22] J II 237. Jataka #268 of the Pali Collection.

and South Africa. While the legal elites in the capital cities of mainland Southeast Asia are busy designing stock markets and joint-venture regimes, older patterns of social control may be preserved upcountry. The monks are back in their village monasteries. The rice fields are still being cultivated. The same old disputes crop up (over inheritance, over agricultural debt, between husband and wife). These were the topics in which *dhammasat* and *rajasat* specialized. Perhaps in the villages upriver, *dhammasat* and *rajasat* are still consulted. In the capital cities of Southeast Asia, however, Buddhist Law has indeed died. If it survives elsewhere, it is as the humblest of normative systems.

CHAPTER 10

Genres and Jurisdictions
Laws Governing Monastic Inheritance in Seventeenth-Century Burma

Christian Lammerts

The interrelationships between Buddhism and law in Southeast Asian history are dynamic and untidy: different legal and scriptural genres borrow from and blend into others; authority is invoked from multiple (and at times seemingly contradictory) sources; jurisdictions of monastic and lay law overlap or conflict. Multiple ideologies of law, their normative expression in texts, or their implementation in practice, are not in any straightforward sense "Buddhist," much less "Theravādan." These latter terms are meant to signify some sort of allegiance to the Pāli *Vinaya* and its Mahāvihārin commentaries. Although these literatures were deeply influential, Southeast Asian historical discourses of Buddhism and Law, and indeed even "Buddhist law" in its strongest definition as *Vinaya*, must be approached as works-in-progress, as contingent convergences, effects of an ongoing dialogue between legists and changing textual, intellectual, and religio-political horizons.

This article examines laws governing the inheritance of monastic property and discourse about such law, expressed in the two principle vernacular and Pāli genres of written law in circulation in seventeenth-century Burma: *Vinaya* and *dhammasattha*.[1] Calling into question any strict divide between lay and monastic legal spheres, it shows that monastic inheritance did not fall under the exclusive jurisdiction of *Vinaya*, and also that *Vinaya* laws regulating monastic partition were appropriated by *dhammasattha* for application to the lay community. The former point underscores the need to historicize *Vinaya* practice and theory as part of broader legal-textual cultures. The latter point addresses the degree to which *Vinaya* might serve as a source of non-monastic law in Southeast Asia. Furthermore, this article examines the eventual recognition of jurisdictional separation and

[1] This term used in Southeast Asia for treatises on the law has several variations: *dhammasat*, *dhammasattha*, *dhammathat*, and *thammasat*.

legal conflict between these two genres. In some quarters, *dhammasattha* laws governing monastic inheritance came to be regarded as contradicting *Vinaya* norms and in need of "purification."

Vinaya Variations in Recorded Decisions on Monastic Inheritance

The *Vinaya Decisions of Sirīsaṅghapāla* (*Decisions*) is a compilation of more than 210 synoptic records of Buddhist monastic legal disputes that were tried by a *Vinaya* jurist (*vinayadhara*) around upper Burma between Wednesday, October 6, 1602 and Tuesday, November 2, 1613. The *Vinaya* jurist heard the majority of the cases in populous towns of considerable importance to the regional economy with close links to the capital at Ava. The name of the adjudicating *vinayadhara* is not stated in all instances, although when it is, he is usually referred to as Sirīsaṅghapāla ("lord of the *saṅgha*"). This monk was an immediate client of the throne; other sources tell us that he was responsible for authoring a *Vinaya* decision (*vinicchaya*) on monastic cloth at the request of King Nyaungyan (r. 1597–1605).[2]

Decisions is prefaced by an introduction that sets forth a number of basic *Vinaya* principles,[3] often through a presentation of brief Pāli citations or pseudo-citations from the *Tipiṭaka*, which are then glossed with a Burmese translation in the form of an interlineated Pāli-Burmese text (*nissaya*). These include the Buddha's rules for the monastic community concerning the forbidden ordination of slaves[4] and thieves,[5] the three categories of monastery and their mode of donation,[6] the solicitation of a preceptor (*upajjhāya*),[7] ordination by five monks in the border regions,[8] the difference between individual and collective monastic lands and property,[9] and dietary restrictions.[10] The introduction ends with a brief citation from the *Vinaya-pācittiya*, perhaps as a warning to anyone who would challenge the authority of the rules or the judgments that follow: "[S]hould any monk knowingly agitate for the reopening of a legal case that has been settled in accordance with the law (*dhamma*), it is an offence requiring expiation."[11]

Among the various rules that are discussed in the introduction to *Decisions*, monastic inheritance receives sustained treatment. Indeed,

[2] Uttamasikkhā, f.kaṃ(v). Uttamasikkhā. c. 1706. *Rhaṅ Tisāsana Achak Anvay Cā Tamḥ* [Treatise on the lineage of Tisāsana]. Ms = NL kaṅḥ 85.

[3] It is 7–9 folios in length in the manuscripts used.

[4] Sirīsaṅghapāla. c. 1614. *Vinaya Decisions of Sirīsaṅghapāla*. Mss = UCL 10716 ff.chau(v)-chaṃ(r)), cf. Vin 1, 74.

[5] UCL 10716 f.jī(r); cf. Vin 1, 74–75.

[6] *Ibid.* ff.chaṃ(r)-chaṃ(v).

[7] *Ibid.* ff.chāḥ(r)-chāḥ(v); Vin 1, 45–46.

[8] *Ibid* f.ja(r); Vin 1, 197.

[9] *Ibid.* ff.ja(r)-(v); Vin 1, 250.

[10] *Ibid.* ff.ji(r)-(v).

[11] *Ibid.* f.ju(v); cf. Vin 4, 126.

approximately half of the cases in the text concern disputes over the partition and succession of monastic property following the death of a monk. The prescriptions of the Pāli *Vinaya* concerning monastic inheritance have been discussed by Robert Lingat in comparison with Brāhmaṇical *dharmaśāstra* and what Lingat calls Southeast Asian "droit laïque."[12] The rules derive ultimately from the brief *Discourse on the Property of the Dead* (*Matasantakakathā*) of the canonical *Vinaya-mahāvagga*, and are explained and elaborated in most major *Vinaya* commentaries and sub-commentaries of the Mahāvihārin tradition.[13] The author of *Decisions* is clearly aware of some of these commentarial works, such as the *Vinayasaṅgaha*, as he explicitly refers to them in other contexts, although his treatment of the law of monastic inheritance echoes only the root text of the *Vinaya* itself, and invokes the *Mahāvagga* by name.

His discussion is organized around three Pāli statements, each of which he elaborates in a vernacular gloss:

> [I.]
>
> Monks, the *saṅgha* is the owner and lord of the bowl and robes of the monk who has died, but yet those who have given support to the sick monk (*gilānupaṭṭhāka*) have performed a virtuous service. I allow the *saṅgha* to give them the three robes and bowl.
>
> [II.]
>
> At that time a certain monk with much property and many requisites died. Whatever light goods (*lahubhaṇḍa*) or light requisites (*lahuparikkhāra*) there are in his residence among his requisites, [I allow] the members of the *saṅgha* who are present (*sammukhībhūta-saṅgha*) to distribute them.
>
> [III.]
>
> Whatever there is among [a dead monk's] requisites in the way of heavy goods (*garubhaṇḍa*) or heavy requisites (*garuparikkhāra*), [I prescribe that] these belong to all past and future monks of the entire *saṅgha* (*cātudisa-saṅgha*), and are not to be divided into shares or apportioned.[14]

[12] Robert Lingat, "Vinaya et droit laïque: Études sur les conflits de la loi religieuse et de la loi laïque dans l'Indochine hinayaniste," *Bulletin de l'École française d'Extrême-Orient* 37 (1937), 415–77.

[13] Vin 1, 303–05; Sp, 1133–34; Sp-ṭ 3, 343; Vjb, 498–500; Pālim, 246–49; Vmv 2, 201–02; Pālim-nṭ 2, 33–36.

[14] Sirīsaṅghapāla, UCL 4893 f.phaṃ(r), UCL 10716 ff.ja(v)-jā(r).

Although they are presented as such, these are not verbatim "citations" of the *Vinaya-mahāvagga* or of any later commentarial restatement of its rules. Here the basic canonical formulae are slightly reworked, perhaps because the author was recalling them from memory rather than copying them from a written text, or perhaps because he was citing written monastic legal compendia or handbooks.

The interlineated gloss (*nissaya*) that serves as a vernacular translation and brief exegesis of these Pāli statements goes on to explain that citation II regulates monastic inheritance of property classified as light goods that are owned by the individual monk (*puggalika*), whereas citation III regulates heavy goods that are owned by the collective fraternity (*saṅghika*). Sirīsaṅghapāla concludes his discussion with a vernacular list of the twenty-five types of heavy goods parallel to that found in *Vinaya-cullavagga*.[15] Twice in the introduction, the making of monastic bequests or wills (*accayadāna*) is expressly prohibited,[16] although the author, following the *Vinaya*, notes that gifts donated during a monk's lifetime remain valid after death. All of this is perfectly consonant with basic rules contained in the root text of the *Vinaya*.

Interestingly, many of the inheritance cases recorded in *Decisions* discuss problems that arose in the context of disputes over who should inherit manuscripts belonging to a dead monk. Embracing the later Pāli commentarial classification of manuscripts as objects of veneration of the dhamma (*dhammacetiya*),[17] Burmese *Vinaya* jurists viewed them and other objects of veneration, such as Buddha images, as a type of property exempt from the usual descriptive classification of light or heavy goods. Another major issue in the disputes concerns the inheritance of monastic property by laypersons aside from those who can be classified as a supporter of the sick (*gilānupaṭṭhāka*), and especially the reversion of property donated to an individual monk by the donor following the monk's death.

Another feature concerns the ownership and inheritance by monks of slaves (*dāsa*; *kyvan*). It is clear that Sirīsaṅghapāla views the monastic ownership of slaves as a breach of monastic law. Slavery is presupposed as an acceptable lay Buddhist practice in Pāli literature, and there are several instances in the *Tipiṭaka* that suggest that the monastic ownership of servants (e.g., *ārāmika*s, *veyyāvaccakara*s) was common and indeed prescribed

15 Vin. 2, 170; Lingat, "Vinaya et droit laïque," 444–45.

16 UCL 10716 f.chaṃ(v); f.ju(r). Cf. Vin 2, 267–68; Lingat, "Vinaya et droit laïque," 461–65.

17 Sp-ṭ 1, 172.

by the Buddha himself.[18] Despite the fact that slavery was a common feature of Burmese monasticism throughout the second millennium, certain Pāli commentaries do appear to forbid the monastic ownership of slaves (*dāsa*) as a category of bonded individual contrasted with other types of servants.[19]

We may cite the following two cases from the collection that exemplify these various concerns:

I.

11th, waning Pyatho, *sakkarāja* 966 [January 4, 1605]. The following judgment in the *Vinaya* dispute between the monk Dhammanandi and the donor of the Golden Monastery was passed at Sagaing by Sirīsaṅghapāla. As for the remaining property of the dead monk which has not been distributed or deeded before death: his heavy property should be retained [as property of the monastery collectively] and the monks of the monastery should distribute his light property and requisites to those who nursed and aided him while he was sick. Since according to the *Vinaya* monks may not possess slaves, it is right that slaves are inherited according to mundane law (*lokavat*). As for the four types of object of veneration (*cetiya*), including manuscript-texts (*cā pe kyamḥ gan*) and Buddha images, these are classified as neither light or heavy property nor as requisites. As Dhammanandi is one among the four types of son [i.e., was his close disciple],[20] and has taken care of the deceased monk, he should receive the manuscripts and Buddha images. As for the heavy property which is not to be separated from the monastery, it may be transferred to anyone in whom the donor of the Golden Monastery has faith. Except for the five root texts of *Vinaya-pāḷi* and the two *Vinaya-aṭṭhakathā*, a total of seven texts, whatever other manuscripts remain are to be considered property belonging to the monastery as before.[21]

II.

4th, waning Tagu, *sakkarāja* 967, Wednesday [March 12, 1605]. Before the Sayadaw [the following judgment was passed at Ava] in the *Vinaya*

[18] Jonathan Silk, *Managing Monks: Administrators and Administrative Roles in Indian Buddhist Monasticism* (New York: Oxford University Press, 2008), ch. 3; Gregory Schopen, *Buddhist Monks and Business Matters* (Honolulu: University of Hawai'i Press, 2004), 193–218; Petra Kieffer-Pülz, "Stretching the Vinaya Rules and Getting Away with It," *Journal of the Pāli Text Society* 29 (2007), 10–35.

[19] Vin 2, 267; Vjb 499.

[20] Cf. Vin 1, 45; Ja, 135.

[21] Sirīsaṅghapāla, UCL 10716, f.jai(v); UCL 4893, f.bī(v).

> dispute between [the monks] Paññāraṃsī and Uttamaraṃsī. As for the light requisites of the deceased monk that were not given or deeded [by him before death], the one who attended him while sick should receive [a share] and the remainder should be distributed among the monks present at his monastery. It is proper that the heavy property remains with the monastery. As for his texts and Buddha images, it is appropriate that Paññāraṃsī and Uttamaraṃsī each receive a share because they were one among the four types of son to the deceased [i.e., were his close disciples] and took care of him. The following texts shall remain as part of the collection of the monastery...[22] Since according to the *Vinaya,* monks may not possess slaves, it is proper that the slaves belonging to the deceased monk are inherited by his lay relatives.[23]

Both of these records typify the inheritance rulings in *Decisions* and are in many respects commensurate with basic *Vinaya* rules governing inheritance outlined in the *Mahāvagga*, except for two departures. The first concerns the judgment in the first case that grants the reversion of the heavy property belonging to a monk to the donor of his monastery following his death. Here the donor is not granted the right of complete ownership, but has the ability to transfer or re-donate the monastic property of the deceased to another monk of the same monastery "in whom he has faith."[24] An issue over which there is considerable divergence from *Vinaya* law concerns how the ownership and inheritance of slaves is handled. Although Sirīsaṅghapāla holds that, according to the *Vinaya*, monks may not possess slaves, he does not expressly forbid them to monks. Rather, he rules that should a monk own slaves, their partition falls under the jurisdiction of mundane law, according to which the dead monk is treated as a member of a family and thus his relatives have a right to inherit the slaves.

Sirīsaṅghapāla's recognition here of what we might call the "two legal bodies" of a monk – his legal identity under supermundane *Vinaya* law and

[22] Fourteen texts in pure Pāli: *Vinaya-pārājika-pāḷi* and *-aṭṭhakathā; Vinaya-parivāra; Greater Vinayasaṅgaha-aṭṭhakathā; Lesser Vinayasaṅgaha-aṭṭhakathā; Sutta Sīlakkhandavagga-aṭṭhakathā; Sutta Mahāvagga-aṭṭhakathā; Sutta Pāthikavagga-pāḷi; Dhammasaṅgaṇī; Vibhaṅga; Dhātukathā; Puggalapaññatti; Abhidhānappadīpikā-ṭīkā; Saddanīti.* The following are bilingual glosses (*nāma*): *Vinaya-pāḷi-nāma;* (*Vinaya-*)*aṭṭhakathā-nāma; Greater Vinayasaṅgaha-aṭṭhakathā-nāma; Sutta Sīlakkhandavagga-aṭṭhakathā-nāma; Sutta Mahāvagga-aṭṭhakathā-nāma; Nyāsa(=Mukhamattadīpanī)-nāma Handbook; Nāma* of *Greater Subcommentaries on the Foundational* (*Curricular*) *Texts.*

[23] Sirīsaṅghapāla, UCL 10716 ff.jaṃ(r)-(v); UCL 4893 f.be(r).

[24] Cf. Schopen, *Buddhist Monks and Business Matters,* 222–23.

under mundane law, respectively – enables a provocative set of reflections. A monk is simultaneously subject to two jurisdictions whose authority in any particular instance is determined by the class of practices in question. Oskar von Hinüber has pointed out that Pāli commentators recognize the authority of royal law over the saṅgha in the case of certain regulations, and it appears that a similar overlapping of jurisdictions is at work here.[25] The inheritance of monastic property that is not governed by *Vinaya* is regulated by mundane law. Contrary to the commonly held assumption that monks simply renounce all family ties and status upon ordination, here we see that for purposes of succession, monks could remain as sons or fathers and their surviving biological relatives had a right to inherit property that was illicit in *Vinaya* terms.

The Early *Dhammasattha* and Their Complex Relationship to *Vinaya*

Pāli *Vinaya* literature is often read as testimony to what Buddhist monastic legal culture was really like in historical Southeast Asia. While in certain cases canonical *Vinaya* texts and their mainstream commentarial treatments may provide a reasonably accurate reflection of juridical realities, it is often difficult or impossible to determine to what extent they are expressions of scholastic or commentarial ideals. As Charles Hallisey and Anne Blackburn have argued, *Vinaya* handbooks and monastic legal rulings – such as *Decisions* – allow us to further historicize the ways in which monastic law was actually negotiated in practical textual, juridical, and pedagogical contexts.[26] Things become increasingly complicated in circumstances where this broad field of *Vinaya*-related legal learning and literature is not the only relevant genre of law bearing on monastics.

The category of "worldly law" that Sirīsaṅghapāla invokes is a reference to the legal genre known as *dhammasattha*, which consists of hundreds of distinct texts that survive in Burmese, Tai, Lao, and Cambodian manuscripts. In Burma, the vernacular term *lokavat*, cognate with Pāli *loka-vatta* – "worldly practices" or "worldly duties" – is used as a

[25] Oskar von Hinüber, "Buddhist Law According to the Theravāda-Vinaya: A Survey of Theory and Practice," *Journal of the International Association of Buddhist Studies* 18 (1995), 7–45.

[26] Charles Hallisey, "Apropos the Pāli Vinaya as a Historical Document," *Journal of the Pāli Text Society* 15 (1990), 197–208; Anne M. Blackburn, "Looking for the *Vinaya*: Monastic Discipline in the Practical Canons of the Theravāda," *Journal of the International Association of Buddhist Studies* 22 (1999), 281–309.

synonym for *dhammasattha* from the early sixteenth century onward. This genre was present in Burma by the mid-thirteenth century and has certain remote parallels with Sanskrit Brāhmaṇical *dharmaśāstra* literature, especially in terms of its overall literary structure. However, while *dharmaśāstra* deals in detail with a range of prescriptions of socio-theological relevance only within a Brāhmaṇical context – such as its rules concerning duties at the different stages of life (*āśrama*), caste purity, and ritual procedure – only the eighteen grounds for litigation (*vyavahārapadas*) find echo in *dhammasattha*.[27]

Although *dhammasattha* texts betray affinities with *Vinaya* and other Pāli canonical and commentarial literatures, this relationship is complex owing to the fact that *dhammasattha* developed largely outside the scholastic tradition that gave rise to successive Theravāda commentaries on monastic law. The genealogy of *dhammasattha* is murky and difficult to reconstruct before the seventeenth century, but it is evident that the Southern Indian and Laṅkān commentators such as Buddhaghosa and Sāriputta, who were responsible for codifications of Mahāvihārin *Vinaya* orthodoxy during the fifth–twelfth centuries CE, were either unaware of *dhammasattha* or unwilling to classify it as a legitimate repository of authentically Buddhist law. In mainland Southeast Asia, however, Pāli *Vinaya* literature and *dhammasattha* circulated in coexistence throughout the second millennium.

This coexistence was not always frictionless, and in seventeenth-century Burma there are cases of monastic authors harshly criticizing *dhammasattha* as a non-Buddhist literature and an obstacle to the path of *nibbāna*.[28] On the one hand, there are instances where surviving *dhammasattha* texts largely agree with parallel legal provisions in the *Vinaya* corpus, or indeed seem to have taken texts of that corpus as a source for its rules. Yet, on the other hand, there are laws concerning which *Vinaya* and *dhammasattha* radically disagree, and such instances of conflict were a cause of significant anxiety in contexts where orthodox textual and jurisprudential purity was a principal concern.

The earliest surviving *dhammasattha* text was written sometime before 1628 CE. This *dhammasattha*, entitled *Dhammavilāsa*, does not contain a separate section that discusses monastic inheritance, although its author

[27] Dietrich Christian Lammerts, "Buddhism and Written Law: Dhammasattha Manuscripts and Texts in Premodern Burma," unpublished Ph.D. dissertation, Cornell University (2010).

[28] Christian Lammerts, "Narratives of Buddhist Legislation: Textual Authority and Legal Heterodoxy in Seventeenth through Nineteenth-Century Burma," *Journal of Southeast Asian Studies* 44.1 (February 2013), 118–44.

is clearly aware of, and in discussions of other matters refers to, the *Vinaya* by name as an authoritative source of the law of theft.[29] It is possible to speculate that the reason for the omission of such a section is because monastic and lay jurisdictions were not regarded by the compiler of the *Dhammavilāsa* as fully separate – that is, laws derived from both *Vinaya* and *dhammasattha* had authority over both lay and monastic communities.

As noted previously, according to the *Discourse on the Property of the Dead* of the *Vinaya* and its commentaries, the supporter of a sick monk (*gilānupaṭṭhāka*) is entitled to receive a share of monastic property following his death. Citing a non-canonical narrative of a judgment attributed in the text to the Buddha himself, the *Dhammavilāsa* extends this rule to apply to all supporters of any sick and dying person, whether monastic or lay.[30] Thus, here we have a case where a *Vinaya* rule concerning monastic inheritance is accommodated within and refashioned by an early Burmese *dhammasattha* text and made applicable to society at large.

There are numerous other examples of the same phenomenon that involve different *Vinaya*-related laws, where *Vinaya* prescriptions initially designed for the monastic community are interpreted as binding on all persons. But it would be wrong to assume that in all cases *Vinaya* and *dhammasattha* were easily commensurable. It is precisely in the context of laws concerning monastic inheritance in later *dhammasattha* treatises that disagreements between the two genres were recognized and the separation of monastic and lay jurisdictions became increasingly exigent.

The *Manusāra Dhammasattha* on Monastic Inheritance

Redacted in Pāli verse and given a prose *nissaya* commentary in 1651, the *Manusāra* is the earliest *dhammasattha* for which we have secure data concerning authorship and the exact year of compilation. For present purposes, it is important because this is the first *dhammasattha* to include an explicit discussion of laws regulating the inheritance of monastic property belonging to the saṅgha as a community whose regulations differ from those of non-monastics. That is, it is the first Burmese legal text to

[29] Dhammavilāsa. c. 1628. *Dhammavilāsa Dhammasat.* Mss = 1386 f.gu(v); UBhS 163/582 f.gaṃ(v); cf. Sp, 304.

[30] Dhammavilāsa, BL Or Add 12249 ff.chai(v)-cho(v); NL 1386 ff.ghāḥ(r-v); UBhS 163/582 ff.cā(r-v); UCL 9926 ff.chau(r-v).

recognize a clear distinction between monastic and lay jurisdictions and their respective authoritative, textual sources. Moreover, in this section of the text, the compilers explicitly affirm that the rules of *dhammasattha* and *Vinaya* regarding monastic inheritance are not in harmony, but in disagreement.

Before citing the passage in question, a few remarks concerning the compilation and overall structure of the text of the *Manusāra* are necessary. The *Manusāra* in fact contains two texts: the *Manusāra-dhammasattha-pāṭha* and the *Manusāra-dhammasat-nissaya*. The latter work is a bilingual Pāli-Burmese interphrasal commentary (*nissaya*) on the former monolingual Pāli verse text (*pāṭha*). In nearly all surviving manuscripts of the *Manusāra*, these two texts are transmitted together, and it is unlikely that at any time since 1651 the Pāli text circulated or was accessed independently of the *nissaya*. The structure of the *nissaya* commentary is conventional: It cites in succession one or occasionally several verses from the Pāli text and then glosses each word or phrase of the verse individually in succession. This interverbal or interphrasal linguistic and semantic gloss is then followed by an all-vernacular section that presents a translation of the meaning (*adhippāya*) of the verse. In many instances, however, the commentary offers far more than simple translation and gives lengthy vernacular digressions on legal topics that are often only distantly related to the verse cited.

The compilers based their recension of the Pāli sections of the *Manusāra* (*Manusāra-pāṭha*) on some preexisting *dhammasattha* text. At present we cannot say whether this earlier text was written in Pāli, Burmese, Mon, or some other language, although the introductory verses do mention a sixteenth-century Mon version that may have served as a prototype. Nor is the extent of the compilers' editorial intervention in the shape of the Pāli text certain, although it would seem, from passages such as the one cited in this chapter, that if they had any disagreements with the legal content of the received text, these were registered only in the commentarial gloss. That is, they did not seek to alter the text or meaning of the *dhammasattha* as they inherited it.

The interlineated Burmese section of the *Manusāra* (*Manusāra-nissaya*), by contrast, was not a received text, but an original commentary written in 1651 by Manurāja, the tax-lord or "Eater" of Kuiṅḥ Village, and the monk Tipiṭakālaṅkāra, both of whom were clients of the royal court at Ava.[31]

[31] Lammerts, "Buddhism and Written Law," 334–56. Manurāja, Kuiṅḥ Cā and Tipiṭakālaṅkāra. 1651. *Manusāra-dhammasattha-pāṭha* and *-nissaya*. Mss = BL Add Or 12241; NL Taṅ 10.

The key passage in question from the *Manusāra-nissaya* commentary follows:

I cite the following verses [from the *Manusāra-pāṭha*] concerning the inheritance of monastic property and requisites (*parikkhāra*):

> Upon the death of the father of a *saṅgha*, a *mahāthera* takes the requisites of going forth, gifts, and offerings. ||
>
> Dividing his slaves and property into four shares, the *mahāthera* takes two. A *thera* of lesser rank takes one. Dividing the remainder into four shares, a newly ordained monk takes three. ||
>
> A novice takes one. A householder takes just the gift [given by the deceased]. If there are none of these, an equal takes the property, since a monk is not a relative of a householder. ||[32]

The vernacular meaning (*adhippāya*) of these verses is as follows:

> When a *mahāthera* who is a parent of a saṅgha dies, it is right that his eight monastic requisites (*parikkhāra*) – the upper robe, outer robe, girdle, lower robe, ladle, razor, bowl, and needle – his gardens and water-tanks, his donative offerings, food, and so forth, are inherited by the highest ranking *mahāthera* among his monastic disciples. If [the deceased] left any specie, slaves, or [other] property (*kyeḥ kyvan uccā*), after dividing it into four shares, it is right that the highest-ranking *mahāthera* among his disciples takes two. A lower-ranking *thera* [who was his disciple] should take one. After apportioning the remaining share into four shares, newly ordained monks (*pañjaṅ sac*), should take three. Novices are entitled to inherit [the remaining] one share. If there are any lay disciples, relatives, or supporters, they are entitled to only as much as has been delivered into their hands, equivalent to their acts of merit. If there are none of these four, then the [general community of] monks who are entitled to the inheritance should take it. Why is this? Because monks are not relatives of laypersons. Such is the law of the *dhammasat*.

However, the law of the *Vinaya* is as follows:

> When a *mahāthera* becomes unwell and is supported by his own disciples or other [monks], [his property after death] should be distributed among those monks in the place of his illness. In apportioning his property in this way the monks who gave support to the sick should receive an additional share. A novice should receive a half-share. Whosoever served as a supporter of the sick monk, whether a monk, novice, or layperson, is entitled to keep whatever they received in their hands [as a gift] from the dying, but only monks are allowed to inherit property that was not transferred [as a gift] before death. If there are any novices who supported the sick monk until

[32] I have omitted the bilingual *nissaya* portion of this passage.

> the very end, they are entitled to inherit only the eight requisites and half a share given to monks. If there are any laypersons who supported the sick monk, they are entitled to inherit a share of the eight requisites, and have no claim over any remaining requisites or property. Why is this? Because only other monks are regarded as relatives [of monks]. If upon death the requisites and property of a dead monk are deposited in another place, only the monks of that place are entitled to inherit.[33]

The *Manusāra-pāṭha* verses cited here by the *nissaya* offer us the earliest record of inheritance laws binding on monastics in Burma that do not parallel the Pāli *Vinaya* regulations. Their model is clearly the structure of succession within the lay family. A senior monk or *mahāthera* is styled as a "father" to members of his monastic community (*saṅghassa pitā*), and the partition of inheritance among his "sons" depends on their ranking. However, whereas the *dhammasattha* system of lay inheritance ranks children for succession purposes according to gender, primogeniture, and legitimacy (as in Brāhmaṇical *dharmaśāstra*), monks are ranked according to their standing as either *mahāthera*, *thera*, *navabhikkhu*, or *sāmaṇera*, institutional titles determined by how many years one has been a member of the saṅgha.[34] The commentators' interpretive gloss of the verses clearly admits the ownership by monks of money, a form of property deemed illicit by the *Vinaya*. In contrast to both *Sirīsaṅghapāla* and *Dhammavilāsa* discussed earlier, the *Manusāra-pāṭha* account excludes the laity from having any possible share in monastic inheritance, even in cases where a layperson may have acted as a supporter of the dying monk. In this regard the *dhammasattha* prescribes even stronger rules against the lay inheritance of monastic property than does the *Vinaya*. Laypersons are entitled only to property that has been given to them by the deceased monk during his lifetime.

In the *adhippāya* section of *Manusāra-nissaya*, the Eater of Kuiṅḥ and the monk Tipiṭakālaṅkāra announce that the *dhammasattha* regulations concerning monastic inheritance in the *pāṭha* text are not in agreement with the *Vinaya*. The content of their reference to *Vinaya* law suggests their familiarity with either the *Vinaya-mahāvagga* itself, or with one or more Mahāvihārin commentaries or handbooks on the canonical *Discourse on the Property of the Dead*. The only stipulation mentioned here that cannot be traced directly to the *Mahāvagga* or the commentaries is that which says novices who have attended a dying monk are entitled to only half a

[33] Manurāja and Tipiṭakālaṅkāra, BL Add Or.12241, ff.cai(v)-cau(r); NL Taṅ 10 ff.ṅe(v)-ṅai(v).

[34] Oskar von Hinüber, "Old Age and Old Monks in Pāli Buddhism" in S. Formanek and S. Linhart (eds.), *Aging: Asian Concepts and Experiences Past and Present* (Vienna: Austrian Academy of Sciences, 1997), 65–78.

monk's share.[35] The fact that this conflict is made explicit signifies an awareness in mid-seventeenth century Burma that certain texts of the inherited *dhammasattha* tradition contained rules that were incommensurable with perceptions of *Vinaya* legal orthodoxy. It is reasonable that Tipiṭakālaṅkāra would have been the one to point out this discrepancy. Several years prior, this monk had compiled the *Vinayālaṅkāraṭīkā*, a normative Mahāvihārin sub-commentary on the *Vinayasaṅgaha*, the twelfth-century *Vinaya* commentary written in Sri Lanka at the request of Parākramabāhu I.

Vinaya and *Dhammasattha* in Conflict

As the examples above demonstrate, monastic law during the seventeenth century was anything but simply commensurate with the dicta of the Pāli *Vinaya*. Nor was the relative jurisdiction of *Vinaya*- or *dhammasattha*-derived laws uniformly articulated by the various materials we have surveyed. Rather, there was a considerable amount of variation in ideas about the authoritative textual sources of monastic law and the separation of distinct lay and monastic jurisdictions. While Sirīsaṅghapāla clearly bases his understanding of monastic inheritance law on the canonical *Discourse on the Property of the Dead*, he nonetheless admits that mundane law – *lokavat* or *dhammasattha* – comprises a legitimate legal corpus that has jurisdiction over the saṅgha in cases not explicitly addressed by the *Vinaya*, such as the inheritance of monastic slaves. *Dhammavilāsa* indicates that a rule seemingly derived from *Vinaya* could be mobilized to regulate lay inheritance outside the monastic context. *Manusāra-pāṭha* forbids lay succession of saṅgha property altogether, yet at the same time presents laws that are entirely unknown to the *Vinaya*, and instead appear to mirror the structure of inheritance within the lay family. The fact that the glossators of *Manusāra* note in their *nissaya* commentary that this rule differs from the canonical account of the *Discourse on the Property of the Dead* points toward a growing awareness during this period of the distance between the sources and jurisdiction of monastic law on the one hand and *dhammasattha* discourse on the other.

This situation of jurisdictional and textual intermingling concerning the partition of monastic property did not persist for long. As Lingat observed, later *dhammasattha* treatises written during the eighteenth and nineteenth centuries, "strictly condemn the old customary rules and prescribe only the

[35] On the *samaka* and *jeṭṭhaka* shares of a novice, cf. Vin I, 305; Sp, 1134; Pālim, 247.

application of canonical rules" in their discussion of monastic inheritance.[36] The most prolific jurisprude of the Konbaung era, Vaṇṇadhamma Kyau Thaṅ, who was responsible for redacting the *Manusāra* and other earlier treatises in versions that became the most widely circulated and influential legal texts in late precolonial Burma, offers lengthy verbatim citations from the Pāli *Vinaya-mahāvagga* to press the point that "the ancient *dhammasats* are not in accordance with the *Vinaya*" on the issue. In his *Legal Judgments Explained* (*Vinicchaya-pakāsanī*) written in 1771, Vaṇṇadhamma begins his discussion of monastic inheritance by citing and glossing the verses of the *Manusāra-pāṭha* discussed earlier, but then cautions:

> Here we note that this is merely what is stated as the law in the mundane *dhammasattha* (*lokiya-nicchaya, loka-dhammasat*) texts, whereas now I shall make known the regulations of the *Vinaya* (*Vinaya-nicchaya*). In the *Vinaya* there is no trace of [the verses] beginning "*mate saṅghassa pitari*" ["upon the death of the father of the saṅgha"], which conflict with *Vinaya* law concerning the partition of monastic inheritance. The testimony of the *dhammasattha* texts *Manusāra*, *Mahārājasat*, and other mundane (*loki*) legal texts, is given here simply to avoid the criticism of having neglected ancient treatises (*cā hoṅḥ*) and traditions (*lamḥ hoṅḥ*). But monks have their own, proper law in the *Vinaya*, which is as follows. . . .[37]

Vaṇṇadhamma goes on to restate in a non-canonical Pāli verse the basic rule from the *Vinaya-mahāvagga*, which provides that the supporter of the sick (*gilānupaṭṭhāka*) may inherit the robes and bowl of the deceased, and then enters into a lengthy enumeration of the orthodox distinction between different types of light and heavy monastic property. He concludes his treatment by advising:

> This is what the texts of the Buddha's teaching (*sāsanā kyamḥ*) instruct regarding monastic inheritance. Extended analysis is given in the *Vinaya Piṭaka*. The ancient [law of] the partition of monastic inheritance [transmitted in the *dhammasattha* corpus] is at odds with these *Vinaya* regulations. For that reason I have purified the text. May my act of purification be cleansed by the clear water of wisdom.[38]

"Purifications" such as these were enjoined across Burmese legal culture during the eighteenth and nineteenth centuries. Throughout this period,

[36] Lingat, "Vinaya et droit laïque," 449, n. 1.
[37] Vaṇṇadhamma Kyau Thaṅ. 1771. *Vinicchaya-pakāsanī* [Legal Judgments Explained]. Mss = UCL 9831 f.che(r); UCL 6526 f.jhaṃ(r).
[38] Vaṇṇadhamma, UCL 6526, f.ññā(r); UCL 9831, ff.chai(r)-chau(v).

law texts and law ways perceived as deviating from normative and jurisprudential ideals represented in the Pāli *Tipiṭaka* and its Mahāvihārin commentaries were either rewritten or rejected. However, we would be wrong to characterize these developments as exclusively driven by royal or elite initiatives, or the motivations inspiring them as essentially uniform.[39] Following nearly three centuries of fragmentation after the decline of Pagan, the establishment of the Nyaungyan Dynasty in 1599 at Ava inaugurated an era of economic expansion and political and cultural consolidation in Upper Burma.[40] The conceptual and literary resources offered by the translocal Pāli imaginary[41] were central to this efflorescence and provided the vocabulary for not only its ritual and devotional expression, but also its social and political manifestation. The lay and monastic jurisprudes of early modern Burma participated in these developments through a hermeneutics of law drawn in increasing levels of scholastic sophistication from the Pāli canon and (especially) its commentaries. This is, of course, not to suggest that this literature arrived or became popular in Upper Burma only in the seventeenth century – the Pāli *Vinaya* as well as certain *Vinaya* commentaries were already transmitted in some form at Pagan.[42] Rather, the economic, political, and cultural changes during this period spurred the patronage of monastic and lay textual and interpretive work, and this corpus served as a vital means for elaborating and reimagining Buddhist visions of law and its relationship to scripture and society.

39 Lammerts, "Narratives of Buddhist Legislation," 141–42.

40 Victor Lieberman, *Strange Parallels: Southeast Asia in Global Context, c.800–1830* vol. 1 (New York: Cambridge University Press, 2003), 158–211.

41 Steven Collins, *Nirvana and Other Buddhist Felicities* (New York: Cambridge University Press, 1998).

42 Gordon H. Luce, "Mon Glosses in the Pahtothamya Temple," *Journal of the Burma Research Society* 18 (1975), 126–35; Than Tun (ed.), *Nhoṅḥ tve. kyok cā myāḥ* (recently discovered inscriptions) (Yangon: Myanmar Historical Commission, 2005), 21–25.

PART III

Buddhism and Law in East Asia

CHAPTER 11

Buddhism and Law in China
The Emergence of Distinctive Patterns in Chinese History

T.H. Barrett

> King Zhao of Wei, wishing to take part in the business of his bureaucrats, announced the fact to his chief minister Lord Mengchang. "If you wish to take part in the business of your bureaucrats' said Lord Mengchang, "why don't you try studying law?" By the time King Zhao had read about a dozen columns of law, he was asleep. The king said: "I can't study these laws!" Of course it's no wonder he fell asleep – not keeping a personal grip on the handles of power and wanting to do what his underlings should have done.[1]

This story about a king who ruled from 295–277 BCE is primarily designed to show the importance of delegation, but it also demonstrates that long before Buddhism reached China, expertise in law, already quite technical and forbidding, formed an indispensable part of the duties of a Chinese bureaucrat. Thus, even at this early stage, the Chinese theorized the nature of bureaucratic control and practiced administrative record keeping. At this point and for a couple of centuries or so after the unification of China by the First Emperor in 221 BCE, such records were written on hard materials such as slips of bamboo, but the invention of paper greatly extended the capacity of the Chinese to create written documentation. This did not prevent the first great period of empire from collapsing into an age of division and foreign invasion in much the same fashion as happened to the classical world of Europe. It did help sustain government from the late sixth century onward by a record-keeping bureaucracy into a new era of integration unparalleled in the West. This era also gave way to one of increasing devolution of power and even briefly complete political fragmentation in the tenth century, but bequeathed to future empires, whether run by Chinese or by invaders, the ability to use woodblock printing technology to multiply the already numerous copies of documents produced by the writing brush on paper. The first observers arriving from Renaissance

[1] Chen Qiyou, *Han Feizi jishi* (Hong Kong: Zhonghua shuju, 1974), 660.

Europe found China a society in which printing was more widespread than their own, although by now the voice of Buddhism had to compete much harder against what outsiders saw as dominant Confucian norms. Even when our sources add up to much less than would be ideal, the interaction of Buddhism and law in China may be traced throughout its historical development in the long term within a relatively detailed historical record. While the introduction of a detailed code expressed in writing in the form of the *Vinaya* might have profoundly affected places in Asia that only had unwritten customary law, in China, Buddhism encountered a continuous tradition of written law requiring specialist knowledge.

This was not because China lacked any knowledge of *Vinaya* rules – in fact, in due course, more versions of the *Vinaya* were translated into Chinese than survive in any other language.[2] But this corpus in its full form was not read outside China's monasteries, save perhaps by some of the monarchs who took seriously their duty to uphold its provisions within the Buddhist monastic orders, since the basic regulations of the *Prātimokṣa* restrict its study to pupils of an ordained master.[3] This communication barrier between religious and secular law means that we should not necessarily expect to see direct reflections of the former in the latter, nor assume Buddhist influence unless it can be demonstrated. Some seemingly Buddhist traditions of clemency within Chinese legal history, for example, are in fact older than Buddhism and eventually withered under regimes more Buddhist than Chinese.[4]

One legal consequence of Buddhism's self-defined religious tradition and a full-time clergy was the appearance of very clear legal provisions in secular government that permitted senior clergy to govern themselves in accordance with their own communal regulations. These provisions were the outcome of a chaotic phase in north China during the early centuries of Buddhism, when new invaders looked to the Buddhist monasteries as surrogates in providing leadership and especially control of labor in local society when they failed to secure the loyalty of Chinese administrators. The monasteries devised codes of conduct for lay people under their control, but were subject to the oversight of and direction from the central

[2] Anne Heirman, "*Vinaya* from India to China," in Anne Heirman and Stephan Peter Bumbacher (eds.), *The Spread of Buddhism* (Leiden and Boston: Brill, 2007), 167–202.

[3] Werner Pachow, *A Comparative Study of the Pratimokṣa on the Basis of its Chinese, Tibetan, Sanskrit and Pāli Versions* (Delhi: Motilal Banarsidass, 2000), 114, vol.6. (27): not all versions are explicit, but Chinese monastic tradition is unambiguous (39).

[4] Brian E. McKnight, *The Quality of Mercy: Amnesties and Traditional Chinese Justice* (Honolulu: University of Hawai'i Press, 1981).

government.[5] Under Chinese rule, the arrival of the Buddhist *saṅgha,* a form of perpetual voluntary corporation unprecedented in East Asian civilization, prompted the codification of regulations designed to control its affairs from the political center. It did not result from any respect for the established South Asian precedents granting substantive internal autonomy to the Buddhist order. Monastic control of laypeople vanished in due course, although not before a clergy that shielded its own rules from public scrutiny turned to other sources of authority – including sources of its own devising – to carry out this task. Control of the clergy by laypeople turned out by contrast to be an abiding reality in Chinese religious life, affecting Daoism also. This long tradition (more than a millennium and a half) of state control of religion remains an important aspect of relations between the state and religious groups in the Chinese world to this day.

Far from bringing major new elements of its own to Chinese law, Buddhism absorbed into its imagery and religious thought legal procedures and concepts of indigenous origin, since in early China, an indigenous tradition of jurisprudence was not only well established, but also informed the religious imagination of the broader population. It is not simply that Imperial China inherited a tradition of criminal law with the unification of China by the First Emperor; some have speculated that even in pre-imperial times the world of the spirits was already conceptualized as one dominated by an unseen empire of bureaucrats as well.[6] Even if some scholars dispute this early date, recently recovered manuscript materials of the first century CE attest to the incorporation of legal terminology in the operations of this unseen empire.[7] In the second century CE, when Buddhist translations began to be made in China, the breakdown of law and order in the visible world caused by the weakening of the central control of the Han Dynasty (206 BCE–220 CE) seems to have had repercussions for human attitudes

[5] For the role for monasteries after the turn away from earlier Chinese administrative norms, see, Xinru Liu, *Ancient India and Ancient China* (Delhi: Oxford University Press, 1988), 139–73; for the role of monasteries in directing labor and the long-term consequences for monastic landholding, see also Jacques Gernet, *Buddhism in Chinese Society*, Franciscus Verellen (trans.) (New York: Columbia University Press, 1995), 94–141 and the review of his work by D.C. Twitchett, "The Monasteries and China's Economy in Medieval Times," *Bulletin of the School of Oriental and African Studies* 19.3 (1957), 526–49, especially 542 for some further references on law.

[6] For an introduction to law in early China from a comparative perspective, see Karen Turner, "Sage Kings and Laws in the Chinese and Greek Traditions" in Paul S. Ropp (ed.), *Heritage of China: Contemporary Perspectives on Chinese Civilization* (Berkeley, Los Angeles, and Oxford: University of California Press, 1990), 86–111. For a summary of the legacy passed on to the imperial age, see Michael Loewe and Edward L. Shaughnessy, *Cambridge History of Ancient China* (Cambridge: Cambridge University Press, 1999), 1003–10.

[7] See Donald Harper, "Contracts with the Spirit World in Han Common Religion: The Xuning Prayer and Sacrifice Documents of A. D. 79," *Cahiers d'Extrême-Asie* 14 (2004), 227–67.

to the world unseen, as priests who presented documents to the powers in the realm of the spirits emerged to take on administrative functions in the visible world also.[8] This development certainly had very important consequences for the emergence of organized groups ancestral to the Daoist church of later times, which preserved materials attributed to the end of the Han that described the lenient legal system imposed on small rustic communities in West China by their priests. Secular historical records note that these autonomous adherents of a new dispensation incorporated the language of the Han scale of penalties, but rejected the harsh penalties of the floundering Han regime by calibrating them to much more humane values, substituting community service for corporal punishment.[9]

We know that these cultists were not the only ones to abandon the laws of the dynasty in favor of alternative and apparently religious codes at this time.[10] Frustratingly, however, information is too sparse for us to see how Buddhism fit into this environment. One of the earliest references to Buddhism, from about 100 CE, comments on the near imperviousness of Buddhist *śramaṇas* to the pulchritude of the emperor's harem, suggesting that from the earliest times the Chinese may have been aware that Buddhist monks were subject to some form of disciplinary code of their own. Or, it may reflect that Chinese saw Buddhist clerical celibacy simply as a bizarre and pointless custom.[11]

The frequent translation during this early period of the Buddhist term *dharma* by the Chinese *fa*, signifying – among other things – a legal norm, also suggested a strong link between Buddhism and law. More cumbersome translations attempted to clarify the possible confusion.[12] It is certainly clear that the Buddhist usage of this Indian term, which suggested a legal sense, gave rise to problems elsewhere that demanded radical solutions from translators. The popular Sogdian translation *nom* (from Greek *nomos*) was eschewed in clerical circles in favor of a transliteration, although the

[8] T.H. Barrett, "Religious Change under the Han and its Successors" in Michael Loewe and Michael Nylan (eds.), *China's Early Empires* (Cambridge: Cambridge University Press, 2009).

[9] For the fullest collection of the surviving depictions of these autonomous communities, see Ōfuchi Ninji, *Shoki no Dōkyō* (Tokyo: Sōbunsha, 1991), 156 and 367–406. For the lenient reputation of this group in secular history, see Lu Bu, *Sanguo zhi jijie* (Beijing: Zhonghus Shuju, 1982), 267–68.44a-b. For the identical terminology but harsher penalties of Han law, see A.F.P. Hulsewé, *Remnants of Han Law* (Leiden: E. J. Brill, 1955) vol. I, 80,124–28.

[10] See Barrett, "Religious Change," 438.

[11] E. Zürcher, *The Buddhist Conquest of China* (Leiden: E. J. Brill, 1958), 29.

[12] On the disyllabic early translation of the term *dharma*, see Tilmann Vetter and Stefano Zacchetti, "On *Jingfa* in Early Chinese Buddhist Translations," *Annual Report of the International Research Institute for Advanced Buddhology at Soka University* 7 (2004), 159–66.

former term had the greater influence over time.[13] Whatever the initial reactions may have been, the evolution of *fa* in Chinese religious usage exhibits no clear link with law in the longer run; the Buddhist title *fashi* or "dharma-master" (as opposed to a specialist in meditation, *chanshi,* or a *Vinaya*-master, *lüshi*) in Daoist circles means something rather different, but ends up as the term for a ritual master commanding various methods of dealing with the supernatural, not an expertise in codified regulations of any sort.[14]

Initially the *Vinaya* was not rendered into Chinese in any written form, but carried as oral literature in the capacious memories of foreign monks. The first secular reference to its existence might be the demand of a southern ruler following the Han, Sun Hao (r. 264–84 CE), to see a monastic code in writing; this was refused, suggesting the operation of the restriction mentioned earlier limiting study of the *Prātimokṣa* to pupils of an ordained master.[15] Nevertheless, it is quite clear from references in other types of earlier Buddhist translated texts, such as the sutras, that local believers knew a fair amount about its characteristics.[16] The effective initial autonomy of the Buddhist community probably had no legal implications for the government at first. The assumption is that Buddhism came to China in association with foreign traders, and it was, after all, a long tradition of allowing autonomy (or rather, devolved responsibility) to foreign merchant communities that eventually gave rise to the modern phenomenon of extraterritoriality.[17] Until the mid-third century CE, Chinese believers were apparently forbidden ordination as monks; ultimate bureaucratic responsibility for Buddhist monks would, therefore, have in all likelihood remained with the organ of government charged with the oversight of foreign relations.[18]

[13] See 110–11 of Xavier Tremblay, "The Spread of Buddhism in Serindia" in Heirman and Bumbacher (eds.), *Spread of Buddhism,* 75–129, and cf. Johannes Elverskog, *Buddhism and Islam on the Silk Road* (Philadelphia: University of Pennsylvania Press, 2010), 137, 295 n. 53.

[14] Edward L. Davis, *Society and the Supernatural in Song China* (Honolulu: University of Hawai'i Press, 2001), 7, 30.

[15] Huijiao, *Gaoseng zhuan,* 1, 326a12–14. At this point, even the ruler is denied access, but since one of the functions of the ideal Buddhist ruler is to monitor the upholding of the *Vinaya,* this extreme position seems to have been tempered.

[16] For a passage in translation that has a Chinese version mentioning (as "laws," *lü*) the *Vinaya* before the end of the second century, see Jan Nattier, *A Few Good Men: The Bodhisattva Path according to the Inquiry of Ugra (Ugrapari pṛcchā)* (Honolulu: University of Hawai'i Press, 2003), 274.

[17] Joseph Fletcher in J.K. Fairbank (ed.), *The Cambridge History of China,* vol. 10, part 1 (Cambridge: Cambridge University Press, 1978), 378.

[18] The prohibition on ordinations is referred to in later sources, although its historicity is not beyond question; see Arthur F. Wright, *Studies in Chinese Buddhism* (New Haven and London: Yale University Press, 1990), 58, 141. Although we have no details confirming bureaucratic responsibility

Mass conversion to Buddhism in the fourth century certainly made this system difficult to maintain, and indeed, over the course of time, regimes in both the northern and southern portions of the divided Chinese world came to a new rapprochement with organized religion in order to bolster their now much less certain legitimacy. It is a stark and simple fact that we know much more about religion than law during the long period until the reunification of China in the late sixth century. Even in the south, where Chinese regimes maintained themselves until this political reintegration, it would seem that legal scholarship had to rely on transmission from memory at one stage, owing to the incomplete state of the manuscript tradition, while for at least a century in the north, the non-Chinese invaders do not appear to have developed the legal aspects of their rule at all.[19] However, one concomitant affecting both Buddhism and its newly coherent Chinese counterpart, Daoism, was that participation in the exercise of imperial government could only be granted to religious organizations capable of guaranteeing their own good order.

In the Buddhist case, this seems to have prompted both the undertaking of full *Vinaya* translations and also the nomination of monks to govern their own disciples as well as the Buddhist community as a whole. The former process resulted in the early fifth century in the production of no less than four written versions of the complete *Vinaya* in China at a time when it was still commonly orally transmitted in South Asia; the latter saw the imposition of state control of the saṅgha in China that had no precedents in the decentralized and autonomous monasteries of the rest of the contemporary Buddhist world.[20] Such was the compromise between religion and the state at this time. Recognition of the legality of well-conducted religions might be granted – although, as we shall see, it might also be revoked – but in return, the authority of the state, and its right to regulate, had to be acknowledged. For this reason Buddhism in East Asia, which followed the Chinese model, has had a somewhat different political complexion from Buddhism elsewhere.

for foreign monks, for an interesting linguistic link between the Han "Department of Foreign Relations" and Buddhism, see Zürcher, *Buddhist Conquest*, 39–40.

[19] These observations are based on the dynastic histories: *Sui shu* 20 (Beijing: Zhonghua shuju, 1973), 697; *Wei shu* 111 (Beijing: Zhonghua shuju, 1974), 2873. What we do know of legal history during this period is incorporated in the study of E. Balazs, *Le traite juridique du "Souei-Chou,"* (Leiden, Brill, 1954) – for the first passage cited here in translation, see 34, 103–05 (*sic*) n. 41.

[20] For the translations, two in the north and two in the south, see Satō Tatsugen, *Chūgoku ni okeru kairitsu no kenkyū* (Tokyo: Mokujisha, 1986), 12. For the origins of centrally appointed monk-officials, see Xie Chongguang and Bai Wengu, *Zhongguo sengguan zhidu shi* (Xining: Qinghai renmin chubanshe, 1990), 10–16; Wang Yonghui, *Zhongguo fojiao sengduan fazhan ji qi guanli yanjiu* (Chengdu: Bashu shushe, 2003), 48–53.

The early Northern Wei Dynasty (386–534 CE), founded by the Tuoba people, was among the first regimes to exercise a specialist form of control over the Buddhist religion by appointing a monk overseer. Later rulers of this dynasty, after a subsequent attempt at suppressing Buddhism in favor of a state-controlled Daoism, returned to lavish patronage of Buddhism in the second half of the fifth century, combined with the introduction of increasingly complex and detailed measures to assert legal control over the Buddhist community.[21] As a result of the administrative vacuum in North China in the fourth century, rulers delegated administrative control of portions of local society to Buddhists and other religious groups, but this expedient fell far short of granting what we would see as autonomy. As the ruling group progressively gained administrative confidence, the responsibility of the government-appointed monk-officials to the secular authorities was stringently enforced. Indeed, from the dynasty's point of view, the more stringently this control was imposed, the better.

The boundaries between secular and religious authority and their responsibilities shifted in each new period, often becoming interwoven and interdependent. This included changes in actual sites for decision-making about the saṅgha, different agents and institutions, and the use and development of various regulations and law codes. For example, a defunct specialized government office from the Northern Wei Dynasty was resurrected to house a central administration for Buddhism. A decree of 508 CE shows that the responsibility for the administration of justice for the saṅgha was removed entirely from the regular bureaucracy, save for cases of murder, or worse.[22] This may seem to recall the benefit of clergy of medieval England, but a law code from 493 CE in forty-seven sections applied to the clergy *in addition to* their own canon law of the *Vinaya* suggests that the autonomy the saṅgha had enjoyed was in fact being progressively compromised.[23] A fragmentary manuscript apparently deriving from a mid-sixth century successor state, the Western Wei (534–50 CE), gives some indication of the stipulations of a new, even more stringent type of legislation. Although it frequently cites Buddhist texts and does not at first glance impose additional legal burdens, its very existence demonstrates that the state wanted to clarify the ultimate administrative subordination of all Buddhists to its rule, even if its power was exercised at this point through intermediaries who

[21] The classic scholarship on Northern Wei Buddhism is listed in Kenneth Ch'en, *Buddhism in China: A Historical Survey* (Princeton, NJ: Princeton University Press, 1964), 518–20; for one important recent study, see n. 23.

[22] *Wei shu* 114, 3040.

[23] *Wei shu* 114, 3039; Moroto Tatsuo, *Chūgoku Bukkyō seidoshi no kenkyū* (Tokyo: Hirakawa shuppansha, 1990), 59–60, suggests, however, that the contents were still at this point determined by monks.

were members of the clergy.[24] The first northern persecution of Buddhism in the mid-fifth century appears as an initial move to supplant Buddhism by recruiting Daoist forces in local society whose legal arrangements – even if they echoed the *Vinaya* – were easier to reconcile with a revival of Han legal institutions. The outright persecution of the late sixth century then makes sense as a move by the state to take over direct control of all parts of local society once more.[25]

It has long been recognized that the institutions of China's next great unified dynasty, the Tang (618–907 CE), derived ultimately from the Northern Wei, and that the success of the Tang further set a legal pattern for other states in East Asia. The legal provisions controlling Buddhism during this epoch are reflected in contemporaneous Japanese legislation, which allows a partial reconstruction of the Tang regulations for the Buddhist and Daoist clergies, the *Daosengge*, although many issues relating to the registration and taxation of monks remain imperfectly understood.[26] The Japanese *Sōniryō* from which our information derives are not, however, "regulations" but "statutes"; that is, more basic provisions of law as codified in Japan, rather than supplementary to the main code.[27] This heightened legal importance reflects the much more destabilizing presence of Buddhist clergy in Japan, a country rapidly developing under continental influences. As a consequence, reconstituting the Chinese regulations from Japanese sources is not a straightforward matter.[28] One element clearly present in the surviving portions of the *Daosengge* that does not derive from the *Vinaya* is an injunction that monks (and Daoist priests) should abstain not simply from alcohol, but also from meat. This prohibition was strongly supported by a number of Mahāyāna texts that had a major impact in China, even if edicts attempting to spread the observance of vegetarianism to the

[24] Moroto, *Chūgoku Bukkyō seidoshi*, 53–107, covers the fragmentary manuscript and its historical environment.

[25] Richard B. Mather, "K'ou Ch'ien-chih and the Taoist Theocracy at the Northern Wei Court, 425–451" in Holmes Welch and Anna Seidel (eds.), *Facets of Taoism* (New Haven, CT: Yale University Press, 1979), 103–22, especially 113; Whalen W. Lai, "The Earliest Folk Buddhist Religion in China" in David W. Chappell (ed.), *Buddhist and Taoist Practice in Medieval Chinese Society* (Honolulu: University of Hawai'i Press, 1987), 11–35, especially 32.

[26] Moroto, *Chūgoku Bukkyō seidoshi*, is essentially a lengthy review of our knowledge of the *Daoseng ge* (8–213); the remainder of his book concerns aspects of state control of the clergy not covered by these regulations.

[27] This terminology is from Denis Twitchett (ed.), *The Cambridge History of China, Volume 3: Sui and Tang China, 589–906*, Part I (Cambridge: Cambridge University Press, 1979), 207, passim.

[28] For the case of the Japanese Buddhist leader Gyōki, see Jonathan Morris Augustine, *Buddhist Hagiography in Early Japan: Images of Compassion in the Gyōki Tradition* (Abingdon: Routledge Curzon, 2005), 45–62, especially 52–55.

populace from the sixth century on had limited results.[29] The Western Wei manuscript further shows that influences on the regulations also derived from apocryphal texts, which are scriptures apparently composed under Chinese cultural influence. These indigenously composed texts tend to express more strongly the Chinese norms of state control over the clergy than those contained in genuine translations from South Asian languages, although counterexamples can also be found.[30]

One of these counterexamples dates to a period in the late eighth century when China's emperors, while still loyal to the Daoist ideological priorities of their forefathers, looked to Buddhism for added ideological support at a time of dynastic weakness. These emperors also showed an active interest in sponsoring discussions among monks on authoritative *Vinaya* interpretation.[31] This may mean that later during the early 840s, when a viciously atavistic reaction in favor of Daoism set in, the emperor of the day may have known that many legal stipulations ostensibly of Buddhist derivation had no *Vinaya* authority. At this point, at any rate, when the bans on taking human and animal life at certain times of the year and on certain days of the month, which were of Buddhist origin, were cancelled in favor of more circumscribed Daoist observances, it turns out that those practices were probably based on texts composed in China, such as *Tiwei boli jing*. This was precisely one of the main scriptures apparently created to provide a code of regulations for laypersons under saṅgha control.[32] As the legal and economic position of Buddhism was eroded, and as new forms of synthesis between Buddhist norms and Chinese values emerged, the *Tiwei boli jing* ceased to be transmitted, even though it remained important to Buddhist scholars into the ninth century.[33]

In its place, new apocryphal scriptures came to the fore in response to new developments, and as always they showed themselves more flexible

[29] For a review of this topic, see John Kieschnick, "Buddhist Vegetarianism in China" in Roel Sterckx (ed.), *Of Tripod and Palate: Food, Politics, and Religion in Traditional China* (Basingstoke: Palgrave Macmillan, 2005), 186–212.

[30] Cf. Moroto, *Chūgoku Bukkyō seidoshi,* 78; Arthur F. Wright, "T'ang T'ai-tsung and Buddhism" in Arthur F. Wright and Denis Twitchett (eds.), *Perspectives on the T'ang* (New Haven and London: Yale University Press, 1973), 239–63, especially 261–26; but cf. also Moroto, *ibid.*, 72–73; Charles D. Orzech, *Politics and Transcendent Wisdom* (University Park: Pennsylvania State University Press, 1998), 287–88.

[31] See Stanley Weinstein, *Buddhism under the T'ang* (Cambridge: Cambridge University Press, 1987), 86–88, 97.

[32] This is the suggestion of Weinstein, *Buddhism under the T'ang,* 122–23, 189 n. 25, 195n.56 and n.58.

[33] Peter N. Gregory, "The Teaching of Men and Gods: The Doctrinal Basis of Lay Buddhist Practice in the Hua-yen Tradition" in Robert M. Gimello and Peter N. Gregory (eds.), *Studies in Ch'an and Hua-yen* (Honolulu: University of Hawai'i Press, 1983), 253–319.

than genuinely translated texts in their accommodation with the Chinese situation. These scriptures demonstrate that the indigenous legal culture that had always formed an important feature of Daoist conceptions of the unseen world, in which litigation was one of the chief delights of the deceased, merged with imported Indian depictions of the sufferings of hell, to produce a spirit world where the corporal punishment that formed a routine part of Chinese justice loomed much larger in death than in life.[34] This quasi-legal way of conceptualizing the afterlife as a potential scene of judicial horror ameliorated by the redemptive possibilities offered by Buddhism became over the long term – and indeed still is – a prominent aspect of Chinese popular belief, as has been most recently demonstrated by Paul Katz.[35] The full history of this long process of development is as yet obscure, but we do know that tales of near-death experiences circulated by Buddhist propagandists routinely depict the coming judgment after death in legal terms from the seventh century onward.[36] Although some canonical translations of the eighth century from Indian sources were clearly modified to present Lord Yama, the Indian Buddhist King of Hell, in Chinese terms as a judge of the dead, the popular and often illustrated apocryphal scriptures most conspicuously embodying Chinese legal terminology in a Buddhist context have been generally excluded from the official canon – not that this hindered their widespread dissemination.[37] No doubt it was the perceived omnipresence of law in both the visible and the invisible realms that gave rise to the legal terminology that eventually was to emerge in Chan (Zen) Buddhism, in which the key term *gong'an* (or *kōan* in Japanese) literally means the documentation used in a court of law; it is possible that the beatings handed out by masters to their students should be construed as judicial punishments also.[38]

[34] For the Daoist conception of the toils of post mortem litigation, see Stephen R. Bokenkamp, *Ancestors and Anxiety: Daoism and the Birth of Rebirth in China* (Berkeley: University of California Press, 2007), 130.

[35] Paul R. Katz, *Divine Justice: Religion and the Development of Chinese Legal Culture* (Abingdon: Routledge, 2009), 40–42.

[36] Frederick Chen, "The Transformation of Concepts of Bureaucratization of the Other World in Early Medieval China from Buddhist Perspectives," unpublished Ph.D. dissertation, St. Cross College, Oxford, (2009); for the miracle tales, see e.g., Valerie Hansen, *Negotiating Daily Life in Traditional China: How Ordinary People Used Contracts 600–1400* (New Haven and London: Yale University Press, 1995), 192–94.

[37] For Yama in Tang translations, see Osabe Kazuo, *Tō-Sō Mikkyō shi ronkō* (Kyoto: Nagata Bunshōdō, 1982), 34–64; for the Ten Kings and legal terminology, see Stephen F. Teiser, *The Scripture on the Ten Kings and the Making of Purgatory in Medieval Chinese Buddhism* (Honolulu: University of Hawai'i Press, 1994), 168.

[38] For the meaning of *gong'an*, see T. Griffith Foulk, "The Form and Function of *Koan* Literature: An Overview" in Steven Heine and Dale S. Wright (eds.), *The Kōan: Texts and Contexts in Zen Buddhism*

The assumption by Zen masters of symbolic judicial powers dates to the tenth century, following the collapse of Tang rule and the spectacular fragmentation of Chinese political power, which resembles the conditions linked to the ascendancy of groups with expertise in the laws of the spirit world in the late Han period. The shouting Zen master may have been no more than the reverse side of the total chaos of the times, which were so out of joint that in one petty kingdom, a Buddhist monk was briefly raised to the position of puppet emperor, perhaps another indication of the temporary bankruptcy of normal political symbolism.[39] In Daoism, too, we may also arguably find an assertion of spiritual power appearing at this time within a vacuum in temporal authority.[40]

The waning of Tang authority, however, is a somewhat complex topic, since following a major rebellion in the mid-eighth century, the dynasty was obliged to resort to methods of control less direct than the uniform centralized bureaucracy that had marked the first half of its existence. Responsibility for the Buddhist clergy, for example, was devolved to special lay commissioners, although monk-officials were also eventually appointed as their subordinates. After struggling to regain more central control over their empire, the Tang supported Daoism to the extent that they even initiated in 845 CE a complete proscription of all but 49 Buddhist institutions and the laicization of all but 800 of China's Buddhist clergy. This proscription was so widely enforced as to inflict untold damage, even though its measures were soon reversed with the accession of a new emperor in the following year.[41] During the early years of the ninth century, as the government was attempting to reassert its grip, its laws controlling Buddhism were at times flagrantly disobeyed by local power holders; in one case, ordination certificates, which granted immunity from normal taxation, were sold to unqualified laymen arriving at a famous pilgrimage center in massive quantities.[42]

The following centuries of imperial rule are much better documented, thanks to the introduction of printing, making the details of the

(New York: Oxford University Press, 2000), 15–45, especially 18. I am indebted to Robert Sharf for the suggestion about beatings. Despite these examples, the legal terminology of the *Scripture on the Ten Kings* does not seem to be prominent in Chan texts.

39 Edward H. Schafer, *The Empire of Min: A South China Kingdom of the Tenth Century* (Rutland: Charles E. Tuttle, 1954), 58–59, 95.

40 T.H. Barrett, "The Emergence of the Taoist Papacy in the T'ang Dynasty," *Asia Major*, Third Series, 7.1, (1994 – distributed 1996), 89–106, especially 105.

41 Stanley Weinstein, *Buddhism under the T'ang*, 85–9, 100–01, 114–44.

42 T.H. Barrett, "Buddhist Precepts in a Lawless World," in William M. Bodiford (ed.), *Going Forth: Visions of Buddhist Vinaya* (Honolulu: University of Hawai'i Press, 2005), 101–23.

relationship between Buddhism and law more apparent. The polities that emerged from the chaos of the early tenth-century Chinese world reverted to the earlier norms of limited state recognition of Buddhism combined with extensive efforts at control, even in the case of regimes such as the Tangut Empire of the Xi Xia in northwest China that made considerable ideological use of Buddhist symbolism.[43] Under the Song Dynasty (960–1279 CE), the internal administration of monasteries fell partly within the scope of secular law. Song Dynasty monasteries were divided between "hereditary" establishments, in which an abbot could pass down the institution to his disciples as spiritual heirs, and "public" monasteries, in which succession to the abbacy required at least government approval, or else more straightforwardly government appointment. Both types of succession were subject to detailed state regulations.[44]

The importance of these regulations may furthermore be gauged by their incorporation into the internal regulations of monasteries. Rules of conduct for Chinese monasteries serving as supplements to the *Vinaya* may be traced a long way back in China, to before the translation of the main *Vinaya* texts themselves. They were either preserved as very concise lists, or else were scattered throughout commentary on the *Vinaya* – where they often incorporated Mahāyāna developments such as vegetarianism – and so were not separately codified.[45] The great Chan (Zen) masters of the Song, however, looked back to a Tang predecessor, Baizhang Huihai (749–814 CE), as having introduced a new code suitable for the innovative movement to which they adhered. The existence of Baizhang's code itself is a myth, which seems to have come into existence upon his death in 814, when his disciples drew up a brief list of five regulations for their own community, in a fashion not unparalleled among similar groups at the time.[46] But this myth legitimated the publication under the Song of extensive monastic codes wherein earlier precedents of this sort – *Vinaya* stipulations, Chinese ritual observances, and state regulations – were all

[43] Evgenii Ivanovich Kychanov, "Buddhism and State in Hsi Hsia from Juridical Aspect," *Acta Orientalia Hungarica* 34.1–3 (1980), 105–11.

[44] Summarized in Morten Schlütter, *How Zen Became Zen: The Dispute Over Enlightenment and the Formation of Chan Buddhism in Song Dynasty China* (Honolulu: University of Hawai'i Press, 2008), 36–41.

[45] Yifa, *The Origins of Buddhist Monastic Codes in China* (Honolulu: University of Hawai'i Press, 2002), 8–28.

[46] In this I follow not Yifa, *Origins of Buddhist Monastic Codes*, 28–35, but Jinhua Jia, *The Hongzhou School of Chan Buddhism* (Albany: State University of New York Press, 2006), 96–101.

brought together into one compendium, often in printed form.[47] Thus, a Song text of this type dating to about 1100 CE survives in no less than six Japanese printed editions, thanks to the adoption of the Chan monastic system in medieval Japan and the consequent demand there for models of monastic organization and conduct.[48]

The overlap in compendia of this sort between the regulations of the state and the rules of conduct drawn up by members of the Buddhist clergy themselves resulted in the publication of a Chan monastic code compiled between 1335 and 1338 by imperial decree under the Mongol Yuan Dynasty (1272–1368 CE).[49] The Mongol period was, however, a somewhat anomalous one in terms of the relationship between Buddhism and the law. The Mongols were happy to rule China without a statutory legal code for years, which sometimes allowed Muslims, for example, to settle disputes according to their own laws.[50] In the case of their Buddhist subjects in China, however, administrative control was centralized in a Mongol imperial government office that also was responsible for Tibet and was headed by a Tibetan cleric.[51] This dignitary, whose office seems to have derived from one in the Tangut state, was also preceptor to the Mongol emperor.[52] As a result, unlike earlier or later Chinese monk-officials, he therefore had a freedom of action quite anomalous in terms of Chinese legal arrangements. It is not surprising that although the arrangement was revived in the Tibetan and Mongol world in the person of the Dalai Lama – a person of some importance to the Manchu emperors – such an innovation did not commend itself to the Chinese themselves.[53]

[47] Yifa, *Origins of Buddhist Monastic Codes,* 53–98, details the origins of assorted elements in one such text, which she translates in full in the second half of her study. As she also shows on 35–37 and 50–52, Chan Buddhists were not the only ones to draw up guidelines for monastic life under the Song and later, but they had the greatest impact, especially overseas; see the next note.

[48] *Ibid.*, 108, cf. 38–43. [49] *Ibid.*, 48–49.

[50] Bettine Birge, "Sources of Law in Mongol-Yuan China (1260–1368): Adjudication in the Absence of a Legal Code" in Denise Aigle, Isabelle Charleux, Vincent Goossaert, and Roberte Hamayon (eds.), *Miscellanea Asiatica: Mélangesen l'honneur de Françoise Aubin/ Festschrift in Honour of Françoise Aubin* (Sankt Augustin: Institut Monumenta Serica, 2010), 387–406, especially 391.

[51] This matter is disputed in China today; cf. the remarks of Eliot Sperling in Anne-Marie Blondeau and Katia Buffetrille, *Authenticating Tibet: Answers to China's 100 Questions* (Berkeley: University of California Press, 2008), 14–16.

[52] The case is made in Ruth Dunnell, "The Hsia Origins of the Yüan Institution of Imperial Preceptor," *Asia Major* 5.1 (1992), 85–111.

[53] For the revival, see Veronika Veit, "The Eastern Steppe: Mongol Regimes after the Yuan (1368–1636)" in Nicola Di Cosmo, Allen J. Frank, and Peter B. Golden (eds.), *The Cambridge History of Inner Asia: The Chinggisid Age* (Cambridge: Cambridge University Press, 2009), 157–81, especially 170–71. For a Manchu clarification of their "Chinese" position on the relationship, see Li Hongzhi, *China Falungong*, rev. ed. (Hong Kong: Falun Fo Fa Publishing Co., 1998).

In fact, the Mongols, who frequently employed outsiders with no ties to the local population as their subordinate officials, delegated the actual administration of local religious affairs in China not to Chinese bureaucrats or even Chinese monks, but to Tibetan clerics, who were also responsible under the imperial preceptor for the administration of their homeland. According to Chinese accounts, this innovation was not a success: clashes between Chinese administrators and Tibetan clerics over matters such as the pardoning of prisoners were not uncommon, for example.[54] Chinese sources depict these ecclesiastics not simply as criminal (which some indubitably were in financial terms), but also in one case utterly debauched, although this may reflect a misunderstanding of Tibetan tantric or other practices unfamiliar to the Chinese.[55]

The restored Chinese rule of the Ming Dynasty (1368–1644 CE) at first continued to employ some foreign monks in nominal fashion as monk-officials, but the administrative arrangements covering religion soon reverted once more to Chinese norms.[56] It actually took a little time for the precise policies of imperial control over Buddhism to reach their eventual form.[57] The principles now governing this relationship were once again clear: even though the Manchus had dealings with the Dalai Lama, the Qianlong Emperor (r. 1736–96 CE) explicitly rejected the Mongol imperial model in which "decrees given by the Teacher of the Emperor had the same force as decrees emanating from the court," and went on at some length to explain how he had authority even over living Buddhas.[58]

The Ming and its successor, the Manchu Qing Dynasty (1644–1911), were the only imperial dynasties well known to Europeans, many of whom arrived in China to promote Christian missionary work. The relationship

[54] Herbert Franke, "Tibetans in Yüan China" in John D. Langlois (ed.), *China under Mongol Rule* (Princeton, NJ: Princeton University Press, 1981), 316.

[55] *Ibid.*, 318–19; see the erudite study of Hirosato Iwai distinguishing between Asian custom of the day and *ius primae noctis,* "The Buddhist Priest and the Ceremony of Attaining Womanhood During the Yüan Dynasty," *Memoirs of the Research Department of the Toyo Bunko* 7 (1935), 105–61, especially 155 suggests a less likely explanation of the source concerned.

[56] For one such foreign monk official of the early Ming who had already held office under the Yuan, see Kuan Guang, "Sahajaśrī: A Fourteenth-Century Indian Buddhist Missionary to China," *Religions of South Asia,* 1.2 (2007), 203–15: note (213) that although he was an eminent *Vinaya* scholar, a translation was elicited from him giving disciplinary prescriptions for laypeople.

[57] Anne Gerritsen, "The Hongwu Legacy: Fifteenth-century Views on Zhu Yuanzhang's Monastic Policies" in Sarah Schneewind (ed.), *Long Live the Emperor! Uses of the Ming Founder Across Six Centuries of East Asian History,* Ming Studies Research Series, vol. 4 (Minneapolis: Society for Ming Studies, 2008), 55–72.

[58] Ferdinand Diedrich Lessing, *Yung-Ho-kung: An Iconography of the Lamaist Cathedral in Peking* vol.1 (Stockholm: Elanders Bocktryckeri Aktiebolao, 1942), 59. "Teacher" represents in Lessing's translation the same term given as preceptor earlier.

between religion and law came to be copiously commented on in European languages – and usually contrasted unfavorably with the situation prevailing in Europe.[59] The somewhat negative view of Chinese justice that dominates Western writing on late imperial China would seem to be echoed also by the continued emphasis on "tormenting the dead" in nineteenth-century depictions of the spirit realm, although these were generally less informed by Buddhist sources and much more by the florid imaginative domain of the Chinese theater.[60] One might conclude that Buddhism in China had waned to the extent that the relationship between Buddhism and law ceased to be an issue in the modern Chinese world – or at least the modern Chinese temporal world. Such is, however, not the case.

59 The most comprehensive work in this vein, which includes detailed accounts of the Ming and Qing legislation affecting Buddhism, is J.J.M. de Groot, *Sectarianism and Religious Persecution in China* (Leiden: E. J. Brill, 1901), especially 81–134.

60 Timothy Brook, Jérôme Bourgon, and Gregory Blue, *Death by a Thousand Cuts* (Cambridge, MA: Harvard University Press, 2008), 122–51.

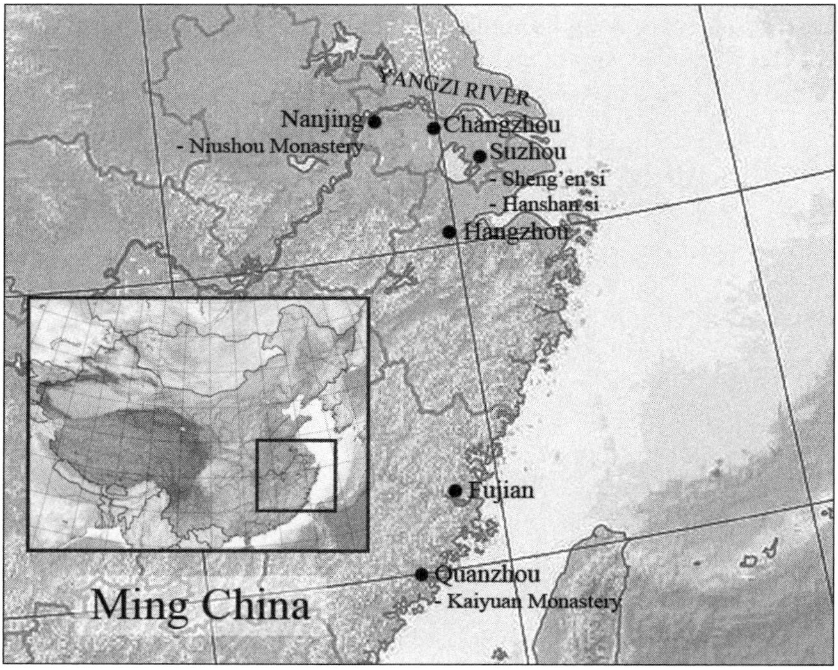

Map of Ming China

CHAPTER 12

The Ownership and Theft of Monastic Land in Ming China

Timothy Brook

Landowning was a universal condition of monastic survival in late-imperial China. Some Buddhists might like to invoke the ancient ideal of begging, but when it came to running a monastery, itinerant almsgiving was inadequate. "When the eating fingers become daily more numerous, begging for food does not meet the need, so the monastery has to have property in land," as a patron put it.[1] Or as an abbot phrased it, "How can a monastery remain secure in the long term with only a little permanent property?"[2] Master Hanshan Deqing (1546–1623) was blunter, declaring that "land is the foundation of a Buddhist abbey."[3]

While the law of monastic property was almost entirely the law of the state in Imperial China, the law of the Buddha had some influence as well. Few contemporaries wrote on ownership of Buddhist property as a general topic, but many were inspired to write about theft, which is why theft will serve as my approach to the legal status of Buddhist property in the Ming Dynasty (1368–1644). Theft looms as a constant threat in the principal sources for this essay, the gazetteers compiled by monasteries to record their history and protect their assets.[4] The monastery that did not lose a significant piece of property was as rare as the monastery that owned none at all. With property the norm and theft the fate, attachment to property was the condition.

Given that landownership is not attested as a virtue in the Buddhist tradition, which prefers to focus on the production and circulation of

[1] Zhao Jiong, *Qixia sizhi* (Gazetteer of Qixia Monastery, 1704), 1.59a, citing a text dated 1703.

[2] *Wuxian zhi* (Gazetteer of Wu county, 1642), 26.2a.

[3] Hanshan Deqing, *Hanshan dashi ji* (Writings of Master Hanshan), ed. Xiexuan (1954; repr., Taipei: Taiwan yinjingchu, 1970), 114.

[4] Timothy Brook, *Geographical Sources of Ming-Qing History* (Ann Arbor: Center for Chinese Studies, University of Michigan, 2002), 31–38; Timothy Brook, *Praying for Power: Buddhism and the Formation of Gentry Society in Late-Ming China* (Cambridge, MA: Council on East Asian Studies, Harvard University, 1993), 178–81.

religious value rather than the extraction of economic rents,[5] we will consider how Buddhists squared landowning with the doctrine of nonattachment. Monks and patrons did so differently because for donors land was a source of merit and for abbots, a source of income. The tension between economic value and religious value – and the curious reversal of values for the actors involved – is the theme of this essay.

Law and Monastic Property

Ming law made little distinction between a monastic and a civilian landowner. Both were treated for tax purposes as "households," liable for taxes on the basis of the number of household members and the size of its holdings. The one difference was an exemption from the service levy for a monk holding an official ordination certificate. Since by the sixteenth century, the service levy was paid in cash rather than as corvée, a monastic "household" bore a lighter tax burden than its civilian counterpart. A monastery might enjoy a further tax reduction through the generosity of the local magistrate.

Buddhist law made a profound distinction between monastic property and private property. Private property was karmically inert, at best; it was owned solely for the purpose of generating wealth. Monastic property, however, because it supported the saṅgha, had the capacity to generate merit, both directly for the donor and indirectly through the rites and works of the monks it supported. This distinction entailed another. Private property could be alienated through gift or sale without karmic effect, whereas monastic property could not. Once land that had been given to the saṅgha was no longer supporting Buddhist practice, the karmic value of the original donation was cancelled. Thus, there were interests on both sides of the monastery-donor relationship to accumulate land and prevent its loss.

The Ming Code includes little regarding the arrangements under which property might be held or transferred. Article 99 of the "Fields and Houses" subsection of the "Laws on Revenue" forbids what it terms "the fraudulent selling" of land, that is, selling by someone who is not its rightful owner; it specifies that this law also applies to land held in pawn. Article 101 enlarges this rule by laying out the tax consequence, which is that the pawn-holder is liable for all taxes pertaining to the transfer and ownership

[5] Gustavo Benavides, "Economy" in Donald Lopez (ed.), *Critical Terms for the Study of Buddhism* (Chicago: University of Chicago Press, 2005), esp. 90–94.

of the land.[6] These laws were designed to stem the practice of engrossment, by which a landholder without any fiscal privilege transferred his property to a landholder who did enjoy fiscal privilege. Some monasteries engaged in this practice by charging fees for permitting donors to avoid taxes and covertly collect rents on donated property. Article 96 of the Ming Code specifically forbids this sort of arrangement, although it cites the example of a ranked official rather than a religious institution.[7] The penalty was the payment of back taxes, a beating of 100 strokes for both parties, and forfeiture of the land. The previous dynasty in fact had instituted a law in 1344 forbidding monasteries from buying civilian land on the grounds that such purchases were "invariably" fraudulent engrossments intended to remove taxable land from the tax registers, but that law was not brought into the Ming Code.[8]

Monastic Landholding

Most Ming monasteries were modest landowners. The great monasteries of earlier dynasties boasted holdings of more than 1,000 hectares, but Mongol occupation in the thirteenth century, the chaos of dynastic transition in the mid-fourteenth century, and the repression of religious institutions toward the end of that century reduced the once vast holdings of the grandest monasteries to well fewer than 100 hectares. The Ming dynastic founder did not explicitly restrict landholding, out of concern that the monasteries would lack the means to support their residents, leaving discharged monks to sow discontent in society at large. His heirs experimented with limits to monastic landholding, but these schemes failed.[9] Nonetheless, the pressures of state control and land competition meant that Ming monasteries no longer possessed the fabled estates, often given by imperial gift, which some had enjoyed in earlier centuries. The long-term effect on monastic landholding in the Ming was severe. An abbot in Hangzhou testified in 1570 that his monastery, then at its lowest ebb, owned less than one percent of the land it had been given in earlier dynasties.[10] Two centuries later, another Hangzhou abbot noted that the rents he collected at the winter

[6] Jiang Yonglin (trans.), *The Great Ming Code : Da Ming lü* (Seattle: University of Washington Press, 2005), 78–80.

[7] Jiang, *The Great Ming Code*, 76–77.

[8] *Zhizheng tiaoge jiaozhu ben*, (The Zhizheng Regulations, annotated edition) (repr., Seoul, 2007), 239.

[9] Timothy Brook, *The Chinese State in Ming Society* (London: Routledge, 2005), 148.

[10] Bichu Guangbin, *Shang tianzhu jiangsi zhi* (Gazetteer of Upper Tianzhu Taching Monastery, 1646, 1897), 10.15b.

solstice from his meager forty *mu* (2.7 hectares) of "permanently owned monastic property for the support of rites" were insufficient to feed his residents.[11] Critics in earlier times complained that Buddhist monasteries monopolized too much land; in later times, that they ended up with too little to survive.

Agricultural land was not the only property of value that Ming monasteries owned. Anything of value that a monastery owned could be stolen, from bells – especially in wartime when metal was in short supply[12] – to buildings and urban real estate.[13] But no target of theft is reported as consistently in Ming sources as farmland. Land was the economic mainstay of most institutions, and sustaining its profitability demanded considerable attention and effort. "What with maintaining support, collecting rents, and dunning for taxes," wrote a patron of a monastery by the Yangzi River, "almost no day passes free of business." These burdens were so heavy that, prior to the appointment of a particularly competent abbot in 1530, "the monk in charge could not fulfill all these tasks, such that before the abbot's seat was warm, he would flee."[14]

The theft of monastic property was greatly encouraged by the growth of the Ming economy. By 1450, the Ming economy was already significantly monetized, but by 1550, money facilitated transactions at all levels of the economy, not all of them legal. Monasteries sold products and services for cash, bought necessities with cash, and collected rents in cash. Money exerted an even stronger presence within a monastery when a building campaign was underway. We see this in 1610 when the elder monks of Nanhua Monastery in northern Guangdong accused their abbot, Hanshan Deqing, of embezzling no less than 8,000 *taels* (2,500 kg.) of silver. The accounting system Master Hanshan created when he moved to Nanhua required receipts for every item of income and expense, which saved him

11 Minglun, *Yunju shengshui sizhi* (Gazetteer of Yunju-Shengshui Monastery, 1773), 1.17b–18a. "Permanently Owned Monastic Property for the Support of Rites" (*changzhu jisi sichan*) was land yielding income to a religious institution.

12 For example, Xingji and Xingyuan, *Huangbo sizhi* (Gazetteer of Huangbo Monastery, 1637), 3.24a; *Lingyin sizhi* (Gazetteer of Lingyin Monastery, 1872), 8.61a.

13 For example, when Qingpu was re-established in 1573 as a county of Songjiang, the prefecture east of Suzhou, those in charge of building the new office for the magistrate decided to cannibalize an old monastery in town. Had influential patrons not stepped in and blocked the move, the monks would have been powerless to halt the loss of their buildings and real estate. See Lu Shusheng, "Yihao jiangsi yougun lou jibei" (Stele record of Yougun Tower at Yihao Teaching Monastery) in Chai Zhiguang and Pan Mingquan (eds.), *Shanghai fojiao beike wenxian ji* (Buddhist epigraphic documents from Shanghai) (Shanghai: Shanghai guji chubanshe, 2004), 138.

14 Wu Shen, "Chongxiu zhaoyin siji" (Record of the restoration of Zhaodai Monastery, 1553) in Xu Guocheng, *Ganlu sizhi* (Gazetteer of Ganlu Monastery, 1599), 19a–b.

from humiliation. When his records were checked, the charge was shown to be malicious.[15]

The examples I will present regarding the legality of possession and theft of monastic land have been drawn principally from historical materials from sixteenth- and seventeenth-century Suzhou. Situated in the heart of the Yangzi Delta west of Shanghai, Suzhou was the commercial and cultural heart of China during the Ming Dynasty. The prefectural seat was a major city whose jurisdiction spread over two county jurisdictions (Wu and Changzhou). It was one of the most prosperous cities in the world, if not the most prosperous.[16] Both the city and the prefecture were famous for their magnificent monasteries that dated well before the Ming Dynasty. And yet Suzhou did not aspire to be a religious center. It aspired to cultural centrality, and the scale and beauty of its religious institutions were understood as demonstrating that centrality. The rise and decline of Suzhou monasteries thus may be taken as describing the larger arc of Suzhou's fortunes in the expanding commercial economy of the Ming. Suzhou has the additional advantage of being well documented by both monastic and county gazetteers.

Sheng'en Monastery: Theft as Commercial Competition

Sheng'en si (Sagely Grace Monastery) was one of Suzhou's most eminent Buddhist institutions in the Ming. Founded in the eighth century, Sheng'en was destroyed in the civil war in the 1360s but underwent reconstruction a decade later. It was restored again in two waves of donations in the early fifteenth and the late sixteenth centuries, followed by a further round of building in the last two decades of the dynasty (and yet another after the Ming, in 1658). When an official returned to his native Suzhou in 1536, he found Sheng'en in the trough between these waves and was concerned. "Even though the Lord Buddha discoursed on the method of cultivating oneself by leaving the world, yet [Buddhists] cannot find a day's rest when protecting their places." In this, he judged, Sheng'en was typical, for no history of a Buddhist monastery can avoid being a history of "decline and prosperity."[17]

15 Fuzheng, *Hanshan dashi nianpu shuzhu* (Annotated chronology of the life of Master Hanshan) (Taipei: Zhenmeishan, 1967), 96. The biographer guesses that the charge was laid by monks who had been pushed down the hierarchy of power by Hanshan's arrival as abbot. Hanshan's donors included gentry from as far away as Suzhou.

16 Michael Marmé, *Suzhou: Where the Goods of All the Provinces Converge* (Stanford: Stanford University Press, 2005), 5.

17 Zhou Yongnian, *Dengwei sheng'en sizhi* (Gazetteer of Sheng'en Monastery on Dengwei Mountain, 1644), Lu's preface (1536), 1b.

Sheng'en was restored during the Wanli era, but the main flood of investment started only in 1628 when Master Sanfeng Fazang became abbot. Fazang set about restoring old buildings, constructing new ones, and acquiring statues and books to put in them, but he needed an endowment for this work and maintenance. Accordingly, lay patrons set about re-establishing the monastery's economic foundation. Discovering that Sheng'en had been a significant landowner in earlier times, they held up that past as grounds for arguing that it should have land again. The compiler of the Sheng'en gazetteer makes no mention of land theft in his basic annals of the monastery's history.[18] The extent of the monastery's loss is only revealed in a series of texts issued by the county magistrate in the penultimate chapter of the gazetteer. They show that the nadir of land loss was reached in the 1560s, by which time local landlords had taken over most of the land.

In 1629, several of the monastery's patrons got together to recover some of this property. They started by seeking a site for a mortuary pagoda for the previous abbot. The site they selected was part of this lost property, and they petitioned the magistrate to restore it to monastic ownership. As the site was then in the hands of a maternal uncle of one of the patrons, transferring the ownership to Sheng'en was not difficult, although the current owner insisted that the nephew and his friends pay him for the land. The patrons also raised funds to buy a separate piece of agricultural land, the rents from which would ensure that the pagoda was properly staffed and maintained in perpetuity. The endowment was intended to create an ongoing security for both investments: an institution in good working order was unlikely to fall into decline so long as it received rental income, and the land from which that income came was unlikely to be stolen so long as the institution thrived.

In response to an appeal from the patrons who arranged for this land to revert to monastic possession, the county magistrate in 1630 issued what would be the first in a series of pronouncements on behalf of the monastery through the 1630s.[19] Three years later, he issued a declaration of legal protection for Sheng'en's newly built Dharma Hall. The magistrate noted that the construction of the hall had been possible because of the financial contributions of "the rural gentry," who donated the hill land on which it stood. He also noted, however, that the hall and land were in the abbot's possession as a trust, and that the abbot was obliged to

[18] The county gazetteer notes only vaguely that parts of the grounds were sold off in the 1560s and 1570s; *Wuxian zhi* (1642), 25.85b.

[19] Zhou Yongnian, *Dengwei sheng'en sizhi*, 7.6b–16b.

pass these properties intact to his dharma heirs. Even though that transfer was imagined in fictive kinship terms, this was fiduciary and not private property and therefore was inalienable.

That same year, the patrons of Sheng'en made another series of appeals to the county office requesting protection of a different sort. These patrons were donating a large amount of agricultural land to the monastery, and they wanted the county to exempt this land from the service levy. The patrons offered several arguments to justify the request: that similar exemptions had been given in the past, that the product of the land was going entirely to the support of the monastery, and that the land was poor in quality and carried a heavy tax burden. They also noted that the monks who received the land had allowed more than 20 percent of it to be used to build a reservoir to irrigate the fields of neighboring landowners, and suggested that a service levy exemption would be an appropriate reward for this sacrifice. The connection between the land grant and the building of the reservoir on that same land could point to a confluence of interest between the donors and the institution. There is no evidence that the donors gifted the land to protect themselves from the tax burden once it was lost to flooding, yet the peculiarity of the request is conspicuous. The magistrate issued his consent the following year, in 1634, decreeing that the land could not be alienated and stipulating that government underlings and tax collectors should not interfere with this privilege.

Four-and-a-half years later, the county magistrate issued yet another declaration of protection for Sheng'en. This document goes back to two cases in which a monk named Tici had illegally sold portions of the monastery's grounds. In the first case, Tici sold a piece of land for 100 *taels* of silver because he needed to pay for the costs of running the monastery and had no other way of raising funds. He was not blamed for this transaction as his sole intention in converting the land into money had been the institution's survival, not his private benefit. In the second case, Tici sold 2.4 *mu* (0.16 hectare) of land behind the Buddha Pavilion to a monk from Hangzhou who wanted to build a small residential chapel for himself. This was done as a favor to an elderly monk, yet it alarmed the patrons, whose religious merit and social prestige were extinguished when their donations left the monastery's possession. Patrons bought the two parcels of land back and wanted them recertified as monastic property. The county magistrate's statement was more of a warning to outsiders not to encroach on monastic property than an admonition to warn monks against selling it. He ordered that an inventory of this land giving its exact measurements and locations be inscribed in stone so that all would know what belonged to Sheng'en Monastery in perpetuity.

The declaration decommodified Sheng'en's land, to use our language. Any attempt to put it back in circulation would be regarded as theft, not as a legitimate reorganizing of institutional assets in response to market forces. The magistrate's intention was to protect the monastery's property against loss, but one might argue that placing it in the hands of a corporate institution increased its exposure to loss. Land on the Yangzi Delta was a profitable and stable investment: it was in high demand and difficult to procure, given the customary expectation that one should look for a buyer inside one's kinship network before selling it outside. All this meant that powerful landowners were in a better position to acquire land than weak ones. When stewardship was weak, fiduciary property was particularly vulnerable. Indeed, to declare land fiduciary was almost an invitation to prey.

And such attacks came. According to a provincial-level declaration of protection issued to Sheng'en Monastery in 1694, over the intervening half-century, "the powerful and strong had schemed in a hundred ways" to get their hands on Sheng'en's property.[20] "The powerful" is the standard term that writings of the late-imperial era use to describe land thieves.[21] The term is pejorative and not socially precise. It tended to be used for large landlords who could exert economic clout and had the social power to intimidate weaker people.[22] Ge Yinliang, the assiduous bureau head in the Nanjing Ministry of Rites who oversaw a complete resurvey of property belonging to monasteries in and around the southern capital in 1603–06, divided threats to monastic property between "powerful families" and "recalcitrant tenants."[23] The latter threatened the flow of merit from monastic property by cheating on their rents and preventing the monastery from reallocating their land, whereas the former engaged in income-getting practices that threatened the very source of that flow. Monasteries found themselves particularly exposed to encroachment when such magnates owned adjacent land, or were looking for prime hill real estate for

20 *Ibid.*, 8.7a-b. Extinguishing competing claims on disputed land was made more difficulty when bodies had been buried in the land under dispute. For an example elsewhere in Suzhou, see Zhenjian Zhiming, *Zhutang sizhi* (Gazetteer of Zhutang Monastery 1917), 15a–16a.

21 References to monastic land theft by such "powerful families" are legion in Ming county gazetteers; e.g., *Wuyuan xianzhi* (Gazetteer of Wuyuan county, 1882), 12.3a.

22 For example, "The Families of the Powerful (*hao*) Take Over Great Amounts of State-owned Reservoir Land for Their Own Profit, Amassing Tracts that Spread From Field to Field"; taken from the Changzhou prefect's declaration in his register of polder lands in the prefecture, quoted in Yun Yingyi, *Gaoshan zhi* (Gazetteer of Gao Mountain, 1608, 1849), 2.19a. *Wuyuan xianzhi* (Gazetteer of Wuyuan county, 1882), 12.3a.

23 Ge Yinliang, *Jinling fancha zhi* (Gazetteer of the monasteries of Nanjing, 1607), 50.9b.

tombs.[24] Also identified by such pejorative terms as "the privileged," "the forceful," or "strongmen," these people dominated their local economies and were feared and despised for the tactics they used to aggrandize their holdings at the expense of others.[25] The law was against them, yet they were rarely brought to justice.

Hanshan Monastery: Theft as Sin

Hanshan si (Cold Mountain Monastery), another prominent Suzhou Buddhist establishment, claimed to have been founded in 976 and to have been the home of the famous Tang monk-poet Hanshan, although the compiler of the 1911 gazetteer acknowledges that there is no evidence the poet ever lived at the monastery.[26] The monastery lay four kilometers outside Suzhou's city wall. Like Sheng'en, Hanshan was destroyed in the 1360s, rebuilt in the 1370s, and restored several times in the fifteenth and sixteenth centuries. It, too, underwent a major reconstruction early in the seventeenth century, starting in 1618, a full decade before Sheng'en. Again, an activist abbot appears to have been pivotal to this renaissance.[27] The only surviving gazetteer was compiled just after the turn of the twentieth century. It lacks information about Hanshan's landholdings in the Ming, as the compiler had only damaged inscriptions three centuries in the past to work from. It does, however, include three texts that the county magistrate ordered carved on stone in response to a request from the monastery for a declaration of protection. In this case, the request came from the abbot rather than his patrons. None of these texts is dated, although they appear to date from the last two decades of the dynasty.[28]

The texts are tantalizingly vague about the circumstances of land theft and recovery. One, by patron Zhang Yandeng, refers to "the battle over the monastery's grounds." He observes that lay people had encroached on Hanshan's property "illegally." It seems that the monastery attempted to

[24] For an instance of encroachment by a contiguous landowner in Nanjing, see Zhou Yun, *Jiuhua shanzhi* (Gazetteer of Jiuhua Mountain, 1900), *jiu xu*, 4b, referring to an incident in 1578. For a Suzhou example of monastic land being used for burial, which made it much more difficult to recover, see Zhenjian Zhiming, *Zhutang sizhi* (Gazetteer of Zhutang Monastery 1917), 15a–16a.

[25] For example, Gao Yifu, *Helin sizhi* (Gazetteer of the monastery on Helin Mountain), 22b, referring to a discovery of encroachment in 1594.

[26] *Ibid.*, 1.3a.

[27] This was also the year in which Kaiyuan Monastery was reconstructed to be "The Finest Monastery in Jiangnan"; Pan Zengyi, *Kaiyuan sizhi* (Gazetteer of Kaiyuan Monastery, 1922), 9b.

[28] Patron Qian Qianyi, was living in retirement in nearby Changshu county during most of the period 1625–44. Patron Zhang Yandeng (*jinshi* 1598) may have been serving in the region, although I am unable to ascertain when.

recover this land by paying a "redemption price" to the people occupying its grounds, only to have the occupiers take the money, but refuse to leave. The seizure of monastic land was bad enough for Zhang Yandeng, but what outraged him was that the problem was not resolved when the money was paid. The payment of money to the occupiers was a generous fiction that should have allowed everyone to pretend that the land was circulating back into the possession of Hanshan Monastery. The money was a polite way of burying any accusation that the land had been stolen in the first place. Zhang was not only annoyed that those who seized the land were not going along with this generous gesture; he was frustrated that the monks did nothing to challenge the theft. Why, he wondered, had the clerical residents of the monastery not reported the situation sooner to the officials?[29]

In a separate text written to protect Hanshan's property, Qian Qianyi (1582–1664), takes a different tack. Rather than condemn the theft of monastic land as a crime against human law, as Zhang Yandeng does, he regards it as an affront to divine justice. "Land that belongs to the Three Jewels," he declared, "is protected by the gods. Those who encroach on it will drop into hell, and disaster will dog their children and grandchildren. Karmic response is utterly clear and so terrifying." Later in the text, Qian repeats the claim that the theft of "Buddhist earth" is a "sin," suggesting that afterlife punishment carries some weight in his moral calculation.[30] Qian's defense enunciates what might be called a vernacular Chinese Buddhist concept of property. That is, the privilege of possessing or transferring property rests ultimately not on what one does in this life, but on the action of karmic recompense. Those who deserve to benefit from good acts done in previous lives do so by gaining access to property and enjoying its fruits. Those who deserve to be punished for their evil acts will experience that punishment in the form of loss of property, an inability to inherit or pass on property through the male line, or some other deprivation.

Property is not just a passive field on which karma pays out its profits and losses, however; it is a field for generating merit through gifts to the saṅgha, and demerit for taking it away. The dual value of land is presented literally in the merit system that the great Buddhist master Yunqi Zhuhong (1535–1615) worked out for his followers in Zhejiang, the province to the south of Suzhou. This system converted acts into spiritual values, at a rate of 100:1;

29 Ye Changchi, *Hanshan sizhi* (Gazetteer of Hanshan Monastery, 1911), 2.5a.

30 *Ibid.* For other commemorative texts by Qian, see *Wuxian zhi* (1642), 24.28b, 39b.

that is, the production of a material benefit or loss valued in the economy at 100 copper cash generated one merit or demerit point. Giving land to a monastery earned the donor one merit point for every hundred cash value of the donation, and as land was typically donated in amounts valued in the tens of *taels* of silver (one *tael* was nominally worth ten merit points), a land gift entailed considerable merit for the donor. Zhuhong credited the same value to efforts to "maintain monastic property," meaning the protection or recovery of monastic land – one merit point for every 100 cash worth of property saved from loss – which I take as reflecting the reality that land recovery was quite as important as land acquisition to the revival of Buddhist institutions during the Wanli era. Zhuhong's system handles theft according to the same calculation: for every 100 cash value of monastic land stolen, the thief collects one demerit point.[31]

The economic reality of the Wanli-era commercial land market was that the acquisition or disposal of land operated in complete indifference to claims to moral or religious benefits accruing to specially designated parcels of land. It seems that the political reality of the land market weighed more heavily on Zhuhong's calculations than its religious significance. This explains why Zhuhong's system did not penalize the theft of monastic land at a rate greater than the theft of non-monastic land. Both are equally expensive on his moral scale. One might have expected the karmic cost of eroding the saṅgha to be higher than the karmic cost of eroding the economic viability of a neighbor. However, the only instance where he imposed a higher penalty on the moral cost of theft was in the case of someone stealing land "because one has the support of the powerful."[32] When *hao* were involved, the theft of land worth 100 cash garnered the thief ten demerit points, not just one. This huge increment seems to reflect the sense of threat that small landowners felt in the face of large landowners, a threat sufficiently general for Zhuhong to apply the increment to all land seizures, not just of monastic land. For him, it seems, what made Buddhist property vulnerable was the political climate of the Wanli era, not the economic environment. The latter was simply an unexceptional fact of institutional existence. The loss of monastic land concerned him, but the power of *hao* to steal any land, monastic included, disturbed him more.

[31] Chün-fang Yü, *The Renewal of Buddhism in China: Chu-hung and the Late Ming Synthesis* (New Haven, CT: Yale University Press, 1981), 238, 250, 252–53.

[32] *Hanshan sizhi* (1911), 249.

Reversing Theft

Recovering stolen monastic property required a concerted effort on the part of abbots, patrons, and local officials. Intervention by one of these actors was in itself unlikely to bring about the desired outcome. Bringing land back under monastic control involved firstly the burden of proving that the land in dispute had previously belonged to the monastery. Then it involved raising the money to buy it back, for it was generally accepted that those who had acquired monastic land, even if they had done so illegally, could not be expected to hand it back to the monastery without compensation. Official backing helped in the recovery of monastic property, but this was not enough to waive the obligation for compensation. For example, two brothers who engaged prominently in Buddhist patronage, Lu Guangzu and Lu Guangzhai, approached the imperial grain commissioner in Suzhou in 1579 to request that land originally belonging to Kaiyuan Monastery be restored. The commissioner's response was to direct a Kaiyuan monk to raise subscriptions for its repurchase. The sale to an imperial eunuch had been illegal, but the current owner had to be compensated. The brothers sponsored the campaign, although their scheme ultimately failed.[33]

The 1570s and 1580s marked an upsurge in monastic patronage. Lu Guangzu and Lu Guangzhai, singly and together, were active figures in campaigns to restore lost property to Buddhist institutions throughout the region, but their initiatives required the support of the local magistrate. If the issue were simply money, patrons could handle that on their own, but many an attempt to restore land foundered because of the legal problems that land recovery involved. Could the land be successfully re-registered as monastic land in the county tax records? Could it remain in the monks' hand without special declarations of state indulgence or protection from the magistrate? Magistrates occasionally had to intervene against monasteries. Monks were certainly not above stealing fiduciary property belonging to other institutions that had fallen into disuse or cadastral ambiguity.[34] So, too, the effective theft of monastic land usually depended on the cooperation of someone within the institution. For every thief from the outside, there was usually one inside.

[33] Pan Zeng, *Kaiyuan sizhi*, 9b; *Wuxian zhi* (1642), 24.24b.

[34] The institutions most vulnerable to theft by monks were schools and private academies that, like monasteries, relied on fiduciary property and required the vigilance of patrons. For some examples of local magistrates who forced monks to return illegally appropriated school or academy land, see *Yinxian zhi* (1788): 11.22a (in Ningbo, Zhejiang, about 1580), 17.26a (in Zhangzhou, Fujian, at the end of the seventeenth century), and 17.46b (in Fuliang, Jiangxi, in the mid-eighteenth century).

What tended to tip the scales in a monastery's favor was the issue of taxes. A common way of referring to the loss of monastic land was to say, as did a patron of one of the monasteries the Lu brothers supported, that the land "had entered the civilian registers."[35] Once re-registered under a lay household, it was gone. Re-registration meant that the new owner had legal certification of his ownership, which he could use to defend himself against an aggrieved monastic claimant. Being in a register was an indicator of ownership as well as a recognition of tax liability. Although landowners liked to shirk taxes, paying them on a particular plot of land confirmed ownership.

Given the thoroughness with which the tax system was administered, battles over landed property were often fought out on the tax registers. The ability of powerful landowners to manipulate the tax registers to their benefit by finding loopholes and bribing the tax clerks contributed to the long, slow deterioration of the Ming state's capacity to assess taxes and collect revenue. The accumulation of these abuses led to a series of tax reforms known by the punning title of the Single Whip Reform (*yitiao bianfa* is more felicitously translated as the Single Filing Reform). Carried out on a national scale in the 1570s, the resurvey uncovered extensive theft of monastic land. The Single Whip may also have been a factor encouraging the wave of donations of land to Buddhist monasteries starting at exactly this time.

The Ming tax system was based on surveys of households entered into the Yellow Registers, and their land recorded in the Fish Scale Registers. Every ten years the county magistrate was required to resurvey all households and land and submit copies of his registers to the national fiscal archive in the southern capital, Nanjing. In practice, when the "Great Compiling Year" came around, most magistrates simply resubmitted the figures from a decade earlier. This was to simplify their administrative lives, but with each survey waived, the abuses mounted to the point at which a magistrate who actually did try to resurvey the land was faced with an impossible mountain of legal conflicts that arose where ownership and registration were found to be inconsistent.

A particularly rich example of this process extends from 1371 to 1442 and then to 1570, the dates in which resurveys occurred on a particular plot of land registered to Niushou Mountain monastery. In 1386, the head abbot of Niushou opted to return to lay life and claimed the land as his own.

35 Lu Shusheng, "Faren si shidi jibei," (Stele of the record of the giving of land to Faren Monastery), 174.

In 1424, his son and nephew, who jointly controlled the land, decided to return it in the form of a trusteeship for then Abbot Dounan who also wanted to keep the land upon his retirement. To accomplish this, Dounan worked out an illegal and hidden arrangement that transferred half of the land to a neighboring landlord – Li Sheng, who was in a completely different canton – in return, presumably, for a regular allowance that was recorded in the decennial land survey of 1442.[36] This arrangement survived until 1570 when a later abbot discovered the fraud in the course of auditing the monastery's land leading up to the Great Compiling of 1572.

In 1570, magistrates throughout the realm began conducting detailed surveys preparatory to the universal implementation of the Single Whip Reform.[37] The Great Compiling of 1572 was the most thorough resurvey of land since 1371 and had a huge impact on monastic property in Suzhou.[38] The thoroughness of the survey was a proximate factor, but two other factors lent it particular force. One was the accumulated effect of several decades of Japanese pirate raids on the Yangzi Delta. Under this pressure, fields were abandoned and tax registers burned, enabling land to slip unregistered into the possession of "powerful families." This disappearance intensified the burden on less-powerful taxpayers, prompting a student in the neighboring prefecture of Songjiang to petition Vice-Prefect Zheng Yuanshao to resurvey the land and redistribute the tax burden equitably. Zheng supported the idea but had to approach his superiors for permission. The court agreed, giving Zheng a special appointment as Assistant Surveillance Commissioner in Charge of Grain Taxes in the Songjiang Region to do it. Zheng carried out a detailed re-survey of all agricultural land in the prefecture by having every plot of land paced out and graded according to quality, then re-assessed for tax purposes. Not surprisingly, the assessors discovered other land that had fallen out of the control of its owners, including monastic land.[39]

36 Sheng Shitai, *Niushou shanzhi* (Gazetteer of Niushou Mountain, 1579), 30b–31a.

37 For two examples of surveys personally conducted by magistrates, one from South Zhili and one from Fujian, see my *The Chinese State in Ming Society*, 45.

38 As it did elsewhere in the region; in Nanjing, the land belonging to Linggu and Qixia monasteries, and probably others as well, was surveyed in 1570; Ge Yinliang, *Jinling fancha zhi*, 50.18a; Sheng Shitai, *Qixia xiaozhi* (Short gazetteer of Qixia Monastery, 1578, 1884), 18a.

39 *Songjiang fuzhi* (Gazetteer of Songjiang prefecture, 1630), 26.21b, 32.42b–43a; the student's name was Zhang Neiyun. On Zheng Yuansao, see *Fuzhou fuzhi*, (Gazetteer of Fuzhou prefecture, 1754), 40.61a (recording his *juren* of 1549) and 50.48b. The case that brought Zheng Yuanshao's resurvey to my attention was a property dispute concerning the five-story pagoda at Chengzhao Monastery. The pagoda, which stood at the edge of Lake Mao, had lost its land, although in this case it was shore erosion that caused the loss; *Louxian zhi*, (Gazetteer of Lou county, 1788), 10.20a. The patrons responsible for setting up a permanent land endowment for Chengzhao Monastery were Lu

Fields of Blessedness and the Road to Desire

Having considered many aspects of the experience of land theft at Ming monasteries, it is now time to consider the impact that Buddhist ownership may have had on this property – for which, curiously, we will need to interview Confucian observers.

Land was fundamental to popular notions of wealth, not just among Chinese, but among Buddhists as much as anyone. Land as metaphor had a place in Buddhist discourse, for Ming Buddhists like to speak of "fields of blessedness" (*futian*). The great Suzhou painter Tang Yin (1470–1524), for instance, in a fundraising appeal for a new bell for Hanshan Monastery, declared that donations would "make Buddhist property magnificent, bring benefits to humans and heaven, cause the sun of wisdom to shine, and ensure that the fields of blessedness are not scanty."[40] Tang meant the final phrase purely metaphorically: He was urging patrons to contribute for a bell, not for land. But others literalized the metaphor and spoke of a plot of land given to a monastery as a field of blessedness, blessing being the religious recompense the donor expected for the gift.

Some Confucians held other views of the Buddhist relationship to landed property. Gao Panlong (1562–1626), an active reformer from the prefecture to the west of Suzhou, was not sympathetic to monasticism, declaring that most monks entered the clergy purely as a way to support themselves and not to pursue a religious vocation. He allowed that Buddhist teachings were useful to the extent that they helped nurture goodness among the masses. In a fundraising appeal he wrote for a Buddhist old-age home, Gao makes an intriguing observation on the nature of landholding: He observes that old-age homes would not be necessary were China still practicing the ancient system of land equalization, in which land was reapportioned every generation in accordance with labor and need. In the Ming economy, Gao suggests that landownership was not simply unequal; it produced land poverty.[41] Those with landed wealth make donations to compensate for the inequality their landownership produced. It was not only land theft that generated moral demerit; so, too, did land acquisition. By conceding that property produces inequality, he accepts donations as morally positive

Shusheng and his brother Lu Shude (close friends of the other Lu brothers, Guangzu and Guangzhai, but no relation). For another case of shore erosion forcing a new survey, see Ge Yinliang, *Jinling fancha zhi* (1607), 15.1a.

40 Ye Changchi, *Hanshan sizhi*, 1.21a.

41 Gao Panlong, *Gao zi yishu* (Surviving Writings of Master Gao), 6.5b, in *Qiankun zhengqi ji* (The Righteous Bearing of Heaven and Earth, 1848), *juan* 263.

and socially necessary to offset the natural impact of a commercial economy in which land was taken away from those who needed it.

Other Confucian critics were even more critical of monastic landownership. Zhang Yue (1492–1553), for instance, regarded the concentration of land as inimical to Buddhism's declared purpose. "Today the Buddha is revered by grand monasteries and the support of fertile land," he notes of his native Fujian, "but this only brings Buddhists further along the road of desire." Arguing that income from property stimulates greed rather than detachment, Zhang attacked the Buddhists on their own terms. He did so as an administrator who regarded monastic landholding as a screen from taxation, as at times it was.[42] He chose to cite the Buddhist theory of attachment because he probably looked upon the conduct of Buddhist monks in his time and place as unworthy of their claim to religious sanctity.

Buddhists regarded the privilege of partial tax exemption on monastic land as justified by the expenditure of effort that monks made on behalf of others. Many could acknowledge Zhang Yue's charge that landownership was a cause of attachment and delusion, but their response was to develop institutional mechanisms, such as bursars or managers specially appointed to handle cash and transactions with tenants, to insulate most monks from the economic processes on which they relied for their livelihood. The goal of land acquisition was adequate wealth, not excessive wealth: perpetuation, not increase.[43] Some gazetteer compilers blamed wealth for institutional decay, as does the chronicler of Luquan Monastery on the Yangzi River, who attributed the near abandonment of the monastery to the success of Luquan's tree nursery. The opposite logic – that poverty, not wealth, promotes institutional decay – was the more conventional explanation.[44] Indeed, the same compiler notes that when property was lost in the fifteenth century, "the monks had nothing by which to support themselves and so fled."[45] A monastery could be damned for having property and damned for losing it. Therein lies the contradiction of monastic landownership: that monks are not allowed to possess land that can be effectively protected only through possession. Law and religious doctrine would strive to interpose

42 Zhang Yue, *Huian xianzhi* (Gazetteer of Huian county, 1530), 6.11a–b.

43 This point is made by a monk who revived a chapel in Suzhou in 1596. He states that his purpose in setting up a land endowment was purely to guarantee the longevity of the mortuary pagoda attached to the chapel; *Wuxian zhi* (1642), 24.40b.

44 For example, Xingji and Xingyuan, *Huangbo sizhi* (1637), 1.1b, which reports that the monks abandoned Huangbo and lost its lands after the monastery was burned down in 1555.

45 Gao Yifu, *Luquan sizhi* (Gazetteer of Luquan Monastery, 1599), 1b–2a.

themselves between the monk and the market, but the market was stronger than either.

Few abbots chose to interpret the Buddhist teaching of nonattachment so literally as to declare land an impediment to religious cultivation. Abbots sensitive to the religious and financial contradictions buried in land could order their monks to farm the fields in the belief that monks who did not labor would become idle and spiritually lax, but by the sixteenth century this was an unconventional defense against the temptation of luxurious living.[46] Most abbots preferred just to enjoin their monks not to own land privately, as monastic rules required, rather than suggest that their institutions do without. A patron in 1533 voices the conventional opinion: "Although Buddhists regard emptiness as their teaching, when it comes to hunger and thirst they are no different than other people. If the bell is to sound and the drum to summon, if [monks are to] hold out their begging bowls and be given food, how is this possible without land?"[47] Land made the religious life possible. At the same time, however, it also generated merit for lay donors, along with social prestige, filial reputation, and political visibility – all of which evaporated when the land was stolen. And so it was Buddhist law rather than state law that ensured the vigilance of donors, but it was state law to which abbots turned when they discovered that their land had been spirited away.

[46] Shanzu Xingfu, *Fushan zhi* (Gazetteer of Fu Mountain, 1680, 1873), 4.23a. It is possible that the cultivators were monks in name only.

[47] Huang Gongzhen, "Fuyuan sitian ji" (Record of the land of Fuyuan Monastery) in *Wuxian zhi* (1642), 26.18b.

CHAPTER 13

Buddhism and Law in China

Qing Dynasty to the Present

Anthony Dicks

Introduction

Law relating to Buddhism in the last period of imperial rule in China embodied much of the legal fabric of earlier periods and, with its unambiguous emphasis on the state control of religion, foreshadowed future legal developments in the Republican and Communist periods. The present chapter surveys the main features of law relating to Buddhism from the Qing Dynasty (1644–1911) through the subsequent era of the Republic of China (1911–49) to the People's Republic of China (1949 to the present day).[1]

The Qing state sought to contain and control both Buddhism and Daoism through a statutory framework, the *Penal Statutes and Sub-statutes of the Great Qing* (*Da Qing lü*, hereafter *Qing Code*), which was largely inherited from the Ming Dynasty. Adopted in 1646, the Qing made only minor changes to their predecessors' code and added some sub-statutes.[2] Additionally, a number of administrative decrees and orders were published either in the vast and elaborate *Qing Administrative Code*[3] or in the departmental rules of the Six Boards, particularly those that were concerned with Buddhism, namely the Boards of Civil Office, Revenue, Rites, and Punishments.

As a result, anyone looking up the criminal and administrative statutes relating to Buddhism in 1900 would have been confronted with several texts that were enacted some 500 years earlier and had hardly changed in

1 Sections of this chapter have been published as parts of the author's paper, "The Ownership of Buddhist Temples and the Civil Status of the Clergy in China" in Clara Bulfoni (ed.), *Tradizioni Religiose e Trasformazioni dell' Asia Contemporanea* (Milan and Rome: Ambrosiana and Bulzoni, 2012).

2 D. Bodde and C. Morris, *Law in Imperial China* (Cambridge, MA: Harvard University Press, 1967), 55–68.

3 *Da Qing huidian shili* (Qing collected statutes with sub-statutes based on precedents), Guangxu edition (1898, reprinted, Taipei: Qiwen chubanshe, 1963).

the intervening centuries. Needless to say, the written law contained in such texts has to be read in a nuanced way if its practical significance in the later centuries of Qing rule is to be properly understood. Furthermore, acknowledging a carefully balanced ambivalence on the part of both Qing rulers and their officials is essential to an understanding of the legal position of Buddhism in the late imperial period. A similar attitude may be discerned on the part of the Chinese government today. The five "accepted" popular religions (two forms of Christianity and Islam have been added to Buddhism and Daoism) are recognized by the state within officially approved spheres, but unorthodox offshoots, such as the Falun Gong (with Buddhist roots), fundamentalist forms of Islam, or radical evangelical Christian sects, are subject to coercion and persecution.

A further related point should be noted. There is little mention in the discussion that follows of the Buddhist laity. The primary reason is that neither the formally admitted lay devotees who form an important part of the Buddhist community nor the much larger Chinese population, huge numbers of which are or were – often in a very loose sense – followers of the religion, are hardly mentioned in Chinese legislation. Lay devotees were the subject of one sub-statute in the Qing period, but are scarcely noticed in Republican or Communist law. Secular law relating to Buddhism up to almost the end of the twentieth century was concerned exclusively with monks and nuns and with the monasteries and temples in which they lived. The general public, in imperial times at least, was to be protected from excessive contact with the Buddhist clergy; they were, in a sense, the prize to be contended for rather than the players. It is only in the Communist legislation on religion, much of it concerned with the congregational faiths of Christianity and Islam, that "followers" of Buddhism are mentioned.

This chapter is laid out in three major sections: the Qing period, the post-Qing Republican period and the Communist period to the present. The general topics discussed within each historical period are: administrative bureaucracies and substantive laws, Buddhist temples and their inhabitants, land and religious property, and taxation.

Buddhism in the Qing

The Qing established an administrative system with ecclesiastical officials at each level of government to control the clergy and to ensure that they followed the *qinggui* ("the rules of purity"). Precedents for such a system go back to the earliest days of Buddhism in China. The first Ming emperor (himself a former Buddhist monk) also adopted this approach as a way to reform religious life and restrict its growth. Although the system of salaried "monk-officials" had degenerated by the end of the Ming, the Manchu rulers were so enthusiastic about it that they adopted the system in their original capital at Mukden (now Shenyang) ten years before their invasion of China.[4] This Registry of Buddhist Monks (*Senglusi*), with its elaborate hierarchy of officials and assistants throughout the empire, remained in the last edition of the *Qing Administrative Code* in 1898.[5] Monk-officials exercised a broad criminal jurisdiction over monks and nuns, except in the most serious cases, such as robbery, homicide, or sexual debauchery, which had to be reported to the local magistrate. Yet in practice, discipline in Buddhist monasteries was usually maintained by the monasteries' own officers. Although various tasks were imposed on monk-officials in the mid-eighteenth century, there is very little evidence that by 1900 they fulfilled any significant function other than issuing (usually selling) the licenses required to become a monk or nun after the Board of Rites ceased to issue these directly in 1739.

The Qing, like their Ming predecessors, sought to contain Buddhism within its existing boundaries through statutes. The principal legislation in this case was the part of the *Qing Code* pertaining to the Board of Revenue and the sub-statutes attached to it. Immediately following the rules on registration of families for tax purposes, the statute curtailed the opportunities for individuals to "leave their families" (a conventional expression in Chinese for entering religious life) and thus cease to be productive members of society. First, it required a person to obtain a permit from the Board of Rites to become a novice monk or nun. Second, the statute prohibited the construction of new Buddhist monasteries, Daoist temples, and Buddhist and Daoist nunneries without imperial permission, with penalties that included 100 blows of the bamboo for the perpetrators, military exile for monks or priests, enslavement of nuns found in such convents, and confiscation of the land and building materials.[6]

A subsequent sub-statute forbade boys to enter religious life once they had attained majority under customary law (sixteen *sui*, which might be as little as fourteen years old), unless they had at least two brothers apparently

[4] The Manchus adopted this rule even before they had established themselves as emperors of China; Decree of Tiancong 6 (1633) in *Da Qing huidian*, 1898, 501.1b (1963 reprint, 15:11735).

[5] W.F. Mayers, *The Chinese Government* (Shanghai: Kelly and Walsh, 1897; reprinted Taipei: Ch'engwen Publishing, 1966), 84–85. There were no such officials at the provincial level of government.

[6] *Da Qing lüli zengxiu tongzuan jicheng* (The comprehensively edited and annotated penal statutes and sub-statutes of the Great Qing) (Shanghai: Wenyuan Shanfang, 1906), 8.12a. Translation in G. Jamieson, *Chinese Family and Commercial Law* (Shanghai: Kelly and Walsh, 1921), 61–62.

to secure the ancestral succession.[7] However, this sub-statute left open another important source of recruitment: the adoption of orphans and foundlings who would grow up to become monks or nuns, a long-standing practice that had tacit government approval. Various other sub-statutes were added by Qing emperors, including one in 1736 that prescribed a procedure for obtaining consent for the establishment of new monasteries and temples. How effective these provisions were is debatable. In his commentary on the *Qing Code* in 1905, a distinguished Qing legal official pronounced this procedure a dead letter.

There were many other offenses scattered throughout the *Qing Code* that applied specifically to the clergy. In some cases, such as the prohibition of marriage for Buddhist monks and nuns,[8] these restrictions were directed at enforcing the rules of the religion. Others were intended to distance the saṅgha from ordinary people. Under the *Qing Code* heading of "Sacrilege," officials, soldiers, and ordinary people were forbidden to allow their wives or daughters to visit monasteries or temples to worship.[9] A sub-statute imposed punishment on monks or priests who lured married women or girls into temples to have sexual relations with them.[10] All of these restrictions formed part of the criminal law and were enforceable by punishments, which usually included 50 or 100 strokes of the bamboo and the forcible return of monks and nuns to lay life. Furthermore, members of the clergy who engaged in adultery, fornication, or other sexual crimes were subject to a punishment two degrees more severe than other offenders.[11]

One criminal statute introduced by the Ming was remarkable for its direct official interference in Buddhist doctrine by requiring all monks and nuns to offer sacrifices to their ancestors when visiting their parents and to observe the same statutory mourning rules as the other members of the family, even though as a matter both of customary law and Buddhist doctrine, they were no longer members.[12] However, there is no evidence that this rule was ever enforced in Qing times. A further rule in the same

7 *Da Qing lü*, 8.12b.

8 *Da Qing lü*, 10.20a. Translation in Jamieson, *Chinese Family and Commercial Law*, 40–41. A translation of the identical provision in the *Da Ming lü* can be found in Jiang Yonglin, *The Great Ming Code* (Seattle: University of Washington Press, 2005), 87.

9 *Da Qing lü*, 16.6a. Identical provisions in the *Da Ming lü* translated in Jiang, *Ming Code*, 112. See also Hui-chen Wang Liu, *The Traditional Chinese Clan Rules* (Locust Valley: J.J. Augustin, 1959), 95–96.

10 *Da Qing lü*, 16.6b.

11 *Da Qing lü*, 33.13b. Original Ming statute translated in Jiang, *Ming Code*, 217. A French translation of the Qing statute and two related sub-statutes can be found in Guy Boulais, *Manuel du code chinois* (1924, reprinted Taipei: Ch'engwen, 1966), 693.

12 *Da Qing lü*, 17. 19a. Ming statute translated in Jiang, 117.

Ming statute requiring the clergy to wear simple cotton clothing, allowing silk only for their ceremonial vestments, was and still remains an almost universal practice.[13]

Although all of these penal statutes remained at least theoretically in force until the end of the Qing period in 1911, none survived after the introduction of Western notions of criminal law in the early twentieth century.[14] Formal discrimination in the application of criminal law between different social groups, whether based on occupation, ethnicity, religion, or otherwise, was abolished in line with Article 5 of the *Provisional Constitution of 1912*.[15]

Despite the absence of any legal concept of corporate personality in Qing times, land could be registered in a variety of names other than those of natural persons, including the names of various institutions. In particular, land was frequently registered in the names of Buddhist monasteries and temples; for many purposes such land was treated as the land of the institution in question, giving these bodies what was, in effect, a quasi-corporate status.[16] Buddhist temples in this period were divided into four broad categories based on function, organization, and ownership. The first category was comprised of the usually large public monasteries, which belonged to the entire saṅgha.[17] The second consisted of the much more widespread hereditary temples, monasteries, and nunneries, each belonging to a religious "family."[18] Third, there were temples, both monasteries and nunneries, which were privately owned by laypeople, typically the members of a local clan or lineage.[19] In the last category were temples that were

13 *Ibid.*

14 See generally M.J. Meijer, *The Introduction of Modern Criminal Law in China* 2nd ed. (Hong Kong: Lung Men Bookstore, 1967).

15 For the English text of the *Provisional Constitution of the Republic of China*, adopted March 11, 1912, see William L. Tung, *The Political Institutions of Modern China* (The Hague: Martinus Nijhoff, 1966), 322–25.

16 In this sense it may be said that such monasteries had the attributes of legal personality – that is to say, they were separate "persons" from the individuals who governed them or belonged to them. However, the Western theory of the corporation with separate legal personality was unknown as a concept in traditional China.

17 The finding of the trial judge in Hong Kong in *To Kan Chi & Others v. Pui Man Yau & Others* (unreported judgment, High Court Miscellaneous Proceedings 562/1992, dated November 26, 1998, http://www.legalref.judiciary.gov.hk) at para 8.9 that a large public monastery was owned by "all people of that faith" was clearly an error, since the expert evidence on which it was based stated that such establishments belonged to the whole clergy of the faith in question. The error was repeated *per incuriam* in the judgments of the Court of Appeal (unreported, para. 61) and Court of Final Appeal [2000].

18 Holmes Welch, *The Practice of Chinese Buddhism* (Cambridge: Harvard University Press, 1967), 276ff.

19 *Ibid.*, 133.

the communal property of villages, which in some cases were Buddhist in character.

In public monasteries, with their well-established procedures for dealing with property and its income, the opportunities for large-scale speculation were no doubt limited. However, in hereditary temples the position was different. In the customary law governing families, the powers of the family head in relation to the alienation of family land were open to different interpretations. While the relationship between monks and nuns and their disciples lacked the absolute authority and duty of obedience that characterized the relationship of father and son, it was still difficult for the junior member to control the activities of the head, particularly when the property of a temple was registered in his or her name.

In principle, the estates of temples were subject to the ordinary taxes on agricultural land, but in practice, many monasteries and temples were able to obtain exemption from the land tax under the legislation of various dynasties. This privilege extended to a wide variety of endowments, not only for Buddhist temples but also for charity, education, family, and clan ancestral worship. This longstanding land tax exemption for institutions was eventually confirmed by a sub-statute, which also provided: "In each province where the literati or ordinary people purchase land to establish public cemeteries or temples, the amount originally fixed for the grain tax may be remitted in full after the circumstances have been reported to the authorities and verified."[20] Newly founded Buddhist temples that received official permission would clearly have had little difficulty in also obtaining the exemption, but it seems that in practice it was available to most temples. It can be surmised that the donors of land found ways of persuading the local officials to grant exemption regardless of the way in which the temple was founded.

The exemption of monastic estates from the grain tax on land in Qing times gave rise to a practice, which seems to have been quite common in some parts of the country, where wealthy landowners registered their own land in the names of temples to shelter it from tax. This practice tended to confuse the distinction between temples that belonged to the saṅgha and those that were the private property of lay families. For example, a government order issued in 1766 by the literary chancellor of Zhejiang province, who had disciplinary powers over the scholarly gentry, denounced degree holders who claimed to be "patrons" of temples but who treated

[20] *Imperially Authorized Statutes and Regulations of the Board of Revenue*, in *Da Qing huidian* 7.16a–16b (1963 reprint, 2:509–510).

the temples' land as their own and engaged in litigation to assert their claims. It concluded: "Landed property donated by gentry or commoners and temples built by them may be managed only by Buddhist monks or nuns or by Daoist priests."[21]

Buddhism in the Republican Period

Following the revolution of 1911, many of the clergy were fearful of a wholesale confiscation of the buildings and lands of Buddhist monasteries.[22] There were, in fact, numerous seizures of temple lands in the aftermath of the revolution, but the *Temple Ordinance of 1915*[23] was more favorable to the Buddhist cause than many had expected.[24] Although it is true that this law restored a system of government supervision and that various features of monastic life had to be registered with local officials,[25] in some ways the *Temple Ordinance of 1915* seems to have been designed to give the saṅgha greater freedom in relation both to monastic organization and to personal status.

The *Temple Ordinance of 1915* first contains a classification of all monasteries and temples in which Buddhist or Daoist clergy resided. Small, privately owned temples are expressly excluded from the operation of the *Temple Ordinance of 1915* altogether. The rest are distinguished in part by function, by method of governance, and by classification. Function refers to "propagating Buddhism" or "initiating the clergy," which extended to Daoists; method of governance refers to the two categories of "ten directions" monasteries (the large institutions); and classification refers to either "dense forests," suggesting numerous monks or nuns, or "branches" of larger convents.[26] What was studiously avoided in these categorizations

[21] Decree dated Qianlong 31 (1767), *Qinding xuezheng quanshu* (Imperially Authorized Complete Manual for Provincial Education Commissioners), 26.16b–17a, (reprinted Taipei: Wenhai chubanshe, 1968), 492–93. See K.C. Hsiao, *Rural China: Imperial Control in the Nineteenth Century* (Seattle: University of Washington Press, 1960), 280.

[22] Holmes Welch, *The Buddhist Revival in China* (Cambridge: Harvard University Press, 1968), Chapter II, passim.

[23] *Guanli simiao tiaoli* (Ordinance on the administration of monasteries and temples), promulgated *Jiaoling* No. 66, October 29, 1915, and amended by *Jiaoling* No. 12, May 20, 1921. *Sifa ligui* (Regulations on justice) (Beijing: Ministry of Justice, 1922, 2 vols.), 1:731–34.

[24] This did not prevent vigorous lobbying against the *Temple Ordinance of 1915* while it was being considered by the legislature. See Welch, *Buddhist Revival*, 38–39.

[25] *Guanli simiao tiaoli*, Articles 6, 7, and 9. Under the terms of this law, each religious institution had to register itself, its property, the appointment of its abbot or superior, and also the school that every monastery and temple was now required to maintain.

[26] *Ibid.*, Article 1.

was any mention of "hereditary" temples, which comprised the vast majority of Buddhist (and Daoist) establishments at the end of the Qing era. The *Temple Ordinance of 1915* also provided that temples and monasteries, as well as the clergy, should receive "the same degree of protection" as the ordinary people, and it prohibited the abolition or dissolution of monasteries or temples.[27]

The *Temple Ordinance of 1915* made clear that the superior of each institution was to have control of the property, subject to safeguards,[28] and provided that the succession of this official was to comply with the custom of the institution in question, "unless the people of the Republic of China (sic) will not accept the succession."[29] A further important development in the earliest years of the Republic was the recognition that temples and monasteries, among other traditional institutions, could possess an independent juridical personality either as corporations or foundations – the latter derived from the German *stiftung* – and were capable, under the new civil law, of owning property in their own names. This innovation was not provided for in the *Temple Ordinance of 1915*, but resulted from the rulings of the *Daliyuan*, the Supreme Court of early Republican China, which applied Western legal principles to the realities of Chinese society on a case-by-case basis.[30]

The *Temple Ordinance of 1915* provided that the religious rules that monks and nuns followed should conform to custom, subject to the limitation that the rules did not contravene public order or public morality.[31] However, the provision goes on to state that "to amend or reform those . . . matters it is proper for the monks or priests of a 'dense forest' to convene an assembly of all the practitioners of the religion," in effect giving coenobitic communities the power to introduce their own rules.[32] The local magistrate could investigate serious breaches of the "rules of the religion" and either exonerate or dismiss individual monks or nuns, including abbots and other officers. However, questions of criminal liability under the modernized *Provisional Criminal Code*[33] had to be referred to the newly established law courts, which also heard civil disputes.[34]

[27] *Ibid.*, Articles 2 and 4. [28] *Ibid.*, Article 10, 11, and 13. [29] *Ibid.*, Article 10.

[30] Brief summaries of these decisions will be found in Guo Wei (ed.), *Daliyuan panjueli quanshu* (Complete judgments of the *Daliyuan*, 1912–1928) (reprinted Taipei: Ch'engwen, 1972). For translations of a number of such summaries, see F.T. Cheng, *The Chinese Supreme Court Decisions* (Peking: Commission on Extraterritoriality, 1923), 8–18.

[31] *Guanli simiao tiaoli*, Article 15. [32] *Ibid.*

[33] *Provisional Criminal Code of the Republic of China*, promulgated March 16, 1912 (Peking: Commission on Extraterritoriality, 1923).

[34] *Guanli simiao tiaoli*, Article 19.

Another provision made an important change by requiring ordination masters to give ordinands a certificate recording personal details, and the date and place of ordination, while reporting the same matters to the civil authority as a matter of record.[35] Clergy who were fully ordained before the *Temple Ordinance of 1915* came into force were issued retrospective certificates.[36] This replacement of the old novice license benefited the saṅgha because it proved that the bearer had undergone the full process of becoming a monk or nun. The old permits enabled many "wild monks" – former novices who dropped out – to pose as ordained monks.

Another provision required monks or nuns who engaged in public preaching to confine themselves to explaining and preaching the religion and morality, transforming society by teaching, and disseminating patriotic ideas.[37] The *Temple Ordinance of 1915* also required all monasteries and temples to open schools that would give a general education as well as a religious one, but there is no suggestion in the text that monks or nuns were expected to become the teachers.[38]

The *Temple Ordinance of 1915* remained in force until 1927, when the new nationalist government of the Guomindang, established in Nanjing, passed new legislation to replace it, which in turn was repealed and replaced at the end of the same year owing to objections by some legislators.[39] The *Temple Ordinance of 1929*[40] was a much shorter document than its 1915 predecessor, neatly illustrating advances made during the previous decade in legislative drafting. Abandoning the cumbrous classification scheme, the *Temple Ordinance of 1929* embraced "all religious buildings where there are resident Buddhist monks or Daoist priests" (implicitly including female as well as male residents), excluding from its operation only monasteries or temples controlled by a local public organization, or those built and controlled by private persons.[41] It retained the supervisory control of the superior of each institution (who now had to be a Chinese national) and required him or her to draw up half-yearly accounts and present them to

[35] *Ibid.*, Article 18. [36] *Ibid.* [37] *Ibid.*, Article 16. [38] *Ibid.*, Article 6.

[39] See Holmes Welch, *Buddhist Revival*, 41–42, who attributes the repeal to successful lobbying by the Chinese Buddhist Association founded in Shanghai in 1929.

[40] *Jiandu simiao tiaoli* (Ordinance for the supervision of monasteries and temples), promulgated December 7, 1929. See Wu Jingxiong (comp.), *Zhonghua minguo liufa liyou panjie huibian* (A collection of the Six Codes of the Republic of China with explanations, judgments, and interpretations) (Revised and enlarged by Guo Wei, Shanghai: Huiwen Tang Xin Jishuju, 1948, 6 volumes), 1:597–605.

[41] *Jiandu simiao tiaoli*, Articles 1 and 3. A judicial interpretation of this provision decided that a Buddhist Association was not a local public organization for this purpose, *Yuanzi* No. 817 (1932), noted in Wu Jingxiong, *Zhonghua panjie huibian*, 1:599.

the local government.[42] The provision on schools was not repeated, but all institutions, according to their financial circumstances, were to engage in public welfare or charitable work.[43] While the Guomindang Party's *Constitution of 1931*[44] continued to guarantee equality regardless of race, class, or religion, there was no provision for freedom of religion, although "freedom of religious belief" did eventually appear as Article 13 of the short-lived *Constitution of 1947*.[45]

The Nanjing government also brought about a profound change in the civil status of the Buddhist clergy, though it seems possible that it happened by accident rather than by design. This change occurred with the enactment of the *Civil Code of the Republic of China* in 1930 and 1931.[46] Although the criminal law was modernized along European lines immediately after the revolution of 1911, the codification of civil law was a more difficult task. Despite several drafts, it was only completed in 1931. During the intervening years, the *Qing Code*, stripped of its criminal provisions, remained in force, under the title of *Civil Law Temporarily in Force*.[47] Alongside it, the Chinese courts continued to apply customary law. The result for Buddhist clergy, as for the population as a whole, was that the law of civil status, family relationships (including the fictitious religious family relationships that underlay the whole organization of the saṅgha), and property remained as it had been in Qing times.

With the enactment of the *Civil Code* in 1930, all of this changed. As a matter of law there was no longer a specific civil status for monks or nuns; as far as their civil rights and capacity were concerned, the clergy were ordinary citizens. Their incapacity to contract a valid marriage, for example, was removed. A much greater change, from the point of traditional Buddhist organization, was the disappearance of the old law supporting the creation of fictitious families by analogy to adoption, none of which was provided for by the *Civil Code*. The inheritance system within the artificial family no longer had legal force.

42 *Ibid.*, Article 9. The accounts were to include a report of "matters effectively accomplished."

43 *Ibid.*, Article 10.

44 *Provisional Constitution of the Republic of China for the Period of Political Tutelage*, promulgated June 1, 1931; see Tung, *Political Institutions*, 344–49.

45 *The Constitution of the Republic of China*, promulgated January 1, 1947; Tung, *Political Institutions*, 350–66.

46 *Civil Code of the Republic of China* (Zhonghua minguo minfa), Parts I, II, and III promulgated between May and November 1929, and Parts IV and V promulgated in 1930. Translation into English by Ching-lin Hsia et al. (Shanghai: Kelly and Walsh, 1931).

47 *Ibid.*, Introduction, ix–x.

In reality, it seems probable that these changes had very little effect on the lives of the saṅgha between their introduction in 1930–31 and the wholesale abolition of the Guomindang legal system in 1949. As with other aspects of law during this period, the extent to which the population as a whole was even aware of legal changes outside a few large cities on the coast and in the Yangzi River Valley was very limited; people simply continued to follow the customary law long after it had lost its validity in the eyes of the state.[48] Additionally, the potential for conflict between these two versions of law does not appear to have given rise to litigation in this period.

However, in the early Republican period, a report produced by the Ministry of Judicial Administration during a national survey of customary law, suggested that the illicit sale of the common property of hereditary temples was a significant problem and that there had been litigation over such matters within recent memory. First, the *Temple Ordinance of 1915* put temple property (including scriptures, paintings, carvings, and other treasures), under the control of the principal resident cleric, but prohibited its hypothecation or alienation. Second, the *Temple Ordinance of 1929* established a tighter regime for all temples, obliging the principal to account twice yearly for income and expenditures, and restricting the latter to certain specified "proper purposes." Land and all other property had to be registered with the government, and although the religious group to which it belonged could by a majority vote resolve to dispose of it or alter it, government permission was also required for such acts. Each of these two statutes gave rise to a considerable amount of litigation, and the Supreme Court issued a number of interpretations to clarify some of the provisions on property.[49] Regardless, the illicit sale or gift of land by members of the clergy continued throughout this period.

After the Republican legislation excluded private temples from its operation, there was a considerable amount of litigation in which lay families and clans tried to establish proprietary claims to Buddhist monasteries and nunneries to which they had in the past donated land, money, or buildings. The courts applied what appears to have been a long-standing rule

48 H. McAleavy, "Some Aspects of Marriage and Divorce in Communist China" in J.N.D. Anderson (ed.), *Family Law in Asia and Africa* (London: Allen and Unwin, 1968), 73–89 at 75.

49 See, for example, *Interpretation Tongzi* No. 726 given by the Daliyuan (Supreme Court at Beijing, 1912–28) to the Superior Court of Henan Province, December 20, 1917, in Guo Wei (ed.), *Daliyuan Jieshili Quanshu* (reprinted Taipei, Ch'engwen, 1972), 398–99; *Interpretation Tongzi* No. 1901, given by the Daliyuan to the Department of Industry of Zhejiang Province, October 17, 1924, *Ibid.*, 1100–01; *Interpretation Yuanzi* No. 3934, given by the Nationalist Judicial Council in 1948, in Wu Jinxiong, *Zhonghua panjie huibian*, 1:909.

of customary law, namely that once land or buildings had been donated to a temple, the donor could not claim it back. Only in cases where it could be demonstrated that a person had used his own assets to build a monastery or temple without any intention of making a donation to the public sphere could it be said that he or his successors were the owners of a private temple. Such an intention was not easy to prove, as shown in the case of the Pumensi, a Buddhist temple in Ningbo, claimed by the Shi clan on the basis of some inscriptions and other documents showing that their ancestors had given land, restored buildings, administered the monastery, and even appointed head monks in the past. However, because the evidence of their involvement did not reach back to the foundation of the monastery, which the court accepted as having occurred in 945 on the basis of a local gazetteer, their claim accordingly failed.[50]

In the Republican period, the liability of monasteries and temples to pay the land tax on their property holdings was restated in the legislation of 1915,[51] and there is some evidence that the practice of wealthy landowners registering their own land with Buddhist temples to avoid taxation survived into the early twentieth century in northern Jiangsu.[52] However, in the People's Republic, the question of tax became irrelevant, both because of the confiscation of the agricultural property of monasteries and because this form of tax ceased to be levied.

The Communist Period to the Present

The Communist Party policy toward Buddhism first appeared in the politics of the land reforms in the areas of the country under Communist control between 1927 and 1949, and later applied at the national level in the early 1950s. Although Article 5 of the *Common Program of the Chinese People's Political Consultative Conference* provided for freedom of religious belief,[53] the new government seems to have moved slowly in establishing its own bureaucratic control of religion. The secretive approach of the Communists toward legislation of all kinds in the first three decades of their regime makes it difficult to be certain of the early history. A

[50] Supreme Court of the Republic of China, Civil Appeal No. 2138, 1935 (*Sifa Gongbao* (Judicial Gazette) No. 182, April 28, 1937; translation in *L'Annee Judiciaire Chinoise*, Year 10, *Affaires Civiles*, 83–86).

[51] *Guanli simiao tiaoli* (Temple ordinance of 1915), Article 8.

[52] Hsiao, *Rural China*, 280.

[53] Promulgated September 29, 1949; A.P. Blaustein, *Fundamental Legal Documents of Communist China* (South Hackensack: Fred. B. Rothman and Co. 1962), 34–53.

State Council decision on the organization of "religious affairs work" in December 1955 suggests a gradualist approach to the establishment of a national religious bureaucracy: setting up small offices of religious affairs in some places, larger ones elsewhere, and requiring local governments to designate a cadre to take the position of secretary of the local "mass organizations" of believers, which were to become a key element in the management of religion in the People's Republic.[54] The Bureau of Religious Affairs of the Central Government oversaw this nationwide bureaucracy and remains in charge of religious affairs at the time of this writing.

Much of the work of the Bureau and its regional offices is carried out through the agency of the five national associations, which in theory "represent" the five officially recognized religions, mediate between their coreligionists and the atheist party-state. For Buddhists, the Chinese Buddhist Association fulfills this role at the national level. Although officially nongovernmental in form, the association is government-subsidized and its chairman, many of its officers, and the officers of its affiliated local Buddhist associations are prominent monks or nuns who have been co-opted. These individuals are selected for these positions in accordance with principles not unlike those laid down for choosing monk-officials in the *Qing Code*. In short, the government of the People's Republic has established an administrative bureaucracy to control Buddhism that is every bit as comprehensive as that of the Qing. Like the Ming and Qing regimes, it uses the clergy to control the clergy, but it does so more subtly through the network of Buddhist associations, many having been formed long before the arrival of the Communists and thus able to claim some degree of authenticity as representatives of the "progressive" Buddhist revival of the early twentieth century.

However, the establishment of the Communist-led People's Republic in October 1949 presented the Buddhist monastic community with more pressing problems than questions about administrative bureaucracy or civil status by inaugurating a period of intense political pressure on the saṅgha, which continued intermittently until 1979. It has been referred to by one scholar as "the decimation of the *saṅgha*."[55] The process was launched before 1949 in Communist-held areas in the course of the land reform. Prior to the land reforms, many Buddhist monasteries, both large and small, had extensive landholdings that were usually leased on long or even

[54] *Notice of the State Council Regarding the Question of the Administration and Organization of Religious Work*, December 1, 1955, *Zhonghua renmin gongheguo fagui huibian*, vol. 2, July–December 1955 (Peking: Legal Publishing House, 1956), 111.

[55] Holmes Welch, *Buddhism under Mao* (Cambridge: Harvard University Press, 1972), chapter 2.

perpetual terms to tenant farmers. Under the *Land Reform Law of 1950*,[56] all rural agricultural land belonging to religious bodies was confiscated for redistribution; not long afterward the same treatment was extended to agricultural land in suburban areas of the cities, leaving only urban land rights unaffected.[57] Additionally, temple buildings were frequently requisitioned for secular purposes.

Many members of the clergy were persuaded to return to lay life when rent from their landholdings, the only source of income for their temples, was cut off in this way. In some places, groups of them were allowed to work the land formerly belonging to their convents as laborers, sometimes forming their own cooperatives. In the words of Liu Shaoqi's report on land reform to the Chinese People's Political Consultative Conference (a Communist Party-appointed assembly of United Front and other non-Party "progressive" organizations and individuals) on June 14, 1950: "Monks, nuns, Daoists and priests in the rural districts ... should be given shares of land and other means of production if they have no other means of livelihood and are willing and able to take up agricultural production, otherwise they will become jobless vagabonds and disturb public order, to the detriment of the interests of the people."[58]

Based on a famous essay of Mao Zedong, the 1950 *Decisions of the Government Administration Council Concerning the Differentiation of Class Status in the Countryside*[59] accompanied land reform and was supplemented by further rules to cover urban residents.[60] Under these rules, monks and nuns in general were classified as "religious practitioners." Some abbots and superiors, however, were classified as landlords and executed.[61] Clerics who took up other occupations might be classified, for example, as poor peasants or agricultural laborers, but some continued to live as caretakers in monasteries and temples, which were ordered to be preserved on grounds of their historical or cultural importance. This latter group appears to

56 *Law on Land Reform of the People's Republic of China*, promulgated by the Central People's Government, June 30, 1950, in Blaustein, *Fundamental Legal Documents*, 276–90 at 276 (Article 3).

57 *Regulations Governing Land Reform in Suburban Areas*, promulgated November 21, 1950, *Zhongyang renmin zhengfu faling huibian* (Collected laws and decrees of the Central People's Government), vol. 1, (September 1949–December 1950), 93–95, Article 4.

58 Liu Shaoqi, then Vice-Chairman of the Central People's Government, report to the Second Session of the Chinese People's Political Consultative Conference, Beijing, June 14, 1950 in J.E.P. Wang (ed.), *Selected Legal Documents of the People's Republic of China*, (Arlington: University Publications of America, 1976), 474.

59 Promulgated August 20, 1950, *Zhongyang renmin zhengfu faling huibian* vol. 1 (1949–50), 73–90. Translation located in Blaustein, *Fundamental Legal Documents*, 291–324 (see Article 10).

60 These extensions are found in numerous supplementary rules issued at the local level.

61 See, e.g., Holmes Welch, *Practice*, 130–31.

have been the nucleus of the coenobitic population that emerged when the successive waves of antireligious policies, campaigns, and persecution finally subsided in the late 1970s. Only then did the Communist Party begin to implement its policy of freedom of religious belief, long embedded both in Article 88 of the *Constitution of 1954*[62] and in Article 28 of the *Constitution of 1975*.[63]

The first public manifestation of legal change was the wording of the post-Cultural Revolution *Constitution of 1982*. Article 36 was left unchanged when the *Constitution of 1982* was amended in 1993, and consequently expresses the current law:

> Article 36. Citizens of the People's Republic of China enjoy freedom of religious belief. No state organ, public organization or individual may compel citizens to believe in, or not to believe in, any religion. The state protects normal religious activities. No one may make use of religion to engage in activities that disrupt public order, impair the health of citizens or interfere with the educational system of the state. Religious bodies and religious affairs are not subject to any foreign domination.[64]

As often happens in Communist China, however, the implementation of the new policy was in full swing before its existence was ceremonially confirmed by legislation. Many famous temples, monasteries, and institutions, which had been previously suppressed but preserved, were reopened to large crowds of worshippers as well as tourists as soon as the Cultural Revolution was over. By the early 1980s, the pent-up demand for religious expression led to a widespread epidemic of temple building.[65]

The legal basis for these developments was slow to emerge as the law-making activities of State Bureau of Religious Affairs were kept secret for many years. Not until 1994 did the People's Republic issue a public statute

[62] *Constitution of the People's Republic of China*, promulgated September 20, 1954, *Zhonghua renmin gongheguo fagui huibian* (Collected laws and regulations of the People's Republic of China), vol. 1, (September 1954–June 1955), 4–31; translated in Blaustein, *Fundamental Legal Documents*, 1–33.

[63] *Constitution of the People's Republic of China*, promulgated January 17, 1975, *Zhonghua renmin gongheguo xianfa* (Constitution of the People's Republic of China) (bilingual pamphlet, Beijing: Commercial Press, 1975). The same wording was used in Article 46 of the subsequent *Constitution of the People's Republic of China*, promulgated March 5, 1978 (pamphlet of the same name, Beijing: Foreign Languages Press, 1978).

[64] *Constitution of the People's Republic of China*, promulgated in amended form, March 29, 1993, in *Zhonghua renmin gongheguo falü fagui quanshu* (Compendium of laws and regulations of the People's Republic of China) (NPP, China Democratic Legal System Publishing House, 1994) vol. 1, 20–29; translation in *The Laws of the People's Republic of China* vol. 5 (1993), (Beijing: Science Press, 1995), 9–41.

[65] "The Indiscriminate Building of Temples in Rural Areas Should be Curbed," *Nanfang ribao*, June 5, 1982, 2; translated in FBIS China Report, Political, Sociological, and Military Affairs No. 318, July 19, 1982, JPRS No. 81310, 21.

on religion, the *Ordinance for the Control of Places of Worship*,[66] to which were added more detailed regulations on registration and inspection of places of worship.[67] There were also regulations forbidding the unlicensed creation of colossal outdoor statues of Buddha[68] and the "chaotic" building of Buddhist and Daoist temples.[69] Prior to the public legislation of 1994, a number of important earlier measures were contained in "internal" or secret documents that have never been made available. In February 1979, for example, the Communist Party Central Committee ordered the release of the frozen bank accounts of the various religious associations, including the Chinese Buddhist Association and its local affiliates.[70]

Special rules for the revival of Buddhist and Daoist monasteries and temples in Han nationality areas were contained in a secret provisional regulation (hereafter *Procedures*) prepared by the Bureau of Religious Affairs in December 1981.[71] These rules permitted the reopening of monasteries and temples throughout the country "in accordance with the needs of believers," including a "suitable number" on the famous sacred mountains,[72] which pilgrims as well as tourists have traditionally visited. Lists of such

66 Promulgated by the State Council, January 31, 1994, *Zhonghua renmin gongheguo guowuyuan gongbao* (Gazette of the State Council of the People's Republic of China), 1984, No. 2, 50–52; translation at http://www.hrw.org/reports/ 1997/china1/, 60–62.

67 *Procedures for the Registration of Places of Worship*, promulgated by the Bureau of Religious Affairs of the State Council, April 13, 1994, *Zhonghua renmin gongheguo guowuyuan bumen guiding 1994* (Departmental Regulations of the State Council of the People's Republic of China, hereafter *Departmental Regulations 1994*) (Beijing: University of Politics and Laws Publishing House, 1996), 1499; translation at http://www.hrw.org/reports/1997/china1/, 62–64. The original text of the rules for annual inspection of places of worship have not been found, but a translation of a document dated May 1, 1994 is at the same website, 64–66.

68 *Notice Prohibiting the Indiscriminate Construction of Open-Air Statues of Buddha*, promulgated by the Bureau of Religious Affairs of the State Council, the Ministry of Construction and the State Bureau of Tourism, September 13, 1994; *Departmental Regulations 1994*, 1503.

69 *Notice of the Bureau of Religious Affairs of the State Council Prohibiting the Indiscriminate Construction of Buddhist and Daoist Monasteries and Temples*, promulgated October 20, 1994; *Departmental Regulations 1994*, 1503–04.

70 *Zhonggong zhongyang zhuanfa zhongyang tongzhanbu "dibaci quanguo zongjiao gongzuo huiyi jiyao" (jielu)* ("Summary of Discussions at the Eighth National Conference on Religious Work" of the United Front department of the Central Committee issued by the Central Committee of the Chinese Communist Party – excerpt), October 2, 1979, in *Fangdichan shenpan shouce* (Handbook for litigation concerning property in buildings and land) (Beijing: Legal Publishing House, n.d., for internal circulation), vol. 2, 1658.

71 *Guanyu Hanzu Diqu Fajiao Daojiao Siguan Guanli Shixing Banfa* (Provisional procedures regarding the administration of Buddhist and Daoist temples in Han nationality areas; hereafter cited as *Procedures*), Bureau of Religious Affairs of the State Council, ratified and issued by the State Council, December 26, 1981, *Jingji fagui huibian*, 1978–84 (Compendium of economic laws and regulations, 1978–84) (*Neibu faxing* (internal distribution), n.d., n.p.p., *Guangzhoushi gongshang xingzhang guanli xuehui*, 2 vols.) 2:600–03.

72 *Procedures*, Article 2(1).

monasteries and temples were compiled by local governments in consultation with the local Buddhist and Daoist associations, but no temples or monasteries were to be reopened or built without official permission.[73] Reopened temples and those in which clergy were already residing were to be placed under "Buddhist or Daoist administration," although subject to the "leadership" (a Communist euphemism for direct control) of the Bureau of Religious Affairs. The upkeep of buildings, "cultural relics," and parks and woodlands was to be a government responsibility.[74]

The further provisions of these secret *Procedures* were of great importance to the life of the saṅgha. Article 5, for instance, sanctions two alternative ways of selecting a superior: (1) "traditional practice," whereby a monk or nun who has "high religious attainments and is patriotic" may "assume the office of superior," or (2) a superior may be chosen by "democratic consultation," so that the clergy of a particular temple may opt for "democratic administration by monks or nuns" and followers of the religions – a phrase that would certainly embrace lay devotees and might possibly extend to a wider "congregation." These provisions suggest that in temples where the consensus favored tradition, the fictitious family system might still determine the succession to the headship of the temple.

Although these *Procedures* appear to have been tolerant of the traditional organization of the saṅgha into religious families, the civil status of the clergy remained exactly the same as that of other citizens, as it was after the enactment of the Republican *Civil Code* (the class ascriptions such as "religious practitioner," "landlord," and "poor peasant," were abolished in 1979).[75] The resulting tension between the traditional customary law observed by the saṅgha and the law of the state was put to the test in a case that the Bureau of Religious Affairs referred to the Supreme People's Court in 1994. The Court said that "in the law of our country as it now stands there are certainly no special provisions for succession to the estate of a person who was a Buddhist monk"; he was an ordinary citizen and his estate must pass to the appropriate members of his natural family, and it continued that the question was a novel one that could only be resolved by legislation. No such legislation appears to have been passed and the legal status of the Buddhist clergy remains unchanged, although within the saṅgha the traditional customs are observed.

[73] *Procedures*, Article 2(3) and (4). [74] *Procedures*, Articles 3(1) and (2), and Article 3(3).

[75] For the significance of this change in terms of Chinese legal theory, see A.R. Dicks, "The Chinese Legal System: Reforms in the Balance," *China Quarterly* 119 (September 1989), 546–48.

Although it was no doubt easy enough to reopen the large and often famous temples that had been protected as cultural relics and tourist attractions, the recovery of possession and property rights in the case of many small institutions was a complex process, often involving the courts. One problem was to get the various state units that had requisitioned many temples to vacate them. There were also complications where monks or nuns had continued to inhabit temples. Some remained celibate and had continued to live a religious life; others who were laicized and married had families with a claim on the property. The Shanghai Municipal Superior People's Court and the Shanghai Municipal Religious Affairs Bureau jointly drafted a series of principles for solving problems of this kind, which was approved by the Supreme People's Court and the Religious Affairs Bureau of the State Council and published as a model.[76] Yet, some of the problems encountered did not fit into the categories set out in this document.

Conclusion: The Current Situation

The position of Buddhism in Chinese law at the present time is governed by the *Ordinance on Religious Affairs*, which was enacted by the State Council on November 30, 2004 and went into effect on March 1, 2005. This *Ordinance*, which applies to all religions, is a codification of some previously promulgated regulations and contains general provisions that make few references to specific religions. It has seven main sections. The first introductory section declares freedom of religious belief, but places that freedom within the context of public order and national unity. Article 5 rehearses the administrative powers of the local departments of religious affairs.

Part II of the *Ordinance* requires religious organizations such as the Chinese Buddhist Association to register with the government, which gives them an independent legal personality as a corporation. This enables them, among other things, to own property. It also contains provisions governing religious publications and their contents, as well as religious education.

Although the *Ordinance* falls short of further delineating the functions of religious organizations, it seems clear that the Chinese Buddhist

[76] "Zuigao renmin fayuan, guohuyuan zongjiao shiwuju quanyu simiao, daoguan fangwuchanguan guishu wentide fuhan" (Responsive letter of the Supreme People's Court and the Bureau of Religious Affairs of the State Council regarding questions of the ownership of the buildings of Buddhist monasteries and temples and Daoist temples), January 27, 1981, with the original report appended, in *Fangdichan shenpan shouce* (Handbook for litigation concerning property in buildings and land), vol. 2, 1663–65.

Association has important normative and disciplinary powers. For example, the Association proposed at the Fourth National Council Meeting in 1983 that Buddhist monks and nuns should no longer be scarred by burning incense on their scalps during ordination and that novices only be accepted at the age of eighteen.[77] The Association's control of ordinations was more recently illustrated in an announcement by the Shaolin Temple in Henan of its intention to hold an ordination ceremony from April 20–May 21, 2010 as "approved by the Buddhist Association of China."[78]

A glimpse of the disciplinary functions of the Association is afforded by a report issued by the New York office of Human Rights in China concerning the expulsion of the abbot of Huacheng Temple in Yichun, Jiangxi province on August 22, 2006. When the abbot refused to accept a notice concerning a monk in his temple who was accused of improper relations with women during the Tiananmen demonstrations and improper relations with three female believers, both the abbot and the monk were taken away by thirty plainclothes policemen.[79]

Part III of the *Ordinance* contains the important provisions for the control of "places of religious activity," defined in the case of Buddhism as monasteries and temples. Qualified religious personnel are expected to preside, to follow appropriate religious doctrines, to obtain licensing and registration certificates with the local religious affairs office, to follow required principles of management, and to aid regular inspection by the religious affairs authorities. Temples are permitted to sell religious articles and publications and to accept donations.

Part IV of the *Ordinance* sets out the conditions under which "religious personnel," qualified in accordance with the rules of the religion and registered with the religious affairs authority, may conduct religious activities. Part V deals with the property of religious organizations and places of religious activity, making it clear that these organizations are fully capable of owning buildings and land use rights, but that these properties cannot be transferred, hypothecated, or used for investment. Part VI of the *Ordinance* sets out the various penalties for infractions of the earlier provisions, and Part VII contains largely formal provisions, including the possibility of

77 "Buddhist Council Proposes Practice, Entry Changes," Xinhua press release, December 11, 1983, in FBIS China Report, Political, Sociological, and Military Affairs, JPRS No. CPS 84–003, January 9, 1984, 12.

78 "Shaolin Temple to Perform Precept – Transmitting Ceremony," http://www.shaolin.org.cn/templates/EN_T_newS_list/index.aspx?nodeid=353&page=ContentPage&contentid=2208. September 20, 2010.

79 "Top Officials Join in Persecution of Activist Monk," http://chinaview.wordpress.com/2006/08/27/top-buddhist-officials-join-in-persecution-of-activist-monk/, May 31, 2013.

further regulations for religious exchanges with Taiwan, Hong Kong, and Macao.

This paper is only a brief introduction into the legislation of several historical Chinese government regimes concerning monastics, ownership of property, ordination, and other legal issues. It is presented in the hope that further research will be done on internal legal procedures of the monasteries, cases that demonstrate how these internal cases were handled, symbolic and visual cues to legal Buddhist rules and processes, the relationship to the local secular authorities and their use of law, and many other topics.

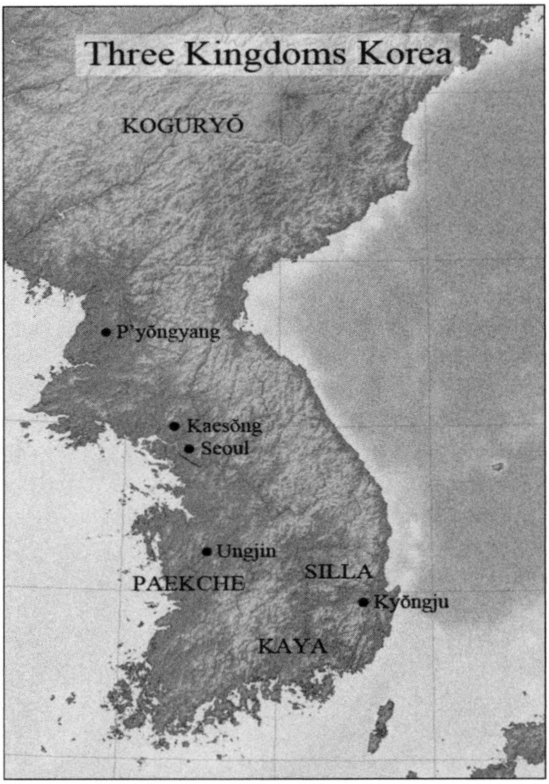

Map of Korea in the Three Kingdoms Period, c. 500 CE

CHAPTER 14

Buddhism and Law in Korean History
From Parallel Transmission to Institutional Divergence

Mark A. Nathan

Introduction

This chapter provides a brief overview of the relationship between Buddhism and law in Korea from transmission in the fourth century CE through the change of dynasties at the turn of the fourteenth century. Given the wide scope of time and the dearth of previous scholarship on this subject, this chapter can do little more than sketch the broad contours of the multifarious ways that Buddhist ideas, texts, institutions, and individuals intersected and interacted with secular law in Korean history. It begins with a consideration of the initial patterns in the transmission of Buddhism and written law to Korea, which roughly coincided, and then examines different aspects of their interconnections as the relationship developed over time. Although Buddhism and law were closely intertwined through much of this period, distinctions were gradually drawn between them leading to greater divergences and the increasing subordination of the former to the latter. Political changes in the late fourteenth century produced an onslaught of laws and legal measures designed to strip the monastic community of much of its property, rights, prestige, and power. The evidence suggests, however, that from a Buddhism and law perspective, the legal tools needed to suppress and marginalize monastic institutions had already been put in place much earlier. In other words, the radical reorientation in saṅgha-state relations at this time did not alter the fundamental structure of the relationship between Buddhism and law, although it did substantially change its character. This suggests that, while the relationship of Buddhism to law was closely related to the relationship of Buddhism to the state, the two were neither identical nor interchangeable.

The author would like to thank Sem Vermeersch, Robert Buswell, Rebecca French, Walter Hakala, and Ramya Sreenivasan for reading draft versions of this chapter at various stages in the writing process and offering helpful comments.

The Transmission of Buddhism and Law to Korea

Buddhism was officially introduced to Korea during the period known as the Three Kingdoms when the peninsula was divided among competing states in varying stages of development. The northernmost kingdom, Koguryŏ, was the earliest to develop and also the first to formally accept Buddhism in 372 CE, followed by Paekche, its main peninsular rival at the time, just twelve years later in 384. A century and a half passed before Silla, which was the last of the three to emerge as an independent power, officially recognized the religion by sanctioning the construction of a Buddhist temple in the second quarter of the sixth century. The introduction of Buddhism and state support for the monastic community in all three of these early Korean kingdoms occurred in conjunction with the importation of other elements of Chinese culture, civilization, law, and statecraft. The contemporaneous Chinese models provided blueprints for consolidating and centralizing authority under a king (*wang*): drawn from a single royal lineage, preferably through father-to-son succession, the ruler stood at the apex of a hierarchical bureaucratic and administrative system codified by written law. The adoption of legal codes and more complex bureaucratic structures appears to have coincided with the acceptance of Buddhism in each of the Korean kingdoms, and both of these moves were in turn closely related to the creation of centralized states out of the tribal and clan-based political configurations that had previously predominated in the peninsula. The fact that these phenomena were nearly simultaneous in Korean history meant that Buddhism and law developed together and overlapped considerably in the beginning.

This convergent transmission of cultural ideas and institutions from China, which included not only Buddhism and codified legal systems, but also Confucian teachings, occurred first in the Koguryŏ kingdom. In the same year that Buddhism was officially introduced to the kingdom by a monk sent to the Koguryŏ court at the behest of the Former Qin (351–94) ruler in northern China, a National Confucian Academy was established, and just one year later, in 373, an administrative law code was promulgated.[1] Because this statutory code is no longer extant, its contents are largely unknown. Nevertheless, as the noted Korean historian Lee Ki-baik points out, "there is no question that it signifies Koguryŏ's initial completion of a

[1] Lee Ki-baik, *A New History of Korea*, Edward W. Wagner (trans.), with Edward J. Shultz (Cambridge, MA: Harvard University Press, 1984), 38.

centralized aristocratic state structure."[2] Chŏng Ki-ung has speculated that the legal code adopted by Koguryŏ at this time bore some resemblance to the Jin code of law, but unfortunately, that code also has been lost.[3] Despite the absence of a surviving copy, a significant amount of information about the legal code can be gleaned from a preface that was preserved in the Jin official history and composed by Zhang Fei, a law specialist and minor official in the Jin's highest legal office.[4] The Jin Code was clearly based on its immediate predecessor, the Wei Code, which had been promulgated just thirty-eight years earlier in 230, as well as the paradigmatic Han Code.[5] It seems likely that the Jin Code combined elements of the Qin Legalist model with Han Confucian concepts and categories, just as its Chinese predecessors had done.[6] While Buddhism admittedly did not play a role in the creation and adoption of secular legal codes in China, the near simultaneous transmission of Buddhism and law in Koguryŏ undoubtedly strengthened the perception that they were intrinsically connected.

Twelve years after Koguryŏ became the first Korean kingdom to welcome a Buddhist monk to its court, another monk of probable Central Asian extraction set out from the southern Chinese state of Eastern Jin (317–420) and was greeted by the king of Paekche on his arrival. The warm reception and immediate support given to both of these foreign monks resulted in the construction of temples for them, the assignment of novice disciples, and the promulgation of edicts exhorting people to follow the Buddhist teachings. Although the date of Paekche's promulgation of a law code is unknown, we can be reasonably certain that the implementation of an administrative legal system based on the available Sinitic models occurred no earlier than 372, which is the year that Paekche began to have direct diplomatic relations with China through a mission to the Eastern Jin court.[7] But it seems unlikely that any statutory law codes were put in place

[2] *Ibid.*

[3] Chŏng Ki-ung, "Samguk sidae Pulgyo ka pŏmnyul munhwa e mich'in yŏnghyang" (Buddhist influence on legal culture in the Three Kingdoms period), *Pŏpsahak yŏn'gu* 19 (1998), 139.

[4] For more, see Benjamin E. Wallacker, "Chang Fei's Preface to the Chin Code of Law," *T'oung Pao*, 72.4/5 (1986), 229–68. For a handy list of the twenty chapters that were contained in this code, see John H. Head and Yanping Wang, *Law Codes in Dynastic China: A Synopsis of Chinese Legal History in the Thirty Centuries from Zhou to Qing* (Durham, NC: Carolina Academic Press, 2005), 110.

[5] Wallacker, "Chang Fei's Preface," 231.

[6] *Ibid.*, 232. Head and Wang state that the code was "prepared by a team of ... Confucianists" and ascribe considerable influence to Confucianism not only in the code's compilation, but also in the way that the law was interpreted and applied, citing Zhang Fei's preface as evidence. See Head and Wang, *Law Codes*, 110.

[7] Jonathan W. Best, "Diplomatic and Cultural Contacts Between Paekche and China," *Harvard Journal of Asiatic Studies*, 42.2 (1982), 453.

around this time. The early sixth century, when substantial moves were being made, especially under King Sŏng (r. 523–54), to strengthen royal authority, centralize power in the kingdom, and establish closer diplomatic ties in Japan and China, seems more plausible. This also happens to be the point at which Paekche kings became truly ardent supporters of Buddhism: "Seemingly concurrent with this royally initiated restructuring and centralizing of political authority in Paekche in the sixth century was a conspicuous increase in the level of the royal patronage of Buddhism."[8]

One tantalizing, but admittedly inconclusive, bit of evidence for the existence of law codes in Paekche based on Sinitic models by at least the mid-sixth century comes from a Chinese historical text containing the biography of Ling Xu, who was active toward the end of the southern Chinese dynasty of Liang (502–57). As Jonathan Best has documented, Paekche had especially close ties with Liang and its ruler, Emperor Wu, who was a famously ardent supporter of Buddhism. Ling Xu, according to Best, was purportedly "sent to the kingdom [of Paekche] in response to a request for a master of ceremonial lore and etiquette (rites)."[9] The Confucian concept of rites (Ch. *li*, Kor. *ye*) has several meanings, but the connection to law in ancient China has been amply demonstrated.[10] Regardless of whether Ling's visit or his expertise were in fact related to law, the evidence concerning other changes taking place in Paekche around this time is strong enough to presume that by the time of Ling's visit in the second quarter of the sixth century, Paekche either possessed a relatively new legal system based in large measure on Chinese legal codes or was in the process of implementing one. This means that the development of secular law in Paekche, much like the case of Koguryŏ, coincided with intensified royal support of Buddhism, the active importation of Confucian teachings and an increase in direct contacts with Chinese states.

Silla's slightly later development as a centralized kingdom can be explained in part by the more isolated position it occupied in the southeastern part of the peninsula. Its greater exposure to seaborne attacks and

[8] Jonathan W. Best, *A History of the Early Korean Kingdom of Paekche* (Cambridge, MA: Harvard University Asia Center, Harvard University Press, 2006), 134. Best notes that the textual and material evidence for Buddhism in Paekche for the century after its introduction is extremely limited.

[9] *Ibid.*, 124. See also Best, "Diplomatic and Cultural Contacts," 466–67.

[10] Yongping Liu, *Origins of Chinese Law: Penal and Administrative Law in its Early Development* (Oxford and New York: Oxford University Press, 1998). As Liu explains, "[s]ome scholars equate the systematic theory of *li*, here called natural *li*, with the concept of natural law" (61). See also Derk Bodde and Clarence Morris, *Law in Imperial China* (Cambridge: Harvard University Press, 1967), 29, where the "Confucianization of law" is defined as "the incorporation of the spirit and sometimes of actual provisions of the Confucian *li* into the legal codes."

raids originating from the Japanese archipelago limited its diplomatic intercourse and exchange with the Chinese mainland prior to the sixth century. In 520, the seventh year of King Pŏphŭng's (r. 514–40) reign, "laws and statutes" (Kor., *yullyŏng*) were promulgated, and within a decade, support for Buddhism within the kingdom had mostly been won. Unlike the other two Korean kingdoms, there was some opposition to Buddhism at first. According to the accounts found in a pair of thirteenth-century Korean texts, the *Samguk yusa* (*Memorabilia of the Three Kingdoms*) and the *Haedong kosŭng chŏn* (*Lives of Eminent Korean Monks*), Pŏphŭng was in favor of founding of a monastery and supporting Buddhism, but his officials, presumably representing the interests of other aristocratic clans, strongly opposed such plans.[11] The impasse was apparently settled only after a minor official named Pak Yŏmch'ok, better known as Ich'adon, gained the king's permission to sacrifice his life for the cause of establishing Buddhism.

Knowing the king's desire to establish a Buddhist monastery and lamenting the obstinacy of his high officials, Ich'adon informed King Pŏphŭng that if he were sentenced to death for constructing a temple, then a miracle would occur causing even the most ardently opposed to Buddhism to recognize its awesome power.[12] Accordingly, he proposed a secret plan, which the king reluctantly accepted, leading to his execution for a crime, and thus allowing the miracle to occur. Although the miraculous aspects of Ich'adon's martyrdom attract considerable attention whenever these events are recounted, the story actually hinges on a legal matter. Ich'adon's crime was not for building a Buddhist temple in violation of any legal prohibitions against Buddhism, for no such law existed so far as we know. According to the account found in the *Lives of Eminent Korean Monks*, which is the most detailed concerning the events leading up to Ich'adon's beheading, he was instead found guilty of forging a royal decree authorizing the work to begin.[13] When the officials demanded to know why a temple was being built without their approval, King Pŏphŭng falsely declared that no royal

[11] For the story of Ich'adon in the *Samguk yusa* (SGYS), see T2039.49.987b3–c16 and also Iryŏn, Tae-Hung Ha and Graftan K. Mintz, *Samguk yusa: Legends and History of the Three Kingdoms of Ancient Korea* (Seoul: Yonsei University Press, 1972), 187–89. For the *Haedong kosŭng chŏn* (HKC) version, see T2065.50.1018c21–1019a25; Kakhun and Peter H. Lee (trans.), *Lives of Eminent Korean Monks* (Cambridge, MA: Harvard University Press, 1969), 58–61.

[12] Ich'adon's death, as predicted, was accompanied by miraculous events. In addition to the strange occurrences in the natural world that are quite common in these types of stories, his decapitated head was said to have flown to the top of a nearby mountain and his blood also flowed milky white.

[13] The SGYS, which is decidedly more interested in the miraculous events surrounding Ich'adon's death rather than the circumstances leading up to it, largely agrees with the HKC concerning the sequence of events, but it merely says that Ich'adon's crime in this case was for disobeying the king's order.

order authorizing it had been issued, at which point Ich'adon confessed to forging the decree.

Interestingly, the contemporaneous Chinese law codes contained a chapter called "fraud and counterfeit" (*zhawei*; Kor., *sawi*), which covered precisely this type of crime.[14] It first appeared as a separate chapter in the Wei Code and was included in all subsequent Chinese codes, including the Jin Code mentioned earlier, as well as the later Tang Code.[15] Among the twenty-seven articles that comprise the identical chapter found in the Tang Code are statutes against the forgery of imperial seals and official documents. If the law code that Silla purportedly adopted less than a decade prior to Ich'adon's execution was based on Chinese models, then it would likely have contained a corresponding *sawi* chapter, thus explaining this aspect of the story. There is no way to be certain, of course, whether the tale of Ich'adon is evidence of this, or whether the precise legal rationale for his execution was embellished or possibly inserted by Kakhun in the thirteenth century. Nevertheless, the story itself does seem to suggest that Buddhists were adept at using the legal system, as well as magic and miracles, to further the interests of the religion. Buddhism was made to fit with the laws of the state, even if the spiritual power of the religion ultimately transcended the reach of secular law in some matters.

Buddhist monastic institutions from the very start in Korea had strong ties to the throne and were closely aligned with the interests of the state and ruling powers. Buddhism provided legitimacy to the throne, giving rulers access to a universal, organized, and powerful religion as a source of authority. Moreover, the creation and continued existence of the monastic community in the peninsula crucially depended on the support received from the throne. All of the earliest monasteries were royally sponsored institutions, often dedicated to deceased kings, located in or around the capitals of the Three Kingdoms, and drew heavily on the aristocratic sons of politically powerful elite clans or the royal family for new recruits. Buddhist monks and institutions were not merely a complementary component of the wider process of cultural and institutional transmission that was taking place; they were in fact integral to the very process of dissemination and important agents of cultural, intellectual, and diplomatic exchange. Because the line between religious emissary and diplomatic envoy was not

[14] For the translation of this term, see Wallace S. Johnson (trans.), *The T'ang Code*, 2 vols. (Princeton, NJ: Princeton University Press, 1979), 2:419.

[15] Wallacker, "Chang Fei's Preface," 231, 233; Geoffrey MacCormack, "The Transmission of Penal Law (*lü*) from the Han to the T'ang: A Contribution to the Study of the Early History of Codification in China," *Revue Internationale des Droits de L'Antiquité* (2004), 76–77.

explicitly drawn and Buddhist monks were among the most literate in society, they were carriers and no doubt interpreters of law in the early period. The dissemination of Buddhism from the ruler of one state to another through official diplomatic channels in conjunction with a wider transmission of culture, people, institutions, and knowledge, including law, also characterizes the way in which King Sŏng of Paekche officially introduced Buddhism to the Yamato ruler in Japan in the sixth century.

Historical Development of Buddhism and Law in Korea

The overlap and interconnections between Buddhism and law that existed in this early period can make it difficult at times to draw clear boundaries between the two in the first few centuries after their introduction. Nevertheless, the absence of a clear distinction does not warrant the assertion, which can occasionally be found, that Buddhism and law in the Three Kingdoms were identical or perhaps interchangeable: "A conspicuous feature of this process [of indigenizing Buddhism in Korea] was that [the] law of Buddha was the law of the state; that is, the non-secular law of Buddha was equated with the secular law of the royalty."[16] Until we know more about Buddhism or law in Korea during this early period, definitive conclusions about the exact relationship between the two will be difficult to reach.

We do know that Buddhist teachings and principles, however, were not foundational in the creation of Chinese law codes, and they were not the basis for the administrative law codes used in Korea, which were modelled on their Chinese counterparts. Despite the confluences between Buddhism and secular law based on their simultaneous transmission, therefore, divergences began to appear over time. These divergences coincided with a distinct increase in the independent growth and autonomy of the saṅgha. This moment in history further corresponds with a sudden need on the part of the Silla state to consolidate its hold on newly acquired territory in the peninsular wars. Although the connections between Buddhism and the state remained strong for many centuries to come, from this point in the second half of the seventh century, Buddhism and law to some degree started working at cross purposes in ways that could potentially be viewed as detrimental to the proper or ideal functioning of one side or the other. While the simultaneous transmission ensured that Buddhism and

[16] Suh Kyung-Soo and Kim Chol-Choon, "Korean Buddhism: A Historical Perspective," in Chun Shin-yong (ed.), *Buddhist Culture in Korea* (Seoul: Si-sa-yong-o-sa, 1982), 121.

law were closely associated and at least initially almost indistinguishable, over time the two branched off in significant ways, resulting in the subordination of the monastic community to secular law and culminating in the legal suppression of Buddhism beginning in the fourteenth century.

Buddhist Doctrines and the Laws of the State

In perhaps the only study of its kind to date in Korea, Chŏng Ki-ung has sought to identify the influences that Buddhist doctrines, rituals, and institutions exerted on the legal culture of the Three Kingdoms. Chŏng points to karma and *Vinaya* as having the most far-reaching effects on the legal culture from the late fourth through the ninth centuries in Korea.[17] Scholars generally presume, with good reason, that the fundamental ideas concerning karma and causality – the recompense of all of one's present actions at a future time – took hold in the Three Kingdoms sooner than some of the more abstruse Buddhist doctrines. As Jonathan Best has remarked in the case of early Paekche Buddhism, "The metaphysical teachings . . . probably did not exceed the elementary causal principles of the doctrine of karma and its useful social corollary that good behavior is duly rewarded and evil punished."[18] Best further speculates that the Paekche rulers at the time may have possessed "an awareness that Buddhism in China served as an important instrument for the generation of sanction and support – both mortal and divine – for the established order of society."[19] The presumption that basic Buddhist concepts surrounding the theory of karma provided a potential source of conceptual, religious, and ideological support for the laws of the state in Korea finds support in certain areas of legal practice.

One way that a belief in karma may have influenced law during the Three Kingdoms lies in the occasional edicts and decrees banning the intentional killing of sentient creatures within the realm. The first mention of this type of royal decree in Korean historical records dates to 529 during King Pŏphŭng's reign, which places it squarely in the pivotal third decade of the sixth century when, as we have seen, both administrative law and Buddhism were being officially promoted in Silla.[20] Another example is the edict promulgated by King Pŏp of Paekche in 599: "The king prohibited the killing of sentient creatures. He commanded that the falcons which people had raised be gathered together and then released. He also

[17] Chŏng, "Samguk sidae," 148–52. [18] Best, *History of Early Paekche*, 84.
[19] *Ibid.*, 83. [20] Chŏng, "Samguk sidae," 147; Best, *History of Early Paekche*, 161.

ordered that the implements of fishing and hunting be burned."[21] Similar instances of legal prohibitions against killing living creatures or setting captive animals free are found in the histories of China and Japan, as well.

In Korea these types of edicts were neither as numerous nor as consequential as the related practice of issuing general amnesties and pardons to criminals. Amnesties were granted for a variety of reasons, some explicitly connected to Buddhism and others less so. Pardons might be given when the king made offerings at the ancestral temple, or when Buddhist priests were called on to pray for rain at times of drought, or at other times of natural disaster and hardship. Confucian officials had long been highly critical of the practice in China, and these amnesties and pardons later became the subject of much legal debate and controversy in Korea during the transition to the Chosŏn dynasty. Officials in the early decades of the dynasty frequently took aim at the Buddhist influence on this longstanding legal practice. Given the piety and personal devotion to Buddhism of many of the early Chosŏn rulers, as well as the ardent commitment to Neo-Confucian values of their bureaucratic officials, the act of pardoning criminals through royal decrees and edicts became a potential flashpoint for ideological and political conflict between the throne and officials tasked with implementing the law.

William Shaw has examined the discourse and policies in the early Chosŏn period concerning the practice of granting royal amnesties for those convicted of or arrested for crimes.[22] For Shaw the issue of leniency and clemency in the administration of law in the Chosŏn period provides a window into the "Neo-Confucian conceptions of the role of laws and punishments in government."[23] In the minds of the Confucian officials, devotion to Buddhism and a belief in the workings of karma were the main culprits in the excessive leniency shown by early Chosŏn kings with respect to pardons and punishments, even though granting general amnesties sprang from a variety of motivations.[24] For these officials, including one of the most important architects of early Chosŏn legal and social

[21] Best, *History of Early Paekche*, 349. Best notes elsewhere that this "could hardly have been more than a pious gesture" aimed at aristocrats who killed animals for sport (161).

[22] William Shaw, "The Neo-Confucian Revolution of Values in Early Yi Korea: Its Implications for Korean Legal Thought," in Brian E. McKnight (ed.), *Law and the State in Traditional East Asia* (Honolulu: University of Hawai'i Press, 1987).

[23] *Ibid.*, 154.

[24] *Ibid.*, 156–58. Shaw remarks that they "occurred on occasions of state celebration, as expressions of benevolent largesse, or conversely in the wake of unusual natural occurrences," but he maintains that the Censorate railed against all such amnesties, "and not merely those which could be specifically linked to Buddhist piety," often using anti-Buddhist language in their arguments.

policies, Chŏng Tojŏn (d. 1398), "whether such leniency took its point of departure in a refined sense of compassion or in a more calculating consideration of retribution in the present or in a future existence, there was a powerful tendency to an unlimited, unconditional clemency which could have repercussions in the social order."[25] As a result, the Censorate officials responsible for remonstrating the king worked to reduce the number and mitigate the effects of large-scale amnesties and pardons, but the practice itself was a legal prerogative that Chosŏn monarchs could choose to exercise.

The Vinaya as a Source for Secular Laws

While the decrees banning the killing of living creatures are undergirded by karmic considerations, they also represent attempts, albeit on a limited scale, to apply Buddhist precepts found in the *Vinaya* to the wider society. The prohibition against killing living creatures (*prāṇa-atipāta*, Kor., *salsaeng*) is the first of the five precepts (*pañcaśīla*, Kor., *ogye*) taken by laypeople. The extent to which elements of the Buddhist monastic legal code were incorporated directly into the state's legal system, or at least applied in some sense to non-monastic members of society, is often taken to be a litmus test for the presence of a "strong" or "weak" Buddhist legal system.

A frequently cited example of this type of crossover in the case of Korea relates to the "five secular precepts" (Kor., *sesok ogye*) issued by Wŏn'gwang, an important Silla monk active from the late sixth to early seventh centuries.[26] However, this example is problematic for two reasons. First, scholars have debated whether these secular precepts represent Buddhist lay precepts or Confucian ethical principles, although, as Pankaj Mohan notes, "they need not be pigeonholed as either essentially Buddhist or Confucian in character."[27] Secondly, the question of who was meant to follow these precepts is also a matter of some debate. Chŏng dubiously asserts that they were intended not solely for the two Silla youths who had requested and received Wŏn'gwang's moral guidance, but rather for the

[25] *Ibid.*, 157.

[26] For a discussion of Wŏn'gwang's dates, which are usually given as 555–638, see Richard D. McBride II, "Silla Buddhism and the *Hwarang*," *Korean Studies*, 34 (2010), 86–87.

[27] Pankaj N. Mohan, "Wŏn'gwang and Chajang in the Formation of Early Silla Buddhism," in Robert E. Buswell, Jr. (ed.), *Religions of Korea in Practice* (Princeton, NJ: Princeton University Press, 2007), 52. The five are: serve the king with loyalty, serve one's parents with filial piety, treat one's friends with trust, do not retreat in battle, do not kill indiscriminately.

people of Silla as a whole.[28] Of equal or greater significance than the actual content of the precepts, however, is Wŏn'gwang's stated rationale for devising them: "The Buddhist vinaya prescribes ten Bodhisattva precepts, but since you are subjects [of the king] and sons, you will not be able to adhere to them."[29] This suggests the recognition of a certain incompatibility of secular life with adherence to the *Vinaya*.

Chŏng identifies two other areas of influence that are tangentially related to the *Vinaya*: the state-sponsored rituals or ceremonies known as the Eight Prohibitions Assembly (*P'algwanhoe*) and the Humane Kings' One-Hundred Seat Assembly (*Inwang paekkojwa hoe*), both of which first began in Silla and were continued in a modified form into the Koryŏ period that followed.[30] The eight prohibitions refer to the five lay precepts together with three more that a portion of the laity sometimes observed on special days, specifically during the fortnightly recitation of the *Prātimokṣa* rules of the *Vinaya* by members of the monastic community, which were known as *poṣadha* days. How closely the Silla and later Koryŏ ceremonies followed either the Chinese or the canonical Indian precedents is difficult to determine, but there is little doubt that it was an important state ceremony in the ritual calendar of Silla and Koryŏ.

Sem Vermeersch maintains that the nature of the ritual changed, however, from Silla to Koryŏ:

> Although it had thus become a state event with a political agenda [in Silla], in these instances it still retained a religious dimension, since the practice of eight prohibitions rituals can be seen as acts of penance or gratitude. The Koryŏ *P'algwanhoe* was of a different character altogether: it bore all the hallmarks of a festival, a celebration rather than a religious ritual.[31]

Whatever the actual character of this ceremony in Korea as it developed over time, these Buddhist rituals were perhaps more relevant to the relationship of Buddhism to the state – or, more accurately, to the throne – than to law. The same might also be said for the final area of influence identified by Chŏng: the ideal of the *cakravartin* or "wheel-turning" ruler that a variety of kings from Silla through the Koryŏ period drew upon symbolically. This

[28] Chŏng, "Samguk sidae," 144. For an English version of the account found in the *Samguk sagi*, see Mohan, "Wŏn'gwang and Chajang," 52. The two youths, Kwisan and Ch'uhang, are often assumed to be members of the *hwarang*, and thus most scholars speculate that the precepts were intended for this order of aristocratic youths. For a brief survey of these claims and their related problems, see McBride, "Silla Buddhism," 67.

[29] Mohan, "Wŏn'gwang and Chajang," 52. [30] Chŏng, "Samguk sidae," 152–54.

[31] Sem Vermeersch, *The Power of the Buddhas: The Politics of Buddhism During the Koryŏ Dynasty (918–1392)* (Cambridge, MA: Harvard University Asia Center, Harvard University Press, 2008), 118.

ideal had potency in terms of enhancing the king's legitimacy and right to rule, and it also had implications for the legal regulation of the monastic community.

The state took an interest in finding ways to ensure that monks and nuns actually upheld their vows and abided by the rules and regulations contained in the *Vinaya*. According to Vermeersch, even though a secular legal code comparable to the Chinese *Daosengge* or Japanese *Sōniryō*, both of which dealt explicitly with the monastic community as a legal and regulatory matter of the state, has not been found in Korea, "even a cursory look at the statutes on Buddhism in the chapters on law in the *Koryŏsa* reveals that the authorities regularly issued decrees on aspects of monks' lives normally covered by the Vinaya."[32]

Bureaucratic Offices, Ordinations, and the Legal Status of Buddhist Monks

Another prominent area of overlap between Buddhism and law in Korean history concerns the relationship of the saṅgha to the administrative and bureaucratic state structures that were created through the written law codes. Buddhist monks were not simply passive objects in the process of cultural transmission and diplomatic exchange in East Asia, as explained earlier. Although we think of them primarily as religious agents in the dissemination of Buddhism, from the very start members of the monastic community had both official and unofficial roles as envoys, diplomatic representatives, political advisors, and even spies on occasion. Rhi Ki-yong interprets "the fact that monks were used as political and military spies" in Koguryŏ and Paekche – activities that he sees as counter to their monastic vows – as evidence that the understanding of Buddhism in those two kingdoms remained elementary at this early stage.[33] An alternative interpretation, however, might be that Buddhist monks were expected to render services to the king or state, whether or not it conflicted with their ethical vows. For example, when the Silla monk Won'gwang, who was "entrusted with the responsibility for drafting all the court's important reports, memorials, and correspondence, and the exchange of state orders," was asked by King Chinp'yŏng to draft a letter in 608 requesting Sui Dynasty military help against Koguryŏ, he famously answered: "To seek

[32] *Ibid.*, 161.

[33] Rhi Ki-yong, "Silla Buddhism: Its Special Features," in Lewis R. Lancaster and C.S. Yu (eds.), *Introduction of Buddhism to Korea: New Cultural Patterns* (Berkeley: Asian Humanities Press, 1989), 190.

one's own profit and destroy others is not the way of a monk. But since I, a poor monk, live on your majesty's land, eat your majesty's grain, and drink your water, how dare I disobey [your command]?"[34] Pankaj Mohan suggests that this statement can be read "as an attempt by the state to domesticate Buddhism and to appropriate the human and material resources of the Buddhist establishment in order to advance the political interests of the state."[35]

Over time a complex monastic bureaucracy emerged, and this seems to suggest the subordination of saṅgha to the secular law of the state, particularly through state-approved ordination procedures and regulation of the monastic community through state-appointed monk-officials. However, there is evidence that the distinction between religious and political offices was not clearly demarcated and that monk-officials played an important role in governing all the people, both monastic and lay, in the first several centuries after Buddhism's arrival. Jonathan Best has pointed out that "the employment of Buddhist clerics as rank-bearing members of the secular official bureaucracy" was "a phenomenon clearly documented in later Paekche history."[36] Sem Vermeersch notes that although an actual monastic bureaucracy was not created in Silla until 785, monks held a variety of official positions in the government before that time, going all the way back to the mid-sixth century, a few decades after Buddhism was accepted. Speculating that the Silla system prior to 785 was modelled on a similar one used by the Northern Wei, Vermeersch posits, "Silla originally did not distinguish between political and religious roles" and that some monks "acted as governing officials rather than officials who governed Buddhism."[37]

Many of the initial moves made in the Silla Dynasty to regularize the monastic bureaucratic system and appoint monks to official positions were solidly established under the Koryŏ Dynasty. The creation of a monastic examination system actually preceded the implementation of a civil service exam in early Koryŏ, and it may have even surpassed the latter in importance and the number of successful candidates.[38] The two highest positions, royal preceptor (Kor., *wangsa*) and state preceptor (Kor., *kuksa*) carried a significant amount of prestige. The latter position was started under the Silla and was based on precedents in China and perhaps even India, while the former was an institution unique to Korea that began under the Koryŏ

[34] Mohan, "Won'gwang and Chajang," 51. The passage Mohan is quoting and translating can be found in the *Samguk sagi* (Chinp'yŏng 30, SKSG 4) and the *Haedong kosŭng chŏn* (T2065.50.1021a23–25).

[35] *Ibid.*, 51–52.

[36] Best, *History of Early Paekche*, 139–40.

[37] Vermeersch, *Power of the Buddhas*, 206–07.

[38] *Ibid.*, 236.

founder, Wang Kŏn.[39] According to Vermeersch, the royal preceptor was the one who "conferred the precepts on the ruler and instructed him in Buddhism," and thus he became "someone invested with the symbolic power to discern and legitimize the true ruler."[40] These positions, as well as the monastic bureaucracy itself, were eventually abolished under the next dynasty, Chosŏn, as part of its effort to eliminate Buddhism as a legitimating symbol of royal and state authority. The monastic examination system and officially approved ordinations were also discarded under the Chosŏn. As products of the state and regulatory mechanisms, their elimination was certainly within the state's power, and it was accompanied by the imposition of even tighter restrictions on becoming a monk or nun.

Property, Landowning, and Donations to Temples

Beginning in the second half of the seventh century, the Silla state began to use legal means in an effort to regulate the construction of Buddhist monasteries and temples and to limit donations of land and other assets to them. Prior to this period, Buddhist temples had been established almost exclusively by the state or royal family and were located in or around the capitals of all three kingdoms. By the mid-seventh century, however, some monks, especially after returning from a period of study in China, began independently to build temples at greater distances away from the capital. Silla was also gaining the upper hand in the peninsular wars with the help of Tang Chinese forces and bringing more territory under its political control around this time. In 664, after defeating Paekche and nearing a total victory over Koguryŏ, King Munmu of Silla issued an edict prohibiting the donation of land or assets for the construction of Buddhist temples, while also establishing official temples in areas away from the capital.[41] At the start of the ninth century, the construction of new temples was banned altogether, but as Vermeersch remarks, "the state was apparently unable to enforce these measures."[42] There are indications, as well, that Silla Buddhist monasteries in the eighth and ninth centuries were able to own, buy, and sell land, and that private ownership of land by Buddhist temples continued after the transition to the Koryŏ Dynasty (918–1392) in the first half of the tenth century.

The founder of the Koryŏ Dynasty, Wang Kŏn, citing the indiscriminate construction of new temples and monasteries as one of the reasons for

[39] *Ibid.*, 239–47. [40] *Ibid.*, 267. [41] Vermeersch, *Power of the Buddhas*, 46.
[42] *Ibid.*, 112.

Silla's downfall, warned his successors in his famous Ten Injunctions "that the royal family, the aristocracy, and the courtiers all may build many [private] temples and monasteries in the future in order to seek Buddha's blessings."[43] Exhorting his descendants to prevent this, he instructed them to follow his example by restricting the establishment of temples to those places previously identified by the monk Tosŏn as propitious based on geomantic principles. As Vermeersch notes, however, this injunction did not preclude the donation of land or money to existing temples, and it was apparently ineffective at stopping the founding of private temples, which can be inferred from the repeated promulgation of laws banning the practice in 985, 1017, and again in 1101.[44] While attempting to regulate the construction of new temples, the state was also endowing a growing number of temples with official status as *pibo-sa* (remedial temple), providing land grants and slaves in diverse ways that then became part of the temples' permanent assets.[45] The amount of land that temples controlled in the Koryŏ Dynasty, perhaps as much as one-sixth of the arable land, presented an inviting target to the founders and architects of the following Chosŏn Dynasty, who clearly needed to find ways to bring more land and free-floating resources under the state's control.[46]

Even before the new dynasty was inaugurated in 1392, Yi Sŏng-gye and his reform-minded supporters had carefully considered what to do about fiscal reform and state resources, which centered on landholding and prebends.[47] The resulting Rank Land Law (Kor., *kwajŏnbŏp*) was promulgated a year prior to Yi Sŏng-gye's ascension and, given the financial problems that plagued the late Koryŏ ruling structure, can almost be considered a prerequisite for putting the new dynasty on firm footing fiscally. One of the provisions of the Rank Land Law made the donation of land to temples and shrines illegal,[48] while another prohibited the "allocation of prebends to the descendants of artisans, merchants, fortune tellers, professional entertainers and monks."[49] The *Great National Code* (*Kyŏngguk taejŏn*), which was promulgated in 1471 after decades of preparation and

[43] Peter H. Lee and William Theodore de Bary (eds.), *Sourcebook of Korean Tradition, Volume One: From Early Times through the Sixteenth Century* (New York: Columbia University Press, 1997), 154.

[44] Vermeersch, *Power of the Buddhas*, 305. Vermeersch explains that dedicating a privately established temple to the state or the throne was a common way to get around the ban.

[45] *Ibid.*, 304, 311. [46] *Ibid.*, 310.

[47] John B. Duncan, *The Origins of the Chosŏn Dynasty* (Seattle and London: University of Washington Press, 2000), 206–07.

[48] Pori Park, *Trial and Error in Modernist Reforms: Korean Buddhism under Colonial Rule* (Berkeley: Institute of East Asian Studies, University of California, Berkeley, 2009), 15.

[49] Duncan, *Origins of Chosŏn Dynasty*, 210.

remained the law of the land for more than four centuries, stipulated that no new monasteries could be built, although repairs to existing temples were allowed.[50] Although nothing less than the total confiscation of monastery lands and assets and laicization of all monks was enough to satisfy many zealous officials, the personal inclinations and religious beliefs of the ruler on the throne, as well as the weight of tradition, prevented this from happening. Nevertheless, the monastic community was legally forced to forfeit to the state much of the land, slaves, and legal privileges it once possessed.

Conclusion

In terms of its intensity, duration, and impact, the severe legal repression that the Korean monastic community suffered beginning in the late fourteenth century appears unprecedented and unparalleled anywhere outside of India up to that time. The Confucian scholar-officials who sought to remake Korean society along the lines of an idealized vision as spelled out by the neo-Confucian reformers of the Song Dynasty in China began a sustained effort to repress and marginalize the Buddhist monastic community, whose prior position in society and close relationship to the throne and state were seen as antithetical to their vision of a well-ordered and moral society. Law was the primary tool through which they sought to accomplish their goals – that is, curtailing or if possible, eliminating the power, prestige, and political influence of the Buddhist establishment.

The precise measures taken under this policy of suppression – the forced closure of countless temples, the massive confiscation of land and slaves, large-scale laicization, the expulsion of monks and nuns from the capital and other cities, and the amalgamation and elimination of separate Buddhist schools – are well known. One aspect of these historical events that seems rather striking, however, is the surprising lack of resistance on the part of the monastic community. Despite the wealth and power that Buddhist temples had acquired by that time, not to mention the ability of large monasteries to maintain armies of slaves and monk-soldiers and their past willingness to use them for political ends occasionally, no violence accompanied the stripping of the monastic community's privileges. The defenses that were offered appealed mainly to philosophical arguments by asserting the underlying commonalities shared by Confucian and Buddhist ethical teachings. One puzzling issue that remains, however, is why the Buddhist

50 Park, *Trial and Error*, 16.

establishment acquiesced in these new policies and refrained from engaging in armed or other forms of resistance.

When we shift our gaze from Buddhist relations with the state to the centuries of interactions between Buddhist institutions and secular legal systems, the fact that the state carried out its suppressive policies through legal measures may offer some clues.[51] This brief survey suggests that the relationship of Buddhism and law had evolved over time and that by the start of the Chosŏn Dynasty, the fundamental structure of that relationship had been well established. This made the policies pursued by Confucian scholar-officials bent on circumscribing the role of Buddhism in society and eliminating it from state rituals or political functions appear harsh perhaps, but entirely within the bounds of the state's power and its recognized legal authority. This represents to some extent the triumph of the Sinitic legal models, which subordinated organized religious groups to the laws of the state, over alternative models that did not distinguish Buddhist law from secular law as emphatically as Chinese states did. To determine whether this hypothesis is correct, however, will require further research.

[51] Another factor could be that these measures were not as severe as they have historically been portrayed. I am grateful to Robert Buswell for pointing this out in a personal communication. Buswell also noted that a similarly muted response on the part of the monastic community also characterized the occasional persecutions in China. I consider this in keeping with parallel models of legal regulation of Buddhism in China and Korea by the fourteenth century and thus expected to some degree.

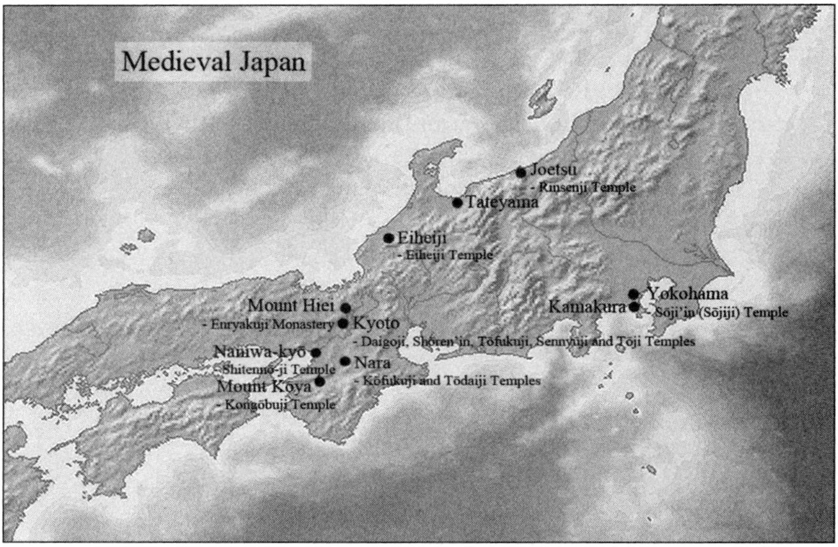

Map of Medieval Japan

CHAPTER 15

Buddhism and Law in Japan

Brian Ruppert

Introduction

The study of the relationship between Buddhism and law in Japan has developed only in the twentieth century. The pioneering work of scholars like Miura Hiroyuki and, especially, Hosokawa Kameichi, attempted to understand Japanese Buddhism within larger historical contexts, but it was not until recently that more extensive examination was undertaken.[1] Given the limited amount of existing scholarship, the lengthy span of Japanese history, and the restrictions of space, this overview is primarily concerned with the developing relationship between Buddhism and law in the medieval era (ca. 950–ca. 1600 CE), providing only a brief consideration of the other historical periods.

Buddhism and Law in Early Japan

The *Ritsuryō* code of 718, patterned partially on Tang legal codes, issued a set of specific guidelines for the behavior of Buddhist monks and nuns in its seventh section entitled "Laws for Monks and Nuns" (*sōniryō*).[2] While prohibiting acts not directly discussed by the Buddhist precepts, such as military training or action, the code also clearly intersected at points with the *Vinaya*, such as subjecting those who make false claims of enlightenment to civil law. In each temple, three monk administrators

[1] Miura Hiroyuki, "Sōni ni kansuru hōsei no kigen" in Miura Hiroyuki (ed.), *Hōseishi no kenkyū* (Tokyo: Iwanami Shoten, 1973 [1919 repr.], 1113–32; Miura Hiroyuki, "Jiin hō shiryō" in Miuru Hiroyuki (ed.), *Zoku hōseishi no kenkyū* (Tokyo: Iwanami Shoten, 1973 [1925 repr.]), 1194–202; and Hosokawa Kameichi, *Nihon chūsei jiin hō sōron* (Tokyo: Ōokayama Shoten, 1933). I would like to thank Kikuchi Hiroki for his extensive consultation regarding research, and express my appreciation to Uejima Susumu and Takahashi Shinichirō for their advice; I would like to thank Helen Hardacre and Hoshino Seiji for their suggestions concerning modern Japan.

[2] See Umeda Yoshihiko, "Bukkyō seido" in Umeda Yoshihiko (ed.), *Nihon shūkyō seido shi, jodai hen* (Tokyo: Tōsen Shuppan, 1971), 226–39; Joan R. Piggott, "Todaiji and the Nara Imperium," Ph.D. dissertation, Stanford University (1987), 267–73.

(*sangō*) were to keep the monastic register and oversee any changes in status, such as a monk's or nun's decision to return to lay life as well as other petitions, most of which required record keeping and government notification; they were, moreover, required to mete out the punishment for infractions – typically, labor on monastery grounds.

Laws proscribing the killing of sentient creatures, repeatedly promulgated since at least the seventh century, may be related to autochthonous concerns and other East Asian religious influences. However, it is important to note the implications of these laws for temples and for lay Buddhists. For temples, such government proclamations seem to have had their roots in notions that monastic grounds, nearby precincts, and practitioners must retain their purity.[3] For lay believers, ritual purity was more of a central concern than the purity of sacred space. Beginning as early as 737, government proscriptions on fishing, hunting, and other forms of taking life were applied specifically to monthly Buddhist abstinence days (Skt., *poṣadha*; Jap., *fusatsu*).[4]

The creation of extensive rules within temples seems to have coincided with the gradual weakening of the *Ritsuryō* state form and, by extension, the weakening of any effective aspects of the *sōniryō* codes. At the same time, as Yoshida Kazuhiko has emphasized, monks and nuns were extremely free figures even at the height of the presumed use of the *sōniryō* codes.[5] So it is difficult – at least in the ninth century – to conclude that the production of temple rules was directly related to the general demise of the *Ritsuryō* system and the *sōniryō* within it, which is thought to have occurred significantly from the tenth century onward.

Established Nara schools, which enjoyed official approval, seemed to have no need to develop temple codes of conduct, whereas the new schools constructed codes to establish discipline and mark their communities as distinct within the system of Japanese Buddhist schools and their temples. Thus, the first set of such codes for monks was authored by Saichō (767–822), founder of the Tendai school, and was directly related to his efforts to establish monastic life at Mount Hiei (Enryakuji temple). Saichō was especially interested in developing codes that would extricate Tendai from the dominant monastic system regulated by the Office of Monastic Affairs.[6]

[3] Taira Masayuki, "Sesshō kindan no rekishiteki tenkai" in Ōyama Kyōhei Kyōju Taikan Kinenkai (ed.), *Nihon shakai no shiteki kōzō: kodai chūsei* (Kyoto: Shibunkaku, 1997), 151–56.

[4] *Ibid.*, 159.

[5] Yoshida Kazuhiko, *Kodai bukkyō o yominaosu* (Tokyo: Yoshikawa Kōbunkan, 2006), 27.

[6] Paul Groner, *Saichō: The Establishment of the Japanese Tendai School* (Honolulu: University of Hawai'i Press, 2000), 267.

The first ordinance of the code he initially proposed begins by clarifying that the ordinands retain their lay registration, excluding them from official monastic registers.[7] Each set of Saichō's codes emphasized that monks were to remain on Mount Hiei in monastic training for twelve years, a rule that was clearly designed to retain Saichō's students and that departed from the *sōniryō* and Buddhist precepts. Just as important was Saichō's proposal in the second of the set of codes that two lay administrators (*zoku bettō*) be appointed by the court to supervise the monastic order and ensure adherence to prohibitions on theft, alcohol, and female entrance to the premises.[8] Saichō seems to have seen his codes as supplementing rather than replacing the Buddhist ordination practice, which he interpreted primarily in terms of the Mahāyāna "perfect precepts" (*endon kai*) based on the *Brahmā Net Sutra* (Ch. *Fan-wang jing*) in place of the traditional *Four-part Vinaya*. Other Japanese schools came to develop their own interpretations of the *Vinaya*;[9] the monastic codes developed in these other schools were also typically seen as supplementing the *Vinaya* precepts rather than at variance with the latter.

In 824, the new leading monks on Hiei put forth the "Prohibitions of Enryakuji Temple" (*Enryakuji kinsei shiki*). These proscriptions focused especially on a range of issues: the proper colors and features of monastic robes and footwear; seating arrangements by seniority based on time since reception of precepts; theft of personal items; the treatment of acolytes; burial of monks and management their effects; offerings made for sūtra recitation; paperwork upon receiving a clerical name; limits on visitation periods by outside monks; arguments and hurtful language; and toilet sanitation. Although punishments included being cast out from the community or ritual space, most common was a combination of obeisance and repentance, a requirement clearly drawn from the temple code of Tiantai patriarch Zhiyi (538–97).[10] Okano Kōji has noted that the inclusion of prohibitions concerning acolyte visitation to areas below Mount Hiei and permissible visitation by outsiders to the complex suggests both the perceived importance of the boundary between the area of the temple and

7 *Ibid.*, 116–23. 8 *Ibid.*, 126–44, 269–71.

9 Among the most prominent of these were the Vinaya school's (Risshū) view that the *Four-Part Vinaya* was harmonious with the perfect precepts, the Pure Land School's (Jōdo shū) ambivalent appropriation of the moral aspect of Saichō's precept teachings, and the Zen traditions' identification of the precepts with esoteric Buddhist initiation. See William M. Bodiford (ed.), *Going Forth: Visions of Buddhist Vinaya* (Kuroda Institute Book; Honolulu: University of Hawai'i Press, 2005), 10–15.

10 Satō Masatoshi, "Enryakuji kinseishiki no kisoteki kōsatsu" in Yoshie Akio (ed.), *Kodai chūsei no shiryō to bungaku* (Tokyo: Yoshikawa Kōbunkan, 2005), 200–02.

the world outside,[11] which demarked entry into the sacred realm, as well as efforts to retain Tendai disciples on Hiei.

The Shingon monk Shinshō's (797–873) last testament offered more than a dozen instructions to guide monastic life at Zenrinji (*Zenrinji shiki*, 868).[12] These emphasize that monks should stay on the premises for six years following reception of the precepts, engage in recitation and repentance without interruption, observe the regular abstinence and confession ceremonies, avoid living in separate quarters, and study and transmit both esoteric and exoteric Buddhism, among other prescriptions. Monks who have left the premises must bathe prior to their return to monastic life, and all monks in the larger monastic meetings (*daishu shū'e*) must be pure when they gather. Finally, the text introduces regular memorial rites (*tsuifuku*) for the deceased masters of the tradition. The effort to require monks' extended residence on the mountain was a common feature of codes given by temple founders.[13]

Space, Cloisters, and Law

As Yamagishi Tsuneto has noted, the Zenrinji Code has additional features that include spatio-ritual distinctions for Buddha halls as well as residential arrangements, which were similar to medieval forms that became prominent from the tenth century onward.[14] The instructions forbid the establishment of personal living quarters separate from the main area, but they go on to permit construction of such quarters in cases where space is unduly limited – an extremely early reference to a cloister (*shi'in*; later called *inge*).[15] Such halls were commonplace in large temple complexes throughout the medieval era, and in their ties to specific familial or Dharma lineages became prominent players in monastic life.

By the early tenth century, Nara temples began to develop their own codes to supplement the *sōniryō*. The abbot Shōbō (832–909), a Shingon monk trained also in Madhyamaka (J. Sanron) Buddhism, made an oath

11 *Tendai kahyō* 5.1 in Takukusu Junjirō and Mochizuki Shinkō (eds.), *Dainihon bukkyō zensho* [DNBZ] 126 (Tokyo: Ushio Shobō, 1931), 522a–524b; Okano Kōji, "Enryakuji no kinseigata jiinhō ni tsuite" in Kawane Yoshiyasu and Fukuda Eijirō (eds.), Enryakuji to chūsei shakai (Kyoto: Hōzōkan, 2004), 17–18.

12 *Heian ibun* 1–156 in Takeuchi Rizō (ed.), *Heian ibun* 14 vols. (Tokyo: Tokyōdō, 1963–76).

13 See Nagamura Makoto, "Chūsei jiin to 'jihō'" in Nagahara Keiji (ed.), *Chūsei no hakken* (Tokyo: Yoshikawa Kōbunkan, 1993), 267–68.

14 Yamagishi Tsuneto, "Jiinhō kara mita naijin/raidō" in Yamagishi Tsuneto (ed.), *Chūsei jiin shakai to butsudō* (Tokyo: Hanawa Shobō, 1990), 109–11.

15 *Ibid.*, 111.

just before his death regarding Tōnan'in, a hall within Tōdaiji; although the oath form was very different from other genres of temple code, the text offered one example of a developing administrative unit (sub-temple) within a larger temple complex.[16] Shōbō's instruction that the abbacy of the hall remain in his monastic lineage was an early example of testamentary succession of a cloister.[17]

The tenth-century code of the Enryakuji abbot Ryōgen (912–85), *Nijūrokkajō kishō* (twenty-six article oath) significantly influenced medieval Japanese Buddhism.[18] The work reflected his effort to strengthen monastic discipline in the wake of the second fire to destroy the Sōji'in, the esoteric Buddhist hall in which Ryōgen expressed special interest, given its connection to Ennin's ritual lineage within the monastery. Ryōgen began the code with a clause prohibiting extravagance of the monks at the relic's assembly. Comportment constitutes a prominent portion of the code, but so do esoteric rites and ordinations, followed by lectures and examinations. While the code refers to Saichō and more recent Tendai leaders, it also quotes from the precepts scripture, *Fan-wang jing*, reminding us that Ryōgen saw it as supplementing the precepts.[19]

Ryōgen later wrote a last testament that clarified his instructions for a series of monks' residential halls on Hiei as well as several manors, ritual implements, and death rite protocols.[20] Ryōgen included in his instructions "exo-esoteric sacred works" (*kenmitsu hōmon*; also called *shōgyō*) of specific halls, offering details such as the scriptural treasury in which these works were to be enshrined, how their lending might occur in the future, and stressing the importance of the sacred works catalog. Sacred works were directly intertwined with testamentary concession and thus have legal roles in addition to their religious place within the traditions.

The creation of all of these codes indicates that the Tendai and Shingon traditions, as well as some of the major Nara temples, faced significant changes in their self-governance and relationship to the Japanese government. The newer Tendai and Shingon schools needed to establish their place as loyal subjects to the royal court while they demonstrated they could govern themselves successfully. Moreover, clear decline by the tenth

16 "Sōjō Shōbō kishōmon," *Heian ibun* 9–4552.

17 See Yamagishi Tsuneto, *Chūsei jiin no sōdan/hō'e/monjo* (Tokyo: Tokyo Daigaku Shuppankai, 2004), 120. The term for such concession typically used in medieval times would be *yuzurijō* or, particularly in the case of temples, *fuzokujō*.

18 "Tendai zasu Ryōgen kishō, nijūkajō kishō," *Heian ibun* no. 303, vol. 2, 431–40.

19 Paul Groner, *Ryōgen and Mount Hiei: Japanese Tendai in the Tenth Century* (Honolulu: University of Hawai'i Press, 2002), 236–39; for Groner's English translation, see 345–66.

20 "Tendai zasu Ryōgen yuigō," *Heian ibun* 2–305; see also Okano, "Enryakuji," 16.

century of the *Ritsuryō* system necessitated that temples expand administrative operations and achieve greater self-governance. Indications of these changes included the increased placing of sons of the nobility in the temple complexes, the development of aristocratic cloisters, as well as increased temple ownership and operation of manors.

Sovereign Law and Buddha Law: The Exo-Esoteric Temple System, Temple Decision-Making, and Power Blocs

Early legal historian Ishii Ryōsuke described the medieval era as being marked by the "mixture" of public and private law – the development of shogunal codes supplementing the *Ritsuryō* and, of course, the ongoing centrality of common law.[21] Nitta Ichirō has called into question whether we can even speak of a central government in the medieval era.[22] It is clear that medieval Japanese temples enjoyed a level of independence that was unique in Japanese history, with the possible exception of the warring provinces era (late fifteenth–late sixteenth centuries), when multiple groups could easily develop their own rules.

To create their own organizational structure, medieval temples developed several documentary genres that legally affected the various levels of monastic organization, their interactions and intersections with each other, and with the newly prominent governing entities of the medieval era – the royal court, the warrior government (shogunate), and other major temple complexes. Although scholars often use the term "temple law" (*jihō, jiinhō*) to refer to the regulations pronounced, this general term was rarely used at the time. Instead, varied terms – often with closely related senses – were used, including *sōto no hō* (monks' rules), *hōrei* (legal instructions), *shikimoku* (regulation list), *shikijō* (regulation clauses), *zōsei* (miscellaneous rules), *kinsei* (rules of prohibition), *shinsei* (new rules), *seishiki/kishiki/hōshiki* (regulations), *seihō* (rules), *seiyaku* (restrictions), *seifu* (prohibition document), and *okibumi* (testamentary stipulations).[23]

By the late eleventh century, the monastic organizations of the major temple complexes, which typically also featured prominent kami-worshipping shrines, wove complicated alliances and rivalries with members of the royal court and major warrior groups. Kuroda Toshio analyzed the development of power blocs, which took three different forms during

[21] Ishii Ryōsuke, *Keibatsu no rekishi* (Tokyo: Akashi Shoten, 1992), 78–82.
[22] See Nitta Ichirō, *Chūsei ni kokka wa atta ka* (Tokyo: Yamakawa Shuppansha, 2004).
[23] For a discussion of these terms, see Nagamura Makoto, "Chūsei jiin to 'jihō,'" 264–65, 278–79.

the medieval era: temple (shrine), nobility, and warrior organizations. Power blocs were organizations that possessed complex systems of self-governance and variously collaborated and vied to increase their wealth, prestige, and power. At minimum, they protected their self-governance wherever possible. The most powerful religious power blocs were temple (shrine) complexes, such as Enryakuji, Kōfukuji, and Tōdaiji, which possessed monastic organizations with the ability to engage in political demonstration. Such power blocs used various modes of symbolic practice – both ritual and written – to promote their respective interpretations of Buddhist doctrine and practice.

Kuroda, in his "Chūsei jisha seiryokuron" (Study of Medieval Temple-Shrine Power), explored the larger monastic meetings as well as the changes that developed in monastic organizations. Kuroda highlighted the connection between the changes and the exo-esoteric Buddhism (*kenmitsu bukkyō*) of the major complexes that combined sūtra study with esoteric Buddhist study and that had the support of the sovereign and his royal court, a relationship referred to typically as "Sovereign Law–Buddha Law mutual dependence" (*ōbō buppō sō'i*). Considering the early example of Ryōgen's role at Mount Hiei, Kuroda particularly took note of two aspects of monastic life. On the one hand, there was the "power bloc" character constituted by scholarly school, the temple-shrine itself (including the larger monastic organization), monastic residences, Buddha halls and reliquaries, and ritual assemblies. On the other hand was the personal level of relations marked by affiliations with a ritual lineage, a lineage chart, and co-residence with a master in a separate residential hall.

It was, in particular, the full development of the coercive power of the temple complexes by the eleventh century that Kuroda identified as corresponding with the consolidation of what he called their "exo-esoteric system" (*kenmitsu taisei*).[24] Temple complexes sometimes used coercive demonstrations, which typically took the form of bringing an object associated with the kami of the shrine from within the complex to a site of contestation. As Mikael Adolphson noted, partisans of Mount Hiei would sometimes take the kami's palanquin down into the capital;[25] those of Kōfukuji connected multiple mirrors to a *sakaki* sacred tree to do so, with the similar threat of kami punishment in the background.[26]

[24] *Kuroda Toshio choshakushū* vol. 3 (Kyoto: Hōzōkan, 1995), 197–205; the study was written in 1975.

[25] Mikael S. Adolphson, *The Gates of Power: Monks, Courtiers, and Warriors in Premodern Japan* (Honolulu: University of Hawai'i Press, 2000), 241–47.

[26] For a discussion of the divine punishment – presented as that of both kami and buddhas – see Katsumata Shigeo, *Ikki* (Tokyo: Iwanami Shoten, 1982), 42–51. Satō Hiroo and others, however,

Some scholars, however, have emphasized a feature of the larger monastic organizations that has often been ignored in historical studies: their use of majority rule in decision-making. Seita Yoshihide has meticulously investigated and demonstrated the use of majority rule as the basic principle in the large temple complexes of the medieval era.[27] Seita distinguishes between three basic patterns of majority-rule decisions within temple complexes, represented respectively by Kōfukuji, Enryakuji (Mount Hiei), and Kongōbuji (Mount Kōya): decision-making almost solely by the larger monastic organization (Kōfukuji), made centrally by the various sub-temples within the complex (Hiei), and undertaken via a complicated mix of deliberations at both the levels of the larger organization and of the sub-temples (Kōya).[28]

Others scholars' research seems to support Seita's conclusions. For example, Inaba Nobumichi has studied *jihen shinsei* (new rules of temple areas) from the late twelfth century onward, which correspond in format to new laws introduced by the nobility and shogunate, and concluded that the larger monastic organization at Kōfukuji created and disseminated them.[29] Shimosaka Mamoru and Kinugawa Satoshi have clarified that while the monastic organization at Enryakuji originally had a role in decision-making as central as those of the various sub-temples in the various valleys of the complex, it became weaker and ceased to have any meaningful role in the decision-making process from the mid-to-late thirteenth century as the sub-temples vastly increased their self-governance.[30] Wada Shūjō's study of Kōya clarified the extremely complicated and fluctuating mix of levels of deliberation there, which developed in connection with and were coordinated by the main "annual administrator" (*nen'yo*), whose chief

have emphasized the particular role of kami as punishers within the Buddha-kami combinatory framework. See Satō Hiroo, "Wrathful Deities and Saving Deities" in Mark Teeuwen and Fabio Rambelli (eds.), *Buddhas and Kami in Japan:* Honji Suijaku *as a Combinatory Paradigm* (New York: Routledge Curzon, 2003), 95–114.

27 See Seita Yoshihide, *Nihon chūsei jiinhō no kenkyū* (Tokyo: Keibundō, 1987) and *Chūsei jiinhō shi no kenkyū: Jiin no tasūketsusei to jiin hōshiki* (Tokyo: Keibundō, 1995). Adolphson, *Gates of Power*, 251–58, writes, "Since no protests were brought to the capital without the approval of the main clergies, there was a democratic aspect to this process" (257). We also take note of a recent study by Fabio Rambelli that has explored the democratic character of temple governance and attempted to connect it to Indian Buddhism in "Buddhist Republican Thought and Institutions in Japan: Preliminary Considerations" in James Baskind (ed.), *Scholars of Buddhism in Japan: Buddhist Studies in the 21st Century* (Kyoto: International Research Center for Japanese Studies, 2009), 127–53.

28 *Ibid.*, 22.

29 Inaba Nobumichi, *Chūsei jiin no kenryoku kōzō* (Tokyo: Iwanami Shoten), 337.

30 Shimosaka Mamoru, *Chūsei jiin shakai no kenkyū* (Kyoto: Shibunkaku, 2001), 211–12; and Kinugawa Satoshi, "Enryakuji no saikyo to jiin kenryoku" in Ōyama Kyōhei (ed.), *Chūsei jiin saikyojō no kenkyū* (Tokyo: Hanawa Shobō, 2008), 476.

function was to call the meetings of the entire monastic organization, record its decisions and distribute its commands, and maintain the records and treasures of the complex. The levels of decision, by the second half of the thirteenth century, included not just that of the larger organization (rarely convened), but also the so-called major and minor meetings of scholastic monks and the developing worker-monk (*gyōnin*) and holy men (*hijiri*) organizations.[31]

These meetings and their documents, of course, do not exhaust the literature of temple law. More than anything else, the fact that the royal court and the warrior government added new regulations, in addition to the traditional *Ritsuryō* codes, influenced relations between society at large and the other power blocs. Noble families and, eventually, warrior families also developed their own family codes.[32] Nobles, the shogunate, and powerful warrior lords sometimes themselves authored temple law as patrons (*dan'otsu*) rather than in official pronouncements.[33]

Suits and Status in Exo-Esoteric Buddhism

Given the development of power blocs and their own systems of governance,[34] it is not surprising that Buddhists, like others in Japanese society, would initiate lawsuits. Some lawsuits alleged that the "Buddha's property" had been improperly appropriated by a temple, its monks, or others for their own use.[35] Most claims were between temples or cloisters, drawing especially on the writings of ancestral masters, historic and symbolic connections with influential masters, documents representing two temples as being in a home-affiliate (*honmatsu*) administrative or doctrinal temple relationship, lineage charts, and other forms of ritual transmission verification.

31 Wada Shūjō, "Chūsei Kōyasan no sōryo shū'e seido" in MIyasaka Yūshō (ed.), *Mikkyō taikei dainanakan, Nihon mikkyō yon* (Kyoto: Hōzōkan, 1995), 355–98.

32 For examples and an overview, see Ishii Susumu et al. (ed.), *Chūsei seiji shakai shisō, jō* (Tokyo: Iwanami Shoten, 1981); also see the six volumes of *Chūsei hōsei shiryō shū*, although vol. 6 is the only volume to specifically include temple-shrine law (*jisha hō*). See Satō Shin'ichi et al. (eds.), *Chūsei hōsei shiryō shū, dairokkan* (Tokyo: Iwanami Shoten, 2005).

33 See, for example, for the Sanbō'in sub-temple of Kongōji temple, "Minamoto Sadahiro senyū jō," *Heian ibun* 8–4017; for Bannaji, "Ashikaga Yoshiuji kudashibumi," in Takeuchi Rizō (ed.), *Kamakura ibun* (Tokyo: Tōkyōdō, 1971–97) 8, no. 5766. Nagamura Makoto includes a series of other examples in "Chūsei jiin to jihō," 268–69.

34 Nitta Ichirō has emphasized the contingent character of law in medieval era and its manifestation in cases of suit. See "Hō to rekishi ninshiki no tenkai" in Karube Tadashi et al. (eds.), *Nihon shisōshi kōza 2: chūsei* (Tokyo: Perikansha, 2012), 128–29.

35 Kasamatsu Hiroshi, "Butsumotsu, sōmotsu, jinmotsu" (Kasamatsu, *Hō to kotoba no chūsei shi*) (Tokyo: Heibonsha, 1984), 117–20.

For example, Tōdaiji attempted to compel Daigoji to submit to the position of "affiliate temple" (*matsuji*). In 1308 the sovereign initially conferred the honorific appellation of Hongaku Daishi on the early Shingon monk Yakushin (827–906) of Tōji and Tōdaiji temples. When rival Enryakuji monks successfully protested this act, Tōdaiji held a meeting of its entire monastic organization (*manji shū'e*) and decided to request its affiliates' participation in protest and written support of its suit to the royal court to have the posthumous name re-conferred. Daigoji refused to participate or sign on as an affiliate temple of Tōdaiji, leading to arguments over the question of whether the two had a home-affiliate relationship. Tōdaiji emphasized its position as an ordination site for Shingon monks, a center for doctrinal study, a temple complex bearing a ritual transmission connection with many Shingon monks, and the monastery where the great Shingon masters Kūkai and Shōbō had once practiced and resided. Tōdaiji also highlighted Daigoji's position as belonging to one of the eight traditional schools of Japanese Buddhism.[36]

Daigoji argued that it was not an affiliate of Tōdaiji because it was founded as a vow temple of the sovereign (*chokuganji*), setting it apart from other temples. Moreover, the royal lineage changed after Shōmu (r. 724–49), who was the sovereign when Tōdaiji was founded, and Daigoji was thus founded by a different royal line. The main temple of Shingon monks, as designated by the government, was Tōji rather than Tōdaiji. Shingon lineages, in addition, prohibited cohabitation with monks of other doctrinal schools, whereas Tōdaiji included multiple groups and so was not an appropriate esoteric Buddhist site. Since Tōdaiji did not currently have esoteric Buddhism, a significant number of Tōdaiji monks had received esoteric initiation under Daigoji monks. Finally, the notion that the doctrinal schools of Tendai (Enryakuji) and Hossō (Kōfukuji, etc.), let alone Shingon, were included among the eight traditional schools and thus under the authority of Tōdaiji, was preposterous.

As Nagamura Makoto has noted, Tōdaiji pressed the home-affiliate claim, especially out of concern over temple status.[37] Tōdaiji had long emphasized its presumed unique position as the original home temple of all provincial temples in the system developed in the Nara period and its possession of the precepts platform in Nara. The success or failure of its

36 This discussion is based on Nagamura Makoto, "'Shingonshū' to Tōdaiji" in Chūsei Jiin Kenkyūkai (ed.), *Chūsei jiin shakai no kenkyū, ge* (Kyoto: Hōzōkan, 1988), 19–28; Inaba Nobumichi, "Tōdaiji honmatsu sōron shiryō: komonjo shū ni" in Kokubungaku Kenkyūshiryōkan (ed.), *Shinpukuji zenpon sōkan daijikkan* [dai niki] (Kyoto: Rinsen Shoten, 2008), 769–73.

37 *Ibid.*, 34.

arguments, along with its place as a major residential monastery and its success at gaining government support for major dharma assemblies, was intimately related to its stature vis-à-vis other temples.

We also find suits between cloisters. One famous series of cases over the course of a century were those filed in connection with the question of both the leadership of the powerful Tendai cloister Shōren'in and the ownership of certain objects. It is important to note that a central feature of these suits was the expressed concern over the fate of the sacred works collection of the cloister, which consisted of a series of doctrinal and ritual manuscripts by former masters of the lineage as well as a broad array of cloister documents. Retired sovereign Fushimi decided in 1314 that the monastic lineages vying for the abbacy had to reconcile, particularly because the monks had neglected their ritual practices and, through their repeated suits, contributed to the decline of the doctrinal school (Tendai), the cloister itself, and the Buddha Dharma.[38]

Suits were thus undertaken at a series of levels within and between power blocs, intersecting with issues of both temple and personal status. Larger monastic organizations were, of course, keenly aware of the dangers of decisions made by sub-groups within the monastery – hence the warnings in some codes against having unauthorized meetings.[39] Thus, while Tōdaiji's organization was concerned with the temple's status vis-à-vis other major complexes, the dharma lineages of the cloisters were also concerned with the personal level, where one's clerical position could be advanced by selection as a "guardian monk" of the sovereign or as a reward for performing rites for the sovereigns, families in the royal court, shogunate, or members of powerful warrior clans. These rewards for ritual service, typically from the royal clan out of gratitude for officiating at one or another major rite, included increased clerical status and later land grants from warriors. These rewards were of such concern to cloisters and temple organizations that records of the major rites performed by monks were often listed in great detail.[40] As with Shingon school's rain-making records, compilations of

[38] Shōwa 3.4.21, in *Mon'yō ki Taishō shinshū daizōkyō zuzōbu* 12 (Tokyo: Taishō Shinshū Daizōkyō Kankōkai, 1978), 403b; also see Taira Masayuki, "Shōren'in no monzeki sōron to Kamakura bakufu" in Kawane Yoshiyasu and Fukuda Eijirō (eds.), *Enryakuji to chūsei shakai* (Kyoto: Hōzōkan, 2004), 90–150, esp. 129–30.

[39] See, for example, "Kaijūsenji shūsō rensho kishōmon" of 1219, *Kamakura ibun*, 4–2481.

[40] Examples include: (1) "Godan hō kenjō [no] koto," *Mon'yō ki, Taishō shinshū daizōkyō zuzōbu*, vol. 11, 346b–350a; (2) *Daidai goki shuhō midokyō tō ki*, Shinpukuji Bunko archives Box 43–71 and *Kujakukyō mi-shuhō ki* in Zokugunsho Ruijū Kanseikai (ed.), *Zokugunsho ruijū nijūgo shū, ge* (Tokyo: Zokugunsho Ruijū Kanseikai, 1933), 345–86; and (3) *Sho mi-shuhō kenjō rei*, Daigoji Shōgyō archives, box 105.18–10.

such works were undoubtedly thought to help protect the ritual prerogative of a particular lineage or school to undertake a particular rite. This prerogative then aided a monk, lineage, school, and, sometimes, a specific temple, to acquire or maintain positions of status. Indeed, as in the case of the networking monk Raishin (1281–1336), who represented Tōdaiji in several suits with Daigoji (1312–17), the success of one's legal arguments was enhanced by the study of Buddhist logic, the possession of initiation documents, and the ability to acquire sacred works.[41] As distinctions between legal and religious authority were remarkably fluid, Buddhist initiations and knowledge, when supported by written materials attesting to their authenticity, were also seen as legally efficacious.

Kamakura "New" Buddhism and the Relationship between Buddhism and Law in Later Eras

By the fourteenth century, a series of newer Buddhist organizations began to develop their own rules and to enter into varied relationships with other power blocs, such as local warrior lords and, eventually, the Tokugawa Shogunate, which would unite Japan under its extensive legal authority in the seventeenth century. As the so-called new Kamakura schools developed, the Zen schools, in particular, incorporated Chan codes and endeavored to develop their own versions. Early on, Dōgen (1200–53) attempted to regulate monastic life at Eiheiji, including a series of instructions concerning arenas such as the monk's hall, monastic officers, meals, and reading practices. Eiheiji developed rules concerning financial practices within the monastery, and Keizan (1264–1325) left behind instructions concerning rules for his lineage.[42] Rinzai's Enni Bennen (1202–80) created several sets of rules for his followers at Tōfukuji. As Harada Masatoshi has stressed, these rules emphasized monks' vigilance in performing rites for the nobles and shogunate, his lineage's continued occupation of the abbacy, and a prohibition against all demonstrations. His codes also required participation in a whole series of regular ceremonies, including prayers for the sovereign, chanting *dhāraṇī* for the shogunate, and memorial rites for earlier masters and for the noble Kujō family and others.[43] Musō Soseki (1275–1351) wrote extensive rules for administration and monastic life for the San'e-in

[41] Makino Atsushi, "Kamakura kōki no jiin shakai to sono bunkateki kankyo," *Chūsei bungaku*, 56 (2011), 14–25.

[42] Martin Collcutt, *Five Mountains: The Rinzai Zen Monastic Institution in Medieval Japan* (Cambridge: Harvard University Press, 1981), 148; Nagamura, "Chūsei jiin to 'jihō,'" 270–73.

[43] Harada Masatoshi, "Kujō Michi'ie no Tōfukuji to Enni," *Kikan Nihon shisōshi*, 68 (2006), 90–91.

sub-temple and his larger Rinsenji temple, which clearly owed a substantial debt to early fourteenth-century Chan codes.[44] Daitokuji instituted several codes, beginning with the instructions given by Shūhō Myōchō (1282–1338) for the satellite nunnery near there, Myōkakuji. The codes generally were concerned with differentiating responsibilities and administration within the monastery.[45]

Nichiren school temples developed their own codes beginning in the mid-fourteenth century. The abbots, who were comparatively strong, typically wrote the codes, which strictly prohibited arms, harmful speech, theft, sale of the Buddha's property, illicit relations with women, and gambling. Likewise, Pure Land School (Jōdoshū) temples developed their codes beginning in the late fifteenth century. Their abbots also usually wrote the codes, which prohibited arguments, fights, the taking of life, cultivation of pungent foods, close interaction with women, unauthorized travel, personal use of the Buddha's property, laxity in rite attendance, and the wearing of any clothing other than monastic robes.[46] The authoritarian character of these codes was clearly related to a variety of difficulties experienced by the newer groups and also the vicissitudes of a period of Japanese history when power was becoming increasingly decentralized throughout the isles.

After the rise of Honganji partisan leagues (*ikkō ikki*) and other leagues in the late fifteenth and sixteenth centuries,[47] the policies undertaken by the early Tokugawa regime began to take shape at the beginning of the seventeenth century. From the seventeenth and into the early eighteenth century, the shogunate introduced temple regulations (*jiin hatto*), the temple affiliation system (*jidan seido*), temple certification (*terauke*), a strict interpretation of the main-affiliate temple hierarchy, monastic positions and status, and a broad set of newer regulations, which remained in place until the nineteenth century.[48] The strict temple regulations fit with the Tokugawa's efforts to maintain a close eye on the Buddhists, which also propelled an extremely vibrant period of Japanese Buddhist studies and, in many ways, for Buddhism in general. Families were required to affiliate,

[44] Collcutt, *Five Mountains*, 149–65; "Rinsen kakun" in Zokugunsho Ruijū Kanseikai (ed.), *Zokugunsho ruijū kyū shū, ge* (Tokyo: Zokugunsho Ruijū Kanseikai, 1932), 530–34.

[45] Seita, *Chūsei jiinhō shi*, 270; Seita Yoshihide, *Chūsei hokke jiinhō shi ron* (Tokyo: Keibundō, 2009), 13–14.

[46] Seita, *Chūsei jiinhō shi*, 416–81; *Ibid.*

[47] See Katsumata Shigeo, *Ikki* (Tokyo: Iwanami Shoten, 1982).

[48] Sonehara Satoshi, "Kinsei kokka to bukkyō" in Sueki Fumihiko (ed.), *Minshū bukkyō no teichaku* (Tokyo: Kōsei, 2010), 81–122; also see Barbara Ambros, *Emplacing a Pilgrimage: The Ōyama Cult and Regional Religion in Early Modern Japan* (Cambridge, MA: Harvard University Asia Center, 2008), 61–63.

but the funerary Buddhist temple was of their own choosing.[49] With the financial support of the shogunate, major Buddhist schools (Jōdo shū, Tendai shū, Jōdo shinshū, Shingon shū, Nichiren shū and, later, Yūzū Nenbutsu shū) developed seminaries called *danrin* and similar training temples, requiring extensive study for monastic certification.[50]

Research on the relationship between Buddhism and law in the Tokugawa period remains limited in its scope, given that few studies have addressed the distinction between "[doctrinal] school law" (*shūha hō*), specific temple law (*kobetsu jihō*), and shogunal temple law (*bakufu jihō*),[51] despite the fact that extant manuscripts are plentiful.[52] We do know, though, that the shogunate gave the leadership of the relevant doctrinal schools, which it had strengthened in the process of constructing a more centralized system of governance over temples, responsibility for handling lawsuits and only intervened if the temple's leaders could not decide. With the exception of the True Pure Land School and the Tōzan branch of Shugendō, the shogunate strictly prohibited sexual relations with women. Possession of a wife could lead to the death penalty, although lower-ranking monks were punished by their local or temple authorities, suffering expulsion in the Pure Land and Shingon orders. In 1770, the shogunate issued a document that gave the Tokugawa government direct authority over the monks and rites of all schools of Buddhism.[53] Even more stringent rules for all religious institutions were introduced by the Meiji government as part of its modernization beginning in the late 1860s.

From that point onward, the development of the modern state was accompanied by the legal transformation of Buddhism into a "religion" (*shūkyō*) subject to a system of national laws. This was a complex process that permanently altered the dynamics of Buddhist life in the Japanese isles.[54] Government legislation in 1872, for example, said that monks and nuns were free to eat meat, marry, and engage in other practices contrary

49 Nam-lin Hur, *Death and Social Order in Tokugawa: Buddhism, Anti-Christianity, and the Danka System* (Cambridge, MA: Harvard University Asia Center, 2007), 228.

50 Nishimura Ryō, "Kyōgaku no shinten to bukkyō kaikaku undō" in Sueki Fumihiko (ed.), *Minshū bukkyō no teichaku* (Tokyo: Kōsei, 2010), 184–95.

51 Kojima Nobuyasu, *Kinsei sensōji no jihō to kōzō* (Tokyo: Sōbunsha, 2008), 72.

52 Also, in premodern research, there remains a major lacuna for study of the legal aspects of local Buddhist life, beyond the specifically "temple" level, as well as that of marginal organizations of *shugenja* and *hijiri*.

53 *Ibid.*, 100–04.

54 For a useful overview of the relationship between modern Buddhism and politics, including legal issues by implication, see Ōtani Eiichi, "Kindai Nihon no 'seiji to bukkyō' no kurosuroodo," (Nanzan Shūkyo Bunka Kenkyūjo) *Kenkyūjohō*, 16 (2006), 35–47. http://nirc.nanzan-u.ac.jp/Shuppanbutsu/Shoho_to_burechin/pdf/S16-Ohtani.pdf.

to the precepts without violating the law, which seemed to condone a lack of discipline. However, the decision was not merely forced on Buddhists as a series of monks were involved in its writing. A multiplicity of voices within and without government helped to shape religious policy, which changed regularly over the next decades, undergoing radical shifts after the Pacific War with the rise of secular democracy.[55]

[55] See Richard M. Jaffe, "Passage of the Nikujiki Saitai Law: The Clergy and the Formation of Meiji Buddhist Policy" in Richard M. Jaffe (ed.), *Neither Monk Nor Layman: Clerical Marriage in Modern Japanese Buddhism* (Princeton, NJ: Princeton University Press, 2002) 95–113.

CHAPTER 16

Relic Theft in Medieval Japan

Bernard Faure

Throughout its history, Buddhism had to adapt to the various legal, political, and social environments it encountered, while developing its own monastic legal system, the *Vinaya*. Among the four *pārājika* rules leading to exclusion from the monastic community, the rule about theft comes second, just after the one about illicit sex and before those about murder and boasting of spiritual powers. Indeed, it seems to have generated as many legalistic commentaries as the rule about illicit sex. Yet, unlike illicit sex and the taking of life (the latter mostly by meat-eating), theft never became a narrative topos. In both China and Japan, stories abound about meat-eating, drinking, and fornicating monks, whereas stealing among monks is not often discussed, and much less justified. Only very few texts consider it as a skillful means (*upāya*).[1] Most references to theft contain dire warnings against stealing the saṅgha's (or, more precisely, the Buddha's) property. Outside the clerical community, however, the Buddhist clergy did not try to legislate on moral and legal issues and to sanction laymen's offenses, as did, for instance, the Church in medieval Europe.

As in the case of other *pārājika* offenses, early Buddhist condemnations of theft reflect an attempt to align the Buddhist community with the larger society and its legal system. However, they also sometimes aim – in the case of medieval Japan, for instance – to protect the property of the monasteries. Since the saṅgha was often identified with the Buddha, any theft of monastic – therefore sacred – property became a sacrilege against the Buddha himself. In addition to this non-juridical method of discouraging theft, doctrinal and ethical justifications also denounced it: it is condemned, for instance, because it results from greed (*rāga*) – one

[1] In the *Futsū jubosatsukai kōshaku* (T. 2381), for instance, illicit sex and stealing, rather than abstention thereof, paradoxically become the precepts. On this text, see Paul Groner, "The *Fan-wang ching* and Monastic Discipline in Japanese Tendai: A Study of Annen's *Futsū jubosatsukai kōshaku*" in Robert E. Buswell, Jr. (ed.), *Chinese Buddhist Apocrypha* (Honolulu: University of Hawai'i Press, 1990), 251–90.

of the "Three Poisons" along with hatred (*dveṣa*) and ignorance (*moha*) – and because it harms others. It is perceived as the structural opposite of gift (*dāna*), whose merit is produced by the act of giving up material possessions.[2]

The *Vinaya* of the Mahāsāṃghika moved beyond pure disciplinary legalism, explaining the negative effects of theft for the spiritual progression of the culprit.[3] The Mahāyāna code does this primarily by emphasizing the intention of the act. The apocryphal *Fanwang jing*, for instance, justifies the rule against theft by the fact that stealing would go against the bodhisattva's duty, which is to make others joyful and happy by always presenting a state of mind that conforms to the buddha nature.[4]

Not only can theft lead to exclusion in the case of a monk or nun, it can also, in the cases of both clerics and laypeople, have far-reaching effects extending beyond this lifetime. The *Āgamas* mention that it leads to retribution in future life and that it affects rebirth. The thief will fall among the hungry ghosts or animals (because of the greed that motivated his act). Even if he is reborn among humans, he will live a miserable existence.[5] The *Dazhidulun* defines ten punishments for theft, in this life and in the next: essentially rebirth in hell and poverty in future lives.[6]

In the Japanese tradition, the *Nihon ryōiki*, provides many examples of punishments of evil deeds, but in only one case does unduly taking other people's possessions result in retribution. Some people receive a violent death for hitting a monk, persecuting a novice, or breaking his alms-bowl; a person is reborn as a monkey for keeping people from seeking the way, another as an ox for having stolen from his own son; people receive retribution for the misuse of temple property, for collecting debts by force, or for lack of filial piety. In this text, retribution intervenes in a quasi-automatic fashion, without any juridical apparatus. Among the crimes listed, theft is practically passed over in silence. Some cases of theft are indeed mentioned in relation to the bodhisattva Myōken ("Wondrous Sight"), a deity of Daoist origin that rules over human destiny and is identified with the Pole Star (and also sometimes with King Yama). In these

2 *Abhidharmakośabhāṣya*, translated into French by Louis de la Vallée Poussin, *L'Abhidharmakośa de Vasubandhu* (1923–31, reprint, Brussels: Institut Belge des Hautes Études Chinoises, 1971), vol. 3, ch. 4, 244.

3 *Mahāsāṃghika Vinaya*, T. 22, no. 1425: 244b.

4 *Fanwang jing*, T. 24, no. 1484. See also *Dazhidulun* in Étienne Lamotte (trans.), *Le traité de la grande vertu de sagesse de Nāgārjuna* (1949, reprint, Louvain-la-Neuve: Université de Louvain, Institut Orientaliste, 1981), vol. 2, 795–96.

5 *Avataṃsaka-sūtra*, T. 9, 278: 549b.

6 *Dazhidulun*, T. 25, no. 1509: 156b; Lamotte, *Traité*, vol. 2, 798.

stories, Myōken's acute vision helps to see hidden human acts and to solve some cases of theft.[7] I will return to this panoptical gaze, which also characterizes Yama and similar deities.

The fear of retribution and hell, which was such a powerful instrument of Buddhist predications in premodern Japan, has been recently adapted to modern audiences. A case in point is an animation picture presented to tourists – mostly schoolchildren – at Tateyama (Toyama Prefecture), a place formerly believed to be the earthly entrance to the Buddhist hells. In this film, the Japanese thief lies to Yama and as punishment gets his tongue pulled out, before being reborn in Avīci Hell. Interestingly, this Buddhist hell is described as a futuristic Japan, a land destroyed by an ecological disaster, a gloomy megalopolis in which no tree remains.

In this story, the culprit has his tongue pulled out because he lied, trying to deny his crimes. The fault is revealed in the great mirror of King Yama, which reflects all human deeds, good and evil. This panoptical device is supplemented by various others, in particular Yama's *danda* staff, also known as the "human-headed staff" because of the one or two talking heads at its top, which tell Yama all the deeds committed by the individual on trial. These two heads are another form of Yama's attendants, Shimei and Shiroku, who record all human acts and report them to Yama. They came to be known in Japan as the *kushōjin*, that is, "deities born together" or at the same time as the individual. This conception, and the notion of a trial in which the two deities act as prosecutor and lawyer, respectively, is probably the closest Buddhism ever came to a juridical conception of individual life. In later developments, in which Jizō becomes the defender of the dead, his acolytes are sometimes described as the Lads of Good and Evil, and play the same role as the "twin-devas." Jizō is himself, particularly in Japan, often identified with Yama.

The judgment, symbolized by the juridico-administrative mechanism represented by Yama and his two acolytes, leads to the emergence of a psychological structure: the accusing conscience. This is similar to the mechanism of confession in Christianity that contributed to the individuation process described by Michel Foucault.[8] The twin figures of the *kushōjin* flanking the accused individual (who is the other face of Yama, the judge) and literally "co-arising" ("co-naissants") is found again, as we

[7] See, for example, *Nihon ryōiki* 1.34, 3.5, and 3.32 in Keikai and Kyoko Motomochi Nakamura (trans. and ed.), *Miraculous Stories from the Japanese Buddhist Tradition: The Nihon Ryōiki of the Monk Kyōkai* (Cambridge, MA: Harvard University Press, 1973), 149, 229, 266–67.

[8] Michel Foucault, *Discipline and Punish: The Birth of the Prison* (New York: Vintage, 1995).

will see shortly, in the medieval cult of the Buddha's relics, with the pair of reliquary guardians formed by the wisdom kings (*vidyārāja*) Aizen (Rāga) and Fudō (Acalanātha).

It seems that Buddhism, rather than translate its "law" (dharma) into juridical practice, tried to impose it in the imaginary realm by instilling the fear of evil – in particular by emphasizing the notions of karmic retribution and of the judgment of the dead. This led to a mythological development of the role of Yama as King of the Law (*dharmarāja*, J. *hōō*), whose motto could have been: *Dura lex, sed lex*. Yama was helped in this task by various attendants, like the aforementioned *kushōjin* as well as various shady beings such as the *ḍākinīs*, who steal the vital essence of humans and thus diminish their life. This shortening of the human lifespan is also, indirectly, the result of the reports made by the *kushōjin* and similar witnesses of human fallibility. We thus arrive at a paradox: crimes of an individual, including theft, lead to his life being, as it were, stolen in turn by such infernal agents – theft justified as legal punishment.

At any rate, the notion of a panoptic power, symbolized by devices such as Yama's mirror, his human-headed staff, and his various informants, led to a Buddhist conception of a moral conscience that parallels – although very differently – that of Christianity, a moral conscience perceived as an alien and enemy presence within oneself.[9] Perhaps this internalization of the offense, and the fear of hell that sustains it, partly results from the internalization of the precepts that characterized the Mahāyānist *Vinaya*.

Relic Theft

While the *Vinaya* is excruciatingly detailed about various forms of theft, it fails to mention one of them, whose object was arguably the most precious that could come to the mind of a Buddhist (if not of the Buddha himself): the theft of the Buddha's relics (*śarīra*). Indeed, relic theft seems to be the blind spot of the panoptical retribution system, and it deserves further scrutiny.

The cult of the Buddha's relics itself has long remained quasi-invisible to the eyes of Buddhist scholars, probably because of its uncanny (and superficial) resemblance with the Christian cult of relics. It has now become a favorite object of research, as shown by the recent publication of several books and numerous articles on the subject. As Gregory Schopen points out, "[r]elics were thought to retain – to be infused with, impregnated

[9] *Ibid.*

with – the qualities that animated and defined the living Buddha . . . The *stūpa* or reliquary was cognitively classified as a 'living person of rank' and . . . [was] a 'juristic personality' and owned property."[10] Thus, "[regardless] of what some canonical texts might occasionally suggest and some scholastic texts definitely state, the Buddha was and continued to be an actual living presence in the midst of the Buddhist community."[11]

Collecting relics for the purpose of worshiping them easily leads to theft (or at least, to a tendency to borrow without returning). Because theft interrupts circulation and exchange, it is the opposite of the gift (in the Maussian sense and in the Buddhist sense of *dāna*, one of the six *pāramitā* or perfections).[12] Stealing is "capitalizing," a harbinger of Pierre-Joseph Proudhon's anti-capitalist slogan that "property is theft."

Although relic theft constitutes a rather special case, it is presented in various sources as a paradigmatic example of theft. According to the *Mahāsāṃghika-vinaya*, for instance, the theft of things belonging to the Three Jewels constitutes one of the most serious offenses.[13] To steal a relic is to steal from the Buddha, because before entering nirvāṇa he has accepted all gifts. These goods are the property of the Buddha and his community.[14] A contrary viewpoint, however, can be found in the *Mahāparinirvāṇa-sūtra*, according to which: "To steal the property of the Buddha is not a sin."[15] In the *Vinaya* of the Sarvāstivāda, the theft of a relic is classified among "serious infractions"; in other words, it is not a *pārājika* offense. If committed with piety and "good faith," it creates no sin.

According to Daoxuan (596–667), the founder of the Chinese *Vinaya* (Lu) school, if the things stolen from the gods or from a stūpa have a guardian, the thief commits a heavy sin toward the Three Jewels; otherwise, it is only an offense toward the donor.[16] We encounter here what we could call the "guardian's paradox." Indeed, as Patrick Geary noted in the Christian case, "the guardian's presence symbolizes the faith, avarice, and apparent contradiction of the entire phenomenon of relic thefts. He knows

[10] Gregory Schopen, "On the Buddha and His Bones: 'The Conception of a Relic in the Inscriptions of Nāgarjunikonda,'" *Journal of the American Oriental Society* 108 (1988), 533. See also Schopen, "Burial 'Ad Sanctos' and the Physical Presence of the Buddha in Early Indian Buddhism: A Study in the Archaeology of Religions," *Religion* 17 (1987), 204.

[11] Schopen, "Burial 'Ad Sanctos,'" 212.

[12] Marcel Mauss, *The Gift: Forms and Functions of Exchange in Archaic Societies*, in Ian Cunninson (trans.) (New York and London: W.W. Norton, 1967).

[13] *Mahāsāṃghika Vinaya*, T. 22, 1425.

[14] Fabio Rambelli, "Buddha's Wrath: Esoteric Buddhism and the Discourse of Divine Punishment," *Japanese Religions* 27 (2002), 41–68.

[15] T. 12, no. 374: 405c. [16] T. 40, no. 1804: 55b.

that he is guarding what can only be stolen by the will of the saint"[17] – or in this case, of the Buddha. And if the latter "wills to be removed, then a mere man will be powerless to prevent it."[18] Thus, Geary concludes, "the impossibility of stealing a relic without permission of the saint is a major means of justifying (or condemning) a theft. The saint is master of his own fate."[19] And even more so, we may add, is the Buddha. Since relics of the Buddha were often believed to have a will of their own, their theft was perceived more like kidnapping. While morally ambiguous, such theft could eventually be condoned if it was committed for the benefit of a community.

Theft was from the start associated with Buddhist relics; it is at the very center of the famous episode of the division of the Buddha's relics by a brahmin named Droṇa. The tale actually involves a double theft, since the relic stolen by Droṇa was in turn stolen by a god (Indra in some versions). Another important relic, the Buddha's eyetooth, is said to have been stolen by a *rākṣasa*, but later retrieved by the god Naḍa (var. Skandha). This particular relic is said to have been returned eventually to the human world, but in a very different location, since it was given by Naḍa to the *Vinaya* master Daoxuan. Once reintroduced in the circuit of worship, it eventually made its way to Japan.[20]

This episode profoundly influenced the Japanese imagination, becoming the source of a Nō play, entitled *Shari* (The Relic), in which a monk visits Sennyūji in Kyoto to worship the relics brought from China. While he is weeping tears of emotion, a villager appears and the two men discuss the Buddhist dharma and the virtues of relics. But suddenly the sky darkens and a strange light appears. Before the astonished monk the villager changes into a demon, grabs the relic, and flies off into the sky. At that moment, the god Idaten (Ch. Weituo tian, a mistaken transcription of Skandha) appears, pursues, and tackles the demon, recovering the relic.[21]

Often, *nāgas*, semi-divine beings, attempt to, or actually, steal relics, since having been entrusted with some of the Buddha's relics, they are known to crave them. Many stories, beginning with the legend of King Aśoka, mention the *nāga*-king's reluctance to part with the relics in their

[17] Patrick Geary, *Furta Sacra: Thefts of Relics in the Central Middle Ages* (Princeton, NJ: Princeton University Press, 1978), 137.
[18] *Ibid.*, 133–34. [19] *Ibid.*, 137.
[20] Bernard Faure, "Dato," in Hubert Durt et al. (eds.), *Hōbōgirin* (Paris: Librairie d'Amerique et d'Orient, and Tokyo: Maison Franco-Japonaise, 2003), vol. 8, 1140–41.
[21] John S. Strong and Sarah Strong, "A Tooth Relic of the Buddha in Japan: An Essay on the Sennyū-ji Tradition and a Translation of Zeami's Nō Play 'Shari'," *Japanese Religions*, 20 (1995), 1–33.

possession. Stealing relics from the *nāgas* is often justified because they are perceived as unworthy for keeping such treasures for themselves. In only one instance, that of the *nāga*-girl mentioned in the *Lotus Sūtra*, does a *nāga* willfully give her jewel (itself the transformation of a former relic) to the Buddha. Unlike other stingy *nāgas*, she is enlightened.[22]

Following Patrick Geary's work on *furta sacra* in the Christian tradition, Kevin Trainor has examined justifications for relic theft in the Pāli tradition in the accounts from Sri Lankan chronicles, such as the *Thūpavaṃsa* (thirteenth century) and the *Dhātuvaṃsa* (circa fourteenth century).[23] He notes that these accounts simultaneously affirm the desirability of relics and explain the orderly movement of these valued objects from one location to another. As he points out, this kind of theft was predicted by the Buddha in order to explain how his relics would eventually land in Sri Lanka. Yet these accounts are problematic in that they appear to endorse the practice of stealing, which is a violation of the *Vinaya*. In response to this problem, Trainor identifies two different models of relic theft, noting that one model is religiously affirmed, while the other is condemned. He concludes:

> It is apparent from these relic theft accounts that the practice of relic veneration has been incorporated into the Theravada tradition in such a way as to reinforce the overarching goal of mental detachment. It is precisely this ideal of non-attachment that makes it possible to affirm, under the proper circumstances, that "a relic theft is not a theft."[24]

In Japan, however, the relics of the Buddha came to acquire a very different symbolic value, and the meaning of relic theft changed accordingly. Next to the relics (*śarīra* or *dhātu*), properly speaking, we find relics in a broader sense – for instance, the mummies of Buddhist masters or "relics of contact," such as the robe (*kaṣāya*) and similar objects. I have discussed elsewhere the case of the alleged mummy of the Chan patriarch Shitou Xiqian (700–90), which a Japanese layman stole from its temple and smuggled out of China during the 1911 Revolution. After many adventures, it was eventually enshrined at Sōjiji in Yokohama, one of the headquarters of the Sōtō Zen school.[25] James Robson has tried to trace the Chinese history of that mummy.[26] Despite the moral reprobation and nationalistic feelings

22 *Miaofa lianhua jing*, T. 9, no. 262: 35b.

23 Kevin Trainor, "When is a Theft Not a Theft?" *Numen* 39 (1992), 1–26.

24 *Ibid.*, 19.

25 Bernard Faure, *The Rhetoric of Immediacy: A Cultural Critique of the Chan/Zen Tradition* (Princeton, NJ: Princeton University Press, 1991), 167–68.

26 James Robson, "A Tang Dynasty Chan Mummy [*roushen*] and a Modern Case of Furta Sacra? Investigating the Contested Bones of Shitou Xiqian," in Bernard Faure (ed.), *Chan Buddhism in Ritual Context* (London: Routledge Curzon, 2003).

among the Chinese over the incident, this relic theft has not caused – nor is it likely to cause – any juridical action (within or outside Buddhism).

Another well-known case is that of the mummy of the sixth Chan patriarch Huineng (d. 713) at Nanhuasi in Guangdong Province, which was described among others by the Jesuit Matteo Ricci. In the Tang period, a Korean monk tried, but failed, to steal its head and was arrested – at least according to the Chinese tradition. Korean sources claim that the head was actually removed and eventually enshrined in a Korean monastery that later became a thriving center. Taiwanese pilgrims, untroubled by the conflicting accounts or the implication of theft, visit both sacred places to worship the integral mummy as well as its severed head.[27]

The patriarchal robe has often been the object of greed, but in most cases, theft is said to have been prevented by a prodigy reflecting the will of the patriarch himself. When someone tried to steal the robe of the fifth patriarch from his successor Huineng (d. 713), that robe became so heavy that the thief could not lift it and, awed by this mysterious power, paid obeisance.[28]

The contemporary Chan master Xuyun claimed that the Buddha's relic at Mt. Ayuwang appeared as either big or small, as one or many, as still or moving, according to each visitor's vision. Its color also varied – it might be blue, yellow, red or white.[29] This metamorphic quality of the relic could, in theory, render it invisible to the eyes of potential thieves. Another interesting case, although slightly different, is that of the mummy of Kūkai (774–835), allegedly preserved in a cave on Mt. Kōya. According to tradition, it was at first invisible to Fujiwara Michinaga, but later became visible to him, although not to his companion, who could only touch it without seeing it.

The mention of Kūkai, the great Shingon master, brings us to an epoch-making development, namely, the transformation of the Buddha's relics into a wish-fulfilling jewel (*cintāmaṇi*). Kūkai himself is said to have fabricated one such jewel with the eighty grains of relics he brought from China, and in his apocryphal "Testament," the *Goyuigō*, he describes the method to fabricate these jewels.[30] As relics and jewels became the main

27 Faure, *Rhetoric of Immediacy*, 162–64; Faure, "Relics and Flesh Bodies: The Creation of Ch'an Pilgrimage Sites," in Susan Naquin and Chün-Fang Yü (eds.), *Pilgrims and Sacred Sites in China* (Berkeley: University of California Press, 1992), 150–89.

28 Anna Seidel, "Denne" in *Hōbōgirin*, vol. 8, 1127–58.

29 Xu Yun and Charles Luk (trans.), *Empty Cloud: The Autobiography of the Chinese Zen Master* (Longmead: Element Books, 1988), 41–44.

30 *Goyuigō*, T. 77, no. 2431: 413a; see also Brian Ruppert, *Jewel in the Ashes: Buddha Relics and Power in Early Medieval Japan* (Cambridge, MA: Harvard University Press, 2000).

objects of worship of one of the major Shingon rituals, the Rite of the Latter Seven Days (*goshichinichi mishiho*), their status gradually changed, becoming powerful symbols in their own right and no longer merely relics of Śākyamuni's body. They transformed into the source and fountainhead of all power, mystical and temporal. As such, they also embodied the *samaya* or "conventional" form of various esoteric deities, such as Butsugen Butsumo, Nyoirin Kannon, or Aizen Myōō.

The case of Aizen also illustrates the value of sacred jewels.[31] This "wisdom king" (Skt. *vidyārāja*, Jpn. *myōō*), sometimes called "Impartial King" (Byōdō-ō), was the main deity (*honzon*) of Byōdō-in, the symbolic center of the Fujiwara Regents in the late Heian period (794–1185). A later medieval Tendai encyclopedia, the *Keiran shūyōshū* claims that: "He holds in his hand the essence of beings, and rules over the world with impartiality."[32] In his representation with six arms, the third left hand, which does not hold any ritual implement or weapon, nevertheless "holds the essence of beings." This essence is said to be that of one's enemies, for whom impartiality seems a pious wish.

According to various sources, Aizen holds a wish-fulfilling jewel (*cintāmaṇi*) in his hand, or again Aizen has the *cintāmaṇi* for its *samaya* or "conventional" form. The *cintāmaṇi* is therefore no longer simply a wish-fulfilling jewel, but a jewel for ruling the world. Elsewhere, we read that what the Aizen of Byōdō-in holds in his left hand is actually the "human yellow" (*ninnō*), that is, the vital essence of humans.[33] If Aizen holds the "human yellow" in his hand, to preserve it or to crush it depending on the case, other deities, the *ḍākinīs* – a kind of female ghoul – feed on this precious substance, from which they derive their supernatural powers.[34] The Buddha's relics and the *cintāmaṇi* were in various ways closely connected with *ḍākinī* rites. Thus, a symbolic network centered on the relics and the *cintāmaṇi*, sometimes in the form of "human yellow," connected heterodox Dakini rites with the Aizen rite of Shingon.

Returning to the question of theft, the *Hōbutsushū* by Taira no Yasuyori (fl. 1190–1200) refers to the theft of relics to illustrate the precept against taking that which is not given. This is included under the general rubric

[31] On Aizen myōō, see Roger Goepper, *Aizen-myōō* (Zürich: Rietberg Museum, 1993).

[32] T. 76, no. 2410: 579b.

[33] *Keiran shūyōshū*, T 76, 2410: 579b, 799c. The term "human yellow" seems patterned after "ox yellow" (*go-ō*, Sk. *gorocāna*, ox bile or bezoar), a substance used in Asian medicine. On this question, see Michel Strickmann, "The Seal of the Law: A Ritual Implement and the Origins of Printing," *Asia Major*, 3rd Series, 6 (1993), 72–73; Iyanaga Nobumi, "Dākinī et l'Empereur: Mystique bouddhique de la royauté dans le Japon médiéval," *Versus: Quaderni di studi semiotici*, 83–84 (1999), 41–111.

[34] Iyanaga, "Dākinī et l'Empereur."

"stealing things of the Buddha."[35] After explaining how the brahmin Droṇa avoided a "war of relics" by distributing the Buddha's relics among eight Northern Indian states, the *Hōbutsushū* tells how the tooth relic was stolen by the god Naḍa.

The dialectical relationship between the *Vinaya* and relic theft, or between the monastic rule and its transgression, is suggested by a Chinese tradition according to which that stolen relic was eventually given by the god to the *Vinaya* master Daoxuan. Relics also played an important role in the Japanese *Vinaya* (Ritsu) school, in particular in the Saidaiji lineage founded by Eizon (var. Eison, 1201–90). Relics were stolen from Shitennōji in 1183 and 1185, which was interpreted by Kujō Kanezane and others as a sign of the impending decline of the Buddhist dharma. The *Hōbutsushū*, however, does not mention relic thefts in Japan, although it was contemporary with the most famous relic theft, which took place in 1191 at Mt. Murō (Nara Prefecture) and which inaugurated a new period for *furta sacra*. Mt. Murō was famous as the site where Kūkai buried the Buddha's relics (or, in a more widespread variant, the Indian wish-fulfilling jewel that he had brought back from China). A Chinese monk by the name of Kūtai, a disciple of the eminent priest Chōgen (1121–1205), stole the relic, and as a result of his action, calamities are said to have struck the province of Yamato, causing the starvation of many people.[36]

What makes this theft so significant, apart from the intrinsic value (or rather, the priceless nature) of the *corpus delicti*, is the fact that it implicated, directly or indirectly, Chōgen, one of the most prominent clerics of the time.[37] Chōgen reconstructed Tōdaiji in Nara after its destruction by fire in 1180. He had also long been interested in relics and reportedly experienced the famous Aśokan relics of Mt. Ayuwang (Mount of King Aśoka), describing how they transformed according to the merits of the beholder. He also claimed to have enshrined more than eighty grains of relics, a number slightly larger than the amount brought from China by Kūkai himself, in the Great Buddha of Tōdaiji. He constructed many five-leveled reliquaries (*gorintō*) and had a close relationship with Shōken, a Shingon master influential in the development of relic worship.

Soon after Kujō Kanezane discovered that relics had been stolen from Mt. Murō, Chōgen came to see him and reported that the culprit was his

35 Ruppert, *Jewel in the Ashes*, 176–77.

36 *Zoku gunsho ruijū* 27: 299. On Kūtai, see Sherry Fowler, *Murōji: Rearranging Art and History at a Japanese Buddhist Temple* (Honolulu: University of Hawai'i Press, 2005), 24–25; Ruppert, *Jewel in the Ashes*.

37 On Chōgen, see Itō Satoshi, "Chōgen to hōju." *Bukkyō bungaku*, 26 (2002), 10–26.

own disciple, who seemed to have temporarily lost his mind, but who had pledged to return the relics. Fearing that Kōfukuji monks, who controlled Mt. Murō, would cause havoc, Kanezane decided to discuss the matter with the retired Emperor Go-Shirakawa. At that point, Chōgen vanished, raising suspicions that he was responsible for the theft. When Shōken arrived in the capital, a meeting took place at court with Go-Shirakawa. Chōgen and his disciple Kūtai finally appeared, bringing with them thirty grains of relics that they gave to the retired Emperor. Kanezane suspected the authenticity of the relics, but Shōken decided to help Chōgen and performed a *cintāmaṇi* ritual with these relics on behalf of Go-Shirakawa. The latter, aging and ill, felt overjoyed to receive relics that might bring him back to health, and declared the matter settled – much to Kanezane's frustration.[38] The relics never returned to Mt. Murō, and were lost to the Kōfukuji and Mt. Murō communities, but Chōgen's status at court, whatever his role in the theft, greatly improved. The event transferred the relics from Mt. Murō to Go-Shirakawa by transforming the theft into a gift for the emperor, a gift of health and legitimacy. Chōgen's increased prestige was the counter-gift from the emperor – not only for Chōgen, but for Taikū as well.[39]

Relics thus become an invaluable commodity, an inexhaustible economic and symbolic capital. They constitute an obscure object of desire, which in turn can, like the *cintāmaṇi* jewel, fulfill all desires. Relics *are* the wish-fulfilling jewel. The monks of Daigoji in Shingon recognized this and Chōgen probably did as well. The latter possibility is suggested by the number of grains he gave to Go-Shirakawa, practically the same number needed to fabricate the wish-fulfilling jewel of Mt. Murō, according to Kūkai's apocryphal *Testament* (*Goyuigō*).[40]

As Brian Ruppert points out, this episode marks the beginning of a series of *furta sacra* that became renown in the capital during the medieval period.[41] Although the historical record is not always as explicit as we might like, these thefts were common enough that rituals to circumvent them were described in manuals like that of the Tōji priest Jingen, who describes rituals centered on Butsugen and other deities associated with the *cintāmaṇi*.

[38] One of these relics was even offered to Mt. Kōya by the imperial consort Senyōmon'in, a daughter of Go-Shirakawa.

[39] Kūtai came to be known as the "Saint who spread the relics of Mt. Murō." Chōgen's interest in relics is attested by the fact that two other of his disciples were accused of lesser relic thefts.

[40] *Goyuigō*, T. 77, 2431: 423a. [41] Ruppert, *Jewel in the Ashes*.

In 1216, for instance, a group of thieves stole Tōji's relics, but they were eventually arrested, allegedly owing to the performance of rituals centered on the buddha Butsugen (Buddhalocanī), the bodhisattva Kokūzō (Ākāśagarbha), and the deva Shōten (Vināyaka).[42] Another theft is mentioned in 1329 in the diary of Emperor Hanazono. Along the same lines, and just as threatening to imperial legitimacy, was the theft of the famous statue of the bodhisattva Kannon from the Futama room, which was adjacent to the room in the imperial palace where the imperial regalia were preserved.

Soon after that event, the question of legitimacy resurfaced with Go-Daigo's attempted restoration of the imperial Kenmu period (1333–36). The relics remained an important element of legitimacy, but, through their identification with the *cintāmaṇi*, they gradually lost their character of bodily remains of the Buddha Śākyamuni, becoming something quite different. And this brings us back to King Yama, or rather to King Aizen, the "Impartial King" (Byodō-ō), who was worshiped at Byōdō-in in Uji (Kyoto Prefecture). This King Aizen, a well-known and powerful *vidyārāja* (Jp. *myōō*), was not only identified with the lord of the underworld Yama, but also with the Sun, and consequently with the cosmic Buddha Vairocana (Jp. Dainichi) and his kami counterpart, the Sun-goddess Amaterasu.

With the sacralization of the Japanese emperor, we have left the realm of law to enter that of magic. In this model, the esoteric priest and the emperor represent two aspects of the *lex incarnata*, the Buddhist law and the imperial law, respectively and are above human laws. These were both united in one single person, as in the famous image of Go-Daigo officiating at an esoteric subjugation ritual. They claim to divest all power to themselves, to literally "steal" the power, the "vital essence" of their political rivals.

At first glance, this model contrasts sharply with that which developed around the same time in Europe based on Christian canon law and the rediscovery of Roman law. However, the contrast should not be exaggerated. As Ernst Kantorowicz and Marc Bloch, among others, have argued, the sacralization of the French and British monarchs, despite being ratified by law, are of an extra-legal origin, whether they are considered survivals from an earlier time, more recent developments, or simply a coexisting notion of kingship.[43] These archaic notions may still be alive in some of

[42] *Azuma kagami*, s.v. Kenpo 4.2.5; in *kokushi taikei* 32,: 720; *Tôbōki*, in *Zoku zoku gunsho ruijū* 12: 44; and *Usuzōshi kuketsu* T. 79, 2535.

[43] Ernst H. Kantorowicz, *The King's Two Bodies: A Study in Medieval Political Theology* (Princeton, NJ: Princeton University Press, 1957); and Marc Bloch, *The Royal Touch: Sacred Monarchy and Scrofula in England and France* (Montreal: McGill-Queen's University Press, 1973).

our modern democracies. In medieval Japan, the sacred ruler clearly takes precedence over the "saintly ruler," a ruler whose model was the *cakravartin* king or the Indian king Aśoka – that is, a ruler whose dignity and legitimacy derived from his scrupulous observance of the Buddhist law. In its effort to support and legitimize the imperial (shogunal) rule, the "law of the strongest," Buddhism had – at least temporarily – forsaken its moral (and legal) dignity. The paradox of the new relic rituals that were thriving in medieval Japan is that they were called *nyohō* ("according to the law") – Nyohō Aizen-hō, Nyohō Butsugen-hō, and so forth.[44] The law they reflect lost its "legalistic" connotation, if it ever had any, apart from the *Vinaya*.

While the Buddhist standpoint in this regard may be specific, theft and its condemnation can perhaps be seen as a broader anthropological phenomenon. Theft disrupts the general reciprocity established by its opposite, the gift or exchange, on which society rests. Relic theft occupies an ambiguous position in this respect, since it can lead to private hoarding and consequently interrupts exchange and the circulation of power; or, conversely, it can return objects to circulation that had been "put aside" by certain groups or individuals. In the case of medieval relics and *cintāmaṇi*, however, the stakes of power were so high that they seem, like a state of urgency, to suspend the norms of customary, ecclesiastic, and civil law. Relic theft constitutes, on the plane of social transactions, the same thing as a coup on the plane of political life. The possession of relics, even if it is unlawful from the standpoint of civil or religious law, becomes a source of legitimacy beyond discussion.

Theft is no longer perceived primarily as material loss, but rather as a loss of spiritual substance. Medieval texts mention the "stealing of the mind or heart" committed by demonic *ḍākinīs*, as well as human fiends through their spells. With the notion of "soul-stealing," we leave the legalistic domain of *Vinaya*, where one could steal only objects, for that of witchcraft; even sanctions or punishment could be subverted by magical counterattack, returning spells to the sender, with the help of powerful rituals centered on deities such as Fudō or Daikokuten (the latter in his Indian, dark form as Mahākāla). Theft has become magical, and consequently the resolution also becomes ritual or magical; it is no longer merely juridical. Theft is one of the activities of a resentful enemy, often represented as a demonic fiend, who must be tamed through powerful subjugation rituals. This, however, does not mean that lawlessness prevails and that the magical has superseded the legal approach, but merely that they have become increasingly intertwined.

[44] It is perhaps worth pointing out that it is the same word that means "law" and "ritual."

The relics' loss of referent transformed medieval relic theft, as well, into something symbolic or "imaginary" and increasingly less liable to a traditional judgment, punishment, or retribution. Having become a currency or a commodity in power relationships, they are inscribed into quasi-monetary circuits; or, on the contrary, they become a kind of "general equivalent" – a gold standard of sorts. They were withdrawn from symbolic circulation, becoming emblems of secrecy.

The Buddhist notion of theft was thus drastically reshaped in Japan by symbolical thought. The Japanese emperor in particular, perceived as a kind of *lex incarnata*, came to be symbolized and empowered by the regalia, the Buddha's relics, and the *cintāmaṇi*. But the latter were associated with shady beings (*ḍākinī*, etc.) that formed the retinue of the Dharma King – Yama and Aizen. The earlier representation symbolized by King Yama and his attendants (the *kushōjin*) marked a shift from the karmic mechanism to a juridical model inspired by Chinese civil law.[45] In medieval Japan, a new shift occurs from that model to a symbolic representation in which the *kushōjin*, symbolized by Aizen and Fudō, become the guardians of the relics and of the *cintāmaṇi* (protecting them, among other things, against theft), while King Yama becomes identified with Aizen. In this new model, the relics, Aizen, and King Yama, are reinterpreted ontologically or epistemologically as metaphors for the *ālaya-vijñāna* or storehouse consciousness.[46] But this is the topic of another essay.[47]

[45] On this question, see Bernard Faure, in John Kieschnick and Meir Shahar (eds.), *Under the Spell of India: Buddhism and the Formation of Medieval Chinese Culture* (Honolulu: University of Hawai'i Press, forthcoming).

[46] *Keiran shūyōshū*, T. 76, no. 2410:579b.

[47] Bernard Faure, *Raging Gods: The Pantheon of Medieval Japan* (forthcoming).

PART FOUR

Buddhism and Law in North Asia and the Himalayan Region

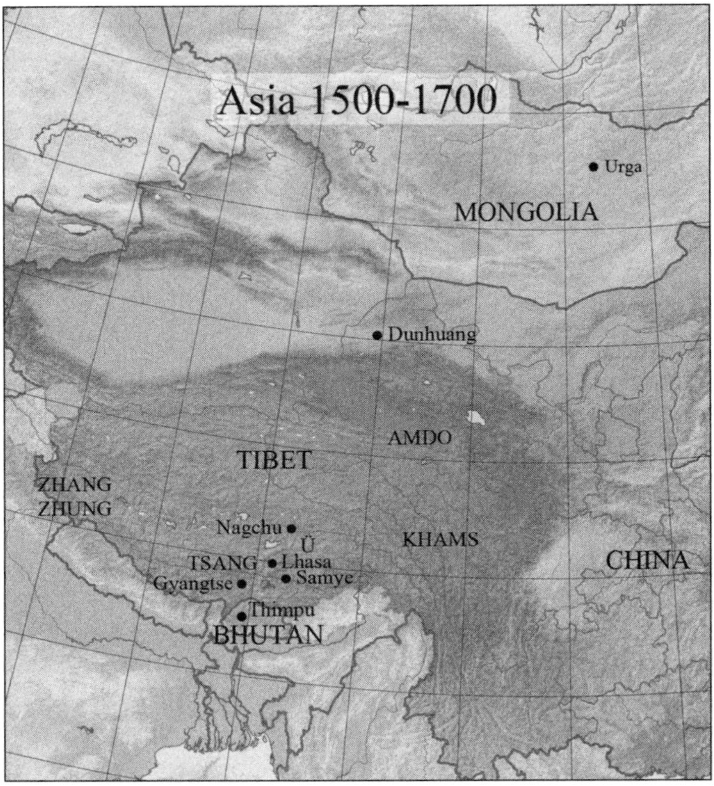

Map of Himalayan Plateau and North Asia

CHAPTER 17

Buddhism and Law in Tibet

Rebecca Redwood French

The Tibetan plateau is an immense high-altitude desert[1] that, except for a few larger towns, was very sparsely populated with agriculturalists, nomadic herders, and merchant traders prior to 1960.[2] The small population and minimal urbanization are the most important distinguishing features of this Buddhist country because concentrated populations are commonly connected to the development of government administration, law, and intellectual production. Despite this, Tibetan culture is known for its long history of enormous production of literary, scholarly, and religious works. Books on Buddhism and other topics from the five traditional classifications of knowledge in Tibet – arts and crafts, medicine, language, logic and Buddhism – were written and printed throughout much of Tibetan history.[3]

When discussing the relationship between law and Buddhism in Tibet, the number of topics and the many historical twists and turns are daunting given the long history, the growth in Tibetan scholarship, and the rich textual resources available. As it is not possible to cover all of Tibetan legal history, this essay will concentrate on four distinct periods, providing a brief political history followed by a discussion of law during each period: (1) the Empire period (c. 600–850), which is the origin of many of the original customary law practices that were codified over the centuries; (2) the First Patron-Priest period (c. 1264–1350) in which a particular political formation, "the patron-priest," resulted in the interweaving of

[1] The landmass of the Tibetan plateau is similar to four times that of France or the seven combined U.S. states of California, Nevada, New Mexico, Colorado, Arizona, Oklahoma and Texas. Charles Bell, a British diplomat in Tibet in the early part of the twentieth century, estimated the entire population of this area as only 2 million and the largest town at 40,000. Charles Alfred Bell, *The People of Tibet* (Oxford: Clarendon Press, 1928).

[2] As a consequence, any legal transactions, documents, or law codes concerned subject matters that related directly to this pastoral and agrarian economy, and the various governments of the people that occupied the plateau.

[3] See Kurt Schaffer, *The Culture of the Book in Tibet*, (New York: Columbia University Press, 2004).

Buddhist principles with legal and political institutions into a "Buddhist government"; (3) the Law Code Drafting period (c. 1618–1705) in which the law codes were developed and took on a very specific form and shape that included Buddhist elements in the prologue, factoring, and forms of reasoning; and (4) the 1940s in Tibet, the period before the Chinese takeover, in which we can look at the daily practice of law as it blends ordinary bureaucratic decision-making with a continuous thread of customary practices from early times and embedded Buddhist concepts.

While necessarily general and overbroad in their depiction, these sections are meant to acquaint the reader with a few brushstrokes of Tibetan law and to demonstrate how it compares to other Buddhist societies in Asia.

The Empire Period (600–850)

King Songtsen Gampo (r. 629–50), who united the plateau into what became the Tibetan Empire, resided in an enormous mobile court comprised of hundreds of tents that moved from a summer to a winter encampment each year. His judiciary moved with him, as well as hundreds of royal guards.[4] While histories attribute to him the introduction of both a script for the Tibetan language and Buddhism, after marrying the widowed Chinese princess of his son, he and his minister Gar Tsongtsen are also credited with crafting bureaucratic governmental and military institutions – Tibetan administrative divisions, military formations, official ranks and powers, measurements of volume and weight, transportation systems, and a law code.[5]

After a conversion experience when he was twenty years old, King Tri Songdetsen (c. 742–97) committed fully to Buddhism and built the first large Tibetan Buddhist monastery at Samye in 779. He is credited with bringing an Indian Buddhist monk sage to quell the local demons throughout the plateau and supporting hundreds of translations of Buddhist texts into Tibetan. The appeal of monastic, clerical Buddhism to the Tibetan imperial court was based on several factors: a ready-made system of organized knowledge and pundits with a mastery of language and reasoning, a universal religion with universal vision, laws and symbols, and the legitimation of an international religious viewpoint prominent in

[4] See Brandon Dotson, *The Old Tibetan Annals: An Annotated Translation of Tibet's First History* , (Wien: Österreichische Akademie der Wissenschaften, 2009), 43.

[5] See Bacot and Toussaint, *Documents de Touen-houang relatifs a l'histoire de Tibet*, (Paris: Libraire orientaliste Paul Geunther, 1940–46); Michael Walters has argued in *Buddhism and Empire: The Political and Religious Culture of Early Tibet*, (Leiden: Brill, 2009) that many of these organizational structures were derived from Central Eurasian models.

all of the surrounding countries – Nepal, India, China, and the Silk Road states.[6] In 763, the Empire's armies invaded the Chinese Tang Empire's capital of Chang'an and held it for fifteen days. Fighting between the Chinese and the Tibetans continued with skirmishes at the borders of the Tibetan plateau and other spots in Central Asia for the rest of the century. In the west, the "red-faced" Tibetan Empire armies marched as far as the current areas of Tajikistan and Uzbekistan.

By the beginning of the ninth century, edicts and inscriptions indicate that Buddhism was already beginning to be a part of Tibetan governmental culture and international relations. However, the economic basis of the empire was waning – some scholars have argued that this was caused by too much money being spent on Buddhism translation colleges and monasteries, while others claim that there were no new lands to conquer and poor local harvests. With the death of the last king in 838, the central government began to collapse. Monks packed up their texts and moved away from the central monasteries to temples in the east and west. Over the next several decades, the former Tibetan Empire fragmented into smaller districts, each with its own government, local laws, and Buddhist monasteries. Both language and historical writing changed after this period from imperial histories in archaic Tibetan to largely religious histories.[7]

A great amount of recent scholarly work has been done on the early Empire period in Tibet based on the collection of documents brought back by Sir Aurel Stein from the caves in Dunhuang on the Silk Road in western China. The legal sources that are available to scholars from as early as the seventh century CE include Tibetan legal and administrative texts, documents and monastic records, general legislative documents, contracts, inscriptions, and legal decisions. Several fragments of old law documents from this period discuss how to handle disputes over contracts, dog bites, yak stampedes, theft, and hunting injuries.[8] Tibetan histories such as the *Tibetan Chronicles* and the *Old Tibetan Annals* as well as other sources provide information about the operation of the legal process.[9]

One interesting aspect of this period from a legal perspective is how many of the original customary law practices in early Tibetan society were

6 See Mathew T. Kapstein, *The Tibetans* (Cambridge: Blackwell, 2006), 71–72.

7 See Sam van Schaik and Lewis Doney, "The Prayer, the Priest and the Tsenpo: An Early Buddhist Narrative from Dunhuang," *Journal of the International Association of Buddhist Studies* 30 (2007), 175–217.

8 See Tsuguhito Takeguchi, *A Study of Old Tibetan Contracts* (Bloomington: Indiana University Press, 1994); Geza Uray, "The Narrative of the Legislation and Organization of the Mkhas pa'i dga ston," *Acta Orientalia Academiae Scientiarum Hungaricae* (1972) 26, 11–68; Hugh Richardson, "Early Tibetan Law Concerning Dog-Bite," *Bulletin of Tibetology* (1989), 3, 5–10.

9 Dotson, *The Old Tibetan Annals*.

retained over the centuries, and then codified. These early legal records set the stage for later Tibetan customary legal concepts such as the ten virtues,[10] the sixteen pure human laws,[11] a graduated restitution system based on a status hierarchy, and the use of dice to decide disputes.[12]

For example, in early Tibetan history, status hierarchy was very important and legal disputes could be based on complaints about order of rank insignia.[13] The *Old Tibetan Annals* contains an extensive list of ranks in the government from horn officials (*ru dpon*), great justices (*zhal ce pa ched po*), and translators of Chinese and Turkish, all the way down to accounts inspectors (*rtsis spyan*) and tally officials and wooden-slip makers (*khram pa/sam mkhan*).[14] This social ranking system is echoed in the graduated hierarchy of payments for murder and injury victims in the Ganden Podrang Law Code that starts with the Dalai Lama, in the highest of the high category, and moves down to bachelors, beggars, blacksmiths, executioners, and hermaphrodites in the lowest of the low. Blood money payments correlated to status ranking was an important aspect of cases in Tibetan law until the 1950s.[15]

Other examples in the early legal fragments include discussions of decisions made by local magistrates by rolling dice and using local deities. As Brandon Dotson has described:

> The connection between the divination text and the legal text reveal that local magistrates employed divination dice and divination manuals to decide legal disputes. . . . The content of the divination text reveals a truly "imperial" pantheon of deities from whose mouths the prognoses come, in that the text names territorial deities of several different regions.[16]

In later law codes and even in the twentieth century, there is much evidence of these legal practices and procedures, including oaths as a form of divination occurring in front of Buddhist deities.

10 These are the ten virtues of the Bodhisattva vow – to abandon acts of the body (murder, stealing, and sexual misconduct), speech (lying, abuse, gossip, and flattery), and mind (greed, anger, and lust) – called the *mi dge ba bcu*.

11 See Rebecca Redwood French, *Golden Yoke: The Legal Cosmology of Buddhist Tibet* (Ithaca: Cornell University Press, 1995), 81–82.

12 Examples of this will reappear in later law codes in the Tsangpa and Ganden Podrang periods.

13 See Cristina Scherrer-Schaub, "Revendications et recours hiérarchique: contribution à l'histoire de Sá cu sous administration tibétaine," in J.P. Drege (ed.), *Études de Dunhuang et Turfan*. (Genève: Librairie Droz, 2007), 257–326.

14 See Dotson, *The Old Tibetan Annals*, 71–73.

15 See the murder case described in French, *Golden Yoke*, 291–305.

16 See Brandon Dotson, "Divination and Law in the Tibetan Empire: The Role of Dice in the Legislation of Loans, Interest, Marital Law and Troop Conscription," in Matthew T. Kapstein and Brandon Dotson (eds.), *Contributions to the Cultural History of Early Tibet*, (Leiden: Brill, 2007), 17

The Patron-Priest Period (1264–1350)

Although Tibet remained politically fragmented from approximately the mid-ninth to the late thirteenth centuries, the plateau was visited during this period by famous Buddhist teachers who taught and worked on translations. Atisha came from India to Toling monastery to teach tantric Buddhism in western Tibet (c. 1042–45) and then traveled to Central Tibet where he stayed for the rest of his life, writing and working on translations, talking to other visiting Indian scholars, and teaching Buddhism. The sectarian lineage of Atisha's teachings, the Kadampa, developed in the smaller western kingdom of Guge, as did the teachings of other well-known teachers in other regional centers. This was the development period for several Tibetan Buddhist sects –the Sakyapa, Kagyupa, and the Zhalungpa.

In 1227, Chinggis Khan conquered the Buddhist Tangut kingdom, a close ally of the Tibetans to the northeast. As the new Mongol Empire began to take over parts of China, a delegation of various local aristocratic Tibetan states requesting to pay tribute was sent to the Mongols. The Khan of the Mongol Empire in 1244 asked the learned Tibetan Buddhist teacher, Saskya Pandita, to come to his court to teach the dharma. This was the beginning of a political relationship called "patron-priest" in which a "patron" country or political leader provided military and foreign protection to a particular priest of a sect of Tibetan Buddhism. These Tibetan Buddhist practitioners, the priests, were able to present the teachings of the Buddha as well as ritual transmissions (*lung*) of tantric texts that were considered magical and potent by the patron Mongols, Manchus, and Chinese.

While different Tibetan Buddhist sects attended to other members of the Mongol royal house, the Sakyapa sect became the tutors for Qubilai Khan. After invading Tibet, the Mongols supported the Sakyapas as rulers of the plateau from 1264–1350. Their army installed Mongolian administrative institutions into a centralized Tibetan government: regional states with district governors (*dzong pon*), taxation, postal system, grades of officials, and a census of households. The population of Tibet at that time was estimated by the Mongolians at 300,000 people.[17] While scholars have mentioned a Sakya-Tibetan law code during this time period, there is little evidence that one was written down, although it is likely that a Mongolian military law code was used. When interviewed in India in the mid-1980s, members of the Sakya royal house stated that there had been no independent, separate Sakya law code during this historical period, so this question remains unsettled.

[17] See Kapstein, *The Tibetans*, 115.

From this point on, the Tibetan population was increasingly devoted to Buddhism. With an estimated quarter of the entire adult male population taking vows, the country was soon typified by mass monasticism. These monasteries came to have enormous social, economic, and political power as institutional centers of commerce, scholarship, and industry. Each of the sects of Tibetan Buddhism had monasteries dependent on connections to one or more wealthy aristocratic families and each was vitally concerned to continue its monastic lineage and essential teachings. The Tibetan language had also shifted from the archaic writing of the empire period into a more sophisticated, standardized literary language that was strongly influenced by Indian culture and Buddhism. Over the centuries, thousands of monks became scholar authors, commentators, scribes, plate carvers, and printers of books as well as librarians for vast holdings of scriptural works in Tibetan and Sanskrit. As landholders, the monasteries of Tibet owned an estimated one half of all of the arable farmland on the plateau from this period and well into the second half of the twentieth century.

The patron-priest relationship (*yon bdag mchod gnas*)[18] became a central principle in Tibetan political ideology under the Sakyapa, producing a distinctive historical pattern. The basis of this dyarchy derives from the practice of the Buddha who gathered his disciples into a monastic unit that needed to be supported by local leaders and a lay population of believers. This created a dependent, reciprocal relationship between, on the one hand, the Buddha (or later, his representative – a monk, spiritual power, priest, or donee) who provided teachings and, on the other hand, the king (or his representative – a lay supporter, temporal power, patron, or donor) who provided food, money, and worldly power. They were the "sun and the moon," with the Buddha as the personal embodiment of religion and the king as the personal embodiment of political power.[19] At times, one member of this dyadic relationship could be much more powerful than the other, or the two positions could be collapsed into one as in the figure of the Dalai Lama, who, as a manifestation of the Bodhisattva Avalokiteśvara, embodied both religious and political power.

As a political pattern, the patron-priest model resulted in the creation of multiple possible centers of power and, at times, political instability. Inside Tibet, royal aristocratic families acted as patrons to their sectarian monasteries and created local patron-priest polities. An external patron

[18] Also *lugs gnyis, chos srid gnyis ldan*, and *chos srid zung 'brel.*

[19] For a recent example of this idea, see Anya Bernstein, "More Alive than all the Living: Bodies and Cosmic Politics in Buddhist Siberia," *Cultural Anthropology* 27 (2012), 261–85.

army backing a particular Tibetan Buddhist lama could devastate the plateau, force a leader to flee into exile, and then set up its own Tibetan Buddhist "priest." The next several centuries were typified by cycles of internal division followed by periods of centralization or fragmented peace. While some invaders proceeded to interfere with internal governmental affairs for a period of time, others did not. The twentieth-century colonial powers, specifically the British and the Chinese, took on somewhat similar roles.

This relationship between religion and the state in Tibet, as it manifested later in the sixteenth and seventeenth centuries, has been termed "Buddhist government" by Yumiko Ishihama. It was a common idea and term in correspondence between three major sovereignties of the time, Tibet, Mongolia, and Manchurian-ruled China.[20] In the context of the Bhutanese government, Ardussi has described it as "the Buddhist equivalent of a 'Social Contract.'"[21] There is little doubt that it was a very distinctive relationship and that it fused religion and secular politics in a special way, which affected the legal system and legal practices.

The Period of Law Code Drafting (c. 1618–1705)

This 100-year period was the central time for the drafting of law codes in Tibet. Many of the extant codes and other administrative texts that were found on the desks of judges when the Chinese took over the plateau were drafted or dated to this period. Our knowledge of these codes and their connection to Buddhism is, therefore, a central subject of concern.

However, the story begins much earlier with a monk, Jangchup Gyeltsen (1303–64), the founder of the Pakmodrupa Dynasty that followed the Sakyapa reign. He built on the Mongolian administrative infrastructure but also tried to Tibetanize the government, and to that end, he created a new law code that was promulgated throughout the kingdom.[22] The

[20] Yumiko Ishihama, "The Notion of 'Buddhist Government' (*chos srid*) shared by Tibet, Mongol and Manchu in the Early Seventeenth Century," in Christoph Cüppers (ed.), *The Relationship between Religion and State (chos srid zung 'brel) in Traditional Tibet*, (Lumbini: Lumbini International Research Institute, 2004), 15–31.

[21] John Ardussi, "Formation of the State of Bhutan (*'Brug gzhung*) in the Seventeenth Century and its Tibetan antecedents," *Ibid.*, 33–48.

[22] See Leonard van der Kuijp, "On the Life and Political Career of Ta'i -si-tu Byangchub rgyal-mtshan (1302?–1364)" in Ernst Steinkellner (ed.), *Tibetan History and Language* (Wien: Arbeitskreis für Tibetische und Buddhistische Studien Universität Wien, 1991).

Pakmodrupa or Neudong Law Code that is attributed to him[23] had an introductory section followed by fifteen substantive law sections.

The introduction of the Neudong Law Code is filled with accumulated wisdom, proverbs, and lists that are important to legal decision-making. For example, the best type of witness for a law case was one with "high victorious speech," which was demonstrated by the four causes, signs, or qualities of greatness. The causes (important paternal ancestors, acts for the country, learning, and great wealth), the signs (presenting tea and beer, wearing silk, lynx or fox, using *zo* animals, and having important guests), and the qualities (taking on a guru, taking care of one's parents or one's relatives and servants, and vanquishing enemies) were marks of a good character – someone who should be trusted in legal proceedings.

The following substantive sections cover both criminal and civil acts without a strong distinction between the two. They include murder,[24] theft, oath taking, adultery, family separation, selling and buying goods, accounts, loans of animals, rules for the chief of the army, rules for those who retreat, and rules regarding the payment of court costs. This general set of categories appears to have remained important as a template for the next 400 years, although much future research on this topic is needed.

A famous cleric, Je Tsongkhapa (1357–1419) lived during this period and was supported by later Pakmodrupa kings. He is renowned as the founder of the Gelukpa sect of Tibetan Buddhism, the sect of the Dalai Lamas, and as a promoter of monastic education, fidelity to the *Vinaya*, and strict morality. Regional kingdoms continued to vie for power with the Pakmodrupa over the next two centuries. In the seventeenth century, the king of the Tsangpa of western Tibet was successful in beating the Pakmodrupa, a fact that is important for our purposes as one of his successors, Karma Tenkyong, commissioned the drafting of the new law code, the Tsangpa Law Code (*Khrims yig chen mo dang zhal lce bcu drug pa sogs bzhugs so*).[25]

[23] There is some disagreement about the dating of this law code. The former Tibetan magistrate that I worked with stated emphatically that this law code was written during the next century and not under this leader.

[24] For example, "The murder section . . . gives a history of the law of murder; the social classes that distinguish the victim compensation payments (these categories were already present in the Empire period); exceptions in the case of the killing of a woman or killing by a child; murder during theft; murder by mob or multiple persons; attempted murder; payments in land instead of money or goods; mitigations in payments; merit payments for the purification of the dead body; payments in the case of cremation and for religious ceremonies; numerous categories of allowances to be paid to all the relatives; reductions resulting from payments; and the form the payments can take." French, *Golden Yoke*, 352, n. 11.

[25] Many copies of this text are available. See *Law Code of the Tsang Kings in Sixteen Sections*, Manuscript Ta.5, 13544 (Dharamsala, India: Library of Tibetan Works and Archives). Also, *Tibetan Legal*

King Karma Tenkyong, a secular ruler aligned with the Karma Kagyu sect, was keenly interested in legal administration. One version of the new code states that the humble compiler, "the donkey with a leopard skin on its back," canvassed Tibetans of many occupations from all areas as well as Buddhist lamas, and also collected all available law texts. The resulting law code, comprised of sixteen sections, included customary legal rules and processes, Buddhist reasoning and ideas, systems of factoring, some proverbs, moral principles, and charts of social statuses. It was preceded by an introduction with offering verses praising the king and Buddhism and concluded with a long section on how to handle foreigners. Gone are the previous law code's discussions of causes, signs, and qualities of greatness; they are replaced by more substantive expositions on how to think about and factor a case or mitigate an offense.[26] In the section on "Establishing Evidence of the Truth through an Oath," it states:

> The one who wins the dice can choose the order of the administration of the oath. Whatever the dice indicate, the judge or conciliator shall read into the ear of the oathtaker the oath document three times, explaining each term one by one in such a manner that it goes well into the realm of the oathtaker's mind.[27]

Within a few decades, the armies of the Mongolian Gushri Khan, a patron of the Gelukpa sect, rode into central Tibet. By 1642, they had established a new government in Lhasa headed by the Fifth Dalai Lama called the Ganden Podrang. The regent commissioned a new law code using the Tsangpa template that began with a prologue describing the relationship between the "sun and the moon," the priest and patron, the Fifth Dalai Lama and Gushri Khan.[28] Legal officials interviewed in the early 1980s could recite sections from this law code and confirmed that they had used it in making decisions as late as the late 1950s. The same status hierarchy for victim compensation in nine parts, now with the Dalai Lama and other lamas at the top, was included.

Similarities in the drafting and structure of these codes raise four points for our consideration of Buddhism and Law. First, these law codes have

Materials, reprint of the Library of Tibetan Works and Archives (Delhi: Dorjee Tsering, M.M. Offset Press,1985). See also R.O. Meisezahl, "Die Handschriften in den city of Liverpool Museum," *Zentralasiastische Studien des Seminars für Sprach und Kulturwissenschaft Zentralasiens* (Weisbaden 1973). Guiseppe Tucci, *Tibetan Painted Scrolls* (Rome: Libreria dello Stato, 1949), 697.

26 See French, *Golden Yoke*, 41–44. 27 *Ibid.*, 129.

28 G. Tucci stated that the Ganden Podrang Law Code was copied from the Neudong code and was just a revision. However, a close look at the documents shows the Tsangpa to be the real template. G. Tucci, *Tibetan Painted Scrolls* (Roma: Libreria dello Stato, 1949), 37.

from twelve to sixteen sections with an introduction and generally similar substantive content. Second, they appear to be primarily local customary rules and procedures blended with administrative procedures. Third, they acknowledge the Buddhist nature of Tibetan society; whether encouraging submission to a guru or lauding a current leader as the manifestation of a Buddhist deity, the religious grounding of Tibetan society in the patron-priest relationship is evident. Fourth, some forms of analysis in the law codes correlate with Buddhist forms of reasoning.

With the exception of these law codes, jurisprudential questions were not the center of the prolific literary scholarship of book production during this or any period of Tibetan literature. Neither comprehensive legal treatises nor legal commentaries appear to have been produced because law was not a highly prized subject matter for creating merit through the production of texts. That said, Dieter Schuh and Hanna Schneider have found, analyzed, and published many examples of seal inscriptions, contracts, loans, decision documents, and legislative and executive edicts from the Ganden Podrang in the last two centuries.[29] Christoph Cuppers has also done fascinating studies of the administrative texts produced during this period, including government handbooks, seating order lists with ranks, letter writing manuals, reminder notes for district officials, decrees, tax collection notices, inventory books, and lists of government offices with salaries.[30]

Ultimately of course, the real question is how these codes and documents were employed. The actual use as opposed to the cultural production of many of these legal texts remains a subject for further research. Some of the recent work by younger Tibetan scholars has been particularly exciting in this area. Alice Travers, for example, has used interviews of Tibetan officials as a database to determine what the legal documents actually

[29] Below are only a few of the books containing the seals and legal documents they have recorded: Dieter Schuh, *Grundlagen tibetischer Siegelkunde: Eine Untersuchung uber tibetische Siegelaufschriften in Phags-pa-Schrift* (Monumenta Tibetica historica) (St. Augustin: VGH Wissenschaftsverlag, 1981); Dieter Schuh, *Urkunden und Sendschreiben aus Zentraltibet, Ladakh und Zanskar* (St. Augustin: VGH Wissenschaftsverlag, 1976). There are many more volumes in this series. See also for example, Hanna Schneider, *Tibetische Handschriften und Blockdrucke: Teil 16: Tibetischsprachige Urkunden aus Sudwesttibet (Spo-Rong, Ding-Ri und Shel-Dkar)* (Stuttgart: Franz Steiner Verlag, 2012).

[30] A few examples are Christoph Cüppers, "Some Aspects of Tibetan Administration Under the dGa'-ldan pho-brang Government" in H. Krasser et al. (eds.), *Tibetan Studies: Proceedings of the 7th Seminar of the International Association for Tibetan Studies*, vol. 1 (Wien: Verlag der Österreichischen Akademie der Wissenschaften, 1997) 189–93; C. Cüppers, "Registers and Account Books of the dGa' ldan pho brang Government" in R. Prats. (ed.), *The Pandita and the Siddha: Tibetan Studies in Honour of E. Gene Smith*, (Dharamsala: Amnye Machen Institute, 2007) 12–15; another excellent source for documents is Nor bu Bsam 'phel, *Gzhung sa dga' ldan pho brang gi chos srid lar rgya dang 'brel ba'i khrims srol rtsa 'dzin dang bca' yig chings dan sogs phyogs gcig tu bsgrigs pa nor bu'i me long zhes bya ba bzhugs so* (Beijing: Mi rigs dpe skrun khang, 2008).

mean, whether or not they reflect actual normative practices, invented traditions, and techniques to preserve family wealth and power or simply practices to achieve status.[31]

The 1940s in Tibet

At the turn of the twentieth century, Tibet was still an agricultural and pastoral society perched on a high-altitude plateau with extreme weather, few wheeled vehicles, and no industrialization. Most inhabitants worked hard in their daily lives and were taxed by the local nobles, monastery, or government for corvée labor, traveling parties, and in-kind produce. Local customs and traditions, local officials, and legal processes varied with the degree of distance from a center of administrative power. Scholars have noted that, given the extensive differences across the plateau, one of the larger intellectual quandaries is "the strong sentiments of affinity and cohesiveness running throughout the Tibetan culture world."[32] Much of this affinity undoubtedly came from Tibetan Buddhism, the most pervasive religious institution in the society, which organized and pervaded much of Tibetan life in terms of holiday rituals, education, art, calendar, medicine, language, logical reasoning, and crafts until the modern period.

The government intrigues in the decades before the Chinese takeover reflect the brittle political institutions that had developed over the previous centuries of Gelukpa rule, a small-scale central government often riven by dissenting factions seeking power. The small Tibetan military trained by the British had limited usefulness. Conservative politically and rejecting of modernizing reforms, the enormous monasteries around the capital city employed their power to maintain the status quo. Added to all of this was the unstable system of incarnation for the replacement of the titular Dalai Lama. With a young child being trained for up to twenty years of interregnum during which regents ruled, the Tibetan governmental system was neither stable nor strong and certainly not extensive in its range.

With the death of an effective leader, the Thirteenth Dalai Lama, in 1933, Tibet experienced another period of instability. Factions strove for power even as the new Dalai Lama was found and took his vows in 1942. An

[31] Alice Travers, "The Careers of the Noble Officials of the Ganden Phodrang (1895–1959): Organisation and Hereditary Divisions within the Service of the State" in Kelsang Norbu Gurung, Tim Myatt, Nicola Schneider, and Alice Travers (eds.), *Revisiting Tibetan Culture and History, Proceedings of the Second International Seminar of Young Tibetologists Vol 1.* (Paris: Revue d'Etudes Tibétaines, 2011) 155–74.

[32] Kapstein, *Tibetans*, 243.

internal fight over power between two regents, Reting and Takdra, and the monks of Sera monastery caused several years of political upheaval in Lhasa with standoffs, imprisonments, coup attempts, and rebellions. With the victory of Mao Zedong in China, the teenage Dalai Lama was confirmed as head of state in 1950. The ensuing negotiations with the Chinese leadership continued through the decade as the intentions of the stronger state became clear. On March 10, 1959, riots broke out in the streets of Lhasa against the Chinese Communist Army that began to shell the capital a week later. The Dalai Lama fled under cover of night for India.

The power politics that play out at the upper reaches of a political system often do not tell us much about the daily practice of legal administration. In Tibet in the 1940s, it was a blend of customary law practices, some from early times, with ordinary bureaucratic decision-making, codified law, government administrative regulations, local politics, and some embedded Buddhist concepts. The Tibetan government had a longstanding formal system of legal documentation, both private and public, with detailed requirements related to language, script style, length and sections for each part of a deed, contract, disposition, decision document, or appeal that was being drafted. They included standardized phrases such as "as long as the precious Buddhist doctrine will remain existent!" Monks and staff trained in drafting these documents were available throughout Tibet and sought after for their services.

The processes of decision-making had likewise been established for a long time from the lowest level of consensus decision-making in a rural village to the central courts of Lhasa. Tibetan refugees interviewed in the 1980s described four different legal processes that were typical in the 1940s–1950s in Lhasa. The first three were: internal dispute settlements that could take many forms, including oaths, ordeals and dice (*sho*); a conciliation (*bar 'dum*) between two parties using a conciliator (*bar mi*); and lastly, showing respect by visiting a judge at home with a present or bribe. A case involving dice recounted by a Tibetan from this period follows:

> A Nepalese man . . . had married a local Tibetan woman and he had thereafter made a false loan document stating that he had given money to four or five families. All the people of the area knew the loan was false . . . Finally, as this was becoming a big dispute, the families asked the man to play dice in front of the community. . . . All the other families got a higher number than he did and the case was decided against him.[33]

[33] See French, *Golden Yoke*, 135. Divination, casting of lots, oaths, and ordeals were also used, see 130–34.

The fourth type – official legal proceedings – also took many forms, of course, but had a ritual structure that was generally followed. The space in which the decision was to be made was divided into a judge's area, a place for a clerk, and an area for a third person to sit.[34] Monks, monk-officials, local leaders, and government officials were all referred to as "judges" (*khrims dpon*) when engaged in deciding a legal case. Court procedure[35] took place against the backdrop of formal monastic debate practices (*rtsod pa*) and the use of customary proverbs and sayings. One former official said this about the use of law codes:

> Although there was no law code provided in our office at that place, I had my own copy from my father and I used it in my office in Changra. Actually I had two of them. . . . Officials in the government all knew that there was a standard code and that when they were sent out to a district, they must know the code.[36]

Conclusion

This chapter has looked at some of the periods in Tibetan history in terms of the movement of Buddhism into society, local customs, politics, law, and government practices that influenced aspects of Tibetan law. On a practical level, a form of Tibetan Buddhist legal consciousness developed from these constant interactions and the natural interdependence between monks, nuns, laypersons, and local authorities. Buddhist holidays and rituals became central to Tibetan society (for example, the sixty-year cycle of the Buddhist *Kalachakra Tantra* calendar was adopted in 1027), reincarnation allowed for transfer of spiritual as well as legal power, and ideas of fairness and legal actions in the Buddhist literature such as the Jātaka tales – former lives of the Buddha – began to appear in dramas, art, and other aspects of Tibetan culture. All of these influenced Tibetan legal consciousness.

In conclusion, a few major points bearing on the relationship between Buddhism and law can be gleaned from these four periods and their themes. First, the importance of Buddhism in Tibet was not questioned after

[34] See French, *Golden Yoke*, 147–54.

[35] See French, *Golden Yoke*, 103 for an outline of court procedure and this comment about the importance of monastic debate in court: "The vigorous questioning and response of judges and petitioners, analysis by factoring, outlining the arguments, truth by consonance, the uniqueness of the case – each of these aspects of the Tibetan legal system reflected monastic recitation and debate. Tibetan[s] often spoke of debate training as the most important factor in their choice of a monk as a legal representative, conciliator or judge, for debate sharpens mental skills, requires a quick wit and trains one in logical analysis."

[36] See French, *Golden Yoke*, 336.

approximately the twelfth century and it remained the majority religion on the plateau without real competition from any other philosophy or religion. While the state never banned or banished Buddhism or worked to suppress it until the second half of the twentieth century, different Tibetan sects did try to gain control over others and acquire assets through political power. Second, Tibet was never colonized by a foreign power with a different religion or anti-Buddhist position until 1950. This is a long period of time. Third, the central political ideology was a dyarchy, the patron-priest relationship that was sometimes conflated into one person. Religion and the state were understood as fused through this dyarchy into a single, harmonious entity with different but complementary roles. Fourth, Tibet had a massive amount of its population dedicated to religious institutions. Monasteries were not entities to be regulated by the state as in China and Korea. Instead, monasteries were full players in politics – often the major players and sometimes pitted against each other. Fifth, no ruler of Tibet tried to use the Buddhist *Vinaya* as a template for creating a secular law code as far as we know. Sixth, a wide variety of legal issues arose in Tibet – inheritance questions, boundaries, land disputes, tax issues, criminal punishments, contracts, religious property, guarantees, loans, and so forth – with respect to both lay and religious institutions and many were handled by both formal and informal legal processes. And finally, law itself was not an honored subject, a respected profession, or a proper subject matter for extended treatises as it created conflict and did not bring about merit.

CHAPTER 18

Buddhist Laws in Mongolia

Vesna A. Wallace

Introduction

Examining the historical relationship between Buddhism and law in Mongolia helps us to understand several aspects of this pastoral society, namely, the Buddhist legal consciousness, the defining characteristics of both religious and secular Buddhist law, the relationship between Buddhism and the state, and the ways in which Buddhism, law, and local customs shaped each other in this society. It also reveals the interdependence that emerged at times between Buddhist monastic and state laws, which took diverse forms in different sociopolitical climates. This interdependence contributed to the diminishing of the boundaries between the two and enabled the Mongol and Manchu Qing rulers to institute Buddhist codes of law as Buddhist monarchs in Mongolia. This was most evident during the Bogd Khaan state when the attempt to make all members of society legally responsible for the conduct and moral condition of monks became a symbolic expression of the communal values of a Buddhist society. General disobedience of such law would result in disintegration of the Buddhist character of the Bogd Khaan's state. On these grounds, the observance of the law was deemed to be one's civil and religious duty.

Buddhist legal codes in Mongolia show the influence of the nomadic and pastoral culture on the Mongolian Buddhist legal tradition, as both Buddhist ethical norms and legal codes became equally conditioned by the social, economic, and political contexts that tied them together. The legal documents that will be discussed in this essay show that the history of socioeconomic development and the structure of the Mongolian Buddhist establishment can be fully understood only in light of the history and character of the Mongolian legal tradition and vice versa. The Buddhist legal tradition in Mongolia developed into a complex social phenomenon and represented an intricate aspect of the Mongolian Buddhist world from the late sixteenth until the early twentieth centuries.

From the time of the Mongols' conversion to Buddhism in the late sixteenth century until the Communist revolution in 1921, different types of Buddhist laws became instituted within Mongolian territories. These were the banner laws, state laws, the laws of individual monasteries, and the laws governing the Great Shavi (Ikh Shavy), the personal estate of the Bogd Gegeen Jebtstundamba (Tib., rJe btsun Dam pa) Khutukhtus. A presence of these types of laws contributed to the legal pluralism among the Mongols. These laws regulated various aspects of secular and religious life in the country and, for those who enacted them, communicated their self-representation.

Ideological Principles of the Premodern Mongolian Political and Legal Traditions

The creation of Buddhist law in Mongolia has its roots in Mongolian political thought, which is rooted in ancient Indian Buddhism and founded on the aforementioned principle of dual law (*qoyar yosun*, Tib., *lugs gnyis*) – the law of dharma and the law of the state. Its propagation by the Mongol rulers began at the time of the second conversion of the Mongols to Buddhism in the late sixteenth century, when Khutukhtu Sechen Khung Taiǰi (1540–86) – the ruler of the Ordos Mongols and a relative of Altan Khan, the ruler of the Tümeds – discovered and circulated the anonymous text *The Sūtra Called the White History of the Dharma with Ten Virtues of the Mongol People* (*Mongγol Ulus-un Arban Buyantu Nom-un Chaγan Teüke Neretü Sudar*), which he dated to the late thirteenth century and ascribed to Qubilai Khaan (1260–94).

The *White History* gives an account of the principle of dual law as being initially implemented in India, then brought into Tibet, and reintroduced in Mongolia in the thirteenth century by Qubilai Khaan on the initiative of his Imperial Preceptor, the great Tibetan *paṇḍita* 'Phags pa bLa ma. It traces the governance based on the policy of dual law among the Mongols to Chinggis Khaan himself, inspiring the Mongolian Buddhist historiographers of the seventeenth and nineteenth centuries, such as Luvsandanzan (bLo bzang bsTan 'dzin) and others, to identify the Golden Clan of Chinggis Khaan with the Golden Clan of the mythical Buddhist king Mahāsammata, who is mentioned in the *White History* as an emanation of the Buddha Samantabhadra. The *White History* speaks of Mahāsammata as the first king to set up the policy of dual law in the land of Magadha in Bodhgayā at the time when the human lifespan was 100 years.

According to the *White History*,[1] it is because of Chinggis Khaan's implementation of the policy of dual law that he became famous in all of the occupied Jambudvīpa as the "Holy Lord, Chinggis Khaan." Reportedly, Chinggis Khaan requested from the Tibetan Sa skya lama the bestowal of the superior power to his successors for all generations and asked for a son who would rule in accordance with the policy of dual law. Hence, three generations later, Qubilai Khaan, known as a "Thousand Golden-Wheel Turner," having established the four great states consisting of five races, declared the following:

> After the ancient India, where two laws were established by Mahāsammata and reintroduced by the Buddha, they were maintained without a failure by the three *cakravartin* kings of Tibet for the next generation. Due to this transmission without a failure, my ancestor Chinggis Khaan, the Great, adopted these laws, governed his state, and ruled his countries properly. Hence, I will follow these two laws.[2]

According to the *White History*, the cornerstone of the sacred religion is the lama, the Lord of Dharma, while the head of secular power is the emperor, the sovereign of terrestrial power. When these two become consolidated, the teaching of the true dharma, like a silken knot, cannot be loosened; and the laws of the powerful ruler, like a golden yoke, cannot be crushed.[3] Hence, where the dual law is enduring, the dharma and the state will be lasting. On these grounds, the *White History* justified a law severely punishing those who transgress their monastic vows and commit crimes by stating that it seeks to ward off corruption of monastic discipline and social ethics. It justifies its concerns by referring to the Buddha, declaring: "My Dharma will not be destroyed by the outsiders, but it will be destroyed only by the misleading insiders."[4]

The text suggests that the seriousness of a crime against the state equals the sin of killing the Buddha or killing one's own *guru*. It relates a perilous karmic retribution to legal punishment in the case of both crimes. It presents the state and the dharma as two fundamental sources of refuge and as the most sacred domains of one's civic and religious duties. A ruler

[1] *Mongol Ulsyn Arvan Buyant Nomyn Tsagaan Tüükh Nert Sudar Orshivoi* (Ulaanbaatar: University of Mongolia, 2006), ch. 2.

[2] *Ibid.*, ch. 3.

[3] Shagdaryn Bira, "Khublai Khan and 'Phagspa Bla-ma," in Ts. Ishdorji and Kh. Purevtogtokh (eds.), *Studies in Mongolian History, Culture and Historiography* vol. 3 (Ulaanbaatar: International Association for Mongol Studies, Mongolian Academy of Sciences, Institute of History International Institute for the Study of Nomadic Civilization, 2001), 314.

[4] *Mongol Ulsyn Arvan Buyant*, ch. 3, 13.

who governs his territory in accordance with the policy of dual law is likened to a bodhisattva, endowed with impartial compassion. In contrast, a ruler who does not conduct himself in the manner of a bodhisattva is unable to adopt the policy of dual law; and in consequence, he falls into the error of favoring the rich and showing no mercy to the poor. As a result of this, his truthful ministers resign, and the liars and informers become promoted.[5]

The principle of the dual law as expressed in the *White History* influenced Mongolian Buddhist political and legal thought and was invoked in the establishment of a new state order. Therefore, in 1911, when Mongolia gained its independence from the Qing Dynasty and the Eighth Bogd Gegeen, Jebtsundamba Khutukhtu (1870–1924), ascended to the throne as an absolute monarch and as "the Holder of the Power of the State and Religion," he was given the name "Olan-a Ergügdegsen," which is the Mongolian rendering of the Sanskrit Mahāsammata. On that occasion, the Eighth Jebtsundamba proclaimed the year of independence (1911) as the Year One of Mahāsammata. With his unified religious and political roles, he exemplified the embodiment of the policy of dual law.

Upon the discovery of the *White History*, whenever the Mongol rulers tried to consolidate and centralize their power, they invoked the principle of dual law, were given the titles of dharma-kings, and were identified as emanations of celestial bodhisattvas by their preceptors. One of the first Mongolian Buddhist laws, the sixteenth-century *Altan Khan's Code of Law* (*Altan Khany Tsaaz*), praises Altan Khan as an emanation of Bodhisattva Āryabala (Avalokiteśvara) and as a protector and pacifier of all beings within the six realms of existence.[6] His code of law depicts the unification of the two laws as the means of facilitating the invincibility of the state and as the khan's method of revealing the path of peace to those living in the deep darkness of ignorance and accumulating sin. The law was to regulate the monastic ranks and to create a new line of nobility at the time when the Chinggis line was in decline.

Another early code of laws, the *Code of the Dharma with Ten Virtues* (*Arvan Buyant Nomiin Tsaaz*), was prepared under the auspices of Khutukhtu Sechen Khung Taiǰi, Altan Khan, and the Third Dalai Lama, bSod nams rGya mtsho around the same time that the *White History* came to light. It was in force until the beginning of the seventeenth century in the

[5] *Ibid.*, ch. 3.

[6] Christopher Attwood, *Encyclopedia of Mongolia and the Mongol Empire* (New York: Facts on Life, 2004), 10–11.

territories of Chakhar and Ordos Mongols.[7] The code prohibited the *hoilgo* practice of burying the servants and animals with the body of a deceased nobleman, and it required that things dedicated to the *hoilgo* rite be given to a Buddhist monastic community for religious activities. It demanded a destruction of Shamanic figurines (*onghoon*) and their replacement with an image of Mahākāla. It also forbade the killing of animals on the first, eighth, and fifteenth days of the month, made a stipulation for fasting on those days, and determined the hierarchy of the monastic degrees, such as *tsorj* (Tib., *chos rje*), *gavj* (Tib., *dka 'bcu*), *gelen* (Tib., *dge long*), and *agramba* (Tib., *snags rams pa*). It introduced penalties for those who would harm a member of a monastic community and punishments for monks who breach their monastic vows.

The Mongolian Buddhist laws bear the features of legal paternalism, expressing the notion that the wellbeing of the individual and society is contingent on a legal system that supports the flourishing of the principles of the Buddha-dharma. The paternalistic character of the Mongolian Buddhist laws is also revealed in their prohibitive expressions and in opening benedictions and colophons. The statutes instituted by Tüsheet Khan and other dignitaries of Khalkha in 1728, which were inserted in the earlier version of the *Khalkha Regulations of the Western Khüree* (*Baruun Khüreenii Khalkh Juram*), explain the motivation for Tüsheet Khan enacting them. By the blessing of the Tenggri of the Golden Clan of Chinggis Khaan, he composed the statutes in accordance with dharma for the sake of making the Buddhist teachings and the state prosper.[8]

Most of Mongolian Buddhist law codes either begin or conclude with expressions of homage to the Buddhas and great Buddhist personages, and with benedictions for the spiritual and social wellbeing of the people. For example, the legal document entitled, *The Great Code of Law of the Monkey Year* (*Bičin Jiliin Ikh Tsaaz*), which was prepared in 1620 at the river Taran, begins with the following benediction:

> I pay homage to the Buddha Śākyamuni, a Tathāgata, who crushed the four demons (Māras) and discovered the two truths.
>
> May the sanctity of the Buddhas of the three times and ten directions shine forth!
>
> May the three qualities of the emperor's body be complete![9]

[7] B. Bayarsaikhan, *Mongolyn Tör, Erkh Züin Tüükh* vol. 1 (Ulaanbaatar: MUIS-iin Huuly Züin Surguuly, Explanation of Terms, 2006).

[8] *Ibid.*, 84. [9] *Ibid.*, 33, 36.

Similarly, *The Great Law of Oirat Mongols* (*Mongol Oiratyn Ikh Tsaaz*), which was instituted in 1640 in the presence of three *khutukhtus* (incarnate lamas)[10] as a customary law for the western Mongols, and later revised in 1709, begins thus:

> O˙ may there be peace!
>
> I pay homage to the *guru* Vajradhara, who has unified the three Bodies, which are splendidly ornamented with all [32] signs and [80] characteristics that have issued from the Dharma-body of emptiness in the middle of the ocean of the two accumulations [of merit and wisdom].
>
> Śākyamuni, the guide of all, please open [the flower of my] originally closed mind in doubt with your warm light.
>
> I bow my head to the feet of the supreme, holy Tsongkhapa, who at this time translated the complete Wheel of Dharma and is a king of Dharma in the succession of the Holy Toin (Śākyamuni).
>
> I pray at the feet of the two holy ones: the protector Dalai Lama, who is a crown-pendant of the Land of Snow, and to the holy Panchen, who has become a reddish-yellow (monastic) form of the Buddha Amitābha for the sake of all living beings.
>
> O, Holy One, whose spirit of enlightenment is without distinction between compassion and emptiness, you who are of the nature of the Victorious Ones, and who have become well known as Khutukhtu Inzan (Yongdzin) Rinpoche, please fulfill a benefit of all sentient beings.[11]

Likewise, in the opening of *The Khalkha Regulations of the Ministry* (Yaamny Khalkh Jurmyn Dürem) and *The Khalkha Regulations of the Western Khüree* (Baruun Khüreenii Khalkh Juram), which governed the Great Shavi, we read the following:

> May the Dharma blaze strongly like the *vajra* feet of the supreme lama, the crown-pendant of living beings. May the lives of benefactors who support it be lengthen [sic]. May the State and nation prosper! May there not be even the slightest mention of the name of a bad deed! May the mind be peaceful! May the pure and good conduct thrive, infinitely gushing forth.[12]

Taking on the role of the guardians of the Buddha-dharma and the state, the Mongol and Manchu lawmakers in Mongolia instituted the laws that protected monastic properties, defined the positions and privileges of Buddhist clergy in society, and regulated the conduct of ordained Buddhists and their interactions with lay communities and state authorities. Legislating

[10] These were Shakyaagiin toin etseg inzan Rinbüche, Angkhobi Manzushiri, and Amuka Siddhi Manzushiri.

[11] *Ibid.*, 38. [12] *Ibid.*, 53, 88.

the monks and laypeople's social and ritual practices that are in accordance with Buddhist teachings and monastic rules, and introducing penal measures for their breaching, they made Buddhist teachings and practices either a regional or a state law. The penal systems they introduced involved severe punishments for both civil crimes and for transgressions of Buddhist precepts and practices. The penal system for transgressing restrictions was built on the clan, pastoral economy, and a nomadic way of life. It was based on property fines, most commonly in livestock, in confiscation of movable property and serfs, in bricks and baskets of tea, animal products, roles of silk, circumambulations around a monastery, and prostrations.

The Khalkha Regulations

The *Khalkha Regulations* (*Khalkh Juram*) were first created under the auspices of Tüsheet Khan (r. 1702–1711) and other Khalkha dignitaries to regulate and administer the Great Shavi of the Öndör Gegeen Zanabazar, the First Jebtsundamba Khutukhtu. Since then, the document underwent a series of revisions and functioned as a code of customary laws for Khalkha Mongols. After 1789 and until nearly 1925, it applied only to the Bogd Gegeens' Great Shavi, which by that time consisted of extensive pasture lands, livestock, and lay and monastic subjects, who supported Bogd Gegeen's monastic establishments through direct annual payments to his treasury, labor services to the monastery, tending of his herds, and so on.[13]

In its original form, the *Khalkha Regulations* contained seven articles with 194 sections. Among other things, they regulated the prerogatives and provisions for Bogd Gegeen, whom they extolled as a refuge of Mongolian people. In its later versions dating from 1676 and 1736, they secured the privilege of the exemption from paying taxes and tributes for monks belonging to the Great Shavi, which was administered by its own office, the chancellery of Erdene Shanzodva (Tib., *shan mdzod pa*), established in 1723, under the decree of the Qing administration as an institution with the authority to bring together state and religious matters and to administer Mongolian monks and high-incarnate lamas.

The *Khalkha Regulations of the Chancellery* (*Shavy Yaamny Halh Juram*) were introduced to regulate the prerogatives and provisions for Bogd Gegeen. The fines for verbally abusing or cursing a monk and for slandering an innocent monk ranged from 4 horses to 300 heads of livestock. The number of animals to be given as the fine for a physical assault on a

[13] Atwood, *Encyclopedia of Mongolia*, 211.

monk depended on the seniority of the assaulted monk – on whether he was a novice, a fully ordained monk, or Bogd Gegeen's messenger. One who wished to receive monastic ordination had to obtain permission from his parents and a banner-prince. If he demonstrated a sincere yearning for the monastic life, the law prohibited his banner-prince from hindering his ordination. Although monks were exempted from compulsory taxes or tributes, in civil affairs they were subject to the laws of their administrative units or banners.

The *Khalkha Regulations of the Chancellery* and the *Khalkha Regulations of Western Khüree* were also to prevent the misconduct of monks and the ill reputation of monastic establishments. In the *Khalkha Regulations of the Chancellery*, a penalty for a person offering alcohol to a monk was a fine of four young horses. If a fully ordained monk was caught consuming alcohol, his penalty was a fine of nine horses, whereas the prescribed penalty for a novice was three horses. A person who saw a monk drinking and reported him to the appropriate authorities was to be rewarded with a horse taken from the imposed fine. In contrast, a person who concealed a monk's drinking was to be given the same penalty as the one who gave alcohol to the monk. A monk who was seen drinking repeatedly was subject to imprisonment for one year.

This document also provided the provisions for the safeguarding of temples and monasteries from attacks and theft. Penalties for the theft of valuable objects and animals belonging to temples were equivalent to those for theft of Bogd Gegeen's private possessions. In addition, attacks on monasteries were punishable by exile and the confiscation of serfs if the offender was a nobleman, and by the death penalty and confiscation of property if the attacker was a commoner. The extent of punitive measures depended on the degree of theft or robbery. Other forms of punishment included confiscation of property, beating, confining, hobbling into a cangue, mutilation, compulsory labor, fine in serfs and family members, and compulsory supply of tea to monasteries.

In cases of theft from the private herds or treasury of the Bogd Gegeen or other nobles, the penalty was the confiscation of the perpetrator's entire property, including his wife and children, a fine in the heads of livestock, and so on. In the earliest version of this legal document, in addition to fines in livestock, everyone involved in theft was subject to punishment by flogging and handcuffing. A thief was also sentenced to circumambulations around monasteries and prostrations, the number of which depended on whether or not this was the first offense of the accused. The number of compulsory circumambulations of monasteries ranged from 100 to 1,000, and the number of prostrations varied from 1 to 10,000. Later amendments to the code introduced more severe physical punishments and higher fines in livestock. The death penalty was carried out only for first-degree robbery and attacks on monasteries, and it was introduced only after 1746, when the amendments to the code were made under the order of the Qing Emperor Kangxi.

Mongolian Code of Laws

While supporting Buddhist monasteries in Mongolia through gifts and required taxes, Qing emperors, in their presumed roles as Buddhist *cakravartins*, tightly controlled Buddhist institutions in Mongolia through their administrative body, the Lifan Yuan, and through the codes of law. One such code of laws, the *Mongolian Code of Laws* (*Mongol tsaazyn bichig, Menggu Luli*),[14] which was first issued by the Qing administration in 1643, began the period of the standardization of the court through consolidation of punitive measures in the Mongolian legal system.

The *Mongolian Code of Laws* reveals the extent to which the Qing administration utilized the Buddhist standards of proper monastic conduct and made them statutory law. It dictated stricter conditions under which someone could receive monastic ordination than those laid out in the *Khalkha Regulations* and in the *Great Law of Oirat Mongols*. In the *Mongolian Code of Laws*, a monastic ordination became also a state matter. It prohibited lamas from ordaining a novice on their own accord, without properly registering him with the Ministry of Affairs. The code also required that a parent whose child became a non-registered novice, as well as a person who sheltered such a novice, be handed over to the Ministry of Affairs, arraigned, and heavily punished.[15] It also prohibited a bestowal of the *upāsaka*[16] vows to a soldier or to a state official, and it provided penalties for violation of this law.

Through the *Mongolian Code of Laws*, the Qing administration also regulated the number of *getsuls* (fully ordained monks) and *gelens* (novice monks) within a monastic congregation that belonged to a Mongolian nobleman. If the number of *gelens* was insufficient, a nobleman had to promote the *getsuls* who were proven to be good in dharma into *gelens* and

[14] The original copy is preserved in the State Central Library in Ulaanbaatar. It consists of twelve chapters containing 205 articles.

[15] A flogging with a plank was primarily utilized in criminal interrogations, and a flogging with a rod was implemented only in certain situations.

[16] An *upāsaka* is a layman who takes the five main Buddhist ethical vows.

to replace them by learned Manchus. The code also prescribed the colors of monks' robes according to their ranks, it regulated their behavior in accordance with the monastic rules, and it prescribed penalties for monks' relations with women. It further regulated the penal dealings with monks who committed crimes and those who sheltered a monk convicted of a crime. It required that the monastic vows be taken away from a monk accused of a crime before his trial. A reason for disrobing a monk prior to his sentencing was that penalties for criminal cases involved various kinds of mutilations and execution, which were inapplicable to a monastically ordained person. If an accused monk was found innocent, he was to be given his monastic vows back; if he was found guilty, his belongings were to be given to the Ministry of Affairs and distributed to the monks of different monasteries as rewards.[17]

A layperson who invited a monk to his home to perform a healing ritual or to read prayers had to request permission from the monastery's head lama and hand the monk over to his head lama upon his return to the monastery. A monk who violated this rule was fined with three sets of nine head of livestock, and the person who received the monk was handed over to a subordinate Ministry of Affairs and arraigned. A monk who spent a night in the home of a woman in the absence of her husband had to be forcefully secularized and subjected to 100 floggings. Similarly, a lama of any rank who allowed a woman to enter the monks' living quarters was subject to a fine in animals, and the woman's husband was handed over to the Ministry of Affairs and punished. Moreover, if a lama engaged in sexual relations with a nun, the nun's monastic vows were to be abolished, and she was to be flogged 100 times. The implicated lama, however, was to be penalized by a fine in animals.[18]

The Laws and Regulations to Actually Follow

Following the decline of the Qing Dynasty, the autonomous Mongolian state was established and the Eighth Bogd Gegeen, Jebtsundamba Khutukhtu, was installed as the head of the Buddhist church and state. He was given the title of the "Holy Emperor Supported by All." With this event, Mongolian statehood was restored to a Buddhist monarchy, and a new government consisting of five ministries was formed under his auspices. The Ministry of Justice consisted of two departments: the Shuukh ("judging") and Ariutgakh ("purifying") departments. The former charged

[17] Bayarsaikhan, *Mongolyn Tör, Erkh Züin Tüükh*, 129–30, 167–68. [18] *Ibid.*

a crime, and the latter decided on sentencing. The name of the sentencing department itself reveals that, in the Buddhist monarchy, sentencing was to be interpreted not as a mere act of punishing, but also as an act of purifying the offender's negative deeds.

The Chancellery of Erdene Shandzodva continued to administer the Bogd Gegeen's Great Shavi, which continued to be exempt from taxes, military service, and corvée labor for the state. During this period, about half of the country's male population, totaling 206,000 monks and laymen, was under the direct control of Buddhist administrative organs.

Many of the statutes of the *Khalkha Regulations of the Chancellery* continued to be applied to the Great Shavi. However, the creation of the new Bogd Khaan state called for reforms in the Mongolian legal system and for new legal codes. In 1911, the records of the Ministry of the All-Governing Court of the Bogd Khaan state, entitled *The Records of Actions Followed by All According to Special Orders and Established by Many Ministries, Starting from the First Year of the State Supported by All*,[19] were inaugurated by the order of the Eighth Jebtsundamba Khutukhtu. One of these records is *The Book of Law Presently Established and Implemented by the Revised Agreement of the Five Ministries*, also known as the *Laws and Regulations to Actually Follow* (*Jinkhene Yavakh Dagaj Khuuly Dürem*), which was enacted between 1913–18. The record regulated the structure and operations of the newly formed monarchical state, the conduct of Buddhist ecclesiastics, criminal and civil law, the penal system, and so on.

The document reflects the legal thought of the transitional period and shows evidence of the cautious strategy of a new government. It introduced a small number of revisions and only changed the previously established measures in an incremental way. It made amendments with regard to the death penalty and certain harsh sentences that had been previously instituted by the *Mongolian Code of Laws*, replacing the death penalty and exile with flogging, imprisonment, and bonding with a cangue. However, armed attacks on monasteries, in which the number of stolen livestock exceeded twenty or thirty, was still punishable by breaking the spine of the perpetrator who orchestrated the robbery. According to Article 1, the official state judicators and investigators had no power to directly interrogate or penalize a fully ordained monk, a novice, or a Buddhist layperson belonging to a monastic college or to one of the monastic administrative organs in the Great Shavi. The Erdene Shanzodva had to be informed first about such

[19] B. Sodovsuren, *Khovysgalyn ömnökh Mongolyn tör ba khuuly tsaaz: 1911–1920* (Ulaanbaatar: no publisher given, 1989), 56.

a case. If a high-ranking lama was accused of some offense, the case had to be reported first to the *khamba nomun han* (the "abbot *dharma-rāja*" of Ikh Khüree), who was authorized either to grant permission for a court hearing or to deny it.

It was stipulated that every monastic division select a chairman, who was to select, with the assistance of the disciplinarian, security guards to keep night watch at the monastery's gates. If a guard failed in his duty, both the chairman who selected him and the disciplinarian who approved his appointment must be penalized. If they were unable to pay their fines, then they were removed from their positions. A convicted disciplinarian was sentenced to performing *pūjas* day and night and 100 daily prostrations for up to 100 days, while a chairman was sentenced to floggings with a stick, cleaning the monastic area, and public humiliation.

The new monarchical government legislated against actions that contradicted monastic rules, and it introduced the prohibitions on gambling, drinking of alcohol, monks' relations with women, and wandering outside of monasteries. The document forbids a monk from leaving the monastic grounds without a required permit, called a "stamped wood" (*temdegt mod*), which could be obtained from one of the seventeen authorized monastic offices. A permit had to provide a reason for leaving, the name of the destination, the date of issue, and the length of one's stay.[20] If a monk had to travel to a remote place, someone from the Erdene Shanzodva's office had to accompany him. If he was going to a marketplace or to circumambulate a shrine in the city, he had to go through the main avenue and return before sunset. If a monk grew his hair or wore layman's clothing, he was disrobed, placed into cangue for forty-five days, flogged with a stick, then ordained again and further penalized with attendance to *pūjas* for 200 days and 100 prostrations for each day of the penalty period.

According to Article 24, no one residing in the capital, be it a layperson or a monk, was allowed to drink or sell alcohol. The penalty for breaching this regulation was bondage in a cangue for forty days and 100 whippings. In the case of a monk, in addition to the aforementioned penalty, 100 *pūjas* and 100 prostrations for each day of the period of punishment was prescribed. When alcohol was needed for a religious ceremony in a monastery, a trusted official who had a permit was allowed to purchase it from herders.[21]

[20] B. Bayarsaikhan (ed.), *Jinkhene Dagaj Yavakh Khuuly Dürem: 1913–1918* (Ulaanbaatar: The University of Mongolia, School of Law, Research Center for Mongolian State and Law History, 2004), 48.

[21] According to the *Laws and Regulations to Actually Follow*, gambling with cards was introduced in Mongolia from Russia and became very popular during the theocratic period.

The penalty for monks caught gambling with cards[22] or dominos varied in accordance with their rank, and it ranged from hobbling in a cangue for forty days and 100 floggings to performing *pūjas* for 100 days, as well as 100 daily prostrations, and a fine in livestock.[23] In the case of laity, punitive measures for gambling included: (1) confiscation of the money involved in gambling, (2) sentencing of gamblers to 100 floggings and forced labor, (3) confiscation of the *ger* and the yard of a person who sheltered gamblers, (4) hobbling in a cangue for six months to a year, as well as 100 floggings for those who provided gamblers with accommodations for gambling, and (5) confiscation of horses and money belonging to those who joined the gamblers.

The document placed more accountability for the misbehavior of monks on all of the members of society than the previous laws did. For example, Article 32 of the *Laws and Regulations to Actually Follow* states:

> From now on, in order to keep these laws and rules valid at every level, all the related officers in the capital will cite all of the established laws and rules to people – to the ordained, laypeople, and women – not leaving a single person out. Sometimes there are certain monks in the capital who are prone to misconduct and escape from the monastic area. From now on, arrest all those who are roaming around without permits or with expired permits. Take them to the appropriate offices for punishments and make sure that no one makes mistakes regarding monastic discipline![24]

The responsibility for the inappropriate behavior of monks residing in Ikh Khüree was placed on the monastic disciplinarians and head lamas, who were to be fined in animals if they failed in their disciplinary duties. Outside the capital, the duty of enforcing monks' proper conduct was placed on the shoulders of the police, town mayors, and other administrators of related provinces, and on local laypeople as well.[25] An inspector or a policeman who fails in his duty was to be harshly penalized in the same way as a monk who breached the law. One who witnessed an official protecting such a monk under his authority by taking a bribe and setting him free must report the case to the related ministry.

In 1921, the People's Revolutionary Government came to power and initiated reforms in the judiciary system. It imposed strict limits on the Bogd Khaan's secular power while granting him unlimited power in religious

[22] Bayarsaikhan (ed.), *Jinkhene Dagaj Yavakh Khuuly Dürem: 1913–1918*, Article 25.

[23] *Ibid.*, Article 26. [24] *Ibid.*, Article 29.

[25] Valentin A. Riasanovsky, *Fundamental Principles of Mongol Law* (Bloomington: Indiana University Press, 1976), 67.

affairs, which he held until his death in 1924. On November 21, 1921, the document entitled the *Agreement Under Oath Concluded between the Bogd Khaan and the Government for the Purpose of Defining Their Mutual Relations* gave him the position of a constitutional monarch with the limited power of veto. According to Article 1, the Bogd Khaan of the Mongol state, Jebtsundamba Khutukhtu, being the Holy Head of the Yellow Religion (dGe lugs pa), could not concern himself with the affairs of the state, but in all matters dealing with religion he was to wield unlimited powers.

Conclusion

This essay has not attempted to determine the degree to which the prohibitive and punitive measures prescribed in the legal documents discussed were carried out in practice. Instead, it has aimed to demonstrate the manner in which these laws embodied the expressions of the political and religious authorities in Mongolia, who aspired to the ideal of dual law within their own socio-political realities. By briefly pointing to the inextricability of the legal and Buddhist systems of thought and practice in Mongolia prior to the Communist revolution, this essay has indirectly proposed that, at least in certain times and particular instances, the category of Buddhism has encompassed a legal tradition in addition to a religious tradition. As a normative social practice, Buddhist law in Mongolia gave rise to both social and religious actions. Buddhist law should be understood not as a mere set of regulations, but analyzed in light of what lawmakers, laden with the responsibility of upholding Buddhist morality, aimed to construct and sought to obtain from it. When the Buddhist tradition embraces law as integral to its operation, it becomes a complex socio-political phenomenon.

Although the main reason for the merging of Buddhism and law in Mongolia was political in nature, this does not diminish the significance of other factors facilitating this occurrence. Buddhism and law are both, in their own respective ways, normative social practices that set standards for desirable behavior and proclaim symbolic expressions of social values. In the Mongolian cultural context, the normative domain of Buddhism is expressed by the term "religious law" (*nomyn khuuly, nom-un khauli*), which also carries the meaning of the "law of dharma." The Mongolian word for law (*khuuly, khauli*) contained in the phrase "the law of dharma" is also used in phrases such as customary law (*khev khuuly*), civil law (*irgenii khuuly*), criminal law (*erüügiin khuuly*), and so forth. Thus, the Mongolian term for "religious law" points to the perception of the Buddha-dharma as bearing a legal aspect. The term encompasses a wide range of Buddhist ethical and social norms and values, whose purpose was to guide the conduct of and set standards for Mongols and as such, influenced other normative domains and practices in Mongolian culture. The legal documents discussed in this essay attest to conscious efforts on the part of their authors to enforce Buddhist norms and practices in Mongolian society.

However, there were other normative orders that also influenced Mongolian Buddhism and its legal tradition, as evidenced in the legal and administrative structure adopted by the Mongolian Buddhist establishments and in the cases where local customs and laws of the steppe overrode Buddhist principles. Through the inclusion of other normative domains that guided the behavior of Mongols – namely, the social conventions and etiquettes of Mongolian nomadic, pastoral life – the dimensions of Buddhist law in Mongolia were extended and gave it a unique character.

CHAPTER 19

Karma, Monastic Law, and Gender Justice

Karma Lekshe Tsomo

This chapter investigates the theory of karma, its relationship to the monastic legal system (*Vinaya*), and the consequences that misinterpreting and unjustly applying the theory in gender relations has for women, particularly with respect to the issue of higher ordination for women.

The theory of karma is basic to an understanding of law for any individual in a Buddhist society, and it undergirds a community's understanding of the results of legal actions in this and the next life. The Buddha Śākyamuni rejected a deterministic interpretation of karma, instead emphasizing individual responsibility, intention, and the primary importance of actions created in the present moment. As the first part of this chapter will demonstrate, the fundamental Buddhist concepts of cause and effect, rebirth, and suffering are all central to an understanding of the Buddhist legal worldview.

The section on gender relations and women begins with the insight that over time, many Buddhists have come to assume that being born a woman represents a lower status and a lesser spiritual potential. The stereotype of a female rebirth as lower than a male has historically resulted in discriminatory attitudes toward women and has been correlated with obstacles to women's education and ordination. This rests on the presumption that women are more suited to devotion than philosophy, teaching, and religious leadership. Yet exclusion and fixed conceptions sit uneasily with Buddhist egalitarian ideals and fundamental teachings on *dukkha* (dissatisfaction), *anitya* (change), and *anātman* (no inherent identity). Using the theory of karma to justify gender bias and exploitation is a travesty against the Buddha's teachings on cause and effect. A careful rethinking of the law of cause and effect, its application to monastic law, and its implications for gender justice and human rights is imperative if the liberating promise of the Buddhist path is to be realized, especially by women.

Karma and Its Fruits

The theory of karma is a fundamental aspect of Buddhist metaphysics and Buddhist ethics, including the monastic codes. Over the course of many rebirths, sentient beings take many forms, including different genders, as a result of actions (karma) of body, speech, and mind. According to this theory, actions are a matter of choice, conditioned by many factors, including thoughts, emotions, knowledge, and past experiences. Just as a seed, under proper conditions, produces a plant of similar type, actions give rise to consequences similar to their causes in this and future lives. The law of cause and effect extends to psychological phenomena and to multiple lifetimes on the path to awakening. Sentient life arises not randomly, but from causes. Beginning during the Buddha's lifetime, precepts (*śīla*) were set forth to help renunciants mindfully regulate their actions of body, speech, and mind. Over time, this body of precepts evolved into monastic codes that were observed and recited on full moon and new moon days by fully ordained Buddhist monks and nuns.

Buddhist ethics originated from the Buddha's observations of the outcomes of actions and mental states over many lifetimes. Because it can be verified through a process of trial and error, the relationship between actions and their consequences is not simply a matter of faith. To the extent that we can directly observe the consequences of actions and mental states, it is possible to verify the theory of karma (cause and effect) through personal experience. It is not possible to observe the workings of karma completely, however, since the consequences of actions do not necessarily follow immediately. The exact correlation between actions and consequences is influenced by a large number of mitigating circumstances that operate over many lifetimes and include different forms of sentient existence, which can only be observed by advanced meditators. It may be especially difficult to verify the results of mental states, since feelings of remorse and regret may not arise until some future time, perhaps even at the time of death.

While connections between actions and consequences had been noted in pre-Buddhist philosophical systems, the Buddha argued against a deterministic interpretation of karma, emphasizing individual responsibility and the motivation behind the action. Intention is pivotal in Buddhist interpretations of karma, affecting the intensity of the action and the seriousness of the consequences. For example, the consequences of inadvertently killing an insect are less serious than stomping the creature deliberately with the intent to kill and then gloating over its death. These differences in intention are also significant in some secular legal settings. Each sentient being's consciousness is unique and distinct from any other and the effects of actions are only experienced directly by that specific individual:

> I am the owner of my karma.
> I inherit my karma.
> I am born of my karma.
> I am related to my karma.
> I live supported by my karma.
> Whatever karma I create, whether good or evil, that I shall inherit.[1]

While the law of cause and effect addresses why bad things happen to good people and why good things happen to bad people, to label people either good or bad is to vastly oversimplify reality. All human beings have positive and negative traits. Buddhists argue against essentializing any phenomenon, since most things are changing all the time. Within moments of characterizing someone as "good" or "bad," that person has changed and could even change radically. The error of assigning fixed attributes to ourselves and others is compounded by the concept of rebirth. Carefully observing the law of cause and effect is said to free the mind of guilt and regret and help human beings "live happily and die without regrets." Remorse can be a healthy corrective, insofar as it causes one to reassess careless, self-interested, and harmful patterns of thought and behavior. Left uncorrected, these destructive patterns can weigh on our minds, leading to unease and even, if left unprocessed, to burdens of guilt.

The whole of Buddhist metaphysics is implicitly assumed in the concept of cause and effect. Although it can be argued that the theory of rebirth was something the Buddha simply inherited from earlier Indian tradition, he affirmed a belief in rebirth numerous times throughout the teachings ascribed to him. While the concept of rebirth was prominent at the time, Gananath Obeyesekere points out that it was the Buddha who elaborated on its ethical implications.[2] Buddhist texts are replete with explanations of the workings of cause and effect and rebirth, yet the specifics of the process are complex; explaining the inner mechanics of an infinite universe with infinite ramifications is not a simple matter. The theory (or "law") of karma is situated within a metaphysics that assumes the existence of multiple lifetimes, as was current in India at the time of the Buddha. According to the principle of cause and

[1] *Upajjhatthana Sutta*, Aṅguttara Nikāya, 57.

[2] Gananath Obeyesekere, *Imagining Karma: Ethical Transformation in Amerindian, Buddhist, and Greek Rebirth* (Berkeley: University of California Press, 2002).

effect, the consequences of actions may ripen in this very lifetime, the next lifetime, or some lifetime after that. Observing this principle is key to achieving happiness in this lifetime, to having a fortunate rebirth next time around, and ultimately to liberating oneself from the tedious and miserable process of rebirth altogether. The consequences of actions are not dictated by any supreme being or cosmic calculator, but are simply natural phenomena that arise in connection with actions. Certain causes are requisite for certain consequences; without performing those actions, there is no reason to expect or fear the consequences.

Yet, there is considerable speculation about how the law of cause and effect actually operates. In one view, each and every phenomenon within time and space is the result of a specific cause. In another view, the law of cause and effect best describes the overall pattern of actions and consequences, usually with the aim of guiding behavior and helping human beings prevent unpleasant conditions and experiences in the future. The first view issues from a rather literal reading of the texts: actions inexorably give rise to consequences of similar nature to their causes. For example, killing a human being may result in being murdered, either in this or some future life. In such an interpretation, a direct correlation exists between actions and their consequences, albeit tempered by numerous factors, especially intention. The second view acknowledges the general workings of cause and effect without prescribing specific results. For example, killing human beings results in unpleasant consequences such as unfortunate rebirths, illness, a short lifespan, and so on. Both views inform the moral worldviews of Buddhists in diverse societies and are applied in practice to avoid creating the causes of suffering.

The existence of past and future rebirths is not merely assumed or believed, however. It is substantiated or ascertained through four lines of reasoning: similar type, substantial cause, prior habitual patterns, and past experience.[3] These lines of reasoning were applicable in monastic legal settings as well, or any legal system with a foundation in Buddhist thought. Reasoning by way of similar type means that a specific rebirth is not simply the result of physical causes, since that would provide inadequate causes for the life force, sense faculties, and consciousness, which must be explained by some other antecedent. Reasoning by way of the substantial cause means that phenomena, such as consciousness, are the result of causes similar to

[3] Geshe Lam Rim, *A Necklace of Good Fortune: A Series of Instructions on Past and Future Lives, Actions and Their Results*, Jampa Gedun, Tsepak Rigzin, and Damdul Namgyal (trans.) (Dharamsala: Library of Tibetan Works and Archives, 1982), 3–9.

themselves, just as a barley sprout is produced by a barley seed and not by a seed of some other type. Reasoning by way of prior habitual patterns means that tendencies toward specific emotions or personality traits, wholesome or unwholesome, such as tendencies toward compassion or anger, can be understood as the result of habituation with these emotions or traits in past lives.

As for reasoning on the basis of past experience, it is possible to directly verify the existence of past lives firsthand through meditation. Certain analogies are given in the scriptures to help explain the existence of and relationship between past and future lives: a sense of familiarity with certain oral teachings, a flame that is transmitted from one lamp to the next, a face in the mirror, the impression of a seal, the image of a magnifying glass, a seed that no longer exists once it sprouts, word associations, and an echo. The interpretations of these eight analogies explain how interdependent causes and conditions function even when they may not function in a linear fashion or be obvious to the unenlightened mind.

The texts explain how an understanding of the workings of cause and effect has both mundane and ultimate benefits. Understanding even the general outlines of the theory helps one to carefully consider both the immediate and long-range consequences of their actions over the course of many lifetimes. By failing to reflect on the long-range consequences of actions, one may create actions that result in an unfortunate rebirth and great suffering for a very long time. An understanding of karma is therefore beneficial both from a worldly perspective and an ultimate perspective, namely, achieving liberation from cyclic existence (*saṃsāra*).

The principle of cause and effect is the basis for Buddhist ethical prescriptions, which are set forth in a variety of formats in the texts. There are general explanations of wholesome and unwholesome actions, often conveyed by the Buddha in dialogue format in the *sūtras*; there are enumerations of the ethical precepts to be observed by laypeople and monastics; and there are innumerable stories that demonstrate the principle. To illustrate the injunction against taking life, killing sentient beings is said to result in hellish sufferings or a short lifespan, whereas saving sentient beings' lives is said to result in long life and good health. Human beings create actions through body, speech, and mind: physical karma, verbal karma, and mental karma. We may create actions directly ourselves or indirectly, by instigating an action (for example, encouraging someone to commit an action, such as killing a human being or animal) or by rejoicing in an action committed by someone else (for example, rejoicing in the hanging of Saddam Hussein). The negative results for the actor occur in addition to the judgment and punishment that happens in any legal proceedings or in court.

The broad outlines of karma are easy to understand, but the details are rather complicated and the precise results of actions are impossible for an ordinary person to predict. Only a fully awakened Buddha can understand karma completely; a Buddha understands karma so completely as to understand the causes of every color of the peacock's tail. The general principle is that wholesome actions give rise to pleasant results, whereas unwholesome actions give rise to unpleasant results. The law of karma is not a matter of simple equivalency, however, because a vast number of contingent factors affect the consequence of actions. Commentaries on the law of cause and effect explain that the results of actions depend on both causes and conditions. Among the influential factors that affect the consequences of actions and were relevant to Buddhist legal reasoning are: the nature of the action, the intention behind the action, the agent of the action, the mindset of the agent, the object of the action, the modus operandi, and the factors or the circumstances surrounding the event. These factors for legal reasoning were even encapsulated in some law codes in Buddhist countries. For example, murder is more unwholesome than other actions; killing intentionally is more serious than killing accidentally; an act of killing by an ordained monastic who has made a commitment not to kill is more serious than an act of killing by a person who has not made such a commitment; killing a human being is more serious than killing an animal; to kill someone cruelly is more culpable than killing indifferently, and so forth. The seriousness of the consequences also depends on whether one commits the action of killing gleefully, viciously, or reluctantly, and whether one derives satisfaction from the act of killing, rejoices, or regrets having done it. If one generates regret, it depends on how quickly one regrets. Further, the consequences depend on whether the action is done once, repeatedly, or habitually.

Understanding the principle of cause and effect is deemed valuable because it is by understanding that wholesome actions bring happiness and that unwholesome actions bring suffering that one will be able to free oneself from dukkha, often translated as suffering, which signifies frustration, and dissatisfactions of all kinds. A thorough understanding of the principle of cause and effect will naturally incline one to engage in wholesome actions and to thereby sow the seeds of happiness. It will also naturally incline one to avoid creating unwholesome actions and to thereby avoid future unpleasantness. Most importantly, because an understanding of cause and effect is essential for all higher attainments, understanding cause and effect provides a sound foundation for higher realizations and for the ultimate attainment of liberation, or putting an end to dukkha.

There are four concomitant principles for a thorough understanding of cause and effect. First, actions unerringly give rise to consequences consistent with the causes. For example, the practice of generosity results in prosperity, whereas stinginess results in poverty. Just as a mango seed will never produce a pepper plant and a pepper seed will never produce a mango plant, virtuous actions will never result in misery and non-virtuous actions will never result in happiness. One can never expect prosperity to result from stinginess, and one need not worry that poverty will result from practicing generosity. Second, actions have many consequences; just as a seed that grows then produces many other seeds, so the results of actions continue to increase. Until and unless the doer of an unwholesome action feels remorse regarding that action, the unfortunate consequences of that action continue and increase. Third, unless an action is created, the consequences of that action will not be experienced. For example, one cannot expect to experience the pleasant consequences of a wholesome action one has not performed, nor need one anticipate experiencing the unpleasant consequences of an unwholesome action one has not performed. Fourth, the consequences of actions never dissipate or disappear. The consequences of actions can be mitigated or alleviated through the practice of wholesome actions, but cannot be completely eliminated. Just as a spoonful of salt in a small glass of water will make the water taste very salty, a spoonful of salt in a huge fresh-water lake will go unnoticed. Similarly, in a huge store of merit, the consequences of a small non-virtuous deed will be negligible.

Tibetan commentaries explain four powers that help mitigate the consequences of non-virtuous actions, and these four powers were recognized in legal transactions as well: recognizing a transgression as a transgression, generating sincere remorse for having committed it, making a commitment not to commit the action again, and performing virtuous actions to help offset the unfortunate consequences of one's action. For example, giving is considered a purifying action. Other actions that Buddhists regard as purifying actions include meditation, the recitation of texts, and saving the lives of sentient beings. It is believed that, if one has accumulated great merit through actions of purification, the consequences of subsequent unwholesome deeds may mature in a less serious form in this life, and one will not suffer a miserable rebirth in an unfortunate realm of existence.

Experiencing the results of one's virtuous actions, such as good health and good fortune, exhausts one's store of merit; it is necessary to sow the seeds of future happiness by creating wholesome actions now.

Living by the Rule: Ancient Codes and Contemporary Life

The theory of karma underpins the Buddhist practice of ethics and the monastic law codes. While the relationship between karma and ethics is fairly straightforward, the link between karma and monastic discipline may be less obvious. Buddhist systems of ethics are regarded as a means to ensure the welfare of individuals by prohibiting harmful actions. Similarly, the monastic codes ensure the welfare of the monastic community by regulating the conduct of renunciants and their interactions with each other and the surrounding lay community. The monastic codes may also be regarded as a means to protect the welfare of society at large, by establishing standards for human conduct and inscribing ethical values. Although laypeople generally take only five precepts, while the monastics take more than 200, monastic protocols and behavior exert a strong influence in lay society.

The law of cause and effect connects each individual's path over many lifetimes, from a beginning in ignorance to ultimate awakening or enlightenment. A celibate monastic lifestyle is thought to be the most conducive circumstance for dedicated practice. Developing concentration and purifying mental defilements are difficult to accomplish when a person has worldly obligations and is subject to emotional entanglements such as desire and attachment. Monastic law prescribes disciplined conduct for members of the saṅgha to create optimal conditions for mental cultivation. Observing the precepts and monastic protocols minimizes selfish desires and aversions and creates an environment that promotes mindful awareness of the workings of cause and effect. Associating with good friends (*kalyāṇamitra*), companions of good character, is recommended for everyone, monastic or lay, and members of the saṅgha are regarded as ideal companions. By setting forth standards of disciplined behavior, the monastic codes help monastics develop an awareness of every action – physical, verbal, and mental – and thereby facilitate their progress toward liberation and awakening.

According to the teachings of the Buddha, the ideal circumstance for treading the path to liberation is to renounce household life and embark on a path of homelessness. In joining the saṅgha, the "assembly" or monastic community, one leaves behind the comforts and security of hearth and home to live in the company of other renunciant seekers. By renouncing family life, one begins to eradicate the desire and attachment that keep one bound within cyclic existence, the wheel of rebirth. In the early years, a fully ordained monk (*bhikṣu*) or a nun (*bhikṣuṇī*) lived a wandering lifestyle. Even today, the ordination rite begins with the formula of the four reliances: relying on alms for food, rags for clothing, trees for shelter, and cow dung and urine for medicine. Gradually, the Buddha agreed that the nuns and monks could accept invitations to meals, donations of robes, more permanent shelter, and additional medicines. After instances of sexual assault against nuns, the Buddha observed that it was not safe for them to take shelter in the forest and instead allowed them to stay in a *vihāra* (monastic dwelling) or temporarily with families. Over time, Buddhist nuns and monks began to settle into monastic communities, usually located near a town or village where they could go for their daily alms. Today, most Buddhist nuns in the world live in nunneries or monasteries. Some live in solitary retreat, either alone or in small retreat communities.

The rules and procedures that govern the lives of Buddhist monastics are contained in the *Vinaya*, the texts of monastic discipline. The official acts of the saṅgha include three rites that are essential for Buddhist monastic life: full ordination (*upasampadā*), the bimonthly recitation of the *Prātimokṣa sūtra* that contains the monastic precepts (*upoṣadha*), and the assembly held at the end of the three-month rainy season retreat (*pavāraṇā*). The rite of full ordination for monks requires the presence of ten bhikṣu precept masters (five in a remote area), whereas the rite of full ordination for nuns requires the presence of both ten bhikṣu and ten bhikṣuṇī precept masters.[4]

The monastic precepts are organized into a number of categories, ranging from serious transgressions entailing expulsion from the order to seemingly minor infractions of behavioral protocol. These precepts can be seen as belonging to three general types: moral injunctions, such as to refrain from lying, killing, stealing, or sexual activity; regulations to help maintain harmony in the monastic community, such as to avoid accumulating unnecessary possessions, hiding others' belongings, or neglecting monastic property; and rules of etiquette, such as to refrain from spitting, wearing the robes askew, or talking with one's mouth full. At least six reasons can be cited for observing the precepts: (1) the precepts support the practice of mindfulness and alertness in everyday actions; (2) they support the development of renunciation by limiting the number of possessions monastics

[4] Twelve bhikṣuṇī precepts masters are required in the Mūlasarvāstivādin tradition practiced by Tibetans.

may keep; (3) they prevent monastics from becoming overly involved in worldly affairs, thereby limiting distractions and allowing more time for mental development; (4) they help foster respect for others; (5) they provide a standard of deportment that inspires the respect and support of the lay community on whom the saṅgha depend for their livelihood; and (6) they encourage restraint of the senses, which is necessary for achieving liberation.

Today, as Buddhism increasingly attracts international attention, age-old assumptions about the primacy of monastic life in Buddhist societies points to a certain cultural and conceptual dissonance between traditional and contemporary values and institutions. Just as religious thought and practice influence social and historical developments, social and historical developments also influence religious thought and practice. On one hand, religious practices inevitably change in new cultural contexts, which is the sign of a vital, responsive tradition. On the other hand, uncritical acculturation of a tradition may transform it into something entirely different, challenging its continuity or compromising its authenticity. This, of course, raises questions about how authenticity can be gauged: whether tradition is intrinsically valuable, what is at stake in preserving tradition, and ultimately what constitutes tradition and authenticity. In other words, what is lost and what is gained with acculturation? For example, many Buddhist teachers in the West today teach what is disparagingly called "feel-good Buddhism," devoid of any mention of ethics, death, rebirth, discipline, or mental control. At the other extreme, orthodox approaches often render Buddhism unapproachable and irrelevant.

In the current climate of acculturation, discussion about the relevance of the monastic law and lifestyle consider such questions as how monastics can get support (almsround? handicrafts?), how they can acquire religious education and training (teachers? role models?), how they gain organizational experience and leadership skills, the relationship between monastics and laity in the contemporary context (clear in traditional Buddhist societies, at least for monks, but quite unclear in contemporary societies, especially Western societies), and the value of the *Vinaya* rules, traditional customs, and deportment in changing societies. Does it matter how many times a day we eat and when we eat our meals? To cling to the minor rules is clearly problematic, but even some of the relatively major ones are being reconsidered. How practical is it to live without money in a non-Buddhist society? How seriously will coming generations take a teacher who is not allowed to sit alone with someone of the opposite gender?

One major area of cultural and conceptual dissonance between traditional and contemporary Buddhist societies and institutions concerns gender issues. Archaic modes of thinking about women's roles and potentials are being seriously challenged. In Thailand, where Theravada orthodoxy strongly opposes the full ordination of women, there are already six communities of *bhikkhunīs* (Skt., *bhikṣuṇī*). Western adherents are often in the vanguard of change. A recent controversy in Australia brought these tensions into the open. In an open letter dated November 1, 2009, addressed to "Buddhist Societies Throughout the World," Wat Nong Pah Pong, a monastery of the Thai Forest Sangha, revoked the status of Ajahn Brahmavamso, the abbot of Buddhinyana Monastery in Perth, for officiating at a bhikkhunī ordination. The international outcry that followed was almost entirely in support of women's right to full ordination.

Women's Rites and Rights: The Ordination of Buddhist Women[5]

According to tradition, the Buddha maintained that the ideal society consists of four communities: monks (*bhikṣus*), nuns (*bhikṣuṇīs*), laymen (*upāsakas*), and laywomen (*upāsikās*). The order of Buddhist monks began soon after the Buddha's awakening, some 2,500 years ago. The order of nuns began five or six years later, when the Buddha's aunt and foster mother Mahāprajāpatī requested permission to join the saṅgha. The Buddha is said to have hesitated at first, which is not surprising given the patriarchal social climate of the time and the radical social changes that such a decision portended. When questioned by his attendant Ānanda as to whether women could achieve the fruits of the Buddhist path, the Buddha is said to have responded that renunciant women who followed the path that he taught were capable of attaining all four stages of the religious path to liberation.[6] This affirmation prompted Ānanda to then request the Buddha to permit his foster mother to enter the renunciant life under his discipline. This marked the beginning of the order of Buddhist nuns that flourished under Mahāprajāpatī's leadership and continued to exist in India for 1,500 years. According to legend, King Aśoka's daughter, Saṅghamitra, took the bhikṣuṇī lineage from India to Sri Lanka in the fourth century BCE. In the fifth century CE, the Sri Lankan nun Devasāra

[5] An earlier version of this section was published as "Women's Rites and Rights: The Ordination of Buddhist Women," *New Woman, New Church* 29 (Fall 2006), 3.

[6] Mohan Wijayaratna, *Buddhist Nuns: The Birth and Development of a Women's Monastic Order* (Kandy: Buddhist Publication Society, 2010), 16.

took the lineage to China and from there it spread to Korea, Vietnam, and Taiwan. Tens of thousands of fully ordained nuns continue to practice in these countries today.

Nevertheless, as Buddhism spread throughout Asia, communities of fully ordained monks were established and thrived, but equal attention was not always paid to establishing communities of nuns. For example, there is no conclusive evidence that the lineage of full ordination for women was established in Burma, Cambodia, Laos, Mongolia, Thailand, or Tibet. The bhikṣuṇī saṅgha died out in India, Nepal, and Sri Lanka around the eleventh century CE, but has been reintroduced in the last twenty years with the help of ordained nuns from Korea and Taiwan. A vibrant international movement to institute full ordination for women in all Buddhist societies is now underway.[7]

The English terms "ordination" and "nun" are used for the sake of convenience, but require explanation, since they do not exactly match their Buddhist counterparts. The first step in becoming a Buddhist nun (or monk) is the "going forth" (*pravrajyā*) or "leaving the household life." According to tradition, she subsequently receives the ten precepts of a novice (*śrāmaṇerikā*),[8] the precepts of a probationary nun (*śikṣamāṇā*), and eventually the more than 300 precepts of a fully ordained nun (bhikṣuṇī). Buddhist monastic communities are organized democratically and the ultimate authority for regulating everyday life is the *Vinaya,* the monastic code or precepts that nuns and monks voluntarily undertake and observe. Nuns' communities function independently from monks' communities in most countries and contexts, but procedures for higher ordination and sanctions for bhikṣuṇīs stipulate the presence of monks, bhikṣus, who are generally invested with final authority. The dual ordination procedure for nuns is reflected in the eight special rules (*gurudharmas*) that Mahāprajāpatī purportedly accepted in exchange for her admission to the saṅgha. These eight special rules vary in the different *Vinaya* schools and their historicity is anything but clear.[9] These rules stipulate the nuns' dependence on

[7] The history and development of this movement are described from a variety of perspectives in Karma Lekshe Tsomo (ed.), *Buddhist Women and Social Justice: Ideals, Challenges, and Achievements* (Albany: State University of New York Press, 2004).

[8] The ten precepts of a novice Buddhist nun or monk are to abstain from: (1) taking life; (2) taking what is not given; (3) sexual intercourse; (4) lying; (5) taking intoxicants; (6) wearing ornaments or cosmetics; (7) singing or dancing; (8) sitting on high or luxurious seats or beds; (9) accepting gold or silver; and (10) taking untimely food.

[9] Bhikkhuni Kusuma discusses the inconsistencies inherent in these rules in her article, "Inaccuracies in Buddhist Women's History" in Karma Lekshe Tsomo (ed.), *Innovative Buddhist*

the order of monks in such important matters as ordination, instruction, and reinstatement, despite the fact that nuns' communities generally function independently of monks' communities. The first *gurudharma*, which requires even the most senior bhikṣuṇī to bow to a brand-new bhikṣu, is particularly grating to the sensibilities of women raised with ideals of gender equity. Even if it could be established that Mahāprajāpatī agreed to abide by these rules, it is still far from clear why all bhikṣuṇīs up to the present day should be obligated to follow them.

The rule that nuns must receive full ordination from both bhikṣuṇīs and bhikṣus means that, in countries where there are no bhikṣuṇīs, women are not able to receive the precepts in their own tradition. This is the situation that currently prevails in the Theravāda and Tibetan traditions, where nuns occupy a liminal or perpetual novice status, respectively. In the present era of improved communications and transportation, however, it is theoretically possible for nuns to receive ordination from bhikṣuṇīs of another tradition. In the present transnational climate, methods for overturning centuries-old obstructions to women's ordination are being vigorously explored by an international, Buddhist women's movement.[10]

Today, Buddhist nuns live in different countries throughout the world, attempting to abide by codes of monastic discipline formulated in ancient India, while simultaneously adapting to local etiquette and contemporary cultural mores. Even in the most traditional Buddhist setting, it is difficult for nuns today to live on alms food and adhere strictly to all the precepts. In modern times, especially for Western women, the most glaring cultural discrepancy is the lack of full ordination for women in certain Buddhist traditions. Although today women's equal potentialities are recognized in virtually every field, male domination persists in Buddhist societies and is inscribed in monastic law. Age-old patriarchal patterns have been replicated in the saṅgha, despite the fact that there is no philosophical justification for male dominance either in the Buddhist monastic community or other social institutions. With a new global ethic of respect for human rights, the legislation of subordinate status for any group of individuals must be seriously questioned. This is, in effect, a global legal standard – human

Women: Swimming Against the Stream (Surrey: Curzon Press, 2000), 5–12. Her research demonstrates that the eight *gurudharmas* are almost certainly later interpolations.

10 A variety of perspectives on these questions, both historical and contemporary, from scholars and practitioners of diverse Buddhist traditions were presented at the International Congress on Women's Role in the Sangha held at Hamburg University in 2007. Thea Mohr and Jampa Tsedroen (eds.), *Dignity & Discipline: Reviving Full Ordination for Buddhist Nuns* (Boston: Wisdom Publications, 2010).

rights – being applied to a religious law code, the *Vinaya*, and to the historical decision-making processes within the religion that have resulted in the exclusion of women from ordination.

Since 1987, Sākyadhitā International Association of Buddhist Women has campaigned continuously for gender equity, especially with respect to education and ordination. Inspired by Sākyadhitā's Biennial International Conferences and grassroots social activism, Buddhist women have begun to work toward making full ordination available in all Buddhist traditions. The first breakthrough came in 1988 when the Nepalese nun Dhammavati and two of her disciples received full bhikṣuṇī ordination in a ceremony conducted at Hsi Lai Temple in Los Angeles.[11] The second breakthrough came in 1996 when Kusuma Devendra and nine nuns from Sri Lanka became bhikṣuṇīs at a ceremony conducted in Sarnath, India.[12] Another twenty Sri Lankan nuns received full ordination in 1996 at a ceremony conducted in Bodhgaya, India. Since then, Sri Lankan bhikṣus have presided over numerous full ordination ceremonies for hundreds of Sri Lankan nuns. Nuns from Burma, Indonesia, Thailand, and other countries have also been ordained in these ceremonies.

There has also been some progress toward achieving full ordination for women in the Tibetan tradition. His Holiness the Fourteenth Dalai Lama has repeatedly expressed his support for the full ordination for women, but states that such a decision must be made by a council of senior bhikṣus and cannot be taken by him alone. Senior Western bhikṣuṇīs practicing in the Tibetan tradition have formed a Committee of Western Nuns to research ways to institute the bhikṣuṇī lineage and to answer the objections of those who oppose it. These nuns have traveled to Hong Kong, Korea, and Taiwan to receive full ordination, but are concerned to open up opportunities for nuns of the Tibetan tradition, who may find it difficult to travel to foreign countries.

The reluctance to institute bhikṣuṇī ordination in the Tibetan tradition revolves primarily around two issues. The first issue concerns the origins of the bhikṣuṇī lineage practiced in China, Korea, Taiwan, and Vietnam, and whether the lineage has been transmitted uninterruptedly

11 Dhammavati's story is told in Sarah LeVine and David N. Gellner, *Rebuilding Buddhism: The Theravada Movement in Twentieth-Century Nepal* (Cambridge: Harvard University Press, 2005), 76–85.

12 These ordinations are described in Ranjani De Silva, "Reclaiming the Robe: Reviving the Bhikkhuni Order in Sri Lanka" in Karma Lekshe Tsomo (ed.), *Buddhist Women and Social Justice* (Albany: State University of New York Press, 2004), 119–35; and Yuchen Li, "Ordination, Legitimacy, and Sisterhood: The International Full Ordination Ceremony in Bodhgaya" in *Innovative Buddhist Women*, 168–98.

since the time of Mahāprajāpatī. This objection has now been resolved by producing a text that documents the unbroken continuity of the Chinese bhikṣuṇī lineage. The second issue concerns the method of conducting the full ordination in traditions that have no living bhikṣuṇī lineage. The Theravāda[13] and Tibetan Buddhist traditions have preserved the bhikṣuṇīs *Vinaya* texts, but do not have living bhikṣuṇīs in their own traditions to conduct ordinations. Therefore, the question is which method of conducting the bhikṣuṇī ordination is preferable and most likely to be considered valid: (1) by bhikṣus alone; (2) by bhikṣus and bhikṣuṇīs who all belong to the Chinese, Korean, or Vietnamese traditions; or (3) by bhikṣus and bhikṣuṇīs who belong to different *Vinaya* traditions (e.g., Tibetan bhikṣus together with bhikṣuṇīs ordained in the Chinese, Korean, or Vietnamese traditions). The third procedure was used to restore the bhikṣuṇī saṅgha in Sri Lanka, with subsequent ordinations conducted by Sri Lankan bhikṣus and bhikṣuṇīs.

Karma and Gender Justice in Historical Perspective

Both Buddhists and feminists around the world have taken an active interest in finding an equitable solution to this dilemma. Buddhists often claim that women and men have equal opportunities to achieve liberation, but the lack of equal opportunities for women to receive full ordination throughout much of Buddhist history up to today contradicts this claim. Buddhist societies are now moving gradually toward greater gender equity, at least in the secular sphere. Marriage and monastery are no longer the only two options for women and religious institutions are no longer the undisputed sources of moral authority. Although Buddhist traditions continue to provide systems of value and meaning for women, Buddhist institutions will go down on the wrong side of history if they do not begin to address issues of gender discrimination. As long as women lack access to full ordination, they lack the optimal conditions for fulfilling their ultimate potential. To paraphrase the rallying call, as long as a Buddhist woman anywhere is deprived, all Buddhist women are deprived. To bring social practice into line with the expressed goal of liberation for all, Buddhists have no choice but to work for women's religious rights and gender equity, beginning with their own traditions. One potential starting point would be to reconsider

[13] The Theravāda tradition relies on the Pāli canon. Theravāda Buddhist countries include Burma, Cambodia, Laos, Thailand, and Sri Lanka. Theravāda communities are also found in Bangladesh, China, India, Indonesia, Malaysia, Nepal, and Vietnam.

the theory of karma and its relation to gender discrimination. If karma plays forward as well as from the past to the present, then all "sons and daughters of good families" ought to be concerned to ensure that human beings of all genders are treated justly, especially in their efforts to achieve the highest goal of enlightenment.

CHAPTER 20

Buddhism and Constitutions in Bhutan

Richard W. Whitecross

Introduction

The subject of Buddhism and constitutionalism, or more specifically constitutions, presents us with a series of questions and challenges. As the other essays in this volume demonstrate, Buddhism adapted itself to the local cultures and polities it encountered as it spread to the north and east from India. So what we mean or understand by the term "Buddhism" is problematic when generalized across South, Southeast, Central, and East Asia. Equally, how are we to define "constitution"? Are we looking for a written constitution, such as in Thailand, or one based on custom and rules that constitute, as in the United Kingdom, an unwritten constitution? We generally understand constitutions as enabling people – citizens – to act and participate in a political system by defining how they can participate and how decisions are made. Typically, constitutions set out laws that are constitutive and laws that are regulative in nature. I understand constitutions as defining the basic powers of a government, and their limits, and the relationship between a government and its citizens, while recognizing that the term "constitution" has no equivalent in Tibet or Bhutan prior to the creation of written constitutions in the second half of the twentieth century.

This chapter will focus on Bhutan, a small landlocked kingdom located in the eastern Himalaya that has sought to balance its traditional values informed by Buddhist teachings with major political and social change. The interrelationship between Buddhism and constitutions has been particularly significant in Bhutan, which moved from an unwritten constitution to a written constitution on July 18, 2008. Central to the constitution enacted in July 2008 are the concepts of a Buddhist monarchy and Gross National Happiness (GNH). For the first time since the unification of Bhutan in the seventeenth century CE, the state-sponsored Central Monk Body has been excluded from the legislature. Moreover, the constitution takes care not to declare Buddhism the official religion of Bhutan. In this, Bhutan mirrors other Buddhist nations, for example, Thailand.[1] The creation and enactment of a written constitution in 2008 highlights the problem of untwining the interrelationship between the religious and secular systems. This chapter suggests that, in the Bhutanese context, it is important not to lose sight of how deeply held values – for example, those held by the individual constitutional drafting committee members – have shaped and defined the constitution.

When the Bhutanese constitution was being drafted, the drafting committee carefully scrutinized those of other countries, and the shape and tenor of the finalized constitution locates it firmly within an international framework underpinned since the mid-1990s by an emphasis on establishing the "rule of law." First, I contextualize the Bhutanese constitution in relation to "constitutions" within the wider Himalayan context. The next section examines the process by which the Bhutanese constitution was created and reflects on how the constitutional drafting committee re-imagined the relationship between law, politics, and religion. The drafting committee members were sensitive to the importance of Buddhism to Bhutan's history and identity. However, a clear separation of powers emerges, underscored by the removal of Buddhist monastic representatives from the legislature.[2] I conclude that the constitution-making process in Bhutan represents a major shift in sovereignty and power, and the firm establishment of the rule of law. The constitution of Bhutan sets out the foundational principles for the newly emerged democratic, constitutional monarchy, which embodies and represents the Buddhist heritage of the kingdom.

Buddhism, the State, and Constitutions: An Overview

In an article on early Buddhist views of the state, Gokhale argues that the Buddhist view of the state, an important consideration when examining the relationship between Buddhism and constitutions, underwent three distinct phases.[3] Initially, as illustrated by the life of the historical Buddha,

[1] See Schonthal in this volume page for a discussion of the ambiguous relationship between Buddhism and the state in Sri Lanka.

[2] The removal of monastic representation in the legislature is significant. Since the mid-1990s there has been a conscious move to locate Bhutanese law and the operation of justice in Bhutan within the context of Bhutan's Buddhist heritage. See Richard Whitecross, "'Keeping the Stream of Justice Pure': The Buddhicisation of Bhutanese Law?" in F. Benda Beckman, K. Benda Beckman, and A. Griffiths (eds.), *Law and Anthropology in a Trans-national World* (Oxford: Berghahn Press, 2009), 199–215.

[3] Balkrishna G. Gokhale, "The Early Buddhist View of the State," *Journal of the American Oriental Society* 89 (1969), 731–38.

royal support was a key factor for the spread of Buddhism in India. The example of powerful kings such as Bimbisāra and Ajātasattu of Magadha, who were supporters of the Buddha, and later the major role of promoting Buddhism attributed to Aśoka, demonstrate the important relationship between early Buddhist communities and local rulers. However, differences arose, and Gokhale argues that the second phase was characterized by a theory of two equal spheres of life: one that was based on *dhamma* (Pāli), understood to mean "righteousness" and equated with impartiality and justice, and the other on *āṇā* (Pāli), which refers to authority or command.

According to Gokhale, Buddhist texts present a paradox in relation to the state. On the one hand, they stress the importance of an orderly human society. The texts indicate that the Buddha himself would, using his authority *(āṇā)*, amend the *Vinaya* rules applying to his followers when necessary, to avoid offending local rulers. However, fearing potential abuse by the state, the texts assert the supremacy of the dhamma. The ideal of the state becomes a vehicle through which dhamma not only contains the power of the state, but also regulates its behavior. In effect, the state becomes an ethical institution drawing its authority from the dhamma and guided by the *saṅgha*.

Of course, how this relationship between dhamma and *āṇā* manifested across Buddhist polities reflected local political and cultural conditions. In the Himalayan region, the intertwining of spiritual and secular authority created a theory of governance known as the dual system (*chos srid gnyis* or *chos srid zung 'brel*).[4] How the dual system was understood and operated varied across the Himalayas. The turbulent religious and political histories of the region illustrate the tensions between creating a state founded on religious and ethical principles and the realpolitik of maintaining effective political power. While law codes illustrate the operation of each regime and how they secured their legitimacy, it is in the monasteries that we find *bca'yig*, texts that are more recognizable to us as written "constitutions."

[4] See John Ardussi, "Formation of the State of Bhutan ('Brug gzhung) in the 17th Century and its Tibetan Antecedents," *Journal of Bhutan Studies* 11 (2004), 10–32. The dual system as a concept appears to have emerged by the late twelfth century as Ardussi notes reference to Tibetan sources on the early Tibetan monarchy. The terms mean "the religious and secular system" or "combination of religious and secular systems." See Melvyn C. Goldstein, T.N. Shelling, and J.T. Surkhang, *The New Tibetan–English Dictionary of Modern Tibetan* (Berkeley: University of California Press, 2001), 379.

In Tibet, as well as Bhutan, most monasteries had *bca'yig*, which is a charter, constitution, or legal document that sets out the basic principles, institutions, roles, and rules governing the organization and the operation of monastic communities.[5] Based on his comparison of fifty-one monastic constitutions written between the fifteenth and twentieth centuries, Ellingson argues that there are essentially three sources for monastic constitutions: historical precedent (drawn from the *arthaśāstra* literature),[6] texts prepared by a specific authority for the monastery, and monastic constitutions based on the *Vinaya* texts.[7] While the monastic constitutions provide interesting information about the administration of the monasteries, they do not define the powers of government nor the relationship between the government and its subjects.

Goldstein notes that "Tibetan politics traditionally was the prerogative of a tiny elite of lay (aristocratic) and monk officials. There was no notion of popular democracy – no political parties and no freedom of political expression . . . Tibet's traditional political ideology was simple and straightforward: the work of governing was not the concern of its subjects."[8] However, following the signing of the Seventeen-Point Agreement between the Peoples' Liberation Army of China and the Tibetan Government in 1951, a non-elite political organization emerged, the People's Association, with the purpose of influencing politics.[9]

The People's Association marked a major change in Tibetan politics, one that illustrated the need for political change. In March 1963, the Tibetan Government-in-Exile promulgated the Constitution of Tibet. Before 1963, the Ganden Podrang government of the Dalai Lamas operated under an unwritten constitution in the sense that there was a structure of government and law codes, which together defined the basic powers of the

5 See José Cabezón, "The Regulations of a Monastery" in D. Lopez (ed.), *Religions of Tibet in Practice* (Princeton, NJ: Princeton University Press, 1997), 335–51. Cabezón describes *bca'yig* as a genre of Tibetan literature that "deal with the rules and regulations of particular monastic institutions" (337).

6 See Roger Boesche, "Kautilya's *Arthaśāstra* on War and Diplomacy in Ancient India," *Journal of Military History* 67 (2003), 9–37. Written about 300 BCE, Kautilya's *Arthaśāstra* was a science of politics intended to "teach a wise king how to govern" (9). Kautilya was the key adviser to the Indian king Chandragupta Maurya (c. 317–293 BCE), founder of the Mauryan Empire in the Indian subcontinent.

7 Ter Ellingson, "Tibetan Monastic Constitutions: The Bca' yig" in Lawrence Epstein and Richard F. Sherburne (eds.), *Reflections on Tibetan Culture: Essays in Memory of Turrel V. Wylie* (Lewiston, NY: E. Mellen Press, 1990), 205–30.

8 Melvyn C. Goldstein, *A History of Modern Tibet: The Calm before the Storm, 1951–1955* (Berkeley: University of California Press, 2007), 314.

9 *Ibid.*

government, even if it was silent on the relationship between government and its subjects.[10]

In the foreword to the 1963 Constitution, the Dalai Lama states that even before he left Tibet in March 1959, he had come to the "conclusion that in the changing circumstances of the modern world the system of governance in Tibet must be so modified and amended as to allow the elected representatives of the people to play a more effective role in guiding and shaping the social and economic policies of the State."[11] The Dalai Lama set out the principles for a draft constitution in October 1961. There followed a period of public consultation with the representatives of the Tibetan exiles, both "lay and religious," during which the details of the constitution were prepared.

The 1963 Constitution of Tibet (*Bod kyi rtsa khrims*) consists of ten chapters with a closing epilogue totalling eighty-six pages. The constitution begins by setting out the fundamental rights and duties of Tibetan citizens before enumerating the directive principles of the Tibetan state (Government-in-Exile). The principles include the provision of social welfare, the promotion of education, and health care. The constitution delineated the roles of the executive, legislature, and judiciary, reflecting the "ideas and ideals of the modern world."[12] We are advised by the Dalai Lama that the constitution similarly "takes into consideration the doctrines enunciated by Lord Buddha, the spiritual and temporal heritage of Tibet."[13] These claims are not specifically explored in either the foreword or in the accompanying text. However, the terms of the foreword to the 1963 Constitution are reminiscent of similar statements found in the preface to the Bhutanese Supreme Law Code, the first modern law code, enacted by the National Assembly of Bhutan in 1958. Chapter Two of the 1963 Constitution outlines the fundamental rights and duties of "all Tibetans." Article 8 states that all Tibetans "shall be equal before the law . . . without discrimination on any ground such as sex, race, language, religion, social origin, property, birth or other status." The subsequent articles confirm the right to life, liberty, and property together with freedom from inhumane treatment, torture, slavery, and forced labor. Article 20 confirms the right to vote for all Tibetans over the age of eighteen.[14] The 1963 Constitution reflects a "distinctive modern political environment" created, for

[10] Rebecca Redwood French, *The Golden Yoke: The Legal Cosmology of Buddhist Tibet* (Ithaca, NY: Cornell University Press, 1995).

[11] Tibetan Government-in-Exile, *Bod kyi rtsa khrims* (Constitution of Tibet) (Calcutta: no publisher, 1963), v.

[12] *Ibid.* [13] *Ibid.* [14] *Ibid.*, 8.

example, by the Universal Declaration of Human Rights, which emerged in the exile community.[15] The emphasis on equality of status and a vision of a united Tibet demonstrate this new political culture. The constitution's underlying rationale is less a matter of condensing Buddhist doctrine than of emphasizing the importance of the rule of law.

Turning to the structure of the Tibetan Government-in-Exile, the executive powers of the state are vested in the Dalai Lama. While the Dalai Lama provides a unifying symbol in exile, the constitution notably makes no specific reservations for monastic representatives on the Kashag (Cabinet). An Ecclesiastical Council of five representatives appointed by the Dalai Lama is responsible for the affairs of all "monasteries and religious institutions in the State under the direct authority of His Holiness the Dalai Lama."[16] In exile, the Tibetan government could no longer only support the Gelugpa religious establishments, and thus the Kagyupa, Sakyapa, Nyingmapa, and Bonpo sects were also represented. The 1963 Constitution appears to maintain the separation of secular and religious affairs, which was a feature of the Ganden Podrang system of government. However, in the composition of the National Assembly, the elected legislative body, seventy-five percent of the members were to be elected directly by the people, ten percent elected by the regional and district councils, five percent appointed directly by the Dalai Lama, and the remaining ten percent elected by the "monasteries and other religious institutions."[17] The next section examines the political and legal development of Tibet's southern neighbor Bhutan from the seventeenth century. As Bhutan emerged from its political isolation in the mid-twentieth century, Tibet lost its independence. The Bhutanese state gradually transformed from an absolute to a constitutional monarchy with a democratically elected parliament. Enshrined in the 2008 Constitution is a key concept that seeks to inform and shape governance in Bhutan: Gross National Happiness.

From "Religious Estate" to Monarchy: Seventeenth to Twentieth Centuries

In 1616, the Zhabdrung,[18] Ngawang Namgyal (1597–1651), a religious hierarch of the Drukpa Kagyu sect of Tibetan Buddhism, fled from Ralung

[15] Ronald D. Schwartz, "Renewal and Resistance: Tibetan Buddhism in the Modern Era," in Ian Harris (ed.), *Buddhism and Politics in Twentieth-Century Asia* (London: Continuum, 1999), 235.
[16] Constitution of Tibet, Article 37(1), 1963: 17.
[17] Constitution of Tibet, Article 39(1)(b), 1963: 18.
[18] *Zhabs drung* (Tibetan/Dzongkha) is an honorific title. It is also spelled Shabdrung.

monastery in south-central Tibet to western Bhutan where he began to create a "religious estate."[19] Tsang Khanchen, the Zhabdrung's biographer, describes the Zhabdrung's intention of creating a new state based on religious laws, as well as the legends and laws of the early Tibetan monarchy. These sources provided "a vocabulary of religious purpose and governing process."[20] Above all, Tsang Khachen states that the Zhabdrung created the "new state for the welfare of its sentient inhabitants."[21]

The Zhabdrung's vision was based on the concept of the dual system that was widespread across the Himalayan region, notably the Ganden Podrang system of the Dalai Lamas in central Tibet. Under the Ganden Podrang model, the ecclesiastical and secular authorities were separate. In Bhutan, there was no clear distinction between religious and secular authority. The Zhabdrung and his reincarnations were the pinnacle of the government. The *Desi*, a subordinate role adapted from Tibetan practice, was responsible for the civil administration of the Drukpa state that emerged during the early seventeenth century, assisted by three regional governors.[22] These lay officials typically assumed a semi-monastic character by taking basic monastic vows.

Although there was no formal written constitution, the Zhabdrung's vision for the governance of Bhutan was intimately linked with the Druk Kagyu tradition. According to the *Lo rgyus*, a chronicle written in the mid-seventeenth century, a key concern for the system of governance established by the Zhabdrung was "upholding, guarding and diffusing the Precious Teachings [of the Buddha] by means of the Dual System . . . Thereafter, if there is no law, happiness will not come to beings."[23] This concern with the happiness and well being of the people is further developed when the writer notes that "in all the broad realms of the subjects and their communities the abundant enjoyment of food and wealth increased and . . . there was an absence of strife."[24] From the perspective of the Bhutanese state, secular and religious laws were intermingled as the "golden yoke of secular law administered according to religious principles . . . devoid of partiality."[25] This system of government continued until the early twentieth century, despite the regional rivalries that emerged in the nineteenth century. A political vacuum appeared in Bhutan when Zhabdrung Jigme Chogyel

[19] Michael Aris, *Sources for the History of Bhutan* (Vienna: Arbeitkreis fur Tibetische und Buddhistische Studien Universitat Wien, 1986), 129.
[20] Ardussi, *Formation of the State of Bhutan*, 16. [21] *Ibid.*, 17.
[22] *sDe srid.* (Tibetan/Dzongkha). [23] Aris, *Sources for the History of Bhutan*, 111–13.
[24] *Ibid.*, 113. [25] *Ibid.*

died in 1904 and the fifty-sixth *Desi*, Yeshe Ngodrup, retired in 1905. The absence of both a religious and secular head of state threatened the stability of the country and paved the way for the election of Ugyen Wangchuck as hereditary monarch in 1907.

Modernization and Decentralization: Bhutan in the Twentieth Century

In 1907, the State Council unanimously elected Ugyen Wangchuck (1907–22) the new hereditary King of Bhutan. His son, the second king, Jigme Wangchuck (1922–52) reformed and centralized the administrative system during the 1930s and 1940s. While the administrative structures of the dual system remained in place, it was recognized that the strife of the nineteenth century stemmed from the lack of effective control. The reigns of the first two kings witnessed the consolidation of royal authority in Bhutan. The transition from the dual system to the monarchy perpetuated the structures of the Zhabdrung's government, and as Aris comments, "the state is still today presented as the church triumphant under the motto 'the Glorious Drukpa Victorious in All Directions.'"[26]

Jigme Dorji Wangchuck (1952–72), the third king, embarked on a major series of reforms of the existing Bhutanese administrative and political system. Among the first acts were the creation of a National Assembly and the abolition of various categories of serfs and slaves in Bhutan. This was carried out in tandem with a policy of land reallocation to the newly freed serfs and slaves, which may have been nearly ten percent of the population, and a re-evaluation of the landholding system. The broader reforms over the next two decades focused on the construction of infrastructure with the assistance and aid of the Indian government.

The third king refined the changes made to the central bureaucracy, which oversaw the wider structural changes in government. New ministries and governmental departments were created and a centralized bureaucracy emerged that offered places for the formally educated Bhutanese. Aspects of the former system remained in evidence, but with the separation of the judiciary under the High Court in 1968, the district officers relinquished their roles as dispensers of justice. Local government continued to draw on pre-existing forms; however, the villages were reorganized into

[26] Michael Aris, "Conflict and Conciliation in Traditional Bhutan" in Michael Hutt (ed.), *Bhutan: Perspectives on Conflict and Dissent* (Gartmore: Kiscadale, 1994), 21–42, 24.

gewog (village block) under the supervision of a *gup* (village headman) and eventually, once membership of the National Assembly was reorganized in the 1960s, the *gewog* were represented by *chimi* (representatives).

A major dimension of this period was the move to break Bhutan's isolation from the international political scene. Bhutan began to cultivate relations in the South Asia region and joined the Colombo Plan in 1962. However, the acceptance to join the United Nations in 1971 was undoubtedly the most significant achievement in terms of marking Bhutan's independence and sovereignty.[27] The sudden death of the third king in 1972 led to the ascension of his son, Jigme Singye Wangchuck (1972–2006), as the fourth king.[28] During the period of direct royal rule (1972–98), two new institutions were created by the fourth king to decentralize the decision-making process: the Dzongkhag Yargye Tshogchung (DYT) (District Development Committees) and the Gewog Yargye Tshogchung (GYT) (Village Block Development Committees).

A DYT was established in each of the twenty districts (*dzongkhag*) between 1976 and 1981. The creation of this new tier of administration reflected the fourth king's plans to begin the process of political and administrative decentralization.[29] The DYT are responsible for developing and implementing development activities in their areas, and their creation delegated these tasks from the central government to each district. In addition to placing responsibility for development at a district level, the DYT offered the local people an opportunity to participate in the planning process.

In 1991, the king, building on the model of the DYT, instituted a third level of administration by setting up a GYT in every village block (*gewog*) across Bhutan. The promotion of the GYT was to generate at the lowest level a sense of participation in local decisions. The GYT are composed of village elders with the *gup* acting as chairman. When the GYT was created in 1991, the *gup* and his staff were elected once every three years by representatives from each household in the *gewog*. However, the methods for election varied across *gewog* and from election to election. A new GYT Act in 2002 radically transformed the method for electing

[27] Under the terms of the Bhutan-India Friendship Treaty of 1949, Bhutan was recognized as an independent country. However, its foreign policy was conducted in consultation with India. This was amended in 2007.

[28] The fourth king abdicated in favor of the Crown Prince in December 2006.

[29] Karma Ura, "Decentralisation and Development in Medieval and Modern Bhutan" in Michael Aris and Michael Hutt (eds.), *Bhutan: Aspects of Culture and Development* (Gartmore: Kiscadale Asia Research Series No.5, 1994), 40.

gups at the *gewog* level. A royal edict issued by the king stated that in the future, all elections for *gup* must be subject to a secret ballot. The first universal suffrage elections at *gewog* level were accordingly held in November 2002. The 2002 *gup* elections were the first experience for Bhutanese with secret ballots and elections among competing candidates, and they were a major political landmark. Elections took place in 199 of the 201 *gewogs*.

The momentum of political, social, and economic change increased sharply during the 1980s and 1990s. Aspects of the changes taking place caused concern that distinct Bhutanese values, traditions, and identity would be lost in the face of these changes and the challenges they created. In the mid-1980s, the government emphasized the importance of Bhutanese culture and traditions, and in 1989 a royal edict re-emphasized a code of etiquette (*driglam namzha*), notably by requiring the wearing of traditional forms of dress. These policies created tensions with the Lhotshampa, the descendants of Nepalese migrants, as well as more recent migrants from Nepal, over a range of citizenship and cultural identity issues. This led to a series of violent clashes with government forces in the early 1990s, which forced about 90,000 Lhotshampa into exile.[30]

At the same time, there was a gradual articulation of a concept that defined the fourth king's vision for Bhutan: Gross National Happiness. The guiding principle of Gross National Happiness is "to maintain a balance between material progress and spiritual well-being."[31] Concerned about the impact of changes occurring in Bhutan, the king argued that Bhutan should seek to develop in a way that reflected its culture, institutions, and spiritual values. Gradually, four pillars were identified as key to GNH: economic development, environmental conservation, cultural preservation, and good governance. Reforms introduced during the 1990s focused on developing and strengthening good governance in Bhutan. Central to the reforms was a focus on the "rule of law." The Chief Justice of the High Court, Lyonpo Sonam Tobgaye appointed in 1992, began a major program of judicial reforms.[32] At the annual judicial conference in

[30] See Michael Hutt, *Unbecoming Citizens: Culture, Nationhood, and the Flight of Refugees from Bhutan* (Delhi: Oxford University Press, 2003).

[31] Lungten Dubgyur, "Law, Justice and Gross National Happiness," *The Parasol of Silken Knot* (Thimphu: High Court of Justice, 2005), 141–54, quote 143.

[32] Alessandro Simoni and Richard Whitecross, "'Gross National Happiness' and the 'Heavenly Stream of Justice': Modernisation and Dispute Resolution in the Kingdom of Bhutan," *American Journal of Comparative Law* 1 (2007), 165–95.

2002, the fourth king emphasized that the average Bhutanese citizen had two essential needs: "health and justice. People need good doctors and medicine when they are ill and they need justice when they are wronged. Governance is good when laws are good and there is justice."[33] As noted earlier, the structures of the dual system established by the Zhabdrung remained in place, although as a school textbook notes, "with the creation of the hereditary monarchy, there was no longer a dual authority in the administration of the state."[34] The same textbook states that the "monastic establishment does not form part of the political structure of Bhutan,"[35] yet when describing the executive and the legislature, it unquestioningly notes monastic representation on the Royal Advisory Council and in the National Assembly. Presenting the monastic body as separate from the political/secular administration of Bhutan was in tension with the role of monks in these administrative bodies, which was restricted to advising on religious matters only. This appears to reflect the third phase outlined by Gokhale[36] in which the state becomes an ethical institution drawing its authority from the dhamma and guided by the saṅgha. This was expressed in a major policy document issued by the Royal Government in 1999, which noted "the importance of the Buddhist tradition . . . recognized in the provision for the guaranteed representation of the monastic establishment in the National Assembly, in the Royal Advisory Council and the Cabinet."[37]

Toward a Written Constitution: From Royal Decree to Royal Enactment

In June 1998, direct royal rule ended by royal decree and a Cabinet of Ministers was appointed. In September 2001, it was announced that a written constitution would be drafted for the country. A drafting committee of thirty-nine members was established under the chairmanship of the Chief Justice. The committee was drawn from a broad cross-section of Bhutanese society and included two representatives of the Central Monk Body,[38] two additional monastic representatives, and one Lhotshampa

[33] Dubgyur, "Law, Justice and Gross National Happiness," 143.

[34] Royal Government of Bhutan, *Bhutan Civics* (Thimphu: Ministry of Education, 1999), 75.

[35] *Ibid.* [36] Gokhale, *Early Buddhist Views of the State.*

[37] Planning Commission, *Bhutan 2020 – A Vision for Peace, Prosperity and Happiness* (Bangkok: Keen Publishing Thailand Co. Ltd, 1999), 76.

[38] The Central Monk Body (*gZhung grwa-tshang*) refers to the monastic body of approximately 600 monks supported by the state.

member. The Chairman, writing in his personal diary in September 2002, expressed his hope that:

> With blessings from the Almighty [*Buddha*], combined with human efforts and sincerity for greater future of Bhutan, I pray that this Constitution will usher in the maintenance of constitutional monarchy for unity . . . and prosperous nation imbedded in Buddhist values. Through this Constitution, I pray that Bhutan shall be a leader in the Buddhist world and a shining example of living and working democracy with enjoyment of liberty, freedom and rights.[39]

A draft constitution, which balanced the transformation of governance in Bhutan with its Buddhist heritage and the monarchy, was prepared during a series of meetings over three years. Numerous international organizations were invited to comment on the draft constitution, notably the United Nations office. One paper submitted to the Chairman noted that

> the present draft is not just a copy of recent constitutions, but blends in a fascinating way "imports" from other constitutions with solutions that are adapted to the specific needs and the specific context of the country. The drafters . . . must be commended for their very innovative and independent approach to constitution making against the background of a traditional (feudal) and strongly Buddhist society. One certainly has to take into account the unique location, history and culture of Bhutan when looking in the draft Constitution.[40]

After undergoing several rounds of revisions, the draft constitution was published on March 26, 2005. The drafting committee held public meetings across all twenty districts with government officials, the king, and the crown prince in attendance. Of the many concerns and key issues addressed was the need to simplify the Dzongkha text of the draft constitution, which ordinary people could not understand. The constitution underwent various revisions before being officially enacted by the fifth king, Jigme Khesar Namgyel Wangchuck, on July 18, 2008 during a ceremony in Thimphu. Consisting of thirty-five articles and four schedules, the 2008 Constitution primarily focuses on the new form of government being established (Articles 10–35). Articles 1–9 cover the monarchy, spiritual heritage, culture, the environment, citizenship (Art. 6), fundamental rights and duties (Arts. 7–8), and finally, the principles of the state (Art. 9).

[39] Lyonpo Sonam Tobgye, personal diary, September 2002 cited by Lungten Dubgyur, unpublished paper, "The Making of Bhutan's Constitution," 17.

[40] *Ibid.*, 12–13.

Cover Image of Bhutanese Constitution Thimphu, Bhutan, 2008

The Constitution of Bhutan: The Dual System Transformed

The constitution begins with a preamble set within a mandala – an outer circle of flames, a *vajra* fence, and a mantra in the stylized Sanskrit script known as *Lentsa* with dharma wheels punctuating the mantras. The preamble declares:

> WE, the People of Bhutan:
>
> *Blessed with the luminous benedictions of the Triple Gem, the protection of our guardian deities, the wisdom of our leaders, the everlasting fortunes of the Pelden Drukpa, and the command of His Majesty the Druk Gyalpo, Jigme Khesar Namgyel Wangchuck;*
>
> *Solemnly pledging ourselves to strengthen the sovereignty of Bhutan, to secure the blessing of liberty, to ensure justice and tranquillity and to enhance the unity, happiness and wellbeing of the people for all time;*
>
> *Do hereby ordain and adopt this Constitution for the Kingdom of Bhutan on this Fifteenth Day of the Fifth Month of the Male Earth Rat Year corresponding to the Eighteenth Day of July, Two Thousand and Eight.*[41]

The declaration of "We, the People of Bhutan" underscores the vesting of legal sovereignty in the people. This phrase is reminiscent of the U.S. Constitution, but it is not immediately followed by "do hereby ordain and

[41] RGOB: 2008.

adopt this Constitution." Rather, the preamble acknowledges and invokes Bhutan's Buddhist heritage, mirroring Buddhist texts by beginning with the objects of refuge, the Three Jewels – the Buddha, the Dharma, and the Sangha – and adjuring the protection of guardian deities.

On the cover of the constitution is an image reminiscent of the royal and national insignia. Enclosed within a circle are two dragons facing each other, with a double *vajra* in a swirling hub representing the Four Noble Truths in the center of the circle resting on a lotus flower. At the apex of the image are the Three Jewels. Below the image, the Dzongkha proclaims, "The Glorious Drukpa Victorious in All Directions," a traditional motto or epithet for Bhutan. The preamble and the seal are highly significant. The image on the front cover and the mandala enclosing the preamble draw on familiar religious iconography, while the text of the preamble echoes traditional invocations and dedications found in other texts, including the first modern law code, the *Thrimszhung Chennmo*, often referred to as the "Supreme Laws," promulgated in 1958–59.[42]

Article 1 locates sovereignty in the people of Bhutan and declares the constitution to be the Supreme Law of Bhutan. While the constitution draws on the international discourses of rights and duties reflected in Articles 7 and 8, it redefines the dual system. Article 2(2) declares that, "The *Chhoe-sid-nyi* [the dual system] of Bhutan shall be unified in the person the Druk Gyalpo who as a Buddhist, shall uphold the *Chhoe-sid.*" Based on this article, it may be argued that the monarch is the embodiment of Buddhism in Bhutan. Article 3(1) acknowledges Buddhism as the "spiritual heritage of Bhutan" that "promotes the principles and values of peace, non-violence, compassion and tolerance." This declaration does not explicitly affirm Buddhism as the official religion of Bhutan. Rather, the monarch will protect all faiths and uphold their right to freedom of belief (Article 7[3]). However, there is a prohibition on proselytizing.

Article 3 on the "Spiritual Heritage" initially provoked calls for Buddhism to be declared the official religion of Bhutan. During public discussions in the capital in October 2005, speakers suggested that the spiritual heritage of Bhutan should be specifically described as "Drukpa Kagyu and Nyingma" rather than the more general, "Buddhism." Such statements reflect the fact that the majority of Bhutanese are members of these two sects of Buddhism. Other speakers argued that there should be no separation of religion and

[42] Richard Whitecross, "The *Thrimzhung Chenmo* and the Emergence of the Contemporary Bhutanese Legal System" in Karma Ura and Sonam Kinga (eds.), *The Spider and the Piglet: Collected Papers on Bhutanese Society* (Thimphu: Centre for Bhutan Studies, 2004), 355–79.

politics, "since Bhutan had prospered throughout history because of the harmony between religion and politics."[43]

However, the Chief Justice, when addressing the assembled people, advised that the drafting committee had sought to consider the long-term future of the constitution and decided that it was not appropriate to mention different sects. Furthermore, it was considered essential on reflection to separate "church from the state" to ensure that religion and politics "flourish without interference from each other."[44] As a concept, the separation of state and church is perhaps familiar to educated Bhutanese, many of whom have studied in India and may be aware of debates around secularism in India. However, for the majority of Bhutanese living in rural communities, secularism and the separation of "church and state" are unfamiliar concepts.

In early 2007, it was announced that lay monks (*gomchen*) and lay nuns (*anim*) would be permitted to vote, but members of the Central Monk Body would not be eligible to vote. In central and eastern Bhutan, the number of *gomchen* is large, with the majority of families having at least one *gomchen* who, in addition to working on the land, may also perform rituals for family and neighbors. Those not permitted to vote included 7,437 monks, 169 lamas, 1,539 lay monks and 88 lay nuns registered with the Monk Body. This, therefore, disenfranchised a significant number of men and women. The issue over the right of religious practitioners to participate in the elections was raised in June 2008. Section 181, chapter 10 of the Election Bill states that religion should remain above politics. The newly elected National Council representative, Tshewang Lhamo, spoke in favor of this clause on the grounds that "innocent villagers can be influenced by religious figures."[45] However, this was challenged by other representatives who argued that allowing members of the Central Monk Body to vote would not politicize the monastic community, provided monks did not stand in elections.

These arguments reveal tensions within Bhutan over the relationship between religion and politics. The Chief Election Commissioner stated that "when a common man becomes a monk he leaves all the worldly things. Religion and politics are two separate entities and we should not mix the two."[46] Yet, these arguments highlight the problems of untwining

[43] "A Constitution for the Future of Bhutan," *Kuensel*, (October 29, 2005). http://www.kuenselonline.com/modules.php?name=News&file=print&sid=6193 (last accessed July 21, 2012).

[44] *Ibid.* [45] *Ibid.* [46] *Ibid.*

the complex interrelationship between religion and the secular state that stemmed from the central role of Buddhism and the monastic body in the development of the Bhutanese state. Until very recently, the Bhutanese were not particularly concerned with articulating the relationship between religion and government. As with Tibet before 1959, there are no Bhutanese texts on legal, or more precisely, constitutional theory that examined and set out the balance between the sacred and the secular.[47] In seeking to separate the sacred from the secular, religion from politics, the Bhutanese Constitution has introduced a major transformation in the character of the Bhutanese state that may take several generations to become embedded and whose consequences cannot yet be predicted.

From interviews conducted with a wide range of Bhutanese, it was striking to note how few people commented on the removal of the Central Monk Body from the executive and legislature. Although concerns over the definition of religious practitioner continue to be expressed, the separation of religion and state appears to have been accepted by the majority of Bhutanese. This may reflect the indirect influence of students educated in India, where the secular nature of the Indian constitution and state is publicly discussed and debated. Also, general knowledge of Western legal and political traditions that set out the separation of powers and of religion from state should not be underestimated.

Under Article 9 the principles of state policy are set out. Of particular interest is Article 9 (2), which declares "the State shall strive to promote those conditions that will enable the successful pursuit of Gross National Happiness." Since the late 1990s, the concept of Gross National Happiness has been developing from an abstract concept into a guiding principle for government. Underlying this concept is an emphasis on self-sufficiency, a gradual approach to change and innovation, and deeply embedded Buddhist beliefs about the transitory nature of the world. This has been used to balance economic indicators with recognition of the spiritual and cultural values that have shaped Bhutanese society. These values have been challenged by the social and economic transformation of the country, especially from the late 1990s onward. More recently, GNH has become linked with environmental concerns that bring together Bhutanese concepts of sacred landscape and the increasing threat from climate change to the glacial lakes that could devastate the main valleys and human settlements.

[47] See Rebecca R. French, "A Conversation with Tibetans? Reconsidering the Relationship between Religious Beliefs and Secular Legal Discourse," *Law and Social Inquiry* 26 (2001), 95–112.

Conclusion

The development of the Bhutanese state since the 1950s reflects a transformation of the political and legal structures that were primarily established by the Zhabdrung in the mid-seventeenth century and later modified by the first two monarchs. The dual system may have since collapsed, but secular and spiritual authority is still shared between the monarch and the Je Khenpo.[48] Buddhism in Bhutan has never been persecuted as it was, for example, in China or Japan; however, just as there were tensions in Meiji Japan between the conservatives and those advocating change, so, too, similar tensions in contemporary Bhutan have appeared.[49] While some may not wish to promote Buddhism, it would be difficult to deny the central importance of Buddhism and its influence on Bhutanese social and cultural values. Nevertheless, the constitutional debates over the role of Buddhism as "the spiritual heritage" or the "official religion" of Bhutan and the removal of the Central Monk Body from the new political institutions mark a major transformation in the relationship between the secular authorities and the monastic establishment.

So, what does the 2008 Constitution reveal about Buddhism, Buddhist principles and values, and constitutionalism? The Bhutanese Constitution illustrates how Buddhist principles and values as understood by the constitutional drafters, government officials, and the people of Bhutan have been interpreted and incorporated into the legal text. They are not explicit, but like the Supreme Law Code enacted in 1958, the spirit of the constitution reflects how ordinary people, not Buddhist scholars, understand the essence of Buddhist teachings. Often this understanding is based on the teachings encountered in the home, village, and by attending religious events. There is an everyday quality to this understanding that makes it elusive and hard to articulate. Ask why a householder is making water offerings in the morning before leaving for work, and the response may be framed in terms of merit-making rather than cultivating *bodhicitta* through the act of giving.

Therefore, if we attempt to narrowly specify what is Buddhist and what is not, we can easily lose sight of how deeply held values shape and define worldviews. In the preparation of the constitution, key principles that reflect and embody Bhutanese values, such as Gross National Happiness and the monarchy, had to be enshrined. Similar to the Tibetan 1963

[48] Michael Aris, *The Raven Crown: The Origins of Buddhist Monarchy in Bhutan* (London: Serindia Press, 1998).

[49] James E. Ketelaar, *Of Heretics and Martyrs in Meiji Japan: Buddhism and Its Persecution* (Princeton, NJ: Princeton University Press, 1990).

Constitution, the Bhutanese Constitution is not an overtly "religious" document. Yet, Bhutanese point out that the fundamental rights, duties, and principles set out flow from Buddhist doctrine and teachings. This understanding reflects the influence of wider, non-local discourses that have aligned Buddhist principles and beliefs with modern rights-based legal and political language and practice.

A Selection of Readings

Aris, Michael. *The Raven Crown: The Origins of Buddhist Monarchy in Bhutan*. London: Serindia Press, 1994.

Atwood, Christopher P. *Encyclopedia of Mongolia and the Mongol Empire*. New York: Facts on File, 2001.

Barrett, Timothy H. *The Woman Who Discovered Printing*. New Haven: Yale University Press, 2008.

Bodiford, William M., ed. *Going Forth: Visions of Buddhist Vinaya*. Honolulu: University of Hawai'i Press, 2005.

Bodde, Derk and Clarence Morris. *Law in Imperial China*. Philadelphia: University of Pennsylvania Press, 1973.

Brook, Timothy. *The Troubled Empire: China in the Yuan and Ming Dynasties*. Cambridge, MA: Harvard University Press, 2010.

Brook, Timothy. *The Chinese State in Ming Society*. London: Routledge, 2005.

Bumbacher, Stephan Peter and Anne Heirman, eds. *The Spread of Buddhism*. Leiden and Boston: Brill, 2007.

Chakravarti, Uma. *The Social Dimensions of Early Buddhism*. Delhi: Oxford University Press, 1987.

Chatterjee, H.N. *The Law of Debt in Ancient India*. Calcutta: Sanskrit College, 1971.

Clarke, Shayne. *Family Matters in Indian Buddhist Monasticism*. Honolulu: University of Hawai'i Press, 2014.

Collins, Steve. *Nirvana and Other Buddhist Felicities: Utopias of the Pali Imaginaire*. Cambridge: Cambridge University Press, 1998.

Elverskog, Johan. *Our Great Qing: The Mongols, Buddhism, and the State in Late Imperial China*. Honolulu: University of Hawai'i Press, 2006.

Evers, Hans-Dieter. *Monks, Priests, and Peasants: A Study of Buddhism and Social Structure in Central Ceylon*. Leiden: E. J. Brill, 1973.

Faure, Bernard. *The Power of Denial: Buddhism, Purity and Gender*. Princeton, NJ: Princeton University Press, 2003.

French, Rebecca Redwood. *The Golden Yoke: The Legal Cosmology of Buddhist Tibet*. Ithaca, NY: Cornell University Press, 1995.

French, Rebecca Redwood. "A Conversation with Tibetans? Reconsidering the Relationship between Religious Beliefs and Secular Legal Discourse." *Law and Social Inquiry* 26.1 (2001), 95–112.

Gethin, Ruppert. *The Foundations of Buddhism*. Oxford and New York: Oxford University Press, 1998.

Goldstein, Melvyn C. *A History of Modern Tibet: Volume 2, The Calm before the Storm, 1951–1955*. Berkeley: University of California Press, 2007.

Goonasekera, Sunil. "The Descent of the Law." *Journal of the Royal Asiatic Society of Sri Lanka, New Series* 55 (2000), 179–188.

Groner, Paul. *Saichō: The Establishment of the Japanese Tendai School*. Honolulu: University of Hawai'i Press, 2000.

Gunawardana, R.A.L.H. *Robe and the Plough: Monasticism and Economic Interest in Early Medieval Sri Lanka*. Tucson, AZ: University of Arizona Press, 1979.

Hansen, Valerie. *Negotiating Daily Life in Traditional China: How Ordinary People Used Contracts, 600–1400*. New Haven and London: Yale University Press, 1995.

Harris, Ian Charles. *Buddhism, Power and Political Order*. London: Routledge, 2007.

Hinüber, Oskar von. "Buddhist Law According to the Theravāda-Vinaya: A Survey of Theory and Practice." *Journal of the International Association of Buddhist Studies* 18.1 (1995), 7–45.

Holt, John Clifford, Jonathan S. Walters, and Jacob N. Kinnard, eds. *Constituting Communities: Theravāda Buddhism and the Religious Cultures of South and Southeast Asia*. Albany: State University of New York Press, 2003.

Hur, Nam-lin. *Death and Social Order in Tokugawa: Buddhism, Anti-Christianity, and the Danka System*. Cambridge: Harvard University Asia Center, Harvard University Press, 2007.

Huxley, Andrew. "The Buddha and the Social Contract." *Journal of Indian Philosophy* 24 (1996), 407–20.

Huxley, Andrew. "Studying Theravāda Legal Literature." *Journal of the International Association of Buddhist Studies* 20.1 (1997), 63–91.

Huxley, Andrew. "Buddhism and Law – The View from Mandalay." *Journal of the International Association of Buddhist Studies* 18.1 (1995), 47–95.

Ishii, Yoneo. *Sangha, State, and Society*. Honolulu: University of Hawai'i Press, 1986.

Jackson, Peter A. *Buddhism, Legitimation, and Conflict: The Political Functions of Urban Thai Buddhism*. Reprint ed. Singapore: Institute of Southeast Asian Studies, 1989.

Kapstein, Matthew T. *The Tibetan Assimilation of Buddhism: Conversion, Contestation, and Memory*. Oxford and New York: Oxford University Press, 2002.

Kapstein, Matthew T. *The Tibetans*. Oxford: Wiley-Blackwell, 2006.

Katz, Paul R. *Divine Justice: Religion and the Development of Chinese Legal Culture*. Abingdon, Oxon: Routledge, 2009.

Kemper, Steven. "The Buddhist Monkhood, the Law, and the State in Colonial Sri Lanka." *Comparative Studies in Society and History* 26.3 (1984), 401–427.

Kieffer-Pülz, Petra. "Stretching the Vinaya Rules and Getting Away with It." *Journal of the Pali Text Society* 29 (2007), 1–51.

Kinnard, Jacob. *The Emergence of Buddhism: Classical Traditions in Contemporary Perspective*. Minneapolis: Fortress Press, 2010.

Lammerts, Dietrich Christian. "Buddhism and Written Law: Dhammasattha Manuscripts and Texts in Premodern Burma." Unpublished PhD diss., Cornell University, 2010.

Lingat, Robert. "Vinaya et droit laïque: Études sur les conflits de la loi religieuse et de la loi laïque dans l'Indochine hinayaniste." *Bulletin de l'École française d'Extrême-Orient* 37 (1937), 415–77.

Lingat, Robert. *The Classical Law of India*. Berkeley: University of California Press, 1973.

Loos, Tamara Lynn. *Subject Siam: Family, Law, and Colonial Modernity in Thailand*. Ithaca: Cornell University Press, 2006.

Malalgoda, Kitsiri. *Buddhism in Sinhalese Society*. Berkeley: University of California Press, 1976.

McKnight, Brian E. *The Quality of Mercy: Amnesties and Traditional Chinese Justice*. Honolulu: University of Hawaii Press, 1981.

Nathan, Mark A. "The Encounter of Buddhism and Law in Early Twentieth-Century Korea." *Journal of Law and Religion* 25.1 (2010), 1–32.

Olivelle, Patrick. *Dharmasūtras: The Law Codes of Āpastamba, Gautama, Baudhāyana, and Vasiṣṭha*. Oxford: Oxford University Press, 1999.

Ralapanawe, Mahinda. *Buddhist Temporalities Ordinance: Inception, Evolution, Present, Future*. Colombo: Sarasavi, 2011.

Reynolds, Frank. "The Two Wheels of Dhamma: A Study of Early Buddhism" in *The Two Wheels of Dhamma: Essays on the Theravada Tradition in India and Ceylon*, Gannanath Obeyesekere, Frank Reynolds, and Bardwell L. Smith, eds. Chambersburg, PA: American Academy of Religion, 1972.

Reynolds, Frank. "Buddhism and Law – Preface." *Journal of the International Association of Buddhist Studies* 18.1 (1995), 1–6.

Riazanovskii, V.A. *Fundamental Principles of Mongol Law*. Bloomington: Indiana University Press, 1965.

Roy, Kumkum. *The Emergence of Monarchy in North India, Eighth-Fourth Centuries BC, as Reflected in the Brahmanical Tradition*. Delhi: Oxford University Press, 1994.

Ruppert, Brian. *Jewel in the Ashes: Buddha Relics and Power in Early Medieval Japan*. Cambridge, MA: Harvard University Press, 2000.

Schaffer, Kurt. *The Culture of the Book in Tibet*, New York: Columbia University Press, 2004.

Schopen, Gregory. *Figments and Fragments of Māhāyana Buddhism in India: More Collected Papers*. University of Hawai'i Press, 2005.

Schopen, Gregory. *Buddhist Monks and Business Matters. Still More Papers on Monastic Buddhism in India*. Honolulu: University of Hawai'i Press, 2004.

Shaw, William. "The Neo-Confucian Revolution of Values in Early Yi Korea: Its Implications for Korean Legal Thought," in *Law and the State in Traditional East Asia*, Brian E. McKnight, ed. Honolulu: University of Hawaii Press, 1987.

Silk, Jonathan. *Managing Monks: Administrators and Administrative Roles in Indian Buddhist Monasticism*. Oxford and New York: Oxford University Press, 2008.

Singh, Upinder. *A History of Ancient and Early Medieval India*. Delhi: Pearson, 2008.

Sizemore, Russell F., and Donald K. Swearer, eds. *Ethics, Wealth, and Salvation: A Study in Buddhist Social Ethics*. Columbia: University of South Carolina Press, 1990.

Smith, Bardwell L., ed. *Religion and Legitimation of Power in Sri Lanka*. Chambersburg, PA: Anima Books, 1978.

Tambiah, Stanley Jeyaraja. *Buddhism Betrayed?: Religion, Politics and Violence in Sri Lanka*. Chicago: University of Chicago Press, 1992.

Tambiah, Stanley Jeyaraja. *World Conqueror and World Renouncer: A Study of Buddhism and Polity in Thailand against a Historical Background*. Cambridge and New York: Cambridge University Press, 1976.

Tsomo, Karma Lekshe, ed. *Buddhist Women and Social Justice: Ideals, Challenges, and Achievements*. Albany: State University of New York Press, 2004.

Vermeersch, Sem. *The Power of the Buddhas: The Politics of Buddhism during the Koryŏ Dynasty (918–1392)*. Cambridge, MA: Harvard University Asia Center, Harvard University Press, 2008.

Wallace, Vesna. "The Legalized Violence: Punitive Measures of Buddhist Khans in Mongolia," in *Buddhist Warfare*, Michael Jerryson and Mark Juergensmeyer, eds. Oxford and New York: Oxford University Press, 2010.

Walser, Joseph. *Nāgārjuna in Context: Mahāyāna Buddhism and early Indian Culture*. New York: Columbia University Press, 2005.

Walters, Jonathan S. *Finding Buddhists in Global History*. Washington, D.C.: American Historical Association, 1998.

Walters, Michael. *Buddhism and Empire: The Political and Religious Culture of Early Tibet*. Leiden: Brill, 2009.

Welch, Holmes. *The Practice of Chinese Buddhism*. Cambridge, MA: Harvard University Press, 1967.

Whitecross, Richard. "Separating Religion and Politics? Buddhism and the Bhutanese Constitution," in *Comparative Constitutionalism in South Asia*, Sunil Khilnani, Vikram Raghavan and Arun Thiruvengadam, eds. New York: Oxford University Press, 2013.

Yifa. *The Origins of Buddhist Monastic Codes in China*. Honolulu: University of Hawaii Press, 2002.

Index

abbot, 212, 217, 219–222, 225, 229, 252, 276, 277, 344
Abhayagiri, 118–120, 122, 139–141
Abhidharma, 9, 56, 63, 66, 84
accounting, 83, 220
adharma, 77
adjudication, 13, 138
Adolphson, Mikael, 279
adultery. *See* crime
Aggañña-sutta, 68–70
agriculture, 3, 38–40, 43, 45
alcohol. *See* crime
Allchin, F.R., 39, 42–43
amnesties, 263–264. *See also* pardons
Anāthapiṇḍika, 82
anātman, 334
animals
  and meat-eating, 288
  as a destination for rebirth, 289
  avoiding the killing or injuring of, 75
  buried with deceased noblemen, 323
  case of a fight between pet rat and pet squirrel, 174
  fines paid in, 325–326, 328, 331
  handling of as a profession, 44
  killing of as less serious than killing a human being, 339
  loans of, 312
  prohibition on the killing of, 122, 209, 263, 323
  religious ceremonies involving the slaughter of, 75
  ritual sacrifice of, 38–39, 75
  set free from captivity, 263
  the wearing or use of as a sign of good legal witness, 312
Āpastamba Dharmasūtra, 36
Aquinas, Thomas, 173
arbitrator, 155
Ardussi, John, 311
Aristotle, 173
Arthaśāstra, 123, 353. *See also dharmaśāstra*
Aśoka, King, 56, 145, 146, 293, 297, 300, 344
  inscriptions of, 33, 38, 41
authority, 10, 34–35, 153, 179, 209, 211, 284, 345, 360
  and responsibility, 331
  Buddha as a legal, 9, 65, 111, 352
  Buddhist sources for political legitimacy and, 151, 260, 268, 352, 360
  civil versus religious, 150
  colonial takeover of legal, 125
  compared to parents, 239
  consolidating royal, 256, 258, 357
  Daoist spiritual, 211
  for case decision is vision of a diety, 290
  from multiple legal sources, 183
  in *Arthaśāstra*, 37
  intertwining of spiritual and secular, 352
  limits of royal, over land grants to monasteries, 121
  lineage, of Japanese Buddhist schools, 282
  monastic *bca 'yig* as, 353
  moral. *See* ethics
  of Brahmin priests, 123
  of Buddha, as new claim to, 35
  of Dalai Lama, in current Tibetan constitution, 355
  of *dhammasatthas*, 191
  of legal transplants, 21
  of monks to influence state, 56, 119, 121
  of *saṅgha* to speak for Buddhism, 163, 164
  of *sūtras* as legal, 35
  of the Buddha as legal, 65
  of the state, to regulate Buddhism and monasteries, 120–121, 152, 164, 203, 206, 214, 271, 286, 325
  of *Vinaya Decisions* text in Burma, 184
  of *Vinaya* over laity, 23, 117
  ordination and registration, 242

authority (*cont.*)
over religious affairs, 252
relationship of religious and political claims to legal, 17, 150, 164, 189, 352, 356, 366
shifting boundaries over time between state and religious, 207
symbols of, 37
Vinaya as legal, 46, 179
violating monastic, 129, 143
wheel of, 144
women and *śudras* as, 36
autonomy
compromise of monastic, 207
of Buddhist monks and institutions, 163, 203, 205, 261
of foreign merchants, 205

Baizhang Huihai. *See* Pure Rules (*qinggui*)
Bangladesh, 167
Bareau, A., 104
Berman, Harold J., 15
Best, Jonathan, 258, 262, 267
bhikhuni-upasaya, 103
bhikkhunūpassaya, 103
bhikkhus
affected by caste in Sri Lanka, 130
as part of administrative bodies under the Buddhist Temporalitites Act, 132
Buddhist education provided by, 127
establishment of Theravāda monastic order in Sri Lanka by, 117
from Siam, 130
guilty of treason put to death, 122, 129–130
limitations of king's authority over, 120–121
mentioned in Kandyan Convention, 131
movement to counter moral decay in saṅgha by, 128
property of after death, 87
purification of the saṅgha by expelling, 121
state regulation of in contemporary Sri Lanka, 156
subject of the laws of the land in Sri Lanka, 122
suppression of on charges of heresy, 118–120
bhikṣu, 46, 342, 345–348
bhikṣuṇī, 10, 46, 99, 112, 342, 344–348
Bhikṣuṇī-vibhaṅga, 92–96, 97, 109, 110, 112, 114
Bhutan, 16, 24, 26–27, 311, **350–367**
Bimbisāra, King, 56, 73, 178–179, 352
Blackburn, Anne, 189
Bloch, Marc, 299
Bodhgayā, 31, 320
Bodhisattva, 14, 72, 123, 145, 289, 299, 308, 310, 322
Bogd Khaan State, 319, 329
Brahmā Net Sūtra (*Fan-wang jing*), 13, 275, 277, 289
Brahmanism, 5, 36, 71, 123
British, 131–132, 154, 157–158, 176, 181, 299, 305, 311, 315
Buddhaghosa, 11, 87, 137, 173–175, 176, 178–179, 190. *See also Samantapāsādikā*
buddhasāsana, 117–118, 121–122, 127, 137, 157, 161, 163
Buddhist Ecclesiastical Law, 157
Buddhist laws, colonial affects on, 181
Bühler, G., 101–102
Bureau of Religious Affairs, 246, 248–250
Burma, 11, 17, 18, 23, 25, 48, 151, 152, 153, 164, **167–182**, **183–197**, 345, 347, 348
Bu-ston, 94

cakkavatti, 144. *See also* cakravartin
cakravartin (wheel-turning king), 5, 70–76, 265, 300, 321, 327
Cambodia, 17, 53, 151, 153, 164, 167, 169–170, 181, 345
cases, 163, 187
activities of lawyers during, 170
appeals and reappeals of, 171
Buddha deciding, 9, 14
by famous Elder Godha, 56
chief monks serving as expert witnesses in, 157
contrasting legal sources for, 195
criminal, 328
definition of law as, 13–15
expulsion of a monk, 120
found in the Burmese Encyclopedia, 172
Greek ideas of equity in, 174
heard by a *Vinaya* jurist, 184
incorporation, 161–162
inheritance. *See* inheritance
involving nuns, 59
king using *Vinaya* in secular, 56
length of time affecting, 170
monks discussing legal, 143
of Ajjuka's legal advice to the laity, 176
of Buddhaghosa's notebook and the broken water jug, 178
of disrespecting a nun, 177
of Hpo Hlaing, 176–179
of monastic inheritance, 185
of monks deciding secular law, 56
of the stolen monk's head, 295
of the water snake and the fish, 73
of theft. *See* crime
on Bad Sex, The Twenty-seven, 168
on monastic succession and incumbency, 153

seeking protection of Buddhism, 162
status ranking in, 308
suits between cloisters in Japan, 283
Supreme Court, 160
Tibetan, 17
Vinaya, 8, 14, 25, 47, 50, 178
casuistry, 47, 49, 52, 54
causality, 3, 5, 262. *See also* cause and effect
cause and effect, 4, 334–340, 341. *See also* causality
celibacy, 204
Central Asia, 51, 167, 257, 307
Central Monk Body (Bhutan), 16, 350, 360, 366
chags rgya, 92–93, 95, 99. *See also* promissory notes
Chaisangsukkul, Pitinai, 169
Chakravarti, Uma, 42–45
Chan monastic codes, 12, 213, 284–285. *See also* Pure Rules
China, 6, 9, 12, 15–16, 22, 24, 25–26, 27, 48, 89, 167, **201–215**, **217–233**, **234–253**, 256–260, 262–263, 266, 267–268, 270, 271, 288, 292–297, 301, 306–307, 309, 311, 315–316, 318, 344–345, 347, 353, 366
Chinggis Khan, 24, 309, 320–321, 323
Chŏng, Ki-ung, 257, 262, 264–265
Christianity, 7, 15, 123–125, 131–132, 158, 160–161, 173, 214, 235, 290–294, 299
Cicero, 173
circumambulations, 325, 326
civil law, 53, 241, 243, 273, 300–301, 329, 332
civil rights, 243
coins, 32–33, 110
collateral, 106, 113–114
Collins, Steven, 72–73, 76
colonialism, 23, 25, 118, 121, 123, 125, 131–132, 154, 158–159, 168, 169–170, 181, 311
commentaries, 26, 123, 178
a *vṛtti* that looks like a *Vibhaṅga*, 97
and monastic inheritance, 191
as expressions of scholastic or commentarial ideals, 189
auto-commentary to Guṇaprabha's *Vinaya-sūtra*, 107
Burmese *nissaya* as, 191–193
case from the *Samantapāsādikā* used in Burmese judicial decisions, 176
classification of manuscripts as objects of veneration in, 186
discussion of theft in, 173
interpretation of the Buddha's rules in, 65
legal, 314
on causality, 5, 339
on Guṇaprabha's *Vinaya-sūtra*, 105
on the *Bhikṣuṇī-vibhaṅga*, 93
on the *Qing Code*, 237
on the sūtras, 66, 179
on the *Vinaya*, 11, 47, 50–51, 53, 54, 56, 60, 61, 63, 66, 89, 183, 185–186, 189–191, 194–195, 197, 212
on theft, 288
ownership of slaves forbidden in, 187
place within the Buddhist canon, 9
references to *katikāvata* in, 136
relationship to *dhammasat*, 190
sub-commentaries, 195
Tibetan, 340
use of in Burma, 197
commerce, 3, 6, 310
commodity loans *(bun 'gyed par byed pa)*, 110
common law, 181, 278
Communism, 234–235, 245–250, 316, 320, 332
Comparative Law, 2, 14, 18–23
confession. *See* punishment
conflicts, 42, 120, 126, 229
Confucianism, 19, 202, 231–232, 256, 258, 263–264, 270–271
constitutional law, 5, 72, 73, 152
contracts, 19, 53, 57, 59, 84, 93, 99–101, 105–106, 109–112, 113–114, 180, 307, 314, 316, 318
corporation, 160, 238
as a legal body, 55, 58
as institutions, 6
incorporation, 160–162, 212
law of, 91
legal personality of, 251
multinational, 159
personality, 238
saṅgha as a, 21, 203
temples as, 241
corpus delicti, 297
corvée labor, 180, 218, 315, 329
courts
abbot could grant or deny hearing in, 330
application of customary law, 174, 243, 244, 332
arguments allowed in. *See* legal reasoning
as part of an administrative body for temples, 132, 275
as source for *rajadhamma*, 168
Buddhist property disputes in, 153, 156–157, 164, 223, 251
cases, 157, 170, 210, 230, 250–251, 339
civil and criminal, 164, 241
conflict of laws, issues in, 175, 207
costs, 312
define how state should protect Buddhism, 163–164

courts (*cont.*)
equity, 173
ethnographic view of, 26
jurisdiction, 11, 55–56, 59, 175, 177, 183, 189, 195, 207, 221, 236
levels or grades of, 58, 126–127, 171, 316, 357
modern, 151, 165, 176
monastic courts, 142
monks and nuns using, 20, 95, 96, 156, 178
procedures, 317
records of, 329
religious and secular, 26
royal, 118, 123, 129, 139, 192, 214, 256–258, 266, 277–278, 281–282, 283, 298, 306, 309
standardization of, 327
Supreme, 157, 160–161, 162–163, 241, 244, 359
the study of, 17–18
trial, 170, 177, 290, 328
crime
amnesty for, 263
and victim compensation, 313
as grave offense, 49, 54, 111
as offense, 54–55, 57, 177, 178, 237
de minimus, 174, 178
Forty-Nine Cases on Theft, 168, 176
fraudulent sale, 218
gambling, 285, 330–331
justified as legal punishment, 291
killing living creatures (*prana-atipata*), 263
law of, 203, 237–238, 243, 332
Mongolian Code of Laws on monastic, 327–328
murder or homicide, 54, 57, 71, 122, 129, 207, 236, 288, 308, 312, 337, 339
of adultery, 58, 129, 237, 312
of alcohol consumption, 54, 208, 275, 326, 330
of carrying arms, 285
of embezzling, 220
of forging a royal decree, 259–260
of robbery, 236, 326, 329
of sale of Buddha's property, 285
of theft, 16, 21, 53–58, 69, 71, 80, 173–178, 191, 217, 220–222, 224, 225, 227, 228–229, 231, 274–276, 285, **288–301**, 307, 312, 325–327
of treason, 122, 128, 129
punishment fits the, 72
sexual, 237, 252, 285, 286, 328, 330
Tibetan law codes on, 312
transgression, 9, 49, 54, 66, 297, 325, 340, 342
Twenty-seven Cases on Bad Sex, 168
wrong-doing, 54
culpability, 114, 339
Cuppers, Christoph, 314
customary law, 195, 202, 236–237, 239, 243–245, 250, 305, 307, 314, 316, 324, 332
Dalai Lama, xvii, 213–214, 308, 310, 313, 315–316, 322, 324, 347, 354–355
dāna (giving), 79, 81, 289, 292
daṇḍa, 37
Daoism, 234–235, 236, 240–241, 242, 247, 249–250, 289
Daoseng ge, 208, 266
Daoxuan, 292, 297
debt, **91–114**
agricultural, 182
and eligibility for ordination, 58, 61
Arthaśāstra discusses, 37
calling in or collecting, 93, 95, 97, 100, 289
case of, 180
debtor, 95
discharging of deceased's by heir, 59
nuns pursuing, 92, 96
petitioning to the king for, 180
promissory note of, 92, 96, 98, 100–101, 109, 114
decision-making, 17, 207, 280, 306, 312, 316, 347, 358
deposition, 178
Derrett, J.D.M., 104
detachment, 78, 232, 294
dhamma, 3, 46, 184, 186, 352, 360. *See also* dharma
dhammasat, 168, 179–182
dhammasattha, 11, 183–184, 189–197
Dhammavilāsa, 190–191, 194–195
dharma, 4, 72, 77, 95, 105, 107, 124, 167, 168, 178, 180, 205, 276, 283, 291, 293, 297, 301, 309, 320–324, 363. *See also* dhamma
Dharmaguptaka-vinaya, 9, 21, 48, 51, 97, 114
Dharmapramāṇa, 35
dharmaśāstra, 37, 104, 106, 185, 190, 194
Dharmasūtras, 34–35, 36, 43, 67, 123
dice (divination, rolling), 308, 313, 316
Dīgha Nikāya, 39
Dīpavaṃsa, 117
discipline
and establishment of codes in Japanese Buddhism, 274, 277
and karma, 341
and the *Vinaya*, 23, 63–64, 117, 177, 341–342, 346
as punishment, 155
as training or putting into practice the teachings, 142, 341, 343
breakdown of in monasteries, 121–122, 140, 147, 287
difficulty of adhering to in modern world, 346
maintenance of, in monasteries, 236, 321, 331
monastic, 64, 331

dispute, 17, 42, 126, 128, 170–173, 174, 176, 186–188, 203, 228, 316
disrobe, 122, 152, 155, 156, 211, 270, 328, 330
divorce. *See* marriage
donation, 20, 155, 184, 218, 221, 223, 227, 231, 245, 252, 268–269
Dotson, Brian, 308
dual law, 319–325, 332, 366. *See also* patron-priest
dukkha, 334, 339
Dunhuang, 307

economy, 16, 37, 131, 168, 170, 179, 184, 220–221, 227, 231, 325
education, 15, 315
 and conversion to Christianity, 126, 132, 162
 and tax exemption, 239
 as a means of enforcing compliance to monastic regulations, 142
 Christian influence upon, in Sri Lanka, 158
 Education Ordinance of 1939, 132
 legal mandates to open schools in Chinese monasteries, 242
 of Bhutanese, 357, 364–365
 of children by Buddhist monks, 127
 of monastics, 343
 of nobility in Sri Lanka, 124, 129
 of women, 334, 347
 promotion of, 155, 158, 312, 354
 standardization of, within monasteries, 152
 state supervision of, 131–132, 163, 248, 251
eight special rules (*gurudharmas*), 10, 345
eighteen grounds for litigation (*vyavahārapadas*), 190
elections, 359, 364
Ellingson, Ter, 353
endowments, 83, 84, 92, 102–107, 109, 111–113, 239
engrossment, 219
enjoined (*samyukta)*, 38, 107, 196
equality, 10, 55, 162, 171, 231, 243, 355
equity, 173–175, 346–348
ethics
 as reflected in monastic or religious law, 86
 Aśoka's dharma as Buddhist, 75
 Buddhist ethical norms in Mongolia, 319
 Buddhist ethical prescriptions, 5
 Buddhist views on kingship grounded in, 5
 causality as basis of Buddhist ethical prescriptions, 338
 Confucian, 264, 270
 connotations of dharma in wider Indian discourses, 4, 36, 72, 75
 discouragement of theft, 288
 ethical behaviors and temple laws, 13
 ethical complications of property, 79–80
 ethical guidelines for attaining, possessing, and giving property, 82
 ethical implications of rebirth, 336
 human rights as global, 346
 lack of mention of, by Buddhist teachers in the west, 343
 monks advising lay-supporters on, 177
 of kingship in *rajadhamma*, 179
 of the Pāli state, 179–181
 origin of in Buddhist teachings, 335–336
 reflected in monastic codes, 341
 service to the king or state as conflicting with ethical vows, 266
 social, 8, 117, 321
 the state as ethical institution, 352, 360
 theory of karma as fundamental aspect of, 335–337, 341
 three separate ethical and legal systems in Pāli Buddhist society, 168
 unethical conversions, 160
Evers, Hans-Dieter, 83
expulsion, 38, 54, 120, 276, 286, 342. *See also* punishment
extraterritoriality, 205

Falk, Nancy, 82
family, 20, 45, 81–82, 98–99, 114, 128, 137, 144, 176–177, 180, 188–189, 194, 195, 237–239, 243, 250–251, 260, 268–269, 281, 284, 312, 315, 326, 342, 364
Fan-wang jing. See Brahmā Net Sūtra
fiduciary property, 224, 228
finances, 6, 20, 92, 101, 108, 112–113
Foucault, Michel, 290
Four Solidarities, 179–181
Four Variables, 173–174
Four-Part Vinaya, 13, 26, 275. *See also Dharmaguptaka-vinaya*
fraternities, 118, 131, 138, 150, 154–155, 157
fraudulent selling. *See* crime
freedom (thought, conscience, religion), 157, 160
fundamental rights, 158–159, 354, 361, 367
funerary rites, 59
furta sacra, 294, 297, 298

gahapati, 39, 44. *See also* householder
Gal Vihāra, 11, 134, 136
gambling, 285, 330–331
gaṇa, 42, 58, 138
Ganden Phodrang, 308, 353, 355–356
Geary, Patrick, 292–294
Geertz, Clifford, 78

Geiger, Wilhelm, 120, 122
Gelugpa, 312–313, 315, 355
gender relations, 170, 334
generosity, 20, 73, 75, 81–83, 98–99, 218, 340
Glenn, Patrick, 19
Gokhale, Balkrishna G., 351–352, 360
Goldstein, Melvyn C., 353
Gombrich, Richard, 74
gong'an (kōan), 210
grave offense, 49, 54. *See also pārājika*
Great Shavi, 320, 324–325, 329
Gross National Happiness, 16, **350–367**
guilds, 33, 55
Gywe, Tha, 174

Hallisey, Charles, 189
Harada, Masatoshi, 284
Harris, Ian, 15, 53
hereditary temples, 238–239, 244
hierarchy, 37, 39, 44, 55, 68, 138, 151–153, 236, 285, 308, 313, 323
Hinüber, Oskar von, 189
Hla, Nai Pan, 169
homelessness, 78, 341
Hosokawa, Kameichi, 273
householder, 39, 43, 74, 89, 95–96, 98, 100, 107–108, 112, 114, 176, 193, 327, 344, 366. *See also* laity
human rights, 15, 159, 252, 334, 346, 355
Huxley, Andrew, 69–70

immunity, 55, 58, 211
Inaba, Nobumichi, 280
independent legal person, 97, 100, 112, 113
Indonesia, 126, 347, 348
inheritance, 171–172, 174
  and colonial powers, 124, 126, 181
  and karma, 226
  and nuns, 59, 114
  and the Buddha, 78
  Arthaśāstra on, 37
  capatio, or legacy hunting, 99
  Civil Code of 1930 and *The Temple Ordinances,* 243–246
  from dying monk by lay person, 194–196
  Khmer *dhammasarts*, the Burmese *dhammathats* and the *Dhammasatthas* on, **167–182**
  land, 11, 126, 186, 189, 193
  monastic, 11, 57, 156, **183–197**, 318
  Mūlasarvāstivāda-vinaya on, 59, 84, 85, 89
  of kingdoms, 172, 177
  of light and heavy monk's property, 196
  of monastic property, 193–197
  of promissory notes, 93
  of slaves, 188, 195
  pupillary succession, 128
  religion of person with, 126
  Theravāda-vinaya and *Mahāsāṃghika-vinaya on*, 59
  Vinaya on, 84, 176, 183, 185, 187–191, 195
intention, 5, 49, 54, 130, 143, 223–224, 245, 252, 289, 334, 336, 337, 339, 356
invocation (*praśasti*), 81, 135, 139, 147
Ishihama, Yumiko, 311
Ishii, Ryōsuke, 278
Islam, 15, 235. *See also* Muslims

Jainism, 5, 39, 71, 123
Japan, 12, 21–23, 26, 48, 208, 213, 230, 258–259, 261, 263, 266, **273–287**, **288–301**, 366
Jäschke, H.A., 92
Jātaka, 72–73, 181, 317
jurisdiction, 11, 55–59, 175, 183, 188, 195, 221, 236
jurisprudence, 118, 203, 314

kami, 278–279, 299
Kandy, 122, 124–128, 130–132, 154
Kantorowicz, Ernst, 299
karma
  and Buddhist ethics, 5, 335–337, 341
  and gender relations, 334, 348–349
  and King Vessantara's generosity, 20
  and kingship, 145
  and property, 226
  and the Buddha's awakening, 3
  and understanding of law in Buddhist societies, 334
  Buddhist understanding of, 338–339
  communal implications of, in Sri Lankan Buddhism, 146
  influence of, on legal culture in Korea, 262–263
  link to monastic discipline, 341
  of rulers seeking to regulate the saṅgha, 144
  of rulers seeking to uphold the law, 77
Karmavācanā, 50, 51
katikāvata, 11, **135–149**, 151
Khutukhtu Mon. (high-ranking incarnate *lamas*), 320, 322–324, 325, 328–329, 332
kingship
  and "social contract" theory within Buddhism, 69–74
  and Aśoka, 145
  and divine-will vs. popular consent, 70
  and *rajadhamma*, 179
  Brāhmanical theory of, 129
  Buddhist views of, 5, 39, 43, 125, 144
  models of correct, 179–180

origin of, within Buddhism, 69
Parākramabāhu, 137, 143–149
sacralization of, 299
Kinugawa, Satoshi, 280
Korea, 12, 22, 23, 26, **255–271**, 295, 318, 345, 347–348
Koryŏsa, 266
kriyākāra, 10, 59
Kublai Khan (Qubilai Khaan), 309, 320–321
Kuroda, Toshio, 278–279

laicization. *See* disrobe
laity
admininstration of monasteries by, 250
and *dhammasattha*, 168, 183, 191–192
and *katikāvata*, 11
and legal hermeneutics, 197
and monastic donations, 83, 113, 156, 177, 222, 233
and monastic inheritance, 183, 188, 191, 193–194, 195
and wealth or property, 107
application of *dhammasattha* to, 11
as actors in legal transplant process, 23
as subjects of the Great Shavi in Mongolia, 325, 329
Buddhist monks giving legal advice to, 176–177
cases of theft, 289
control of the clergy in China by, 203
descriptions of customary practices in temples by, 157
disciplinary prescriptions for, by a *Vinaya* scholar, 213–214
encroaching on monastic property, 225
ethical implications of wealth or property, 82
ethical impolications of wealth or property, 82
forcible return of monastics to lay life, 237
immunity from secular law upon ordination, 57
improper use of temple land by, 154
influence of *Vinaya* upon, 8, 11, 23, 25, 46, 117, 195, 341
lack of mention of, in Chinese law, 235
laws of as overlapping with or separate from monastic law, 11, 89, 183, 191, 195
laws proscribing the killing of sentient creatures, 274
lay administrators, 275
lay commissioners, 211
lay monks and nuns in Bhutan, 364
lay officials, 353, 356
lay registration in Japan, 275
lay trustees, 154, 155
lay wardens of Buddhist monasteries, 128
legal actions against monastics by, 156, 163, 244
legal issues in Tibet affecting, 318
lending on interest to, 113
mentioned in *katikāvata*, 61
monastic control of, 202, 203, 267
monastic donations, 80–81
notions of property defined in relation to, 19
ownership of temples by, 238, 239
precepts for, 264–265
punishment for gambling, 331
recommendations to associate with good friends (*kalyāṇamitra*), 341
relation to monastic institutions, 6
relationship of, to the saṅgha, 3, 5, 8, 10, 11, 18, 23, 26, 37, 83, 130, 138, 142–143, 151, 158, 177, 310, 324, 341, 343
return to lay life, 229, 247, 274. *See also* disrobe
ritual purity as important for, 274
slavery as acceptable Buddhist practice for, 186
social categories of, in India, 44
taking Bodhisattva precepts, 12
theft of monastic property by, 229
Tibetan lay exiles, 354
wealth or property given by, 79
within the division of society, 175
land
abandonment of, and reversion to the state, 121
accumulation of, 218
agricultural and pasture, 39, 42, 219, 222–223, 239, 246–247, 310, 364
as a source of merit, 217–219
as belonging to the king, 267
as impediment to religious cultivation, 233
as necessary for monastic survival, 217, 220, 232–233
Buddhist Temporalities Act for, 132
commercial market for, 16, 227
concentration of, as inimical to Buddhism's purpose, 232
confiscation or misappropriation of, 124, 140, 158, 236, 239, 246, 269–271, 281
different types of, 39, 184
donation or gift of, 3, 20, 39, 81, 121, 128, 218, 223, 226, 229, 244, 268–269, 271
exemption of, from service levy, 223
fiduciary for, 224, 228
Fish Scale Registers, 229
forfeiture of, 219
fraudulent use of, 218, 230, 244
held in pawn, 218
improper use of, 154
inheritance of. *See* inheritance

land (*cont.*)
Land Reform Law of 1950, 247
landowners, 38, 44, 217–222, 228–230, 232, 239
loss of, 228
monastic, 16, 83, 120–122, 128, 153–157, 163, 217–219, 223–228, 231–233, 237–239, 244, 247, 251, 266–269, 310
ownerless, 119
prohibition against the sale or transfer of, 155, 252
Rank Land Law, 268–270
reforms and equalization of, 231, 245–247, 357
registration of, 229, 238, 244
reversion to monastic possession of, 222, 228
sale of, 223
state regulation of monastic, 153–156, 244
surveys, 229–230
taxation of, 132, 228, 232, 238–240, 244–246
temple, 132, 152, 165, 237–240, 268–270
Temple Ordinance of 1915, 240–244
theft of, 221–222, 224, 225, 226, 229, 231. *See also* crime, of theft
working the, 247
land grants, 103, 223, 269, 283
land reform, 245, 247
landowners. *See* land
Laos, 17, 151, 153, 167, 168, 181, 189, 345, 348
law codes
as creating administrative structures, 266
as legal transplants, 21
based on Buddhist texts, 261
Buddhist benedictions in, 323
Buddhist teachings not the basis for, 261
codification of, 3, 18, 31, 34–38, 181, 203, 243, 251
dating of, 257, 311–315
definition of law using, 13
differences between, and constitutions, 353
drafting periods of, 306
karma as basis for, 341
monastic. *See* monastic codes
of Bhutan, 366–367
of Burma, **167–182**, **183–197**
of China, 22, 26, **199–215**, **217–233**, **234–253**
of Korea, **257–260**
of Mongolia, **319–333**
of Tibet, 26, **305–318**
Vinaya as Buddhist, 1, 3, 46–62
laws, conflict of, 175–176, 178. *See also* jurisdiction
lawyers
and legal profession, 17–18, 151, 170, 181, 318
dieties as, 290
English, 175
in Burma, 18, 170–174
in Sri Lanka, 159, 164
monks as, 83, 84
monks forbidden to be, 163
regulating religion, 159
Southeast Asian, 180
layman (*upāsaka*), 58, 74, 96, 138, 175–177, 294, 327, 330
laywoman (*upāsikā*), 344. *See also* laity
Lee, Ki-baik, 256
legal consciousness, 17, 317, 319
legal reasoning
Buddhaghosa's text on, 11. *See also* Buddhaghosa
Buddhist, 5, 313–314, 337–341
legal concepts and, 308
Pāli Buddhist, 170–173, 179–181
ten forms of argument, 172
legalis homo, 96–97
legitimacy, 21, 24, 35, 124–125, 135, 150–151, 194, 206, 260, 266, 298–300, 352
Legrand, Pierre, 22
Lhasa, 17, 313, 316
liability, 174, 229, 241, 245
liberation, 3, 65, 76, 338, 340–341, 343–344, 348
lineage, 129, 145, 148, 238, 256, 277, 279, 281–284, 297, 309–310, 344–345, 347
Lingat, Robert, 185, 195
litigation, 170, 172, 178, 190, 210, 240, 244
loan contracts. *See* contracts

Magadha, 40, 73, 178, 320, 352
magic, 260, 299–300, 309
Mahābhārata, 69–70, 77
mahājanapada, 32, 40
Mahāsāṃghikas, 46, 49, 51–53, 59–60
Mahāsāṃghika-vinaya, 48
Mahāsammata, 145, 146, 320–321
Mahāsaṅghika-vinaya, 97, 114, 289
Mahāvaṃsa, 51, 117, 120, 122, 140
Mahāvihāra, 118–121, 139–141, 145–146, 177
Mahāyāna
and vegetarianism, 212
influence in Sri Lanka, 119, 123
ordination platforms in East Asia, 12
perspective on awakening, 140, 145
precepts, 13, 275
sūtras and texts, 12, 64, 208
Mahinda, 117–118
Mahīśāsakas, 60
Mahīśāsaka-vinaya, 48, 51
majjhimadesa, 32, 38
majority, 55, 236, 244, 280
Malaysia, 167–168, 348
Mānavadharmaśāstra, 37

Manusāra. *See dhammasattha*
marriage
  adultery. *See* crime
  Arthaśāstra on, 37
  divorce, 53
  for Buddhist monks and nuns, 237, 243
  no longer only option besides nun, 348
Maung, Aye, 179–180
meat-eating. *See* animals
meditation, 69, 75, 141–142, 148, 205, 338, 340
merit
  and acts of purification, 340
  and immunity from prosecution, 55
  and kingship, 145–147
  fields of, 3
  generation of, through donations, 3, 20, 79, 81–82, 98, 106, 218, 223, 226, 289, 366
  generation of, through the production of texts, 314
  inheritance based on, 193
  law does not bring, 318
  making, 95
  mentioned in a law code, 324
  mitigating the consequences through, 340
  property or land as a source of, 218, 224, 226, 233
Milindapañha (Questions of King Milinda), 81–82
Miura, Hiroyuki, 273
Mohan, Pankaj, 264, 267
monastic codes, 4, 26, 48, 52, 79, 212, 275, 335, 341
monastic complexes, three main, in Sri Lanka, 139
monastic disputes, 118, 121, 164
monastic inheritance. *See* inheritance
monastic life, 8, 78, 152, 213, 240, 274–276, 279, 284, 326, 342–343
monastic property, 11, 16, 20, 21, 121, 128, 142, 156, 183, 185, 186, 188–189, 191–193, 194, 195–196, 217–218, 220, 223–224, 227–228, 230, 342
monasticism, 1, 6–8, 9, 18, 47, 58, 83, 91, 125, 187, 231, 310
Mong, Sai Kham, 169
Mongolia, 23–24, 26, 48, 309, 311, 313, **319–333**, 345, 369
Mongols, 213–214, 309, **319–333**, 369
monk officials, 206, 207, 211, 213–214, 236, 246, 267, 317, 353
morality, 71, 75–76, 123, 180, 241–242, 312, 332. *See also* ethics
Mūlasarvāstivāda-vinaya, 9, 20, 26, 48, 50–52, 55, 58–60, 83, 87, 88, 91–94, 103, 104–106, 108, 114
Mūlasarvāstivādins, 49, 51–53, 61, 97, 113
mundane law (*lokavat*), 187–188, 195. *See also* secular law
murder. *See* crime
Muslims, 125, 127, 159, 164, 213. *See also* Islam
Myanmar. *See* Burma
myth, 20, 24, 71, 74–75, 212, 320

Nagamura, Makoto, 282
Nālandā, 6
natural law, 180
Nepal, 2, 31, 103, 307, 316, 345, 347, 359
Nikāyas, 63
Nirvāṇa, 46, 72, 75, 84, 292, 369
nissaya (apprenticeship), 142
nissaya (commentary), 186, 192–193
Nitta, Ichirō, 278
non-attachment, 79, 218, 233, 294
novice, 143, 155, 193, 236, 242, 257, 289, 326–327, 329, 345–346
nuns, **91–114**, **334–349**
  active as donors, 91
  and ordination procedures in China, 252
  and the *Vinaya*, 9–10, 12, 25, 46, 49, 57–58, 67, 93, 94, 97, 101, 108, 114
  as independent legal persons, 97, 113
  as invisible in *Dharmaśāstra* literature, 97
  as part of the saṅgha, 3, 5
  as subordinate to monks, 8, 10, 20, 113–114, 342, 345
  communities of, as independent from monks, 345
  difficulty adhering to all of the precepts today, 346
  engaging in monetary transactions, 109, 111
  enslavement, 236
  establishment of the order of, 344
  identity cards for non-ordained, in Sri Lanka, 156
  in inscriptions, 108
  inscriptional references to institutions connected with, 102
  lay nuns in Bhutan, 364
  legal processes in monasteries recorded by, 18
  lending on interest, 110–111
  ordination of women, 347–348
  orphans growing up to become, 237
  prohibited from making loans to the poor, 106
  prohibition of marriage, 237
  prohibitions concerning, 60–61
  prosecuting for seizure of a debt, 96–97, 100–101
  Qing Code on, 236–237
  relationship to disciples, 239

nuns (*cont.*)
required by law to offer sacrifices to ancestors, 237
secular law relating to in China, 235
status under Chinese law, 243, 247
subject to decisions by the Elder Godha, 177
threat of sexual assault against, 342
use of courts by, 178
use of financial instruments, 113
use of permanent endowments, 103
use of promissory notes by, 92

offenses, 37, 54–55, 57, 177–178, 237
Office of Monastic Affairs, 274
Okano, Kōji, 275
Okudaira, Ryuji, 169
Old Tibetan Annals, 307–308
Olivelle, Patrick, 3, 35–36
ordination
and establishment of the dispensation, 137
and immunity from secular law, 58
and Japanese monastic codes, 277
and rules about property in *Vinaya*, 84–85
and vows to uphold *Vinaya* rules, 10
as a legal matter in China, 253
certificates, 211, 218, 242
chapter on, in *Vinaya*, 58
control of, by the Chinese Buddhist Association, 252
elimination of, officially approved in Korea, 268
examinations, 138, 142
exclusion from, 61, 184
formulas in *Vinaya*, 51
issues surrounding, for women, 334, 342, 344–349
licenses, 236
lineages, 148
permission for, in Mongolian law, 326
platforms, 12, 282
practice in Japan, 275
practice, interpretation of, 13
problems concerning, in Sri Lanka, 128
reestablishment of higher, in Sri Lanka, 129–130, 148
register of higher, in Sri Lanka, 155
renunciation of family ties upon, 189
restricted only to those of noble birth, 130
restrictions upon, in early China, 205
rite, 342
state control of, in Korea, 267
state control of, in Mongolia under the Qing, 327
origins of society, 67–69
otherworldliness, 6
ownership, 8, 20, 58, 83–84, 86, 88, 91, 121, 163, 186, 188, 194, 218, 222, 229–231, 238, 251, 253, 268, 278, 283

Pagan, 197
Pāli Buddhist Law Reports, 178
Pāli Buddhist legal tradition, 167
Pāli canon, 9, 10, 25, 78, 197, 348
Pāli *Vinaya*, 11, 85–87, 97, 103, 114, 183, 185, 189–190, 194–197
pañcaśīla. *See* precepts
paradigms, 144, 147
pārājika, 49, 54, 57, 288, 292
Parākramabāhu I, 11, 120, 135–136, 140–141, 147–148, 195
pardons, 130, 214, 263–264
partition, 11, 183–185, 188, 194–196
Pātaliputra, 33, 40
pāṭha, 192–196
Pātimokkha, 142
patralekhya, 93, 96
patronage, 118, 197, 207, 228, 258
patron-priest, 305, 309–311, 313–314, 318. *See also* dual law
Patton, Laurie L., 37
pavidi, 117
pawn, 218
permanent endowment, 102–103, 107, 110, 113
political party of Buddhist monks, 161
politics, monastic involvement in, 133
Pollock, Sheldon, 34
possession, 20, 79, 82, 84, 88, 156, 221–223, 226, 230, 232, 251, 282–284, 294, 300
Prasenajit, King, 68
Prātimokṣa, 10, 24, 47, 49, 51–54, 57, 61, 94, 97, 99–101, 109, 265, 342
precedents, 89, 117, 147–148, 163, 203, 206, 212, 265, 267
preceptors, 128, 138, 141, 143, 184, 213–214, 267–268, 320, 322, 342
precepts, 3, 6, 20, 26, 39, 65–66, 76, 138, 156, 265, 268, 273, 275–277, 287, 291, 296, 325, 335, 338, 341–342, 345–346
Bodhisattva, 12, 21, 265
five lay (*pañcaśīla*), 80, 123, 264–265, 341
of a probationary nun, 345
platform, 282
reasons for observing, 342
ten, of a novice, 345
precious commodities. *See* commodity loans (*bun 'gyed par byed pa*)
primogeniture, 194
private law, 19–20, 278

private property, 125, 128, 218, 223, 239
prohibition on ("laws prescribing") killing living creatures (*prana-atipata*), 263
promissory notes, 92–94, 96–98, 99, 109, 114. *See also chags rgya*
negotiable, of debt, 93
property. *See* land
Property Law, 20
Proudhon, Pierre-Joseph, 292
public law, 19
public monasteries, 238–239
pudgalika (*puggalika*), 156, 186
punishment
Āpastamba Dharmasūtra, 37
Arthaśāstra, 37
as retribution, 290
Aśokan, 74–76
at origin of society, 69
beatings by masters as, 210
by breaking the spine, 329
by confiscation of the family and every possession of the perpetrator, 326
by death penalty, 75, 122, 129, 286, 327, 329
by expulsion, 38, 49, 54, 120, 252, 270, 275, 286, 342
by fine, 34
by fines in livestock, 326
by handcuffing and flogging, 75, 326, 329
by mutilations, 326, 328
by obeisance and repentance, 275
corporal, 34, 326
Dharmasūtra, 67
dictated by great elders, 138
enforcement by king, 37
fits the crime, 72
for breaching monastic vows, 321–323, 325
for misconduct and escape of monks, 331
for theft, *Dazhidulun* ten, 289
general criminal, 318
leniency by kings with respect to, 263
monastic institutions regulating through, 6
Mongolian, 326–332
Neo-Confucian views of, 263
of blood money payments by status level, 308
of branding and banishment, 122
of confession, 49, 276
of disrobing, 122, 328
of evil deeds in the *Nihon ryōiki*, 289
Prātimokṣa, 48–50
Qing Board of, 234, 237
subverted by magical counter-attack, 301
theft as, 291
to ward off corruption, severe, 321
tongue pulled out as, 290
victim compensation as, 313
Vinaya, 8, 53, 117
violent, as wrong, 72
pupillary succession, 128
Pure Rules *(qinggui)*, 12, 212
purity, 11, 14, 59, 83, 144, 190, 235, 274

Qing Code, 234, 236–237, 243, 246
Qing state, 16, 234
Qubilai Khaan. *See* Kublai Khan

rajadhamma, 11, 168, 175, 179
Rājagṛha, 40, 65
Ratnagar, Shereen, 33, 38, 41
real property, 124–126
rebirth, 145, 289, 334, 336–338, 340–343
Registry of Buddhist Monks (*Senglusi*), 236
relics
and decline of the Dharma, 297
as element of legitimacy, 299
as invaluable commodities and symbolic capital, 298
as living Buddha, 291
burial of by Kūkai, 297
changing nature of, 295
Christian cult of, 291
collection of for worship, 292
cultural, 250–251
identification with wish-fulfilling jewels, 298
medieval cult of in Japan, 291
of contact, 294
of mummified monk, 295
of the patriarch's robe, 295
relics assembly in Japanese Tendai, 277
theft of, 21, 288–301
theft of, two models, 294
Tooth Relic, 132, 293, 297
worship of, 297
religion and the state, 15, 206, 311
religion, establishment of, 158–165
religion, official, 16, 350, 363, 366
religions, state-sanctioned, 125
religious corporation, 21
religious governance, 151
renunciant, 341, 344
renunciation, 76–77, 79, 81, 342
requisites, 143, 185, 187–188, 193–194
responsibility, 69, 114, 138, 141, 143, 146, 157, 205, 207, 250, 266, 286, 331–332, 334–335, 358
Reynolds, Frank, 4, 14, 81
Rhi, Ki-yong, 266
rider, 111
Ritchu, Sarup, 169

Ritsuryō, 273–274, 277–278, 281
rituals, 3, 34, 130, 155, 262, 265, 271, 296, 298–300, 315, 317, 364
robbery. *See* crime
robes, 79, 83–88, 156, 185, 196, 275, 285, 328, 342
Robson, James, 294
Roerich, Y.N., 92
Roman law, 14, 21, 99
Ruppert, Brian, 298

sacrifice, 38, 45, 68, 75, 179–180, 259
Saichō, 13, 274, 277
Said, Edward, 14
Sakyapa sect, 309
sale and purchase, 39
Samantabhadra, 24, 320
Samantapāsādikā, 11, 53, 56, 87, 137, 173, 176. *See also* commentaries
saṃsāra, 338
Sangha, 151, 344, 363
Sangha Act, 152
saṅghāvaśeṣa, 99–100
Sarnath, 347
sāsana-katikāvata, 10, 60
Schneider, Hanna, 314
Schopen, Gregory, 84, 87–89, 291
Schuh, Dieter, 314
secular law, 8, 10–11, 14, 24, 26–27, 47, 52–53, 55–58, 67, 76, 87, 90, 119, 202, 212, 255, 258, 260–261, 267, 271, 318, 356
secularize, 132
Seita, Yoshihide, 280
seizure, prosecution for, 96, 100–101
self-governance, 277, 279–280
service levy exemption, 223
seṭṭhi, 44
settlements, 17, 32, 40, 57, 143, 316, 365
Sharma, Ram Sharan, 38–39, 41, 45
Shaw, William, 263
Shimosaka, Mamoru, 280
Siam. *See* Thailand
Silk Road, 307
sīmā, 53, 59
Skandhakas, 10, 48–50, 61
skillful means (*upāya*), 288
slavery, 37–39, 45, 47, 61, 128, 184, 186–188, 193, 195, 269–270, 354, 357
social stratification, 43, 307–308, 313
Sogdian, 204
Sŏng, King, 22, 261
Sōniryō, 208, 266, 273–276
Śrāvastī, 40, 95, 98, 109
Sri Lanka, 10–11, 17, 23, 25, 48, 50–51, 53, 60, 80, 89, **117–133**, **135–149**, **150–165**, 168, 177–178, 195, 294, 344–345, 347–348
status, 8, 20, 22, 35–36, 42, 64, 91, 100, 114, 121, 127, 131–132, 154, 157, 159–160, 189, 217, 238, 240, 243, 246, 250, 269, 274, 282–283, 285, 296, 298, 308, 313–315, 334, 344, 346, 354
statutes, 13, 17, 126, 151, 156, 234, 236–238, 244, 259–260, 266, 323, 329
Stein, Aurel, 307
suffering, 3, 74, 78, 81, 146, 286, 334, 337–339
supporter of a sick monk (*gilānupaṭṭhāka*), 185, 191, 193
Sūtra Piṭaka, 63–64, 67, 71–76
sūtras (suttas), 7, 12, 34–35, 39, 64, 175, 179, 338
Sūtravibhaṅga, 10
suttas. *See* sūtras
Suzhou, 221, 225–226, 228, 230–231

Taiwan, 253, 345, 347
Tajikistan, 307
Takeuchi, T., 92
Tambiah, Stanley J., 78
Tangut, 212–213, 309
Tantrayāna, 140
taxation, 73, 132, 208, 211, 232, 235, 239, 245, 309
temple lands. *See* land
temple regulations, 285
ten forms of argument. *See* legal reasoning
testament, 277. *See also* inheritance
Thailand, 17, 48, 129–130, 148, 151–153, 164, 167, 168–171, 175, 181, 189, 344–345, 347–348, 350–351
thammasats, 168–169. *See also dhammasattha*
theft. *See* crime
Theravāda, 11, 17, 53, 57–58, 61, 63, 66, 117, 119, 123, 131, 139, 144, 148, 151–153, 164, 167, 190, 294, 346, 348
Theravāda-vinaya, 9, 25, 48, 50–51, 53, 56, 58, 60
Theravādins, 48, 52–53, 60
Three Jewels, 175, 226, 292, 363
Tibet, 9, 16–17, 19, 23–24, 26–27, 48, 51, 89, 213–214, **305–318**, 320–321, 340, 345–348, 350, 353–356, 365–366
Tibetan Chronicles, 307
tipiṭaka, 46, 119
Tipiṭakālaṅkāra, 192, 194
Tiwei boli jing, 209
trade, 6, 22, 43, 45, 140–141
Trainor, Kevin, 294
translation
  and the dating of the *Vinayas*, 51
  excessive funds spent on, 307
  from Sogdian into Chinese, 204

genuine versus apocryphal, in China, 209
into Burmese, 184, 186, 192
into Tibetan, 92–93, 107, 306
modifications made to the original through, 210
of Buddhist texts into Chinese, 203
of dharma as law, 4
of dharma by the Chinese *fa*, 204
of the Āgamas into Chinese, 63
of the *Bhikṣuṇī-Prātimokṣa-sūtra* into Tibetan, 97, 99
of the *Bhikṣuṇī-vibhaṅga* into Tibetan, 94
of the Sūtra Pīṭaka into Chinese and Tibetan, 63
of the *Vinayas* into Chinese, 52, 206, 212
of *Vinayas* into Chinese and Tibetan, 48
transmission (cultural, religious), 6, 21–22, 25, 51, 206, 255–257, 260–261, 266, 281–282, 321
Travers, Alice, 314
treason. *See* crime
tripiṭaka, 46, 63
trusts, 154, 222
Tsomo, Karma Lekshe, 99

Uttaragrantha, 105–108

Vaiśālī, 40, 105, 107
vajra, 324, 362–363
varṇa, 37, 43, 67
Vedic, 31, 35–37, 39, 43, 74–75, 123, 179
Vermeersch, Sem, 265–269
vernacular, 137
Vessantara, King, 20, 81
Vibhaṅga, 47, 48, 61, 94, 97, 99–100, 107–108, 111–113, 188
victim compensation, 313
Vietnam, 167, 345, 347–348
vihāra, 10, 112–113, 120, 122, 127, 154, 342
vihāra-katikāvata, 10, 60
vihārasvāmin, 58, 113
Vinaya Decisions of Sirīsaṅghapāla, 184–189
vinayadhara, 11, 184
Vinayasaṅgaha, 185, 188, 195
Vinayavastu, 94
vote, 55, 244, 354, 364
vow temple of the sovereign, 282

Wada, Shūjō, 280
Watson, Alan, 21
White History of the Dharma, 320–322
wills. *See* written will
Wisdom-kings (*vidyārāja*), 291
women, illicit relations with, 252, 285–286, 328, 330
worldly law. *See dhammasattha*
worship, 105, 107, 123, 126, 153, 157, 160–161, 237, 239, 249, 293, 295–297
writ petition, 163
written law, 183, 202, 235, 255–256, 266
written will (*patrābhilikhita*), 89, 93. *See also* inheritance

Yama, 210, 289–291, 299, 301
Yamagishi, Tsuneto, 276
Yunqi Zhuhong, 16, 226

Zan, Myint, 172